The American Political System

INTRODUCTORY READINGS

The
American Political System

INTRODUCTORY READINGS

GEORGE S. MASANNAT • VERNON MARTIN

WESTERN KENTUCKY UNIVERSITY

CHARLES SCRIBNER'S SONS

NEW YORK

CONTRIBUTORS

GABRIEL A. ALMOND

STEPHEN K. BAILEY

BERNARD BERELSON

WILLIAM P. BUNDY

JOSEPH S. CLARK

ROBERT A. DAHL

JAMES C. DAVIES

DWIGHT G. DEAN

J. WILLIAM FULBRIGHT

JOHN KENNETH GALBRAITH

NATHAN GLAZER

HENRY F. GRAFF

FRED J. GREENSTEIN

PAUL J. HOFFMAN

MORRIS JANOWITZ

WILBER G. KATZ

V. O. KEY, JR.

MILTON R. KONVITZ

ROBERT E. LANE

NORMAN R. LUTTBEG

HERBERT McCLOSKY

GEORGE McGOVERN

WARREN E. MILLER

RALPH NADER

GAYLORD NELSON

RICHARD M. NIXON

LOUIS NIZER

ROSEMARY O'HARA

SAUL K. PADOVER

NELSON W. POLSBY

MORRIS ROSENBERG

BAYARD RUSTIN

THEODORE C. SORENSEN

HAROLD P. SOUTHERLAND

DONALD E. STOKES

DAVID B. TRUMAN

SIDNEY VERBA

CLEMENT E. VOSE

TOM WICKER

AARON B. WILDAVSKY

HARMON ZEIGLER

PREFACE

This volume is intended to supplement the standard textbooks used in introductory courses in American government. We have selected readings that will stimulate the reader's interest and sharpen his understanding of the American political system. To do this we have included timely articles on the politics of violence and the politics of ecology as well as fresh material on more traditional topics such as Congress and the presidency.

The readings are divided into eleven parts: 1) The Political Culture; 2) Political Participation and Alienation; 3) Civil Rights and Liberties; 4) The Politics of Violence: The Challenge to the Status Quo; 5) The Politics of Ecology; 6) Political Dynamics: Public Opinion, Pressure Groups and Political Parties; 7) The Electoral Process; 8) The Congress; 9) The Presidency; 10) The Judiciary; and 11) United States Foreign Policy. Each part opens with an introduction that supplies the political and analytical context for the readings and identifies their salient aspects. The selected bibliography and the study questions at the end of each part are intended to provoke further reading, class questions and discussion. We are confident that the material we have assembled in this text will meet the needs of both students and instructors.

The editors are grateful to Western Kentucky University for making its various facilities available in the preparation of this manuscript.

GEORGE S. MASANNAT
VERNON MARTIN

CONTENTS

Political Parties

PART SEVEN

The Electoral Process

PART EIGHT

The Congress

PART NINE

The Presidency

PART TEN

The Judiciary

PART ELEVEN

United States Foreign Policy

The American Political System

INTRODUCTORY READINGS

PART ONE

The
Political Culture

"Every political system," writes Gabriel A. Almond, "is embedded in a particular pattern of orientations to political action. I have found it useful to refer to this as the *political culture*." [1] The concept of political culture places great emphasis upon political attitudes, beliefs, expectations, and symbols held by the individual. The process of transmitting the political culture from one generation to another is known as *political socialization*. It is through the political socialization process that the traditional political values, norms, and attitudes are learned by children and carried by them through adulthood, where they become significant to the performance of roles in the political system.

The concept of political culture assumes the individual must learn and incorporate into his own attitudinal dispositions and behavior patterns the traditions of society and identify himself with its institutions, historical experience, and politics. Among the various agencies of political socialization are the family, the peer group, the church, and the school. The readings in this section attempt to examine the socialization process of children and the idea of consensus and ideology in American politics.

In the first article James C. Davies discusses the role of the family in forming the individual's political attitudes. The child tends to identify with his parents and adopt their outlook toward the political system. The father is the center of authority and thereby initiates the child's views of political authority. The political socialization process, at least in the United States, is basically complete when the child is about thirteen. As the child moves from the stage of dependence to that of autonomy, he is likely to develop into a mature and responsible citizen. When he suffers physical and emotional deprivation,

[1] Gabriel A. Almond, "Comparative Political Systems," *Journal of Politics*, 18 (August 1956), 396.

he is likely to establish a pattern of chronic dependence that includes the political. When conflict generates between his own emerging needs, the family pattern of satisfying them, and the demands of society, the growing child is in mental turmoil. Only gradually, then, can he change from hierarchized to equalized patterns of political behavior in which he can responsibly share power with other citizens and acquire a sense of security, responsibility, and autonomy in the family and the polity.

In the second article Fred I. Greenstein examines children's images of political authority. His study shows the differences between adult and children's orientations to political authority. For instance, adult orientation to political authority is characterized as ambivalent while that of children as sympathetic. Children are at least as likely as adults to perceive high political roles as being important. Greenstein states that the benevolent image of political leaders to children (President, Governor, and Mayor) declines with age. For example, the study shows that widespread political distrust and cynicism does not seem to have developed by the eighth grade (age 13). Finally, Greenstein discusses the significance of the child's view of political authority and suggests further research in the development of political behavior.

In the third article Herbert McClosky attempts to find empirically the degree of consensus in American democracy. Although the term "consensus" has been defined by scholars in many different ways, McClosky states that consensus has to do with shared beliefs such as accountability, consent, limited government, equality before the law, and religious toleration.

McClosky's study shows that political elites exhibit a far greater understanding of the fundamental ideas and principles on which the American democratic system rests than the masses or electorate. However, on items expressing abstract statements of democratic belief in freedom of speech and opinion, both the political influentials and the electorate strongly support these values. Moreover, the study shows that the political elites exhibit stronger support for specific application of free speech and procedural rights than the electorate. The political elites not only register higher scores on all pro-democratic scales but also are more likely to reject anti-democratic sentiments. They disdain extremism and authoritarianism.

The political articulates and the electorate are sharply divided on equalitarian values. As McClosky writes, both the leader and the electorate "are uncertain and ambivalent about equality." Also, his research shows that Americans accept the political system as legitimate and shy away from extreme movements. Americans are, at least verbally, confused and divided in their reaction to the political system and yet a high percentage express confidence that the government will do what is right. While the electorate expresses a sense of political futility, the political elites exhibit a sense of optimism. Moreover, the political elites are more partisan and consistent in their views on political issues than is the electorate.

McClosky concludes that a democratic society can survive despite widespread disagreement and misunderstanding about fundamental democratic and constitutional values. A case in point is the American political system. He claims that the responsibility for keeping the political system going falls mainly on the articulate classes.

THE FAMILY'S ROLE IN POLITICAL SOCIALIZATION

JAMES C. DAVIES

The family provides the major means for transforming the mentally naked infant organism into the adult, fully clothed in its own personality. And most of the individual's political personality—his tendencies to think and act politically in particular ways—have been determined at home, several years before he can take part in politics as an ordinary adult citizen or as a political prominent.

The politicizing process starts early. Easton and Hess have indicated that in America it begins at about the age of three and is basically completed by the age of thirteen. And it usually remains stable, at least in terms of party loyalty, for life. These statements suggest the strength of family influences on political behavior. In what follows I will try to indicate why and how the family influence is so strong, among both ordinary citizens and political prominents and in polities that are either relatively stable and constitutional or unstable and nonconstitutional.

THE MOTHER, THE FATHER, AND THE CHILD'S BASIC NEEDS

There are at least four basic needs that appear to be innate and therefore common to all human beings—the physical needs for food, clothing, shelter, health, and safety from bodily harm; the need for love and affection, which antiseptically may be called the social need; the need for establishing the identity or selfhood that Maslow calls self-esteem; and the need for self-actualization.[1] The ways in which these needs are met—during the longest matu-

[1] This listing of needs is borrowed directly from Abraham H. Maslow, "A Theory of Human Motivation," *Psychological Review*, 50 (July 1943), pp. 370–396, who lists a fifth need (for secu-

SOURCE: James C. Davies, "The Family's Role in Political Socialization," *The Annals of the American Academy of Political and Social Science*, 361 (September 1965), 10–19. Reprinted by permission. Some footnotes have been deleted.

ration process required by any species—expose the human organism to a range and intensity of conditioning that are unique. The family provides the individual initially with all his environment for need satisfactions and throughout his entire life is the locus for most of them.

As the initial provider for the new-born child, the mother constitutes the biggest portion of his environment. She is—as Freud indicated—indistinguishable in the infant's primitive mental processes from himself. He and his mother are the same. As he grows, the infant begins gradually to distinguish himself from her and other aspects of the environment. As this distinction emerges, the child nurtured with food, warmth, and affection begins the process of establishing his own identity and at the same time begins the process of deciding with whom he wants to identify. This internal dialogue, beginning before the child can talk, continues through his later life, so that he must forever not only establish his distinct self but relate that self to others whom he would like to be, to be like, or, minimally, to be with. Even the aged citizen who freely and secretly casts his last ballot in an election that presents free alternatives to him is never quite free of those people who have influenced him —most particularly his childhood family. And the political leader, like all others, likewise remains under the influence of his family background—if not in the content, then at least in the style, of his rule. Throughout his presidency, Woodrow Wilson remained a preacher and remained in unconscious rebellion against his Presbyterian preacher father.

The basic, innate, organic needs appear to emerge generally in the order stated above: first, the physical; then the social; then the self-esteem; and lastly the self-actualization needs. The family is the most prominent environmental source not only of what may be deemed its inherent function of providing affection but also of satisfying other needs. This is probably the central reason that the individual comes to think and act like his family more than he thinks and acts like those who are less regularly relevant to his need satisfactions. In the process of fulfilling his needs, the individual establishes who he is and whom he is like. In short, he thus establishes his identity.[2] This definition emphasizes the continuing purposes, the continuing functions, which his lifelong interaction with others serves.

There is a dearth of research on the relationship between the family as a source of physical deprivation, and no great amount of research on the politi-

---

rity) that I regard as a need for being secure in the satisfaction of the physical, social, self-esteem, and self-actualization needs. See J. C. Davies, *Human Nature in Politics* (New York: John Wiley & Sons, 1963), chap. 1.

[2] A closely reasoned and comprehensive analysis of the family's role in the identification process defines it as "the more or less lasting influence of one person on another," in Robert F. Winch, *Identification and Its Familial Determinants* (Indianapolis, Ind.: Bobbs-Merrill, 1962), p. 3. Identification may be more casually defined as the process by which an individual is influenced in his behavior in the course of satisfying each of his basic needs.

cal consequences of physical deprivation itself. The research on brainwashing clearly establishes the (usually transitory) political pliancy that occurs when the victim realizes that his very existence depends on his conformity to his captors' (his pseudo parents') ideology.[3]

Dependency is a very common reaction to physical deprivation, but we may thus far only hypothesize that such dependency associated with the family will heighten the tendency to conform to the familial political outlook. This hypothesis helps explain the greater tendency of wives in America to conform to their husbands' politics than vice versa, because the husband is usually the breadwinner.[4]

Social deprivation arising from maternal deprivation has been examined empirically and throws light by inference on the political consequences of the individual's failure to receive normal affection during his early years. The profundity of the consequences of affection deprivation is indicated by research both with primates and with human beings.

Harlow has compared monkeys raised with mechanical mothers—devices to which a nursing bottle is attached—to ones raised under the normal care of their natural mothers. Some of the monkeys raised with mother-surrogates would rage at passers-by or, internalizing their tension, would rage at themselves by biting or picking at their own bodies. Others displayed deep apathy. At the age of six months, they could not play normally with normally raised monkeys or with one another. When they became adults and were placed together with other monkeys that were breeding, they were incapable of normal sexual activity. These "childhood" deprivations had permanently abnormalized the behavior of the mature monkeys.[5]

Comparably systematic but nonexperimental research by Spitz has indicated the consequences of maternal deprivation among infants. He was able to compare infants raised by their own mothers in a nursery home with infants raised in a foundling home without mothers. All the former category were still alive at the age of two years. Among the ninety-one raised without mothers, over a third had died. All but a couple of cases in the foundling home became "human wrecks who behaved either in the manner of agitated or of apathetic idiots." [6] The same polarization between hyperexcitability and apathy occurred in the behavior of the Harlow monkeys and the Spitz children.

---

[3] Among the many reports, a most penetrating analysis is Robert Jay Lifton, *Thought Reform and the Psychology of Totalism* (New York: W. W. Norton, 1961).

[4] See Angus Campbell *et al.*, *The Voter Decides* (Evanston, Ill.: Row, Peterson, 1954). Table C.3, p. 205.

[5] Harry F. Harlow, "The Nature of Love," *The American Psychologist*, 13 (December 1958), pp. 673–685 and H. F. and M. K. Harlow, "Social Deprivation in Monkeys," *Scientific American*, 207 (November 1962), pp. 136–146.

[6] R. A. Spitz, "The Role of Ecological Factors in Emotional Development in Infancy," *Child Development*, 20 (September 1949), pp. 145–155.

One of the major discontinuities in the research in political socialization lies between the degree and kind of physical and social nurturance or deprivation of the child within the family and the degree and kind of politicization of the adult. We can not yet report systematically any such research that might establish ties between these phenomena and political socialization. It is again only possible to hypothesize that the general political apathy (and transient hyperexcitability)—the lack of politicization—that still prevails in most of the world is traceable to the apathy (and transient hyperexcitability) resulting from childhood deprivation of these basic needs within the family.

ACHIEVING POLITICAL IDENTITY
THROUGH THE FAMILY

The minimal normal family unit consists of mother, father, and child, but this unit is by no means the universal one. There are both larger and smaller ones. At one extreme are the extended families in which various combinations of nuclear family units are (usually) intergenerationally combined. Research on the politicization consequences of extended family experience for the growing child is again lacking, despite some analysis of the quasi-extended family units in the Israeli kibbutzim. But these novel social units have not been in existence long enough to predict what are the political consequences for kibbutz-raised adults.

But there is the opposite extreme of the minimal and subnormal family unit, typically consisting of the mother and child. On this phenomenon there is some evidence, including some that relates to politicization. One study compared children raised in normal nuclear families with children of families in which the fathers were sailors absent from home for long and irregular periods. Among the findings were these: the father-absent boys, compared with those raised with both parents, strove more to identify with their fathers and at the same time were uncertain of their own masculine identification and tried to act more masculine. Both the boys and girls in father-absent families remained more dependent on their mothers.[7]

In an intensive study of Japanese youth experiencing the profound emotional crisis of their country after its first resounding national defeat in the Second World War, Lifton made comparable observations. Although the fathers were physically present, Japanese youth were very dependent on their mothers. Fathers often were incapable of managing the tensions of young Japanese in cultural transition from a still semifeudal and authoritarian family structure to a still unstabilized new set of interpersonal relationships. They consequently have withdrawn into ineffectual noninvolvement. The mother has remained as the source for satisfying a basic need for stable affection quite

---

[7] David B. Lynn and William L. Sawrey, "The Effects of Father-Absence on Norwegian Boys and Girls," *Journal of Abnormal and Social Psychology*, 59 (September 1959), pp. 258–262.

without ideological or other cultural content. The great intergenerational gap has been bridgeable emotionally only with the mother. The political consequence has been a high anxiety level among the youth and a tendency to oscillate between quiescence and extreme activity that has involved engaging in massive demonstrations in which the individual finds strong extra-familial social identification and release from his own private tensions.[8]

Langton, in comparing maternal with two-parent families in Jamaica, has found that authoritarianism in maternal families is higher and both political interest and a sense of political efficacy are lower. The effect is more pronounced among male than female children, and the relationship, with some exceptions, holds regardless of the social class of the children studied.[9]

Even in the relatively more equalitarian father-mother authority relationships that prevail in American families, the father is generally more dominant. On the more specific question of the father's political influence, Langton has found that in Jamaican father-present families it is the father, by a ratio of better than two to one over the mother, who is looked to for political advice and influence.[10]

The reasons for this preponderant influence of fathers in family decision-making, including political decisions, remain imperfectly explored. It is not adequate to explain the phenomenon in such altogether environmental terms as authoritarianism or father-centered cultures. There is the possibility that, in addition to environmental forces, organic ones may be operating. A study of 27 males and 27 females for whom data were gathered from childhood (ages 3–10) and adulthood found a change that was strikingly different as between the men and women. The boys and girls had been rather alike in their emotional dependence on parents and their tendency to withdraw passively from problem situations. As adults, the males showed a pronounced reduction in these tendencies; females were much less likely to change.[11] This finding may be one link in a still unformed and long chain of explanation for the fact that fathers and husbands are more politically influential in the family than mothers and wives.

The causes for family influence on political socialization do remain very largely unexplored. Even the detailed knowledge of the early life of Lee Harvey Oswald, Kennedy's probable assassin, does not adequately explain his unique political behavior. But there is enough provocative description of just

[8] Robert Jay Lifton, "Youth and History: Individual Change in Postwar Japan," *Daedalus*, 91 (Winter 1962), pp. 172–197.

[9] Kenneth P. Langton, *The Political Socialization Process: The Case of Secondary School Students in Jamaica* (Unpublished Ph.D. dissertation, University of Oregon, 1965), pp. 113, 115–117.

[10] *Ibid.*, p. 118.

[11] Jerome Kagan and Howard A. Moss, "The Stability of Passive and Dependent Behavior from Childhood through Adulthood," *Child Development*, 31 (September 1960), pp. 577–591. The authors' speculative explanation is environmental, but it does not seem to preclude an organic inference that is no more speculative.

what happens politically in childhood to promise that more analytical, casually oriented work may be done in the future.

Easton and Hess have indicated that one decade is the critical period for basic politicization, starting at the age of three. Just how the first filaments of political identification are formed is not quite clear, but these first ties, well established by the age of seven, are to the broad political community, on an emotional basis that starts with a warm and positive attachment to schools, the "beauty of their country," and "the goodness and cleanliness of its people."

These relatively concrete attachments to community are followed by similar ties to the wielders and visible symbols of public authority, represented by the President of the United States, the local policeman, and the flag. The attachment to the flag becomes almost religious and the flag salute almost a prayer to God. As the child grows, his attitudes toward political authority become increasingly impersonal.

To his quasi-religious set of political attachments, which reach some sort of plateau by the age of nine or ten, is added a more abstract set of identifications with such concepts as democracy, voting, and various aspects of civic liberty. An awareness develops of people as citizens and of one's obligations as a future citizen.[12]

How much of this politicization derives from the family is uncertain, but the likeness between the child's positive, warm appraisal of his own father and the President is clear and may relate to the relatively generous, benign, and nonauthoritarian behavior that is deemed fairly common in American fatherhood. Greenstein emphasizes another characteristic of children's appraisal of the President, namely, that they are remarkably lacking in cynicism about him and other political leaders. Part of this is attributed to the tendency of parents to protect their children from harsh realities of the adult political world and part to the tendency of children to establish a univalent picture free of unpleasant coloration.[13]

The reasons for the warm and trusting attitude toward political authority remain speculative but are seen by Easton and others as relating to the child's anxiety about his dependency on his parents. We can add an explanatory link by again suggesting that the child identifies with both parents because they are the early and the continuing primary source for his need satisfactions. And he identifies more with the father than the mother as an authority figure because—for surely cultural and also perhaps organic reasons—the father is typically the prime exerciser of authority in the family.

---

[12] David Easton and Robert D. Hess, "The Child's Political World," *Midwest Journal of Political Science*, 6 (August 1962), pp. 229–246, notably at pp. 236–239. For a very preliminary cross-national research report, see R. D. Hess, "The Socialization of Attitudes toward Political Authority: Some Cross-National Comparisons," *International Social Science Journal*, 15 (4: 1963), pp. 542–559.

[13] Fred I. Greenstein, "The Benevolent Leader: Children's Images of Political Authority," *American Political Science Review*, 54 (December 1960), pp. 934–943.

The research of Sigel in analyzing both child and adult responses to the assassination of President Kennedy in November 1963 extends earlier research. She found that the younger the child, the greater the emotional shock and the worry about what would happen after the sudden removal of the central power figure. The President's death produced a reaction that he was not quite so powerful after all, because the presidency and the government continued without interruption after he died. But the younger children more often were unconcerned with the rule of law, more often approving the murder of the assassin. And in a response that may reflect what Greenstein described, the younger children were more inclined to regard the assassination as the act of a single specific individual and not of a conspiracy.[14]

CHANGES FROM POLITICAL IDENTIFICATION WITH PARENTS

The high degree of conformity in America to the political system has been attributed by Lane and others to the lack of deep political controversy, because the system and its parts generally work well.[15] But quite aside from the system's effectiveness, most of the forces *internal* to the family tend strongly to produce a likeness in political attitudes and action from generation to generation. Correlatively, when the child becomes alienated from its parents, it tends also to become politically alienated.[16] One cause for this alienation (which is in any case a common phenomenon of adolescence) is strict parental control, which has been found to make some children more conforming and others more deviant politically.[17] And in families that are highly politicized, politics is "available as an object of protest." [18]

Intrafamilial sources of change from political identification with parents inevitably ramify into extrafamilial influences. Perhaps the most important of these operate in schools, where it is the peer group of students and the tall authority figure of teachers that interpose and superimpose their influence on the strong family forces. And a young man's change in political orientation may reflect a change in socioeconomic or ethnic status from that of his parents. The Irishman, the Jew, the Negro, the Ainu, or the Untouchable who is becoming integrated into the great society is likely to abandon the views of

---

[14] Roberta S. Sigel, "Some Explorations into Political Socialization: School Children's Reaction to the Death of a President," *Children and the Death of a President*, ed. Martha Wolfenstein and Gilbert Kliman (Garden City, N.Y.: Doubleday, 1965).

[15] Robert E. Lane, "Fathers and Sons: Foundations of Political Belief," *American Sociological Review*, 24 (August 1959), pp. 502–511 or Lane, *Political Ideology* (New York: Free Press of Glencoe, 1962), chap. 17.

[16] Herbert McClosky and Harold E. Dahlgren, "Primary Group Influence on Party Loyalty," *American Political Science Review*, 53 (September 1959), pp. 757–776, at 766.

[17] Eleanor E. Maccoby *et al.*, "Youth and Political Change," *Public Opinion Quarterly*, 18 (Spring 1954), pp. 23–39.

[18] Langton, *op. cit.*, Table 27, p. 140 and p. 223.

his parents, as these derive from any political ties that were established on an ethnic and social-class basis.

Such changes reflect a measure of tension resulting from mental conflict within the individual child as he grows and his needs emerge. Changes that are extrafamilial in origin involve the family as the arena where outside forces operate. Long-lasting stability in the social and political system reinforces the custom-conserving familial forces. During times of rapid social and political change the conflicting intra- and extra-familial influences interact most vigorously on the growing individual. And these relate not only to the forces exogenous to the individual (within and without the family) but also to those generated by his own organism as his own needs and other mental processes emerge, change, and grow.

THE IMPACT OF EXTERNAL CRISIS

External threats to members of a family produce a variety of responses in the individual member. Severe economic crisis poses a threat to the physical well-being of the growing child. As Bakke and others have indicated, when the father becomes unemployed, his role as provider of food, clothing, and shelter is so diminished as to affect his role as the chief authority figure in the family.[19]

Natural disaster, like explosion or tornado, does not have necessarily the same effect as economic crisis in altering the power structure within the family, but it does have the remarkable consequence of breaking down ties to the larger community. People hit by such catastrophe have the initial impulse to protect and be protected by their immediate family and to quite forget the broader community welfare.

In a nuclear or extended family in a preindustrial and predemocratic society, the process may be different. We may suppose that there is little of the politicization process that has been described as taking place in industrialized and democratic societies. The large community in the former case is not characteristically national, perhaps not even regional, but is more likely to be bounded by the local village or large rural estate.

When such premodern societies are in transition, the forces for economic, social, and political change probably operate qualitatively the same as in industrialized but still-changing societies. But they are far more widespread and intense, traumatizing the family more severely than natural or economic disaster in a modern society. They both draw the family together and pull it apart.

Within the family arena two contradictory politicizing functions develop, as the growing child begins the move from the traditional to the modern. One family function is to serve as the shield protecting its members from external forces that threaten not only its traditional roles but also its high degree of autonomy and integrity. When the family acts thus as a shield against external

[19] L. Wight Bakke, *Citizens without Work* (New Haven: Yale University Press, 1940), chap. 6. . . .

threats, one consequence is likely to be concerted hostility to the regime itself or—more likely, if the threat is severe—of withdrawal from any kind of political activity whatever.

When the external forces are seen by the young not as a threat but as an opportunity, there is likely to be conflict between parents and children and therefore a long-lasting reduction in the role the family plays in the politicization process and a correlative increase in the role of school, of the young person's age-mates, and of youth organizations which directly demand the loyalty of the young to the government rather than to the family. Many of the needs, including the dependency needs, that hitherto had been largely met within the family are now met outside it.

This crisis to the family in a society in transition may diminish with time, as exemplified in the growing emphasis in the Soviet Union—more than a generation after the 1917 revolution—on loyalty and obedience to family. But the "concluding" stable familial state is unlikely to be like the one before the transition began. It is likely to include an acceptance by the family that its politicization role, while still perhaps the strongest, is not exclusive and that other social groups, notably schools, have relatively free access to the growing children. And renewed crisis, whether it be economic, as in the Great Depression of the 1930's, or social, as in the American civil rights crisis of the 1950's and 1960's or the profound postwar crisis in Japan, or more directly political, as in the foreign-policy crisis in America of the 1960's, is likely to reactivate intrafamilial tensions as the youth diverge from familial political loyalties and outlook.

THE FAMILY AND THE PRODUCTION
OF POLITICAL PROMINENTS

For lack of systematic research, it is here possible only to outline the role of the family in producing that small portion of the citizenry who emerge from the great genetic and social pool of infancy and obscurity to mature prominence as national leaders. There are some psychologically insightful biographies, like Huizinga's of Erasmus, Erikson's of Luther, the Herndon and Charnwood biographies of Lincoln, and, perhaps, Bullock's of Hitler. But this field of study is so undertilled that any outlines of general principles governing the development of national leaders remain fragmentary.

About the only generalization that may have universal validity is that political leaders are, psychologically speaking, marginal men. That is to say, whatever their particular genetic make-up, circumstances have pushed them to various boundaries—between old eras and new, traditional and static social status and modern fluid social status, and, more deeply, between the mental insecurity of alienation from parents and identification with new social and political movements affecting the great society whose profound change they experience and interact with.

Whatever their idiosyncratic characteristics, leaders all seem to experience profound conflict as to their own identifications with others and as to their own identity. They do not quite know to whom and what they belong and who and what they are, and they spend their political lives in a never-quite-ending search for resolution of this manifest conflict and its deeply hidden tensions. In this they probably do not differ in kind from their fellow citizens but do differ in the intensity of their response. Their intensity may be a consequence of greater ego strength—of ability to resolve the conflict rather than to withdraw from it into passivity or insanity—and of an extraordinarily high energy level. But these remain only hypothetical suggestions helping to explain the acute marginality of political prominents.

THE FAMILY, POLITICAL CHILDHOOD AND MATURITY

The child is nurtured in all ways primarily within the family. Until he reaches maturity, he remains in a condition of dependency on the family. However, his achievement of political maturity depends not only on the family but also on other social influences. And in the contemporary world, which for the most part remains politically apathetic, dependent, and immature, neither the political system nor the family is sufficiently prepared to insure that the transition to maturity will be made with less than enormous turmoil in the minds of both the child and the parents. Tribal and feudal societies generally contain family power relationships in which the child is regarded less as a potential equal than as a person who must learn to conform and to rise only slowly in the hierarchy and who must never expect to live in other than superior and subordinate relationships with others.

The retarding influence of autocratic and authoritarian social relationships, within and without the family, is usually accompanied by circumstances of endemic physical deprivation during which the growing child must quickly learn how to provide physically for himself, then his parents, and then his children. Without the potentially leveling, antihierarchizing influences of modern integrated and industrialized society, the child is likely to move from authoritarian dependency to authoritarian support of those dependent on him. He is unable to learn adequately anything other than authoritarian ways of acting and reacting and therefore unable to achieve with any facility the transition from dependency to autonomy. So he uneasily remains authoritarian within the family and in his political relationships.

As he starts the transition from tribal or feudal to modern society, he shifts his dependency on parents to a dependency on a new national movement and new political father figure. There is, perhaps, more often than not, some net gain, because the authority influence of the political father cannot, over a prolonged period, be so strong as the proximal familial influence. In consequence, when the transition has progressed somewhat, he is less likely to be as dependent as he was previously on either familial or political father and, in that case, has achieved the beginnings of his own autonomy. In turn, he is likely to be less authoritarian toward his own dependent children than his father was and so to facilitate both the broad social transition and the internal transition of the single growing individual.

The transition period is heavy with anxiety, chronic in the individual and endemic in the society, but as the dialogue of change develops and stabilizes, the loyalties to family become re-established on a new basis and new ties to other groups develop—including ones to party, leadership, nation, and the social institutions of an increasingly pluralistic society. As the universal, residual social unit, the family can thus serve not only authoritarian social and political functions, in which the individual's value derives from his status as a subordinate or a superior, but equalitarian functions in which the individual's value becomes equal to that of others as he acquires the sense of security, responsibility, and autonomy of a mature member of the family and the democratic polity.

Families as the major matrix for individual political maturation have endured intact a centuries-long transition from feudalism to pluralism and individualism in the Western world. And individuals in transition have similarly remained intact. There is no reason to assume that the experience thus accumulated will not both facilitate and accelerate the process in the rest of the world.

THE BENEVOLENT LEADER: CHILDREN'S IMAGES OF POLITICAL AUTHORITY

FRED I. GREENSTEIN

Society's training of the young, including formal and informal citizenship instruction, character training, and the processes which lead to the development of different personality types, has been seen as an important determinant of adult political behavior by theorists since Plato. In addition, much of our traditional folklore, not to mention much twentieth century literature on personality development, national character, authoritarianism, and electoral preference, points to the utility of examining the individual's early years as one means of illuminating his mature actions.[1]

[1] The first thoroughgoing consideration of the problems in studying political socialization, including a summary of much past research which is germane to understanding political development, is Herbert Hyman's *Political Socialization* (Glencoe, 1959). Emphasis on the socialization

SOURCE: Fred I. Greenstein, "The Benevolent Leader: Children's Images of Political Authority," *The American Political Science Review*, 54 (December 1969), 934–943. Reprinted by permission. Some footnotes have been deleted.

The present paper considers one aspect of the child's political development—the genesis of his attitudes toward political leaders and the possible ways that this developmental process may affect his adult responses to the formal wielders of power. Citizens' orientations to political authority have a complex and imperfectly understood, but obviously important, bearing on the equilibrium of a body politic.

Two classes of data will be considered: survey literature giving some indication of how adults respond to political leaders, and results of a study of 659 New Haven public and private school children of widely varying socio-economic status, ranging from fourth- through eighth-graders (about nine to thirteen years of age). Paper-and-pencil questionnaires were administered to this sample between January and March of 1958. Findings from these sources are supplemented by a smaller collection of prolonged interviews with individual children and many informal encounters with groups of school children and teachers over a period of about two years.[2]

I. ADULT ORIENTATIONS TO POLITICAL
LEADERS: AMBIVALENCE

Adult orientations to political leaders display a curious inconsistency, which must be noted to give meaning to my New Haven pre-adult findings. To begin with, political roles, such as Senator, Mayor, Governor, and Judge, are in general highly esteemed by adults in the United States. Over the years, the many studies of occupational prestige have shown that people rank these roles well above all but an occasional civilian role (such as physician) in terms of impor-

---

process as a determinant of adult behavior does not, of course, carry the implication that "only . . . childhood events determine adult behavior." *Cf.* Nathan Leites, "Psycho-Cultural Hypotheses about Political Acts," *World Politics,* Vol. 1 (1948), pp. 102–19.

[2] For a full report of the larger study from which these findings are drawn, along with a more detailed discussion of its methodology, see Fred I. Greenstein, *Children's Political Perspectives: A Study of the Development of Political Awareness and Preferences among Pre-adolescents,* unpublished doctoral dissertation, Yale University Library. The major methodological point which should be noted here is that the respondents consist of the populations of three public and one private school, rather than a probability sample of New Haven children. As a rough means of compensating for this difficulty, socio-economic status was controlled in the data analysis. However, since SES differences are not relevant to the present discussion, data for all respondents are presented combined.

When data are reported by age, systematic variations between the younger and older age groups are treated as evidence of developmental changes. It is always possible, however, in a cross-sectional study that some other variable is reponsible for apparent age differences. Therefore, further validation of statements about development by longitudinal procedures is desirable. For a discussion of the relative merits of cross-sectional and longitudinal research, see the articles by John B. Anderson and Margaret Mead in Leonard Carmichael, *Manual of Child Psychology* (New York 1954).

I am deeply indebted to Robert E. Lane for his thoughtful criticism at every stage of this project. Earlier drafts of this paper profited from comments by James David Barber, Harold D. Lasswell, Richard D. Schwartz, and Jerome H. Skolnick.

tance and status. On the other hand, responses are much more variable when people are asked to rate individual public officials. The best barometer of this variation is probably the American Institute of Public Opinion's monthly estimates of presidential popularity. For over two decades, national cross-sections have been asked questions such as the following:

> Do you approve or disapprove of the way President X has been handling his job?

During his first term in office, favorable responses to President Truman ranged from 87 percent to 32 percent. Roosevelt and Eisenhower also fluctuated in popularity, although not as sharply.

Perhaps as a function of this blend of respect for high political roles and more qualified opinions toward the men who fill these positions, the mere fact of incumbency seems to have a positive effect on a leader's popularity. Thus it has been found that shortly after a president is elected people who were hitherto opposed to him upgrade their evaluations. This probably is a specific case of what has more generally been called the *fait accompli* effect. For example, support for a law increases after it has been passed and, conversely, people are less likely to back policy proposals if they are told that it will be necessary to change a law, or amend the constitution, to achieve this goal.

But this is not the whole story. As is well known, distinctly anti-"politician" and anti-"politics" views are widespread in the population. The survey literature abounds with evidence that substantial groups of people agree that "It is almost impossible for a man to stay honest if he goes into politics," that it is at best dubious for a young man to make politics his career, and so forth. Unsympathetic images of politics and the politician also are revealed by a great many adults in responses to various questions about the individual's political efficacy, as measured for example by willingness to agree with the statement "I don't think public officials care much what people like me think." [7]

The seeming inconsistency between this set of attitudes and responses to individual political leaders and roles has led one recent commentator to write of "the ambivalent social status of the American politician." [8]

II. CHILDREN'S ORIENTATIONS TO POLITICAL
LEADERS: UNQUALIFIED SYMPATHY

Possibly the most striking outcome of the New Haven study was the finding that the prevailing adult skepticism and distrust of politics and the politician simply did not seem to be present in the grade school sample. In spite of a variety of attempts to evoke such responses during my preliminary interviewing and pretesting, there was no evidence even of a frame of reference which

[7] Angus Campbell et al., *The Voter Decides* (Evanston, 1954), pp. 187–94.
[8] William C. Mitchell, in the *Western Political Quarterly*, Vol. 12 (1959), pp. 683–98.

would make it possible to use questionnaire items tapping the dimension of political cynicism. Moreover, although the final New Haven questionnaires contained a number of items which might have evoked spontaneous references to the malignancy of politicians, only one or two of the 659 children made statements which could be construed in this way.

Let us now note some more specific findings.

1. Children are like adults in their ranking of high political roles. Members of the New Haven sample were asked to tell which of a number of adult roles are "most important." Choices offered included the President and Mayor, authority figures of the immediate environment such as school principals and teachers, as well as physicians, clergymen, police chiefs, and judges. At every age level, there were more references to the President and Mayor than to any of the other roles.

●　●　●

The younger New Haven children were almost devoid of political knowledge. All but a handful of them knew the names of the President and Mayor, but few knew much more than this. Within the brief age span of this sample, the level of political information increases considerably. But the structure of cognitive information is erected on a foundation of feelings, assessments, and opinions; and the development of critical faculties waits on a later stage. Estimates of the importance of political leaders, incidentally, follow the same developmental course as another adult orientation—party identification. New Haven children described themselves as Republicans or Democrats long before they were able to make any meaningful statements about the parties, or even to link the party labels with the names of conspicuous leaders such as the President and Mayor.[10]

2. Another point at which the New Haven children's orientations can be compared, at least tentatively, with adult responses, is in their ratings of individual political leaders. Following the various information items which called, for example, for descriptions of the duties of the Mayor, Governor, and President, the children were asked to evaluate these leaders on a four-point scale ranging from "very good" to "bad."

●　●　●

Here children's responses did not merely reflect what might be expected from comparable adult samples. Their modal assessment of each of the three incumbents was in the highest possible category—"very good." Judging from the way national cross-sections of adults responded to the opportunity to rate President Eisenhower during the (shortly post-sputnik) months of this survey,

[10] Moreover, they expressed the party identification which was "appropriate" for their demographic group. The children's reports of familial party preferences support the familiar thesis that membership in American political parties is "inherited." . . .

children's views of political leaders are substantially more favorable than those of their elders. [Greenstein contrasts] the New Haven responses with the American Institute of Public Opinion's February 1958 report of the President's popularity. Needless to say, this juxtaposition of New Haven findings with national survey data must be treated as suggestive, rather than conclusive. However, differences between these groups in evaluation of the President are considerable. Adults seemed to be about five times more willing to criticize the chief executive.

● ● ●

New Haven responses to items dealing with political efficacy also suggest that children are far more positive in their political orientations than adults. Less than two percent of the children said that they would not vote when they reached twenty-one. And over two-thirds agreed that "it makes much difference who wins an election," in contrast to the markedly smaller proportions of adult samples making such statements.

3. I have already noted that various items in the New Haven questionnaire might have stimulated spontaneous references to graft, corruption, political immorality, and so forth, if these images were important in children's perception of politics, and that such references were not made. However, a totally different set of orientations did emerge spontaneously in response to several of the open-ended items.

These were the six items asking for descriptions of the duties of local, state, and federal executives and legislative bodies. The items were quite unstructured, simply asking, "What sorts of things does the Mayor (etc.) do?" As might be expected, most of the children who were able to respond made rather straightforward factual assertions—"The Mayor runs the city"; "Congress makes laws"; etc. What was surprising, however, was that a conspicuous minority of the children volunteered affective or affectively-toned responses —especially in descriptions of the Mayor and President. As noted above, only one or two of these statements were unsympathetic. Several classes of response are worth examining in more detail.

A. *Services to children.* About ten percent of the respondents eschewed reference to more widely recognized duties of the mayor and mentioned child-related portions of his role. For example:

> [The Mayor] makes parks and swings. (Fifth grade girl)
> [The Mayor] repairs the parks, roads, schools, and takes the snow off the roads when it snows. (Fifth grade boy)

It is a reasonable assumption that when a child's first image of a political leader is in terms of pork-barrel indulgences to the child, his image is a favorable one.

B. *General benevolence.* More generally, children tended to describe political leaders as "helping," "taking care of," and "protecting" people. Benevolent perceptions of this sort were especially evident in descriptions of the President and Mayor, but also occasionally were apparent in descriptions of the Governor and of legislative bodies. For example:

> [The President] deals with foreign countries and takes care of the U.S. (Eighth grade boy)
> [The Mayor] helps people to live in safety. . . . The President is doing a very good job of making people be safe. (Fourth grade girl)
> [The President] gives us freedom. (Eighth grade girl)
> [The Board of Aldermen] gives us needs so we could live well. (Fourth grade girl)
> In a few cases children went so far as to perceive political authority as a direct source of economic support:
> [The Mayor] pays working people like banks. (Fifth grade boy)
> [The Mayor] sees that schools have what they need and stores and other places too. (Fifth grade girl)
> [The Mayor] helps everyone to have nice homes and jobs. (Fourth grade boy)

C. *Normative role.* In addition, some children characterized political leaders in positive normative terms—either as people who "do good things," or as people who are specialists in making moral judgments:

> [The President does] good work. (Sixth grade boy)
> [The Mayor] sends men to build parks for us and make our city be a good one. (Fourth grade girl)
> [The President] makes peace with every country but bad. (Fifth grade boy)
> [The Mayor] talks business to all the people and says what's wrong or bad. (Fourth grade girl)
> I think that he [the President] has the right to stop bad things before they start. (Fifth grade girl)

The frequency of "child-related" references to the Mayor, and of generally "benevolent" and "normative" references to the Mayor and President [was calculated]. Here we see that statements of this sort were made by some children at every age level, but that benevolent imagery declines with age. What is remarkable is that any images of this sort are expressed in answer to such bland, unstructured stimulus questions. Moreover, there were additional descriptions of political leaders with favorable connotations which do not fit as readily into a few simple categories. For example, some children placed emphasis on the wisdom, capability, and solicitousness of public officials:

> [The President] is in charge of the United States and has many wise men to tell him what is best. (Sixth grade boy)
> [The President] worries about all the problems of all the 48 states.

Takes care of threatening wars by holding peace conferences. (Seventh grade boy)

[The Mayor] has to keep track of everything that happens in New Haven. (Sixth grade boy)

The spontaneous appearance of these images suggests that appropriately structured questions would show the imagery of benevolence to be considerably more common among grade school children than [the data] indicates.

● ● ●

The New Haven findings may be summarized as follows: children are at least as likely as adults to perceive high political roles as being important; they seem to be more sympathetic to individual political leaders (and, in general, to politics) than are adults; in at least some cases their actual images of political leaders are qualitatively different from the images one would expect adults to hold, especially in the emphasis on benignancy; and, most important, the widespread adult political cynicism and distrust does not seem to have developed by eighth grade (age 13). Each of these observations rests on a limited sample of respondents, and several are based on fortuitous findings, or comparisons which can only be made tentatively. They are internally consistent and seem to be convincing, but further verification (using more varied and refined techniques) clearly is necessary. However, in this discussion which follows I shall for the moment assume their validity and consider their potential significance.

III. THE CHILD'S VIEW OF POLITICAL AUTHORITY: ITS SIGNIFICANCE

Two questions are raised by the foregoing data: (1) Why is the child's early view of political authority so strikingly favorable? (2) What, if any, effect does this aspect of an individual's development have on his adult political behavior?

Fully convincing answers to these questions, particularly the second, are not available. This is so not only because the New Haven data are limited, but also because the existing body of generalizations linking childhood experience to adult behavior is quite rudimentary. Speculative answers, however, are a necessary first step to designing research which will extend our understanding of the dynamics of citizens' orientations toward political leaders.

1. Although many lasting political orientations are acquired before adolescence—for instance, attitudes about the importance of major governmental roles and identifications with parties—early political learning seems to be quite casual. Young children, including the nine- and ten-year-olds who make up the youngest groups in this sample, have few interests beyond the environment of their immediate circle. And in New Haven there seemed to be little

formal adult effort to shape the political information and attitudes of grade school children. Social studies curriculum guides, for example, do not suggest teaching until the sixth grade the subject matter which once was known as civics. Only in eighth grade is there mandatory provision for such training.

Nevertheless, political learning progresses during the preadolescent years. This learning has many sources. The most important of them—at least as a determinant of attitudes—undoubtedly is the family. Here (though I have no data based on direct observation) much of the learning probably is inadvertent and incidental to normal family activities. Similarly, inadvertent learning surely takes place in the schools, even in the absence of formal requirements for civic instruction, if only through politically related experiences such as patriotic observances. Among other sources of political learning, the mass media seem to be extremely important, especially during election campaigns.

One antecedent of the highly idealized childhood political images may be whatever political communications are intentionally transmitted to children by their agents of socialization. Even parents and teachers who are personally vehement in their castigation of "politicians" may soften or sugar-coat the political explanations they pass on to children. However, it is likely that the socializing agents pass on something considerably more important than specific political attitudes—namely, general orientations toward the adult world. The child, through the entirety of his experiences with adults, acquires a frame of reference within which to place an especially important class of adult—the political leaders. This seems to be the best way to explain the remarkable lack of political cynicism among children. Children certainly cannot be completely insulated from adult attitudes of distrust toward politics. Rather, it may be hypothesized that, having learned to see adults as many times life size, children simply misperceive and otherwise screen out the discordant negative elements in the adult political environment.

Psychoanalytic theory suggests an integral connection between the feelings one develops toward figures in the primary environment (such as parents) and one's later responses to individuals in the secondary environment (such as politicians). The latter relationships become invested with deep personal feelings, sometimes in the form of direct reflections of primary group relationships, sometimes in the form of compensating reactions to them. This notion is now quite familiar and in fact has been thoroughly vulgarized in the form of popular journalistic references to political "father figures." Vulgarizations notwithstanding, it may have considerable empirical substance. At any rate, a degree of clinical evidence supporting the hypothesis has accumulated. That young children's descriptions of political leaders reflect imagery of benevolence, protectiveness, exceptional sagacity, etc., also is consistent with this hypothesis, although this is scarcely "proof" that an unconscious linking of primary and secondary figures has taken place.

As we have seen, the child's glowing political imagery shows signs of attrition (mainly in the use of "benevolent" language), during the five-year span of this sample. But the greatest change away from political euphoria probably is during adolescence. Disillusionment, following increased realistic political understanding, might produce such changes. Another likely cause would be the adolescent's need to assume adult mannerisms, including in some cases an inside dopester's appraisal of politics. Adolescence is, at any rate, a time for felling idols and perceiving the commanding figures of one's adult environment in a more fallible light.

2. How does knowledge that the political learning sequence is from childhood idealism to adult realism and cynicism add to our understanding of citizens' responses to political authority? To answer this some further remarks on adult orientations to political leaders are necessary.

The cynical imagery of Americans seems to be less functionally relevant to their political behavior than the positive side of their responses—their respect for high political leaders and their frequent willingness to hold individual leaders in great esteem. This is evident not merely from such relatively narrow mechanisms as the *fait accompli* effect and the general willingness to accept the verdict of elections. The oft-proclaimed stability of the American political system—in spite of a remarkably heterogeneous population—suggests more broadly that powerful psychological mechanisms encouraging political obedience are present in the citizenry. These mechanisms may be as important as many of the more familiar historical, political, economic, and social factors which are drawn on to explain the complex phenomenon of political stability.

Psychologists of various schools, ranging from psychoanalysis to learning theory, have argued that "learning which takes place early in life should have especially great influence on lasting personality characteristics." [22] It also may be that political and social orientations which are acquired early will be particularly influential in adult behavior. As we have seen, the more negative attitudes toward political leaders are chronologically late arrivals, whereas the firm impression that leaders are important people emerges early and almost unconsciously—years before the child has more than a smattering of factual political information. Thus when the adult is in conflict between his two inconsistent assessments of political leaders, the longest held of these would be most likely to influence his response. In this respect it is worth noting that party identification, which also is acquired before the age of political reasoning, is a more important determinant of adult electoral choice than other motivating variables.

The uniquely positive conceptions and misconceptions of leaders displayed by New Haven respondents, statements such as "The Mayor pays working people like banks," certainly are not important in the conscious political imagery of adults. But even here the fact that they once existed may be of some

[22] Irvin L. Child, "Socialization," in Gardner Lindzey, *Handbook of Social Psychology* (Cambridge, 1954), p. 678.

importance in understanding adult political behavior. If the psychoanalytic hypotheses linking political imagery to the primary group relationships which are vital in molding the personality are valid, it could follow that some early political images exercise an unconscious effect on adult choices. To the degree that responses to political authority are deeply rooted in the personality additional predictions might be made. For example, clinical experience suggests that in times of personal or community crisis individuals might tend to resume their earlier ways of viewing authority.

IV. RESEARCH PROSPECTS

So far I have attempted to relate two aspects of the way orientations toward political leaders develop, to the likelihood that these orientations will be influential in adult life. I have suggested that if the orientation is learned early, or if it becomes tied to intimate primary group experiences, it should have an especially strong effect on later behavior. To this a single more specific hypothesis about the possibility of regression has been added. Further theorizing and research is necessary to generate more in the way of specific, testable hypotheses. At present the general theories of development which have been spun out by Freud, Piaget, Sullivan, and Erikson, for example, have received only limited empirical verification and are poorly correlated with the empirical norms of development reported by child psychologists and the little which is known about the genesis of political and social orientations.

Theory building and hypothesis elaboration might best proceed in the context of concrete research, since little is known in detail at present about how political behavior develops. The following are some of the *desiderata* of such research:

A. We need to know more about children's political images. The data presented in this paper are no more than a first approximation of how children perceive political authority. Do they differentiate between a wider range of political roles than those presented in the New Haven questionnaire? How do their responses vary over time and space? How prevalent are responses of the sort which arose spontaneously in the present study—imagery of benevolence, for example? New instruments will have to be developed to explore these responses in further detail.

B. We need information on the types of independent variables which are related to differences in childhood political response. Do images of political leaders vary with the child's personality type? Do they vary with his family structure? In view of the continuing interest of social scientists in a number of disciplines in relationships between personality, culture, and social organization, there should be increasing possibilities for interdisciplinary collaboration.

Broader sampling of demographic groups will furnish insight into additional independent variables. Here the speculations about the political stability of nations earlier in this paper suggest that cross-cultural investigation may be promising. Recent studies of children's responses to (non-political) authority figures by Gladys and Harold Anderson show substantial national differences in such perspectives as the expectation of punishment for a misdemeanor.[26]

C. Most important (and most difficult), we need ways of determining in some more precise manner than has been possible here what effects early orientations have on later political behavior. Here progress will be slowest, but by the same token validated propositions will be most rewarding. To a considerable extent advances will be dependent upon accomplishments in basic socialization research. This is an area of investigation in which experiments are not normally possible and knowledge accumulates somewhat uncertainly on the basis of correlational studies. Again, collaboration with ongoing research in other disciplines is both desirable and possible. For example, there have been many longitudinal projects which followed the same samples of children over varying periods of time. Other procedures short of the longitudinal study also exist for studying socialization.

As inevitably slow as the early stages of such research may be, the long run possibilities are exciting. For, as John Dollard has commented, if "the life of the individual is a single connected whole," it will be necessary, in order to enrich our understanding of adult political existence, "to peer down the long avenue of the individual life to see how the present-day event matured." [29]

CONSENSUS AND IDEOLOGY IN AMERICAN POLITICS*

HERBERT McCLOSKY

The belief that consensus is a prerequisite of democracy has, since deTocqueville, so often been taken for granted that it is refreshing to find the notion

[26] A bibliography of portions of this study which have been published is contained in Harold H. Anderson et al., "Image of the Teacher by Adolescent Children in Four Countries: Germany, England, Mexico, United States," Journal of Social Psychology, Vol. 50 (1959), pp. 47–55. The Andersons have kindly made available to me unpublished portions of their data.

[29] Criteria for the Life History (New Haven, 1935), p. 27.

* This is a revised version of a paper initially prepared for delivery at the Annual Meeting of the American Political Science Association, Washington D. C., September 1962.

SOURCE: Herbert McClosky, "Consensus and Ideology in American Politics," The American Political Science Review, 58 (June 1964), 361–382. Reprinted by permission.

now being challenged. Prothro and Grigg,[1] for example, have questioned whether agreement on "fundamentals" actually exists among the electorate, and have furnished data which indicate that it may not. Dahl,[2] reviewing his study of community decision-makers, has inferred that political stability does not depend upon widespread belief in the superiority of democratic norms and procedures, but only upon their *acceptance*. From the findings turned up by Stouffer,[3] and by Prothro and Grigg, he further conjectures that agreement on democratic norms is greater among the politically active and aware—the "political stratum" as he calls them—than among the voters in general. V. O. Key,[4] going a step further, suggests that the viability of a democracy may depend less upon popular opinion than upon the activities and values of an "aristocratic" strain whose members are set off from the mass by their political influence, their attention to public affairs, and their active role as society's policy makers. "If so, any assessment of the vitality of a democratic system should rest on an examination of the outlook, the sense of purpose, and the beliefs of this sector of society."

Writers who hold consensus to be necessary to a free society have commonly failed to define it precisely or to specify what it must include. Even Tocqueville[5] does not go deeply enough into the matter to satisfy these needs. He tells us that a society can exist and, *a fortiori*, prosper only when "the minds of all the citizens [are] rallied and held together by certain predominant ideas; . . . when a great number of men consider a great number of things from the same aspect, when they hold the same opinions upon many subjects, and when the same occurrences suggest the same thoughts and impressions to their minds"—and he follows this pronouncement with a list of general principles he believes Americans hold in common. Elsewhere, he speaks of the "customs" of the American nation (its "habits, opinions, usages, and beliefs") as "the peculiar cause which renders that people able to support a democratic government." But nowhere does he set forth explicitly the na-

---

[1] James W. Prothro and C. W. Grigg, "Fundamental Principles of Democracy: Bases of Agreement and Disagreement," *Journal of Politics*, Vol. 22 (Spring, 1960), pp. 276–94.

[2] Robert A. Dahl, *Who Governs?* (New Haven, 1961), ch. 28.

[3] Samuel A. Stouffer, *Communism, Conformity, and Civil Liberties* (New York, 1955).

[4] V. O. Key, "Public Opinion and the Decay of Democracy," *Virginia Q. Rev.*, Vol. 37 (Autumn, 1961), pp. 481–94. See also David B. Truman, "The American System in Crisis," *Political Science Quarterly*, Vol. 74 (Dec., 1959), pp. 481–97. John Plamenatz, "Cultural Prerequisites to a Successfully Functioning Democracy: a Symposium," this *Review*, Vol. 50 (March, 1956), p. 123.

[5] Alexis deTocqueville, *Democracy in America* (ed. Phillips Bradley, New York, 1945), II, p. 8; I, pp. 392, 322. The difficulty of specifying the values which underlie democracy, and on which consensus is presumed to be required, is illustrated in the exchange between Ernest S. Griffith, John Plamenatz, and J. Roland Pennock, cited above, pp. 101–37. The problem of certifying the "fundamentals" of democratic consensus is directly discussed by Pennock, pp. 132–3. See also Peter Bachrach, "Elite Consensus and Democracy," *Journal of Politics*, Vol. 24 (August, 1962), pp. 449–52.

ture of the agreement upon which a democratic society presumably depends.

Later commentators have not clarified matters much. Some, like A. Lawrence Lowell,[6] have avoided Tocqueville's emphasis upon shared ideas, customs, and opinions in favor of the less demanding view that popular government requires agreement mainly "in regard to the legitimate character of the ruling authority and its right to decide the questions that arise." Consensus, in this view, becomes merely a synonym for legitimacy. Others speak of consensus as a sense of solidarity or social cohesion arising from a common ethos or heritage, which unites men into a community.[7] Political scientists have most frequently employed the term to designate a state of agreement about the "fundamental values" or "rules of the game" considered essential for constitutional government. Rarely, however, have writers on consensus attempted to state what the fundamentals must include, how extensive the agreement must be, and *who* must agree. Is agreement required among all men or only among certain of them? Among the entire electorate or only those who actively participate in public affairs? Is the same type of consensus essential for all democracies at all times, or is a firmer and more sweeping consensus needed for periods of crisis than for periods of calm, for newer, developing democracies than for older stable ones?

While certain of these questions are beyond the scope of this paper (no one, in any event, has done the systematic historical and comparative research needed to answer them satisfactorily), something might be learned about the relation of ideological consensus to democracy by investigating the subject in at least one major democracy, the United States. In the present paper I wish to explore further some of the questions raised by the writers I have cited and to present research findings on several hypotheses relating to those questions.

I. HYPOTHESES AND DEFINITIONS

We expected the data to furnish support for the following hypotheses, among others:

> That the American electorate is often divided on "fundamental" democratic values and procedural "rules of the game" and that its understanding of politics and of political ideas is in any event too rudimentary at present to speak of ideological "consensus" among its members.

[6] A. L. Lowell, *Public Opinion and Popular Government* (New York, 1926), p. 9.

[7] *Cf.*, for example, Louis Wirth, *Community Life and Social Policy* (Chicago, 1956), pp. 201–3, 381–2. For a critique of "consensus theory" and the several definitions of consensus see Irving L. Horowitz, "Consensus, Conflict, and Cooperation: a Sociological Inventory," *Social Forces*, Vol. 41 (Dec., 1962), pp. 177–188.

That, as Prothro and Grigg report for their samples, the electorate exhibits greater support for general, abstract statements of democratic belief than for their specific applications.

That the constituent ideas of American democratic ideology are principally held by the more "articulate" segments of the population, including the political influentials; and that people in these ranks will exhibit a more meaningful and far reaching consensus on democratic and constitutional values than will the general population.

That consensus is far from perfect even among the articulate classes, and will be evidenced on political questions more than on economic ones, on procedural rights more than on public policies, and on freedom more than equality.

That whatever increases the level of political articulateness—education, S.E.S., urban residence, intellectuality, political activity, etc.—strengthens consensus and support for American political ideology and institutions.

Whether a word like ideology can properly be employed in the American context depends, in part, on which of its many connotations one chooses to emphasize. Agreement on the meaning of the term is far from universal, but a tendency can be discerned among contemporary writers to regard ideologies as *systems* of belief that are elaborate, integrated, and coherent, that justify the exercise of power, explain and judge historical events, identify political right and wrong, set forth the interconnections (causal and moral) between politics and other spheres of activity, and furnish guides for action.[8] While liberal democracy does not fulfill perfectly the terms of this definition, it comes close enough, in my opinion, to be considered an ideology.[9] The elements of liberal democratic thought are not nearly so vague as they are sometimes made out to be, and their coalescence into a single body of belief is by no means fortuitous. American democratic "ideology" possesses an elaborately defined theory, a body of interrelated assumptions, axioms, and principles, and a set of ideals that serve as guides for action. Its tenets, postulates, sentiments, and values inspired the great revolutions of the seventeenth and eighteenth centuries, and have been repeatedly and explicitly set forth in funda-

[8] Cf. Daniel Bell, The End of Ideology (Glencoe, 1960), pp. 369–75; Edward Shils, "Ideology and Civility: on the Politics of the Intellectual," Sewanee Review, Vol. 66 (Summer, 1958), pp. 450–1; Louis Wirth, op. cit., pp. 202–3.

[9] A persuasive case for considering liberal democracy as an ideology is made by Bernard Williams, "Democracy and Ideology," Political Science Quarterly, Vol. 32 (October–December, 1961), pp. 374–84. The nature of ideology in America and some of the other questions addressed in the present paper are discussed by Robert G. McCloskey, "The American Ideology," in Marian D. Irish (ed.), Continuing Crisis in American Politics (Englewood Cliffs, N. J., 1963), pp. 10–25.

mental documents, such as the Constitution, the Declaration, and the Federalist Papers. They have been restated with remarkable unanimity in the messages of Presidents, in political speeches, in the pronouncements of judges and constitutional commentators, and in the writings of political theorists, historians, and publicists. They are so familiar that we are likely to see them not as a coherent union of ideas and principles embodying a well-defined political tendency, but as a miscellany of slogans and noble sentiments to be trotted out on ceremonial occasions.

Although scholars or Supreme Court justices might argue over fine points of interpretation, they would uniformly recognize as elements of American democratic ideology such concepts as consent, accountability, limited or constitutional government, representation, majority rule, minority rights, the principle of political opposition, freedom of thought, speech, press, and assembly, equality of opportunity, religious toleration, equality before the law, the rights of juridical defense, and individual self-determination over a broad range of personal affairs. How widely such elements of American liberal democracy are approved, by whom and with what measure of understanding, is another question—indeed, it is the central question to be addressed in this paper. But that they form an integrated body of ideas which has become part of the American inheritance seems scarcely open to debate.[10]

The term consensus will be employed in this paper to designate a state of agreement concerning the aforementioned values. It has principally to do with shared beliefs and not with feelings of solidarity, the willingness to live together, to obey the laws, or to accept the existing government as legitimate. Nor does it refer to an abstract or universal state of mind, but to a measurable state of concurrence around values that can be specified. Consensus exists in degree and can be expressed in quantitative form. No one, of course, can say how close one must come to unanimity before consensus is achieved, for the cutting point, as with any continuous variable, is arbitrary. Still, the term in ordinary usage has been reserved for fairly substantial measures of correspondence, and we shall take as a minimal requirement for consensus a level of agreement reaching 75 per cent. This figure, while also arbitrary, recommends itself by being realistically modest (falling as it does midway between a bare majority and unanimity), and by having been designated in this country and elsewhere as the extraordinary majority required for certain constitutional purposes.

Since I shall in subsequent pages frequently (and interchangeably) employ

---

[10] See Gunnar Myrdal, *An American Dilemma: The Negro Problem and American Democracy* (New York, 1944), ch. 1. For a comprehensive review of the American value system and evidence concerning its stability over time, see Clyde Kluckhohn, "Have There Been Discernible Shifts in American Values during the Past Generation?" in E. E. Morison (ed.), *The American Style: Essays in Value and Performance* (New York, 1958), pp. 145–217. Kluckhohn concludes (p. 152) that despite some changes, the American value system has been "remarkably stable" since the 18th century and remains "highly influential in the life of the United States."

TABLE I.

Political Influentials vs. the Electorate: Response to Items
Expressing "Rules of the Game." *

Items	Political Influentials (N = 3020)	General Electorate (N = 1484)
	% Agree	
There are times when it almost seems better for the people to take the law into their own hands rather than wait for the machinery of government to act.	13.3	26.9
The majority has the right to abolish minorities if it wants to.	6.8	28.4
We might as well make up our minds that in order to make the world better a lot of innocent people will have to suffer.	27.2	41.6
If congressional committees stuck strictly to the rules and gave every witness his rights, they would never succeed in exposing the many dangerous subversives they have turned up.	24.7	47.4
I don't mind a politician's methods if he manages to get the right things done.	25.6	42.4
Almost any unfairness or brutality may have to be justified when some great purpose is being carried out.	13.3	32.8
Politicians have to cut a few corners if they are going to get anywhere.	29.4	43.2
People ought to be allowed to vote even if they can't do so intelligently.	65.6	47.6
To bring about great changes for the benefit of mankind often requires cruelty and even ruthlessness.	19.4	31.3
Very few politicians have clean records, so why get excited about the mudslinging that sometimes goes on?	14.8	38.1
It is all right to get around the law if you don't actually break it.	21.2	30.2
The true American way of life is disappearing so fast that we may have to use force to save it.	12.8	34.6

* Since respondents were forced to make a choice on each item, the number of omitted or "don't know" responses was, on the average, fewer than one percent, and thus has little influence on the direction or magnitude of the results reported in this and subsequent tables.

such terms as the "articulate minority," the "political class," the "political elite," the "political influentials," and the "political stratum," I should also clarify what they are intended to signify. I mean them to refer to those people who occupy themselves with public affairs to an unusual degree, such as government officials, elected office holders, active party members, publicists, officers of voluntary associations, and opinion leaders. The terms do not apply to any definable social class in the usual sense, nor to a particular status group or profession. Although the people they designate can be distinguished from other citizens by their activity and concerns, they are in no sense a community, they do not act as a body, and they do not necessarily possess identical or even harmonious interests. "Articulates" or "influentials" can be found scattered throughout the society, at all income levels, in all classes, occupations, ethnic groups, and communities, although some segments of the population will doubtless yield a higher proportion of them than others. I scarcely need to add that the line between the "articulates" and the rest of the population cannot always be sharply drawn, for the qualities that distinguish them vary in form and degree and no single criterion of classification will satisfy every contingency.

The data for the present inquiry have been taken from a national study of political actives and supporters carried out in 1957–58. I have in a previous paper described the procedures of that study in some detail,[11] and will not trouble to repeat that description here. Perhaps it will suffice for present purposes merely to note the following: national surveys were carried out on two separate samples, the first a sample of over 3,000 political "actives" or "leaders" drawn from the delegates and alternates who had attended the Democratic and Republican conventions of 1956; the second a representative national sample of approximately 1,500 adults in the general population drawn by the American Institute of Public Opinion (Gallup Poll). Gallup interviewers also delivered and introduced the questionnaire to all respondents, discussed its contents with them, and furnished both oral and written instructions for its self-administration and completion.

The party actives may be considered an especially pure sample of the "political stratum," for every person in the sample has marked himself off from the average citizen by his greater political involvement. Although the general population sample may be regarded as a sample of "inarticulates," to be compared with the sample of leaders, there are within it, of course, many persons who by virtue of education, profession, organizational activities, etc. can be classified as "articulates." We shall for certain purposes consider them in this light in order to provide further tests for our hypotheses.

Both samples received the same questionnaire—a lengthy instrument containing questions on personal background, political experience, values, atti-

---

[11] Herbert McClosky, Paul J. Hoffmann, and Rosemary O'Hara, "Issue Conflict and Consensus Among Party Leaders and Followers," this *Review*, Vol. 44 (June, 1960), pp. 406–27.

TABLE II.

*Political Influentials vs. the Electorate: Responses to Items Expressing Support
for General Statements of Free Speech and Opinion*

Items	Political Influentials (N = 3020) % Agree	General Electorate (N = 1484) % Agree
People who hate our way of life should still have a chance to talk and be heard.	86.9	81.8
No matter what a person's political beliefs are, he is entitled to the same legal rights and protections as anyone else.	96.4	94.3
I believe in free speech for all no matter what their views might be.	89.4	88.9
Nobody has a right to tell another person what he should and should not read.	81.4	80.7
You can't really be sure whether an opinion is true or not unless people are free to argue against it.	94.9	90.8
Unless there is freedom for many points of view to be presented, there is little chance that the truth can ever be known.	90.6	85.2
I would not trust any person or group to decide what opinions can be freely expressed and what must be silenced.	79.1	64.6
Freedom of conscience should mean freedom to be an atheist as well as freedom to worship in the church of one's choice.	87.8	77.0

tudes, opinions, political and economic orientation, party outlooks, and personality characteristics. Many of the questions were direct inquiries in the standard form, but most were single sentence "items" with which the respondent was compelled to express his agreement or disagreement. While each of these items can stand alone and be regarded in its own right as an indicator of a person's opinions or attitudes, each of them is simultaneously an integral element of one of the 47 "scales" that was expressly fashioned to afford a more refined and reliable assessment of the attitude and personality predispositions of every respondent. Each of the scales (averaging approximately nine items) has been independently validated either by empirical validation procedures employing appropriate criterion groups, or by a modified Guttman reproducibility procedure (supplemented, in some instances, by a "face validity" procedure utilizing item ratings by experts).

Data on the *scale* scores are presented in Table IV and are to be distinguished from the "percentage agree" scores for *individual items* presented in the remaining tables.

II. FINDINGS

"Rules of the game" and democratic values. Although the so-called "rules of the game" are often separated from other democratic values, the distinction is to some extent arbitrary. One might, for example, reasonably regard as "rules of the game" many of the norms governing free speech, press, social and political equality, political toleration, and the enforcement of justice. For convenience, nevertheless, we shall treat separately those responses that stand out from the general body of democratic attitudes by their particular emphasis upon fair play, respect for legal procedures, and consideration for the rights of others. A sample of items expressing these values is presented in Table I.

The responses to these items show plainly that while a majority of the electorate support the "rules of the game," approval of such values is significantly greater and more uniform among the influentials. The latter have achieved consensus (as we have defined it) on eight of the twelve items and near consensus on three of the remaining four items. The electorate, by contrast, does not meet the criterion for consensus on a single item.

Although the *scales* (as distinguished from individual *items*) cannot appropriately be used to measure *consensus*, comparison of the scores on those scales which most nearly embody the "rules of the game" furnishes additional evidence that the political class responds to such norms more favorably than does the electorate. The proportion scoring high[12] on a scale of "faith in direct action" (a scale measuring the inclination to take the law into one's own hands) is 26.1 per cent for the active political minority and 42.5 per cent for the general population. On a scale assessing the willingness to flout the rules of political integrity, the proportions scoring high are 12.2 per cent and 30.6 per cent respectively. On "totalitarianism," a scale measuring the readiness to subordinate the rights of others to the pursuit of some collective political purpose, only 9.7 per cent of the political actives score high compared with 33.8 per cent of the general population.

These and other results which could be cited support the claim advanced by earlier investigators like Prothro and Grigg, and Hyman and Sheatsley,[13] that a large proportion of the electorate has failed to grasp certain of the underlying ideas and principles on which the American political system rests.

---

[12] "High" refers to a score made by the upper third of the popular distribution on the scale in question. For example, in the case of the "political indulgence" scale approximately one-third (actually 30.6%) received scores of five or above. Hence, anyone making a score of five or above on this scale is considered to have scored high on "political indulgence." "Low" refers to scores made by the lower third of the distribution.

[13] Prothro and Grigg, *loc. cit.*; Herbert Hyman and Paul B. Sheatsley, "The Current Status of American Public Opinion," in Daniel Katz *et al.* (eds.), *Public Opinion and Propaganda* (New York, 1954), pp. 33–48.

TABLE III.

Political Influentials vs. the Electorate: Response to Items Expressing Support for Specific Applications of Free Speech and Procedure Rights

Items	Political Influentials (N = 3020)	General Electorate (N = 1484)
	% Agree	
Freedom does not give anyone the right to teach foreign ideas in our schools.	45.5	56.7
A man oughtn't to be allowed to speak if he doesn't know what he's talking about.	17.3	36.7
A book that contains wrong political views cannot be a good book and does not deserve to be published.	17.9	50.3
When the country is in great danger, we may have to force people to testify against themselves even if it violates their rights.	28.5	36.3
No matter what crime a person is accused of, he should never be convicted unless he has been given the right to face and question his accusers.	90.1	88.1
If a person is convicted of a crime by illegal evidence, he should be set free and the evidence thrown out of court.	79.6	66.1
If someone is suspected of treason or other serious crimes, he shouldn't be entitled to be let out on bail.	33.3	68.9
Any person who hides behind the laws when he is questioned about his activities doesn't deserve much consideration.	55.9	75.7
In dealing with dangerous enemies like the Communists, we can't afford to depend on the courts, the laws and their slow and unreliable methods.	7.4	25.5

Endorsement of these ideas is not unanimous among the political elite either, but is in every instance greater than that exhibited by the masses.

The picture changes somewhat when we turn from "rules of the game" to items which in a broad, general way express belief in freedom of speech and opinion. As can be seen from Table II, support for these values is remarkably high for both samples. Both groups, in fact, respond so overwhelmingly to abstract statements about freedom that one is tempted to conclude that for these values, at least, a far-reaching consensus has been achieved.[14] These re-

---

[14] *Cf.* Robert Lane's report on his "Eastport" sample, in *Political Ideology* (New York, 1962), pp. 461–2.

sults become even more striking when we consider that the items in the table are not mere clichés but statements which in some instances closely paraphrase the arguments developed in Mill's essay, *On Liberty*. We cannot, therefore, dismiss them as mere responses to familiar, abstract sentiments which commit the respondent to nothing in particular.

TABLE IV.

Political Influentials vs. the Electorate: Percentages Scoring High and Low on Democratic and Anti-Democratic Attitude Scales*

Scale	Political Influentials (N = 3020)	General Electorate (N = 1484)	Scale	Political Influentials (N = 3020)	General Electorate (N = 1484)
	(%s down)			(%s down)	
Faith in Democracy			Elitism		
% High*	40.1	18.5	% High	22.8	38.7
% Low	14.4	29.7	% Low	41.0	22.4
Procedural Rights			Totalitarianism		
% High	58.1	24.1	% High	9.7	33.8
% Low	12.3	31.3	% Low	60.1	28.4
Tolerance			Right Wing		
% High	61.3	43.1	% High	17.5	33.1
% Low	16.4	33.2	% Low	45.3	28.9
Faith in Freedom			Left Wing		
% High	63.0	48.4	% High	6.7	27.8
% Low	17.1	28.4	% Low	68.7	39.3
Ethnocentrism			California F-Scale		
% High	27.5	36.5	% High	14.7	33.5
% Low	46.9	36.3	% Low	48.0	23.5

* For explanation of % High and Low see footnote 12. The middle group has been omitted from this table. Differences between the influentials and the electorate on all the scales in this table are, by Kolmogorov-Smirnov and chi-square tests, statistically significant at or beyond the .01 percent level of significance.

Still, as can readily be discerned from the items in Table III, previous investigators have been partially correct, at least, in observing that the principles of freedom and democracy are less widely and enthusiastically favored when they are confronted in their specific, or applied, forms.[15] As Dahl remarks, it is a "common tendency of mankind . . . to qualify universals in ap-

[15] See Hyman and Sheatsley, *op. cit.*, pp. 40–2; Prothro and Grigg, *op. cit.*

TABLE V.

Political Influentials vs. the Electorate: Responses to Items Expressing
Belief in Equality

Items	Political Influentials (N = 3020)	General Electorate (N = 1484)
	% Agree	
Political Equality		
The main trouble with democracy is that most people don't really know what's best for them.	40.8	58.0
Few people really know what is in their own best interest in the long run.	42.6	61.1
"Issues" and "arguments" are beyond the understanding of most voters.	37.5	62.3
Most people don't have enough sense to pick their own leaders wisely.	28.0	47.8
It will always be necessary to have a few strong, able people actually running everything.	42.5	56.2
Social and Ethnic Equality		
We have to teach children that all men are created equal but almost everyone knows that some are better than others.	54.7	58.3
Just as is true of fine race horses, some breeds of people are just naturally better than others.	46.0	46.3
Regardless of what some people say, there are certain races in the world that just won't mix with Americans.	37.2	50.4
When it comes to the things that count most, all races are certainly not equal.	45.3	49.0
The trouble with letting certain minority groups into a nice neighborhood is that they gradually give it their own atmosphere.	49.8	57.7
Economic Equality		
Labor does not get its fair share of what it produces.	20.8	44.8
Every person should have a good house, even if the government has to build it for him.	14.9	28.2
I think the government should give a person work if he can't find another job.	23.5	47.3
The government ought to make sure that everyone has a good standard of living.	34.4	55.9
There will always be poverty, so people might as well get used to the idea.	40.4	59.4

plication while leaving them intact in rhetoric." [16] This observation, of course, also holds for the political articulates, but to a lesser degree. Not only do they exhibit stronger support for democratic values than does the electorate, but they are also more consistent in applying the general principle to the specific instance.[17] The average citizen has greater difficulty appreciating the importance of certain procedural or juridical rights, especially when he believes the country's internal security is at stake.

Findings which underscore and amplify these conclusions are yielded by a comparison of the scale scores. The data presented in Table IV confirm that the influentials not only register higher scores on all the pro-democratic scales (faith in freedom, faith in democracy, procedural rights, tolerance), but are more likely to reject anti-democratic sentiments as well. Although they are themselves an elite of a sort, they display greater faith in the capacity of the mass of men to govern themselves, they believe more firmly in political equality, and they more often disdain the "extreme" beliefs embodied in the Right Wing, Left Wing, totalitarian, elitist, and authoritarian scales. Their repudiation of anti-democratic attitudes is by no means unanimous either, but their responses are more uniformly democratic than are those expressed by the electorate.

Equalitarian values. If Americans concur most strongly about liberty in the abstract, they disagree most strongly about equality. Examples of equalitarian values are presented in Table V. Both the political stratum and the public divide sharply on these values, a finding which holds for political, as well as for social and economic equality. Both are torn not only on the empirical question of whether men are *in fact* equal but also on the normative issue of whether they should be *regarded* as equal. Neither comes close to achieving consensus on such questions as the ability of the people to rule themselves, to know their best interests in the long run, to understand the issues, or to pick their own leaders wisely. Support for these equalitarian features of "popular" democracy, however, is greater among the elite than among the masses.

The reverse is true for the values of economic equality. Among the political stratum, indeed, the weight of opinion is against equality—a result strongly though not exclusively influenced by the pronounced economic conservatism of the Republican leaders in the sample. Support for economic equality is only slightly greater among the electorate. The pattern, furthermore, is extremely spotty, with some policies strongly favored and others as strongly rejected. Thus approval is widespread for public policies (such as social security) that are designed to overcome gross inequalities, but is equally strong for certain features of economic life that promote inequality, such as private en-

---

[16] Robert A. Dahl, *loc. cit.* For data on the failure of some people to perceive the relevance of democratic principles for concrete situations see G. D. Wiebe, "The Army-McCarthy Hearings and the Public Conscience," *Public Opinion Quarterly,* Vol. 22 (Winter 1958–59), pp. 490–502.

[17] See also Stouffer, *op. cit.,* ch. 2.

TABLE VI.

Political Influentials vs. the Electorate: Responses to Items Expressing Cynicism toward Government and Politics

Items	Political Influentials (N = 3020)	General Electorate (N = 1484)
	% Agree	
Most politicians are looking out for themselves above all else.	36.3	54.3
Both major parties in this country are controlled by the wealthy and are run for their benefit.	7.9	32.1
Many politicians are bought off by some private interest.	43.0	65.3
I avoid dealing with public officials as much as I can.	7.8	39.3
Most politicians can be trusted to do what they think is best for the country.	77.1	58.9
I usually have confidence that the government will do what is right.	81.6	89.6
The people who really "run" the country do not even get known to the voters.	40.2	60.5
The laws of this country are supposed to benefit all of us equally, but the fact is that they're almost all "rich-man's laws."	8.4	33.3
No matter what the people think, a few people will always run things anyway.	30.0	53.8
Most politicians don't seem to me to really mean what they say.	24.7	55.1
There is practically no connection between what a politician says and what he will do once he gets elected.	21.4	54.0
A poor man doesn't have the chance he deserves in the law courts.	20.3	42.9
Most political parties care only about winning elections and nothing more.	28.3	46.2
All politics is controlled by political bosses.	15.6	45.9

terprise, economic competition, and unlimited pursuit of profit.[18] On social and ethnic equality, both samples are deeply split.

In short, both the public and its leaders are uncertain and ambivalent about equality. The reason, I suspect, lies partly in the fact that the egalitarian as-

---

[18] These inferences are drawn not only from the few items presented in Table V, but from data previously reported by H. McClosky, P. J. Hoffmann, and R. O'Hara, *op. cit.*, p. 413; and from the responses to dozens of items in the present study that express attitudes and opinions toward

pects of democratic theory have been less adequately thought through than other aspects, and partly in the complications connected with the concept itself. One such complication arises from the historical association of democracy with capitalism, a commingling of egalitarian and inegalitarian elements that has never been (and perhaps never can be) perfectly reconciled. Another complication lies in the diffuse and variegated nature of the concept, a result of its application to at least four separate domains: political (*e.g.,* universal suffrage), legal (*e.g.,* equality before the law), economic (*e.g.,* equal distribution of property or opportunity), and moral (*e.g.,* every man's right to be treated as an end and not as a means). Accompanying these are the confusions which result from the common failure to distinguish equality as a *fact* from equality as a *norm.* ("All men are created equal," for example, is taken by some as an empirical statement, by others as a normative one.) Still other complications arise from the differential rewards and opportunities inevitable in any complex society, from the differences in the initial endowment individuals bring into the world, and from the symbolism and fears that so often attend the division of men into ethnic compartments. All these confound the effort to develop a satisfactory theory of democratic equality, and further serve to frustrate the realization of consensus around egalitarian values.

Faith in the political system. Another perspective on the state of ideology and consensus in America may be obtained by observing how people respond to the political system. How do Americans feel about the political and social institutions by which they are ruled? Do they perceive the system as one they can reach and influence? Are they satisfied that it will govern justly and for the common good?

Sample items relating to these questions are contained in Tables VI and VII. An assessment of the responses, however, is confounded by an ambivalence in our tradition. Few will question that Americans are patriotic and loyal, that they accept the political system as legitimate, and that they are inclined to shy away from radical or extreme movements which aim to alter or to overthrow the constitutional foundations of the system. Yet Americans are also presumed to have a longstanding suspicion of government—a state of mind which some historians trace back to the depredations of George III and to the habits of self-reliance forced upon our ancestors by frontier life.[19]

It is impossible in the present context to determine the extent to which the scores contained in these tables signify genuine frustration and political disil-

---

the private enterprise system, taxes, private property, profits, socialism, etc. On the whole, little enthusiasm is registered among either the elite or the masses for a drastic revision of the economy or a major redistribution of the wealth.

[19] Evidence is accumulating that the distrust of politics, often thought to be peculiar to the United States, is also found in many other countries. In fact, Gabriel Almond and Sidney Verba report in their cross-cultural study of citizenship that political interest is higher in the United States than it is in the four other countries they studied (United Kingdom, West Germany, Italy, and Mexico); and that Americans, if anything, are less negative toward politics than are the citizens of the other countries. See *The Civic Culture* (1963), chs. III–IV.

lusionment and the extent to which they represent familiar and largely ritual-
istic responses. It is plain, however, that Americans are, verbally at least, both
confused and divided in their reactions to the political system. Many feel
themselves hopelessly ineffectual politically. Approximately half perceive
government and politicians as remote, inaccessible, and largely unresponsive
to the electorate's needs or opinions.[20] About the same proportion regard poli-

TABLE VII.

*Political Influentials vs. the Electorate: Responses to Items Expressing
a Sense of Political Futility*

Items	Political Influentials (N = 3020)	General Electorate (N = 1484)
	% Agree	
It's no use worrying my head about public affairs; I can't do anything about them anyhow.	2.3	20.5
The people who really "run" the country do not even get known to the voters.	40.2	60.5
I feel that my political leaders hardly care what people like myself think or want.	10.9	39.0
Nothing I ever do seems to have any effect upon what happens in politics.	8.4	61.5
Political parties are so big that the average member hasn't got much to say about what goes on.	37.8	67.5
There doesn't seem to be much connection between what I want and what my representative does.	24.0	43.7
It seems to me that whoever you vote for, things go on pretty much the same.	21.1	51.3

tics as squalid and seamy, as an activity in which the participants habitually
practice deception, expediency, and self-aggrandizement. Yet by a curious inconsistency which so frequently frustrates the investigator searching the data
for regularities, 89.6 per cent express confidence that the government will do
what is right. However strongly they mistrust the men and the procedures
through which public policies are fashioned, most voters seem not to be
greatly dissatisfied with the outcome. They may be cynical about the operation of the political system, but they do not question its legitimacy.[21]
    Although the influentials do not unanimously endorse American political

[20] See also the Michigan data on voters' sense of "political efficacy" in Angus Campbell, Gerald
Gurin, and Warren E. Miller, *The Voter Decides* (Evanston, 1954), pp. 187–94.
    [21] For other data on ambivalent attitudes toward government, see Hyman and Sheatsley, *op. cit.*

practices either, they are substantially less suspicious and cynical than is the electorate. Indeed, they have achieved consensus or come close to achieving it on most of the items in the two tables. These results are further borne out by the *scale* scores: only 10.1 per cent of the articulates score "high" on the political cynicism scale, as contrasted with 31.3 per cent of the general population; on political suspiciousness the scores are 9.0 per cent high versus 26.7 per cent; on pessimism they are 12.6 per cent versus 26.7 per cent; and on sense of political futility the influentials score (understandably enough) only 3.1 per cent high compared with 30.2 per cent high for the electorate. The active minority also exhibits a stronger sense of social responsibility than the people do (their respective percentage high scores are 40.7 per cent versus 25.8 per cent) and, as previously noted, they are less tolerant of infractions against ethical political procedures.

Should we not, however, have expected these results as a matter of course, considering that the influentials were selected for study precisely because of their political experience and involvement? Possibly, except that similar (though less pronounced) differences emerge when we distinguish articulates from inarticulates by criteria other than actual political activity. Voters, for example, who have been to college, attained high status occupations or professions, or developed strong intellectual interests are, by a significant margin, also likely to possess more affirmative attitudes toward government, politics, and politicians.[22] They display a greater sense of social and political responsibility, are more optimistic, and are less indulgent of shoddy political methods. The political actives who are highly educated exhibit these attitudes even more strongly. Familiarity, it seems, far from breeding contempt, greatly increases respect, hope and support for the nation's political institutions and practices. Inferential support for this generalization is available from the findings turned up by Almond and Verba in all five countries they investigated in their comparative study of citizenship.[23]

Coherence and consistency of attitudes. So far we have explored the question of ideology and consensus mainly from the point of view of agreement on particular values. This, however, is a minimum criterion. Before one can say that a class or group or nation has achieved consensus around an ideology, one should be satisfied that they understand its values in a coherent and correct way. It is a poor consensus in which generalities and slogans are merely echoed with little appreciation of their significance. It seemed appropriate,

---

[22] Similar findings are reported by Robert E. Agger, Marshall N. Goldstein and Stanley A. Pearl, "Political Cynicism: Measurement and Meaning," *Journal of Politics*, Vol. 23 (1961), pp. 477–506.

[23] Almond and Verba, *op. cit.*, ch. IV. One can, of course, imagine circumstances, such as political disorganization or revolutionary crises, in which the generalization would not hold—in which, indeed, the political elite might lead the struggle *against* the existing governing institutions. I am speaking, in the present context, of politics under "normal" conditions in established democracies.

therefore, to compare the influentials and voters concerning their information and understanding, the relation of their opinions to their party preferences, and the consistency of their views on public affairs.

To begin with, the influentials are more likely than the electorate to have opinions on public questions. For example, 28 per cent of the public are unable (though a few may only be *unwilling*) to classify themselves as liberal, middle of the road, or conservative; while only 1.1 per cent of the articulates fail to make this classification. Forty-eight per cent of the voters, compared to 15 per cent of the actives, do not know in which direction they would turn if the parties were reorganized to reflect ideological differences more clearly. Forty-five per cent of the electorate but only 10.2 per cent of the influentials cannot name any issue that divides the parties. By ratios of approximately three or four to one the electorate is less likely to know which level of government they are mainly interested in, whether they prefer their party to control Congress or the presidency, whether they believe in party discipline and of what type, whether control of the parties should rest at the national or local levels, and so on.

As these and other of our findings suggest, active political involvement heightens one's sense of intellectual order and commitment. This inference is further supported by the data on partisanship. One example may suffice to illustrate the point: when the articulates and the electorate are ranged on a scale assessing their orientation toward 14 current liberal-conservative issues, the political actives tend to bunch up at the extreme ends of the distribution (the Democratic actives at the "liberal" end, the Republican actives at the "conservative" end), while the rank and file supporters of both parties fall more frequently into the middle or conflicted category. The political influentials, in short, display issue orientations that are more partisan and more consistent with their party preferences.

Essentially the same effect is achieved among the general population by increases in education, economic status, or other factors that raise the level of articulateness. College-educated Democrats and Republicans, for example, disagree more sharply on issues than grade school Democrats and Republicans do. Partisan differences are greater between the informed than between the uninformed, between the upper-class supporters of the two parties than between the lower-class supporters, between the "intellectuals" in both parties than between those who rank low on "intellectuality."

Increases in political knowledge or involvement, hence, cause men not so much to waver as to choose sides and to identify more unswervingly with one political tendency or its opposite. Inarticulateness and distance from the sources of political decision increase intellectual uncertainty and evoke political responses that are random rather than systematic. We are thus led by the findings to a pair of conclusions that may at first appear contradictory but that in reality are not: the political class is more united than the electorate on fundamental political values but divides more sharply by party affiliation on the issues which separate the two parties.[24] Both facts—the greater consensus in the one instance and the sharper cleavage in the other—testify to its superior ideological sophistication.

Not only are the articulates more partisan, but they are also more consistent in their views. Their responses to a wide range of political stimuli are to a greater extent intellectually patterned and informed. They are, for example, better able to name reference groups that correspond with their party affiliation and doctrinal orientation: approximately twice as many active Democrats as ordinary Democratic voters name liberal, Democratically oriented organizations as groups they would seek advice from (e.g., trade unions, Farmers Union, etc.); and by equally large or larger ratios they *reject* as sources of advice such conservative or Republican oriented organizations as the NAM, the Farm Bureau, and the Chamber of Commerce. With some variations, similar findings emerge when Republican leaders are compared with Republican voters. If we also take into account the liberal or conservative issue-orientation of the respondents, the differential ability of party leaders and followers to recognize reference groups becomes even more pronounced. Clearly, the political stratum has a better idea than the public has of who its ideological friends and enemies are. The capacity to recognize sympathetic or hostile reference groups is not highly developed among the public at large.

Compared with the influentials, ordinary voters also show up poorly in their ability to classify themselves politically. For example, among Democratic actives who score as "liberals" in their views on issues, 82.2 per cent correctly describe themselves as "liberals," while 16.7 per cent call themselves "middle of the roaders" and only 1.1 per cent misclassify themselves as "conservatives." Among Democratic *voters* who actually hold liberal views, only 37.0 per cent are able to label themselves correctly. The disparity is less striking between Republican leaders and followers but bears out no less conclusively that most voters lack the sophistication to recognize and label accurately the tendency of their own political views. Even their choice of party is frequently discrepant with their actual ideological views: as we reported in a previous paper,[25] not only do Democratic and Republican voters hold fairly similar opinions on issues, but the latter's opinions are closer to the opinions of Democratic leaders than to those of their own leaders.

Data we have gathered on patterns of support for individual political leaders yield similar conclusions: the articulates are far better able than the electorate to select leaders whose political philosophy they share. Often, in fact, voters simultaneously approve of two or more leaders who represent widely different outlooks—for example, Joseph McCarthy and Dwight D. Eisen-

---

[24] See also V. O. Key, *Public Opinion and Democracy* (New York, 1961), pp. 51–2.
[25] McClosky, Hoffmann, and O'Hara, *op. cit.*

hower. In a similar vein, a surprisingly large number of voters simultaneously score high on a Right Wing scale and a liberal issues scale, or hold other "discrepant" outlooks. Such inconsistencies are not unknown among the political actives either, but they are much less frequent. Not only does the public have less information than the political class but it does not succeed as well in sorting out and relating the information it does possess.[26]

Most of the relationships reported in the foregoing have been tested with education, occupation, and sometimes with other demographic variables controlled, but the introduction of these factors does not change the direction of the findings, although it sometimes affects the magnitude of the scores.

Comparisons of scores for the two samples have also been made with "acquiescent" response-set controlled. Acquiescence affects the results, but does not eliminate the differences reported or alter the direction or significance of the findings.

III. SUMMARY AND DISCUSSION

Several observations can be offered by way of summarizing and commenting upon the data just reported:

1. American politics is widely thought to be innocent of ideology, but this opinion more appropriately describes the electorate than the active political minority. If American ideology is defined as that cluster of axioms, values and beliefs which have given form and substance to American democracy and the Constitution, the political influentials manifest by comparison with ordinary voters a more developed sense of ideology and a firmer grasp of its essentials. This is evidenced in their stronger approval of democratic ideas, their greater tolerance and regard for proper procedures and citizen rights, their superior understanding and acceptance of the "rules of the game," and their more affirmative attitudes toward the political system in general. The electorate displays a substantial measure of unity chiefly in its support of freedom in the abstract; on most other features of democratic belief and practice it is sharply divided.

The political views of the influentials are relatively ordered and coherent. As liberals and conservatives, Democrats and Republicans, they take stands on issues, choose reference groups, and express preferences for leaders that are far more consistent than the attitudes and preferences exhibited by the electorate. The latter's opinions do not entirely lack order but are insufficiently integrated to meet the requirements of an ideology.[27] In contrast to

[26] For other findings on the state of ideological development amcng the electorate, see Angus Campbell, Philip E. Converse, Warren E. Miller and Donald E. Stokes, *The American Voter* (New York, 1960), chs. 8–10.

[27] For a similar conclusion on this point, see V. O. Key, *Public Opinion and American Democracy* (New York, 1961), pp. 41, 49. The second chapter of this volume contains an excellent discussion of opinion consensus among the electorate, and touches on a number of the points dealt with in this paper. Evidence on the infrequency of "ideological" thinking among the voters is

the political elite, which tends to be united on basic values but divided on issues by party affiliation (both of which testify to a measure of ideological sophistication), the voters divide on many basic political values and adopt stands on issues with little reference to their party affiliation.

The evidence suggests that it is the articulate classes rather than the public who serve as the major repositories of the public conscience and as the carriers of the Creed. Responsibility for keeping the system going, hence, falls most heavily upon them.[28]

2. Why should consensus and support for democratic ideology be stronger among the political stratum than among the electorate? The answer plainly has to do with the differences in their political activity, involvement and articulateness.

Some observers complain that Americans have little interest in political ideas because they are exclusively concerned with their own personal affairs. Evidence is becoming available, however, that political apathy and ignorance are also widespread among the populations of other countries and may well be endemic in all societies larger than a city-state. It is difficult to imagine any circumstance, short of war or revolutionary crisis, in which the mass of men will evince more interest in the community's affairs than in their own concerns. This is not because they are selfish, thoughtless, or morally deficient, but because the stimuli they receive from public affairs are relatively remote and intangible. One can scarcely expect ordinary men to respond to them as intensely as they respond to the more palpable stimuli in their own everyday lives, which impinge upon them directly and in ways they can understand and do something about. The aphorism which holds man to be a political animal may be supportable on normative grounds but is scarcely defensible as a description of reality. Political apathy seems for most men the more "natural" state. Although political matters are in a sense "everyone's concern", it is just as unreasonable to hope that all men will sustain a lively interest in politics as it would be to expect everyone to become addicted to chamber music, electronics, poetry, or baseball. Since many voters lack education, opportunity, or even tangible and compelling reasons for busying themselves with political ideas, they respond to political stimuli (if they respond at all) without much reflection or consistency. Their life-styles, furthermore, tend to perpetuate this state of affairs, for they are likely to associate with people like themselves whose political opinions are no more informed or consistent than their own. As inarticulates, they are also inclined to avoid the very activities by which they might overcome their indifference and develop a more coherent point of view.

Many voters, in addition, feel remote from the centers of political decision

---

presented in Campbell, Converse, Miller and Stokes, *op. cit.*, p. 249. By the criteria used the authors were able to classify only 3.5% of the voters as "ideologues" and 12% as "near-ideologues."

[28] V. O. Key, "Public Opinion and the Decay of Democracy," *loc. cit.*

and experience an acute sense of political futility. They know the political world only as a bewildering labyrinth of procedures and unceasing turmoil in which it is difficult to distinguish the just from the wicked, the deserving from the undeserving. The political questions about which they are asked to have opinions are complex and thorny; every solution is imperfect and exacts its price; measures that benefit some groups invariably aggrieve others. The principles which govern the political process seem vague, recondite and impossible to relate to actual events. All this obviously deters voters from developing ideologically, from acquiring insights into the subtleties of the democratic process, and from achieving consensus even on fundamental values.

Although the influentials face some of the same obstacles, they are better able to overcome them. As a group they are distinguished from the mass of the electorate by their above-average education and economic status, their greater political interest and awareness, and their more immediate access to the command posts of community decision. Many of them participate not only in politics but in other public activities as well. This affords them, among other benefits, a more sophisticated understanding of how the society is run and a more intimate association with other men and women who are alert to political ideas and values. Political concepts and abstractions, alien to the vocabulary of many voters, are for the elite familiar items of everyday discourse.

Consider also that the political stratum is, by almost every social criterion we have examined, more homogeneous than the electorate. This promotes communication among them and increases their chances of converging around a common body of attitudes.[29] As Newcomb[30] has remarked, "The actual consequences of communication, as well as the intended ones, are consensus—increasing." Among many segments of the general population, however, communication on matters of political belief either occurs not at all or is so random and cacophonous as to have little utility for the reinforcement of political values. If Louis Wirth is correct in observing that "the limits of consensus are marked by the range of effective communication," [31] it becomes easier to understand why the active minority achieves consensus more often than the voters do.

Compared with the electorate, whose ordinary members are submerged in an ideological babble of poorly informed and discordant opinions, the members of the political minority inhabit a world in which political ideas are vastly more salient, intellectual consistency is more frequently demanded, attitudes are related to principles, actions are connected to beliefs, "correct" opinions are rewarded and "incorrect" opinions are punished. In addition, as partici-

[29] For additional data on the homogeneity of social characteristics and values among American elite groups, see James N. Rosenau, "Consensus-Building in the American National Community: Hypotheses and Supporting Data," *Journal of Politics*, Vol. 24 (November, 1962), pp. 639–661.

[30] Theodore M. Newcomb, "The Study of Consensus," in R. K. Merton *et al.* (eds.), *Sociology Today* (New York, 1959), pp. 277–92.

[31] *Op. cit.*, p. 201.

pants in political roles, the actives are compelled (contrary to stereotype) to adopt opinions, to take stands on issues, and to evaluate ideas and events. As *articulates* they are unavoidably exposed to the liberal democratic values which form the main current of our political heritage. The net effect of these influences is to heighten their sensitivity to political ideas and to unite them more firmly behind the values of the American tradition. They may, as a result, be better equipped for the role they are called upon to play in a democracy than the citizens are for *their* role.

The findings furnish little comfort for those who wish to believe that a passion for freedom, tolerance, justice and other democratic values springs spontaneously from the lower depths of the society, and that the plain, homespun, uninitiated yeoman, worker and farmer are the natural hosts of democratic ideology. The mystique of the simple, unworldly, "natural" democrat has been with us since at least the rise of Christianity, and has been assiduously cultivated by Rousseau, Tolstoy, Marx, and numerous lesser writers and social reformers. Usually, the simpler the man, the lower his station in life, and the greater his objective need for equality, the more we have endowed him with a capacity for understanding democracy. We are thus inclined to give the nod to the farmer over the city man, the unlearned over the educated, the poor man over the man of wealth, the "people" over their leaders, the unsophisticated over the sophisticated. Yet everyone of these intuitive expectations turns out, upon investigation, to be questionable or false. Democratic beliefs and habits are obviously not "natural" but must be learned; and they are learned more slowly by men and women whose lives are circumscribed by apathy, ignorance, provincialism and social or physical distance from the centers of intellectual activity. In the absence of knowledge and experience—as we can readily observe from the fidgety course of growth in the newly emerging nations—the presuppositions and complex obligations of democracy, the rights it grants and the self-restraints it imposes, cannot be quickly comprehended. Even in a highly developed democratic nation like the United States, millions of people continue to possess only the most rudimentary understanding of democratic ideology.

3. While the active political minority affirms the underlying values of democracy more enthusiastically than the people do, consensus among them is far from perfect, and we might well inquire why this is so.

Despite the many forces impelling influentials toward agreement on basic ideological values, counteracting forces are also at work to divide them. Not all influentials are able to comprehend democratic ideas, to apply them to concrete contexts, or to thread their way through the complexities of modern political life. Nor is communication perfect among them either, despite their greater homogeneity. Many things divide them, not least of which are differences in education, conflicting economic and group interests, party competition, factional cleavages and personal political ambitions.

In demonstrating that the influentials are better prepared than the masses to receive and reflect upon political ideas, we run the risk of overstating the case and of exaggerating their capacity for ideological reasoning. Some members of the political class obviously have no more intellectual concern with politics than the masses do; they are in it for "the game," for personal reasons, or for almost any reason except ideology.

Then, too, while most democratic ideas are in their most general form simple enough for almost all members of the elite to understand, they become considerably more puzzling when one sets out to explicate them, to relate them to each other, or to apply them to concrete cases. Only a few of the complications need to be cited to illustrate the point: several of the ideas, such as equality, are either inherently vague or mean different things in different contexts. Some democratic (or constitutional) values turn out in certain situations to be incompatible with other democratic values (e.g., the majority's right to make and enforce the laws at times clashes with individual rights, such as the right to stand on one's religious conscience). As this suggests, democratic ideas and rules of the game are ordinarily encountered not in pure form or in isolation but in substantive contexts that are bound to influence the ways in which we react to them.[32] Many businessmen who consider the regulation of business as an unconstitutional invasion of freedom look upon the regulation of trade unions as a justifiable curb upon lawlessness; trade unionists, needless to say, lean to the opposite view.

Consider, too, what a heavy burden we place upon a man's normal impulses by asking him to submit unconditionally to democratic values and procedures. Compliance with democratic rules of the game often demands an extraordinary measure of forbearance and self-discipline, a willingness to place constraints upon the use of our collective power and to suffer opinions, actions, and groups we regard as repugnant. The need for such self-restraint is for many people intrinsically difficult to comprehend and still more difficult to honor. Small wonder, then, that consensus around democratic values is imperfect, even among the political influentials who are well situated to appreciate their importance.

4. We turn now to the most crucial question suggested by the research findings, namely, what significance must be assigned to the fact that democratic ideology and consensus are poorly developed among the electorate and only imperfectly realized among the political influentials?

Our first and most obvious conclusion is that, contrary to the familiar claim, a democratic society can survive despite widespread popular misunderstanding and disagreement about basic democratic and constitutional values. The American political system survives and even flourishes under precisely these conditions, and so, we have reason to think, do other viable democra-

---

[32] For a discussion of this point, see Peter Bachrach, "Elite Consensus and Democracy," *Journal of Politics*, Vol. 24 (August, 1962), pp. 439–52.

cies. What makes this possible is a more conjectural question, though several observations can be offered by way of answering it.

Democratic viability is, to begin with, saved by the fact that those who are most confused about democratic ideas are also likely to be politically apathetic and without significant influence. Their role in the nation's decision process is so small that their "misguided" opinions or non-opinions have little practical consequence for stability. If they contribute little to the vitality of the system, neither are they likely to do much harm. Lipset[33] has pointed out that "apathy undermines consensus," but to this one may add the corollary observation that apathy also furnishes its own partial corrective by keeping the doubters from acting upon their differences. In the United States, at least, their disagreements are *passive* rather than *active*, more the result of political ignorance and indifference than of intellectual conviction or conscious identification with an "alien" political tendency. Most seem not even to be aware of their deviations from the established values. This suggests that there may, after all, be some utility in achieving agreement on large, abstract political sentiments, for it may satisfy men that they share common values when in fact they do not. Not only can this keep conflicts from erupting, but it also permits men who disagree to continue to communicate and thus perhaps to convert their pseudo-consensus on democratic values into a genuine consensus.

I do not mean to suggest, of course, that a nation runs no risks when a large number of its citizens fail to grasp the essential principles on which its constitution is founded. Among Americans, however, the principal danger is not that they will reject democratic ideals in favor of some hostile ideology, but that they will fail to understand the very institutions they believe themselves to be defending and may end up undermining rather than safeguarding them. Our research on "McCarthyism," for example, strongly suggests that popular support for the Senator represented less a conscious rejection of American democratic ideals than a misguided effort to defend them. We found few McCarthy supporters who genuinely shared the attitudes and values associated with his name.[34]

Whether consensus among the influentials is either a necessary or sufficient condition for democratic stability is not really known. Since the influentials act, make public decisions, are more organized, and take political ideas more seriously, agreement among them on constitutional values is widely thought to be essential for viability. At present, however, we do not have enough information (or at least we do not have it in appropriately organized form) to

[33] Seymour Martin Lipset, *Political Man* (New York, 1960), p. 27. Chapter I of this volume provides a stimulating and valuable discussion of the relation of conflict and consensus to the operation of democracy.

[34] Herbert McClosky, "McCarthyism: The Myth and the Reality," unpublished paper delivered at the American Psychological Association, New York, September, 1957. See also Wiebe, *loc. cit.*

state with satisfactory precision what the actual relation is between elite consensus and democratic stability. Some democratic governments, *e.g.*, Weimar Germany, crumbled when faced with ideological conflicts among their political classes; others, *e.g.*, post-war Italy and France, have until now managed to weather pronounced ideological cleavages. The opinion has long prevailed that consensus is needed to achieve stability, but the converse may be the more correct formulation, *i.e.*, that so long as conditions remain stable, consensus is not required; it becomes essential only when social conditions are disorganized. Consensus may strengthen democratic viability, but its absence in an otherwise stable society need not be fatal or even particularly damaging.

It should also be kept in mind that the existence of intellectual disagreements—even among the influentials—does not necessarily mean that they will be expressed or acted upon. In the United States (and doubtless elsewhere as well), numerous influences are at work to prevent ideological cleavages from assuming an important role in the nation's political life. This is certainly the tendency of such political institutions as federalism, checks and balances, separation of powers, bicameralism, the congressional committee system, the judiciary's practice of accommodating one discrepant law to another, and a system of elections more often fought around local issues and personalities than around urgent national questions. Our two-party system also functions to disguise or soften the genuine disagreements that distinguish active Democrats from active Republicans. The American social system contributes to the same end, for it is a model of the pluralistic society, a profuse collection of diverse groups, interests and organizations spread over a vast and variegated territory. Consensus in such a society becomes difficult to achieve, but by the same token its absence can also more easily be survived. The complexities of a highly pluralistic social and political order tend to diminish the impact of intellectual differences, to compel compromise, and to discourage the holders of divergent views from crystallizing into intransigent doctrinal camps. Thus it seems, paradoxically enough, that the need for consensus on democratic rules of the game increases as the conflict among competing political tendencies becomes sharper, and declines as their differences become more diffused. Italy, by this reasoning, has greater need of consensus than the United States, but has less chance of achieving it. A democratic nation may wisely prefer the American model to the Italian, though what is ideally desired, as Lipset observes,[35] is a balance between cleavage and consensus—the one to give reality and force to the principle of opposition, the other to furnish the secure framework within which that principle might be made continuously effective. Countervailing power within a structure of shared political values would, by this logic, be the optimal condition for the maintenance of a democratic society.

5. But even giving this much weight to consensus may exaggerate the role

---

[35] Lipset, *op. cit.*, pp. 21–2.

which intellectual factors play in the attainment of democratic stability. The temptation to assign a controlling influence to the place of ideas in the operation of democracy is very great. Partly this results from our tendency to confuse the textbook model of democracy with the reality and to assume the high order of rationality in the system that the model presupposes (*e.g.*, an alert citizenry aware of its rights and duties, cognizant of the basic rules, exercising consent, enjoying perfect information and choosing governers after carefully weighing their qualifications, deliberating over the issues, etc.). It is not my purpose to ridicule this model but to underscore the observation that it can easily mislead us into placing more weight than the facts warrant upon cognitive elements—upon ideas, values, rational choice, consensus, etc.—as the cementing forces of a democratic society. An *ad hominem* consideration may also be relevant here: as intellectuals and students of politics, we are disposed both by training and sensibility to take political ideas seriously and to assign central importance to them in the operation of the state. We are therefore prone to forget that most people take them less seriously than we do, that they pay little attention to issues, rarely worry about the consistency of their opinions, and spend little or no time thinking about the values, presuppositions, and implications which distinguish one political orientation from another. If the viability of a democracy were to depend upon the satisfaction of these intellectual activities, the prognosis would be very grim indeed.

Research from many different lines of inquiry confirms unequivocally that the role heretofore assigned to ideas and to intellectual processes in general has been greatly exaggerated and cannot adequately explain many political phenomena which, on *a priori* grounds, we have expected them to explain. Witness, for example, the research on the non-rational factors which govern the voting decision, on the effects—or rather the non-effects—of ideology on the loyalty and fighting effectiveness of German and American soldiers, on the differences between the views of party leaders and followers, on the influence of personality on political belief, and on group determinants of perception.[36] We now have evidence that patriotism and the strength of one's attachment to a political community need not depend upon one's approval of its intellectual, cultural, or political values. Indeed, our present research clearly confirms that the men and women who express "patriotism" in extreme or chauvinistic form usually have the least knowledge and understanding of American democratic ideals, institutions, and practices.

Abundant anecdotal data from the observation of dictatorial and other nations further corroborates the conclusion that men may become attached to a

---

[36] *Cf.*, for example, Campbell, *et al., op. cit.;* Bernard R. Berelson, Paul F. Lazarsfeld, and William N. McPhee, *Voting* (Chicago, 1954), especially ch. 14; Edward A. Shils and Morris Janowitz, "Cohesion and Disintegration in the German Wehrmacht in World War II," *Public Opinion Quarterly*, Vol. 12 (1948), pp. 280–315; Herbert McClosky, "Conservatism and Personality," this REVIEW, Vol. 52 (March, 1958), pp. 27–45; T. W. Adorno, *et al., The Authoritarian Personality* (New York, 1950), ch. XVII; Richard Crutchfield, "Conformity and Character," *American Psychologist*, Vol. 10 (1955), pp. 191–198.

party, a community, or a nation by forces that have nothing to do with ideology or consensus. Many of these forces are so commonplace that we often neglect them, for they include family, friends, home, employment, property, religion, ethnic attachments, a common language, and familiar surroundings and customs. These may lack the uplifting power of some political doctrines, but their ability to bind men to a society and its government may nevertheless be great. This observation, of course, is less likely to hold for the intelligentsia than for the inarticulates, but even the political behavior of intellectuals is never governed exclusively by appeals to the mind.

The effect of ideas on democratic viability may also be diminished by the obvious reluctance of most men to press their intellectual differences to the margin and to debate questions that may tear the community apart. So long as no urgent reason arises for bringing such differences to the surface, most men will be satisfied to have them remain dormant. Although there are men and women who are exceptions to this generalization, and who cannot bear to leave basic questions unresolved, they are likely to be few, for both the principles and practices of an "open society" strongly reinforce tolerance for variety, contingency and ambiguity in matters of belief and conscience. As our data on freedom of opinion suggest, few Americans expect everyone to value the same things or to hold identical views on public questions. The tendency to ignore, tolerate, or play down differences helps to create an illusion of consensus which for many purposes can be as serviceable as the reality.[37]

6. To conclude, as we have in effect, that ideological awareness and consensus are overvalued as determinants of democratic viability is not to imply that they are of no importance. While disagreements among Americans on fundamental values have tended to be passive and, owing to apathy and the relative placidity of our politics, easily tolerated; while they do not follow party lines and are rarely insinuated into the party struggle; and while no extremist movement has yet grown large enough to challenge effectively the governing principles of the American Constitution, this happy state of affairs is not permanently guaranteed. Fundamental differences could *become* activated by political and economic crises; party differences could *develop* around fundamental constitutional questions, as they have in France and other democracies; and powerful extremist movements are too familiar a phenomenon of modern political life to take for granted their eternal absence from the American scene.

----

[37] Robert G. McCloskey, *loc. cit.*, suggests that the American political tradition is marked by "ambivalence" toward certain of our fundamental values and that this may discourage the achievement of "consensus" in the usual sense. He believes, however, that Americans have learned to live with, and even to ignore, inconsistencies in the value system, in keeping with our "pragmatic spirit." Whether this ability is uniquely American or whether it is characteristic of all "open," democratic societies is a question well worth investigating. It could, conceivably, be a natural outgrowth of democratic ideology itself, no element of which can be conceived and enforced absolutely without infringing other elements. On this last point, see Sidney Hook, *The Paradoxes of Freedom* (Berkeley, 1962), pp. 14–62.

Obviously a democratic nation also pays a price for an electorate that is weakly developed ideologically. Lacking the intellectual equipment to assess complex political events accurately, the unsophisticated may give support to causes that are contrary to their own or to the national interest. In the name of freedom, democracy, and the Constitution, they may favor a McCarthy, join the John Birch Society, or agitate for the impeachment of a Supreme Court Justice who has worked unstintingly to uphold their constitutional liberties. They may also have difficulty discriminating political integrity from demagoguery, maturity and balanced judgment from fanaticism, honest causes from counterfeits. Our findings on the attitudes shown by ordinary Americans toward "extreme" political beliefs (Left Wing beliefs, Right Wing beliefs, totalitarianism, isolationism, etc.) verify that the possibilities just cited are not merely hypothetical. Those who have the least understanding of American politics subscribe least enthusiastically to its principles, and are most frequently "misled" into attacking constitutional values while acting (as they see it) to defend them.

There is, however, reason to believe that ideological sophistication and the general acceptance of liberal democratic values are increasing rather than declining in the United States. Extreme ideological politics of the type associated with Marxism, fascism and other doctrinaire networks of opinion may be waning, as many sociologists believe,[38] but the same observation does not hold for the influence of democratic ideas. On the contrary, democratic ideology in the United States, linked as it is with the articulate classes, gives promise of growing as the articulate class grows. Many developments in recent American life point to an increase in "articulateness": the extraordinary spread of education, rapid social mobility, urbanization, the proliferation of mass media that disseminate public information, the expansion of the middle class, the decline in the size and number of isolated rural groups, the reduction in the proportion of people with submarginal living standards, the incorporation of foreign and minority groups into the culture and their increasing entrance into the professions, and so on. While these developments may on the one side have the effect of reducing the tensions and conflicts on which extreme ideologies feed, they are likely on the other side to beget a more articulate population and a more numerous class of political influentials, committed to liberal democracy and aware of the rights and obligations which attend that commitment.

● ● ●

Study Questions

1. Political socialization is the process of transmitting political values, attitudes, norms, and expectations. This process may preserve traditional political norms. Ex-

[38] Cf. Daniel Bell, *The End of Ideology* (Glencoe, 1960), pp. 369–375; S. M. Lipset, *op. cit.*, pp. 403–17; Edward Shils, *loc. cit.*

plain how the socialization process can be used as an agency of political and social change.

2. Compare and contrast the attitudes of political influentials with that of the electorate toward the political system and political practices.

3. Discuss the relationship between education and occupation on the one hand and political attitudes and involvement on the other.

4. There is ambiguity in Americans' attitudes toward democracy. For although there is almost unanimous support for the basic principles of democracy, often this unanimous support disappears when specific applications of democratic principles are made. What are the reasons for this? Explain fully and critically.

Suggestions for Further Reading

Boorstin, Daniel J. *The Genius of American Politics*. Chicago: University of Chicago Press, 1953.

Brogan, Denis W. *The American Character*. New York: Alfred A. Knopf, 1944.

Coleman, James S. (ed.) *Education and Political Development*. Princeton: Princeton University Press, 1965.

Commager, Henry Steele. *The American Mind*. New Haven: Yale University Press, 1950.

Dawson, Richard E. and Kenneth Prewitt, *Political Socialization*. Boston: Little, Brown and Company, 1969.

Easton, David. *A Systems Analysis of Political Life*. New York: John Wiley & Sons, Inc., 1965.

Eisenstadt, S. N. *From Generation to Generation*. New York: The Free Press, 1956.

Elkin, Frederick. *The Child and Society: The Process of Socialization*. New York: Random House, 1960.

Gorer, Geoffrey. *The American People: A Study in National Character*. New York: W. W. Norton & Company, 1948.

Greenstein, Fred I. *Children and Politics*. New Haven: Yale University Press, 1965.

Hess, Robert D. and Judith V. Torney. *The Development of Political Attitudes in Children*. Chicago: Aldine Publishing Company, 1967.

Hyman, Herbert H. *Political Socialization: A Study in the Psychology of Political Behavior*. New York: The Free Press, 1959.

Key, V. O. *Public Opinion and American Democracy*. New York: Alfred A. Knopf, 1961.

Kornhauser, William. *The Politics of Mass Society*. New York: The Free Press, 1959.

Lambert, Wallace E. and Otto Klineberg. *Children's Views of Foreign Peoples*. New York: Appleton-Century-Crofts, 1966.

Lane, Robert E. *Political Ideology*. New York: The Free Press, 1962.

Lane, Robert E. *Political Life: Why People Get Involved in Politics*. New York: The Free Press, 1959.

Lipset, Martin S. *Political Man*. Garden City, New York: Doubleday and Company, 1959.

Marrick, Dwaine. (ed.). *Political Decision-Makers*. New York: The Free Press, 1961.

Matthews, Donald R. *The Social Background of Political Decision-Makers*. Garden City, New York: Doubleday and Company, 1954.

Mayo, Henry B. *An Introduction to Democratic Theory.* New York: Oxford University Press, 1960.

Mitchell, William C. *The American Polity.* New York: The Free Press, 1962.

McGiffert, Michael. *The Character of Americans.* Homewood, Illinois: Dorsey Press, 1964.

Pye, Lucian W. and Sidney Verba (eds.) *Political Culture and Political Development.* Princeton: Princeton University Press, 1965.

Santayana, George. *Character and Opinion in the United States.* Garden City, New York: Doubleday and Company, 1956.

Tocqueville, Alexis de. *Democracy in America.* New York: Vintage Books, 1955.

PART TWO

Political
Participation and Alienation

American political culture may be described as participatory; that is, participants are oriented toward both the input and output aspects of the political system. Orientation of oneself as participant in the political system leads to three important questions: (1) How competent does the individual feel in influencing the formation and implementation of public policies? (2) How much trust does he have in the political system? and (3) Does he consider the political system as basically harmonious or contentious?

The democratic view of government expects the individual to be informed about the major issues of the day, to participate in public affairs by casting his vote on the basis of rational judgment, and to be interested in and motivated by the political and social orders. This view, to be sure, is a normative rather than a descriptive model of politics. In politics, we should bear in mind, theory and ideals do not always describe the actual situation or reality. The gap between the ideal and reality is often found wider than at first believed. In short, we find that there is a gap between the expectation of normative political theorists and political reality.

Gabriel Almond and Sidney Verba discuss the role of the subject in the political system. The subject obeys the law but he does not shape it. In the democratic system the subject is not only expected to obey the law and be loyal but also to play some role in the formation of decisions. Democracy rests upon active participation of the ordinary man in governmental affairs. The fact that he does not live up to this ideal has led to criticism of his passivity and apathy.

Almond and Verba discuss the attitudes of people toward participation within the local community and point out two structural differences that are important: (1) the degree of local autonomy and (2) the degree to which local

56

structures encourage participation. They discuss the differences in the degrees of local autonomy in the United States, Britain, Germany, Mexico, and Italy and the opportunity for the individual to participate in decisions. They state that "the norms to which an individual adheres are largely determined by the role that the system allows him to play." These norms in turn have a feedback effect upon the political structure.

The study shows that the image of the citizen as participant is more widespread in some countries than in others. It also shows that a substantial number of respondents in Mexico, Germany, and particularly Italy, admitted no sense of local civic obligation. Moreover, the study shows that respondents with a higher education and from the middle class express adherence to the norms of participation.

In his discussion of the determinants of political apathy Morris Rosenberg points out that his respondents feared presenting their political views freely. Their fears tended to be of a social and psychological nature rather than of a political nature. To a considerable extent political participation involves *interpersonal interaction*. Political discussion may pose a threat to interpersonal harmony, occupational success, and self-esteem. People impose self-censorship on their political expressions to avert threatening consequences.

Another contributing factor to political apathy is the feeling that political activity is futile. Rosenberg discusses this factor in detail, citing several examples. He states that many respondents felt that they lost control over the political decision-making process and that political powers are unresponsive to their pressure. The citizen felt a lack of control over the political system. Rosenberg also discusses the absence of factors which appeal to or offer the individual any gratification. For many people political matters still remain dull, remote, and uninspiring. There is also the absence of direct or immediate satisfaction to be derived from the activity itself. Finally, most people are concerned about their immediate and urgent needs and do not conceive political action as a means for satisfying these needs.

In the concluding article, Dwight G. Dean discusses the meaning of alienation and its various components—Powerlessness, Normlessness and Social Isolation. Dean also discusses the relationship between alienation and political apathy. His study shows that there is little credence to the hypothesis "that a sense of Powerlessness is related to Political Apathy." Moreover, his study shows that there is little evidence to support the suggestions that Normlessness and Social Isolation are related to Political Apathy or nonvoting.

THE OBLIGATION TO PARTICIPATE

GABRIEL A. ALMOND AND SIDNEY VERBA

The citizen, unlike the subject, is an active participant in the political input process—the process by which political decisions are made. But the citizen role, as we have suggested, does not replace the subject role or the parochial role: it is added to them. Only the rare individual considers his role as citizen more important and salient than his role as subject or parochial; for whom politics is a matter of first priority. This has been corroborated in many surveys of political opinion. When asked general questions about what worries them, or what they consider important, people usually mention family problems, job problems, economic problems, but rarely political problems.[1] Furthermore, if the ordinary man is interested in political matters, he is more likely to be interested in the output than in the input process. He is concerned about who wins the election, not about how it is carried on; he cares about who is benefited by legislation, not about how legislation is passed. Even in relation to his vote—an act that is designed to make him an active participant in the decision-making processes of his nation—he may behave routinely, voting for a party because of traditional allegiance or for other reasons not connected with a desire to guide the course of policy.

That most men orient themselves more as subjects than as citizens is a familiar theme. Much has been written describing this fact, sometimes deploring it. Interest in the criticism of the role of the ordinary man in his political system is especially characteristic of those writers and thinkers concerned with the problems of democracy—from the ancient Greeks to current writers on American civic affairs; for it is in a democracy that the role of the ordinary man as a participant in the political affairs of his country is significant. The man whose relation to his government is that of a subject—a passive beneficiary or victim of routine governmental actions—would not be found wanting

[1] In our survey, when respondents were asked what they spent their free time on, no more than three per cent in any of the five nations mentioned something to do with politics; and in most cases the percentage was smaller. Other survey results show almost universally that politics is not uppermost in the minds of people.

SOURCE: Gabriel A. Almond and Sidney Verba, Chapter 6 from *The Civic Culture: Political Attitudes and Democracy in Five Nations* (Princeton: Princeton University Press, 1963), pp. 161–179. Copyright © by Princeton University Press, for the Center of International Studies, Princeton University. Reprinted by permission.

in a traditional, nondemocratic society. Moreover, this relationship would exhaust what is expected of him. What the government does affects him, but why or how the government decides to do what it does is outside his sphere of competence. He has obligations, but the obligations are passive—he should be loyal and respectful of authority. "All that is necessary for salvation is contained in two virtues, *faith* in Christ and *obedience* to laws." [2] As a subject he may be more or less competent, but his competence will be "subject competence." He will not attempt to influence the decisions of his government, but will try to see that he is treated properly once the decision is made. It is not in his sphere of competence to say what taxes should be levied, but once these are decided the competent subject will see that he is treated fairly within the boundaries of that decision. The law is something he obeys, not something he helps shape. If he is competent, he knows the law, knows what he must do, and what is due him.

In democratic societies, on the other hand, his role as subject does not exhaust what is expected of him. He is expected to have the virtues of the subject—to obey the law, to be loyal—but he is also expected to take some part in the formation of decisions. The common thread running through the many definitions of democracy is that a democracy is a society in which ". . . ordinary citizens exert a relatively high degree of control over leaders." [3] Democracy is thus characterized by the fact that power over significant authoritative decisions in a society is distributed among the population. The ordinary man is expected to take an active part in governmental affairs, to be aware of how decisions are made, and to make his views known.

The fact that the ordinary man does not live up to the ideal set by the normative theory of democracy has led to much criticism of his passivity and indifference. Our goal is to describe and analyze, however, and not to assign praise or blame. In any case, normative questions about the role of the individual in his political system are by no means unrelated to more descriptive and analytic questions. Certainly the political moralist in describing what an individual *should* do will probably not be unaffected by what individuals actually *do*, and certainly he will consider what he believes they *can* do. The three types of questions are not identical, but they affect one another. This is especially the case if we switch our perspective to that of the ordinary man himself. So far we have talked about the gap between what scholars, philosophers, and teachers have said the ordinary man ought to do in a democracy and what in fact he does. But what about the ordinary man himself? What does *he* think he *should* do? And how does this compare with what he thinks he *can* do and with what he does?

This [essay] will deal with the first question: What does the ordinary man think he should do? Philosophers and democratic ideologists have written at

---

[2] Thomas Hobbes, *Leviathan*, London, 1945, Book III, p. 385.
[3] Robert A. Dahl, *A Preface to Democratic Theory*, Chicago, 1956, p. 3.

length about the obligations of the citizen, but what is the ordinary man's conception of his role in politics? If the model democratic citizen is active, participating, and influential, is this what the ordinary man aspires to be? And, what may be more important, does he think of himself as capable of influencing and participating in the decisions of his government? . . .

WHAT IS THE GOOD CITIZEN?

The good citizen does not equal the good man. No zealous advocate of good citizenship would argue that political participation ought to be pursued at the neglect of all other obligations. The active influential citizen described in normative political theory is not excused from the obligations of the subject. If he participates in the making of the law, he is also expected to obey the law. It has, in fact, been argued that he has greater obligation to obey because of his participation. Nor would one want his civic activity to be at the expense of his private obligations. Surely the lady described by Riesman who left her screaming children locked in their room while she attended a meeting of a neighborhood improvement association does not represent the ideal toward which the advocates of good citizenship are striving.[4] There will, of course, always be conflicts between the demands of different roles, but the obligations of one role do not replace those of another.

This point is stressed here because it introduces a complexity into our attempt to measure the extent to which the ideal of the participating citizen exists in the minds of men; for the man who believes that he should be upright in his personal life—work for the good of his family or, to quote one of our respondents, "If he is a carpenter, he should be a good carpenter"—may also believe that he should be a participating and active citizen. Similarly, the man who believes that he should pay taxes and obey the laws is a "good subject." The same man may also be a "good citizen." It is only when the individual thinks of his family's advantage as the only goal to pursue, or conceives of his role in the political system in familistic terms, that he is a parochial and not also a citizen. And it is only when an individual thinks of his relationship to his state as being exhausted by his role as subject that he is subject and not also citizen.

Attempting to see how much the role of participant has been added to those of parochial and subject in our five countries, we examined our respondents' relations with their local community. We were interested in the extent to which respondents considered themselves to have some sort of responsibility to be active in their community—either in a formal or informal way; either in relation to local government or in relation to fellow citizens. The local community seemed to be a good place to begin, since political and governmental problems tend to be more understandable, the organs of government less dis-

[4] David Riesman, *Faces in the Crowd*, New Haven, 1952, pp. 82–83.

tant, the chances of effective participation for the individual citizen greater on the local level than on the level of national government. It has, in fact, often been argued that effective democracy rests on the ability of the individual to participate locally, for it is only here that he can develop some sense of mastery over political affairs. As Bryce put it (and as defenders of local autonomy have constantly argued), "An essential ingredient of a satisfactory democracy is that a considerable proportion should have experience of active participation in the work of small self-governing groups, whether in connection with local government, trade unions, cooperatives or other forms of activity." [5]

NATIONAL DIFFERENCES IN THE CHARACTERISTICS OF LOCAL GOVERNMENT

In this [essay], . . . we shall deal with attitudes toward the local government. In interpreting the responses to questions about the local government, we are faced with the problem that the structures of local government differ from nation to nation and within the nations as well. And these differences in structure partially explain differences in attitudes found among the nations. . . . It is important that these differences be kept in mind. While it would be impossible to describe fully the patterns of local government within the five nations—there are numerous levels of local government in all five nations and substantial variation among regions—one can specify certain similarities and differences among them.

In the first place, all five nations have some form of local government. (It is important to note here that we are dealing with the most local governmental units: units below the level of state, or *Land*, or province.) And the local unit, whether it be a commune, *municipio*, *Gemeinde*, township, or noncounty borough, almost invariably has some sort of locally elected council or set of officials. Thus in each country there is a set of locally elected units on which we can focus.

But despite this similarity, local government differs sharply among the five nations. From the point of view of respondents' attitudes toward participation within the local community, there are two types of structural differences that are particularly significant: the degree of local autonomy and the degree to which local structures foster citizen participation. It is difficult to measure precisely the extent of autonomy of local governmental units within nations; there are variations within nations, the criteria of autonomy are not clear, and the data are often lacking. Nevertheless, the five nations do differ so substantially in this respect—and the variations among the nations are generally larger than the variations within each nation—that one can rank the nations with some confidence in terms of local autonomy. It is clear that at one ex-

[5] James Bryce, *Modern Democracies*, New York, 1921, I, p. 132. (See below, chap. 7.)

treme the pattern of local government in the United States represents the greatest amount of local autonomy. The range of subject matter over which the local communities have control—the police and schools are two important examples (and the communities not only handle administration of the schools, but in many cases they actually formulate educational policy)—as well as the extent of the local governments' freedom from external control appear to be much greater in the United States than elsewhere.

It would appear that Great Britain ranks next to the United States in degree of local autonomy. The range of issues over which the local government has control is smaller—educational policy, for instance, is controlled by central government agencies to a much larger degree—and within the unitary British system of government, local autonomy is not provided for formally by home rule provisions, as it is in the constitutions of a number of American states. Nevertheless, the British have a long tradition of local self-government. And local councils are active in administrative work as well as in some limited areas of legislation where permission is given by the central government.[6]

It is difficult to rank the other three nations precisely. In terms of the formal structure of local government, however, it is relatively easy to specify which ranks lowest. The existence of the prefect system in Italy limits substantially any opportunity for local self-government. The communes in Italy have locally elected councils, but they have little freedom of action. All acts must be submitted to the centrally appointed prefect of the province, who passes on their legality; and certain significant matters, such as the municipal budget and the levying of taxes, must be approved by the provincial administrative committee (*Giunta Provinciale Amministrativa*), which passes on both the legality and the merit of the act. It is quite unlikely that a local government structure of this sort, in which there is a centrally appointed official with powers to oversee the activities of the locality, would foster a high level of autonomous local activity. Though there is some evidence of more local autonomy than one would expect, given the formal structure, the degree of autonomy is probably least of all the five nations.[7]

As in most cases when one is trying to array a series of units along a scale, it is the units near the middle of the scale that present the more difficult problems in categorization. In terms of the degree of local governmental auton-

[6] See, for instance, W. Eric Jackson, *Local Government in England and Wales*, London, 1960. This is not to argue that in the United States and Britain there is no external control over local government. There is obviously a large amount of external control and this control is steadily growing—a point whose implications will be discussed below. But relatively speaking, local government in these two nations has a vigor missing in the other three.

[7] See Samuel Humes and Eileen M. Martin, *The Structure of Local Governments Throughout the World*, The Hague, 1961, pp. 319–24; Harold Zink et al., *Rural Local Government in Sweden, Italy and India*, London, 1957, and Edward Banfield, *The Moral Basis of a Backward Society*, Glencoe, Ill., 1958. See, also, Robert C. Fried, *The Italian Prefects*, unpublished Ph.D. dissertation, Yale University, 1961.

omy, it is probably accurate to place Germany and Mexico between the United States and Britain on the one hand and Italy on the other. But one must approach the characterization of these two nations with somewhat more caution. One reason is the wide range of variation possible within a federal system, a situation heightened in Germany by differing regional traditions and by the somewhat different heritages from the three occupying powers. There is in many areas of Germany a strong tradition of local autonomy, as well as a tendency for local communities to engage in a wide range of activities. This is especially true among many of the older northern German cities, which have long histories of local self-government.[8] It is, however, difficult to estimate in any precise way the extent to which local self-government is firmly entrenched in other areas in Germany.

Mexico, unlike Italy but like the other three nations, has legal provision for relatively autonomous local governments on the level of the *municipio*. In actual practice, however, these local governments have been relatively uninfluential and relatively nonautonomous. This has been largely due to central control over local finances and the pervasive influence of the PRI, the single important Mexican political party. Local government in Mexico has rarely been of great significance.[9]

The nations also differ in the extent to which the local decision-making apparatus is accessible to participation by local residents. In some communities— and again this varies within nations, but perhaps more sharply among nations —there will be greater opportunity for the individual to participate in decisions. It is somewhat more difficult to compare the nations in this respect than it was to compare them in respect to local autonomy. There are fewer studies of the degree to which individuals actually participate in local affairs, for such participation depends largely upon informal as well as formal channels of participation. . . . In general, one would expect that the extent to which the local government is open to citizen participation in decisions would be closely related to the extent of local autonomy; and impressions of community life in these five nations . . . support this proposition.[10]

[8] See, for instance, Lorenz Fischer and Peter Van Hauten, "Cologne," in William A. Robson (ed.), *Great Cities of the World*, London, 1957, pp. 645–82.

[9] For a consideration of the influence of the PRI in the politics of one Mexican city, see Scott, *Mexican Government in Transition*, pp. 44–55; and William H. Form and William V. d'Antonio, "Integration and Cleavage Among Community Influentials in Two Border Cities," *American Sociological Review*, xxiv (1959), pp. 804–14. If our knowledge of and ability to measure this dimension were more precise it is possible that we might rank Mexico close to, or even below, Italy. However, more precise descriptions will depend on more precise research.

[10] But the degree of local self-government and the degree to which individuals can participate within that government may be independent of each other. It would be possible, for instance, to draw the conclusion from John Gimbel's study of *A German Community Under American Occupation: Marburg, 1945–1952*, Stanford, 1961, that the American Occupation's attempt to introduce local democracy failed for the simple reason that, though they gave power to local elites, these elites were not committed to furthering citizen participation.

Consequently, in interpreting the data in this [essay], we shall have to keep in mind that one reason why individuals differ in the frequency with which they adhere to participatory norms is that the structure of government and community organization changes from one nation to another. This does not make the attitudinal data any less significant. As we have suggested earlier, even if the attitudes we describe are in part determined by the structure of government and social system in each nation, this does not remove the fact that these attitudes in turn affect these same structures. The norms to which an individual adheres are largely determined by the role that the system allows him to play (though the fit between norms and structure will rarely be perfect); but these norms in turn have a feedback effect on the structure, reinforcing the structure if the fit between norms and structure is a good one; introducing strain into the system if norms and structure fit less well. And lastly, as we shall attempt to demonstrate below, attitudes toward the local government cannot be explained solely by the relation between the individual and the local governmental structure (and the same point can and will be made about the national government as well). We shall attempt to show, for instance, that the extent to which individuals believe they can influence the government, and in particular the ways in which they would attempt to exert that influence, depend, not only on the governmental system, but upon certain social and attitudinal characteristics of the individuals.

NATIONAL DIFFERENCES IN SENSE OF CIVIC OBLIGATION

Our question to the respondents dealt with participation in local affairs. We were interested, not only in political participation, but in any sort of outgoing activity the individual might mention. We wanted to know the extent to which individuals believe they have any sort of obligation to the community —to care about more than the personal problems of the family life and job.[11]

Table I summarizes the responses we received as to the role individuals should play within their local community.

We have classified our respondents into those who believe that the ordinary man should take some active part in his community (this includes those who say the ordinary man should attend meetings, join organizations involved in community affairs, and the like); those who believe that one ought to participate more passively in community activities (for example: one ought to be interested in local affairs, try to understand them and keep informed, vote);

[11] The question read: "We know that the ordinary person has many problems that take his time. In view of this, what part do you think the ordinary person ought to play in the local affairs of his town or district?" The interviewer attempted to find out as closely as possible what the respondent specifically felt one ought to do in his community.

those who feel that the ordinary man ought to participate only in church and religious activities; and those who do not think the ordinary man has any responsibility that involves him in the affairs of his community (here we include the respondents who feel that the ordinary man ought to maintain an upright personal life; who say that he ought to take no part in the affairs of his community; and who do not know what role the individual ought to play in his community).

TABLE 1.

How Active Should the Ordinary Man Be in His Local Community, by Nation
(in per cent)

Per Cent Who Say the Ordinary Man Should	U.S.	U.K.	Germany	Italy	Mexico
Be active in his community	51	39	22	10	26
Only participate passively*	27	31	38	22	33
Only participate in church affairs*	5	2	1	*	—
Total who mention some outgoing activity	83	72	61	32	59
Only be upright in personal life*	1	1	11	15	2
Do nothing in local community	3	6	7	11	2
Don't know	11	17	21	35	30
Other	2	5	1	7	7
Total per cent	100	100	100	100	100
Total number of cases	970	963	955	995	1,007

* Multiple answers were possible, but we have eliminated them from this table by listing respondents' *most active* response only (i.e., the response that would fall highest on the table). Thus an individual who mentioned active as well as passive participation would be listed under active participation only; one who mentioned church activities as well as an upright private life would be listed under the former and not the latter.

Clearly from this table, the image of the citizen-as-participant is more widespread in some countries than in others. In the United States and Britain a large number of respondents believe that the individual should be an active participant in the affairs of his community. Half of the Americans interviewed and 39 per cent of the British mention some active role that the individual ought to play. In Italy, at the other extreme, there are few who conceive of the citizen as active participant. Only one in ten Italians believes that the ordinary man has an obligation to take an active role in his community. The proportions of German and Mexican respondents who have some image of the active citizen lie in-between the American and British proportions on the one hand and the Italian on the other. One out of five of our German respondents and one out of four of our Mexicans conceive of the ordinary man as having some obligation to participate.[12]

"One ought at least to take an interest in what goes on in the community"; or, "One ought to be active in church and religious affairs": if we consider these statements an indicator (albeit a weaker one) of the existence of some norm of participation, then the contrasts among the nations are still striking. In the United States 83 per cent of the respondents talk of the ordinary man as having some commitment to his community that takes him out of involvement in purely personal affairs—even if the responsibility is minimal. The proportion in Britain is somewhat smaller at 72 per cent; in Mexico and Germany about 60 per cent talk of some outgoing role for the individual, while in Italy only 32 per cent do.

What sorts of community activities do our respondents have in mind when they say the ordinary man ought to play some part in his local community? As Table 2 shows, only a small number of respondents in each country mention partisan activity as the responsibility of the individual to his community. In the United States and Britain respondents frequently mention taking part in local government bodies, attending meetings, and the like. In Germany and Mexico this is less frequently mentioned, but is mentioned more frequently than in Italy. Active community participation in a nongovernmental sense—participation in civic groups and organizations, or informal activity to help the community—is quite frequently mentioned in the United States. Such nongovernmental activity is again least mentioned in Italy, with Germany and Mexico trailing Britain. In terms of active participation, then, the five countries can be roughly grouped: the United States and Britain are the countries in which the image of the active participating citizen is most often the normative ideal; in Germany and Mexico the ideal receives mention, but less often; and in Italy this ideal is least widespread.

Some illustrations may be useful in making explicit the specific areas of activity respondents had in mind:

> *A British Housewife:*
> "He should take some part in public life and have a say in town-planning, education, and religion."
> *An American Housewife:*
> "Everyone should take part in church and community affairs. . . . We should take an active part in making our schools better."

[12] The Mexican pattern is interesting here, and we shall return to it later. Mexican respondents mention an obligation to participate more frequently than do German respondents and much more frequently than do Italian respondents. This relatively high sense of obligation, coupled, as we shall discuss, with lower activity and information, is an aspect of the civic aspirational tendency among the Mexicans.

TABLE 2.

What Role Should the Ordinary Man Play in His Local Community, by Nation
(in per cent)

Per Cent Who Choose	U.S.	U.K.	Germany	Italy	Mexico
ACTIVE PARTICIPATION IN LOCAL COMMUNITY[a]					
Take part in activities of local government	21	22	13	5	11
Take part in activities of political parties	6	4	4	1	5
Take part in nongovernmental activity and in organizations interested in local affairs	32	17	9	5	10
MORE PASSIVE COMMUNITY ACTIVITIES[b]					
Try to understand and keep informed	21	11	24	6	29
Vote	40	18	15	2	1
Take an interest in what is going on	3	13	6	15	4
PARTICIPATION IN CHURCH AND RELIGIOUS ACTIVITIES[a]	12	2	2	—	—
Total percentage of respondents who mention some outgoing activity[b]	83	72	61	32	59
Total number of respondents	970	963	955	995	1,007

[a] The percentages in these categories are somewhat larger than in Table 1, since this table contains all the responses of individuals, rather than their most active responses.

[b] Total percentages are less than the total of the individual cells, since the latter involve multiple responses.

A Mexican Housewife:
"People should have diversion, but have enough free time to occupy themselves with political and social things."

A German Worker:
"Organizations should be formed that would enable [people] to discuss their problems together—for instance, parents' advisory councils [*Eltembeiräte*] at schools."

An Italian Teacher:
"Each individual should be interested in an active way and should criticize justly and severely when it is necessary."

An American Postmaster:

"A citizen should play an active part. . . . He might hold a local office. Other civic work such as drives, such as Red Cross. Here we have a volunteer fire company; he could help out with that."

The last quotation, from an American postmaster, suggests how the existence of structures in which one can participate affects the norms of participation that individuals hold. One would certainly not expect an individual to feel an obligation to participate in such activities as "drives," the Red Cross, and volunteer fire companies in communities where such activities were nonexistent.

One theme running through many of the answers that stress active participation in the local community—a theme found largely among activists in the United States and Britain—is that the individual ought to be active as a participant in decisions; that he ought, in a rather independent way, to take part in the running of the community:

> *An English Female Worker:*
> "Everyone should take a part. . . . They should get together and give opinions as to why and how this and that should be worked."
> *An American Housewife:*
> "I think a person should vote. If there are any town meetings he should attend them. . . . If everyone does things in his own small way, it would add up to something big. Many people sit back and let others do things for them, then complain."
> *A German Farmer:*
> "He should discuss politics, but shouldn't just accept everything, but [should] speak up too."

On the other hand, local activity means for some respondents more informal social participation, perhaps to help out one's neighbors:

> *A German Chauffeur:*
> "He should not just talk, but should act too. For instance, during hay harvesting time, one should not just stick his hands in his pockets and watch the farmers exerting themselves, but should pitch in. After all, it's a matter of community welfare."
> *An English Businessman:*
> "He should help in local organizations—children's clubs, boy scouts. He should help his neighbors and be a good living person."

A number of respondents, as shown in Table 2, thought of the individual as having a more passive sort of obligation to participate in his community; this usually involved some obligation to be informed of what is going on or to be interested in it:

> *A Mexican Housewife:*
> "[He should] be interested in how the government is formed, and be active by studying books and newspapers."

An English Housewife:
"He ought to know what is going on. Go to the occasional meeting to find out."
An Italian Worker:
"Simply be interested."

Though the degree of autonomy of local government differs from nation to nation, in all five nations there are elections for some sort of local or communal council. For many respondents, as Table 2 indicates, voting in these elections was considered a responsibility of the individual to his community. But insofar as the individual considered his local responsibility to be exhausted by the act of voting, we have listed this as a relatively passive form of participation in community life—though a form of participation it certainly is. In some cases, particularly among those German respondents who mention voting as an obligation, this interpretation is made explicit. The responsibility to vote is explicitly stated as exhausting the individual's responsibility and, in fact, is invoked as an act that absolves one of all other community responsibilities:

An American Disabled Worker:
"I think they should do their part. Outside of voting there isn't too much the average fellow can do. . . . You ought to vote and then support any worthwhile thing your community is trying to do."
An Italian Veterinarian:
"What should an individual do? Elect his representatives. That's all."
A German Retired Worker:
"Choose a mayor at election time. That's all one need to do. The mayor takes care of everything."
A German House Painter:
"He should vote—that's the most important thing. But he should not be politically active himself."
A German Housewife:
"I don't understand that. We have to work. The people in the council are cleverer after all. They'll do a good job. You just have to vote for the right ones."

As was pointed out earlier, not all respondents think of the individual as having any outgoing responsibility within his local community. As Table 1 indicated, there were a substantial number of respondents in Germany and Mexico, and particularly in Italy, who admitted to no sense of local civic obligation. In this sense, the norms that they accept in relation to their community are certainly not those of the participating citizen. They are quite probably oriented to their communities as subjects or parochials. These can be found in all five nations, but they are most frequent in Italy (where 15 per cent of the respondents invoke these parochial values—a larger group than those who think the individual ought to be an active participant) and in Ger-

many (where 11 per cent of the respondents talk of such parochial values).
The following are some examples of the ways in which one's responsibility to
the community is interpreted as an essentially parochial or subject responsibility to one's personal life:

> *An English Housewife:*
> "It's as much as my husband can do to go to work, never mind taking
> part in local affairs. We appoint councillors and leave everything to
> them."
> *A German Mechanic:*
> "Take care of one's family by working. Make one's children into decent
> people."
> *A German Farmer:*
> "I pay my taxes, go to my church, and do my work as a farmer."
> *A German Mechanic:*
> "Work and support one's family decently. If everyone did that, the state
> would have less trouble and expense."
> *A German Housewife:*
> "Everyone should do his work."
> *An Italian Worker:*
> "[He] should attend to his work . . . be a good citizen, and take care of
> [his] family."
> *An Italian Artisan:*
> "[He should be] honest and concerned about his work."

One important point about the relationship among civic, subject, and parochial norms is suggested by the data in Table 2. If the values of active participation are widespread in a country, this does not mean that the valuation of
more passive participation is missing, or that subject and parochial values are
missing. In the United States, for instance, where active participation is most
frequently mentioned, the more passive political participation of voting is also
frequently mentioned, as is participation in church and religious activities.
And many respondents who mention active participation also mention the
more parochial norms. This accords with our notion that the citizen role is
built on but does not replace the roles of subject and parochial.

Our data clearly suggest sharp differences among the nations in the roles
that respondents think individuals ought to play in their local communities.
However, our data do not suggest that all those who think the individual
ought to take an active part do in fact take such active roles. The gap between civic norms and civic behavior is, as we all know, large. As one American businessman who stressed the obligation to participate actively put it,
"I'm saying what he ought to do, not what I do." We are not saying that one
out of every two Americans is an active participant in the affairs of his local
community or that four out of ten Britons are. Rather, we suggest that in
these countries the norm of active citizenship is widespread. And this is con-

gruent with the structure of government. The actual opportunities to partici-pate and the norms that one ought to participate mutually reinforce each other to foster a high level of citizen participation. In Italy, on the other hand, the relative lack of opportunity to participate in an autonomous local commu-nity is accompanied [by] the absence of a set of norms favoring such partici-pation.

Demographic Patterns

Who within each country hold to the ideal of the citizen as participant? The middle class? or those with higher education? As Table 3 indicates, in each of the five nations it is those with some higher education who are most likely to express adherence to the norms of participation; and the least likely

TABLE 3.

Per Cent Who Say the Ordinary Man Should be Active in His Local Community, by Nation and Education

Nation	Total (%)	(No.)*	Prim. or Less (%)	(No.)	Some Sec. (%)	(No.)	Some Univ. (%)	(No.)
United States	51	(970)	35	(339)	56	(443)	66	(188)
Great Britain	39	(963)	37	(593)	42	(322)	42	(24)
Germany	22	(955)	21	(792)	32	(123)	38	(26)
Italy	10	(995)	7	(692)	17	(245)	22	(54)
Mexico	26	(1,007)	24	(877)	37	(103)	38	(24)

* Numbers in parentheses refer to the bases upon which percentages are calculated.

to report that the individual has some responsibility to participate actively in his local community are those with primary school education or less. Never-theless, despite the fact that the distribution of adherence to participatory norms is similar in the five nations, the differences in absolute levels of such expressed adherence are still great even within similiar education groups. And within each educational group the relationship among the nations is roughly the same—American respondents tend most frequently to express adherence to such norms, followed by British, Mexican, German, and Italian respondents in that order. Furthermore, unlike some other variables, where the differences among nations tend to disappear when the all-important characteristic of edu-cation is controlled, differences still remain in the frequency of adherence to the norms of participation. In fact, a university-educated person in Germany or Mexico is no more likely to express adherence to these norms than is a pri-mary-educated person in the United States or Britain; and the Italian univer-sity-educated respondent is less likely.

In regard to occupational groups (see Table 4), there is a tendency in the

United States for the acceptance of the norm to be more general among those
with higher-status occupations. In the other countries the relationship between occupation and belief in the norm is relatively weak, but it does tend
to be in the same direction. Thus in all countries, save Mexico, white-collar
workers are more likely than unskilled or skilled workers to believe that the
ordinary man should be an active participant in his local community.

TABLE 4.

*Per Cent Who Say the Ordinary Man Should be Active in His Local Community,
by Nation and Occupation of Family Breadwinner*

Nation	Total (%)	(No.)*	Unskilled (%)	(No.)	Skilled (%)	(No.)	White Collar (%)	(No.)	Professional & Managerial (%)	(No.)
United States	51	(970)	34	(208)	52	(177)	59	(194)	73	(101)
Great Britain	39	(963)	31	(224)	43	(289)	50	(123)	42	(106)
Germany	12	(955)	18	(141)	20	(203)	31	(143)	33	(45)
Italy	10	(995)	8	(223)	6	(77)	24	(142)	14	(57)
Mexico	26	(1,007)	26	(120)	25	(294)	25	(148)	42	(59)

* Numbers in parentheses refer to the bases upon which percentages are calculated.

Lastly, if one compares the sexes (see Table 5) in terms of the degree to
which they hold participatory norms, it becomes clear that in all countries except the United States these norms are more frequently held by men than by
women. Thus the extent to which the norms are widespread differs from nation to nation, but the patterns of who accepts the norms are the same in all
the nations.

TABLE 5.

*Per Cent Who Say the Ordinary Man Should be Active in His Local Community,
by Nation and Sex*

Nation	Total (%)	(No.)*	Male (%)	(No.)	Female (%)	(No.)
United States	51	(970)	52	(455)	50	(515)
Great Britain	39	(963)	43	(460)	36	(503)
Germany	22	(955)	31	(449)	16	(506)
Italy	10	(995)	14	(471)	6	(524)
Mexico	26	(1,007)	31	(355)	24	(652)

* Numbers in parentheses refer to the bases upon which percentages are calculated.

If a democratic political system is one in which the ordinary citizen participates in political decisions, a democratic political culture should consist of a set of beliefs, attitudes, norms, perceptions, and the like, that support participation. Of course, the frequency of adherence to this norm will be affected by the structures of the local community. But if the norm of participation is not widespread, institutional change in the direction of fostering participation will not in itself create a participatory democracy.

It is impossible to say what is the requisite level of participatory norms and of participation in political affairs for an effective democracy. Americans more often accept norms of participation than do individuals in the other four countries, yet they have often been accused of not being civic enough. But while our findings cannot tell us whether the level of participation in the United States or Britain is "good enough," they do tell us that it is certainly higher than in Germany, Mexico, and Italy. And as this and other data on participation will suggest, where norms of participation, perceived ability to participate, and actual participation are high, effective democracy is more likely to flourish.

That an individual believes he ought to participate in the political life of his community or nation does not mean that he will in fact do so. Before the norm that one ought to participate can be translated into the act itself, the individual will probably have to perceive that he is able to act. And though the two are related, they are by no means identical. One can believe he ought to participate, but perceive himself as unable to do so. Or one can perceive himself as able to participate but not feel any obligation to do so. Certainly a great source of political discontent is the acceptance of the norms of participation coupled with the belief that one cannot in fact participate. This, it has been suggested, is the danger of overselling the norms of political democracy in the schools. When the myth of democracy comes into serious conflict with the realities of politics, the results are cynicism. The society in which individuals do in fact participate in decisions—that is, the democratic society—is likely to be the society in which individuals believe they ought to participate. It is also likely to be the society in which they think they can participate and know how to go about it.

SOME DETERMINANTS OF
POLITICAL APATHY

MORRIS ROSENBERG

It has been observed that political apathy is a very widespread phenomenon in American culture.[1] Whether one measures apathy by the criterion of political involvement, knowledge or activity, the number of people who satisfy the culturally defined desiderata of participation is small.

There are those who consider this a serious malfunctioning of democracy.[2] If men are to maintain control over their political destinies, they must be aware of what is going on, and must take a hand in determining public policy. On the other hand, there are some political theorists who find such apathy a favorable, rather than an unfavorable, sign. They interpret it to mean that the society is fundamentally contented, is characterized by consensus rather than by broad cleavages, and is basically stable.

If we accept the view that the democratic ideal encourages political interest and participation, then the question naturally arises: what are the factors which bring about this absence of political interest and activity? In order to cast some light on this question, an exploratory study, designed to reveal the range and variation of factors which contribute to political apathy, was undertaken. Seventy qualitative interviews were conducted with a non-random sample of respondents most of whom resided in Ithaca, New York. The interviews were of an unstructured type, designed to encourage the respondent to reveal his views regarding the political process with a minimum of direction and a maximum of spontaneity.[3] We did not undertake to obtain statistically

[1] Cf., for example, Gordon Connelly and Harry Field, "The Non-Voter—Who He Is, What He Thinks," *Public Opinion Quarterly*, VIII (1944), 175–87; Paul F. Lazarsfeld, Bernard Berelson and Hazel Gaudet, *The People's Choice*, 2nd edition (New York: Columbia University Press, 1948), pp. 40–51; Louis Bean, *How to Predict Elections* (New York: Alfred A. Knopf, 1948), Chap. 5; Richard Centers, *The Psychology of Social Classes* (Princeton, N.J.: Princeton University Press, 1949).

[2] For example, in his examination of the accepted norms of political behavior in America, Bernard Berelson, "Democratic Theory and Public Opinion," *Public Opinion Quarterly*, XVI (1952), 316, notes; "Political interest or apathy is not permitted, or at least not approved."

[3] The author is profoundly indebted to the students in his class in Political Sociology at Cornell University, who not only conducted the interviews, but also offered many illuminating insights in the discussions of the data. In particular, this study owes a great deal to Jay C. Greenfield.

SOURCE: Morris Rosenberg, "Some Determinants of Political Apathy," *Public Opinion Quarterly*, 18 (Winter 1954–55), 349–366. Reprinted by permission.

reliable data but, rather, sought to gather ideas and hypotheses for more systematic research. The results presented here, therefore, lay no claim to representing scientific proof, but are designed to serve as suggestive hypotheses.

Limitations of space prohibit a discussion of the total range of factors which were revealed in these interviews and which appeared to contribute to political indifference and inactivity, but three general factors merit discussion: (1) the threatening consequences of political activity, (2) the futility of political activity, and (3) the absence of spurs to interest and participation. Let us note how these factors are expressed concretely in the interviews.

THE THREATENING CONSEQUENCES OF
POLITICAL ACTIVITY

It is generally felt that any restriction[4] on the individual's right to express his political views freely represents a violation of the value of freedom of speech. It is assumed that the uninhibited airing of ideas, viewpoints, and facts is conducive to the attainment of rational democratic decisions. It may thus be argued that loyalty investigations which frighten innocent people into silence represent a limitation on freedom of speech.

The issue of freedom of speech is usually posed in terms of whether the *government* applies pressure on the individual to restrain him from expressing his political views. Yet there are social factors which may be far more significant than governmental restraint in limiting the expression of social and political ideas. The sociological issue of freedom of speech boils down to the question of whether one is willing to take the *consequences* of expressing one's political ideas and working in their behalf; governmental restraint, expressed in physical coercion, is only *one* such possible consequence.

Our predominantly middle-class respondents expressed many fears of presenting their own political views freely, but very rarely were these fears of political authority. In view of the present congressional investigations, it was surprising how few respondents seemed reluctant to reveal their political attitudes openly out of fear of governmental action. One respondent, it is true, carefully checked on the identity of the interviewer; he was reluctant to express his political views frankly to an unknown person who, for all he knew, might actually be an official investigator trying to draw him out. This is a telling commentary on how the current governmental investigations may immobilize certain people from the very minimum of political action. But such peo-

---

[4] Within certain minor limitations, such as, the prohibition against slanderous or defamatory statements; the ban on the use of obscene, profane or other socially unacceptable language or references in the mass entertainment industries; the prohibition against incitement to panic, such as falsely crying "fire" in a crowded theater; the ban on revealing classified government information; and so on. As such, these prohibitions involve no limitation on the expression of one's political point of view.

ple proved to be rarities. The reason probably is that in any society, authoritarian or democratic, the individual is always free to stand up and express his views frankly in favor of the government; it is only when people desire to express views which challenge constituted authority that freedom of speech becomes an issue. Most of our respondents were Republicans or Democrats, and it did not appear to occur to them that *their* rights might be threatened by such investigations. Whether different results would appear among a more representative sample of respondents is a question requiring further research.

Our particular respondents, however, did express many fears of uninhibitedly expressing their political views, but the threats they mentioned tended to be of a social or psychological sort rather than of a political nature. The point to be stressed here is that political participation does not simply involve the relationship of the citizen to his government. Political participation may to a considerable extent involve *interpersonal interaction.* Consequently the dynamics of interpersonal relationships may have important implications for the operation of the democratic process.

In this paper we will use the term "political activity" in a broad sense to include political discussion, consumption of political communications, interest, voting, and participation in political organizations. It would be important in future investigations to analyze these manifestations of activity separately.

Threats to interpersonal harmony. One of the characteristics of politics in a democracy is that they are *controversial.* This establishes potentialities for interpersonal disagreement which may threaten the individual in many ways— particularly when the individual has an image of himself as a likeable, agreeable personality. Similarly, there are those who are so insecure that they are terrified of aggression or hostility of any sort directed against them.[5]

Political discussion may threaten to alienate one's friends and neighbors.

> Some of my friends are (active in politics). Some are avid Democrats, but most of my friends are not active. We don't discuss politics much. I think it's sort of like religion. It's personal, and I don't like to get into arguments. . . . When politics comes up in conversation, I always say— "Let's talk about something else," . . . especially when ———— is around. She's such a Democrat and gets so riled up.

Political discussion posed threats to a recent marriage:

> I personally want to be informed because my husband holds different political beliefs. We don't discuss politics very often because when we

---

[5] This reaction is particularly characteristic of the self-effacing, or compliant, type described by Karen Horney in *Neurosis and Human Growth* (New York: W. W. Norton, 1950), Chap. 9.

do we are likely to disagree violently. Right now I want to avoid friction—*we were just married last June*—so we try not to get into political discussions."

Political discussion may endanger one's position in a group and threaten one's sense of belongingness. For example, a woman who was very much wrapped up in the ——— organization feared that political discussion might jeopardize her position there. When asked why she did not discuss politics more, she replied: "Well, you see, a lot of local political wives are in ——— and I have to be careful."

The manner in which social pressure may be applied to insure political conformity in a small community is illustrated in the following story:

> I remember one time going to a city council meeting when I was back in Minnesota. I was disagreeing with one of the commissioners on an important town issue. Why, the next day I received calls and a visitor asking me what exactly it was all about and what I was up to. After that I just didn't go to meetings of that sort.

Thus people may impose a powerful self-censorship on political expression in order to avoid threats to friendship, marriage relationships, and group solidarity. While they are legally free to say what they please, many are unwilling to face the interpersonal consequences of such expression. Whether the situation is actually threatening or whether it is simply interpreted as such by the individual, the effect is the same.

Threats to occupational success. The economic processes of production and exchange in a complex industrial-commercial society involve interpersonal relations at almost every point. If political discussion has a potentially divisive and disharmonious interpersonal effect, then it may be avoided because of its threats to the important area of occupational success. This is particularly likely to occur among those engaged in the sale of products where the salesman must maintain harmonious relations with his customer; it is not, however, restricted to this area. In brief, politics fosters argument and dispute, whereas business success thrives on harmony and good will. Consequently, people may fear to talk politics because of the threat it poses to their occupational success.

Political discussion may threaten the harmonious relations essential to economic production.

One respondent refused to tell the interviewer how he had voted. When asked for his reason, he replied:

> Well, it's a personal subject. . . . You see, in my field, there is no harm in avoiding unnecessary conflicts, and politics are subject to strong sentiments. . . . I have to maintain relations among employees and management, and I try to avoid trouble points. I've always felt it wise policy to be quiet about how I vote.

One respondent, a manager of a plant, was asked whether he had helped any candidates in the most recent campaign. He replied:

> No, because I never like to express my political views in public. . . . Since I have to deal with so many men, both in the plant and in the buying of (raw materials), there is no sense in making people angry at you over a local election.

One respondent was asked directly whether the fact that he conducted his business in a small town did not make public support of a candidate or party an economic danger. He replied:

> Absolutely; for that reason I register *No Mark*. Actually I'm a Republican. But in the case of ———, it's different. He's a friend of mine . . . and *everybody* knew I'd support him anyway. Besides, he lives in ——— where I have my business, and (his opponent) is over in ——— (a different town). *I don't sell much over there anyway.*

In other words, the man engaged in commerce cannot afford to alienate *either* Democrats or Republicans; in this sense business is not merely apolitical but anti-political. Similarly an employer may be reluctant to alienate his workers, and a worker may be unwilling to jeopardize his job, in defense of his political principles. These factors may be extremely significant deterrents to the free expression of political ideas.

Threat of ego-deflation. While political discussion may ostensibly represent a form of intellectual intercourse designed to evaluate alternative principles, it cannot escape implicating the self. An attack on a man's principles may often be seen as a blow to his self-esteem.[6] While some people may enhance their egos through victory in political argument, there are others who, facing the prospect of revealing factual ignorance or committing gross logical errors, seek to avoid the feeling of defeat, abashment, humiliation, or other discomfiture by staying far away from such discussions. An individual with a highly vulnerable ego may impose a censorship upon himself which is as rigid as any imposed in an authoritarian state.

One woman, observing that her husband and in-laws discussed politics, was asked whether she joined in these discussions. "No, since I don't understand too much about politics, I just keep my mouth closed." When asked if she discussed politics with anyone, she answered: "Very little, because . . . well, I really don't understand too much about politics. People should know what they are talking about and this takes an education which goes beyond the high-school level."

> I don't think I'm capable enough to take an active part (in politics). I just feel I lack the ability. . . . I don't know what would be required of me.

---

[6] See Muzafer Sherif and Hadley Cantril, *The Psychology of Ego-Involvements* (New York: John Wiley & Sons, 1947).

My husband and I talk it over, of course, but I don't talk about it in public because I don't know enough. I wish I knew more. Sometimes I'd like to say something.

Although these statements reflected a faith in expertism, combined with a rational insistence that a person should have some basis for his expressed opinions, they suggest that an individual may prefer to avert the danger of exposing himself to public ridicule rather than to freely and openly express his political ideas.

To summarize, the democratic right of freedom of speech does not insure that people will feel free to express their political convictions publicly at all times. Threats of governmental action will deter some. Others will be blocked from talking or acting in behalf of their political beliefs out of fear of losing friends, alienating neighbors, endangering marriages, jeopardizing their positions in groups, losing business, jeopardizing their jobs, endangering production in their plants, facing community pressures, or exposing their feelings of self-esteem to threat. These are consequences which many people are unwilling to face and, to avoid these consequences, they impose a self-censorship on their political expression, participation, and even emotional involvement. One factor in the political structure which sets the conditions for these results is the multi-party system. In a democratic society, politics are *controversial,* and controversiality, while it may encourage interest, also has potential interpersonal consequences which may foster political inactivity.

THE FUTILITY OF POLITICAL ACTIVITY

In most cases a precondition for political activity is the conviction that what one does will make a difference, will have an effect of some sort. It is true, of course, that people may engage in some noninstrumental, goal activity such as political discussion simply because they are interested in the subject and enjoy talking about it. In most cases, however, political participation beyond the level of discussion probably has the aim of *getting one's will translated into political action.* But, people tend to be motivated to action only if they feel that this action leads to the desired goal.

One general factor contributing to political apathy is the feeling that activity is futile. The individual feels that even if he were active, the political results he desires would probably not come to pass. There is consequently no point in doing anything.

In expressing this sense of futility, the individual can focus on either the subject or the object of action. On the one hand, he can focus on certain characteristics of himself; e.g., he is insignificant, powerless, or incompetent. On the other hand, he can focus on the characteristics of the objects to be influenced; e.g., political representatives pay no attention to him, political machines run things just as they please, and so on. But if his representative pays

no attention to him, this may be either because *he* is too unimportant or because *the representative* is unresponsive to the public will. In other words,
each "reason" for feeling that political activity is futile implies both a characteristic of the individual effort and a characteristic of the agents to be influenced. For analytical purposes it is important to distinguish between reasons phrased in terms of the self and those phrased in terms of the nature of
the political structure, although these should not be interpreted as representing alternative reasons.

Futility based on the sense of personal inadequacy. It is rather easy to see
why, in a mass society characterized by broad disparities in power, an individual may tend to develop a sense of personal insignficance and weakness.

The feeling of the futility of action, deriving from a sense of personal insignificance, is likely to be particularly strong when the individual feels himself
to be either (a) only one in relation to a great many, or (b) a weak person in
relation to strong and powerful forces.

Simmel has noted that as the size of the group increases, each individual
alone makes less of a difference to the totality.[7] Although the proportion of
potential voters who actually go to the polls in the United States is relatively
small, the absolute number is extremely large; the 1952 national elections attracted over sixty million voters. Many of our respondents appeared overwhelmed by this huge number of participants and felt that their vote would
have little effect on the outcome of the election one way or the other.

> Voting doesn't make that much difference. What can an individual do
> about it? He can't really do much.

> My vote will always count, yet one vote one way or the other doesn't
> make much difference.

One respondent considered herself politically unimportant for the following unexpected reason:

> One vote doesn't mean much. The way it is set up now with the elec-
> trical or electoral college, I can't see we actually vote a person into
> office. I don't know too much about it. I think we should have each per-
> son voting and his vote counted separately. We should have just straight
> balloting.

This sense of political impotence was expressed still more clearly by this respondent when she said:

> There is no real justice in the present system. You don't have too
> much to say, right or wrong. You can feel or think, but that's about all.

People may also tend to consider any serious political efforts on their part
as futile because they feel that they have very little individual power. They

---

[7] *The Sociology of Georg Simmel*, tr. and ed. by Kurt H. Wolff (Glencoe, Ill.: The Free Press,
1950), Part II.

feel that their own voices are too weak, their own strength too puny, to make much political difference.

One respondent felt that politics are

> all right, but it is always the big guy he (the politician) is interested in helping. . . . The only thing I have against them is that they are too damn narrow-minded (and that politics) keep the little man down.

Switching his attention to cities, this respondent felt that there was too much vote-buying in cities and that

> the little man in cities is afraid to go against the party. He either votes right, or he doesn't vote.

He felt the courts, too, were not fair; witnesses were bought off. "It's the same as in politics. . . . The little guy has nothing to do about it."

Another respondent was asked what part the average man played in politics. "Not much of a part," he replied; "the little man votes and that's all. . . . The party usually takes over pretty much. They don't think too much about the little man."

> What does the working man care about politics, anyway? What can he do, even if he did care? That's probably it. . . . What can he do? Nothing should bother him anyway. The country will still go on just the same for the average working man.

One respondent, asked how much influence people like her had on the way the government was run, answered: "None—well, that isn't the right answer. I vote; is that what you mean by it?"

> Well, it seems almost useless to do a lot of work for the national group when there are so many other people for it and when you really won't have much to say about what happens anyway. A lot of those people are a lot better than I am, and a lot of them have more pull.

In some cases, the *individual's self-image* does not correspond to his picture of the requirements of political activity. His sense of inadequacy is based on special personality characteristics.

One respondent was asked whether he would care about campaigning. "No, I don't think so. Unless I felt strongly enough about something, I would. I'm not much of a salesman. I never cared about buttonholing."

"I don't really go in for it that much. I don't know. I guess I'm more of a listener in that line."

The unmanageability of political forces. Many of the respondents who expressed a sense of futility that their own political action would culminate in a desired political result placed less stress on their own impotence and more on the unresponsiveness of political powers to their pressure. The feeling was that in (1) the political representative, (2) the political machine, (3) the "government," or (4) some anonymous agencies of power simply ignored the will of the people; they made their own decisions almost completely uninfluenced by the people.

Under these circumstances, political activity was viewed as futile. Respondents expressing these views tended to feel that they had lost control over the political decision-making process; their political destinies lay in the hands of others.

Many people felt that their *elected representatives* were unconcerned with, and unresponsive to, the will of the people.

> Once they (the politicians) get elected, they don't give a god-damn. You got to know the man who does good, not your friend. You could be a good man but if the people don't like you, it's no good. You say to a guy, "I don't like you; I'm not going to vote for you." He says, "If you vote for me I'm your friend, and if you don't vote for me, I'm still your friend." But if he get elected, he don't do nothing for you.
> . . . This politics is really a funny thing.

Many respondents appear to feel that once the *political machines* gain power, the citizens' control over the political process tends to be lost.

> The machine is too strong to do what you want.
> The machines run things all around. . . . Working to stop the machine could go on and on and still get no place. They'll always be there.

The centralization and concentration of government may produce a sense of remoteness from the decision-making process. The individual feels that he cannot maintain control over political decisions made by powerful figures hundreds and even thousands of miles away.

This phenomenon was highlighted by the respondents who contrasted the type of effectiveness he could have at the local level with his potential influence at the national level.

> In local government, if things aren't really clear, you can usually find out the facts. Go back to knowing persons. You can't say that I can't get something out of some aldermen I know. If something is going wrong in the city, I can see one of them. In the case of senators, I can't go down to Washington and see my senator every time something goes wrong. In local, I think I can find out, whereas in national government, I don't feel I can.

One respondent was asked whether world peace was important to him. He replied:

> It's an important problem, yes, but there isn't much we can do about it in a meeting downtown. We're concerned about it, naturally, everyone is; but just about all we can do is sit by and watch what happens.

Washington does all the deciding, and we've put men there for the purpose. . . . I know what it entails to pick up garbage, but I haven't the foggiest notion of what it takes to put over a treaty between two countries. I don't know whether the men in Washington are doing the best possible job or not.

Finally, there are some people who feel that action is futile because the basic political decisions are in the hands of certain *powerful anonymous forces*. The citizen cannot influence them, not simply because they are remote or unresponsive, but because he does not even know who they are.

The masses feel it's controlled by certain groups.

We say we live in a democracy because we elect our representatives. But if the people we elect are in turn chosen by people who are outside our control, then our democracy is only relative and not as pure as we think it is. . . . I think that the higher levels of party organization are closed to ordinary citizens.

Today most of the platforms of both major parties are about the same. The people it really matters to are those who are looking for special favors. Just take the issue of tidelands' oil and take a list of the visitors of the General the day before he signed the bill!

A couple of men get together in some room . . . and when they come out, the party nomination has been made. You never know.

Thus some people feel it is futile to seek to influence those who make political decisions, because they feel that the locus of power lies in the hands of unknown powerful forces.[8]

It is relevant to note the influence of the time factor in politics. At election time the citizen's sense of power and incentive for action is likely to be maximal. If the individual wishes to get his will translated into political action, he can do something about it, secure in the conviction that he is making some contribution toward that end. Not only may he vote for the candidate who propounds his views and position, but he may also seek to persuade others to do the same. He may thus feel some sense of control over the political process.

However, the *periodicity* of American elections requires the citizen to exercise his power at arbitrarily predetermined times, not when it suits his mood. Thus the individual who is angry at an incumbent or enthusiastic about a candidate may often have to wait a year or more before he can vote again. It is difficult for the human organism to maintain a high level of emotional ardor

---

[8] Although seemingly similar, the apathy of these people differs from that of David Riesman's "inside-dopester" type. The inside-dopester is satisfied to know what goes on in the inner circles, whereas the type described above is apathetic because he feels hopeless about influencing the decision-makers. See David Riesman, *The Lonely Crowd* (New Haven, Conn.: Yale University Press, 1950).

and involvement over a long period of time. The more characteristic reaction, therefore, is to withdraw one's emotional involvement from politics. Once emotion is withdrawn, of course, vigorous political activity becomes difficult. In other words, *electoral periodicity is not resonant with human reactions.* The individual has power at election time but tends to consider action futile at other times.

> Anyway, politics has really stopped until next fall. We won't start till next fall. A guy figures "what the hell?" People aren't interested when there's no election.
>
> Once a man is elected and he turns out no good, it is too late to do anything about it. They might not do what they say. Either they can't do it, or they say, "I'm in now, so I don't have to do it."

The citizen thus feels a *discontinuous* sense of control over the political process. He has some power at the periodic intervals of election time, but most of the time he sees no relationship between his desires and action and actual political results. In addition, he cannot work to translate his will into action immediately, but must "save up" his irritations, desires, or enthusiasms until the next election. This characteristic of the political structure may often cause him to feel that there is no point in getting excited or doing anything about political matters, i.e., it encourages apathy. It is true, of course, that citizens can write to their Congressmen or participate in pressure groups, but these alternatives seldom appeared to have occurred to our respondents.

The foregone conclusion. The sense of futility generated by activity designed to translate one's will into action is likely to be strongest, of course, when one has reason to believe that such action will never come to pass. When a party has no more than a theoretical chance of victory, when the election is a foregone conclusion, then the rather vague incentive of an "impressive defeat" is little spur to vigorous political activity.

The individual feels that no matter how hard he works, the candidate he supports will not be elected in any case. This is particularly likely to be the case when a state or local community has a well-established and virtually unchangeable tradition of electing candidates from one party. Many people prefer to remain inactive, or at least uninvolved, rather than to face the frustration stemming from the certain defeat of their candidates or principles.

This is the situation in Ithaca. The town normally registers and votes overwhelmingly Republican. The Democrats often encounter difficulty in obtaining a slate of candidates, and the Liberal Party characteristically supports the Democratic candidate. A Democrat was elected mayor some years ago, but died before taking office (the cause being, it is facetiously rumored, the terrible shock of his victory). Usually, however, a primarily Republican slate is returned.

> Nobody realizes how hard the Democratic Party around here does work. We'd like to get a higher caliber man to run but it's just impossi-

ble. Everybody knows the Republican will win and nobody wants to waste his time.

Everyone votes Republican here whether they are good, bad or inefficient (sic). . . . In many town, local and county elections, one party dominates the area. There is not enough spirit of competition to arouse interest.

The gap between ideal and reality. Thus far we have focused on the individual's feeling of futility regarding the possibility of attaining some practical political goal. It is also possible, however, that if the goal itself is too remote or too difficult to attain, the individual will give up hope of trying to reach it. The level of social aspiration may be so very high that, rather than serving as an incentive to action, it may discourage and immobilize the individual.

For example, some people may sincerely embrace the social values of democracy, honesty in government, etc. We might thus expect them to be politically active in behalf of these principles. However, these values may be so high and pure, and the facts of political life so low and base, that they abandon any hope of bridging the gap between the normative and factual orders. Indeed it is often precisely the people who embrace the value of democracy most fervently who suffer the greatest disillusionment. One respondent explained:

> You gotta realize, life doesn't go the way you learn it in high school, or college, or the Constitution—It isn't that way.

This gap between the factual and normative orders of society is expressed clearly in this respondent's pungent statement: "The United States is great on paper."

> Everyone who goes to the polls wants democracy. They all consider themselves democrats with a small d. By the time the idea is represented, it ends up far afield from the original ideals. . . . Unfortunately, in spite of the need to vote, not only in America but in any democratic country, very rarely is the democratic objective accomplished.

It is true, of course, that even where the ideal is very low, the reality may be considered so remote from it as to render an effort to bridge the gap futile. The wider this gap, however, the more discouraged the individual is likely to be.

In sum, many people may be deterred from political activity by the conviction that their efforts will be futile.[9] An individual may feel that he is but one

---

[9] Gosnell has observed: "An analysis of the American presidential elections of 1920 and 1924 by states shows that the proportion of adult citizens that come to the polls varies inversely with the strength of the winning party in that state. In other words, as the proportion of the vote received by the winning party in a given state approaches one-half, the greater is the percentage of the eligible vote cast in that state." Harold F. Gosnell, *Why Europe Votes* (Chicago: University of Chicago Press, 1930), p. 199.

among so many; that he is a very "little man" compared with very much more powerful agents; that the agents of political decision—representatives, machines, "the government," certain powerful anonymous forces—are unable or unwilling to heed his voice or follow his will; that the political reality is hopelessly remote from the ideal; or that the hopelessness of political victory makes any effort pointless. It may be observed that these consequences of apathy derive from the particular nature of the social and political structure. The *mass nature of the society,* characterized by wide disparities of power, promotes the sense of personal insignificance; the *centralization of government* fosters a sense of remoteness from the key decision-making processes; the *periodic elections* produce a discontinuous exercise of power; the *system of representation* draws power from the citizen and grants it to the representative; and so on. In other words, a political structure established with the aim of implementing democracy may unwittingly establish the conditions for political apathy.

ABSENCE OF SPURS TO ACTION

In illustrating the fact that people may be reluctant to be political participants out of fear of the potential dangers of such activity or because they consider it futile, we have stressed the *deterrents* to participation. However, it is also relevant to examine the question of apathy in the light of the absence of influences, stimuli, or appeals which might encourage participation. Theoretically there is no limit to the number of factors which can *fail* to stimulate an individual to political activity. Nevertheless, it seems relevant to cite certain factors, as they appeared in the interviews, which might have been influential in stimulating participation.

It would appear appropriate to analyze this section in terms of the concept of *attributes* and *influences.*[10] Under the heading of "attributes" would be included those reasons given by respondents which indicated that it was some characteristic of politics which lacked appeal or which did not seem to offer any gratification. Certain factors which appeared among some of our respondents are: (1) The fact that the subject-matter of politics is not psychologically compelling; (2) the act or process of political activity lacks noninstrumental gratifications, fails to offer immediate satisfactions; and (3) the instrumental *results* of political activity do not appear to satisfy urgent and direct needs or provide important satisfactions. Under the heading of "influences," we refer to those cases in which people or groups fail, either by direct thrust or by shining example, to activate or inspire the respondent. Obviously these attributes and influences are not alternative determinants of apathy; for purposes of analysis, however, it is essential to consider them separately.

[10] Paul F. Lazarsfeld has emphasized the importance of looking for influences, attributes and impulses in the study of actions. See "The Art of Asking 'Why,'" *National Marketing Review* (Summer 1935).

The subject matter of politics is often not psychologically compelling. Since the political institution deals with problems of the total society, involving subjects of general interest and concern, it tends to have an *abstract* or *impersonal* quality. However much the mass media seek to concretize and personalize political matters, they still remain, for many people, dull, remote and uninspiring.

One respondent mentioned that he did not pay much attention to national politics in the newspapers. When asked why, he replied:

> Well, I'm not interested enough. I don't take the time to read such matters. I like to read more exciting things, such as kidnap cases, and I also like the sports section a lot.

Another respondent cited the many newspapers and news magazines he read. Asked what he read first, he replied: "Well, I always read the sports first, since that's what I'm most interested in."

> People like to be entertained . . . and get away from the troubles of the day; and if you get them to start worrying about England and France and everything else in the world, they're just not interested. They've got enough troubles of their own without carrying the weight of the world.

> Well, I would say politics are dull in comparison to other news.

When asked to be more specific, this respondent pointed to the local newspaper.

> Well, like this here—I see much more excitement in this story about the plane crashes than in this story about Eisenhower and the story on farm supports.

In other words, for many people the relatively abstract, impersonal, serious, and often complex, subject matter of politics cannot compete successfully with the simple, personal, emotional appeal and excitement of kidnapping and sports and more entertaining subjects of the mass media.

Absence of noninstrumental gratifications. The individual's incentive to political activity is often dulled by the absence of direct and immediate satisfactions to be derived from the activity itself. Just as people may engage in work not exclusively for the prestige and monetary rewards to be obtained from it but also because the work itself is satisfying, so people might conceivably engage in political activity because they enjoyed it, even if the goals they sought were not attained. Many people, however, find their current activities much more directly gratifying than political activity.

One respondent compared the gratifications she obtained by working with the Girl Scouts with the gratifications to be anticipated from political work. When asked, "Do you think your work as a Girl Scout leader more worthwhile than political work would be?" she replied:

Yes, I think it's better to do something which has direct results. I don't know how party politics go or anything, and maybe I'm wrong, but it seems that you end up doing little things like telephoning or licking stamps. You don't have any control over things because everything is decided by party leaders, and you don't have much to say about what goes on. You don't get any direct results. In Girl Scouts, you see these results; you have a chance to shape the characters of the girls. I think that's more important.

One respondent was asked why she happened to miss the campaign speeches.

R. I didn't have the time. If I had had the time, I would have been more interested. I work each day at the Community Center and it takes up most of my free time. I also devote many evenings to work there. I feel my work there is much more important than politics.

I. Can you say why?

R. I feel I'm really able to help people directly through my work at the Center, but I don't think I have much power to help others through politics.

Political results meet few direct and urgent needs. Most people, concerned with the immediate and imperative needs and exigencies of day-to-day life, do not conceive of political action as a vehicle for the satisfaction of these needs. Politics may be viewed as a moderately interesting spectacle, but one that is remote from the direct concerns of daily life. The man who wants an apartment usually does not attempt to get one by lobbying vigorously for federal housing projects; rather, he consults agents, newspapers or friends. A woman who wants lower food prices ordinarily does not attempt to achieve it by joining a citizens' committee striving to apply pressure on Congress to restore price controls; rather, she goes several blocks out of her way to shop at a supermarket whose prices are lower than those of the neighborhood grocer. Lack of concern with politics is understandable when viewed in this light.

One woman, asked if she were interested in politics, said: "I don't follow the news too much. I feel the world will go on without me, no matter." At a later point, asked if she felt that politics had any importance in her life, she replied: "No, we go on and politics has nothing to do with us. . . . I think most people go along from day to day and take what comes. I don't think they are much interested."

One respondent said: "Most of our serious issues are voted on in town meetings." Asked if he attended, he replied: "Only once in a while, for laughs. They really don't accomplish much, but they are nice to have around."

Another respondent, asked what effect she thought politics had on her everyday life, replied, "Don't think it has any, to tell the truth."

"I don't think politics or election results will or do affect my own life very much. Regardless of who is in power, I'll keep my job and my home."

> I realize that politics does affect me, but it still doesn't seem to really touch me. I think we must be educated to a degree to think about it as something personal. . . . I think the fundamental thing is that we don't feel directly related or affected. . . . It doesn't concern us inwardly.

The following conversation occurred with a Republican who was a member of the school board:

> I. Do you think the Republican Party is as important as the school board?
> R. Goodness, no!
> I. Why?
> R. Because the school board directly affects my children.

To many people, then, governmental action is considered irrelevant to their lives. They do not conceive of the government as an agent which can solve their immediate and pressing problems. It is, then, no wonder that these people fail to feel any urgent incentive to participate actively in political affairs.

People often lack a personal thrust to action. Empirical studies of politics have shown that personal influence may be of great importance in determining political attitudes and behavior.[11] Our data suggest that the interpersonal factor may operate in several different ways to promote apathy or discourage participation.

Potential participants may not be contacted by friends or party organizations.

One respondent claims that she would have been active had the stimulus been available. She was the friendly, cooperative type, always willing to lend a hand. When she was asked whether she had worked, she said:

> No, I wasn't asked to do anything. Many of my friends were asked to help—ring doorbells, stamp envelopes, and things like that. But I wasn't asked to do anything. Had I been asked, I would have been glad to help.

Another respondent said that she wasn't interested in politics, but that she would be active if asked to because, "I like to cooperate. It's like the school. I cooperate with them, too."

> Well, I might have helped if they'd really wanted me to, and if it didn't take too much time. . . . Besides, no one asked me to help out, so I didn't volunteer. I could have worked a little, though.

These respondents were certainly apathetic at the outset, but, as relatively compliant personalities, they might have been induced to participate. Such

---

[11] Lazarsfeld, Paul F., Bernard Berelson and Hazel Gaudet, *op. cit.*, Chaps. XV and XVI.

activity might in turn have led to increased interest. The absence of initial personal stimulation, however, ruled out the possibility that a start toward participation would be made.

Those who might consider it a social responsibility to participate politically may be reassured by the observation that most other people are apathetic. It also provides a very convenient rationalization for apathy.

> You can probably class me as apathetic, except when it's brought right to my attention, but I think most people are the same way. They are not aware of, or they ignore, corruption in government until a McCarthy-type seizes it and makes a big thing out of it.

Another respondent was asked about the political interest of her friends.

> Well, a few of our friends belong to some political groups. But I wouldn't call them our most intimate friends. Not many of our close friends belong.
>
> As a matter of fact, besides the professors' wives, I don't think too many women know much about politics. Even though a lot of them are active on the election board—canvassing and things like that—they still don't seem to know too much about politics—especially national politics.
>
> I guess everyone else is even more passive than I am. They're all busy with household things.

Thus, many people are not motivated because of the absence of a shining example by others. Furthermore, whatever guilt they feel may be assuaged by the observation that others (including the most respectable) are equally apathetic. It is reasonable to speculate, incidentally, that an individual who might be ready for action would be discouraged by the spectacle of such widespread apathy; he might feel that he could not carry the burden with so little help. Thus apathy may become self-reinforcing.

People may be members of groups in which apathy is a positive group norm. A young person became associated with a group of cynics who considered concern with political affairs an expression of philistine conformism. She remained inactive partly out of fear of the scorn and ridicule which would greet any manifestation of social responsibility.[12]

Thus, interpersonal factors may operate in several ways to promote political apathy. In the first place, the individual may receive no positive encouragement from others to participate. In the second place, the guilt feelings arising from an individual's inactivity may be assuaged by the observation that others in the community are also inactive. An individual, ready for action, may be discouraged by the observation that the apathy of other people increases his own burden of political work. Finally, the individual may be a

---

[12] I am indebted to Mr. Jay C. Greenfield for this example.

member of a group in which political apathy is a *positive group norm*—a group which would discourage political action.

Apathy may thus be circular and self-reinforcing. The apathetic individual is not encouraged, and actually may be discouraged, from being politically active. Each individual may thus be reassured and reinforced in his political non-participation by the observation that others behave in a similar fashion. Thus the individual who, by virtue of his own apathy, encourages apathy in others, may also be influenced in a similar fashion by them.

AREAS FOR FURTHER RESEARCH

In this paper we have suggested several factors which in some cases contribute to political apathy. That these factors have some significance is clearly suggested by the data, but their relative importance, their statistical distribution among various population sub-groups, and their interrelationships must remain subjects for more systematic research.

Space limitations prevent us from discussing in detail a number of additional factors which our data suggest might contribute to political apathy. It appears worth noting, however, that some people are apathetic because they feel there is no need to do anything; they are contented with the social and political system, have faith in their representatives, and see no need for change. This basic contentment tends to be linked with a confidence in the basic stability of the society.[13] There are others who would favor change, but who feel that there is no real difference between the two major parties; the outcome of elections, therefore, lacks significance. Some people do not participate actively because of the incertitude of their political convictions; to them politics may be confused, complicated, contradictory; political communications may be rejected as propaganda; or the individuals may be uncertain regarding their own political activity. Others may be too exhausted by the pressure of other activities to pay much attention to it. Certain women express the attitude that political activity would be out of keeping with their social roles. Some people's reluctance to think about political matters ranges from a certain degree of mental laziness to a phobia toward serious thought which borders on the pathological. These and other factors would have to be examined before an adequate understanding of the determinants of political apathy could be achieved.

It is also necessary to bear in mind that apathy is a variable rather than a dichotomous attribute. Thus the reason a non-voter does not go to the polls is likely to be quite different from the reason a party worker who devotes his weekday evenings to the cause does not spend his weekends at it too. Further analysis would require an examination of the obstacles to action as it operates differentially at these various levels.

[13] This point was brought to our attention by Prof. Clinton L. Rossiter and has received empirical confirmation in our data.

To those who consider political apathy a symptom of the malfunctioning of democracy, the important next question would be: What can be done about it? This is obviously a crucial area for social research. It is our conviction, however, that the phenomenon must first be thoroughly understood before fruitful research for its solution can be undertaken.

Finally, of course, the common observation that many people are not politically apathetic, that they do not participate actively, virtually dictates an investigation into the factors which induce them to participate as much as they do.

ALIENATION AND POLITICAL APATHY

DWIGHT G. DEAN

In recent years the concept of Alienation has been frequently and variously utilized in explaining social phenomena ranging from authoritarianism to suicide. Nisbet has commented:

> At the present time, in all the social sciences the various synonyms of alienation have a foremost place in studies of human relations. Investigations of the "unattached," the "marginal," the "obsessive," the "normless," and the "isolated" individual all testify to the central place occupied by the hypothesis of alienation in contemporary social science. . . . It has become nearly as prevalent as the doctrine of enlightened self-interest was two generations ago. It is more than a hypothesis; it is a perspective.[1]

Only recently has empirical work appeared dealing with the topic, and authors frequently use different connotations of the term.[2]

[1] Robert A. Nisbet, *The Quest for Community* (New York: Oxford University Press, 1953), p. 15.

[2] See, for example, Anthony Davids, "Alienation, Social Apperception and Ego Structure," *Journal of Consulting Psychology*, XIX (February 1955), 21–27 and "Generality and Consistency of Relations Between the Alienation Syndrome and Cognitive Processes," *Journal of Abnormal and Social Psychology*, LI (July 1955), 61–67; Allan H. Roberts and Milton Rokeach, "Anomie, Authoritarianism and Prejudice: A Replication," *American Journal of Sociology*, LVI (January 1956), 355–358; Gwynn Nettler, "A Measure of Alienation," *American Sociological Review*, 22 (December 1957), 670–677; and Leo Stole, Social Dysfunction, Personality and Social Distance Attitudes, paper read before the American Sociological Society (Chicago, 1951), mimeographed.

SOURCE: Dwight G. Dean, "Alienation and Political Apathy," *Social Forces*, 38 (March 1960), 185–189. Reprinted by permission.

The manifold references to Alienation may, for the sake of clarification, be classified under three subtypes: Powerlessness, Normlessness and Social Isolation. Hegel and Marx first described powerlessness as the "separation of the worker from the tools of production." [3] Weber[4] extended Marx's concept to the "separation" of the modern professional worker as well.

Numerous references might be cited to illustrate the widespread use of the Powerlessness concept, but perhaps Gouldner's comment is most succinct:

> By "alienation" is meant that men pursue goals, and use means in their pursuit, determined either by social entities with which they do not feel intimately identified or by forces which they may be unable to recognize at all. Thus no man "wants" war, yet two are fought on a world-wide scale within a quarter-century. Practically everyone desires economic security, yet our society encountered its most devastating depression during the thirties, and fears still another. These are but two dramatic indications that social forces are abroad which most men little understand, to say nothing of master. The growth of alienation implies that the range of choice open to the ordinary individual, the area of discretion available to him, is declining.[5]

The second component, Normlessness, may be illustrated by reference to Durkheim's suggestion that in sudden economic loss or gain previous values cannot remain unchanged, "the calibration is turned topsy-turvy . . . yet no new graduation can be quickly improvised." [6]

Normlessness may be either a lack of clear norms or a conflict among norms. For example, Karen Horney[7] has described the difficulties of an indi-

[3] Herbert Marcuse, *Reason and Revolution* (New York: Oxford University Press, 1941), p. 34; see also p. 273.

[4] Hans H. Gerth and C. Wright Mills, *From Weber: Essays in Sociology* (New York: Oxford University Press, 1946), p. 50.

[5] Alvin W. Gouldner (ed.), *Studies in Leadership* (New York: Harper and Brothers, 1950), p. 86. See also Sebastian deGrazia, *The Political Community: A Study of Anomie* (Chicago: University of Chicago Press, 1948), esp. pp. 8–20 and 115–122; Ernest Kris and Nathan Leites, "Trends in Twentieth Century Propaganda," in *Reader in Public Opinion*, edited by Bernard Berelson and Morris Janowitz (Glencoe, Illinois: The Free Press, 1950), p. 283; Erich Fromm, *Escape From Freedom* (New York: Farrar and Rinehart, 1940); Robert Merton, *Mass Persuasion* (New York: Harper and Brothers, 1947), p. 143; C. Wright Mills, *White Collar* (New York: Oxford University Press, 1951), p. 184; Erich Fromm, *The Sane Society* (New York: Rinehart and Company, 1955), p. 120; Karen Horney, *Neurosis and Human Growth* (New York: W. W. Norton and Company, Inc., 1950), p. 155; Theodor W. Adorno *et al., The Authoritarian Personality* (New York: Harper and Brothers, 1950), p. 618; Morris Rosenberg, "The Meaning of Politics in Mass Society," *Public Opinion Quarterly*, XV (Spring 1951), 5–15; David Riesman and Nathan Glazer, "Criteria for Political Apathy," in *Studies in Leadership*, edited by Alvin W. Gouldner (New York: Harper and Brothers, 1950), pp. 505–559.

[6] DeGrazia, *op. cit.*, p. 5.

[7] Karen W. Horney, "Culture and Neurosis," in *Sociological Analysis*, edited by Logan Wilson and William L. Kolb (New York: Harcourt, Brace and Company, 1949), pp. 248–251.

vidual who incorporates in his personality conflicting norms, such as Christianity versus the success imperative, the stimulation toward a high material standard of living versus the practical denial of that standard for many people, and the alleged freedom of the individual versus his factual limitations. DeGrazia[8] has written of the conflict between the Competitive and the Cooperative Directives and the conflict between the Activist and the Quietist Directives in our society.

The third component, Social Isolation, is the perception of losing effective contact with significant and supporting groups. One who is low in Social Isolation would sense warm, friendly, personal relationships; have community identification, and have confidence in the dependability of his acquaintances, as opposed to feelings of rejection, loneliness, and impersonality.[9]

In order to test the effects of Alienation empirically, it was decided to investigate its relationship to Political Apathy. In a democracy, it is an anomaly that only 50 percent to 65 percent of the adult citizens participate even to the minimum extent of voting in presidential elections. There exists a considerable amount of literature concerning political behavior, which has been admirably summed up by Lipset et al.[10]

We are indebted to three authors in particular for relating the Alienation syndrome to political apathy. Rosenberg, for example, has stated that the sense of powerlessness leads to political apathy:

> Politics is avoided because of feelings of psychological inadequacy or weakness. . . . Other factors in the world view of the individual which discourage political action are powerlessness and fatalism. In our complex urban mass society, individuals devote themselves to minute, specialized tasks woven into the complex fabric of our economy. The great economic and power blocs, typified by giant corporations and unions,

[8] DeGrazia, op. cit., chap. III, "Conflict Between Belief Systems," pp. 47–72. For further examples, see Robert M. MacIver, The Ramparts We Guard (New York: The Macmillan Company, 1950), pp. 84–87; Arnold W. Green, "Social Values and Psychotherapy," Journal of Personality, XIV (March 1946), 199–228; Martin Gumpert, "The Physicians of Warsaw," The American Scholar, XVIII, 285–290; Bruno Bettelheim, "Individual and Mass Behavior in Extreme Situations," Journal of Abnormal Psychology, XXXVII (October 1943), 418–526; Jurgen Ruesch, "Social Technique, Social Status, and Social Change in Illness," in Personality in Nature, Society and Culture, edited by Clyde Kluckhohn and Henry A. Murray (New York: Alfred A. Knopf, 1950), p. 125; and William Peterson, "Is America Still the Land of Opportunity?" Commentary, VI (November 1953), 477–486.

[9] This concept has been used in such studies as Ruth S. Cavan, Suicide (Chicago: University of Chicago Press, 1928); E. Gartley Jaco, "The Social Isolation Hypothesis and Schizophrenia," American Sociological Review, XIX (October 1954), 577–584; Melvin L. Kohn and John A. Clausen, "Social Isolation and Schizophrenia," American Sociological Review, XX (June 1955), 265–273.

[10] Seymour M. Lipset, et al., "The Psychology of Voting: An Analysis of Political Behavior," in Handbook of Social Psychology, edited by Gardner Lindzey (Cambridge, Massachusetts: Addison-Wesley Publishing Company, 1954), chap. 30, pp. 1124–1177.

thrust the individual about with pressures too great to resist. As a consequence, the individual is likely to feel overwhelmed and powerless. Given this feeling, the idea that his puny strength can match the giants is absurd, and he feels that a lonely individual can do nothing to change the way the world is run. Raising his weak voice against the massive roar of the mass media and the political giants is futile. For this reason, many people with political convictions do nothing but vote, convinced that they can have no substantial effect on any event.[11]

Lazarsfeld has directly tied in the phenomenon of conflict (a subtype of our "anomie") with nonvoting, for he has shown that "cross-pressures" (between the "predisposing" factors of religious affiliation, economic status, and place of residence) tend to delay and reduce the incidence of voting. Further,

> When people desire and shun a course of action in about equal degree, they often do not decide for or against it but rather change the subject or avoid the matter altogether. For many clashes of interest, the easy way out of the uncomfortable situation is simply to discount its importance and to give up the conflict as not worth the bother.[12]

Lubell [13] has suggested the same possibility in regard to voting, mentioning that nonvoting is not always due to apathy, but that it may be a result of the voter's inability to decide.

The possible relationship between the Social Isolation component of Alienation and political apathy has been suggested by Lazarsfeld:

> . . . personal contacts can get a voter to the polls without affecting at all his comprehension of the issues of the elections—something the formal media can rarely do.[14]

Again, he indicates that people who in our definition would be normless may have their problems solved for them through contact with others:

> . . . the party changers—relatively, the people whose votes still remained to be definitely determined during the last stages of the campaign, the people who could swing an election during those last days— were, so to speak, available to the person who saw them last before Election Day. The notion that the people who switch parties during the campaign are mainly the reasoned, thoughtful, conscientious people who were convinced by the issues of the election is just plain wrong. Actually, they were mainly just the opposite.[15]

[11] Morris Rosenberg, "The Meaning of Politics in Mass Society," *Public Opinion Quarterly*, XV (Spring 1951), 5–15.

[12] Paul F. Lazarsfeld, Bernard Berelson and Hazel Gaudet, *The People's Choice* (New York: Duell, Sloan and Pearce, 1944), p. 45.

[13] Samuel Lubell, *The Future of American Politics* (New York: Harper and Brothers, 1952).

[14] Paul F. Lazarsfeld *et al.*, *op. cit.*, p. 157.

[15] Paul F. Lazarsfeld *et al.*, "Time of Final Decision," in *Reader in Public Opinion and Communication*, edited by Bernard Berelson and Morris Janowitz (Glencoe, Illinois: The Free Press, 1950), p. 113.

Political Apathy has generally been defined simply as voting or nonvoting; most of the generalizations which have been advanced have been based on studies using this single criterion,[16] though Campbell et al.,[17] Lazarsfeld,[18] Robinson,[19] Showel,[20] and Heard [21] have attempted further refinements. None, however, has utilized another's scale in subsequent research.

For this reason, we developed scales to measure Interest Apathy (lack of personal involvement in political interests), Influence Apathy (lack of interest in influencing others), Behavior Apathy (the summed score of the first two), and Voting Apathy (a score assigned in inverse ratio to actual voting records over a span of 12 consecutive election occasions).[22] Reliability was tested by the "split-half" technique and found to be .85 (N 384), .81, and .84 respectively, when corrected. The Voting Apathy was, of course, not tested for reliability as it was the record of actual voting.

HYPOTHESES

The hypotheses of this study are: There are positive correlations between Powerlessness, Normlessness, Social Isolation (and the summed score of these three, Alienation) and Political Apathy scores on scales developed here to measure Interest Apathy, Influence Apathy, Behavior Apathy, and Voting Apathy.

PROCEDURE

In order to develop scales to measure Alienation and its components, 139 items were gleaned from the literature. To validate the scale, these were then

[16] Typical of these studies are: Gordon M. Connelly and Harry N. Field, "The Non-Voter: Who He Is, What He Thinks," *Public Opinion Quarterly*, VIII (Summer 1944), 175–187; Harold F. Gosnell, "Does Campaigning Make a Difference?" *Public Opinion Quarterly*, XIV (Fall 1951), 413–418; Alice S. Kitt and David B. Gleicher, "Determinants of Voting Behavior," *Public Opinion Quarterly*, XIV (Fall 1951), 393–412; Mongo Miller, "The Waukegan Study of Voter Turnout Prediction," *Public Opinion Quarterly*, XVI (Fall 1952), 381–398; Seymour M. Lipset et al., "The Psychology of Voting: An Analysis of Political Behavior," in *Handbook of Social Psychology*, edited by Gardner Lindzey (Cambridge, Massachusetts: Addison-Wesley Company, 1944).

[17] Angus Campbell, Gerald Gurin and Warren E. Miller, *The Voter Decides* (Evanston, Illinois: Row, Peterson and Company, 1954).

[18] Paul F. Lazarsfeld, Bernard Berelson and Hazel Gaudet, *The People's Choice* (New York: Duell, Sloan and Pearce, 1944).

[19] W. S. Robinson, "The Motivational Structure of Political Participation," *American Sociological Review*, XVII (April 1952), 151–156.

[20] Morris Showel, "Political Consciousness and Attitudes in the State of Washington," *Public Opinion Quarterly*, XVII (Fall 1953), 394–400.

[21] Alexander Heard et al., "A Study of Political Participation in Two North Carolina Counties," *Research Previews*, III (February, 1955), 1–8.

[22] This portion of the research is to be reported elsewhere.

submitted with one-page descriptions of the three component types, to seven experts (sociologists at The Ohio State University). These judges were instructed to decide whether or not each of the 139 items referred specifically and only to Powerlessness. They then were given a new set of cards to judge the items in regard to Normlessness, and, finally, a set for judging in regard to Social Isolation. For retention of an item, agreement on specific placement was required from at least five of the seven judges.[23]

When this was completed, the usual "differentiating power" test was applied to determine which of the "valid" items were to be retained. The scales were tested for reliability by the "split-half" method, with the following results (N 384): Powerlessness .78; Normlessness .73; Social Isolation .83; and (total) Alienation .78, corrected for attentuation by the Spearman-Brown prophecy formula for full length of the scale.

THE SAMPLE

When it was decided to use actual voting records as one criterion for Political Apathy, it became necessary to collect data by wards. Four of Columbus' (Ohio) 19 wards were selected on the following bases: (1) The proportions of actual to estimated eligible voters should be approximately equal; (2) the voting ratios should not represent the extremes of voting or nonvoting; (3) the wards should represent the several social classes; and (4) for replicative purposes, two wards should be approximately equal on both voting "percentage" and socio-economic status. Within the designated wards, random sampling was used for selection of precincts; and, within the precincts, for the individuals. To control the sex and race variables, only white males were utilized. Of 1,108 questionnaires presumably delivered, 433 or 38.8 percent responses were obtained.

In three of the four wards, our respondents had a higher median education than the general population for that area; in all wards, respondents had a higher income and averaged somewhat older than the general population for that area. Further, respondents had a significantly lower "Voter Apathy" score than nonrespondents. The mean score for respondents was 2.42 compared to 3.95 for nonrespondents (CR 6.22). To the extent that respondents were more likely to vote, the correlation coefficients between Alienation and Political Apathy may have been depressed.

FINDINGS

While the correlation coefficients between the Alienation and the Political Apathy scales reached statistical significance in many instances, the general

---

[23] This method is adapted from John K. Hemphill and Charles M. Westie, "The Measurement of Group Dimensions," in *The Language of Social Research* edited by Paul Lazarsfeld *et al.* (Glencoe, Illinois: The Free Press, 1950), pp. 325 f.

level was so low that for practical purposes we conclude that the hypotheses were not sustained. The correlation coefficients between the Alienation scales and the Political Apathy scales are given in Table 1.

TABLE 1.

Correlations between Alienation and Political Apathy
(Columbus, Ohio, Sample of 384)

Alienation Component	Interest Apathy	Influence Apathy	Behavior Apathy	Voting Apathy
Powerlessness	.10*	.13**	.13**	.03
Normlessness	.10*	.15**	.19**	.05
Social Isolation	.17**	.17**	.18**	.14**
Alienation	.15**	.16**	.17**	.07

* Significant at the .05 level of confidence.
** Significant at the .01 level of confidence.

In order to determine the possible effects of certain socio-economic variables, partial correlations were computed between each of the Alienation subscales and each of the Political Apathy subscales for five major background variables: (1) Occupational Prestige (as measured by the North-Hatt scale); (2) Size of community in which the respondent had spent his youth; (3) Educational attainment; (4) Income; and (5) Age. In no instance were the original correlations changed to any noticeable extent. In Table 2 are summa-

TABLE 2.

Partial Correlations between Alienation and Political Apathy, with the Effect
of Five Background Variables Controlled (N 384)

	Political Apathy			
Variable Controlled	Interest Apathy	Influence Apathy	Behavior Apathy	Voting Apathy
Occupational Prestige	.13**	.15**	.15**	.07
Community Size	.14**	.15**	.17**	.06
Education	.12*	.14**	.16**	.06
Income	.14**	.11*	.15**	.06
Age	.23**	.19**	.24**	.11*

* Significant at the .05 level of confidence.
** Significant at the .01 level of confidence.

rized the correlations between Alienation and Political Apathy, with the designated variables controlled.

CONCLUSIONS

The hypotheses which predicted a positive correlation between Powerlessness, Normlessness, Social Isolation, and (total) Alienation on the one hand, and Interest Apathy, Influence Apathy, and Behavior Apathy on the other, were statistically sustained but because of the uniformly low magnitude of the correlation coefficients, practically rejected. The hypotheses regarding Alienation and Voting Apathy must be rejected. These latter are, in a way, the most crucial tests since the Alienation scales are correlated with actual behavior and not with questionnaire response.

These uniformly low coefficients between Alienation and its components and the Political Apathy scales lend little credence to the hypothesis of Rosenberg[24] that a sense of Powerlessness is related to Political Apathy; nor do they support the oblique suggestions of Lazarsfeld[25] and Lubell[26] that what we have termed Normlessness is related to Political Apathy, nor the suggestion of Lazarsfeld[27] that Social Isolation is highly related to nonvoting.

Perhaps the low correlations between the Alienation scales (especially the Powerlessness component) and the Political Apathy scales may be explained by Adorno's suggestion[28] that when the individual feels overwhelmed, he may "personalize" politics. That is, one who feels powerless may project power onto some father figure. However, until a scale is developed to measure "personalization of politics," one can only speculate. In regard to the Normlessness component, one recalls the suggestion of Riesman and Glazer[29] that the highly alienated individuals may frantically indulge in politics for *apolitical* motivations such as conformity, or use it as a "phobic sector" for psychopathological needs. Our scales do not provide information on which to judge this possibility.

Further, one may raise the question as to whether Alienation is a generic "trait," or whether it must be considered as a situationally-related variable. It might be profitable to develop—instead of a general Alienation scale—scales to be specifically applied to various institutional areas of social life.[30] An individual might have a "high alienation" score, for example, in the political aspect, but a "low" one in regard to religion. Thus, the adherents of Fundamen-

[24] Morris Rosenberg, "The Meaning of Politics in Mass Society," *Public Opinion Quarterly*, XV (Spring 1951), 5–15.

[25] Paul F. Lazarsfeld *et al., op. cit.,* pp. 53 and 62.

[26] Samuel Lubell, *The Future of American Politics* (New York: Harper and Brothers, 1952).

[27] Paul F. Lazarsfeld, *et al., op. cit.,* p. 157.

[28] Theodor Adorno, *op. cit.,* p. 618.

[29] David Riesman and Nathan Glazer, *op. cit.,* pp. 505–559.

[30] For a scale developed with regard to a voluntary association, see Wayne E. Thompson and John Horton, "Alienation and Political Apathy," pp. 190–195 in this issue, and John P. Clark,

talism might very well be politically apathetic because they believe that international crises and other political and social problems cannot be solved by man, but that the world can only be "saved" by the direct and personal intervention of God. In any event, our results raise serious questions as to the utility of the concept of Alienation as it has been used. Certainly much more needs to be done before the theoretical writings referred to above can be empirically substantiated as analytical tools for "the science of society."

Study Questions

1. Compare and contrast Almond and Verba, Rosenberg, and Dean's views of the image of the citizen as participant in the political system.
2. The gaps between the democratic ideal and what actually exists and between promises and rising frustrations tend to deepen cynical attitudes and apathy toward life and particularly toward politics. How can we alter this situation and bring the passive and alienated individual into the mainstream of political life? Discuss fully and critically.
3. Comment on the statement that democratic theory seems to require a high level of political mass participation in the political system for the maximization of its values. However, lack of active political participation is not necessarily bad because it indicates a high degree of political and social satisfaction. Moreover, the non-voters tend to show some anti-democratic tendencies and to bring them to the polls would be of no service to democracy. Discuss fully and critically the validity of this statement.

Suggestions for Further Reading

Agger, Robert E., Marshall Goldstein, and Stanley Pearl, "Political Cynicism: Measurement and Meaning," The Journal of Politics, XXIII (August, 1961), 477–506.

Almond, Gabriel, The Appeals of Communism. Princeton, New Jersey: Princeton University Press, 1954.

Almond, Gabriel A. and Verba, Sidney. The Civic Culture: Political Attitudes and Democracy in Five Nations. Princeton, New Jersey: Princeton University Press, 1963.

Campbell, Angus, Phillip Converse, Warren Miller, and Donald Stokes, The American Voter. New York: John Wiley & Sons, 1960.

Cantril, Hadley. Human Nature and Political Systems. New Brunswick, New Jersey: Rutgers University Press, 1961.

Cantril, Hadley. The Politics of Despair. New York: Basic Books, 1958.

Davies, James. Human Nature in Politics. New York : John Wiley & Sons, 1963.

Eulau, Heinz, and Peter Schneider, "Dimensions of Political Involvement," Public Opinion Quarterly, XX (Spring, 1956), 128–142.

Fromm, Erich. The Sane Society. New York: Holt, Rinehart and Winston, 1955.

Grodzins, Morton. The Loyal and the Disloyal. Chicago: University of Chicago Press, 1956.

"Measuring Alienation Within a Social System," American Sociological Review, 24 (December 1959), pp. 848–852.

Heard, Alexander. *The Costs of Democracy.* Chapel Hill: University of North Carolina Press, 1960.

Hoffer, Eric. *The True Believer.* New York: New American Library, 1951.

Levin, Murray. *The Alienated Voter.* New York: Holt, Rinehart and Winston, 1960.

Lippit, Gordon, and Drexel Sprecher, "Factors Motivating Citizens to Become Active in Politics as Seen by Practical Politicians," *Journal of Social Issues,* XXVI (No. 1, 1960), 11–18.

Milbrath, Lester W. *Political Participation: How and Why Do People Get Involved in Politics?* Chicago: Rand McNally, 1965.

Mills, C. Wright. *White Collar.* New York: Oxford University Press, 1951.

Neumann, Franz. *The Democratic and the Authoritarian State.* New York: The Free Press of Glencoe, 1957.

Riesman, David. *The Lonely Crowd.* New Haven: Yale University Press, 1950.

Rokeach, Milton. *The Open and Closed Mind.* New York: Basic Books, 1960.

Rose, Arnold M., "Alienation and Participation: A Comparison of Group Leaders and the 'Mass'," *American Sociological Review,* XXVII (December, 1962), 834–838.

Thompson, Wayne E., and John E. Horton, "Political Alienation as a Force in Political Action," *Social Forces,* XXXVIII (March, 1960), 190–195.

Whyte, William H. Jr. *The Organization Man.* New York: Simon and Schuster, 1956.

PART THREE

Civil Rights and Liberties

The Declaration of Independence states that all men are endowed by their creator with certain inalienable rights and that among these are life, liberty, and the pursuit of happiness. The American Revolution was fought to secure these rights and in a broader sense, the "Revolution" continues because these rights have not been extended to all Americans.

The movement toward greater equality has been one of the major features of American democracy in action. This movement has been accompanied by a continuing dialogue about the meaning of equality and the proper means of securing it. In the first essay, Robert A. Lane discusses the movement toward greater equality and its meaning for the working and lower middle class. Lane's study of this group indicates that although they are committed to the principle of equality there is a fear of it in the extreme, particularly if it means leveling everyone to the lowest common denominator. His investigation indicates that the working class supports the class structure and defends the unequal status of persons as being rational and just and that the rewards each receives are usually commensurate with his contribution. The working class, rather than looking forward to the Marxist millennium of "from each according to his ability and to each according to his needs," views it with suspicion and alarm.

The Declaration of Independence also states that government exists to protect individual rights. One of the most important of these rights is that of religious freedom. The best evidence of religious freedom is the existence of many different sects protected in their right to worship according to their own dictates, or, in other words, religious pluralism. Wilbur G. Katz and Harold P. Southerland examine, in the second article, the Supreme Court's defense of religious pluralism in America. Religious pluralism is manifested by a situation in which religious groups are not only willing to defend their own beliefs but also willing to defend those of other groups as well. The Supreme Court, according to Katz and Southerland, has not practiced absolute neutrality in the religious area, but has handed down decisions which promote and defend religious pluralism. The Court, they believe, has manifested this commitment "by holding that the establishment clause does not forbid special provisions for religion of a type that may be called 'neutralizing' aids."

The government's policy of providing chaplains for the armed forces is an instance of government not promoting religion but protecting religious pluralism by compensating for a restriction upon religious freedom that might result from its secular activities. The taking of persons from their homes and religious communities to serve in the armed services constitutes a restriction upon their religious freedom which government attempts to compensate for by providing chaplains. Other "neutralizing aids" are discussed by Katz and Southerland in the essay.

In the third essay Milton R. Konvitz develops the thesis that for their protection civil liberties require political institutions based upon certain moral principles. A stated commitment to democratic principles, however, is not sufficient since even totalitarian countries make the same profession. A nation's commitment to these principles must be determined, says Konvitz, by a factual examination of the degree to which it lives up to its ideas.

In the concluding article, Bayard Rustin discusses the position of the Negro in American society. He believes that the McCone Report which examined the conditions in Watts leading up to the riots failed to explain adequately the problems confronted by the black inhabitants. The first error in the McCone Report, Rustin says, was the belief that "the rioters seem to have been caught up in an insensate rage of destruction." The evidence indicated that the rioting was directed primarily at those businesses engaged in exploitation of Negroes and that most of those arrested were not habitual criminals. Of those, most were arrested not for arson or shooting but for looting. The Commission fails to understand, he asserts, that employment of Negroes is necessary to change their attitudes and "when what they see in unemployment and their economic opportunity programs being manipulated in behalf of politicians, their attitudes will remain realistically cynical."

Rustin believes that it is incredible that the United States with its tremendous wealth has allowed the conditions in Watts to reach such an explosive state, and that there needs to be a commitment "to build a genuinely great society that will put an end to these deprivations." Failure to make this effort will mean that in effect "we may well continue to teach impoverished, segregated, and ignorant Negroes that the only way they can get the ear of America is to rise up in violence."

Translating the principle that all men are created equal into a living reality remains this nation's most important unfinished business. As long as people remain impoverished and remain second class citizens and are denied their rights to the good things of life, the goals and objectives outlined in the Declaration of Independence remain unfulfilled and the "Revolution" will and must continue.

THE FEAR OF EQUALITY

ROBERT E. LANE

We move in equalitarian directions; the distribution of income flattens out; the floor beneath the poorest paid and least secure is raised and made more substantial. Since the demise of Newport and Tuxedo Park, the very rich have shunned ostentatious display. The equality of opportunity, the chance to rise in the world is at least as great today as it was thirty years ago. The likelihood of declining status is less. Where does the energy for this movement come from? Who is behind it?

Since 1848, it has been assumed that the drive for a more equalitarian society, its effective social force, would come from the stratum of society with the most to gain, the working classes. This was thought to be the revolutionary force in the world—the demand of workers for a classless society sparked by their hostility to the owning classes. It was to be the elite among the workers, not the *lumpenproletariat*, not the "scum," who were to advance this movement. Just as "liberty" was the central slogan of the bourgeois revolution, so "equality" was the central concept in the working class movement. Hence it was natural to assume that whatever gains have been made in equalizing the income and status of men in our society came about largely from working class pressure.

But on closer investigation the demands for greater liberty or "freedom" turn out to have been of an ambiguous nature. The middle classes sought freedom of speech and action in large part for the economic gains that this would give them, and moralized their action with the theology of freedom. But the freedom that they gained was frightening, for it deprived them of the solidary social relationships and the ideological certainty which often gave order to their lives. On occasion, then, they sought to "escape from freedom." [2] The older unfree order had a value which the earlier social commentators did not appreciate.

There is a parallel here with the movement toward a more equalitarian society. The upper working class, and the lower middle class, support specific measures embraced in the formula "welfare state," which have equalitarian consequences. But, so I shall argue, many members of the working classes do

[2] Erich Fromm, *Escape from Freedom* (New York: Rinehart, 1941).

SOURCE: Robert E. Lane, "The Fear of Equality," *The American Political Science Review*, 53 (March 1959), 35–51. Reprinted by permission. Some footnotes have been deleted.

not want equality. They are afraid of it. In some ways they already seek to escape from it. Equality for the working classes, like freedom for the middle classes, is a worrisome, partially rejected, by-product of the demand for more specific measures. Inequality has values to them which have been overlooked. It is these attitudes on status and equality that I shall explore here.

I. EXTENDED INTERVIEWS WITH FIFTEEN MEN

This discussion is based upon extended interviews of from ten to fifteen hours each (in from four to seven sessions) with a sample of American urban male voters. The sample is a random selection from the white members on a list of 220 registered voters in a moderate income (not low income) housing development where income is permitted to range between $4,000 and $6,500, according to the number of dependents in the family. Out of fifteen asked to participate, fifteen agreed, for a modest cash consideration. The characteristics of the sample, then, are as follows:

They are all men, white, married, fathers, urban, Eastern seaboard.
Their incomes range from $2,400 to $6,300 (except for one who had just moved from the project. His income was $10,000 in 1957.)
Ten had working class (blue collar) occupations such as painter, plumber, oiler, railroad fireman, policeman, machine operator.
Five had white collar occupations such as salesman, bookkeeper, supply clerk.
Their ages ranged from 25 to 54; most are in their thirties.
Twelve are Catholic, two are Protestants, one is Jewish.
All are native born; their nationality backgrounds are: six Italian, five Irish, one Polish, one Swedish, one Russian, one Yankee. Most are second or third generation Americans.
All were employed at the time of the interviews.
Their educational distribution was: three had only grammar school education; eight had some high school; two finished high school; one had some college; one completed graduate training.

The interviews with these men were taped, with the permission of the interviewees, and transcribed. They were conducted by means of a schedule of questions and topics followed by conversational improvised probes to discover the underlying meanings of the answers given. The kinds of questions employed to uncover the material to be reported are illustrated by the following: "What do you think the phrase 'All men are created equal' means?" "How would you feel if everyone received the same income no matter what his job?" "Sometimes one hears the term 'social class'—as in working class or middle class. What do you think this term 'social class' means?" "What class do you belong to?" "How do you feel about it?" There were also a number of questions dealing with status, private utopias, feelings of privilege or lack of privilege, and other topics, throughout the interview schedule which sometimes elicited responses bearing on the question of social and economic equality.

II. HOW TO ACCOUNT FOR ONE'S OWN STATUS?

It is my thesis that attitudes toward equality rest in the first instance upon one's attitude towards one's own status. Like a large number of social beliefs, attitudes towards equality take their direction from beliefs about the self, the status of the self, one's self-esteem or lack thereof. It is necessary, therefore, first to explore how people see themselves in American hierarchical society.

The American culture and the democratic dogma have given to the American public the notion that "all men are created equal." Even more insistently, the American culture tells its members: "achieve," "compete," "be better, smarter, quicker, richer than your fellow men"; in short, "be unequal." The men I interviewed had received these inequalitarian messages, some eagerly, some with foreboding. Having heard them, they must account for their status, higher than some, lower than others. They must ask themselves, for example, "Why didn't I rise out of the working class, or out of the 'housing project class,' or out of the underpaid office help class?" And, on the other hand, "Why am I better off than my parents? or than the fellows down the road in the low rental project? or the fellows on relief?" Men confronted with these questions adopt a variety of interesting answers.

Is It Up To Me?

The problem of accounting for status is personally important for these men only if they think that their decisions, effort, and energy make a difference in their position in life. Most of my subjects accepted the view that America opens up opportunity to all people; if not in equal proportions, then at least enough so that a person must assume responsibility for his own status. Thus O'Hara, a maintenance oiler in a factory, in a typical response, comments that the rich man's son and the poor man's son "have equal opportunity to be President . . . if they've got the education and the know how." But, he goes on to say, "some of them have a little more help than others." This is the constant theme: "all men can better themselves," the circumstances of American life do not imprison men in their class or station—if there is such a prison, the iron bars are within each man.

There were a few, of course, who stressed the differences of opportunity at birth, the mockery of the phrase "all men are created equal." Here, as only rarely in the interviews, a head of steam builds up which might feed radical social movements—but this is true for only a few of the sample. Three or four angry young or middle aged men deny the Jeffersonian phrase. Rapuano, an auto parts supply man, says:

> How could you say we were born equal when, for instance, when I was
> born, I was born in a family that were pretty poor. You get another
> baby born in a family that has millions.

And Kuchinsky, a house painter, says:

> Are we created equal? I don't believe we are, because everybody's got
> much more than one another and it's not right, I think. Of course, ah,
> we have no choice. I mean we can't do nothing about it. So we're not as
> equal as the next party, that's for sure.

And Ferrera, a salesman, says:

> All men created equal? Ah, very hypocritical, cause all men are not
> created equal—and—I don't know—you really pick some beauties
> don't you? . . . The birth of an individual in a [social] class sort of dis-
> putes this.

To these men, then, subordination and life position is attributable not so
much to the efforts of the individual, something for which he must assume responsibility, as to the circumstances of birth, over which he has no control.
Yet for each of those men the channels of advancement were seen as only
partly blocked. Rapuano, for example, says elsewhere that income is generally
proportionate to ability. Like the theme of "moral equality," the theme of
differential life chances from birth is easily available. What is surprising is not
that it is used at all, but rather that it is used so infrequently.

III. REDUCING THE IMPORTANCE OF THE STRUGGLE

When something is painful to examine, people look away, or, if they look at it,
they see only the parts they want to see. They deny that it is an important
something. So is it often with a person's class status when the reference is upward, when people must account not for the strength of their position, but for
its weakness. How do they do this?

In the first place they may *insulate themselves,* limit their outlook and
range of comparisons. Ferrera, an insurance salesman, who says, "It's pretty
hard for me to think there is anyone in the upper class and I'm not in the
upper class," slides into a prepared position of insulated defense:

> I think a lot of people place a lot of stress on the importance of social
> classes [but] I feel that I have a job to do, I have my own little unit to
> take care of. If I can do it to the best ability that is instilled in me at
> birth or progress through the years, I feel that I rightly deserve the high-
> est classification you can get. I don't particularly like the headings,
> "upper, middle, working, and lower."

It is a resentful narrowing of focus in this case: two years at an inferior college
may have led to ambitions which life then failed to fulfill. Contrast this to

Woodside, a policeman with a Middlewestern rural background, who accepts the "categories" of social class rather willingly. He says, after dealing with the moral and intangible aspects of equality:

> ["Are there any people whom you regard as not equal to you?"] Well, that is a tough question. Well, in fairness, I'd say all people are equal to one another in his own category. When I say category, I mean you couldn't exactly expect a person that had very little knowledge to be, we'll say, should have a position where a person with a lot more education had it.

Equality must be treated within classes, not between them, to be meaningful —and in this way the problem of placing oneself becomes tolerable, or sometimes rather gratifying.

A second device for reducing the importance of class position is to *deny its importance.* This is not to deny the importance of getting ahead, but to limit this to the problem of job classification, or occupational choice—nothing so damaging to the self-esteem as an ordering of persons on a class scale. Rapuano, resisting the class concept, says:

> I don't think it [social class] is important. I mean whenever I went and asked for a job, the boss never asked me what class I was in. They just wanted to know if I knew my business. Oh yes, and I don't think in politics it makes any difference.

Others maintain that for other countries social class is important, but not for Americans. There are rich and poor, perhaps, but not status, class, or deference levels to be accounted for.

A third device for reducing the significance of the struggle for status and "success" is *resignation,* a reluctant acceptance of one's fate. When some men assume this posture of resignation one senses a pose; their secret hopes and ambitions will not down. For others it rings true. When Dempsey, a factory operative, speaks of his situation at the age of 54, one believes him:

> It's hard, very hard. We seem to be struggling along now, as it is, right here, to try and get above our level, to get out of the rut, as you might say, that we're probably in right now. . . . [But] After you get to a certain age, there, you stop—and you say, "Well, I can't go any further." I think I've gotten to that point now.

But when Sokolsky reports that he is contented with his station in life, it does not seem authentic:

> Being in the average group [He wouldn't assign himself a class status] doesn't bother me. I know I make a living—as long as I make a living, and I'm happy and I have what I want—try to give my family what they want. It doesn't bother me—no. I'm satisfied.

But then he adds: "I hope to God my children will do better than their father did."

Contrast these views with those of Johnson, a plumber, who says, "I feel someday I'll be better off. I feel that way because I believe I have it within me to do it"; and with Flynn, a white collar worker, who answers:

No, I'm nowhere near satisfied. It seems to me every time I start to move up a little bit, all the levels move up one step ahead of me. I can't ever get out of this area. I have a certain desire and willingness to do something extra.

IV. THE WORKING CLASS GETS ITS SHARE

When comparing their status with those lower on the scale, however each man may define it, it is easy to point with pride to achievement, material well-being, standing in the community. But satisfaction with one's self and one's friends depends on seeing some advantage in one's situation *vis-à-vis* those who live and work on a higher status level. At first, this seems to be a difficult task, but in many simple ways it can be easily done. Our sample, for example, found ways of ascribing greater happiness, power, and even income to the working class than would be found in the upper class.

The equality of happiness is a fruitful vein. Lower income and status is more tolerable when one can believe that the rich are not receiving a happiness income commensurate with their money income. "Are the rich happier than people who are just average?" O'Hara does not think so:

I think lots of times they're never happy, because one thing is, the majority of them that are rich have got more worries. You see a lot more of them sick than you do, I think, the average. I think a lot of your mental strain is a lot greater in the higher class—in the rich class—than in the other.

And Johnson, a maintenance plumber, says:

Well, even though this rich man can go places and do things that others can't afford, there's only certain things in life that I think make people happy. For instance, having children, and having a place to live—no matter where it is, it's your home . . . the majority of these big men—I don't think they devote as much time and get a thrill out of the little things in life that the average guy gets, which I think is a lot of thrills.

Indeed, hardly a man thought the rich were happier. And yet, O'Hara says, on another occasion, "What is the most important thing that money can buy? Happiness, when you come down to it." Perhaps he means that money buys happiness for the average man, but not for the rich. But more likely he means ["I can take care of a gnawing and illegitimate envy by appropriating happiness for me and my kind."] [4]

[4] Brackets are used here and below to distinguish inferred meanings or imputed statements from direct quotations.

Power, like happiness, is awarded to the working (or lower middle) class. The sheer fact of numbers gives a sense of strength and importance. Costa, a factory operative, says, for example, "People like you [the interviewer] are the minority and people like me are the majority, so we get taken care of in the long run." Whether a person sees himself as middle class or working class, he is likely to believe that most people belong to his class. This being true, his class, people like him, become the most important force in electoral decisions. O'Hara puts it this way:

> The biggest part of the people in this country are working class. And I think they've got the most to do with—they've got a big part to do with running this country—because the lower class, a lot of them don't vote, when you come down to it, they don't have the education to vote, and your upper class isn't that much—isn't as great as the other, so really when you come down to it, it's your working class that's deciding one way or the other.

Not only do they "have the biggest part to do with running the country," they are crucial for the economy. This is not only as producers—indeed no one mentioned the theme which romantic writers on the laboring man and the immigrant have often employed—"they cleared the land and built the cities." Rather it is because of their power to shatter the economy and their power to survive in a depression that they are important. Kuchinsky explains this as follows:

> I think the lower class of people are the important people. I think so because of the business end of it. Without us, I don't think the businessman could survive. I mean if we don't work—of course, they have the money, but, ah, a lot of times during the crash which was an awful thing, too, I think a lot of 'em lived so high that they couldn't stand it any more when they went broke, and they committed a lot of suicides there. But we were used to living that way, it didn't bother us.

Today, as perhaps never before, the working class man can see his status loss compared to white collar workers compensated by income advantages. Thus, De Angelo, a factory operative and shop steward, reports:

> You got people working in offices, they might consider themselves upper class, y'know, a little better than the working man. But nine times out of ten the working man is making more money than he is.

And in the same vein, Rapuano says:

> I certainly would hate like hell to be a white collar worker in the middle class and making the money that the white collar worker does. I would rather be a worker in the lower class, and making their money, see?

Of course, this assignment of income advantages to the working class hinges upon a narrowing of the range of competition—but this is the range that makes a difference for these men.

V. MORAL EQUALITY

Another device for dealing with subordination in a society where invidious comparison with others is constantly invited represents, in effect, a borrowing from an older classical or religious tradition—an emphasis upon the intangible and immeasurable (and therefore comfortingly vague) spiritual and moral qualities. The only clearly adequate expression of this religious view was given by McNamara, a gentle and compassionate bookkeeper, who said "All men are created equal? That's our belief as Catholics," implying some sort of religious equality, perhaps such an idea as is captured in the phrase "equality of the soul." Woodside, a Protestant policeman, takes, in a way, a secular 18th Century version of this view when he says that men are equal "not financially, not in influence, but equal to one another as to being a person." Being a person, then, is enough to qualify for equal claims of some undefined kind.

But it seems probable that when men assert their own equality in this vague sense, typically phrased in something like O'Hara's terms: "I think I'm just as good as anybody else. I don't think there's any of them that I would say are better," something other than moral or spiritual equality is at issue. These moral qualities are what the educated commentator reads into the statement, but O'Hara means, if I may put words in his mouth ["Don't put on airs around me," "I'm trying to preserve my self-respect in a world that challenges it; I therefore assert my equality with all." "I won't be pushed around." "I know my rights," and, to the interviewer: "Just because you're a professor and I'm an oiler, it doesn't mean you can patronize me."] And when Sokolsky, a machine operator and part-time janitor, says, in the interview, "The rich guy—because he's got money he's no better than I am. I mean that's the way I feel," he is not talking about moral or spiritual qualities. He is saying, in effect to his prosperous older brother and his snobbish wife, ["Don't look down on me,"] and to the world at large: ["I may be small, but I will protect my self-esteem."] These men are posting notices similar to the motto on the early American colonies' flags: "Don't tread on me."

Speaking of moral virtues, we must observe how easy it would have been to take the view that the morality of the middle levels of society was superior because the rich received their wealth illegitimately. None of my clients did this. Nor did they stress the immoral lives of the wealthy classes, as did Merton's sample[5] some thirteen years ago—a commentary, perhaps, upon changing attitudes toward the upper classes taking place over this period. The psychic defenses against subordination available in stressing moral equality or superiority were used—but only rarely.

[5] Robert K. Merton, *Mass Persuasion; The Social Psychology of a War Bond Drive* (New York: Harper, 1946).

VI. PEOPLE DESERVE THEIR STATUS

If one accepts the view that this is a land of opportunity in which merit will find a way, one is encouraged to accept the status differences of society. But it is more than logic which impels our men to accept these differences. There are satisfactions of identification with the going social order; it is easier to accept differences which one calls "just" than those that appear "unjust"; there are the very substantial self-congratulatory satisfactions of comparison with those lower on the scale. Thus this theme of "just desserts" applies to one's own group, those higher, and those lower.

So Kuchinsky says: "If you're a professor, I think you're entitled to get what you deserve. I'm a painter and I shouldn't be getting what you're getting." Furthermore, confidence in the general equity of the social order suggests that the rewards of one's own life are proportionate to ability, effort, and the wisdom of previous decisions. On ability, Costa, a machine operator, says:

> I believe anybody that has the potential to become a scientific man, or a professor, or a lawyer, or a doctor, should have the opportunity to pursue it, but there's a lot of us that are just made to run a machine in a factory. No matter what opportunities some of us might have had, we would never have reached the point where we could become people of that kind. I mean everybody isn't Joe DiMaggio.

And on the wisdom of earlier decisions, Johnson, a plumber, says:

> I don't consider myself the lower class. In between someplace. But I could have been a lot better off but through my own foolishness, I'm not. [Here he refers back to an earlier account of his life.] What causes poverty? Foolishness. When I came out of the service, my wife had saved a few dollars and I had a few bucks. I wanted to have a good time. I'm throwing money away like water. Believe me, had I used my head right, I could have had a house. I don't feel sorry for myself—what happened, happened, you know. Of course you pay for it.

But the most usual mistake or deficiency accounting for the relatively humble position is failure to continue one's education due to lack of family pressure ("they should have made me"), or youthful indiscretion, or the demands of the family for money, or the depression of the thirties.

The Upper Classes Deserve to Be Upper

Just as they regard their own status as deserved, so also do they regard the status of the more eminently successful as appropriate to their talents. Rapuano, an auto parts supply man, reports:

> Your income—if you're smart, and your ability calls for a certain income, that's what you should earn. If your ability is so low, why hell,

then you should earn the low income. ["Do you think income is proportionate to ability now?"] I would say so. Yes.

But there is a suggestion in many of the interviews that even if the income is divorced from talent and effort, in some sense it is appropriate. Consider Sokolsky again, a machine operator and part-time janitor, discussing the tax situation:

> Personally, I think taxes are too hard. I mean a man makes, let's say $150,000. Well, my God, he has to give up half of that to the government—which I don't think is right. For instance if a man is fortunate enough to win the Irish Sweepstakes, he gets 150—I think he has about $45,000 left. I don't think that's right.

Even if life is a lottery, the winner should keep his winnings. And De Angelo, a machine operator, comes spontaneously to the same conclusion:

> I think everybody needs a little [tax] relief. I mean, I know one thing, if I made a million dollars and the government took nine-tenths of it— boy, I'd cry the blues. I can't see that. If a man is smart enough to make that much, damn it, he's got a right to holler. I'm with the guy all the way.

Because he is "smart enough" to make the money, it is rightfully his. Surely, beyond the grave, there is a spectre haunting Marx.

The concept of "education" is the key to much of the thinking on social class and personal status. In a sense, it is a "natural" because it fits so neatly into the American myth of opportunity and equality, and provides a rationale for success and failure which does minimum damage to the souls of those who did not go to college. Thus in justifying their own positions, sometimes with reference to the interview situation, my clients imply, "If I had gone to college (like you) I would be higher up in this world." . . .

● ● ●

VII. WHAT IF THERE WERE GREATER EQUALITY OF OPPORTUNITY AND INCOME?

We have examined here the working (and lower middle) class defenses of the present order. They are well organized and solidly built. By and large these people believe that the field is open, merit will tell. They may then deprecate the importance of class, limit their perspectives, accept their situation reluctantly or with satisfaction. They may see the benefits of society flowing to their own class, however they define it. They tend to believe that each person's status is in some way deserved.

How would these lower middle and working class men feel about a change in the social order such that they and their friends might suddenly be equal to others now higher or lower in the social order? Most of them wouldn't like it. They would fear and resent this kind of equality.

Abandonment of a Rationale

Changing ideas is a strain not to be lightly incurred, particularly when these ideas are intimately related to one's self-esteem. The less education one has, the harder it is to change such ideas. Painfully these men have elaborated an explanation for their situation in life; it helps explain things to their wives who take their status from them; it permits their growing children to account for relative social status in school; it offers to each man the satisfactions of social identity and a measure of social worth. Their rationales are endowed with moral qualities; the distribution of values in the society is seen as just and natural. While it gives satisfactions of an obvious kind to those who contemplate those beneath them, it also gives order and a kind of reassurance, oddly enough, to those who glance upwards towards "society" or "the four hundred." This reassurance is not unlike the reassurance provided by the belief in a Just God while injustices rain upon one's head. The feudal serf, the Polish peasant, the Mexican peon believed that theirs was a moral and a "natural order"—so also the American working man.

The Problem of Social Adjustment

Equality would pose problems of social adjustments, of manners, of how to behave. Here is Sokolsky, unprepossessing, uneducated, and nervous, with a more prosperous brother in the same town. "I'm not going to go over there," he says, "because every time I go there I feel uncomfortable." On the question of rising from one social class to another, his views reflect this personal situation:

> I think it's hard. Let's say—let's take me, for instance. Supposing I came into a lot of money, and I moved into a nice neighborhood—class— maybe I wouldn't know how to act then. I think it's very hard, because people know that you just—word gets around that you . . . never had it before you got it now. Well, maybe they wouldn't like you . . . maybe you don't know how to act.

The kind of equality with others which would mean a rapid rise in his own status is a matter of concern, mixed, of course, with pleasant anticipation at the thought of "telling off" his brother.

Consider the possibility of social equality including genuine fraternization, without economic equality. Sullivan, a railroad fireman, deals with this in graphic terms:

> What is the basis of social class? Well, things that people have in common . . . Money is one, for instance, like I wouldn't feel very comforta-

ble going around with a millionaire, we'll say . . . He could do a lot and say a lot—mention places he'd been and so on—I mean I wouldn't be able to keep up with him . . . and he wouldn't have to watch his money, and I'd have to be pinching mine to see if I had enough for another beer, or something.

And, along the lines of Sokolsky's comments, Sullivan believes that moving upwards in the social scale is easier if one moves to a new place where one has not been known in the old connection. Flynn holds that having the right interests and conversational topics for the new and higher social group will make it possible—but otherwise it could be painful. Kuchinsky, the house painter, says "I suppose it would feel funny to get into a higher class, but I don't believe I would change. I wouldn't just disregard my friends if I came into any money." Clinging to old friends would give some security in that dazzling new world.

De Angelo, a factory operative, also considers the question of whether the higher status people will accept the *arriviste*, but for himself, he dismisses it:

> I wouldn't worry much about whether they would accept or they wouldn't accept. I would move into another class. I mean—I mean—I don't worry much about that stuff. If people don't want to bother with me, I don't bother with them, that's all.

These fears, while plausible and all too human on the face of it, emerged unexpectedly from the interview material designed to capture ideas and emotions on other aspects of class status. They highlight a resistance to equalitarian movements that might bring the working class and this rejecting superior class—whether it is imaginary or not—in close association. If these were revolutionaries, one might phrase their anxieties: "Will my victims accept me?" But they are not revolutionaries.

These are problems of rising in status to meet the upper classes face to face. But there is another risk in opening the gates so that those of moderate circumstances can rise to higher status. Equality of opportunity, it appears, is inherently dangerous in this respect: there is the risk that friends, neighbors, or subordinates will surpass one in status. O'Hara has this on his mind. Some of the people who rise in status are nice, but:

> You get other ones, the minute they get a little, they get big-headed and they think they're better than the other ones—where they're still—to me they're worse than the middle class. I mean, they should get down, because they're just showing their illiteracy—that's all they're doing.

Sokolsky worries about this possibility, too, having been exposed to the slights of his brother's family. But the worry over being passed by is not important, not salient. It is only rarely mentioned.

Deprivation of a Meritorious Elite

It is comforting to have the "natural leaders" of a society well entrenched in their proper place. If there were equality there would no longer be such an elite to supervise and take care of people—especially "me." Thus Woodside, our policeman, reports:

> I think anybody that has money—I think their interest is much wider than the regular working man. . . . And therefore I think that the man with the money is a little bit more educated, for the simple reason he has the money, and he has a much wider view of life—because he's in the knowledge of it all the time.

Here and elsewhere in the interview, one senses that Woodside is glad to have such educated, broad-gauged men in eminent positions. He certainly opposes the notion of equality of income. Something similar creeps into Johnson's discussion of social classes. He feels that the upper classes, who "seem to be very nice people," are "willing to lend a helping hand—to listen to you. I would say they'd help you out more than the middle class [man] would help you out even if he was in a position to help you out." Equality, then, would deprive society, and oneself, of a group of friendly, wise, and helpful people who occupy the social eminences.

The Loss of the Goals of Life

But most important of all, equality, at least equality of income, would deprive people of the goals of life. Every one of the fifteen clients with whom I spent my evenings for seven months believed that equality of income would deprive men of their incentive to work, achieve, and develop their skills. These answers ranged, in their sophistication and approach, across a broad field. The most highly educated man in the sample, Farrel, answers the question "How would you feel if everyone received the same income in our society?" by saying:

> I think it would be kind of silly . . . Society, by using income as a reward technique, can often insure that the individuals will put forth their best efforts.

He does not believe, for himself, that status or income are central to motivation—but for others, they are. Woodside, our policeman, whose main concern is not the vistas of wealth and opportunity of the American dream, but rather whether he can get a good pension if he should have to retire early, comes forward as follows:

> I'd say that [equal income]—that is something that's pretty—I think it would be a dull thing, because life would be accepted—or it would—rather we'd go stale. There would be no initiative to be a little different, or go ahead.

Like Woodside, Flynn, a white collar worker, responds with a feeling of personal loss—the idea of such an equality of income would make him feel "very mad." Costa, whose ambitions in life are most modest, holds that equality of income "would eliminate the basic thing about the wonderful opportunity you have in this country." Then, for a moment the notion of his income equalling that of the professional man passes pleasantly through his mind: "don't misunderstand me—I like the idea"; then again, "I think it eliminates the main reason why people become engineers and professors and doctors."

Rapuano, whose worries have given him ulcers, projects himself into a situation where everyone receives the same income, in this case a high one:

> If everyone had the same income of a man that's earning $50,000 a year, and he went to, let's say 10 years of college to do that, why hell, I'd just as soon sit on my ass as go to college and wait till I could earn $50,000 a year, too. Of course, what the hell am I going to do to earn $50,000 a year—now that's another question.

But however the question is answered, he is clear that guaranteed equal incomes would encourage people to sit around on their anatomy and wait for their pay checks. But he would like to see some levelling, particularly if doctors, whom he hates, were to have their fees and incomes substantially reduced. . . .

● ● ●

The World Would Collapse

As a corollary to the view that life would lose its vigor and its savor with equality of income, there is the image of an equalitarian society as a world running down, a chaotic and disorganized place to live. The professions would be decimated: "People pursue the higher educational levels for a reason—there's a lot of rewards, either financial or social," says Costa. Sullivan says, "Why should people take the headaches of responsible jobs if the pay didn't meet the responsibilities?" For the general society, Flynn, a white collar man, believes that "if there were no monetary incentive involved, I think there'd be a complete loss. It would stop all development—there's no doubt about it." McNamara, a bookkeeper, sees people then reduced to a dead level of worth: with equal income "the efforts would be equal and pretty soon we would be worth the same thing." In two contrasting views, both suggesting economic disorganization, Woodside believes "I think you'd find too many men digging ditches, and no doctors," while Rapuano believes men would fail to dig ditches or sewers "and where the hell would we be when we wanted to go to the toilet?"

Only a few took up the possible inference that this was an attractive, but impractical ideal—and almost none followed up the suggestion that some equalization of income, if not complete equality, would be desirable. The fact of the matter is that these men, by and large, prefer an inequalitarian society, and even prefer a society graced by some men of great wealth. As they look out upon the social scene, they feel that an equalitarian society would present them with too many problems of moral adjustment, interpersonal social adjustment, and motivational adjustment which they fear and dislike. But perhaps, most important, their life goals are structured around achievement and success in monetary terms. If these were taken away, life would be a desert. These men view the possibility of an equalitarian world as a paraphrased version of Swinburne's lines on Jesus Christ, "Thou hast conquered, oh pale equalitarian, and the world has grown gray with thy breath."

VIII. SOME THEORETICAL IMPLICATIONS

Like any findings on the nature of men's social attitudes and beliefs, even in such a culture-bound inquiry as this one, the new information implies certain theoretical propositions which may be incorporated into the main body of political theory. Let us consider seven such propositions growing more or less directly out of our findings on the fear of equality:

1. The greater the emphasis in a society upon the availability of "equal opportunity for all," the greater the need for members of that society to develop an acceptable rationalization for their own social status.

2. The greater the strain on a person's self-esteem implied by a relatively low status in an open society, the greater the necessity to explain this status as "natural" and "proper" in the social order. Lower status people generally find it less punishing to think of themselves as correctly placed by a just society than to think of themselves as exploited, or victimized by an unjust society.

3. The greater the emphasis in a society upon equality of opportunity, the greater the tendency for those of marginal status to denigrate those lower than themselves. This view seems to such people to have the factual or even moral justification that if the lower classes "cared" enough they could be better off. It has a psychological "justification" in that it draws attention to one's own relatively better status and one's own relatively greater initiative and virtue.

4. People tend to care less about *equality* of opportunity than about the availability of *some* opportunity. Men do not need the same life chances as everybody else, indeed they usually care very little about that. They need only chances (preferably with unknown odds) for a slightly better life than they now have. Thus: Popular satisfaction with one's own status is related less to equality of opportunity than to the breadth of distribution of some opportunity for all, however unequal this distribution may be. A man who can improve his position one rung does not resent the man who starts on a different ladder half way up.

These propositions are conservative in their implications. The psychological roots of this conservatism must be explored elsewhere, as must the many exceptions which may be observed when the fabric of a social order is so torn that the leaders, the rich and powerful, are seen as illegitimate—and hence "appropriately" interpreted as exploiters of the poor. I maintain, however, that these propositions hold generally for the American culture over most of its history—and also, that the propositions hold for most of the world most of the time. This is so even though they fly in the face of much social theory—theory often generalized from more specialized studies of radicalism and revolution. Incidentally, one must observe that it is as important to explain why revolutions and radical social movements do *not* happen as it is to explain why they do.

The more I observed the psychological and physical drain placed upon my sample by the pressures to consume—and therefore to scratch in the corners of the economy for extra income—the more it appeared that competitive consumption was not a stimulus to class conflict, as might have been expected, but was a substitute for or a sublimation of it. Thus we would say:

5. The more emphasis a society places upon consumption—through advertising, development of new products, and easy installment buying—the more will social dissatisfaction be channeled into intra-class consumption rivalry instead of inter-class resentment and conflict. The Great American Medicine Show creates consumer unrest, working wives, and dual-jobholding, not antagonism toward the "owning classes."

As a corollary of this view:

6. The more emphasis a society places upon consumption, the more will labor unions focus upon the "bread and butter" aspects of unionism, as contrasted to its ideological elements.

We come, finally, to a hypothesis which arises from this inquiry into the fear of equality but goes much beyond the focus of the present study. I mention it here in a speculative frame of mind, undogmatically, and even regretfully:

7. The ideals of the French Revolution, liberty and equality, have been advanced because of the accidental correspondence between these ideals and needs of the bourgeoisie for freedom of economic action and the demands of the working class, very simply, for "more." Ideas have an autonomy of their own, however, in the sense that once moralized they persist even if the social forces which brought them to the fore decline in strength. They become "myths"—but myths erode without support from some major social stratum. Neither the commercial classes nor the working classes, the historical beneficiaries of these two moralized ideas (ideals or myths), have much affection for the ideals in their universal forms. On the other hand, the professional classes, particularly the lawyers, ministers, and teachers of a society, very often do have such an affection. It is they, in the democratic West, who serve as the "hard core" of democratic defenders, in so far as there is one. It is they, more frequently than others, who are supportive of the generalized application of the ideals of freedom and equality to all men. This is not virtue, but rather a different organization of interests and a different training. Whatever

the reason, however, it is not to "The People," not to the business class, not to the working class, that we must look for the consistent and relatively unqualified defense of freedom and equality. The professional class, at least in the American culture, serves as the staunchest defender of democracy's two greatest ideals.

RELIGIOUS PLURALISM AND THE
SUPREME COURT

WILBUR G. KATZ AND HAROLD P. SOUTHERLAND

I

This essay examines the pattern of religious pluralism in the United States and the role that the Supreme Court has played in its development. *Pluralism* is a term of many meanings: A society characterized by strife, hostility, and devisiveness may be called pluralistic. In this essay, the term will be used in a sense that expresses hope rather than fear, unity rather than fragmentation. Pluralism, in this sense, describes a society in which there prevails an attitude toward differences that reinforces and contributes to social cohesiveness.

A religiously pluralistic society, then, is one in which the principal religious groups not only claim freedom for themselves, but affirm equal freedom for others, whatever their beliefs may be. In such a society, these groups have also an internal freedom which is reflected in tolerance of criticism and openness to new insights. Individuals are free to doubt and to believe. This freedom is affirmed because of a realization of the need for dialogue, because groups and individuals have a stake—a religous stake—in the freedom of others. The model pluralism is also one in which there is a sensitivity to the differing needs of various groups and a disposition to accommodate these needs. Such a society need not embody perfection; it may contain groups that do not believe in or practice religious freedom. But a society can approximate the model pluralism if such groups are no great threat to freedom, if a trust in the common commitment to religious freedom prevails among the principal groups.

In this essay, the recent work of the Supreme Court will be interpreted as

SOURCE: Wilbur G. Katz and Harold P. Southerland, "Religious Pluralism and the Supreme Court," *Daedalus*, 96 (Winter 1967), 180–192. Reprinted by permission from *Daedalus*, Journal of the American Academy of Arts and Sciences, Boston, Massachusetts. Some footnotes have been deleted.

expanding religious freedom and thus creating a legal structure favorable to the maturing of this kind of religious pluralism. This interpretation may be debatable, legally and historically; but however the Court's work is interpreted, the influence of its decisions on American religious culture can be neither ignored nor minimized.

Controversy in church-state matters centers on the First Amendment's cryptic injunction that "Congress shall make no law respecting an establishment of religion, or prohibiting the free exercise thereof." This provision is now held to bind also the state legislatures by virtue of the due-process clause of the Fourteenth Amendment. The historical meaning of the quoted words is at best obscure. But there is general agreement that they were designed to accomplish some kind of separation of church and state. When inquiry is made, however, as to the degree and kind of separation required, agreement disappears—with respect both to historical meaning and to policy objectives. It is here submitted that the Court has made it clear that the church-state separation required by the Constitution is not one that insulates government from contacts with religion, but rather one that maximizes religious freedom through a policy of government neutrality. The Constitution does not limit religious freedom to the freedom compatible with strict separation; it requires only the separation compatible with maximum freedom. (Religious freedom has, of course, its limits, as the courts have made clear in cases dealing with polygamy, blood transfusion, snake handling, and compulsory education.)

The Supreme Court has expanded freedom in two principal ways. It has insisted upon a policy of neutrality that forbids government promotion or sponsorship of religious beliefs. By this insistence, the Court has not merely protected the freedom of those who hold different beliefs; it has protected the freedom of commitment to favored beliefs from being compromised by government sponsorship. In the second place, the Court has also expanded religious freedom by permitting, and sometimes requiring, special provisions to be made for religion where this is necessary to neutralize the otherwise restrictive effects of government's expanding activities.

These actions have not always been viewed as actions expanding religious freedom, nor have the Court's opinions always been couched in these terms. But for the study of religion and American culture, the prime significance of the Court's recent work has been its creation of broadly libertarian structures for the religious pluralism of the future.

II

The outlines of neutrality, the dominant theme in the Court's church-state decisions, began to emerge in 1947 in *Everson* v. *Board of Education*,[1] the first of the Court's controversial decisions in this area. In this case, New Jersey's provision for bus transportation for parochial-school students was attacked as

---

[1] *Everson v. Board of Education*, 330 U.S. 1, 18 (1947).

a "law respecting an establishment of religion" prohibited by the First Amendment. Although the opinion sustaining the statute was primarily a discussion of the limits of separation, it included a statement that the First Amendment requires the state to be neutral—not only neutral toward sects but also neutral toward "groups of religious believers and non-believers."

The meaning of neutrality became much clearer in 1961 when the Court unanimously struck down a historic provision of the Maryland constitution requiring a declaration of belief in the existence of God as a prerequisite to holding public office.[2] The plaintiff was a member of the American Humanist Association who had precipitated the test by applying for a commission as a notary public. In holding that the test oath requirement violated his "freedom of belief and religion," the Court declared, in effect, that the state may not discriminate on grounds of religion, regardless of whether the discrimination favors a particular belief or favors all who believe in God at the expense of non-theists. In this case, the Court departed for the first time from traditional usage of the word *religion*, referring to "religions . . . which do not teach what would generally be considered a belief in the existence of God" and citing "Ethical Culture and Secular Humanism."

In the 1962 and the 1963 cases on public-school devotions, the plaintiffs included both sectarians who objected to the particular kind of worship that was sponsored and secularists who objected to any religious devotions. In all of the cases, the Court held that public-school authorities may not sponsor practices which imply the taking of sides in relation to religion. In the *Regents' Prayer* case,[3] the emphasis was on the impropriety of the Regents' action in promulgating an official prayer, notwithstanding its nonsectarian character and the broad approval given it by Jewish and Christian spokesmen.

In the *Schempp* case,[4] the neutrality doctrine received repeated emphasis. The Court stated a test: To avoid violating the "no-establishment" clause, an action of a public agency must not be designed to promote (or inhibit) religious beliefs or practices. In the words of one of the justices, neutrality requires "the extension of evenhanded treatment to all who believe, doubt, or disbelieve—a refusal on the part of the State to weight the scales of private choice." [5] All but one of the justices considered official sponsorship of daily devotions to be inconsistent with neutrality.

Some of the Court's critics have argued that toleration is all that a religious minority (including those who profess no religion) can reasonably expect. Erwin N. Griswold, for example, wrote in his criticism of the *Regents' Prayer* case:

> The child of a nonconforming or minority group is, to be sure, different in his beliefs. That is what it means to be a member of a minor-

---

[2] *Torcaso v. Watkins,* 367 U.S. 488 (1961).
[3] *Engel v. Vitale,* 370 U.S. 421 (1962).
[4] *Abington School Dist. v. Schempp,* 374 U.S. 203 (1963).
[5] *Ibid.,* p. 317.

ity. Is it not desirable, and educational, for him to learn and observe this, in the atmosphere of the school—not so much that he is different, as that other children are different from him? And is it not desirable that, at the same time, he experience and learn the fact that his difference is tolerated and accepted? No compulsion is put upon him. He need not participate. But he, too, has the opportunity to be tolerant. He allows the majority of the group to follow their own tradition, perhaps coming to understand and to respect what they feel is significant to them.[6]

This view is incompatible with the kind of pluralism envisaged by the Court, a pluralism based not on tolerance but on equal freedom. As Mark De-Wolfe Howe has said, leaders in the formative period of our government aimed at "converting the liberal principle of tolerance into the radical principle of liberty" and "believed that it might be achieved by prohibiting the governmental establishment of religion and guaranteeing religious freedom to all persons." [7]

The case of the humanist notary made it clear that the protection of the neutrality principle extends to those who do not believe in God. The 1965 conscientious-objector decisions had, therefore, been foreshadowed. Exemption from military service for conscientious objectors has traditionally been predicated on opposition to war stemming from religious training and belief. In 1948, Congress added the qualification that religious belief for this purpose means "belief in relation to a Supreme Being," to the exclusion of moral, philosophical, or other views. But, in *United States* v. *Seeger*,[8] the Supreme Court held that the exemption covers an agnostic whose opposition to war is based on "belief in the devotion to goodness and virtue for their own sakes, and a religious faith in a purely ethical creed." The Court refused to attribute to Congress any narrow or parochial concept of religious belief, although it seems quite likely that a narrow concept had been intended. The test, the Court said, was "whether a given belief that is sincere and meaningful occupies a place in the life of its possessor parallel to that filled by the orthodox belief in God of one who clearly qualifies for the exemption." Citing an impressive array of theological authorities, the Court stated that its interpretation embraced "the ever broadening understanding of the modern religious community."

Thus far, this section has dealt with the way in which the neutrality doctrine protects the freedom of those who hold a particular belief from governmental action penalizing them or promoting other beliefs. But the promoting

[6] Erwin N. Griswold, "Absolute Is in the Dark," *Utah Law Review*, Vol. 8 (Summer, 1963), pp. 167, 177.

[7] Mark DeWolfe Howe, review of Stokes, *Church and State in the United States, Harvard Law Review*, Vol. 64 (November, 1950), pp. 170–72.

[8] *United States v. Seeger*, 380 U.S. 163 (1965).

of religious beliefs or practices by government would impair also the freedom of those who hold the favored beliefs. The neutrality rule protects the freedom of religious commitment from the devitalizing effects of government sponsorship.

Recent observers of American religious culture have seen that "establishment" can be a threat to free religion even where there is no established church. Peter L. Berger has written of "the religious establishment in America" as the principal threat to the vitality of Christian commitment.[9] The danger is that churches may become captive institutions submerged in a culture religion identified with the American Way of Life. Berger called the public schools "the principal agency representing the politically established culture religion." From this point of view, one can readily see at least symbolic importance in what the Court has done in checking the use of the public schools to propagate this faith.

● ● ●

Varying reactions of "believers" to the public-school prayer decisions give clues to varying attitudes toward this internal religious freedom. Initial comments of religious spokesmen were largely critical of the decisions. They often interpreted them as restrictions of the religious freedom of the majority and rejected the Court's assertion that free exercise of religion "has never meant that a majority could use the machinery of the State to practice its beliefs." [12] Second thoughts brought many religious leaders to defend the Court and to oppose efforts to nullify its decision by amendment of the constitution. Some of the second thoughts were induced by concern over the peculiar religiosity of many of the demands for Constitutional amendment. They had an almost hysterical quality that seemed to reflect a fear of genuine religious freedom that was masked behind an insistence that religious belief have the support of agencies of government. Church leaders came to see the dangers of civic religion as a substitute for other religious commitment. They came to see government sponsorship of religion as a threat to the prophetic witness of the churches and a threat to religious freedom. According to one witness at the Congressional hearings, "the threat is not the secularization of our schools but the secularization of our religion." The Court's insistence on neutrality came to be seen as a protection against this threat.

Critics of the Court often claim that the prayer and Bible reading decisions are hostile to traditional religion and amount to an establishment of secularism. These claims ignore not only the point just developed, but also the Court's careful assurances that neutrality toward religion does not mean the elimination from public education of all study of religious beliefs and practices. On the contrary, the Court warned:

[9] Peter L. Berger, *The Noise of Solemn Assemblies,* (Garden City, N. Y., 1961).
[12] *Abington School Dist. v. Schempp,* 374 U.S. 203, 226 (1963).

It might well be said that one's education is not complete without a study of comparative religion or the history of religion and its relationship to the advancement of civilization. It certainly may be said that the Bible is worthy of study for its literary and historic qualities. Nothing we have said here indicates that such study of the Bible or of religion, when presented objectively as part of a secular program of education, may not be effected consistent with the First Amendment.[13]

Educators are beginning to struggle with the practical problems inherent in such "objective" study of religion. The difficulties in maintaining neutrality are formidable. There must be no "teaching for commitment"; the teaching must be "about" religion and not "of" religion. Furthermore, even in a community with a large Protestant majority, it would not be neutral to limit the instruction to beliefs of Protestant churches. There may be even greater difficulty in maintaining neutrality toward traditional religious beliefs and other views of man and his relationships. There is always a danger that teaching about representative faiths (Protestant, Catholic, and Jewish) will carry the implication that this tri-faith pluralism is the American religion, that all good Americans are at least nominally committed to one of these faiths.

Perfect neutrality, however, is not required. In one area, at least, the Court has tolerated what Mark DeWolfe Howe has called "*de-facto* establishment." [14] The Court has refused to upset traditional Sunday-closing laws. Notwithstanding the admittedly religious roots of these laws and the religious language in which some of them are still cast, the Court found that Sunday laws are now designed to serve the secular purpose of providing a uniform day of rest and recreation.[15]

III

The Court has also protected religious freedom by holding that the establishment clause does not forbid special provisions for religion of a type that may be called "neutralizing" aids. These are provisions made to neutralize the restrictions of religious freedom that would otherwise result from government's secular activities. The classic example of such provisions is the chaplaincy program in the armed services. This program is designed not to promote religion, but to promote religious freedom. When the government separates men from ordinary opportunities for worship and pastoral care, it may properly provide substitute opportunities. Such action accords with a policy of neutrality and is therefore not forbidden by the establishment clause. This assertion may be made with confidence although the chaplaincy program has never been before the Court.

[13] *Ibid.*, p. 225.
[14] Mark DeWolfe Howe, *The Garden and the Wilderness*, p. 11.
[15] *McGowan v. Maryland*, 366 U.S. 420 (1961).

Religious exemptions furnish other examples of neutralizing aids. A familiar case is that of the draft exemption of religious conscientious objectors. In the 1918 *Selective Draft Law Cases*,[16] the Court brushed aside a contention that the exemptions were invalid under the "no-establishment" clause, and the recent cases reaffirm this view. This does not mean that Congress might not constitutionally abolish all exemptions for conscientious objectors. The result is that conscription is an area where the effective scope of religious freedom depends upon action by Congress, subject only to a constitutional duty to avoid discrimination.

In certain other areas, however, religious exemptions may be mandatory. This has recently been the Court's ruling with respect to unemployment-compensation laws. These laws provide compensation only for persons willing to accept employment, and for most workers this means willingness to take a job requiring work on Saturday. In 1963, the Supreme Court held that the Constitution requires that a Seventh Day Adventist be exempted from this requirement.[17] This result, the Court said, "reflects nothing more than the governmental obligation of neutrality in the face of religious differences, and does not represent that involvement of religious with secular institutions which it is the object of the Establishment Clause to forestall."

Even more striking is the decision of the California Supreme Court that the First Amendment requires exempting from narcotics laws the traditional use of peyote in religious ceremonies. The court assumed that non-religious use of peyote might be proscribed. The dominant consideration in requiring the exemption was apparently the court's view of the value of cultural pluralism:

> In a mass society, which presses at every point toward conformity, the protection of a self-expression, however unique, of the individual and the group becomes ever more important. The varying currents of the sub-cultures that flow into the mainstream of our national life give it depth and beauty. We preserve a greater value than an ancient tradition when we protect the rights of the Indians who honestly practiced an old religion in using peyote one night at a meeting in a desert hogan near Needles, California.[18]

Exemptions for Sabbatarians are often written into Sunday-closing laws. While these exemptions are not mandatory, they have been upheld by the Court as not involving "establishment." Special exemptions for other religious groups are increasingly common. For example, the recent amendments to the Social Security Act exempt from social-security taxes the members of religious groups that are conscientiously opposed to insurance and that make adequate provision for their own dependent members. These are examples of what Jus-

---

[16] *Selective Draft Law Cases*, 245 U.S. 366, 389–90 (1918).
[17] *Sherbert v. Verner*, 374 U.S. 398 (1963).
[18] *People v. Woody*, 61 Cal. 2d 716, 394 P. 2d 813, 821–22 (1964).

tice Harlan called the "many areas in which the pervasive activities of the State justify some special provision for religion to prevent it from being submerged in an all-embracing secularism." [19]

All of these illustrations show that an insulating type of church-state separation is not required. Avoiding religious controversies is not the prime objective of church-state policy. If all religious exemptions were outlawed, legislative bodies would, to be sure, be protected from troublesome involvement in religious disputes. But this protection would be at the expense of religious freedom. It is for this reason that the Court has held that such insulation is not required by the First Amendment. The Court apparently believes that the health of American religious pluralism is such that issues concerning religious exemptions need not be kept out of the public forum.

Permissible aids for religion are not limited to aids in the form of exemptions, as the case of the chaplaincy program makes clear. But can the use of public funds for education in religious schools be defended as a neutralizing aid, a means of promoting freedom of religious choice? This question is the principal item of unfinished church-state business faced by the Supreme Court. To understand the question one must begin with an impressive fact: the enormous cost of public education. This cost is properly assessed upon all taxpayers, whether or not they patronize the public schools. But the burden of this cost, in the absence of neutralizing aids, greatly reduces the practical freedom to choose a school that combines general education with religious training. The Constitution guarantees the rights to conduct and to patronize religious schools if they meet general standards,[20] but taxes for public education hamper the freedom to enjoy this right. The position taken in this paper is that in a religiously pluralistic society freedom of religious choice is a matter of general sympathetic concern, and that the legal structures for such a society ought, therefore, to permit financial aids to be voted in order to neutralize restraints on such freedom.

Many educational aids have already been provided by both federal and state governments. Among the more important federal statutes are the National Defense Education Act, the Higher Education Facilities Act, and notably the Elementary and Secondary Education Act of 1965. State aids include not only provisions for transportation, standard textbooks, and various auxiliary services, but also appropriations for college scholarships and tuition grants. Aids at the college level raise less controversy than those for elementary and secondary education. Proposals for aid at the lower levels bring out deep-rooted oppositions to private schools in general and Roman Catholic schools in particular.

Even at the elementary-school level, however, there is widening recognition among religious leaders of the strength of the case for government aid as

[19] *Sherbert v. Verner*, 374 U.S. 398, 422 (1963).
[20] *Pierce v. Society of Sisters*, 268 U.S. 510 (1925).

a feature of free pluralism. Dr. F. Ernest Johnson, long an education expert of the National Council of Churches, wrote that he considers opposition to transportation and textbook aid to be unfair and "a conspicuous example of the fact that Americans seem readier to accept the idea of cultural pluralism than to accept its consequences." [21] Recently, Milton Himmelfarb has challenged the "wall of separation" position from which American Jews have traditionally opposed aids to religious schools.[22] He developed the case for government aid not only in terms of fairness and of national educational policy, but also as a means of preserving a vigorous pluralism as a safeguard of freedom.

These views have increasing support because of increasing trust in the commitment of American Catholics to religious freedom. The declaration of Vatican II on this subject and the new openness of Roman Catholicism to other religious groups have combined to create a new climate for American religious pluralism.

The Supreme Court has spoken twice on the subject of educational aids. Twenty years ago, the Court upheld in the *Everson* case the constitutionality of a state statute providing reimbursement of the cost of bus transportation to parochial schools. The Court stated the neutrality rule in language already quoted and said also:

> We must be careful, in protecting the citizens of New Jersey from state-established churches, to be sure that we do not inadvertently prohibit New Jersey from extending its general state law benefits to all its citizens without regard to their religious belief.[23]

The same opinion, however, included also a general statement against aid to religion which is often cited by advocates of strict separation. The actual decision in *Everson* can be regarded as settled since the Court voted in 1961 in a similar case not to permit reargument of the question.[24]

It is possible, of course, to distinguish between costs of transportation and costs more directly related to education; many other distinctions might conceivably be drawn. The type of aid provided by the federal education act of 1965 furnishes a convenient focus for considering the general problem. This statute provides that projects submitted by local public-school authorities must include arrangements such as dual enrollment in which children in private schools can participate. Dual enrollment (or "shared time") refers to an arrangement by which parochial-school pupils also attend the public school on a part-time basis. Such arrangements have long been in operation for subjects such as industrial arts and home economics; they have been held con-

---

[21] F. Ernest Johnson, "A Problem of Culture," *Religion and the Schools* (Fund for the Republic, 1959), p. 71.

[22] Milton Himmelfarb, "Church and State: How High a Wall?" *Commentary*, Vol. 42 (July, 1966), p. 23.

[23] *Everson v. Board of Education*, 330 U.S. 1, 16 (1947).

[24] *Snyder v. Town of Newton*, 365 U.S. 299 (1961).

stitutional in the only case in which a test has been made.[25] The use of dual enrollment has recently been extended to instruction in sciences, languages, and other subjects not always available in religious schools.

A second title of the education act authorizes grants for textbooks and school-library resources. State authorities receiving funds under this title must give assurances that such books and resources will be provided on an equitable basis for the use of children and teachers in private schools.

Both of these provisions for private schools are questioned by those who are committed to an insulation type of church-state separation. The American Civil Liberties Union, for example, has declared that dual-enrollment programs "present grave constitutional and civil liberties problems under the Establishment Clause . . . because of the substantial benefit that [they] confer upon sectarian schools and because of the joint involvement by secular and church authorities."

Much of the Congressional debate on the education act centered on the so-called "child-benefit" theory, under which it was contended that the bill granted aid only to children and not to religious schools. On this theory, so the argument runs, these aids furnish no precedent for other, more substantial types of aid, such as grants for purchase of scientific equipment. This child-benefit distinction is highly unsatisfactory since all these aids benefit both the children and their schools. All such aids can be defended, however, as neutralizing aids designed to promote freedom in the choice of school.

While prophecy in constitutional law is foolhardy, we hazard the prediction that the Court will not adopt a broad prohibition of programs that help religious schools meet the costs of standard education. None of the bases on which such a prohibition might conceivably be rested seems likely to appeal to the Court. It is highly unlikely that the Court, after its careful exposition of the neutrality principle, will ever take "absolute separation" as a major premise. Nor does it seem likely that the Court will say that separate school systems are so undesirable in a pluralistic society that the establishment clause should be construed as forbidding neutralizing aids. It is also unlikely that the Court will support the claim of opponents of parochial schools that their religious freedom includes freedom from taxes levied to protect freedom of educational choice. Nor is it likely that the Court will follow the fear-inspired logic of those who believe that Roman Catholic attitudes toward religious freedom are still ambivalent, notwithstanding the declarations of Vatican II.

Finally, one may trust that the Court will not consider questions of educational aids to be so hot that they must at all costs be kept off the agendas of Congress and state legislatures. These are issues that can be left to the democratic process because of the healthy vigor of American religious pluralism: a pluralism that is finding its unity in a spreading trust in the common belief in religious freedom.

[25] *Commonwealth ex rel. v. School Dist. of Altoona*, 241 Pa. St. 224 (1913).

IV

Decisions of the Supreme Court have here been interpreted as creating a legal structure within which religious life in the United States can move toward a mature pluralism that reflects an active commitment to religious freedom. Discussion has focused on two applications of a general principle of neutrality. The structure created by the Court is partly permissive. Government may aid religion in ways which protect religious freedom in the context of government's own pervasive activities. But part of the Court's structure is restrictive. Government may not take sides in religious matters; it may not promote religious beliefs—either specific beliefs or religion in general.

It is easy to belittle the practical importance of these restrictions. In the public-school cases, for example, did the Court actually add to the freedom of minorities? Did it actually increase the freedom with which beliefs are held by the majority? It is easy to give a negative answer, and it is easy also to criticize the Court's "absolutist" rhetoric. But such judgments miss an important point. The principal importance of the Court's decisions in this field is symbolic. The Court is commending to citizens of a country with many faiths the ideal of an expanding and deepening religious freedom. In doing so, it is not surprising that the Court uses high-sounding rhetoric. As in the cases on desegregation, if the Court succeeds, it will be through its influence on changing attitudes.

It is not impossible that cultural development in the United States will be toward a pattern in which religious life is sustained more by the vitality of inner freedom than by the pressures of social establishment. It is not impossible that development will be toward a pluralism in which minorities are accorded not the grace of toleration but the right of equal freedom. If these developments do take place, future historians may assign some of the credit to the Supreme Court.

CIVIL LIBERTIES

MILTON R. KONVITZ

In his recent study of the Hebrew Scriptures, Erich Fromm describes one of the functions of the prophets as follows:

SOURCE: Milton R. Konvitz, "Civil Liberties," *The Annals of the American Academy of Political and Social Science*, 371 (May 1967), 39–58. Reprinted by permission. Some footnotes have been deleted.

They do not think in terms of individual salvation only, but believe that individual salvation is bound up with the salvation of society. Their concern is with the establishment of a society governed by love, justice and truth. They insist that politics must be judged by moral values, and that the function of political life is the realization of these values.[1]

OUR FUNDAMENTAL VALUES, GOALS
OR PRESUPPOSITIONS

Today it is doubtful if, in the light of our experience of states, governments, and nations, we can accept, without serious qualifications, the prophetic belief "that politics must be judged by moral values, and that the function of political life is the realization of these [moral] values." We would be much more inclined to agree with Reinhold Niebuhr, whose political realism clearly recognizes and accommodates itself to the limits of morality in political life and accepts the fact that

> political realities are power realities and that power must be countered by power; that self-interest is the primary datum in the actions of all groups and nations.[2]

But this extreme statement also needs qualifications. For politics and morals are not altogether separate. There is room for the moral judgment of political action, provided that the moral principles are not kept and used as pure abstractions; provided that our judgment takes into account the indescribable complexities of social life; provided that our thinking is far removed from utopian commitments and fanatic claims; provided, in a word, that our judgment proceeds from humility in the face of the complexity of forces, recognition of the small role left for creative action, and obligation to try to accommodate and harmonize competing values.

These considerations make the moral judgment harder than was, I suspect, apparent to the prophets of the Hebrew Scriptures, or to Jesus when he preached the Beatitudes; but when hedged in these ways, the moral judgment is inseparable from political action that is more than naked tribalism or a front for the narrowest form of selfishness.[3] With these qualifications, the moral judgment may even be said to be basic in the sense that it is the indispensable condition for the social life of man—who is, we assume, in his social character more than a social insect.[4]

[1] Erich Fromm, *You Shall Be as Gods: A Radical Interpretation of the Old Testament and Its Tradition* (New York: Holt, Rinehart and Winston, 1966), pp. 117–118.

[2] Gordon Harland, *The Thought of Reinhold Niebuhr* (New York: Oxford University Press, 1960), p. 180.

[3] Cf. Reinhold Niebuhr, "Moralists and Politics," in Niebuhr's *Essays in Applied Christianity*, ed. D. B. Robertson (New York: Meridian Books, 1959), p. 78.

[4] Sidney Hook, *Political Power and Personal Freedom* (New York: S. G. Phillips, 1959), p. 94.

In one of his many attempts to translate biblical insights and ideas into modern conceptions, Niebuhr has said that the first problem, in the creation of community and the establishment of justice, is the recognition of the following three presuppositions:

1. Recognition must be given to the dignity of man which assures that in the ultimate instance he is regarded as an end in himself and not merely as an instrument in a social or political process. . . .

2. The law of love must be presupposed as the law of human existence.

3. At the same time the perennial force of self-love and self-interest must be taken for granted.[5]

These "presuppositions" are not essentially different from the prophetic ideals of love, justice, and truth. Indeed, Niebuhr's first presupposition—the dignity of man—may be said to encompass the ideals of love, justice, and truth; or love may be thought to entail human dignity, justice, and truth. No matter; for what is important for us is that, once we recognize, with the prophets, that "politics must be judged by moral values," it becomes necessary for a community to assume that its existence presupposes certain broad and basic moral values or ideals; for "nations do become the bearers of values which transcend their national interests." [6] These values may comprise the vision which keeps a people from perishing.

●　　●　　●

There are, obviously, different ways of stating what these great and important values are, where to find them, and their order. Even so conservative a jurist as Justice Sutherland spoke of those "fundamental principles of liberty and justice which lie at the base of all our civil and political institutions." [9] This would imply that our civil and political institutions are not the only values; for there are values that transcend them and which serve as their foundation, and these values can be summarized in the concepts "liberty" and "justice."

While "justice" and "liberty" are terms used in the Preamble to the Constitution of the United States, and "liberty" is used in the Fifth and Fourteenth Amendments, "justice" is not used anywhere in the body of the Constitution. Yet it is often referred to as one of our great and fundamental values.

Justices of the Supreme Court have not restricted their catalogue of American ideals to those expressly enumerated in the Constitution. The Declaration of Independence speaks prominently of the "pursuit of happiness." Yet "hap-

---

[5] Reinhold Niebuhr, "The Cultural Crisis of Our Age," *Harvard Business Review* (January-February 1954), p. 33, at p. 36.

[6] Reinhold Niebuhr, *op. cit., supra,* note 2, at p. 181.

[9] *Powell* v. *Alabama,* 287, U.S. 45, 67 (1932), quoting from *Hebert* v. *Louisiana,* 272 U.S. 312, 316 (1926).

piness" is not a word that one will find in the Constitution. This, however, was no obstacle to constitutional interpretation as practiced by Justice Brandeis, as evidenced by, for example, the following passage from his important opinion in *Olmstead* v. *United States,* in which he argued for the constitutional right of privacy:

> The makers of our Constitution undertook to secure conditions favorable to the pursuit of happiness. They recognized the significance of man's spiritual nature, of his feelings and of his intellect. They knew that only a part of the pain, pleasure and satisfactions of life are to be found in material things. They sought to protect Americans in their beliefs, their thoughts, their emotions and their sensations. They conferred, as against the government, the right to be let alone—the most comprehensive of rights and the right most valued by civilized man.[10]

But in *Whitney* v. *California,* a case involving the constitutionality of a criminal syndicalism statute, Justice Brandeis made happiness a part of liberty:

> Those who won our independence believed that the final end of the State was to make men free to develop their faculties. . . . They valued liberty both as an end and as a means. They believed liberty to be the secret of happiness. . . .[11]

These passages are quoted to point up the fact that the words of the Constitution—what Justice Cardozo spoke of as the "great generalities of the Constitution" [12]—as important as they are, cannot be taken as an exhaustive compendium of constitutional rights and liberties. "It is," said Justice Frankfurter,

> an inadmissibly narrow conception of American constitutional law to confine it to the words of the Constitution. . . .[13]

In a number of recent cases, the Supreme Court recognized and protected liberties which, the Court itself acknowledged, are not to be found in the words of the Constitution, for, said the Court, liberties expressly mentioned in the Constitution need "breathing space to survive." [14]

---

[10] *Olmstead* v. *United States,* 277 U.S. 438, 478 (1928), dissenting opinion.

[11] *Whitney* v. *California,* 274 U.S. 357, 275 (1927) concurring opinion.

[12] Benjamin Cardozo, *Nature of the Judicial Process* (New Haven, Conn.: Yale University Press, 1921), p. 17.

[13] *Youngstown Sheet & Tube Company* v. *Sawyer,* 343 U.S. 579, 610 (1952), concurring opinion.

[14] *N.A.A.C.P.* v. *Button,* 371 U.S. 415, 430 (1963), opinion by Justice Brennan. The reference was specifically to the First Amendment freedoms, but nothing was said that would necessarily limit the principle to these freedoms. See also *New York Times Co.* v. *Sullivan,* 376 U.S. 254, 272 (1964), opinion also by Justice Brennan.

In the Court's opinion by Justice Douglas in *Griswold* v. *Connecticut*,[15] the Court re-interpreted certain constitutional guarantees as "emanations," "penumbras," "zones," or "facets" of "privacy." Thus, the First Amendment freedoms are derivative from "privacy," the more ultimate or fundamental conception or ideal. So, too, said the Court, other constitutional liberties flow out of "privacy," are "emanations" from "privacy," such as the prohibition in the Third Amendment against the quartering of soldiers in any house in time of peace without the owner's consent; the affirmation in the Fourth Amendment of the "right of the people to be secure in their persons, houses, papers, and effects, against unreasonable searches and seizures"; and the guarantee against self-incrimination in the Fifth Amendment.

But just as express constitutional liberties flow out of the more fundamental but unwritten right of privacy, so the express constitutional liberties themselves generate other unwritten liberties. Thus, the First Amendment freedoms have a "penumbra" in which "freedom to associate" and "privacy in one's associations" are to be found. So, too, the First Amendment freedoms generate the right to educate one's children as one chooses; the right to study foreign languages in a private school; the right to distribute publications, to receive publications, to read, to teach, to pursue inquiry. So, too, the constitutional amendments generate protection of the intimate aspects of the marital relation and of the relation of husband and wife and their physician—these fall into a "zone of privacy created by several fundamental constitutional guarantees." The Constitution does not mention these zones of privacy, but the express provisions "create zones of privacy."

Thus, privacy is the mother of express constitutional guarantees, which in turn become the mother of other zones of privacy.

One is tempted to question the logic of these circular generative processes, but no one should undertake to criticize the logic unless he can produce a more appealing or convincing conceptual scheme. Adapting a passage from Justice Holmes in the Gompers case, I would say that the provisions of the Constitution cannot be read as abstractly as one reads a mathematical formula; they are organic, living institutions; their significance is not formal but vital.[16] We constantly need to be careful not to mistake "the form in which an idea was cast for the substance of the idea." [17]

We have noted that Justice Brandeis found happiness to be a part of liberty. So, too, Justice Douglas found property to be a part of liberty. For in the Heart of Atlanta Motel case, the Court had to meet the challenge that the Civil Rights Act of 1964, by forbidding racial discrimination or segregation by a motel, deprived the owner of his liberty and property without due process of law. Justice Douglas, concurring in the Court's decision upholding the con-

[15] *Griswold* v. *Connecticut*, 381 U.S. 479 (1965).

[16] *Gompers* v. *U.S.*, 233 U.S. 604, 610 (1914).

[17] Chief Justice Vinson in *American Communications Association, CIO* v. *Douds*, 339 U.S. 382 (1950).

stitutionality of the act as a proper exercise of the commerce power, added that Congress also had the power to enact the legislation under the Fourteenth Amendment; and in part resolved the conflict between property and liberty—both of which receive equal mention and dignity in the Due Process Clause—by maintaining that property is an instrumental value serving liberty. It is a means to an end. He quoted approvingly the following passage from the Senate Committee report on the act:

> But there are stronger and more persuasive reasons [than the commerce power] for not allowing concepts of private property to defeat public accommodations legislation. The institution of private property exists for the purpose of enhancing the individual freedom and liberty of human beings. . . .
> Is this time-honored means to freedom and liberty [i.e., property] now to be twisted so as to defeat individual freedom and liberty [by allowing segregation]? [18]

Thus, one might say, in the clash between liberty and property under the Due Process Clause, liberty won out, not because it is "preferred," but because property is only a means to liberty, which is the end.

Justice Goldberg, concurring in the decision, chose to use a concept of even greater reach than liberty, though it is not a term to be found in the Constitution. The primary purpose of the Civil Rights Act of 1964, he said, is "the vindication of human dignity and not mere economics [the regulation of commerce]." [19]

The most candid admission that the Court may look for constitutional liberties outside the Constitution itself came from Justice Goldberg. In his concurring opinion in Griswold, he argued that

> The "liberty" protected by the Fifth and Fourteenth Amendments . . . is not restricted to rights specifically mentioned in the first eight amendments. . . . There are fundamental personal rights . . . which are protected from abridgment by the Government though not specifically mentioned in the Constitution.[20]

Summary

We have seen that political institutions and values are not ultimate but are subject to moral criticism and moral judgment. As Sidney Hook has said, "The moral question is primary and it cuts across all categories." [21] Our civil and political institutions presuppose or are based on certain fundamental

---

[18] *Heart of Atlanta Motel* v. *U.S.*, 379 U.S. 241, 285 (1964).

[19] *Ibid*, at p. 291.

[20] Case cited *supra*, note 15, at pp. 493, 496. Justice Goldberg contended that the Ninth Amendment "lends strong support" to his view, p. 493.

[21] See note 4, *supra*.

moral principles, ideals, or values. Some of them are specifically stated in the Constitution, especially in the First Amendment. But the statement of the principles in the Constitution does not exhaust their meaning or reach. These principles need "breathing space"; thus, for example, there is freedom of association, though it is not mentioned in the Constitution, for without it the freedoms specifically enumerated in the First Amendment could not be fully enjoyed. In turn, freedom of association also needs "breathing space"—without the assurance of "privacy in one's associations," one would not be secure in one's "freedom to associate."

Then, too, the freedoms expressly stated in the Constitution may be interpreted as exemplifications or expressions of even more fundamental values. Thus, privacy is more fundamental than the First Amendment freedoms. The latter may, then, be read as "emanations" of privacy. The First Amendment may then be read as guaranteeing the fundamental right of privacy. But, then, the First Amendment and the other provisions of the Constitution will be read as exemplifying and as implementing some "facets" or "emanations" of this right; however, they do not exhaust the meaning, reach, or power of what the Constitution will protect as the right of privacy.

But even privacy may not be the ultimate value. It may be only an "emanation" or "facet" of a value found to be more fundamental, more encompassing, and more generative, just as happiness may be only a "facet" of liberty, and property only an aspect of liberty.

Finally, as our discussion has demonstrated, there are values, goals, ideals, that our Constitution protects which are not specifically mentioned in the Constitution. They are such as may be found in the "traditions and [collective] conscience of our people." [22]

The words of the Constitution are a "form." The "substance" of the ideas often transcends the form. The relationship of the form to the substance, as Plato discovered, can be described only allegorically: the terms of the Constitution are only "shadows," which the fire that is the substance throws on the opposite wall of the cave.[23] Just as "astronomy compels the soul to look upwards and leads us from this world to another," [24] so constitutional interpretation forces us to read the text but to look beyond it and to see further.

It is this process of transcendence that keeps the Constitution, and especially the Bill of Rights, from being "merely a literary composition" instead of "an organism." [25] It is this process that has made it possible for the Constitution to survive. This principle frees the Constitution from the paralysis of literalism and the disabling effect of narrow historicism.[26] The ideals of the Con-

---

[22] Case cited *supra*, note 15, at p. 493, quoted by Justice Goldberg.

[23] Plato, *The Republic*, Book VII.

[24] *Ibid.*

[25] Justice Frankfurter in *Burstyn v. Wilson*, 343 U.S. 495, 518 (1952).

[26] Justice Black is perhaps the only member of the Court who would attack this proposition. It is not relevant to our purpose to discuss Justice Black's position.

stitution, as important as they are, point beyond themselves to ever richer, greater goals, which become our national values and our constitutional presuppositions. The law, even the law of the Bill of Rights, points to a "higher" law.

THE INTERACTION OF GOALS AND FACTS

We started with the proposition that there is room for the moral judgment or the higher law in the social-political realm, provided that the moral principles are not kept as mere abstractions and are not used as if they provide simple answers to complex questions. Abstractionist and simplistic reasoning are often the trouble of sermonizing and moralizing. Yet sometimes goals or ideals need to be affirmed and vindicated *as if* the facts could make no difference: facts must then accommodate themselves to the values, and the latter will not give an inch. We sometimes say: "Let justice be done though the heavens fall."

We cannot always be concerned with consequences. Aristotle noted the fact that good things at times have harmful consequences. Wealth is a good thing, but some people have been ruined by it. Courage is a virtue, but in some cases courage has cost men their lives. Now, if wealth always meant ruin of the rich man's life or character, if courage always meant death, we would not think of these values as virtues or goods. We must, therefore, be content if, in dealing with premises that are uncertain, we succeed in only "a broad outline of the truth: when our subjects and our premises are mere generalities, it is enough if we arrive at generally valid conclusions." [27]

●   ●   ●

For, certainly, good things may have harmful consequences; but this is no argument against freedom of speech or any of the other freedoms guaranteed by the First Amendment. Freedom of religion is, we believe, a good thing even if it means the creation or spread of religions that may do more harm than good. Freedom of the press is, we believe, a good thing even if we may also believe, with Luther, that "the multitude of books is a great evil," that some books are downright wicked—for example, Hitler's *Mein Kampf*— and that most books are mere scribble and a waste of precious time and substance. A Negro family have a right to move into the house they have purchased even if their white neighbors may become a lawless mob which would try to keep them out. James H. Meredith had a right to be admitted into the University of Mississippi even if the enforcement of his right took 5,000 soldiers and National Guardsmen to accomplish.

From this standpoint, it probably would have been better if the Supreme

[27] Aristotle, *Nicomachean Ethics*, I, iii.

Court in *Brown* v. *Board of Education*[29] had left out the controversial footnote 11, in which the Court referred to certain psychological and sociological studies; for the constitutional question was not whether racial segregation in the schools was in 1954—or in 1896, when *Plessy* v. *Ferguson*[30] was decided —good or bad for all the people, or for the white race, or for the Negro race.[31] What scientific studies were available in 1865 to prove that slavery was bad for Negroes or for the Nation, so that it should be outlawed by a constitutional amendment? When, in 1920, we adopted the Nineteenth Amendment, outlawing discrimination in voting rights on account of sex, how much did we know about women that had not been known to the previous generations of Americans? Many things certainly were different in the United States of 1920 from the United States of 1820, but it is doubtful if among the differences we could cite a greater amount of knowledge about the nature of women. Is it their superior knowledge of women that is the basis of women's suffrage in Uganda, as contrasted with the ignorance of the Swiss, who deny to their women the right to vote? [32]

In recent years there have been published monographs and tracts on the "costs of discrimination." [33] It would be interesting to find out, if one could, how many people have been persuaded by the argument on "costs" to come over to the side of civil rights. I suspect that those who were committed to racial segregation—in the United States, in South Africa, in Rhodesia—would say, with righteous indignation, that segregation was a matter of "principle," a question of a way of life, so what does "cost" matter? Is it an argument on behalf of Protestantism that it "costs" more to be a Roman Catholic?

All that I have said is not intended as an argument against empirical studies of problems connected with civil liberties or civil rights. I mean, however, to point up several considerations:

1. It should by no means be assumed that we know in advance that empirical data should or will influence the ultimate value judgment. Facts and values may each be on their own street, and the streets may or may not intersect.

An individual or a nation may place such stress on an ideal that everything else in relation to it becomes incommensurable. "For what does it profit a man to gain the whole world and lose his soul?" [34] Facts were of no avail against Socrates or Thomas More in prison, to persuade either to change his mind. "I can do no other," said Luther at the Diet of Worms—*Ich kann nicht anders.* Many martyrs and heroes, and many peoples, have said the same; and they have all, in their various ways, followed the counsel of Emerson:

[29] *Brown* v. *Board of Education*, 347 U.S. 438 (1954).

[30] *Plessy* v. *Ferguson*, 163 U.S. 537 (1896).

[31] See M. R. Konvitz, "The Use of the Intelligence in Advancement of Civil Rights," *Aspects of Liberty*, ed. M. R. Konvitz and Clinton Rossiter (New York: Johnson Reprints, 1958), p. 79.

[32] In Switzerland, women vote in three (out of twenty-two) cantons. A (male) referendum in 1954 rejected women's suffrage for the federal republic.

[33] For example, Bucklin Moon, *The High Cost of Prejudice* (New York: Julian Messner, 1947).

[34] Mark 8:36.

Give all to love:
Obey thy heart.
Friends, kindred, days,
Estate, good fame,
Plans, credit, and the Muse,
Nothing refuse. . . .
Follow it utterly. . . .

Hume stressed the distance between values and facts, between the *is* and the *ought*. It is not, he said, "contrary to reason to prefer the destruction of the whole world to the scratching of my finger. . . . 'Tis as little contrary to reason to prefer my own acknowledg'd lesser good to my greater, and have a more ardent affection for the former than the latter." [35]

2. But Hume went perhaps too far in keeping values and facts separate and apart. He concluded from their differences and separation that values, which he significantly called "passions," cannot be ruled by reason. "Nothing," he said, "can oppose or retard the impulse of passion, but a contrary impulse." A passion can be replaced by another—similar or contrary—passion, but not by an argument, not by a chain of reasoning. "Abstract or demonstrative reasoning, therefore, never influences any of our actions, but only as it directs our judgment concerning causes and effects." Passions provide us with our goals; reason and considerations of fact may help us in our choice of means— "Reason is, and ought only to be the slave of the passions, and can never pretend to any other office than to serve and obey them." [36]

Empirical studies, for example, may show that it is probable that poverty breeds disease and crime. If men want to reduce or eliminate disease and crime, then they may be influenced by these studies to fight against poverty as a means to their goal. But the demonstration of a probable causal relationship between means and end will not itself produce a commitment to seek to achieve that end. If we are interested in the end, then we may be interested in finding the best means; but if we are not really interested in the end, discussion of means is a waste of time.

But, as I have said, Hume perhaps went too far to keep facts and values— or "reason" and "passion"—separate and apart. *They may cross and interact.* The mind and character of man are complex, and their ways are indescribably subtle.

Suppose, for example, empirical studies were to show that the poor have diseases that are relatively peculiar to poverty and that the rich also have diseases, such as are peculiar to their ways of life, and that on balance there was not much to choose between them: that in the end, both the rich and the poor end up in the doctor's office and in the hospital. Suppose, too, it could be shown that while the poor contribute a major proportion of criminals who

[35] David Hume, *A Treatise of Human Nature* (1734–1740), Book II., Part III, Sec. III.
[36] *Ibid.*

committed certain types of crime, the same could be shown of the rich with respect to other types, so that, on balance, again there was not much to choose between them. . . .

Concern with such empirical investigations and with the problem of means and ends may, however, lead to the conclusion that our real concern with poverty is not that it may be the cause of certain tangible, even measurable, evils, such as disease or crime, but that, regardless of such considerations, it is in itself—like disease or crime—an evil which society should seek to mitigate or end. . . .

Separate consideration of means and ends may help to clarify our understanding of what our ends *really* are, and empirical investigations may contribute to an exposure of our misconceptions. When we get all through with our research, we may suddenly discover that we are not really seeking what we purported to be seeking. The illumination might have come without the great expenditure of time, resources, thought and effort, but our common experience is that often it comes the hard way.

Some abolitionists probably thought that they could demonstrate the evil of slavery by showing, with empirical data, that slavery breeds sickness and criminality. Suppose, however, that their investigations disclosed that slaves enjoyed longer life than their masters, and that they were relatively healthier men and women (after all, slaves were valuable property, which deserved concern and care) and that, when judged by the standards of the criminal law, slaves were better behaved than their masters (after all, they had less exposure to temptation to commit embezzlement, fraud, adultery, arson for profit, and many other offenses; besides, the risk to them, if caught, was much greater). After reviewing their findings, it might come to the investigators to cry out to themselves: "Can it be that we really, at one time, thought that slavery was a great evil *because* we could consider it a cause of sickness and crime? Did we want to abolish slavery *because* we thought that it breeds these evils? How foolish could we be?"

Hume, therefore, exaggerated when he claimed that

> Reason is wholly inactive and can never be the source of so active a principle as conscience, or a sense or morals.[39]

Empirical investigations of questions of fact may help explicate and may illumine values and value judgments; and such investigations, even when based on hypotheses which prove to be misconceived, have value in compelling deeper criticism of the ends to which they may be related.

3. Hume performed a great service for philosophy, law, politics, and science when he sharply differentiated ideal and fact, "passion" and "reason." But a bridge had to be built to connect them, and that connection may be described in words adapted from Kant—who was awakened out of his dogmatic

---

[39] Hume, *op. cit.*, *supra*, note 35, at Book III, Part I, Sec. I.

slumbers by Hume: *Ideals without facts are empty, and facts without ideals are blind.*

Thus, for example, the ideal of equality before the law could be only a pious fraud unless we made the effort to find out the disparity between rich and poor defendants in the availability of defense counsel, transcripts of records for appeal, bail, and related rights.

As far back as 1865, Massachusetts placed on its books a civil rights law that banned discrimination on account of color or race in places of public accommodation. This pioneering law introduced an "activist" principle into our legal order, for the law presupposed the principle that a state has a *positive* role to play in race relations, to protect one race against the stronger, dominating will of the other; to prevent the development of a caste system based on race or color; to make the suffering of a public indignity on account of race or color an offense against the public order. By 1964, when Congress enacted the Civil Rights Act, there were thirty additional states with laws forbidding racial discrimination in places of public accommodation.[40] But how much have we ever known about the effectiveness of our state civil rights acts? Those who were concerned with such questions knew, in a general way, that the promise of these laws far outran the performance,[41] but there were no broad studies, no empirical data to inform the judgment. The ideals on which the laws were based remained, to a degree no one can say authoritatively, abstract from the facts of life.

4. There is a large area where values need to be asserted, where moral positions need to be taken, with the realization, however, that the inexpressibly complex situations make it practically impossible to prove or disprove cause-effect relations between values and facts, between the *ought* and the *is.* . . .

With respect to some broad, complex questions, we shall need to be satisfied—at least for the foreseeable future—with only the "probable conclusions" which Aristotle allowed the orator. Thus, we are not to expect anyone to demonstrate that the nonviolent civil disobedience demonstrations in the civil rights movement had the effect of increasing or decreasing respect for law, legal process, and authority; or that they prevented race riots by serving as safety valves; or, on the contrary, that they acted to stimulate race riots by accustoming young people to take their demands to the streets and other public places. We must be reconciled to the possession of only fragmentary knowledge, or perhaps almost total ignorance, with respect to some highly significant issues involving relations between values and facts.

5. There is, however, the danger that many questions of fact will not be investigated simply on the exaggerated assumption that the facts and their rela-

[40] See M. R. Konvitz, *Expanding Liberties: Freedom's Gains in Postwar America* (New York: Viking Press, 1965), pp. 255–256; M. R. Konvitz and Theodore Leskes, *A Century of Civil Rights* (New York: Columbia University Press, 1961), chap. 6.

[41] See Konvitz and Leskes, *op. cit., supra,* note 40, at pp. 159–168; M. R. Konvitz, *The Constitution and Civil Rights* (New York: Columbia University Press, 1947), pp. 121–123.

tions make such a "big, blooming, buzzing confusion" that the mind cannot penetrate them or reduce them to an intelligible order; and so there will be no commerce between the realm of *is* and the realm of *ought*. Each will flourish in its own impenetrable kingdom. This would give up more than may be warranted.

Consider how little we really know about academic freedom. In the case decided by the Supreme Court in 1967 in which the Court, by 5-to-4, struck down three antisubversion laws of New York, including the Feinberg Law, Justice Brennan, for the majority, said:

> It would be a bold teacher who would not stay as far as possible from utterance or acts which might jeopardize his living by enmeshing him in this intricate [statutory and administrative] machinery. . . . The result must be to stifle "that free play of the spirit which all teachers ought especially to cultivate and practice." [51]

"The result must be . . .," said the Court, but Justice Brennan did not stop to document this proposition. Later in the opinion, the Court said:

> The stifling effect on the academic mind from curtailing freedom of association in such measure [as is accomplished by the Feinberg Law] is manifest, and has been documented in recent studies.

And here the Court cited a half-dozen studies, most of them of a general nature and several—perhaps no more than two—that may pass as empirical studies.

Admittedly, it is difficult to find out what effects teacher loyalty oaths and regulations may have on the teachers and their work. We know that in the school and college system of New York City, some four hundred teachers and other employees have been dismissed or have terminated their services as a result of inquiries under the Feinberg Law. Most were dismissed for refusal to answer questions about themselves.[52] There are those, however, who contend that "a bold teacher" is always bold; that bold teachers were not silenced or curtailed in their freedom even in the McCarthy period; that timid teachers are timid even in an atmosphere of freedom. We should try to find out more about such matters than we have done in the past. We may not be able to establish much, but we have not thus far really tried to establish anything. What shall be the indicators of academic freedom? Surely the absence of loyalty oath and similar laws and regulations must signify something or there would not be so much emotion generated by their existence; but we have here a matter to which we have not tried to give "that amount of precision which belongs to its subject matter."

A similar point may be made about the law of obscenity. We know that the

[51] *Keyishian* v. *Board of Regents*, 87 S. Ct. 675 (1967).
[52] Article by Mary Hornaday in *Christian Science Monitor*, January 26, 1967.

Supreme Court has avoided saying that obscene publications may be prohibited *because* they have evil effects on those who read them, or on the youth, or on some other special group—that such publications may be prohibited because they create a "clear and present danger" to certain "substantive evils" which a state may have a right to prevent.[53] The Court has, however, said that obscene publications are outside the protection of the First Amendment because they are "utterly without redeeming social importance." [54] Suppose that reliable studies were to show that such publications "often" achieve "beneficial" effects and only "seldom" achieve "evil" effects. It may then well be that the Court, the legislatures, and the informed public generally would change their attitude. In 1963 the [London] *Times Literary Supplement* called upon the Home Secretary to

> institute a thorough study of the effects which different types of supposedly pernicious literature . . . can have on more or less susceptible readers. For the first essential is that we should all stop simply speculating one way or another on this head. At present the whole question is based on guess work.[55]

There have been some factual studies of the problem, but they barely scratch the surface.[56] One should not, of course, underestimate the difficulties involved in setting up and pursuing such empirical, and even experimental, inquiries, but more difficult tasks have been accomplished.

It should be added that the value of empirical studies in such an area would be considerably lessened if they were not set up on a continuing basis; for we live in a time in which moral standards are rapidly shifting. The reactions of a generation to whom *Fanny Hill, Tropic of Cancer,* and *Playboy* magazine are readily available and who assume such publications as a matter of course must be different from a generation to whom they were as unthinkable as they were unseeable. The changes are rapid and deep; for example, the National Catholic Office for Motion Pictures, formerly the National Legion of Decency, made its 1966 awards to *Georgy Girl* as one of the two best pictures of the year, and the Broadcasting and Film Commission of the National Council of Churches made one of its awards to *Who's Afraid of Virginia Woolf?* [57] The time dimension would need to fit prominently in any investigations; this will make general conclusions more hazardous; still, considerable room may be left for significant empirical analysis, which may interact with our relevant constitutional or other principles.

6. The recent case of *Kent* v. *United States*[58] poignantly calls attention to

---

[53] See Konvitz, *Expanding Liberties, op. cit., supra,* note 48, at pp. 117, 168–242.

[54] *Ibid.,* at p. 185.

[55] *Ibid.,* quoted at p. 229.

[56] See some of the literature cited *ibid* at p. 405, note 4.

[57] *New York Times,* February 3, 1967.

[58] *Kent* v. *U.S.,* 58 S. Ct. 1045 (1966).

another aspect of the problem of connection between goals and indicators. The case involved the waiver of jurisdiction over a juvenile delinquent by a juvenile court without a hearing and without stated reasons for the waiver, thereby subjecting the child to the possibility of a death sentence instead of treatment for a maximum of five years. In unanimously reversing and remanding the case, the Supreme Court, in an opinion by Justice Fortas, said that studies and critiques in recent years raised serious questions as to whether the actual performance of juvenile courts

> measures well enough against the critical purpose to make tolerable the immunity of the [juvenile court] process from the reach of constitutional guarantees applicable to adults. There is much evidence that some juvenile courts . . . lack the personnel, facilities and techniques to perform adequately as representatives of the State in a *parens patriae* capacity, at least with respect to children charged with law violation. There is evidence, in fact, that there may be grounds for concern that the child receives the worst of both worlds: that he gets neither the protections accorded to adults nor the solicitous care and regenerative treatment postulated for children.[59]

This indictment of our juvenile courts—an institution of which most Americans could naturally assume we could be justly proud as evidence of our great concern over the welfare of children—underscores the fact that some of our institutions are praiseworthy only if we judge them by their façade. When we open them for inspection, we get quite a different picture, and even a different smell. In recent years we have become aware of the low quality of education provided for millions of our children in the public and the parochial schools; hardly a day passes when we are not reminded of the shabbiness of the performance inside our attractive-looking hospitals. What Florence Nightingale is reported to have said of hospitals may, unfortunately, be said of many of our institutions of which we are—sometimes insufferably—proud: "The least you can expect of a hospital," she said, "is that it should not spread disease!"

For years, the evidence was available that the way legislative apportionment worked, our much-vaunted democracy was only the barest approximation of the democratic ideal; yet hardly anyone stirred before the Supreme Court, in 1962,[60] opened the door for judicial review of apportionment and made relief possible. For years, the evidence was available that the "separate but equal" principle was a cheat and a fraud; yet hardly anyone cared before the Court exploded the fiction in the face of the American people in the 1954 decision.[61]

[59] *Ibid.*, at p. 1054.
[60] *Baker* v. *Carr*, 369 U.S. 186 (1962).
[61] Case cited *supra*, note 29.

Surely, for years, it was no secret that in criminal cases, defendants who were too poor to engage legal counsel often failed to receive a fair trial; yet Americans went about their work and business and undoubtedly often remarked that in totalitarian countries, like the Soviet Union, men could not be sure that they would, when in trouble, receive a fair trial. The Irish proverb that "the hills look green that are far away" must often be reversed: the hills look green that are near. Again, we waited for the Supreme Court, in 1963, to correct our vision. "That government hires lawyers to prosecute and defendants who have the money hire lawyers to defend are," said the Court,

> the strongest indications of the widespread belief that lawyers in criminal courts are necessities, not luxuries. The right of one charged with crime to counsel may not be deemed fundamental and essential for fair trials in some countries, but it is in ours. . . . This noble ideal [of fair trials before impartial tribunals in which every defendant stands equal before the law] cannot be realized if the poor man charged with crime has to face his accusers without a lawyer to assist him.[62]

These are only a few instances of shocking discrepancies between our noble ideals and our practices, where for years the practices have been known to exist, and yet the American people were, on the whole, indifferent and pretended innocence. We tend to sweep under the rug our inconsistencies and failures. As the civil rights demonstrations dramatically showed, we are as a people prone to believe that once we have approved an ideal, nothing further remains to be done: the ideal is assumed to be self-fulfilling; yet there is hardly an aspect of our ideals of which we can truthfully say that it has been fully, or even substantially, achieved.

Summary

It is not enough for a nation to profess to be a democracy. East Germany calls itself the German *Democratic* Republic, and North Vietnam calls itself the Democratic Republic of Vietnam. Nor is it enough for a nation to have a constitution and a bill of rights. Stalin gave the Soviet Union in 1936 a constitution with provision for universal, direct suffrage, with secret ballot, and with a bill of rights that professes to guarantee freedom of conscience, freedom of speech, the press, assembly, mass meetings, street processions and demonstrations, and the inviolability of homes and privacy of correspondence.[63] The statement and affirmance of ideals are important: for while nations—like St. Paul [64]—follow the worse, their bills of rights are admissions against interest, admissions that they see the better; they are the tribute that vice pays to

[62] *Gideon* v. *Wainwright*, 372 U.S. 335, 344 (1963); opinion of Justice Black for the Court.
[63] United Nations, *Yearbook on Human Rights for 1946* (New York: United Nations, 1947), pp. 315–316.
[64] Romans 7:19.

virtue. And as our own case has shown, there is no telling when—sometimes even after the passage of a century or more—a provision of a bill of rights gets called in like a promissory note, and we are told by a court, or by a group of college and high school students in a demonstration, that we either put up or shut up.

For a nation honestly to estimate the degree to which it lives by its vision and its self-image, it must look at the facts. If the facts are not apparent, it must set up machinery to get at the facts, for ideals without facts, consistent with the ideals, are empty.

In looking for the facts, it is necessary to keep in mind different situations. I have dealt, in the second part of this paper, with only six different situations. There are, I am sure, many others, but these should suffice to point up the complex question of the relation between goals and indicators as the question touches fundamental rights and liberties. The different situations touched on were the following:

1. There are values that seem to demand vindication without regard to the proofs of what they may produce; for example, starting in 1954, our federal courts have been ordering and compelling desegregation of universities and schools and will not listen to arguments about hardships, unrest, and violent resistance.[65]

2. Investigations of fact, even when directed toward hypotheses which prove to have been misconceived, may have value in throwing light upon values which may have been misunderstood, disregarded, or falsely estimated. For example, I think that many of the attempts to establish that poverty is a source of this evil or that are not likely to prove successful; yet the attention focused on poverty is itself justified as possibly contributing to an intensified sensitivity to poverty as in itself an evil: an evil not because it leads to other evils, but simply because the state of poverty is by itself an evil. Empirical investigations may contribute to a refinement of our sense of values and may be a process out of which new values may emerge.

3. We lack the knowledge of how our ideals are effective, or even if they are at all effective in life; for example, many states had civil rights acts, fair employment practice acts, fair housing acts, fair educational practices acts, but we seemed satisfied that we have done our duty fully when we enacted these laws and provided some enforcement agencies. These steps may, as a matter of fact, have had the bad effect of soothing our consciences—prematurely. We made almost no effort to find out how effective—or ineffective—these statutes and agencies in fact were.

4. Some questions seem to be too large and too complex for fruitful empirical inquiry; for example: Have the civil rights nonviolent demonstrations contributed to a greater respect for law and the rule of law, or to an increase in

[65] *Cooper* v. *Aaron*, 358 U.S. 1 (1958).

criminality, a proneness to rioting, and a general disrespect for authority? Has the privacy statute of New York State had good or bad effects on the ideal of freedom of the press? Questions of such complexity—at least in the present state of the tools and methods of social science—had better be left unexplored as likely to be fruitless or impossible. But eventually the tools may be sharpened, and the methods may become more sophisticated. In any case, we can look only for "that amount of precision which belongs to its subject matter" and make no exaggerated claims.

5. There are vast stretches of unexplored regions; for example, we have little reliable knowledge of the effects of obscenity or pornography. We know little about the extent to which teachers and professors use the academic freedom that they are supposed to have, and the extent to which laws, regulations, practices, or traditions impinge upon or curtail their freedom.

6. We have, on the one hand, values, more or less clearly defined, and, on the other hand, a considerable amount of data which show how inadequately these values are fulfilled in our society; for example, studies of legislative malapportionment were available for years before *Baker* v. *Carr*. There is in our society and in our governmental system often an unconscionable lag of time between proof of the existence of an institutional disease or malfunction and the cure: the values seem to exist in compartments which are effectively insulated from the facts of life. The problem is how to get those who can do something about an evil to recognize its existence "with all deliberate speed" —to get the guardians of our goals to read the indicators.

QUIS CUSTODIET IPSOS CUSTODES?

There is the danger that the government of the United States—or of any nation—will naturally pretend that its goals are the purest and most noble and that its conduct has been most virtuous. Politics tend to corrupt the highest values—generally not by direct attack but by pretending that the government or the administration or the party is better than it is. "The devil is always an angel who pretends to be God. Therefore, while egoism is the driving force of sin, dishonesty is its final expression." [66] We may grant, and continue to assume, that a nation or government "is not as virtuous as it pretends to be; and also less virtuous than it might be if it made fewer pretensions." [67]

There are, however, enough instances of honest governmental reporting to warrant our feeling that the risks are calculated risks which prudently may be taken. Let me cite a number of examples in support of this feeling:

1. Soon after Congress enacted the Immigration and Nationality Act of

[66] Reinhold Neibuhr, *An Interpretation of Christian Ethics* (New York: Meridian Books, 1935), p. 83.

[67] *Ibid.*, at p. 85.

1952 (the McCarran-Walter Act) over President Truman's veto, the President appointed the President's Commission on Immigration and Naturalization to study and evaluate the immigration and naturalization policies and to make recommendations. The Commission's report, *Whom We Shall Welcome*,[68] is a model of candor, sincerity, and truth. No outside, even foreign, group could have made a more honest report. It is free of any taint of cant, hypocrisy, or sugar-coating. This report had to wait some twelve years for its full vindication; but it was vindicated when President Johnson signed, on October 3, 1965, the act of Congress that provided for the elimination of the national-origins system of quotas.

2. In the spring of 1946, after the last of the relocation centers had been closed, the War Relocation Authority (WRA) issued ten reports on the tragedy that hit the Japanese-American people immediately following the attack on Pearl Harbor. The integrity of this official study, published by the United States Department of the Interior, may be measured by this passage from the final—tenth—volume:

> But perhaps the most disturbing results are the least tangible ones— the pattern we have established for undemocratic behavior, the stain on our national record in the eyes of freedom-loving peoples throughout the world, and the physical discomfort and mental anguish we have brought upon thousands of sincere, well disciplined and patriotic people. If we had learned to judge people by their individual worth instead of by the pigmentation of their skin and the slant of their eyes, these things would not have happened and we would be a prouder, more widely respected Nation today.[69]

3. The historic report of 1947 by President Truman's Committee on Civil Rights cannot be praised too highly. Had it been prepared by a tribunal of foreigners, with Bertrand Russell at their head, it could not have been more critical. The stance and tenor of this report—*To Secure These Rights*—may be sensed from the following general recommendation of the Committee:

> In general: The elimination of segregation, based on race, color, creed, or national origin, from American life. The separate but equal doctrine has failed in three important respects. First, it is inconsistent with the fundamental equalitarianism of the American way of life in that it marks groups with the brand of inferior status. Secondly, where it has been followed, the results have been separate but unequal facilities

---

[68] U.S., President's Commission on Immigration and Naturalization, *Whom We Shall Welcome*. The report was submitted to President Truman on January 1, 1953, just before he left office. Philip B. Perlman, one-time Solicitor General of the United States, was chairman; Harry N. Rosenfield was executive director.

[69] *WRA: A Story of Human Conservation* (1946), p. 190. J. A. Krug was Secretary of the Interior. D. S. Myer was Director of the War Relocation Authority.

for minority peoples. Finally, it has kept people apart despite incontrovertible evidence that an environment favorable to civil rights is fostered whenever groups are permitted to live and work together. There is no adequate defense of segregation.[70]

It should be underscored that this was said seven years before the Supreme Court overruled its "separate but equal" rule and ten years before Congress enacted the first civil rights act in eighty-two years.[71] On the whole, the reports of the United States Commission on Civil Rights, starting with the report published in 1959, have been up to the standard set by the 1947 report.

Indeed, one may venture to suggest that by now the United States enjoys something of a "tradition" of honest and courageous governmental reporting. A significant older document that is evidence of this "tradition" is the famous report on the Chicago strike of 1894, made by a commission appointed by President Cleveland to examine into the causes of the Pullman strike. The commission looked at the facts without fear or favor, and its most important recommendations had to wait for some thirty to forty years for adoption by Congress.[72] I think that when a historian investigates the history of governmental reporting, he will find many reports that he will want to list in his honor roll.[73]

Our society is not, however, completely dependent on governmental agencies for periodic examination and reporting of national goals. Private watchdog organizations are indispensable for the progress of civil liberties and civil rights. We could not sleep or be awake securely without private organizations that neither slumber nor sleep—such as the American Civil Liberties Union, the National Association for the Advancement of Colored People, the American Jewish Congress, the American Jewish Committee, the B'nai B'rith Anti-Defamation League, and the Association on American Indian Affairs. Such organizations are important as long as they are led by persons who are totally dedicated to the pursuit of their organizations' goals and programs, maintain their organizations in complete independence of government, administration, and party, and are not afraid of antagonizing public opinion and even a large segment of their own membership. I would submit that the record of these organizations bears out the judgment that they have been loyal to their purposes with exemplary dedication and courage.

Fortunately, too, watchdogs are built into our system of government. There are many notable veto messages by the President which have the prophetic quality. They remind the Congress and the nation of the permanent ideals

---

[70] U.S., President's Committee on Civil Rights, *To Secure These Rights* (1947), p. 166. Charles E. Wilson was chairman. Robert K. Carr was executive director.

[71] Civil Rights Act of 1957, 71 Stat. 634 (1957).

[72] Railway Labor Act of 1926 and National Labor Relations Act of 1935.

[73] He would, I think, make special mention of the reports of the National Resources Planning Board, created in 1939, and abolished in 1943.

which threaten to be weakened or destroyed. President Truman's veto of the Internal Security Act of 1950 (the McCarran Act)[74] is an instance of this important Presidential power. There are numerous opinions of the United States Supreme Court—opinions of the Court, as in the School Desegregation Cases of 1954; dissenting opinions, as that of Justice Stone in the first Flag-salute case;[75] sometimes even a footnote[76]—that serve to raise our sights.

There are examples, too, of solitary, unofficial voices crying out and being heard. One thinks readily of the article on privacy by Warren and Brandeis,[77] John Steinbeck's *The Grapes of Wrath* (1939), and the more recent *The Other America: Poverty in the United States* (1962) by Michael Harrington. Who can estimate the great influence of the writings by the late Zechariah Chafee, Jr.? We live in an age of noise and mass media; but the power of the still small voice, before or after the fire, is not to be belittled.

There is a crying need, however, for a privately financed, independent agency for research in civil liberties. Perhaps the recently established Center for Research and Education in American Liberties, at Columbia University,[78] will achieve the financial resources and the moral support to become the great institution in this area that other institutions have become for research in the biological sciences, mathematics, aeronautics, and almost all other aspects of our technological civilization.

I would stress, as a caveat, the importance of the precaution that private research in civil liberties be conducted only by agencies which are exclusively or primarily committed to these liberties. If the agency is interested, for example in judicial administration generally, or in the sociology of law, it may be tempted to study the jury by the use of concealed microphones in the jury room.[79] As in other fields of human interest and concern, so also in civil liberties: the frontiers of our knowledge can best be attained by an exclusive— perhaps even obsessive—dedication of the mind to one end. American liberties are far too important for research in them to be entrusted to anyone other than civil libertarians.

[74] U.S., 81st Congress, 2nd Session, House Doc. No. 708, September 22, 1950.

[75] *Minersville School District* v. *Gobitis*, 310 U.S. 586 (1940). Cf. *W. Virginia State Board of Education* v. *Barnette*, 319 U.S. 624 (1943).

[76] For example, the footnote in *U.S.* v. *Carolene Products Co.*, 304 U.S. 144, 152, note 4 (1938), which has played an important role in the discussion over the "preferred position" of certain constitutional freedoms.

[77] "The Right to Privacy," 4 *Harvard Law Review* 193 (1890).

[78] The Center was established in January 1965. It is under the direction of Professor Alan F. Westin.

[79] See F. L. Strodtbeck, "Social Process, the Law, and Jury Functioning," *Law and Sociology*, ed. Wm. M. Evan (New York: Free Press, 1962), p. 151, note 8.

THE WATTS "MANIFESTO" &
THE McCONE REPORT

BAYARD RUSTIN

The riots in the Watts section of Los Angeles last August continued for six days, during which 34 persons were killed, 1,032 were injured, and some 3,952 were arrested. Viewed by many of the rioters themselves as their "manifesto," the uprising of the Watts Negroes brought out in the open, as no other aspect of the Negro protest has done, the despair and hatred that continue to brew in the Northern ghettoes despite the civil-rights legislation of recent years and the advent of "the war on poverty." With national attention focused on Los Angeles, Governor Edward P. Brown created a commission of prominent local citizens, headed by John A. McCone, to investigate the causes of the riots and to prescribe remedies against any such outbreaks in the future. Just as the violent confrontation on the burning streets of Watts told us much about the underlying realities of race and class relations in America —summed up best, perhaps, by the words of Los Angeles Police Chief William Parker, "We're on top and they're on the bottom"—so does the McCone Report, published under the title *Violence in the City–An End or a Beginning?*, tell us much about the response of our political and economic institutions to the Watts "manifesto."

Like the much-discussed Moynihan Report, the McCone Report is a bold departure from the standard government paper on social problems. It goes beyond the mere recital of statistics to discuss, somewhat sympathetically, the real problems of the Watts community—problems like unemployment, inadequate schools, dilapidated housing—and it seems at first glance to be leading toward constructive programs. It never reaches them, however, for, again like the Moynihan Report, it is ambivalent about the basic reforms that are needed to solve these problems and therefore shies away from spelling them out too explicitly. Thus, while it calls for the creation of 50,000 new jobs to compensate for the "spiral of failure" that it finds among the Watts Negroes,

SOURCE: Bayard Rustin, "The Watts 'Manifesto' & the McCone Report," *Commentary*, 41 (March 1966), 29–35. Reprinted from *Commentary* by permission; Copyright © 1966 by the American Jewish Committee.

the McCone Report does not tell us how these jobs are to be created or obtained and instead recommends existing programs which have already shown themselves to be inadequate. The Moynihan Report, similarly, by emphasizing the breakdown of the Negro family, also steers clear of confronting the thorny issues of Negro unemployment as such.

By appearing to provide new viewpoints and fresh initiatives while at the same time repeating, if in more sophisticated and compassionate terms, the standard white stereotypes and shibboleths about Negroes, the two reports have become controversial on both sides of the Negro question. On the one hand, civil-rights leaders can point to the recognition in these reports of the need for jobs and training, and for other economic and social programs to aid the Negro family, while conservatives can find confirmed in their pages the Negro penchant for violence, the excessive agitation against law and order by the civil-rights movement, or the high rates of crime and illegitimacy in the Negro community; on the other hand, both sides have criticized the reports for feeding ammunition to the opposition. Unfortunately, but inevitably, the emphasis on *Negro* behavior in both reports has stirred up an abstract debate over the interpretation of data rather than suggesting programs for dealing with the existing and very concrete situation in which American Negroes find themselves. For example, neither report is concerned about segregation and both tacitly assume that the Civil Rights Acts of 1964 and 1965 are already destroying this system. In the case of the McCone Report, this leaves the writers free to discuss the problems of Negro housing, education, and unemployment in great detail without attacking the conditions of de facto segregation that underly them.

The errors and misconceptions of the McCone Report are particularly revealing because it purports to deal with the realities of the Watts riots rather than with the abstractions of the Negro family. The first distortion of these realities occurs in the opening chapter—"The Crisis: An Overview"—where, after briefly discussing the looting and beatings, the writers conclude that "The rioters seem to have been caught up in an insensate rage of destruction." Such an image may reflect the fear of the white community that Watts had run amok during six days in August, but it does not accurately describe the major motive and mood of the riots, as subsequent data in the report itself indicate. While it is true that Negroes in the past have often turned the violence inflicted on them by society in upon themselves—"insensate rage" would perhaps have been an appropriate phrase for the third day of the 1964 Harlem riots—the whole point of the outbreak in Watts was that it marked the first major rebellion of Negroes against their own masochism and was carried on with the express purpose of asserting that they would no longer quietly submit to the deprivation of slum life.

This message came home to me over and over again when I talked with the young people in Watts during and after the riots, as it will have come home to those who watched the various television documentaries in which the Negroes of the community were permitted to speak for themselves. At a street-corner meeting in Watts when the riots were over, an unemployed youth of about twenty said to me, "We won." I asked him: "How have you won? Homes have been destroyed, Negroes are lying dead in the streets, the stores from which you buy food and clothes are destroyed, and people are bringing you relief." His reply was significant: "We won because we made the whole world pay attention to us. The police chief never came here before; the mayor always stayed uptown. We made them come." Clearly it was no accident that the riots proceeded along an almost direct path to City Hall.

Nor was the violence along the way random and "insensate." Wherever a store-owner identified himself as a "poor working Negro trying to make a business" or as a "Blood Brother," the mob passed the store by. It even spared a few white businesses that allowed credit or time purchases, and it made a point of looting and destroying stores that were notorious for their high prices and hostile manners. The McCone Report itself observes that "the rioters concentrated on food markets, liquor stores, clothing stores, department stores, and pawn shops." The authors "note with interest that no residences were deliberately burned, that damage to schools, libraries, public buildings was minimal and that certain types of business establishments, notably service stations and automobile dealers, were for the most part unharmed." It is also worth noting that the rioters were much more inclined to destroy the stock of the liquor stores they broke into than to steal it, and that according to the McCone Report, "there is no evidence that the rioters made any attempt to steal narcotics from pharmacies . . . which were looted and burned."

This is hardly a description of a Negro community that has run amok. The largest number of arrests were for looting—not for arson or shooting. Most of the people involved were not habitual thieves; they were members of a deprived group who seized a chance to possess things that all the dinning affluence of Los Angeles had never given them. There were innumerable touching examples of this behavior. One married couple in their sixties was seen carrying a couch to their home, and when its weight became too much for them, they sat down and rested on it until they could pick it up again. Langston Hughes tells of another woman who was dragging a sofa through the streets and who stopped at each intersection and waited for the traffic light to turn green. A third woman went out with her children to get a kitchen set, and after bringing it home, she discovered they needed one more chair in order to feed the whole family together; they went back to get the chair and all of them were arrested.

If the McCone Report misses the point of the Watts riots, it shows even less understanding of their causes. To place these in perspective, the authors begin by reviewing the various outbursts in the Negro ghettoes since the summer of 1964 and quickly come up with the following explanations: "Not enough jobs to go around, and within this scarcity not enough by a wide margin of a character which the untrained Negro could fill. . . . Not enough schooling to meet the special needs of the disadvantaged Negro child whose environment from infancy onward places him under a serious handicap." Finally, "a resentment, even hatred, of the police as a symbol of authority."

For the members of the special commission these are the fundamental causes of the current Negro plight and protest, which are glibly summed up in the ensuing paragraph by the statement that "Many Negroes moved to the city in the last generation and are totally unprepared to meet the conditions of city life." I shall be discussing these "causes" in detail as we go along, but it should be noted here that the burden of responsibility has already been placed on these hapless migrants to the cities. There is not one word about the conditions, economic as well as social, that have pushed Negroes out of the rural areas; nor is there one word about whether the cities have been willing and able to meet the demand for jobs, adequate housing, proper schools. After all, one could as well say that it is the *cities* which have been "totally unprepared" to meet the "conditions of *Negro* life," but the moralistic bias of the McCone Report, involving as it does an emphasis on the decisions of men rather than the pressure of social forces, continually operates in the other direction.

The same failure of awareness is evident in the report's description of the Los Angeles situation (the Negro areas of Los Angeles "are not urban gems, neither are they slums," the Negro population "has exploded," etc.). The authors do concede that the Los Angeles transportation system is the "least adequate of any major city," but even here they fail to draw the full consequences of their findings. Good, cheap transportation is essential to a segregated working-class population in a big city. In Los Angeles a domestic worker, for example, must spend about $1.50 and $1\frac{1}{2}$ to 2 hours to get to a job that pays $6 or $7 a day. This both discourages efforts to find work and exacerbates the feeling of isolation.

A neighborhood such as Watts may seem beautiful when compared to much of Harlem (which, in turn, is an improvement over the Negro section of Mobile, Alabama)—but it is still a ghetto. The housing is run-down, public services are inferior, the listless penned-in atmosphere of segregation is oppressive. Absentee landlords are the rule, and most of the businesses are owned by whites: neglect and exploitation reign by day, and at night, as one Watts Negro tersely put it, "There's just the cops and us."

The McCone Report, significantly, also ignores the political atmosphere of Los Angeles. It refers, for example, to the repeal in 1964 of the Rumford Act —the California fair-housing law—in these words: "In addition, many Negroes here felt and were encouraged to feel that they had been affronted by the passage of Proposition 14." Affronted, indeed! The largest state in the Union, by a three-to-one majority, abolishes one of its own laws against dis-

crimination and Negroes are described as regarding this as they might the failure of a friend to keep an engagement. What they did feel—and without any
need of encouragement—was that while the rest of the North was passing
civil-rights laws and improving opportunities for Negroes, their own state and
city were rushing to reinforce the barriers against them.

The McCone Report goes on to mention two other "aggravating events in
the twelve months prior to the riot." One was the failure of the poverty program to "live up to [its] press notices," combined with reports of "controversy
and bickering" in Los Angeles over administering the program. The second
"aggravating event" is summed up by the report in these words:

> Throughout the nation unpunished violence and disobedience to law
> were widely reported, and almost daily there were exhortations here
> and elsewhere, to take the most extreme and illegal remedies to right a
> wide variety of wrongs, real and supposed.

It would be hard to frame a more insidiously equivocal statement of the
Negro grievance concerning law enforcement during a period that included
the release of the suspects in the murder of the three civil-rights workers in
Mississippi, the failure to obtain convictions against the suspected murderers
of Medgar Evers and Mrs. Violet Liuzzo, the Gilligan incident in New York,
the murder of Reverend James Reeb, and the police violence in Selma, Alabama—to mention only a few of the more notorious cases. And surely it
would have been more to the point to mention that throughout the nation
Negro demonstrations have almost invariably been non-violent, and that the
major influence on the Negro community of the civil-rights movement has
been the strategy of discipline and dignity. Obsessed by the few prophets of
violent resistance, the McCone Commission ignores the fact that never before
has an American group sent so many people to jail or been so severely punished for trying to uphold the law of the land.

It is not stretching things too far to find a connection between these matters
and the treatment of the controversy concerning the role of the Los Angeles
police. The report goes into this question at great length, finally giving no credence to the charge that the police may have contributed to the spread of the
riots through the use of excessive force. Yet this conclusion is arrived at not
from the point of view of the Watts Negroes, but from that of the city officials
and the police. Thus, the report informs us, in judicial hearings that were held
on 32 of the 35 deaths which occurred, 26 were ruled justifiable homicides,
but the report—which includes such details as the precise time Mayor Yorty
called Police Chief Parker and when exactly the National Guard was sum-
moned—never tells us what a "justifiable homicide" is considered to be. It
tells us that "of the 35 killed, one was a fireman, one was a deputy sheriff, and
one was a Long Beach policeman," but it does not tell us how many Negroes
were killed or injured by police or National Guardsmen. (Harry Fleischman of

the American Jewish Committee reports that the fireman was killed by a falling wall; the deputy sheriff, by another sheriff's bullet; and the policeman, by another policeman's bullet.) We learn that of the 1,032 people reported injured, 90 were police officers, 36 were firemen, 10 were National Guardsman, 23 were from government agencies. To find out that about 85 per cent of the injured were Negroes, we have to do our own arithmetic. The report contains no information as to how many of these were victims of police force, but one can surmise from the general pattern of the riots that few could have been victims of Negro violence.

The report gives credence to Chief Parker's assertion that the rioters were the "criminal element in Watts" yet informs us that of the 3,438 adults arrested, 1,164 had only minor criminal records and 1,232 had never been arrested before. Moreover, such statistics are always misleading. Most Negroes, at one time or another, have been picked up and placed in jail. I myself have been arrested twice in Harlem on charges that had no basis in fact: once for trying to stop a police officer from arresting the wrong man; the second time for asking an officer who was throwing several young men into a paddy wagon what they had done. Both times I was charged with interfering with an arrest and kept overnight in jail until the judge recognized me and dismissed the charges. Most Negroes are not fortunate enough to be recognized by judges.

Having accepted Chief Parker's view of the riots, the report goes on to absolve him of the charge of discrimination: "Chief Parker's statements to us and collateral evidence, such as his fairness to Negro officers, are inconsistent with his having such an attitude ['deep hatred of Negroes']. Despite the depth of feeling against Chief Parker expressed to us by so many witnesses, he is recognized even by many of his vocal critics as a capable Chief who directs an efficient police force and serves well this entire community."

I am not going to stress the usual argument that the police habitually mistreat Negroes. Every Negro knows this. There is scarcely any black man, woman, or child in the land who at some point or other has not been mistreated by a policeman. (A young man in Watts said, "The riots will continue because I, as a Negro, am immediately considered to be a criminal by the police and, if I have a pretty woman with me, she is a tramp even if she is my wife or mother.") Police Chief Parker, however, goes beyond the usual bounds. He does not recognize that he is prejudiced, and being both naïve and zealous about law and order, he is given to a dangerous fanaticism. His reference to the Negro rioters as "monkeys," and his "top . . . and bottom" description of the riots, speak for themselves, and they could only have further enraged and encouraged the rioters. His insistence on dealing with the outbreak in Watts as though it were the random work of a "criminal element" threatened to lead the community, as Martin Luther King remarked after the meeting he and I had with Chief Parker, "into potential holocaust." Though Dr. King and I have had considerable experience in talking with public officials who do not understand the Negro community, our discussions with

Chief Parker and Mayor Samuel Yorty left us completely nonplussed. They both denied, for example, that there was any prejudice in Los Angeles. When we pointed to the very heavy vote in the city for Proposition 14, they replied, "That's no indication of prejudice. That's personal choice." When I asked Chief Parker about his choice of language, he implied that this was the only language Negroes understood.

The impression of "blind intransigence and ignorance of the social forces involved" which Dr. King carried away from our meeting with Chief Parker is borne out by other indications. The cast of his political beliefs, for example, was evidenced during his appearance last May on the Manion Forum, one of the leading platforms of the radical right, in which (according to newspaper reports) he offered his "considered opinion that America today is in reality more than half pagan" and that "we have moved our form of government to a socialist form of government." Such opinions have a good deal of currency today within the Los Angeles police department. About a month before the riots, a leaflet describing Dr. King as a liar and a Communist was posted on the bulletin board of a Los Angeles police station, and only after the concerted efforts of various Negro organizations was this scurrilous pamphlet removed.

Certainly these were "aggravating factors" that the McCone Report should properly have mentioned. But what is more important to understand is that even if every policeman in every black ghetto behaved like an angel and were trained in the most progressive of police academies, the conflict would still exist. This is so because the ghetto is a place where Negroes do not want to be and are fighting to get out of. When someone with a billy club and a gun tells you to behave yourself amid these terrible circumstances, he becomes a zoo keeper, demanding of you, as one of "these monkeys" (to use Chief Parker's phrase), that you accept abhorrent conditions. He is brutalizing you by insisting that you tolerate what you cannot, and ought not, tolerate.

In its blithe ignorance of such feelings, the McCone Report offers as one of its principal suggestions that speakers be sent to Negro schools to teach the students that the police are their friends and that their interests are best served by respect for law and order. Such public-relations gimmicks, of course, are futile—it is hardly a lack of contact with the police that creates the problem. Nor, as I have suggested, is it only a matter of prejudice. The fact is that when Negroes are deprived of work, they resort to selling numbers, women, or dope to earn a living; they must gamble and work in poolrooms. And when the policeman upholds the law, he is depriving them of their livelihood. A clever criminal in the Negro ghettoes is not unlike a clever "operator" in the white business world, and so long as Negroes are denied legitimate opportunities, no exhortations to obey the rules of the society and to regard the police as friends will have any effect.

This is not to say that relations between the police and the Negroes of

Watts could not be improved. Mayor Yorty and Police Chief Parker might have headed off a full-scale riot had they refrained from denouncing the Negro leaders and agreed to meet with them early on. Over and over again— to repeat the point with which we began—the rioters claimed that violence was the only way they could get these officials to listen to them. The McCone Commission, however, rejects the proposal for an independent police review board and instead recommends that the post of Inspector General be established—under the authority of the Chief of Police—to handle grievances.

The conditions of Negro life in Watts are not, of course, ignored by the McCone Report. Their basic structure is outlined in a section entitled "Dull, Devastating Spiral of Failure." Here we find that the Negro's "homelife destroys incentive"; that he lacks "experience with words and ideas"; that he is "unready and unprepared" in school; and that, "unprepared and unready," he "*slips* into the ranks of the unemployed" (my italics).

I would say, *is shoved*. It is time that we began to understand this "dull, devastating spiral of failure" and that we stopped attributing it to this or that characteristic of Negro life. In 1940, Edward Wight Bakke described the effects of unemployment on family structure in terms of the following model: The jobless man no longer provides, credit runs out, the woman is forced to take a job; if relief then becomes necessary, the woman is regarded even more as the center of the family; the man is dependent on her, the children are bewildered, and the stability of the family is threatened and often shattered. Bakke's research dealt strictly with white families. The fact that Negro social scientists like E. Franklin Frazier and Kenneth Clark have shown that this pattern is typical among the Negro poor does not mean, then, that it stems from some inherent Negro trait or is the ineluctable product of Negro social history. If Negroes suffer more than others from the problems of family instability today, it is not because they are Negro but because they are so disproportionately unemployed, underemployed, and ill-paid.

Anyone looking for historical patterns would do well to consider the labor market for Negroes since the Emancipation. He will find that Negro men have consistently been denied the opportunity to enter the labor force in anything like proportionate numbers, have been concentrated in the unskilled and marginal labor and service occupations, and have generally required wartime emergencies to make any advances in employment, job quality, and security. Such advances are then largely wiped out when the economy slumps again.

In 1948, for example, the rates of Negro and white unemployment were roughly equal. During the next decade, however, Negro unemployment was consistently double that of whites, and among Negro teenagers it remained at the disastrously high figure which prevailed for the entire population during the Depression. It is true that the nation's improved economic performance in recent years has reduced the percentage of jobless Negroes from 12.6 per cent, which it reached in 1958 (12.5 per cent in 1961) to roughly 8.1 per cent today. Despite this progress, the rate of Negro unemployment continues to be twice as high as white (8.13 per cent as against 4.2 per cent). In other words, job discrimination remains constant. These statistics, moreover, conceal the persistence of Negro youth unemployment: in 1961, 24.7 per cent of those Negro teenagers not in school were out of work and it is estimated that in 1966 this incredible rate will only decline to 23.2 per cent. What this figure tells us is that the rise in Negro employment has largely resulted from the calling of men with previous experience back to work. This is an ominous trend, for it is estimated that in the coming year, 20 per cent of the new entrants into the labor force will be Negro (almost twice as high as the Negro percentage of the population). Approximately half of these young Negroes will not have the equivalent of a high-school education and they will be competing in an economy in which the demand for skill and training is increasing sharply.

Thus there is bound to be a further deterioration of the Negro's economic —and hence social—position, despite the important political victories being achieved by the civil-rights movement. For many young Negroes, who are learning that economic servitude can be as effective an instrument of discrimination as racist laws, the new "freedom" has already become a bitter thing indeed. No wonder that the men of Watts were incensed by reports that the poverty program was being obstructed in Los Angeles by administrative wrangling. (As I write this, the New York *Times* reports that political rivalries and ambitions have now virtually paralyzed the program in that area.)

How does the McCone Report propose to halt this "dull, devastating spiral of failure"? First, through education—"our fundamental resource." The commission's analysis begins with a comparison of class size in white and Negro areas (the latter are referred to throughout as "disadvantaged areas" and Negro schools, as "disadvantaged schools"). It immediately notes that classes in the disadvantaged schools are slightly smaller; on the other hand, the more experienced teachers are likely to be found in the *non*-disadvantaged areas, and there is tremendous overcrowding in the disadvantaged schools because of double sessions. The buildings in the "disadvantaged areas are in better repair"; on the other hand, there are "cafeterias in the advantaged schools" but not in the disadvantaged schools, which also have no libraries. This random balance sheet of "resources" shows no sense of priorities; moreover, despite the alarming deficiencies it uncovers in the "disadvantaged schools," the McCone Report, in consistent fashion, places its emphasis on the Negro child's "deficiency in environmental experiences" and on "his home life [which] all too often fails to give him incentive. . . ."

The two major recommendations of the commission in this area will hardly serve to correct the imbalances revealed. The first is that elementary and junior high schools in the "disadvantaged areas" which have achievement levels substantially below the city average should be designated "Emergency

Schools." In each of these schools an emergency literacy program is to be established with a maximum of 22 students in each class and an enlarged and supportive corps of teachers. The second recommendation is to establish a permanent pre-school program to help prepare three- and four-year-old children to read and write.

W. T. Bassett, executive secretary of the Los Angeles AFL-CIO, has criticized the report for its failure to deal with education and training for adolescents and adults who are no longer in school. Another glaring omission is of a specific plan to decrease school segregation. While most of us now agree that the major goal of American education must be that of quality integrated schools, we cannot, as even the report suggests, achieve the quality without at the same time moving toward integration. The stated goal of the McCone Commission, however, is to "reverse the trend of de facto segregation" by improving the quality of the Negro schools: in short, separate but equal schools that do not disturb the existing social patterns which isolate the Negro child in his "disadvantaged areas."

That the commission's explicit concern for Negro problems falls short of its implicit concern for the status quo is also evident in its proposals for housing. It calls for the liberalization of credit and FHA-insured loans in "disadvantaged areas," the implementation of rehabilitation measures and other urban-renewal programs and, as its particular innovation, the creation of a "wide area data bank." Meanwhile it refuses to discuss, much less to criticize, the effect of Proposition 14 or to recommend a new fair-housing code. To protect the Negro against discrimination, the McCone Report supports the creation of a Commission on Human Relations, but does not present any proposals that would enable it to do more than collect information and conduct public-relations campaigns.

The most crucial section of the report is the one on employment and, not unexpectedly, it is also the most ignorant, unimaginative, and conservative— despite its dramatic recommendation that 50,000 new jobs be created. On the matter of youth unemployment, the report suggests that the existing federal projects initiate a series of "attitudinal training" programs to help young Negroes develop the necessary motivation to hold on to these new jobs which are to come from somewhere that the commission keeps secret. This is just another example of the commission's continued reliance on public relations, and of its preoccupation with the "dull, devastating spiral" of Negro failure. The truth of the matter is that Negro youths cannot change their attitudes until they see that they can get jobs. When what they see is unemployment and their Economic Opportunity programs being manipulated in behalf of politicians, their attitudes will remain realistically cynical.

Once again, let me try to cut through the obscuratism which has increasingly come to cloud this issue of Negro attitudes. I am on a committee which administers the Apprenticeship Training Program of the Workers Defense

League. For many years the League had heard that there were not enough Negro applicants to fill the various openings for apprenticeship training and had also repeatedly been told by vocational-school counselors that Negro students could not pay attention to key subjects such as English and mathematics. The League began its own recruitment and placement program two years ago and now has more than 500 apprentice applicants on file. When, last fall, Local 28 of the Sheetmetal Workers Union—to take one example—announced that a new admission test for apprentices was to be given soon, the League contacted those applicants who had indicated an interest in sheetmetal work. The young men came to the office, filled out a 10-page application form, filed a ten-dollar fee, and returned it to the Local 28 office. Then, five nights a week for three weeks, they came to Harlem, in many cases from Brooklyn and Queens, to be tutored. Most of the young men showed up for all fifteen sessions, and scored well on the test. At their interviews they were poised and confident. Eleven of these men finally were admitted to a class of 33. The WDL doesn't attribute this success to a miraculous program; it merely knows that when young people are told that at the end of a given period of study those who perform well will obtain decent work, then their attitudes will be markedly different from those who are sent off to a work camp with vague promises.

To cut the cost of job training programs, the McCone Commission avers that compensation "should not be necessary for those trainees who are receiving welfare support." Earlier in the report the authors point out that welfare services tend to destroy family life by giving more money to a woman who lives alone; yet they have the audacity to ask that the practice of not allowing men who are on family relief to earn an additional income be maintained for young men who are working and being trained. How is a young man to be adequately motivated if he cannot feel that his work is meaningful and necessary? The McCone Report would have us say to him, "There, there, young man, we're going to keep you off the streets—just putter around doing this make-work." But the young man knows that he can collect welfare checks and also hustle on street corners to increase his earnings. A man's share of a welfare allotment is pitifully small, but more than that, he should be paid for his work; and if one is interested in his morale, he should not be treated as a charity case.

Continuing with the problem of employment, the report recommends that "there should immediately be developed in the affected area a job training and placement center through the combined efforts of Negroes, employers, labor unions and government." In the absence of actual jobs, this would mean merely setting up a new division, albeit voluntary, of the unemployment insurance program. "Federal and state governments should seek to insure through development of new facilities and additional means of communication that advantage is taken of government and private training programs and employment opportunities in our disadvantaged communities." Perhaps the only thing the Job Corps program doesn't lack is publicity: last summer it received ten times as many applications as it could handle. Nor can new types of information centers and questionnaires provide 50,000 new jobs. They may provide positions for social workers and vocational counselors, but very few of them will be unemployed Negroes.

The report goes on: "Legislation should be enacted requiring employers with more than 250 employees and all labor unions to report annually to the state Fair Employment Practices Commission, the racial composition of the work force and membership." But an FEP Commission that merely collects information and propaganda is powerless. And even with the fullest cooperation of labor and management to promote equality of opportunity, the fact remains that there are not enough jobs in the Los Angeles area to go around, even for those who are fortunate enough to be included in the retraining programs. As long as unions cannot find work for many of their own members, there is not much they can do to help unemployed Negroes. And the McCone Report places much of its hope in private enterprise, whose response so far has been meager. The highest estimate of the number of jobs given to Los Angeles Negroes since the Watts crisis is less than 1,000.

The Negro slums today are ghettoes of despair. In Watts, as elsewhere, there are the unemployable poor: the children, the aging, the permanently handicapped. No measure of employment or of economic growth will put an end to their misery, and only government programs can provide them with a decent way of life. The care of these people could be made a major area of job growth. Los Angeles officials could immediately train and put to work women and unemployed youths as school attendants, recreation counselors, practical nurses, and community workers. The federal government and the state of California could aid the people of Watts by beginning a massive public-works program to build needed housing, schools, hospitals, neighborhood centers, and transportation facilities: this, too, would create new jobs. In short, they could begin to develop the $100-billion freedom budget advocated by A. Philip Randolph.

Such proposals may seem impractical and even incredible. But what is truly impractical and incredible is that America, with its enormous wealth, has allowed Watts to become what it is and that a commission empowered to study this explosive situation should come up with answers that boil down to voluntary actions by business and labor, new public-relations campaigns for municipal agencies, and information-gathering for housing, fair-employment, and welfare departments. The Watts manifesto is a response to realities that the McCone Report is barely beginning to grasp. Like the liberal consensus which it embodies and reflects, the commission's imagination and political intelligence appear paralyzed by the hard facts of Negro deprivation it has unearthed, and it lacks the political will to demand that the vast resources of contemporary America be used to build a genuinely great society that will finally put an end to these deprivations. And what is most impractical and incredible of all is that we may very well continue to teach impoverished, segregated, and ignored Negroes that the only way they can get the ear of America is to rise up in violence.

Study Questions

1. Why is there so much confusion about the meaning of equality? Does the working class, according to Lane, have an understanding of equality which is consistent with democratic principles?
2. Katz maintains that the Supreme Court has not practiced neutrality in protecting religious freedom, but instead has promoted religious pluralism. What is religious pluralism, and how has the Supreme Court promoted it? Do you regard this approach by the Court as the best means of protecting religious freedom?
3. Why does Konvitz believe that it is necessary for the protection of individual rights that political institutions be based upon moral principles? How is it possible to determine whether moral principles undergird political institutions?
4. What remedies does Rustin suggest for dealing with riots by racial groups?

Suggestions for Further Reading

Becker, Carl. *Freedom and Responsibility in the American Way of Life.* New York: Alfred A. Knopf, 1943.

Burns, Walter. *Freedom, Virtue, and the First Amendment.* Baton Rouge, Louisiana: Louisiana State University Press, 1957.

Broderick, Francis L., and August Meier (eds.) *Negro Protest Thought in the Twentieth Century.* Indianapolis, Indiana: Bobbs-Merrill Company, Inc., 1965.

Chafee, Zechariah. *Free Speech in the United States.* Cambridge, Massachusetts: Harvard University Press, 1941.

Carr, Robert K. *Federal Protection of Civil Rights.* Ithaca, New York: Cornell University Press, 1947.

Fellman, David. *The Defendants Rights.* New York: Holt, Rinehart and Winston, Inc., 1958.

Greenberg, Jack. *Race Relations and American Law.* New York: Columbia University Press, 1959.

Hayden, Tom. *Rebellion in Newark: Official Violence and Ghetto Response.* New York: Random House, Inc., 1967.

Isinsberg, Morris. *On Justice in Society.* Baltimore, Maryland: Penguin Books, 1965.

Lasswell, Harold D. *National Security and Individual Freedom.* New York: McGraw-Hill Book Company, Inc., 1950.

Long, Edward V. *The Intruders: The Invasion of Privacy by Government and Industry.* New York: Frederick A. Praeger, 1967.

Meiklejohn, Alexander. *Free Speech and Its Relation to Self-Government.* New York: Harper & Brothers, 1948.

Mill, John Stuart. *On Liberty.* New York: Appleton-Century-Crofts, 1947.

Murphy, Walter F. *Wiretapping on Trial.* New York: Random House, 1965.

Myrdal, Gunnar. *An American Dilemma*. New York: Harper & Row, Publishers, 1944.

Pritchett, C. Herman. *The Political Offender and the Warren Court*. Boston: Boston University Press, 1958.

Pfeffer, Len. *Church, State and Freedom*. Boston: Beacon Press, 1966.

Russell, Bertrand. *Authority and the Individual*. New York: Simon and Schuster, Inc., 1949.

Thoreau, Henry D. *On the Duty of Civil Disobedience*. New Haven, Connecticut: Yale University Press, 1928.

Woodward, C. Vann. *The Strange Case of Jim Crow*. 2nd rev. ed. New York: Oxford University Press, 1938.

PART FOUR

The Politics of Violence: The Challenge to the Status Quo

Government exists to provide, among other things, a framework of order. To accomplish this objective it must regulate and harmonize the various competing and conflicting interests in society. Democratic government, to survive, must be able to provide the means and create a desire upon the part of the people to resolve their disputes in a peaceful nonviolent manner. The violence and disorder which have erupted in the 1960s have presented democratic government in America with one of its greatest challenges. This decade has witnessed the outbreak of massive urban rioting in the metropolitan centers of Detroit, Cleveland, Newark, Los Angeles, and New Brunswick. Student unrest has occurred in many universities across the country, adding to problems already confronting established authority.

In order to probe the causes of the disorder and violence threatening society, the National Advisory Commission on Civil Disorders was established by the President in 1967 after the outbreak of violence in the cities' black ghettos. The report of this Commission, issued March 1, 1968, stated that the causes of the disorders were many and complex and could be attributed to economic, social and political factors in American society. These conditions stem from the historical pattern of black-white relations in America.

Although the factors contributing to the violence are complex and might vary from city to city and from one year to another, the Commission reported that certain basic characteristics are manifested. The most significant is "the racial attitude and behavior of white Americans toward black Americans." In other words, "white racism" was primarily responsible for the disorders. The recommendations of the Commission for dealing with the causes of the riot will be discussed in the essay.

The second important subject discussed in this Part is student dissent. We should bear in mind that there are students who have a desire to modify the

American system and bring practice more in line with ideas, but there are the few who are determined to destroy existing social institutions. Nathan Glazer examines this movement in his essay. Glazer believes that student liberals fail to understand the ultimate objectives of the radicals and are willing to accept tactical positions at face value. Radicals advocate reforms in universities to gain student support and to create unrest and revolutionary fever. Glazer states that radicals oppose reform because it undermines their desire for revolution. Liberals who say that they are opposed to the means but support the goals of the radicals misunderstand their goals.

Riots and protests in the 1960s have received extensive and intensive coverage by mass media. It has been suggested that the mass media has not only covered these events, but has also helped to mold them. The article on Mass Media and Violence explores this issue. Morris Janowitz states in this article that mass media has had a limited impact upon the social values and upon personal control necessary to maintain order in society. He further states that mass media has popularized riots and their leaders, thus encouraging acts of violence.

The three articles in this section illustrate vividly that one of the major problems facing American democracy is that of maintaining a just social order.

CIVIL DISORDERS

The National Advisory Commission on Civil Disorders

INTRODUCTION

The summer of 1967 again brought racial disorders to American cities, and with them shock, fear, and bewilderment to the Nation.

The worst came during a 2-week period in July, first in Newark and then in Detroit. Each set off a chain reaction in neighboring communities.

On July 28, 1967, the President of the United States established this Commission and directed us to answer three basic questions:

What happened?
Why did it happen?
What can be done to prevent it from happening again?

To respond to these questions, we have undertaken a broad range of studies and investigations. We have visited the riot cities; we have heard many witnesses; we have sought the counsel of experts across the country.

SOURCE: Summary of Report of The National Advisory Commission on Civil Disorders, U.S. Government Printing Office, March 1, 1968, pp. 1–13.

This is our basic conclusion: Our Nation is moving toward two societies, one black, one white—separate and unequal.

Reaction to last summer's disorders has quickened the movement and deepened the division. Discrimination and segregation have long permeated much of American life; they now threaten the future of every American.

This deepening racial division is not inevitable. The movement apart can be reversed. Choice is still possible. Our principal task is to define that choice and to press for a national resolution.

To pursue our present course will involve the continuing polarization of the American community and, ultimately, the destruction of basic democratic values.

The alternative is not blind repression or capitulation to lawlessness. It is the realization of common opportunities for all within a single society.

This alternative will require a commitment to national action—compassionate, massive, and sustained, backed by the resources of the most powerful and the richest nation on this earth. From every American it will require new attitudes, new understanding, and, above all, new will.

The vital needs of the Nation must be met; hard choices must be made, and, if necessary, new taxes enacted.

Violence cannot build a better society. Disruption and disorder nourish repression, not justice. They strike at the freedom of every citizen. The community cannot—it will not—tolerate coercion and mob rule.

Violence and destruction must be ended—in the streets of the ghetto and in the lives of people.

Segregation and poverty have created in the racial ghetto a destructive environment totally unknown to most white Americans.

What white Americans have never fully understood—but what the Negro can never forget—is that white society is deeply implicated in the ghetto. White institutions created it, white institutions maintain it, and white society condones it.

It is time now to turn with all the purpose at our command to the major unfinished business of this Nation. It is time to adopt strategies for action that will produce quick and visible progress. It is time to make good the promises of American democracy to all citizens—urban and rural, white and black, Spanish-surname, American Indian, and every minority group.

Our recommendations embrace three basic principles:

- To mount programs on a scale equal to the dimension of the problems;
- To aim these programs for high impact in the immediate future in order to close the gap between promise and performance;
- To undertake new initiatives and experiments that can change the system of failure and frustration that now dominates the ghetto and weakens our society.

These programs will require unprecedented levels of funding and performance, but they neither probe deeper nor demand more than the problems which called them forth. There can be no higher priority for national action and no higher claim on the Nation's conscience.

We issue this report now, 5 months before the date called for by the President. Much remains that can be learned. Continued study is essential.

As Commissioners we have worked together with a sense of the greatest urgency and have sought to compose whatever differences exist among us. Some differences remain. But the gravity of the problem and the pressing need for action are too clear to allow further delay in the issuance of this report.

I. WHAT HAPPENED?

Profiles of Disorder
The report contains profiles of a selection of the disorders that took place during the summer of 1967. These profiles are designed to indicate how the disorders happened, who participated in them, and how local officials, police forces, and the National Guard responded. Illustrative excerpts follow:

NEWARK. . . . It was decided to attempt to channel the energies of the people into a nonviolent protest. While Lofton promised the crowd that a full investigation would be made of the Smith incident, the other Negro leaders began urging those on the scene to form a line of march toward the city hall.

Some persons joined the line of march. Others milled about in the narrow street. From the dark grounds of the housing project came a barrage of rocks. Some of them fell among the crowd. Others hit persons in the line of march. Many smashed the windows of the police station. The rock throwing, it was believed, was the work of youngsters; approximately 2,500 children lived in the housing project.

Almost at the same time, an old car was set afire in a parking lot. The line of march began to disintegrate. The police, their heads protected by World War I-type helmets, sallied forth to disperse the crowd. A fire engine, arriving on the scene, was pelted with rocks. As police drove people away from the station, they scattered in all directions.

A few minutes later a nearby liquor store was broken into. Some persons, seeing a caravan of cabs appear at city hall to protest Smith's arrest, interpreted this as evidence that the disturbance had been organized, and generated rumors to that effect.

However, only a few stores were looted. Within a short period of time, the disorder appeared to have run its course.

● ● ●

. . . On Saturday, July 15, [Director of Police Dominick] Spina received a report of snipers in a housing project. When he arrived he saw approximately 100 National Guardsmen and police officers crouching behind vehicles, hiding in corners, and lying on the ground around the edge of the courtyard.

Since everything appeared quiet and it was broad daylight, Spina walked directly down the middle of the street. Nothing happened. As he came to the last building of the complex, he heard a shot. All around him the troopers jumped, believing themselves to be under sniper fire. A moment later a young Guardsman ran from behind a building.

The director of police went over and asked him if he had fired the shot. The soldier said "Yes," he had fired to scare a man away from a window; that his orders were to keep everyone away from windows.

Spina said he told the soldier: "Do you know what you just did? You have now created a state of hysteria. Every Guardsman up and down this street and every state policeman and every city policeman that is present thinks that somebody just fired a shot and that it is probably a sniper."

A short time later more "gunshots" were heard. Investigating, Spina came upon a Puerto Rican sitting on a wall. In reply to a question as to whether he knew "where the firing is coming from?" the man said:

"That's no firing. That's fireworks. If you look up to the fourth floor, you will see the people who are throwing down these cherry bombs."

By this time four truckloads of National Guardsmen had arrived and troopers and policemen were again crouched everywhere looking for a sniper. The director of police remained at the scene for 3 hours, and the only shot fired was the one by the Guardsman.

Nevertheless, at 6 o'clock that evening two columns of National Guardsmen and State troopers were directing mass fire at the Hayes housing project in response to what they believed were snipers. . . .

DETROIT. . . . A spirit of carefree nihilism was taking hold. To riot and destroy appeared more and more to become ends in themselves. Late Sunday afternoon it appeared to one observer that the young people were "dancing amidst the flames."

A Negro plainclothes officer was standing at an intersection when a man threw a Molotov cocktail into a business establishment at the corner. In the heat of the afternoon, fanned by the 20 to 25 miles per hour winds of both Sunday and Monday, the fire reached the home next door within minutes. As residents uselessly sprayed the flames with garden hoses, the fire jumped from roof to roof of adjacent two- and three-story buildings. Within the hour the entire block was in flames. The ninth house in the burning row belonged to the arsonist who had thrown the Molotov cocktail. . . .

● ● ●

. . . Employed as a private guard, 55-year-old Julius L. Dorsey, a Negro, was standing in front of a market when accosted by two Negro men and a woman. They demanded he permit them to loot the market. He ignored their demands. They began to berate him. He asked a neighbor to call the police. As the argument grew more heated, Dorsey fired three shots from his pistol into the air.

The police radio reported: "Looters—they have rifles." A patrol car driven by a police officer and carrying three National Guardsmen arrived. As the looters fled, the law-enforcement personnel opened fire. When the firing ceased, one person lay dead.

He was Julius L. Dorsey. . . .

● ● ●

. . . As the riot alternately waxed and waned, one area of the ghetto remained insulated. On the northeast side the residents of some 150 square blocks inhabited by 21,000 persons had, in 1966, banded together in the Positive Neighborhood Action Committee (PNAC). With professional help from the Institute of Urban Dynamics, they had organized block clubs and made plans for the improvement of the neighborhood. . . .

When the riot broke out, the residents, through the block clubs, were able to organize quickly. Youngsters, agreeing to stay in the neighborhood, participated in detouring traffic. While many persons reportedly sympathized with the idea of a rebellion against the "system" only two small fires were set—one in an empty building.

● ● ●

. . . According to Lieutenant General Throckmorton and Colonel Bolling, the city, at this time, was saturated with fear. The National Guardsmen were afraid, the citizens were afraid, and the police were afraid. Numerous persons, the majority of them Negroes, were being injured by gunshots of undetermined origin. The general and his staff felt that the major task of the troops was to reduce the fear and restore an air of normalcy.

In order to accomplish this, every effort was made to establish contact and rapport between the troops and the residents. The soldiers—20 percent of whom were Negro—began helping to clean up the streets, collect garbage, and trace persons who had disappeared in the confusion. Residents in the neighborhoods responded with soup and sandwiches for the troops. In areas where the National Guard tried to establish rapport with the citizens, there was a similar response.

NEW BRUNSWICK. . . . A short time later, elements of the crowd—an older and rougher one than the night before—appeared in front of the police station. The participants wanted to see the mayor.

Mayor [Patricia] Sheehan went out onto the steps of the station. Using a bull horn, she talked to the people and asked that she be given an opportunity to correct conditions. The crowd was boisterous. Some persons challenged the mayor. But, finally, the opinion, "She's new! Give her a chance!" prevailed.

A demand was issued by people in the crowd that all persons arrested the previous night be released. Told that this already had been done, the people were suspicious. They asked to be allowed to inspect the jail cells.

It was agreed to permit representatives of the people to look in the cells to satisfy themselves that everyone had been released.

The crowd dispersed. The New Brunswick riot had failed to materialize.

Patterns of Disorder

The "typical" riot did not take place. The disorders of 1967 were unusual, irregular, complex, and unpredictable social processes. Like most human events, they did not unfold in an orderly sequence. However, an analysis of our survey information leads to some conclusions about the riot process.

In general:

- The civil disorders of 1967 involved Negroes acting against local symbols of white American society, authority, and property in Negro neighborhoods—rather than against white persons.
- Of 164 disorders reported during the first nine months of 1967, eight (5 percent) were major in terms of violence and damage; 33 (20 percent) were serious but not major; 123 (75 percent) were minor and undoubtedly would not have received national attention as riots had the Nation not been sensitized by the more serious outbreaks.
- In the 75 disorders studied by a Senate subcommittee, 83 deaths were reported. Eighty-two percent of the deaths and more than half the injuries occurred in Newark and Detroit. About 10 percent of the dead and 36 percent of the injured were public employees, primarily law officers and firemen. The overwhelming majority of the persons killed or injured in all the disorders were Negro civilians.
- Initial damage estimates were greatly exaggerated. In Detroit, newspaper damage estimates at first ranged from $200 to $500 million; the highest recent estimate is $45 million. In Newark, early estimates ranged from $15 to $25 million. A month later damage was estimated at $10.2 million, 80 percent in inventory losses.

In the 24 disorders in 23 cities which we surveyed:

- The final incident before the outbreak of disorder, and the initial violence itself, generally took place in the evening or at night at a place in which it was normal for many people to be on the streets.
- Violence usually occurred almost immediately following the occurrence of the final precipitating incident, and then escalated rapidly.

With but few exceptions, violence subsided during the day, and flared rapidly again at night. The night-day cycles continued through the early period of the major disorders.

• Disorder generally began with rock and bottle throwing and window breaking. Once store windows were broken, looting usually followed.

• Disorder did not erupt as a result of a single "triggering" or "precipitating" incident. Instead, it was generated out of an increasingly disturbed social atmosphere, in which typically a series of tension-heightening incidents over a period of weeks or months became linked in the minds of many in the Negro community with a reservoir of underlying grievances. At some point in the mounting tension, a further incident— in itself often routine or trivial—became the breaking point and the tension spilled over into violence.

• "Prior" incidents, which increased tensions and ultimately led to violence, were police actions in almost half the cases; police actions were "final" incidents before the outbreak of violence in 12 of the 24 surveyed disorders.

• No particular control tactic was successful in every situation. The varied effectiveness of control techniques emphasizes the need for advance training, planning, adequate intelligence systems, and knowledge of the ghetto community.

• Negotiations between Negroes—including young militants as well as older Negro leaders—and white officials concerning "terms of peace" occurred during virtually all the disorders surveyed. In many cases, these negotiations involved discussion of underlying grievances as well as the handling of the disorder by control authorities.

• The typical rioter was a teenager or young adult, a lifelong resident of the city in which he rioted, a high school dropout; he was, nevertheless, somewhat better educated than his nonrioting Negro neighbor, and was usually underemployed or employed in a menial job. He was proud of his race, extremely hostile to both whites and middle-class Negroes and, although informed about politics, highly distrustful of the political system.

A Detroit survey revealed that approximately 11 percent of the total residents of two riot areas admitted participation in the rioting, 20 to 25 percent identified themselves as "bystanders," over 16 percent identified themselves as "counterrioters" who urged rioters to "cool it," and the remaining 48 to 53 percent said they were at home or elsewhere and did not participate. In a survey of Negro males between the ages of 15 and 35 residing in the disturbance area in Newark, about 45 percent identified themselves as rioters, and about 55 percent as "noninvolved."

• Most rioters were young Negro males. Nearly 53 percent of arrestees were between 15 and 24 years of age; nearly 81 percent between 15 and 35.

• In Detroit and Newark about 74 percent of the rioters were brought up in the North. In contrast, of the noninvolved, 36 percent in Detroit and 52 percent in Newark were brought up in the North.

• What the rioters appeared to be seeking was fuller participation in the social order and the material benefits enjoyed by the majority of American citizens. Rather than rejecting the American system, they were anxious to obtain a place for themselves in it.

• Numerous Negro counterrioters walked the streets urging rioters to "cool it." The typical counterrioter was better educated and had higher income than either the rioter or the noninvolved.

• The proportion of Negroes in local government was substantially smaller than the Negro proportion of population. Only three of the 20 cities studied had more than one Negro legislator; none had ever had a Negro mayor or city manager. In only four cities did Negroes hold other important policy-making positions or serve as heads of municipal departments.

• Although almost all cities had some sort of formal grievance mechanism for handling citizen complaints, this typically was regarded by Negroes as ineffective and was generally ignored.

• Although specific grievances varied from city to city, at least 12 deeply held grievances can be identified and ranked into three levels of relative intensity:

First level of intensity:
    1. Police practices.
    2. Unemployment and underemployment.
    3. Inadequate housing.

Second level of intensity:
    4. Inadequate education.
    5. Poor recreation facilities and programs.
    6. Ineffectiveness of the political structure and grievance mechanisms.

Third level of intensity:
    7. Disrespectful white attitudes.
    8. Discriminatory administration of justice.
    9. Inadequacy of Federal programs.
    10. Inadequacy of municipal services.
    11. Discriminatory consumer and credit practices.
    12. Inadequate welfare programs.

• The results of a three-city survey of various Federal programs—manpower, education, housing, welfare and community action—indicate that, despite substantial expenditures, the number of persons assisted constituted only a fraction of those in need.

The background of disorder is often as complex and difficult to analyze as the disorder itself. But we find that certain general conclusions can be drawn:

- Social and economic conditions in the riot cities constituted a clear pattern of severe disadvantage for Negroes compared with whites, whether the Negroes lived in the area where the riot took place or outside it. Negroes had completed fewer years of education and fewer had attended high school. Negroes were twice as likely to be unemployed and three times as likely to be in unskilled and service jobs. Negroes averaged 70 percent of the income earned by whites and were more than twice as likely to be living in poverty. Although housing cost Negroes relatively more, they had worse housing—three times as likely to be overcrowded and substandard. When compared to white suburbs, the relative disadvantage was even more pronounced.

A study of the aftermath of disorder leads to disturbing conclusions. We find that, despite the institution of some postriot programs:

- Little basic change in the conditions underlying the outbreak of disorder has taken place. Actions to ameliorate Negro grievances have been limited and sporadic; with but few exceptions, they have not significantly reduced tensions.
- In several cities, the principal official response has been to train and equip the police with more sophisticated weapons.
- In several cities, increasing polarization is evident, with continuing breakdown of interracial communication, and growth of white segregationist or black separatist groups.

Organized Activity

The President directed the Commission to investigate "to what extent, if any, there has been planning or organization in any of the riots."

To carry out this part of the President's charge, the Commission established a special investigative staff supplementing the field teams that made the general examination of the riots in 23 cities. The unit examined data collected by Federal agencies and congressional committees, including thousands of documents supplied by the Federal Bureau of Investigation, gathered and evaluated information from local and state law enforcement agencies and officials, and conducted its own field investigation in selected cities.

On the basis of all the information collected, the Commission concludes that:

> The urban disorders of the summer of 1967 were not caused by, nor were they the consequence of, any organized plan or "conspiracy."

Specifically, the Commission has found no evidence that all or any of the disorders or the incidents that led to them were planned or directed by any organization or group, international, national, or local.

Militant organizations, local and national, and individual agitators, who repeatedly forecast and called for violence, were active in the spring and summer of 1967. We believe that they sought to encourage violence, and that they helped to create an atmosphere that contributed to the outbreak of disorder.

We recognize that the continuation of disorders and the polarization of the races would provide fertile ground for organized exploitation in the future.

Investigations of organized activity are continuing at all levels of government, including committees of Congress. These investigations relate not only to the disorders of 1967 but also to the actions of groups and individuals, particularly in schools and colleges, during this last fall and winter. The Commission has cooperated in these investigations. They should continue.

II. WHY DID IT HAPPEN?

The Basic Causes

In addressing the question "Why did it happen?" we shift our focus from the local to the national scene, from the particular events of the summer of 1967 to the factors within the society at large that created a mood of violence among many urban Negroes.

These factors are complex and interacting; they vary significantly in their effect from city to city and from year to year; and the consequences of one disorder, generating new grievances and new demands, become the causes of the next. Thus was created the "thicket of tension, conflicting evidence, and extreme opinions" cited by the President.

Despite these complexities, certain fundamental matters are clear. Of these, the most fundamental is the racial attitude and behavior of white Americans toward black Americans.

Race prejudice has shaped our history decisively; it now threatens to affect our future.

White racism is essentially responsible for the explosive mixture which has been accumulating in our cities since the end of World War II. Among the ingredients of this mixture are:

- *Pervasive discrimination and segregation* in employment, education, and housing, which have resulted in the continuing exclusion of great numbers of Negroes from the benefits of economic progress.
- *Black in-migration and white exodus*, which have produced the massive and growing concentrations of impoverished Negroes in our major cities, creating a growing crisis of deteriorating facilities and services and unmet human needs.
- *The black ghettos*, where segregation and poverty converge on the young to destroy opportunity and enforce failure. Crime, drug addiction, dependency on welfare, and bitterness and resentment against society in general and white society in particular are the result.

At the same time, most whites and some Negroes outside the ghetto have prospered to a degree unparalleled in the history of civilization. Through television and other media, this affluence has been flaunted before the eyes of the Negro poor and the jobless ghetto youth.

Yet these facts alone cannot be said to have caused the disorders. Recently, other powerful ingredients have begun to catalyze the mixture:

- *Frustrated hopes* are the residue of the unfulfilled expectations aroused by the great judicial and legislative victories of the civil rights movement and the dramatic struggle for equal rights in the South.
- *A climate that tends toward approval and encouragement of violence* as a form of protest has been created by white terrorism directed against nonviolent protest; by the open defiance of law and Federal authority by state and local officials resisting desegregation; and by some protest groups engaging in civil disobedience who turn their backs on nonviolence, go beyond the constitutionally protected rights of petition and free assembly, and resort to violence to attempt to compel alteration of laws and policies with which they disagree.
- *The frustrations of powerlessness* have led some Negroes to the conviction that there is no effective alternative to violence as a means of achieving redress of grievances, and of "moving the system." These frustrations are reflected in alienation and hostility toward the institutions of law and government and the white society which controls them, and in the reach toward racial consciousness and solidarity reflected in the slogan "Black Power."
- *A new mood* has sprung up among Negroes, particularly among the young, in which self-esteem and enhanced racial pride are replacing apathy and submission to "the system."
- *The police are not merely a "spark" factor.* To some Negroes police have come to symbolize white power, white racism, and white repression. And the fact is that many police do reflect and express these white attitudes. The atmosphere of hostility and cynicism is reinforced by a widespread belief among Negroes in the existence of police brutality and in a "double standard" of justice and protection—one for Negroes and one for whites.

● ● ●

To this point, we have attempted only to identify the prime components of the "explosive mixture." In the chapters that follow we seek to analyze them in the perspective of history. Their meaning, however, is clear:

In the summer of 1967, we have seen in our cities a chain reaction of racial violence. If we are heedless, none of us shall escape the consequences.

•   •   •

III. WHAT CAN BE DONE?

The Community Response

Our investigation of the 1967 riot cities establishes that virtually every major episode of violence was foreshadowed by an accumulation of unresolved grievances and by widespread dissatisfaction among Negroes with the unwillingness or inability of local government to respond.

Overcoming these conditions is essential for community support of law enforcement and civil order. City governments need new and more vital channels of communication to the residents of the ghetto; they need to improve their capacity to respond effectively to community needs before they become community grievances; and they need to provide opportunity for meaningful involvement of ghetto residents in shaping policies and programs which affect the community.

The Commission recommends that local governments:

• Develop Neighborhood Action Task Forces as joint community-government efforts through which more effective communication can be achieved, and the delivery of city services to ghetto residents improved.
• Establish comprehensive grievance-response mechanisms in order to bring all public agencies under public scrutiny.
• Bring the institutions of local government closer to the people they serve by establishing neighborhood outlets for local, state, and Federal administrative and public service agencies.
• Expand opportunities for ghetto residents to participate in the formulation of public policy and the implementation of programs affecting them through improved political representation, creation of institutional channels for community action, expansion of legal services, and legislative hearings on ghetto problems.

In this effort, city governments will require State and Federal support. The Commission recommends:

• State and Federal financial assistance for mayors and city councils to support the research, consultants, staff, and other resources needed to respond effectively to Federal program initiatives.
• State cooperation in providing municipalities with the jurisdictional tools needed to deal with their problems; a fuller measure of financial aid to urban areas; and the focusing of the interests of suburban communities on the physical, social, and cultural environment of the central city.

Police and the Community

The abrasive relationship between the police and minority communities has been a major—and explosive—source of grievance, tension, and disorder. The blame must be shared by the total society.

The police are faced with demands for increased protection and service in the ghetto. Yet the aggressive patrol practices thought necessary to meet these demands themselves create tension and hostility. The resulting grievances have been further aggravated by the lack of effective mechanisms for handling complaints against the police. Special programs for bettering police-community relations have been instituted, but these alone are not enough. Police administrators, with the guidance of public officials, and the support of the entire community, must take vigorous action to improve law enforcement and to decrease the potential for disorder.

The Commission recommends that city government and police authorities:

- Review police operations in the ghetto to ensure proper conduct by police officers, and eliminate abrasive practices.
- Provide more adequate police protection to ghetto residents to eliminate their high sense of insecurity and the belief in the existence of a dual standard of law enforcement.
- Establish fair and effective mechanisms for the redress of grievances against the police and other municipal employees.
- Develop and adopt policy guidelines to assist officers in making critical decisions in areas where police conduct can create tension.
- Develop and use innovative programs to insure widespread community support for law enforcement.
- Recruit more Negroes into the regular police force, and review promotion policies to insure fair promotion for Negro officers.
- Establish a "Community Service Officer" program to attract ghetto youths between the ages of 17 and 21 to police work. These junior officers would perform duties in ghetto neighborhoods, but would not have full police authority. The Federal Government should provide support equal to 90 percent of the costs of employing CSO's on the basis of one for every 10 regular officers.

Control of Disorder

Preserving civil peace is the first responsibility of government. Unless the rule of law prevails, our society will lack not only order but also the environment essential to social and economic progress.

The maintenance of civil order cannot be left to the police alone. The police need guidance, as well as support, from mayors and other public officials. It is the responsibility of public officials to determine proper police policies, support adequate police standards for personnel and performance, and participate in planning for the control of disorders.

To maintain control of incidents which could lead to disorders, the Commission recommends that local officials:

- Assign seasoned, well-trained policemen and supervisory officers to patrol ghetto areas, and to respond to disturbances.
- Develop plans which will quickly muster maximum police manpower and highly qualified senior commanders at the outbreak of disorders.
- Provide special training in the prevention of disorders, and prepare police for riot control and for operation in units, with adequate command and control and field communication for proper discipline and effectiveness.
- Develop guidelines governing the use of control equipment and provide alternatives to the use of lethal weapons. Federal support for research in this area is needed.
- Establish an intelligence system to provide police and other public officials with reliable information that may help to prevent the outbreak of a disorder and to institute effective control measures in the event a riot erupts.
- Develop continuing contacts with ghetto residents to make use of the forces for order which exist within the community.
- Establish machinery for neutralizing rumors, and enabling Negro leaders and residents to obtain the facts. Create special rumor details to collect, evaluate, and dispel rumors that may lead to a civil disorder.

The Commission believes there is a grave danger that some communities may resort to the indiscriminate and excessive use of force. The harmful effects of overreaction are incalculable. The Commission condemns moves to equip police departments with mass destruction weapons, such as automatic rifles, machine guns, and tanks. Weapons which are designed to destroy, not to control, have no place in densely populated urban communities.

The Commission recommends that the Federal Government share in the financing of programs for improvement of police forces, both in their normal law enforcement activities as well as in their response to civil disorders.

To assist government authorities in planning their response to civil disorder, this report contains a Supplement on Control of Disorder. It deals with specific problems encountered during riot control operations, and includes:

- Assessment of the present capabilities of police, National Guard and Army forces to control major riots, and recommendations for improvement.
- Recommended means by which the control operations of those forces may be coordinated with the response of other agencies, such as fire departments, and with the community at large.
- Recommendations for review and revision of Federal, state and local laws needed to provide the framework for control efforts and for the callup and interrelated action of public safety forces.

The Administration of Justice Under Emergency Conditions

In many of the cities which experienced disorders last summer, there were recurring breakdowns in the mechanisms for processing, prosecuting, and protecting arrested persons. These resulted mainly from long-standing structural deficiencies in criminal court systems, and from the failure of communities to anticipate and plan for the emergency demands of civil disorders.

In part, because of this, there were few successful prosecutions for serious crimes committed during the riots. In those cities where mass arrests occurred, many arrestees were deprived of basic legal rights.

The Commission recommends that the cities and states:

- Undertake reform of the lower courts so as to improve the quality of justice rendered under normal conditions.
- Plan comprehensive measures by which the criminal justice system may be supplemented during civil disorders so that its deliberative functions are protected, and the quality of justice is maintained.

Such emergency plans require broad community participation and dedicated leadership by the bench and bar. They should include:

- Laws sufficient to deter and punish riot conduct.
- Additional judges, bail and probation officers, and clerical staff.
- Arrangements for volunteer lawyers to help prosecutors and to represent riot defendants at every stage of proceedings.
- Policies to insure proper and individual bail, arraignment, pretrial, trial, and sentencing proceedings.
- Adequate emergency processing and detention facilities.

Damages: Repair and Compensation

The Commission recommends that the Federal Government:

- Amend the Federal Disaster Act—which now applies only to natural disasters—to permit Federal emergency food and medical assistance to cities during major civil disorders, and provide long-term economic assistance afterwards.
- With the cooperation of the states, create incentives for the private insurance industry to provide more adequate property insurance coverage in inner-city areas.

The Commission endorses the report of the National Advisory Panel on Insurance in Riot-Affected Areas: "Meeting the Insurance Crisis of our Cities."

The News Media and the Disorders

In his charge to the Commission, the President asked: "What effect do the mass media have on the riots?"

The Commission determined that the answer to the President's question did not lie solely in the performance of the press and broadcasters in reporting the riots. Our analysis had to consider also the overall treatment by the media of the Negro ghettos, community relations, racial attitudes, and poverty—day by day and month by month, year in and year out.

A wide range of interviews with Government officials, law enforcement authorities, media personnel and other citizens, including ghetto residents, as well as a quantitative analysis of riot coverage and a special conference with industry representatives, leads us to conclude that:

- Despite instances of sensationalism, inaccuracy and distortion, newspapers, radio and television tried on the whole to give a balanced, factual account of the 1967 disorders.
- Elements of the news media failed to portray accurately the scale and character of the violence that occurred last summer. The overall effect was, we believe, an exaggeration of both mood and event.
- Important segments of the media failed to report adequately on the causes and consequences of civil disorders and on the underlying problems of race relations. They have not communicated to the majority of their audience—which is white—a sense of the degradation, misery, and hopelessness of life in the ghetto.

These failings must be corrected, and the improvement must come from within the industry. Freedom of the press is not the issue. Any effort to impose governmental restrictions would be inconsistent with fundamental constitutional precepts.

We have seen evidence that the news media are becoming aware of and concerned about their performance in this field. As that concern grows, coverage will improve. But much more must be done, and it must be done soon.

The Commission recommends that the media:

- Expand coverage of the Negro community and of race problems through permanent assignment of reporters familiar with urban and racial affairs, and through establishment of more and better links with the Negro community.
- Integrate Negroes and Negro activities into all aspects of coverage and content, including newspaper articles and television programing. The news media must publish newspapers and produce programs that recognize the existence and activities of Negroes as a group within the community and as a part of the larger community.
- Recruit more Negroes into journalism and broadcasting and promote those who are qualified to positions of significant responsibility. Recruitment should begin in high schools and continue through college; where necessary, aid for training should be provided.
- Improve coordination with police in reporting riot news through advance planning, and cooperate with the police in the designation of po-

lice information officers, establishment of information centers, and development of mutually acceptable guidelines for riot reporting and the conduct of media personnel.

• Accelerate efforts to insure accurate and responsible reporting of riot and racial news, through adoption by all news-gathering organizations of stringent internal staff guidelines.

• Cooperate in the establishment of a privately organized and funded Institute of Urban Communications to train and educate journalists in urban affairs, recruit and train more Negro journalists, develop methods for improving police-press relations, review coverage of riots and racial issues, and support continuing research in the urban field.

The Future of the Cities

By 1985, the Negro population in central cities is expected to increase by 68 percent to approximately 20.3 million. Coupled with the continued exodus of white families to the suburbs, this growth will produce majority Negro populations in many of the Nation's largest cities.

The future of these cities, and of their burgeoning Negro populations, is grim. Most new employment opportunities are being created in suburbs and outlying areas. This trend will continue unless important changes in public policy are made.

In prospect, therefore, is further deterioration of already inadequate municipal tax bases in the face of increasing demands for public services, and continuing unemployment and poverty among the urban Negro population:

Three choices are open to the Nation:

• We can maintain present policies, continuing both the proportion of the Nation's resources now allocated to programs for the unemployed and the disadvantaged, and the inadequate and failing effort to achieve an integrated society.

• We can adopt a policy of "enrichment" aimed at improving dramatically the quality of ghetto life while abandoning integration as a goal.

• We can pursue integration by combining ghetto "enrichment" with policies which will encourage Negro movement out of central city areas.

The first choice, continuance of present policies, has ominous consequences for our society. The share of the Nation's resources now allocated to programs for the disadvantaged is insufficient to arrest the deterioration of life in central-city ghettos. Under such conditions, a rising proportion of Negroes may come to see in the deprivation and segregation they experience, a justification for violent protest, or for extending support to now isolated extremists who advocate civil disruption. Large-scale and continuing violence could result, followed by white retaliation, and, ultimately, the separation of the two communities in a garrison state.

Even if violence does not occur, the consequences are unacceptable. Development of a racially integrated society, extraordinarily difficult today, will be virtually impossible when the present black central-city population of 12.1 million has grown to almost 21 million.

To continue present policies is to make permanent the division of our country into two societies: one, largely Negro and poor, located in the central cities; the other, predominantly white and affluent, located in the suburbs and in outlying areas.

The second choice, ghetto enrichment coupled with abandonment of integration, is also unacceptable. It is another way of choosing a permanently divided country. Moreover, equality cannot be achieved under conditions of nearly complete separation. In a country where the economy, and particularly the resources of employment, are predominantly white, a policy of separation can only relegate Negroes to a permanently inferior economic status.

We believe that the only possible choice for America is the third—a policy which combines ghetto enrichment with programs designed to encourage integration of substantial numbers of Negroes into the society outside the ghetto.

Enrichment must be an important adjunct to integration, for no matter how ambitious or energetic the program, few Negroes now living in central cities can be quickly integrated. In the meantime, large-scale improvement in the quality of ghetto life is essential.

But this can be no more than an interim strategy. Programs must be developed which will permit substantial Negro movement out of the ghettos. The primary goal must be a single society, in which every citizen will be free to live and work according to his capabilities and desires, not his color.

Recommendations for National Action

INTRODUCTION. No American—white or black—can escape the consequences of the continuing social and economic decay of our major cities.

Only a commitment to national action on an unprecedented scale can shape a future compatible with the historic ideals of American society.

The great productivity of our economy, and a Federal revenue system which is highly responsive to economic growth, can provide the resources.

The major need is to generate new will—the will to tax ourselves to the extent necessary to meet the vital needs of the Nation.

We have set forth goals and proposed strategies to reach those goals. We discuss and recommend programs not to commit each of us to specific parts of such programs, but to illustrate the type and dimension of action needed.

The major goal is the creation of a true union—a single society and a single American identity. Toward that goal, we propose the following objectives for national action:

- Opening up opportunities to those who are restricted by racial segregation and discrimination, and eliminating all barriers to their choice of jobs, education, and housing.

• Removing the frustration of powerlessness among the disadvantaged by providing the means for them to deal with the problems that affect their own lives and by increasing the capacity of our public and private institutions to respond to these problems.

• Increasing communication across racial lines to destroy stereotypes, halt polarization, end distrust and hostility, and create common ground for efforts toward public order and social justice.

We propose these aims to fulfill our pledge of equality and to meet the fundamental needs of a democratic and civilized society—domestic peace and social justice.

EMPLOYMENT. Pervasive unemployment and underemployment are the most persistent and serious grievances in minority areas. They are inextricably linked to the problem of civil disorder.

Despite growing Federal expenditures for manpower development and training programs, and sustained general economic prosperity and increasing demands for skilled workers, about 2 million—white and nonwhite—are permanently unemployed. About 10 million are underemployed, of whom 6.5 million work full time for wages below the poverty line.

The 500,000 "hard-core" unemployed in the central cities who lack a basic education and are unable to hold a steady job are made up in large part of Negro males between the ages of 18 and 25. In the riot cities which we surveyed, Negroes were three times as likely as whites to hold unskilled jobs, which are often part time, seasonal, low paying and "dead end."

Negro males between the ages of 15 and 25 predominated among the rioters. More than 20 percent of the rioters were unemployed, and many who were employed held intermittent, low status, unskilled jobs which they regarded as below their education and ability.

The Commission recommends that the Federal Government:

• Undertake joint efforts with cities and states to consolidate existing manpower programs to avoid fragmentation and duplication.

• Take immediate action to create 2 million new jobs over the next 3 years—1 million in the public sector and 1 million in the private sector —to absorb the hard-core unemployed and materially reduce the level of underemployment for all workers, black and white. We propose 250,000 public sector and 300,000 private sector jobs in the first year.

• Provide on-the-job training by both public and private employers with reimbursement to private employers for the extra costs of training the hard-core unemployed, by contract or by tax credits.

• Provide tax and other incentives to investment in rural as well as urban poverty areas in order to offer to the rural poor an alternative to migration to urban centers.

• Take new and vigorous action to remove artificial barriers to employment and promotion, including not only racial discrimination but, in certain cases, arrest records or lack of a high school diploma. Strengthen those agencies such as the Equal Employment Opportunity Commission, charged with eliminating discriminatory practices, and provide full support for Title VI of the 1964 Civil Rights Act allowing Federal grant-in-aid funds to be withheld from activities which discriminate on grounds of color or race.

The Commission commends the recent public commitment of the National Council of the Building and Construction Trades Unions, AFL-CIO, to encourage and recruit Negro membership in apprenticeship programs. This commitment should be intensified and implemented.

EDUCATION. Education in a democratic society must equip children to develop their potential and to participate fully in American life. For the community at large, the schools have discharged this responsibility well. But for many minorities, and particularly for the children of the ghetto, the schools have failed to provide the educational experience which could overcome the effects of discrimination and deprivation.

This failure is one of the persistent sources of grievance and resentment within the Negro community. The hostility of Negro parents and students toward the school system is generating increasing conflict and causing disruption within many city school districts. But the most dramatic evidence of the relationship between educational practices and civil disorders lies in the high incidence of riot participation by ghetto youth who have not completed high school.

The bleak record of public education for ghetto children is growing worse. In the critical skills—verbal and reading ability—Negro students are falling further behind whites with each year of school completed. The high unemployment and underemployment rate for Negro youth is evidence, in part, of the growing educational crisis.

We support integration as the priority education strategy; it is essential to the future of American society. In this last summer's disorders we have seen the consequences of racial isolation at all levels, and of attitudes toward race, on both sides, produced by three centuries of myth, ignorance, and bias. It is indispensable that opportunities for interaction between the races be expanded.

We recognize that the growing dominance of pupils from disadvantaged minorities in city school populations will not soon be reversed. No matter how great the effort toward desegregation, many children of the ghetto will not, within their school careers, attend integrated schools.

If existing disadvantages are not to be perpetuated, we must drastically improve the quality of ghetto education. Equality of results with all-white schools must be the goal.

To implement these strategies, the Commission recommends:

- Sharply increased efforts to eliminate de facto segregation in our schools through substantial federal aid to school systems seeking to desegregate either within the system or in cooperation with neighboring school systems.

• Elimination of racial discrimination in Northern as well as Southern schools by vigorous application of Title VI of the Civil Rights Act of 1964.

• Extension of quality early childhood education to every disadvantaged child in the country.

• Efforts to improve dramatically schools serving disadvantaged children through substantial federal funding of year-round quality compensatory education programs, improved teaching, and expanded experimentation and research.

• Elimination of illiteracy through greater Federal support for adult basic education.

• Enlarged opportunities for parent and community participation in the public schools.

• Reoriented vocational education emphasizing work-experience training and the involvement of business and industry.

• Expanded opportunities for higher education through increased federal assistance to disadvantaged students.

• Revision of state aid formulas to assure more per student aid to districts having a high proportion of disadvantaged school age children.

THE WELFARE SYSTEM. Our present system of public welfare is designed to save money instead of people, and tragically ends up doing neither. This system has two critical deficiencies:

First, it excludes large numbers of persons who are in great need, and who, if provided a decent level of support, might be able to become more productive and self-sufficient. No Federal funds are available for millions of unemployed and underemployed men and women who are needy but neither aged, handicapped nor the parents of minor children.

Second, for those included, the system provides assistance well below the minimum necessary for a decent level of existence, and imposes restrictions that encourage continued dependency on welfare and undermine self-respect.

A welter of statutory requirements and administrative practices and regulations operate to remind recipients that they are considered untrustworthy, promiscuous, and lazy. Residence requirements prevent assistance to people in need who are newly arrived in the state. Searches of recipients' homes violate privacy. Inadequate social services compound the problems.

The Commission recommends that the Federal Government, acting with state and local governments where necessary, reform the existing welfare system to:

• Establish, for recipients in existing welfare categories, uniform national standards of assistance at least as high as the annual "poverty level" of income, now set by the Social Security Administration at $3,335 per year for an urban family of four.

• Require that all states receiving Federal welfare contributions participate in the Aid to Families with Dependent Children-Unemployed Parents Program (AFDC-UP) that permits assistance to families with both father and mother in the home, thus aiding the family while it is still intact.

• Bear a substantially greater portion of all welfare costs—at least 90 percent of total payments.

• Increase incentives for seeking employment and job training, but remove restrictions recently enacted by the Congress that would compel mothers of young children to work.

• Provide more adequate social services through neighborhood centers and family-planning program.

• Remove the freeze placed by the 1967 welfare amendments on the percentage of children in a State that can be covered by Federal assistance.

• Eliminate residence requirements.

As a long-range goal, the Commission recommends that the Federal Government seek to develop a national system of income supplementation based strictly on need with two broad and basic purposes:

• To provide, for those who can work or who do work, any necessary supplements in such a way as to develop incentives for fuller employment.

• To provide, for those who cannot work and for mothers who decide to remain with their children, a minimum standard of decent living, and to aid in saving children from the prison of poverty that has held their parents.

A broad system of supplementation would involve substantially greater Federal expenditures than anything now contemplated. The cost will range widely depending on the standard of need accepted as the "basic allowance" to individuals and families, and on the rate at which additional income above this level is taxed. Yet if the deepening cycle of poverty and dependence on welfare can be broken, if the children of the poor can be given the opportunity to scale the wall that now separates them from the rest of society, the return on this investment will be great indeed.

HOUSING. After more than three decades of fragmented and grossly underfunded Federal housing programs, nearly 6 million substandard housing units remain occupied in the United States.

The housing problem is particularly acute in the minority ghettos. Nearly two-thirds of all nonwhite families living in the central cities today live in neighborhoods marked by substandard housing and general urban blight. Two major factors are responsible:

First: Many ghetto residents simply cannot pay the rent necessary to support decent housing. In Detroit, for example, over 40 percent of the non-white-occupied units in 1960 required rent of over 35 percent of the tenants' income.

Second: Discrimination prevents access to many nonslum areas, particularly the suburbs, where good housing exists. In addition, by creating a "back pressure" in the racial ghettos, it makes it possible for landlords to break up apartments for denser occupancy, and keeps prices and rents of deteriorated ghetto housing higher than they would be in a truly free market.

To date, Federal programs have been able to do comparatively little to provide housing for the disadvantaged. In the 31-year history of subsidized Federal housing, only about 800,000 units have been constructed, with recent production averaging about 50,000 units a year. By comparison, over a period only 3 years longer, FHA insurance guarantees have made possible the construction of over 10 million middle and upper income units.

Two points are fundamental to the Commission's recommendations:

First: Federal housing programs must be given a new thrust aimed at overcoming the prevailing patterns of racial segregation. If this is not done, those programs will continue to concentrate the most impoverished and dependent segments of the population into the central-city ghettos where there is already a critical gap between the needs of the population and the public resources to deal with them.

Second: The private sector must be brought into the production and financing of low and moderate-rental housing to supply the capabilities and capital necessary to meet the housing needs of the Nation.

The Commission recommends that the Federal Government:

- Enact a comprehensive and enforceable Federal open-housing law to cover the sale or rental of all housing, including single-family homes.
- Reorient Federal housing programs to place more low- and moderate-income housing outside of ghetto areas.
- Bring within the reach of low- and moderate-income families within the next 5 years 6 million new and existing units of decent housing, beginning with 600,000 units in the next year.

To reach this goal we recommend:

- Expansion and modification of the rent supplement program to permit use of supplements for existing housing, thus greatly increasing the reach of the program.
- Expansion and modification of the below-market interest rate program to enlarge the interest subsidy to all sponsors, provide interest-free loans to nonprofit sponsors to cover preconstruction costs, and permit sale of projects to nonprofit corporations, co-operatives, or condominiums.

• Creation of an ownership supplement program similar to present rent supplements, to make home ownership possible for low-income families.
• Federal writedown of interest rates on loans to private builders constructing moderate-rent housing.
• Expansion of the public housing program, with emphasis on small units on scattered sites, and leasing and "turnkey" programs.
• Expansion of the Model Cities program.
• Expansion and reorientation of the urban renewal program to give priority to projects directly assisting low-income households to obtain adequate housing.

Conclusion

One of the first witnesses to be invited to appear before this Commission was Dr. Kenneth B. Clark, a distinguished and perceptive scholar. Referring to the reports of earlier riot commissions, he said:

> I read that report . . . of the 1919 riot in Chicago, and it is as if I were reading the report of the investigating committee on the Harlem riot of '35, the report of the investigating committee on the Harlem riot of '43, the report of the McCone Commission on the Watts riot.
>
> I must again in candor say to you members of this Commission—it is a kind of Alice in Wonderland—with the same moving picture reshown over and over again, the same analysis, the same recommendations, and the same inaction.

These words come to our minds as we conclude this report.

We have provided an honest beginning. We have learned much. But we have uncovered no startling truths, no unique insights, no simple solutions. The destruction and the bitterness of racial disorder, the harsh polemics of black revolt and white repression have been seen and heard before in this country.

It is time now to end the destruction and the violence, not only in the streets of the ghetto but in the lives of people.

STUDENT POLITICS AND THE UNIVERSITY

NATHAN GLAZER

It is scarcely possible to write anything about students and the university crisis now without looking back at what one has written over the past five years

SOURCE: Nathan Glazer, "Student Politics and the University," *The Atlantic*, 244 (July 1969), 43–53. Copyright © 1969, by the Atlantic Monthly Company, Boston, Mass. Reprinted with permission.

—and I began to write on this subject in December, 1964, reviewing the first climax of the Berkeley student crisis.

This has the usual sobering effect on human presumption. It turns out one was about half wrong and half right. Both the areas where one was wrong and the areas where one was right are of some interest.

Where I was right: at the beginning I, and others, argued that the issue at Berkeley (and elsewhere) was not one of free speech. Free speech existed at Berkeley, and we argued that very early in the first crisis two other issues had in effect replaced it. One was, would the university become the protected recruiting and launching ground for radical political activity directed to various ends, among them the overthrow of the basic system of operation of a democratic society? And second, would the student tactics of disruption, mild as they appear now in the perspective of four and a half years of increasing escalation, be applied to the basic concerns of the university itself (teaching and research), as well as to such peripheral matters as the political activities permitted on campus?

Those of us who by December, 1964, had decided the free-speech issue was solved, and was then spurious, considered these two issues the dominant ones; those who opposed us thought we were ridiculously exaggerating the most distant possible dangers to free speech, free research, and free teaching. They emphasized on the contrary the facts (with which we all agreed) that the student rebels themselves strongly resisted any tendency toward totalitarianism or even central control in their own movement; that the student leaders had found their political orientation in fighting for the rights of Negroes in the South, and for job opportunities for them in the Bay Area; and that young radical civil libertarians, not Communists, were the center of the radical movement. And they pointed out—and this was a very powerful argument indeed—that the young rebels had brought a refreshing sense of community, one that joined students and faculty as well as student with student, into an institution that had been marked by a far too strong concern simply with professional and academic standards, and which had done almost nothing to feed essential needs for close sharing with others, participation, joint action, and common facing of dangers.

These were certainly serious arguments in those distant days, and I doubt that those who in the end voted *against* a faculty resolution which sanctioned the student revolution felt at all easy with their position. Could one really believe that these attractive young people, many of whom had risked their lives in the South, who had taken up so many causes without concern for their own personal future, themselves carried any possible danger to free speech, free teaching, free research? In the end, both sides consulted their feelings—those who had felt the chill of a conformity flowing from an ostensible commitment to freedom voted one way; those who felt the warmth of a community united in common action voted the other. (This is extravagant, of course; there were many other reasons for going one way or another.)

After these chaotic four and a half years, I have no doubt that on this point my friends and I were right. The Free Speech Movement, which stands at the beginning of the student rebellion in this country, seems now almost to mock its subsequent course. In recent years, the issue has been how to *defend* the speech, and the necessary associated actions, of others. The right of unpopular political figures to speak without disruption on campus; the right of professors to give courses and lectures without disruption that makes it impossible for others to listen or to engage in open discussion; the right of professors to engage in research they have freely chosen; the right of government and the corporations to come onto the campus to give information and to recruit personnel; the right of students to prepare themselves as officers on the campus: all these have been attacked by the young apostles of freedom and their heirs.

The organizations that defend academic freedom, the AAUP and the ACLU, and the others, which have so long pointed their heavy guns toward the outside—for defense against conservative trustees, newspapers, legislators, and vigilante communities—are now with some reluctance swinging them around so they face inward. Anyone who has experienced the concrete situation in American universities knows that the threat to free speech, free teaching, free research, comes from radical white students, from militant black students, and from their faculty defenders. The trustees of the University of California may deny credit to a course in which Eldridge Cleaver is the chief lecturer, but radical students in many places (including campuses of the University of California) have effectively intimidated professors so they cannot give courses they were prepared to give. It is a peculiar sign of the times that the denial of credit seems to many a more monstrous act than the denial of freedom to teach.

Thus, we were right in pointing to the dangers. Where were we wrong? Our gravest mistake was that we did not see what strength and plausibility would soon be attached to the argument that this country was ruled by a cruel and selfish oligarchy devoted to the extension of the power and privileges of the few and denying liberty and even life to the many; and to the further assertion that the university was an integral part of this evil system. It was not possible to predict, in December, 1964, that the spring of 1965 would see an enormous expansion of the American role in Vietnam, and would involve us in a large-scale war that was to be fought by this country with unparalleled, one-sided devastation of an innocent civilian population and its land. We had never been in this position before. Where we were overwhelmingly powerful—as against Spain in 1898—there was no occasion or opportunity or capacity to engage in such horrible destruction; where we were horribly destructive—as in Europe and Japan in 1944 and 1945—it was against powerful opponents who had, in the eyes of most Americans, well merited destruction. There were some excuses even for the atom bombs of Hiroshima and Nagasaki. There were some mitigating circumstances. There were hardly any in Vietnam, unfortunately, except for the arguments, which became less and less impressive over time, that we were after all a democratic society, and had gotten involved in such a war through democratic processes; and the further arguments that our strategy was designed to save a small nation from subversion, and our tactics were intended to save American lives.

THE SPLIT BETWEEN LIBERALS AND RADICALS

We have to examine this moment in American history with the greatest care if we are ever to understand what happened afterward, why Berkeley 1964 did not remain an isolated incident, and why the nascent split that appeared there between liberals and radicals became a chasm which has divided American intellectuals more severely even than the issue of Stalinism and Communism in the thirties and forties. What happened to professors at Berkeley happened to liberals and radicals everywhere. And since intellectuals, including professors, played a far larger role in American society in the sixties than in the thirties and forties, this split became far more important than any possible argument among the intellectuals and their associated professors twenty-five years earlier. (One of the differences between the two periods was that so many intellectuals of the sixties, as against the earlier period, were *in* the universities. Compare the writers, circulation, and influence of *Partisan Review* with that of the *New York Review of Books*.)

It may be argued that no split *really* developed in 1964; that the intellectuals who approved of the United States were ambushed by new events that did not fit into their approach, and by an uprising of suppressed intellectuals who had been silenced by McCarthy, who had harbored for a long time some version of the Marxist view of the United States, and who now—by a series of disasters, mistakes, or demonstrations of the country's basic character and tendencies, take your pick—had been given their chance. This is in large measure true. But we forget how closely those who were to become so divided were linked before 1964.

Some political events of those days now seem so unlikely as to be hallucinatory; thus Paul Jacobs (who was to run in 1968 as a candidate for the Peace and Freedom Party), S. M. Lipset (the liberal sociologist of pluralism, now at Harvard), and Philip Selznick (the Berkeley sociologist who was to become one of the strong defenders of student protest at Berkeley) were linked in defending dissident members of Harry Bridges' union in San Francisco and in attacking what they considered the Communist proclivities of various groups in the Bay Area. Lewis Feuer, who became one of the most forceful critics of student radicalism (in his article in the *Atlantic* and in his book *The Conflict of Generations*), was in 1960 the chairman of a committee to defend the students who had put on a vocal (and, it was charged, a disruptive) demonstration against the House Un-American Activities Committee in San Francisco— this event is considered one of the important precursors of the Berkeley student rebellion. Or, if we want to mount a larger stage, consider who wrote for the *New York Review of Books* in its trial issues of 1963, and consider how many of them now see each other as political enemies.

Thus, to my mind, if we are to understand the student rebellion, we must go back to 1965 and reconstruct the enormous impact of Vietnam, and we will see that the same lines that began to divide friends on student rebellion reappeared to divide them on Vietnam.

Among all those who were horrified by the beginning of the bombing of the North, and by the increasingly destructive tactics in the South—the heavy bombing, the burning of villages, the defoliation of the countryside—a fissure rapidly developed. It could be seen when, for example, Berkeley radicals sat down in front of trains bringing recruits to the Oakland induction station. Those of us who opposed such tactics argued they would alienate the moderate potential opponents of the war, whose support was needed to bring a change in policy. We argued that to equate Johnson with Hitler and America with Nazi Germany would make it impossible to develop a wide alliance against the war. But actually, the principled basis of our opposition was more important. We did believe there were profound differences between this country and Nazi Germany, Johnson and Hitler, that we lived in a democracy, and that the authority of a democratic government, despite what it was engaged in in Vietnam, should not be undermined, because only worse would follow: from the right, most likely, but also possibly from a general anarchy. Perhaps we were wrong. The reaction from the right was remarkably moderate. The radical tactics did reach large numbers and played finally a major role in changing American policy in Vietnam. But all the returns are not yet in: conceivably the erosion of the legitimacy of a democratic government is a greater loss than what was gained. Conceivably, too, a movement oriented to gaining wide support—along the lines of early SANE—might have been even more effective.

At Berkeley, the liberal split on Vietnam replicated the liberal split on student rebellion in the university and was paralleled by splits on the question of the summer riots and the whole problem of black violence. Again and again the issues were posed in terms of tactics—yes, we are for university reform of political rules, but we are against sit-ins and the degradation of university authorities; yes, we are against the war in Vietnam, but we will not attack or undermine the legitimacy of a democratic government; yes, we are for expanded opportunities and increased power and wealth for Negroes, but we are against violence and destruction to get them. But of course the split was not really over tactics.

Behind that there was a more basic disagreement. What kind of society, government, and university did we have?, what was owed to them?, to what extent were they capable of reform and change without resort to civil disobedience, disruption, and violence? The history and analysis of this basic division have scarcely been begun. But there is hardly any question as to which side has won among intellectual youth. We have witnessed in the past four or five years one of the greatest and most rapid intellectual victories in history. In the press addressed to the young (whether that press is elite or mass or agitational) a single view of the society and what is needed to change it is presented. Violence is extolled in the *New York Review of Books,* which began with only literary ambitions; Tom Hayden, who urges his audiences to kill policemen, is treated as a hero by *Esquire;* Eldridge Cleaver merits an adulatory *Playboy* interview; and so it goes, all the way, I imagine, down to *Eye.*

THE POWER OF RADICAL THINKING

When I say *we* were wrong, I mean that we never dreamed that a radical critique of American society and government could develop such enormous power, to the point where it becomes simply the new convention. Even in the fraternities and sororities, conservative opinion has gone underground; the formerly hip conservatism of the *National Review* is as unfashionable on the campus as the intellectualism of *Commentary.* We were not only wrong in totally underestimating the power of radical thinking to seize large masses again; we were also in the position of William Phillips sputtering to Kenneth Tynan, "I know the answer to that, but I've forgotten it." We had forgotten the answers, it was so long ago. When the questions came up again—imperialism, capitalism, exploitation, alienation—those of us who believed that the Marxist and anarchist critiques of contemporary society were fundamentally wrong could not, it seems, find the answers—at least the ones that worked.

Of course, some of the intellectuals of the forties and fifties had never forgotten the old questions (Paul Goodman, Hannah Arendt), and while they looked with some distance, even from the beginning, at the new recruits to their old concerns, they managed with amazing intellectual success the precarious task of combining basic criticism of a liberal society with basic support of the liberal values of free development, human variety, and protection for the individual. Those who had *really* forgotten nothing, neither the problems nor the answers, such as Herbert Marcuse, have been, of course, even more successful in relating to radical youth.

But were we wrong only in underestimating the appeal of old and outworn political ideologies, or were we wrong in considering them outworn, inadequate explanations of the world? In other words, was the issue really some fundamental bent in American society that added up to military adventurism abroad, lack of concern with the rights or lives of those of other skin color, the overwhelming dominance of mindless bureaucracies in determining economic and political policies, the human meaninglessness of the roles these bureaucracies prescribed for people, and the inability of the society and the state to

correct these bents under any pressures short of violence, destruction, and rebellion?

THE UNIVERSITY AS PART OF SOCIETY

One must begin, I am afraid, with these larger questions in speaking about the
university today. One's attitude toward it, the role of students within it, and
the danger of its possible destruction, as a collection of physical facilities and
as an institution, can scarcely be determined without attention to these larger
questions. For the university *is* implicated in the society. It is a rare university
that can for any period of time stand aside from a society, following a totally
independent and critical course. Universities are almost always to some extent
independent (one wonders, though, about Russia, China, and Cuba), but their
insatiable demands for resources inevitably impose on them the need to relate
themselves to the major concerns and interests of the society.

Yet at the same time a university's work *is* in large measure quite independent of the faults or characteristics of any state or government. There is a
realm of scholarship beyond political stands and divisions. The science that is
taught in the United States is not very different from the science that is taught
in the Soviet Union, or in Cuba, or even in China—though at that point we
reach the limits of my generalization. Even the scholarship of the humanities
bears a great deal in common. I have often been surprised by the degree to
which the work of the universities is common across radically different political frontiers. The passion of the Russians and Chinese, under Communism,
for archaeology, for the exact restoration of early buildings and structures,
and for early philology is evidence of the scholarly and scientific validity and
usefulness of archaeology, linguistic reconstruction, art history.

It is only when one approaches the social sciences that the cross-political
scientific validity of research and teaching can successfully be challenged, for
we do find enormous variations between social science under one political
outlook and another. History is perhaps worst off. Consider how Russians or
Americans, and among Americans, established or revisionist historians, interpret our past. Sociology is almost as badly off. Yet some parts of it (for example, the statistical methodology of opinion research) seem to have developed
wide acceptance across disparate political and cultural frontiers. Economics
seems to share some of the universal acceptance of the natural sciences.

I record these truisms to emphasize that the university is not *simply* the
creature of social and political systems, and that scientific and scholarly investigation and teaching have some general value divorced from politics, since
totally opposed and distinct social systems accept its importance and give it
support and prestige. (China is the one great society to break with this general acceptance, and we don't know whether this is only the aberration of a
few years.) But certainly the university is in large measure the creature of distinct social and political systems. The degree to which higher education is

considered a right of all; the degree to which its credentials are considered essential for jobs and positions of all kinds; the degree to which its research is affected by state determination and the availability of state support; the degree to which university education is seen as part of a service to the state, and to which it is integrated with other kinds of service, such as military service: all these show considerable variation between states, but most modern states tend to converge in answering these questions, and the convergence is in the form of a closer and more complex relationship between university, society, and state. And if one is impressed by fatal flaws in the society and state, one may not be overly impressed with whatever measure of university function is independent of deep involvement with a given society and a given political system. At that point, one may well see the university as only the soft underbelly of the society.

ANGER AGAINST THE STATE

What the liberal critics of student disruption in 1964 did not see was that a storm of violent antipathy to the United States—and indeed to any stable industrial society, which raises other questions—could be aroused in the youth and the intellectuals, and that it could be maintained and strengthened year after year until it became the underpinning of the dominant style, political and cultural, among the youth. The question I find harder to answer is whether we failed to see fundamental defects and faults both in the society and state and the associated universities which had inevitably to lead anyone committed to life and freedom to such a ferocious anger.

Vietnam, of course, could justify anything. And yet the same ferocity can be seen in countries such as Germany, Italy, and Japan, which are really scarcely involved, allies though they are in other respects, in our war in Vietnam, and in a country like France, which actively disapproves of our role. Undoubtedly Vietnam has enormously strengthened the movement of antipathy and anger, and not only because our powerful nation was engaged in the destruction—whatever the reasons for it—of a small and poor one. There were other reasons. Vietnam placed youth in a morally insupportable position. The poor and the black were disproportionately subjected to the draft. The well-favored, as long as they stayed in school, and even out of it, were freed from it. The fortunate middle-class youth, with strong emotional and ideological reasons to oppose violently our war in Vietnam, could escape as long as they stayed in college, just as prisoners could escape as long as they were in jail. They undoubtedly felt guilty because those with whom they wanted to be allied, whom they hoped to help, had to go and fight in Vietnam. In this ridiculous moral position, the university became to many a repulsive prison, and prison riots were almost inevitable—whatever else contributed to them.

And yet, where there was no Vietnam, students could create their own, as in France, or the real Vietnam could serve to make them just as angry at their own, in this case hardly guilty, government.

But the question remains: how do we evaluate the role of Vietnam in directly creating frustrations that led to anger at the university? Did Vietnam serve to teach or remind students, with the assistance of critics of capitalism, that they lived in a corrupt society? Or was it itself the major irritant? How was Vietnam related to the larger society? Was it an appropriate symbol or summary of its major trends or characteristics? Or was it itself an aberration, correctable without "major social change"? The dominant tone of student radicalism was increasingly to take the first position—it reflected the society, and could be used as an issue to mobilize people against it.

Those of us who took the position we did in 1964 have stuck with it, and are stuck with it. We took a position of the defense of institutions that we thought worked well enough, which could be changed, and which in the face of radical attack could and would crumble, to be replaced with something worse. I will not defend this position here—I have done so elsewhere (in "The New Left and Its Limits," *Commentary*, July, 1968). I will admit to some discomfort with it. We seem to find it impossible to modify our inhuman tactics in Vietnam (even though I understand we adopt them to save American lives), we seem to find it impossible to reduce the enormous military budget or to make effective steps in reducing the atomic arms race (though I am aware another side is involved too), we seem to find it difficult or impossible to move rapidly in the reform of certain inadequate institutions—for example, the system of punishment, the welfare system, the public schools, the universities, the police—without the spur of the disruption and violence I decry. But the disruption and violence, even if they produce reforms, will in the end, I believe, produce a society that we would find less human than the unreformed society. So I have stuck to this not fully adequate position, for I find it sounder, more adapted to reality, and more congenial than the alternative: the despairing view that we have solved no problems, that selfish and overwhelmingly powerful forces prevent us from solving any, that the society and its institutions respond only to disruption and violence.

Of course, this position has never been one that was uncritical of universities and colleges. Many who defend universities and the institutions of a democratic society against the radicals—for example, Daniel Bell and David Riesman—have been among the most forceful critics of colleges and universities. (I myself wrote, a year or two before Berkeley, an article critical of college and university education, and joined the small band of educational reformers when I came to Berkeley in 1963.) But rarely was the main force of these critics linked to a basic criticism of the society. Their criticism was directed at the structure of the university or college; it spoke of the university as an educational institution and faulted it for educational failure. What this criticism did *not* do was to subordinate the educational criticism to a devastating criticism of the *society*, its distribution of power, forms of socialization, its role in the world.

UNIVERSITY REFORM

Early in the American student revolt it seemed reasonable that educational issues were at the heart of the matter. People spoke of the size of Berkeley, the anonymity of the student, the dominance of education by the disciplines, and the graduate departments and their needs. But there was a key difference between the critics of higher education and the student radicals: to the critics educational reform was, if not of major or exclusive concern, a matter of some significance in itself, worth taking seriously on its own terms; to the student radicals, it was immediately subordinated to the larger social criticism—educational reform was valuable if it meant the universities could be moved toward becoming a training ground for revolutionaries, or if it meant that revolutionaries would achieve greater power within it, or if it meant that the university could be used so as to produce "radicalizing confrontations" with "reactionary" forces.

In other words, university reform was a tactic. I make the distinction too sharply, of course, because to many of the student radicals, university reform was not a tactic; it was a goal of value in itself. Among the student radicals were, and are, to be found many serious students and critics of university education, with strong commitment to change and experiment. And yet again and again the *tactical* use of educational change became dominant.

Thus, consider the case of the course in which Eldridge Cleaver was to lecture at Berkeley, a course organized under the liberalized procedures that permitted students to initiate courses of interest to them. The Regents moved, against this course, that lecturers not members of the regular faculty could give only one guest lecture a quarter in a given course. If the students wanted to hear Eldridge Cleaver give his planned nine lectures, they would have to take the course without credit.

This led to the occupation of the building housing the offices of the College of Letters and Science and the philosophy department by unreconciled radicals (including the ubiquitous Tom Hayden, who can add to his honors his presence in Moses Hall at Berkeley as well as in the mathematics building at Columbia), and to considerable damage. The "revolutionary" slogan, the demands for which the radicals fought, were summed up on a button, "For credit, on campus, as planned!" It would be hard to argue that the radical students were moved by the opportunity to hear Eldridge Cleaver on campus, an opportunity that was available to them every day, if Cleaver had enough time or energy, and it seems quite clear that this educational innovation was now becoming a tactic, a counter in the revolutionary struggle that would (hopefully) activate the students to strike, to occupy buildings, and to disrupt the university.

If we go across the country, we can find a similar development in the enormously successful course that radical students conduct under the auspices of the social relations department of Harvard University, for credit. Some members of the department preferred to move the course elsewhere, into social sciences. The faculty member under whose formal authority the course was given denounced this as an effort to destroy the course, and he and those conducting sections in the course organized to fight the move, insisting it was political, and issued threats as to what would happen if the social relations department tried to disengage itself from this albatross. Thus, it was suggested, other social relations courses would be disrupted in protest.

Everything can be explained, if we are so inclined, as the effort of students devoted to education to save an experimental and rewarding course from destruction, and this certainly was part of the motivation. Reading the statements, I cannot escape the cynical conclusion that the course was being used as a club to threaten a "conservative" department, and the threat was being used to organize and radicalize students. There is enough to suggest that this objective loomed far larger in the minds of the organizers of the course than any concern with education as such.

Of course the organizers would argue, as student radicals argue everywhere, that there is no difference between radicalization and education. Everything else is "miseducation." To understand properly the nature of social relations, or power relations, of the structure of the society, the political system, and the economy is to become radical, and become imbued with the passion to destroy the status quo. Thus, they argue, any so-called "objective" or "scientific" education is really a fraud—if it's not educating people to overthrow the status quo, then it must be educating people to support it, for even inaction (when one could be active against) is a form of support. Thus, the outraged defenders of Social Relations 149 argued that all the other courses were conservative (clearly, for they weren't formally "radical"), and therefore their own radical course was a necessary and valuable effort to redress the balance.

The argument is not new. It is in effect the argument that was fought out in Russia over the question of whether all education and all science must reflect "dialectical materialism," and whether any scholarship that did not was by that fact alone "counterrevolutionary" and "bourgeois." Or the battle that was fought out in Nazi Germany over "Aryan" science and "non-Aryan" (and therefore "Jewish" science). It is understandable why we sputter, "I know the answers, but I've forgotten them." For these positions became so outrageous and untenable in the eyes of Western intellectuals that to have to defend again the possibility and reality of objective science and scholarship means to call into play parts of our minds that have long lain quiescent and unused. But called into play they must be, because the possibility of pursuing and disseminating knowledge freely is now quite seriously threatened.

THE ATTACKS ON FREEDOM

We have to learn the answers to the arguments that are now used to defend attacks on freedom—they are widely used, and in the present cultural atmosphere are repeated in the same form on a hundred campuses. Thus, if ROTC is prevented from operating, and the argument is that students should be free to take it if they wish, the answer is, "But the South Vietnamese are not allowed their freedom—why should students be allowed the freedom to join ROTC and the armed forces, which deny the South Vietnamese their freedom?" If a faculty member is not allowed to give the course he has scheduled, and faculty members criticize the black students who have prevented him from teaching, the answer is, "But this has been a racist institution for a long time, and 'academic freedom' is only a ploy to defend racism and the status quo." If some students engage in violence against others, the argument is, "But the violence of the police at Chicago is far greater, and what about the silent violence of starvation in the South, not to mention the violence of ghetto merchants who overcharge, and of social investigators who ask degrading questions?" We must remember what we have forgotten—for example, the old joke about the man who is being shown the wonderful new Moscow subway, and after a while asks, "But where are the trains?" The Russian answers, "But what about lynching in the South?" It's no joke any longer.

In other words, when I think of the student rebellion today, and of the disasters threatening and in some measure already actual on the campuses today—the massed battles between students and police, the destruction of card catalogues and lecture halls (and the threat to major research libraries), the destruction of computer tapes and research notes, the arming of many black students and the terrorization in many cases of other black and white students—I do not think initially in terms of the major reforms that are required on the university campus, but I think of the politics, and even the tactics, that would defend the university. For I have made some commitments: that an orderly democracy is better than government by the expressive and violent outbursts of the most committed; that the university embodies values that transcend the given characteristics of a society or the specific disasters of an administration; that the faults of our society, grave as they are, do not require—indeed, would in no way be advanced by—the destruction of those fragile institutions which have been developed over centuries to transmit and expand knowledge. These are strongly held commitments, so strongly that my first reaction to student disruption—and it is not only an emotional one—is to consider how the disrupters can be isolated and weakened, how their influence, which is now enormous among students, can be reduced, how dissension among them can be encouraged, and how they can be finally removed from a community they wish to destroy.

I know the faults of the universities as well as any of its critics do, and have worked and continue to work to correct them. But I take this position because I do not believe the character of the university as an institution—its teaching, its research, its government—is really the fundamental issue raised by student radicalism on the campus, or that changes in the government and education and research of the university, important as they are on many grounds, will do much to mitigate or deflect the radical onslaught. Again and again we have seen *political* uprisings on the campus—*political* acts based on a certain interpretation of American society to which one can either adhere or not, as one wishes, in the university—and in response to these political acts, we have seen an effort to shape a response in the *educational* or *administrative* area. This, I suggest, is a completely inappropriate and ineffective response.

Thus, if students attack Columbia for its ties to IDA and its building of a gymnasium in a park adjacent to Harlem, we end up by "restructuring" Columbia, with endless committees, with elected student representatives, with student participation being argued over in every setting, and all the rest—the university turned into committees and tribunals. Now, the fact is that the cause of the uprising was not dissatisfaction with the government of Columbia. The cause was the ceaseless search of the SDS to find means of attacking the basic character and mode of operation of a society and government they wished to transform, "by any means possible," to use the prevailing rhetoric. IDA and the gymnasium we have been told by SDS activists—and we must take this seriously—were *tactical.*

The cause of the uprising at Columbia was not the system of government, for *any* system of government for that university might in the fifties and sixties have involved ties with IDA and might have undertaken the building of a gymnasium in the park. (Who, after all, objected to these things when they were begun?) And indeed, even Columbia's system of government, archaic as it was, was quite capable of responding to changed attitudes, and was engaged in the process of cutting the ties to IDA, before the student uprising. As to the gymnasium, the fact was that aside from the protests of defenders of New York parkland and design (I am among them), who objected violently to the gymnasium, there was little other protest. Even the Harlem community was either indifferent to or actually supported the project.

With IDA and the gymnasium alone, as we all now know, the SDS at Columbia would have gotten nowhere. But then there comes the illegal seizure, the successful confrontation, the battle with the police, and *new* issues arise. The radicals are now joined by the liberals. The latter are concerned with due process, with government, with participation, with education. The liberals are much less concerned with the revolutionary change in the society that the radicals insist is necessary. The liberals demand amnesty for the protesters, due process before punishment, a new role for students and faculty, a change in "governance."

The script was played out before Columbia, at Berkeley in 1964 and 1966, and it is now being played out at Harvard. In 1966 at Berkeley, radical students blocked military recruiters. Police were called onto the campus to eject and arrest them. What was the faculty's response? To set up a commission on governance.

MAKING NEW RADICALS

The logic of these events is truly wonderful. The blocking of recruiters on campus has nothing to do with the governance of an educational institution. Whether it was run by the state, the trustees, the faculty, the students, or the janitors, any university might consider it reasonable to give space for recruiters to talk to students, and if these were blocked, any administration might well decide at some point to call police. But then the liberal students and faculty move into action. First, shocked at the calling of police, they demand that new governance arrangements be created. Then, because they dislike the tactics chosen to remove the disrupters, they demand amnesty for them. Finally, because they have been forced into a tactical alliance with the disrupters—after all, the liberals are defending them against the administration—they begin to find the original positions of the disrupters, with which the liberals had very possibly originally disagreed, more attractive.

We are all aware that calling in the police radicalizes the students and faculty (so aware that many students and faculty protesting President Pusey's action at Harvard said, "Why did he do it, he knows it radicalizes us"—they spoke as if they knew that, according to the scenario, they were *supposed* to be outraged, and they were). We are less aware that the radicalization extends not only to the police issue and the governance issue but to the content of the original demands. A demand to which one can remain indifferent or opposed suddenly gains enormously greater moral authority after one has been hit on the head by the police for it. Thus, the first mass meeting of the moderate student element after the police bust, in Memorial Church, refused to take a position on ROTC and asked only for a student referendum, and referenda, as we know, generally turn out in favor of retaining ROTC in some form on campus. It is for this as well as for other reasons that SDS denounces votes and majority rule as "counterrevolutionary." But the second meeting of the moderate students, in the Soldiers Field Stadium a few days later, adopted a far more stringent position, hardly different from SDS's. And a few days after that, the distinguished faculty, which had devoted such lengthy attention to ROTC only a short time before, returned to discuss it again, and also took a more severe position.

The recourse to violence by the radical students at Harvard was therefore successful. The issue of ROTC, which was apparently closed, was reopened. The issue of university expansion, which excited few people, became a major one. The issue of black studies, which everyone had thought had been settled for a time, and decently, with the acceptance of the Rosovsky report, was reopened by the black students. It might have been anyway, but certainly the SDS action encouraged the reopening.

The SDS takes the position that these are no victories—by the nature of their analysis of the structure of society, government, and university in this country, there can be no victories, short of the final, indefinable "basic social change." Thus, the fact that the university faculty and corporation have now adopted a resolution which will remove the ROTC from campus entirely (even the rental of facilities, according to the mover of the new faculty resolution, would be improper) demonstrates, according to SDS, that the university has not given an inch. Why? Because the resolution says the university will facilitate student efforts to take ROTC as an outside activity, off campus, presumably in the way it facilitates student efforts to find jobs or nearby churches. "Abolish ROTC," the SDS ROTC slogan, it now appears, means that not only must students not be allowed to take ROTC on campus; the university must not give them the address where they might take it off campus. One can be sure that if this "facilitating" clause were not in the resolution, the SDS would find other means of claiming that the university is intransigent—by definition, the power structure must be—and that there has been no victory.

On university expansion, the corporation and the various schools of the university have come up with the most detailed account to demonstrate that the direct impact of the university on housing has been minor and moderated. The indirect impact is hardly controllable—psychoanalysts want to live in Cambridge, millionaires' children want to live in Cambridge (and some of those after all contribute to radicals' causes), students want to live there, and faculty members want to live there. Any reasonable attempt to moderate the situation—as, for example, Harvard's effort to build low-cost or moderate-cost housing—is denounced by the radicals. Could there be any more convincing demonstration that the demands are tactical, not designed to improve the housing situation (if it were, it might prevent the anger that hopefully leads to the revolution), but to serve as a rallying slogan whereby liberals can be turned into radicals?

The issue of the black demands is a different matter; these are raised by the black students and are not tactical. They are deeply felt, if often misguided. Thus, the key demand of formal student equality in recruiting faculty goes against one of the basic and most deeply held principles of the university—that the faculty consists of a body of scholars who recruit themselves without outside interference, whether from government, trustees, or students. For the purpose of maintaining a body of scholars, students *are* an "outside" force—they are *not* part of the body of scholars. But if the black demands are not raised tactically by the black students, they are adopted tactically by the white radicals—as they were at Harvard, with the indescribably simple phrase, "accept all Afro demands."

Once again, this is the kind of slogan that is guaranteed to create the broadest measure of disruption, disorder, and radicalization. Just as in the case of "abolish ROTC" or "no expansion," "accept all Afro demands" has a wonderful accordion-like character, so that no matter what the university does in response, the SDS can insist that nothing really has been accomplished, the ruling class and the corporation still stand supreme, and the work of building toward the revolution must continue.

There is only one result of a radical action that means success for the radicals—making new radicals. In this sense, the Harvard action has been an enormous success. Those who know something of the history of Marxism and Leninism will be surprised to see this rather esoteric definition of success for true radical movements now emerging full-blown in the midst of the SDS, which began so proudly only a few years ago by breaking with all previous ideology and dogma. "Build the cadres" was the old slogan: "build the cadres," because any *reform* will only make the peasants and workers happier or more content with their lot, and will thus delay the final and inevitable revolution.

The aim of action, therefore, is never its ostensible end—the slogan is only a tactic—but further radicalization, "building the cadres," now "the movement." The terrible effect of such an approach is to introduce corruption into the heart of the movement, and into the hearts of those who work for it, because the "insiders" know that the *ostensible* slogans are only tactical, that one can demand anything no matter how nonsensical, self-contradictory, and destructive, because the aim is not the fulfillment of demands, but the creation of new radicals who result from the process that follows the putting forward of such demands: violence by the revolutionaries, counterviolence by the authorities, radicalization therefore of the bystanders, and the further "building of the movement."

What justifies this process, of course, is the irredeemable corruption of the society and all its institutions, and therefore the legitimacy of any means to bring it all down.

THE FAILURE OF THE LIBERALS

Liberals like to make the distinction between themselves and radicals by saying to radicals, "We approve of your aims but disapprove of your means." This in effect is what the liberal student body and faculty of Harvard did. It disagreed with the occupation of University Hall, the physical ejection of the deans, the breaking into the files. But it said, in effect, by its actions, we think the issues you raised are legitimate ones. Thus, we will revise our carefully thought out position on ROTC, and we will change our position on black studies.

On university expansion, the faculty acted just as a faculty should; it accepted the proposals of a committee that had been set up some time before, a committee on the university and the city, chaired by Professor James Q. Wilson. It followed its agenda and its procedures rather than the agenda set for it by the radicals. It received neither more nor less abuse for this action than for its efforts to accommodate radical demands on ROTC. I think the proper liberal response was: "We disagree totally with your means, which we find abhorrent, we disagree totally with your ends, which are the destruction of any free and civil society; some of the slogans you have raised to advance your ends nevertheless point to real faults which should be corrected by this institution, which has shown by its past actions on various issues that it is capable of rational change without the assistance of violence from those who wish to destroy it, and we will consider them."

Oddly enough, the discussion of the ostensible aims, even though the liberal position was that the aims *were* valid, was terribly muted. The liberals were hampered in their discussion first by lack of knowledge of the issues (how many had gone into the intricacies of relocation and the provision of housing for the poor?), and second by the feeling that some of these issues were not really the business of the faculty. In the case of ROTC, the key issue, the faculty tried to find an "educational" component to justify the action that might assuage the passions of student radicals. Thus, the argument on ROTC was carefully separated from any position on the Vietnam War, and a resolution was passed ostensibly for educational purposes, simply because it had been determined that ROTC did not have any place in a university.

This was nonsense. The educational reasons for action against ROTC were settled when it was determined the courses should not get academic credit and the ROTC instructors should not get faculty standing. Why was it necessary to go on and specify that no facilities should be provided? Space is given or rented for all sorts of noneducational purposes on the campus—religious, athletic, social, and so on. What had happened was that under the guise of responding as an educational body to political demands, the faculty had accepted a good part of the political demands, and implicitly a good part of the political analysis, that led to them. It would have been more honest to denounce the Vietnam War than to remove ROTC. After all, what role has ROTC played in getting us into that quagmire? It was civilians, such as Presidents Kennedy and Johnson, who did that.

By denying to students the right previously established to take military training on the campus, the faculty was in effect taking the position that all the works of the United States government, and in particular its military branches, are abhorrent, which is exactly the position that SDS wishes to establish. It wishes to alienate students from their society and government to the point that they do not consider how it can be reformed, how it can be changed, how it can be prevented from making mistakes and doing evil, but only how people can be made to hate it.

This may appear an extravagant view of the action of the Harvard College faculty, and yet the fact is that there was little faculty debate on the demands. The liberals implicitly took the stand, "We agree with your aims, we disagree only with your tactics," and in taking this stand were themselves then required to figure out how by their procedures they could reach those aims without violence.

But the aims themselves were really never discussed. The "Abolish ROTC" slogan was never analyzed by the faculty. It was only acted upon. All the interesting things wrapped up in that slogan were left unexplored: the rejection of majority rule (explicit in SDS's rejection of the legitimacy of a referendum on ROTC); the implication that American foreign policy is made by the military; the assumption that the American military is engaged in only vile actions; the hope that by denying the government access to the campus it can be turned into a pariah—and once we manage to turn someone by our actions into a pariah, we can be sure the proper emotions will follow.

The expansion demand was never really discussed, or at any rate insufficiently discussed. It never became clear how different elements contributed to the housing shortage and to the rise of rents in Cambridge. It was never pointed out that the popular demand for rent control would inevitably mean under-the-table operations in which the wealthier Harvard students and faculty could continue to outbid the aged and the workers. The issues of the inevitable conflicts over alternative land uses, and the means whereby they could be justly and rationally resolved, were never taken up.

The faculty did most to argue against the new demand for equal student participation in the committee developing the program of Afro-American studies and recruiting faculty. Even there, one can hardly be impressed with the scale and detail of the faculty discussion, though individual statements, such as Henry Rosovsky's speech, were impressive and persuasive. The key questions of the nature of a university, the role of students within it, the inevitable limits that must be set on democracy and participation if an institution designed to achieve the best, in scholarship and in teaching, is to carry out its functions—all these played hardly any role in the discussion. The students were not educated. To their eyes, reasonable and sensible demands were imposed by force on a reluctant faculty. They were right about the force. This was hardly a manly posture for the faculty—at least they should have argued.

There was thus to my mind a serious educational failure at Harvard. All the education, after the occupation and the police bust, was carried on by the radicals. They spoke to the issues they had raised; others did not, or countered them poorly. They established that these issues were important, and thus in the minds of many students their tactics were justified. By student, faculty, and corporation response, their view that the university reacts only to violent tactics was given credence. If this was a failure, of course the chief blame must rest on the faculty. It is their function to educate the students, and the corporation follows their lead and their analysis, when they give one.

There were of course administration failures, too, in not consulting sufficiently widely with students and faculty, and perhaps in calling the police. But these did not justify the faculty in its failure to analyze and argue with the radical demands, and in giving up positions it had just adopted.

I agree with the SDS that the issues should have been discussed—ROTC, campus expansion, black demands. But more than that should have been discussed. The reasons SDS had raised the issues should have been discussed. The basic analysis they present of society and government should have been discussed. The consequences of their analysis and the actions they take to achieve their demands should have been discussed. They should have been engaged in debate. They were not. Instead, they were given an open field and all possible facilities for spreading their view of the world, a view that to my mind is deficient in logic, based on ignorance and passion, contradictory, committed to unattainable aims, and one in which a free university could not possibly operate.

The university now suffers from the consequences of an untempered and irrational attack on American society, government, and university, one to which we as academics have contributed, and on which we have failed to give much light. The students who sat in, threw out the deans, and fought with the police have, after all, been taught by American academics such as C. Wright Mills, Herbert Marcuse, Noam Chomsky, and many, many others. All these explained how the world operated, and we failed to answer effectively. Or we had forgotten the answers. We have to start remembering and start answering.

MASS MEDIA AND VIOLENCE

MORRIS JANOWITZ

[An] important institution of social control that has special relevance for collective racial violence is the mass media. A debate on this issue has raged among social scientists since the early 1930's when the Payne Foundation underwrote a group of University of Chicago social scientists in the first large-scale study of the impact of the mass media, in this case, the consequences of movies for young people.[30]

The mass media both reflect the values of the larger society and at the same time are agents of change and devices for molding tastes and values. It is a complex task to discern their impact because they are at the same time both cause and effect. Controversies about the mass media focus particularly on the issue of their contribution to crime and delinquency and to an atmosphere

[30] See W. W. Charter, *Motion Pictures and Youth* (New York: Macmillan, 1933).

SOURCE: Morris Janowitz, from "Patterns of Collective Racial Violence," in *Violence in America: Historical and Comparative Perspectives,* A Staff Report to The National Commission on the Causes and Prevention of Violence, (Washington, D.C.: United States Government Printing Office, June, 1969), pp. 333–337.

of lawlessness. Among social scientists, it is generally agreed that consequences of the mass media are secondary as compared with the influence of family, technology, and the organization of modern society. But differences in the meaning and importance attributed to this "secondary factor" among social scientists are great. "Secondary" can mean still important enough to require constructive social policy, or "secondary" can mean that a factor is trivial and unimportant.

Two separate but closely linked issues require attention. First, what are the consequences of the mass media, with its high component of violence, on popular attitudes toward authority and on conditioning and acceptance of violence in social relations? Second, what have been the specific consequences of the manner in which the mass media have handled escalated rioting since the period of Watts? The managers of the mass media run their enterprises on a profit basis and one result has been that the content of channels of communication, especially television, in the United States have a distinct "violence flavor" as contrasted with other nations. This content emphasis continued to persist as of the end of 1968 despite all the public discussion about this standard of the mass media.[31] In this respect, self-regulation of the mass media has not been effective except to some extent in the comic book industry.

In my judgment, the cumulative evidence collected by social scientists over the last 30 years has pointed to a discernible, but limited, negative impact of the media on social values and on personal controls required to inhibit individual disposition into aggressive actions. Other students of the same data have concluded that their impact is so small as not to constitute a social problem.

Many studies on media impact are based on limited amounts of exposure, as contrasted to the continuous expose of real life. Other studies made use of ex post facto sample surveys that are too superficial to probe the psychological depths of these issues. More recent research employing rigorous experimental methods has strengthened the conclusion that high exposure to violence content in the mass media weakens personal and social controls.[32] These new findings are based on probing fantasy and psychological responses of young people after exposure to violence content. They have special importance for lower class groups because of the high exposure of these groups to television. These lower class groups have less involvement in printed media, which has less violence material.

The issue runs deeper than the concentration of materials on violence in the mass media. It involves an assessment of the mass media's performance in disseminating a portrayal of the Negro and social change in depth. It also in-

[31] See *Christian Science Monitor*, Oct. 4, 1968 for details of a survey conducted by that newspaper's staff.

[32] Leonard Berkowitz, Ronald Corwin, and Mark Heironimus, "Film Violence and Subsequent Aggressive Tendencies," *Public Opinion Quarterly*, vol. XXVII (Summer 1963), pp. 217–229.

volves the access that the mass media extends to the creative talent of the Negro community. The Kerner Commission emphasized the lack of effective coverage of the problems of minority groups by the mass media and the absence of minority group members, especially Negroes, in operating and supervisory positions in these enterprises. The events of the riots and the recommendations of the Kerner Commission on this aspect of the mass media produced "crash" programs to recruit and train minority group personnel. The contents of the media have become more integrated, including advertising, and a long-run impact on public opinion is likely to be felt, especially in younger persons.

It is also necessary to assess the coverage of the riots themselves by television and the impact of this coverage on social control. For example, the National Advisory Commission on Civil Disorders sought to probe the immediate impact of the mass media coverage of the riots of the summer of 1967 both on the Negro community and on the nation as a whole. They commissioned a systematic content analysis study which, despite its quantitative approach, did not effectively penetrate the issue or even satisfy the Commission itself. The content study sought to determine if "the media had sensationalized the disturbances, consistently overplaying violence and giving disproportionate amounts of time to emotional events and militant leaders." [33] The conclusion was negative because of findings that, of 837 television sequences of riot and racial news examined, 494 were classified as calm, 262 as emotional, and 81 as normal. "Only a small proportion of all scenes analyzed showed actual mob action, people looting, sniping, setting fires or being killed or injured." In addition, moderate Negro leaders were shown on television more frequently than were militant leaders. Equivalent findings were reported for the printed media.

But such a statistical balance is no indicator of the impact of the presentation. Even calm and moral presentations of the riots could have had effect on both black and white communities; more certainly, persistent presentation of "hot" messages, even though they constitute only a part of the coverage, would have an impact. Therefore, the Commission modified and in effect rejected its own statistical findings and more appropriately concluded that in (1) "there were instances of gross flaws in presenting news of the 1967 riots"; and (2) the cumulative effect was important in that it "heightened reaction." "What the public saw and read last summer thus produced emotional reactions and left vivid impressions not wholly attributable to the material itself." The Commission concluded that "the main failure of the media last summer was that the totality of its coverage was not as representative as it should have been to be accurate."

The national crisis produced by escalated riots warranted massive coverage according to existing standards of mass media performance. The coverage was

---

[33] National Advisory Commission on Civil Disorders, p. 202.

so extensive that there was an imbalance in presentation of the total scene in the United States, and in particular, a failure to cover successful accomplishments by community leaders and law enforcement agencies. In fact, there were overtones in the coverage of racial violence which conformed to the "crime wave" pattern of news. The result was to bring into the scope of coverage violent events that would not have been reported under "normal" circumstances.

Television has served as the main instrument for impressing the grim realities of the riots onto the mass consciousness of the nation. On-the-spot reportage of the details of the minor riots and their aftermath was extensive and was buttressed by elaborate commentaries. If the fullest coverage of these events is deemed to be necessary as a basis for developing constructive social policy, the costs of such media coverage should not be overlooked. It is impossible to rule out the strong contention that detailed coverage of riots has had an effect on potential rioters. Such a contention does not rest on the occasional instance in which the television camera focused on the riot scene and led either rioters or police to play to the television audience. Of greater importance is the impact of pictures of the rioting on a wider audience. Again we are dealing with a process of social learning, especially for potential participants. Rioting is based on contagion, the process by which the mood and attitudes of those who are actually caught up in the riot are disseminated to a larger audience on the basis of direct contact. Television images serve to spread the contagion pattern throughout urban areas and the nation. Large audiences see the details of riots, the manner in which people participate in them, and especially the ferment associated with looting and obtaining commodities which was so much at the heart of riot behavior. Television presents detailed information about the tactics of participation and the gratifications that were derived.

A direct and realistic account of the tactical role of the mass media, in particular television, can be seen from specific case studies, such as reported in depth by Anthony Oberschall on the Watts riot. He writes:

> The success of the store breakers, arsonists, and looters in eluding the police can in part be put down to the role of the mass media during the riot week. The Los Angeles riot was the first one in which rioters were able to watch their actions on television. The concentration and movements of the police in the area were well reported on the air, better than that of the rioters themselves. By listening to the continuous radio and TV coverage, it was possible to deduce that the police were moving toward or away from a particular neighborhood. Those who were active in raiding stores could choose when and where to strike, and still have ample time for retreat. The entire curfew area is a very extended one.[34]

[34] Oberschall, Anthony, "The Los Angeles Riot of August 1965," Social Problems, pp. 335–336.

The media disseminate the rationalizations and symbols of identification used by the rioters. The mass media serve to reenforce and spread a feeling of consciousness among those who participate or sympathize with extremist actions, regardless of the actions' origins. In particular, television offers them a mass audience far beyond their most optimistic aspirations. Knowledge of the riot would spread in any case, but immediate extensive and detailed coverage both speeds up the process and gives it a special reality. On balance, I would argue that these images serve to reenforce predispositions to participate and even to legitimate participation. To be able to generate mass media coverage, especially television coverage, becomes an element in the motivation of the rioters. The sheer ability of the rioters to command mass media attention is an ingredient in developing legitimacy. In selected highbrow intellectual circles in the United States, a language of rationalization of violence has developed. The mass media serve to disseminate a popular version of such justification. The commentaries on television were filled with pseudo-sociological interpretations and the rioters themselves given ample opportunity to offer a set of suitable rationalizations.

In the past, when rioting was of the contested area variety, the newspapers were the major mass media. In many areas they developed an operational code, informally and formally, to deal with news about rioting. The practice was to apply an embargo on news about a riot during the actual period of the riot. After the event, it would be covered. The goal was to prevent the newspapers from serving as a means for mobilizing rioters, as was the case in the riots of Chicago in 1919. With the growth of television and the intensification of competition between the press and television, this practice broke down.

It is difficult to estimate the short- and long-term effects of the mass media portrayal of riots on white and Negro opinions. However, the riots projected a new element in the mass media imagery of the Negro, if only for a limited period of time. In the past, the mass media served to reenforce the system of segregation by casting the Negro exclusively in a minority position as well as by describing and characterizing him as weak. The portrait of the Negro as weak in the mass media served to mobilize and reenforce aggressive sentiments and emotions against these groups. The extremely prejudiced person is more disposed to release his aggression if he believes that the object of his aggression is too weak to respond to his hostile feelings and emotions.[35]

Since the end of World War II, the mass media have been helping to modify the imagery of the Negro and thereby to weaken the prejudiced symbolism. The advances of the Negro in economic, social, and political life have supplied a basis by which the mass media could project a more realistic and more favorable picture of the Negro. The reasoned and moral arguments in defense of racial equality by black and white leaders provide the subject for

[35] For a discussion of this psychological mechanism, see Bruno Bettelheim and Morris Janowitz, *Social Change and Prejudice* (New York: The Free Press, 1964).

extensive editorial commentary in the mass media. Mass media images of the Negro were enhanced by the role of Negro troops in the Korean conflict and by the increasing presentation of the Negro as policemen. Regardless of Negro leadership opinion on the war in South Vietnam, the Negro soldier's role has served to modify in a positive direction the image of the Negro in both white and Negro communities. The early phase of the civil-rights movement, with its emphasis on orderly and controlled demonstrations, served also to alter the symbolism of the Negro from that of a weak, powerless figure. The climax of this phase of change, as presented by the mass media, was the dramatic March on Washington led by the late Dr. Martin Luther King, Jr. As an event in the mass media, it was unique. The national media were focused on a predominantly black assemblage moving in an orderly and powerful fashion. In a real sense, it was a symbolic incorporation of the Negro into American society, because of the heavy emphasis on religion and the setting in the nation's capital.

In the elimination of prejudiced imagery, the Negro in the United States obviously has had to face much greater psychological barriers than any other minority group. Hostility and prejudice formed on the axis of color runs deep. Nevertheless, the secular trend in negative stereotypes toward the Negro from 1945 to 1965 has shown a dramatic decline, and the mass media have had an effect in this trend.

Even in the absence of adequate psychological studies in depth, some speculation is possible about the image projected by the riots. The view of Negroes as a group growing in strength and direction was for the moment shattered. Instead, a partial image of explosive irrationality has been dramatized. The use of sheer strength for destructive purposes rather than to achieve a goal that the white population could define as reasonable and worthwhile has served only to mobilize counter hostility and counteraggression. No doubt these images fade away as the mass media focus on reporting in depth the realities of the black community and the processes of social change that are at work.

● ● ●

Study Questions

1. It is said that America is becoming a society divided into two hostile groups—black and white. If this is true, what remedial actions would you recommend?
2. In recent years there has been an increase in the amount of violence by blacks. Why has the black responded violently after being non-violent for so many years? If the position of the black has improved in recent years, why has the level of violence increased?
3. Glazer states that it is necessary that a distinction be made between radical and liberal students. How do these groups differ? What should the response be to each of these groups?

4. What are the limitations of assuming that there is a simple division between events and the reporting thereof? Can the media contribute to violence by the manner in which they report these events? What can the media do to reduce the level of violence in society?

Suggestions for Further Reading

A Staff Report to the National Commission on the Causes and Prevention of Violence, Prepared by Hugh Davis and Ted Robert Gurr, *Violence in America: Historical and Comparative Perspectives.* Vol. I and II, Washington, D.C., United States Government Printing Office, 1969.

Abernathy, Glenn. *The Right of Assembly and Association.* Columbia, South Carolina: The University of South Carolina Press, 1961.

Adams, Jane. *The Spirit of Youth and the City Streets.* New York: The Macmillan Company, 1911.

Barton, Allan H. *Studying the Effects of College Education: A Methodological Examination of "Changing Values in College."* New Haven, Connecticut: W. Hazen Foundation, 1959.

Barzun, Jacques. *The House of Intellect.* New York: Harper & Row, 1959.

Bell, Daniel (ed.) *The New American Right.* New York: Criterion Books, 1955.

Bourne, Ralph S. *Youth and Life.* Boston: Houghton-Mifflin, 1913.

Coser, Lewis A. *Continuities in the Study of Social Conflict.* New York: E. P. Dutton and Company, 1968.

Crawley, Malcolm. *Exile's Return.* New York: Viking Press, 1961.

Dewey, John. *Democracy and Education.* New York: The Macmillan Company, 1961.

Freud, Sigmund. *Civilization and Its Discontents.* Garden City: Doubleday and Company, 1930.

Goodman, Paul. *Growing Up Absurd.* New York: Random House, 1960.

Hoffer, Eric. *The True Believer.* New York: Harper & Row, 1951.

Hutchins, Robert Maynard. *Some Observations on American Education.* New York: Cambridge University Press, 1956.

Jaspers, Karl. *The Idea of the University.* trans. H. A. T. Reiche and H. F. Vanderschmidt. Boston: Beacon Press, 1959.

Kerr, Clark. *The Uses of the University.* Cambridge: Harvard University Press, 1963.

Lasch, Christopher. *The New Radicalism in America 1889–1963.* New York: Random House, 1967.

Lipset, Seymour Martin. *Revolution and Counterrevolution: Change and Persistence in Social Structures.* New York: Basic Books, Inc., 1968.

Lipset, Seymour and Sheldon S. Wolin (eds.) *The Berkeley Student Revolt: Facts and Interpretations.* Garden City, New York: Anchor Books, 1963.

Marcuse, Herbert. *Eras and Civilization.* Boston: Beacon Press, 1955.

Nevins, Allen. *The State Universities and Democracy.* Urbana: University of Illinois Press, 1962.

Resek, Carl (ed.) *War and the Intellectuals, Essays by Ralph Bourne.* New York: Harper & Row, 1964.

Ross, Edward A. *Social Control: A Survey of the Foundations of Order.* New York: The Macmillan Company, 1916.

Rovere, Richard. *The American Establishment.* New York: Harcourt, Brace and World, 1962.

Thoreau, Henry D. *On the Duty of Civil Disobedience.* New Haven, Connecticut: Yale University Press, 1928.

Whitlock, Brad. *Forty Years of It.* New York: D. Appleton, 1914.

PART FIVE

The Politics of Ecology

One of the major issues of the 1970s will be that of saving our environment. This promises to be one of the most discussed and hotly debated topics for many years to come. There seems to be universal agreement that mankind has been with increasing speed and improving skill making this planet an unfit place for human habitation.

For most of man's history upon this planet, he has taken his environment for granted. He has assumed that there would always be an unlimited and abundant supply of land, clean air, and pure water. Concentrating upon the development of productive forces which he hoped would improve his standard of living and enable him to achieve the good life, he gave little thought to the possible adverse byproducts of this advancement.

It has now become obvious that land, air and water are vulnerable—that they can no longer be taken for granted. The world has gone through three revolutions important to ecology. The first involved the substitution of steam and electrical power for muscle, which enabled mankind to increase his productive power and was hailed as a great advancement. Along with this change, however, came certain side effects, such as air pollution, which rather than contributing to the ennobling of mankind served and continues to add to the degrading of human existence. The second revolution involved the mass production of "things." This also added to man's enjoyment of life, but not, however, without certain undesirable side effects, namely the solid-waste problem. The development of industrial chemistry, the third revolution, made possible the application of a wide variety of chemicals to be used, for example, as pesticides. These chemicals, however, have contributed to the poisoning and polluting of waters and the destruction of sea-life.

The problems of ecology are not confined to any particular country—it is a world problem. An examination of Soviet publications reveal that pollution of their waters is widespread and that the dumping of chemicals, oils, and acids into streams and rivers is creating problems of major proportions. The Soviet government is taking action to deal with the situation, but it will require tremendous capital investment over a period of many years.

Within a relatively brief period of time the ecological dilemma has burst forth in the American and world scene. Student dissent which had seemed to be almost exclusively concerned with the war in Southeast Asia and in constant conflicts with the "establishment," now is focused, too, upon the ecological issue. Persons of all political persuasions have sounded the clarion call. Even business and labor leaders agree upon the need for action to deal with the environmental problem. Members of the communications media have bombarded the public with information about the nature of the problem and have suggested solutions for dealing with it. Never before has there been such a high degree of consensus that if man is to survive upon this planet he must change his attitude and approach to the environment.

The enormity and the complexity of the problem staggers the imagination. Public understanding of the problem will require great effort and determination. The articles in this section are presented in an attempt to stimulate discussion about one of the major issues confronting mankind in the 1970s and beyond.

The National Environmental Act of 1969 clearly delineates our national environmental policy. The Act requires an annual Environmental Report from the President and establishes in the Executive Office of the President a Council on Environmental Quality. This Council is composed of three members appointed by the President with the advice and consent of the Senate. The Council is to assist the President in the preparation of the Environmental Quality Report. Moreover, it is authorized to gather information, analyze and interpret such information, and make recommendations to the President to improve and foster the environmental quality. The Council is to undertake research, studies, and investigations and consult with state and local governments, and representatives of science, industry, labor, agriculture, and other groups as it deems advisable.

In his message to Congress on the Environmental Quality on February 10, 1970, President Nixon discussed the problems which are gnawing at the quality of life for Americans. He called for greater citizen involvement and for new programs to ensure that government, industry, and individuals carry their share not only in doing the job but also by paying the cost. The President outlined a comprehensive 37-point program in the areas of water pollution control, air pollution control, solid waste management, parklands and public recreation and organization for action. In his message the President examined in detail what needs to be done in each of the five above mentioned areas. The President's program on environmental quality clearly represented a far-reaching commitment on the part of the Federal Government to improve our polluted environment. His program called not only for increased spending but also for more research, better coordination of activities and stricter enforcement measures.

Ralph Nader states that corporations are the main contributors to the long-term destruction of the environment. He suggests and discusses eight areas in which policies must be changed in order to bring pressure to bear on corporations and their officers to cease their destruction of the environment. He concludes by saying that we must preserve "the natural integrity of land, air, and water."

In the last article Gaylord A. Nelson examines in depth the cost of intervention in nature. It is difficult for anyone to do anything at all without affecting the well-being of others. Nelson discusses the cost of intervention in nature by giving several examples. He concludes that "the real loser in man's greedy drive is the youth of this country and the world. Because of the stupidity of their elders, the children of today face an ugly world in the near future, with dangerously and deadly polluted air and water; overcrowded development; festering mounds of debris; and an insufficient amount of open space to get away from it all."

NATIONAL ENVIRONMENTAL POLICY ACT OF 1969

Purpose
The purposes of this Act are: To declare a national policy which will encourage productive and enjoyable harmony between man and his environment; to promote efforts which will prevent or eliminate damage to the environment and biosphere and stimulate the health and welfare of man; to enrich the understanding of the ecological systems and natural resources important to the Nation; and to establish a Council on Environmental Quality.

TITLE I

Declaration of National Environmental Policy
Sec. 101. (a) The Congress, recognizing the profound impact of man's activity on the interrelations of all components of the natural environment, particularly the profound influences of population growth, high-density urbaniza-

SOURCE: The National Environmental Policy Act of 1969, House of Representatives, 91st Congress, 1st Session, Report No. 91–765, pp. 1–6.

tion, industrial expansion, resource exploitation, and new and expanding technological advances and recognizing further the critical importance of restoring and maintaining environmental quality to the overall welfare and development of man, declares that it is the continuing policy of the Federal Government, in cooperation with State and local governments, and other concerned public and private organizations, to use all practicable means and measures, including financial and technical assistance, in a manner calculated to foster and promote the general welfare, to create and maintain conditions under which man and nature can exist in productive harmony, and fulfill the social, economic, and other requirements of present and future generations of Americans.

(b) In order to carry out the policy set forth in this Act, it is the continuing responsibility of the Federal Government to use all practicable means, consistent with other essential considerations of national policy, to improve and coordinate Federal plans, functions, programs, and resources to the end that the Nation may—

1. fulfill the responsibilities of each generation as trustee of the environment for succeeding generations;

2. assure for all Americans safe, healthful, productive, and esthetically and culturally pleasing surroundings;

3. attain the widest range of beneficial uses of the environment without degradation, risk to health or safety, or other undesirable and unintended consequences;

4. preserve important historic, cultural, and natural aspects of our national heritage, and maintain, wherever possible, an environment which supports diversity and variety of individual choice;

5. achieve a balance between population and resource use which will permit high standards of living and a wide sharing of life's amenities; and

6. enhance the quality of renewable resources and approach the maximum attainable recycling of depletable resources.

(c) The Congress recognizes that each person should enjoy a healthful environment and that each person has a responsibility to contribute to the preservation and enhancement of the environment.

SEC. 102. The Congress authorizes and directs that, to the fullest extent possible: (1) the policies, regulations, and public laws of the United States shall be interpreted and administered in accordance with the policies set forth in this Act, and (2) all agencies of the Federal Government shall—

A. utilize a systematic, interdisciplinary approach which will insure the integrated use of the natural and social sciences and the environmental design arts in planning and in decisionmaking which may have an impact on man's environment;

B. identify and develop methods and procedures, in consultation with the Council on Environmental Quality established by title II of this Act, *which will insure that presently unquantified environmental amenities and values may be given appropriate consideration in decisionmaking along with economic and technical considerations;*

C. include in every recommendation or report on proposals for legislation and other major Federal actions significantly affecting the quality of the human environment, a detailed statement by the responsible official on—

i. the environmental impact of the proposed action,

ii. any adverse environmental effects which cannot be avoided should the proposal be implemented,

iii. alternatives to the proposed action,

iv. the relationship between local short-term uses of man's environment and the maintenance and enhancement of long-term productivity, and

v. any irreversible and irretrievable commitments of resources which would be involved in the proposed action should it be implemented.

Prior to making any detailed statement, the responsible Federal official shall consult with and obtain the comments of any Federal agency which has jurisdiction by law or special expertise with respect to any environmental impact involved. Copies of such statement and the comments and views of the appropriate Federal, State, and local agencies, which are authorized to develop and enforce environmental standards, shall be made available to the President, the Council on Environmental Quality and to the public;

D. study, develop, and describe appropriate alternatives to recommended courses of action in any proposal which involves unresolved conflicts concerning alternative uses of available resources;

E. recognize the worldwide and long-range character of environmental problems and, where consistent with the foreign policy of the United States, lend appropriate support to initiatives, resolutions, and programs designed to maximize international cooperation in anticipating and preventing a decline in the quality of mankind's world environment;

F. make available to States, counties, municipalities, institutions, and individuals, advice and information useful in restoring, maintaining, and enhancing the quality of the environment;

G. initiate and utilize ecological information in the planning and development of resource-oriented projects; and

H. assist the Council on Environmental Quality established by title II of this Act.

SEC. 103. *All agencies of the Federal Government shall review their present statutory authority, administrative regulations, and current policies and procedures for the purpose of determining whether there are any deficiencies or inconsistencies therein which prohibit full compliance with the purposes and provisions of this Act and shall propose to the President not later than July 1, 1971, such measures as may be necessary to bring their authority and policies into conformity with the intent, purposes, and procedures set forth in this Act.*

SEC. 104. *Nothing in Section 102 or 103 shall in any way affect the specific statutory obligations of any Federal agency (1) to comply with criteria or standards of environmental quality, (2) to coordinate or consult with any other Federal or State agency, or (3) to act, or refrain from acting contingent upon the recommendations or certification of any other Federal or State agency.*

SEC. 105. *The policies and goals set forth in this Act are supplementary to those set forth in existing authorizations of Federal agencies.*

TITLE II

Council on Environmental Quality

SEC. 201. *The President shall transmit to the Congress annually beginning July 1, 1970, an Environmental Quality Report (hereinafter referred to as the "report") which shall set forth (1) the status and condition of the major natural, manmade, or altered environmental classes of the Nation, including, but not limited to, the air, the aquatic, including marine, estuarine, and fresh water, and the terrestrial environment, including, but not limited to, the forest, dryland, wetland, range, urban, suburban, and rural environment; (2) current and foreseeable trends in the quality, management and utilization of such environments and the effects of those trends on the social, economic, and other requirements of the Nation; (3) the adequacy of available natural resources for fulfilling human and economic requirements of the Nation in the light of expected population pressures; (4) a review of the programs and activities (including regulatory activities) of the Federal Government, the State and local governments, and nongovernmental entities or individuals, with particular reference to their effect on the environment and on the conservation, development and utilization of natural resources; and (5) a program for remedying the deficiencies of existing programs and activities, together with recommendations for legislation.*

SEC. 202. *There is created in the Executive Office of the President a Council on Environmental Quality (hereinafter referred to as the "Council"). The Council shall be composed of three members who shall be appointed by the President to serve at his pleasure, by and with the advice and consent of the Senate. The President shall designate one of the members of the Council to serve as Chairman. Each member shall be a person who, as a result of his training, experience, and attainments, is exceptionally well qualified to analyze and interpret environmental trends and information of all kinds; to appraise programs and activities of the Federal Government in the light of the policy set forth in title I of this Act; to be conscious of and responsive to the scientific, economic, social, esthetic, and cultural needs and interests of the*

Nation; and to formulate and recommend national policies to promote the improvement of the quality of the environment.

SEC. 203. *The Council may employ such officers and employees as may be necessary to carry out its functions under this Act. In addition, the Council may employ and fix the compensation of such experts and consultants as may be necessary for the carrying out of its functions under this Act.*

SEC. 204. *It shall be the duty and function of the Council—*

1. *to assist and advise the President in the preparation of the Environmental Quality Report required by Section 201;*

2. *to gather timely and authoritative information concerning the conditions and trends in the quality of the environment both current and prospective, to analyze and interpret such information for the purpose of determining whether such conditions and trends are interfering, or are likely to interfere, with the achievement of the policy set forth in title I of this Act, and to compile and submit to the President studies relating to such conditions and trends;*

3. *to review and appraise the various programs and activities of the Federal Government in the light of the policy set forth in title I of this Act for the purpose of determining the extent to which such programs and activities are contributing to the achievement of such policy, and to make recommendations to the President with respect thereto;*

4. *to develop and recommend to the President national policies to foster and promote the improvement of environmental quality to meet the conservation, social, economic, health, and other requirements and goals of the Nation;*

5. *to conduct investigations, studies, surveys, research, and analyses relating to ecological systems and environmental quality;*

6. *to document and define changes in the natural environment, including the plant and animal systems, and to accumulate necessary data and other information for a continuing analysis of these changes or trends and an interpretation of their underlying causes;*

7. *to report at least once each year to the President on the state and condition of the environment; and*

8. *to make and furnish such studies, reports thereon, and recommendations with respect to matters of policy and legislation as the President may request.*

SEC. 205. *In exercising its powers, functions, and duties under this Act, the Council shall—*

1. *consult with the Citizens' Advisory Committee on Environmental Quality established by Executive Order numbered 11472, dated May 29, 1969, and with such representatives of science, industry, agriculture, labor, conservation organizations, State and local governments, and other groups, as it deems advisable; and,*

2. *utilize, to the fullest extent possible, the services, facilities, and in-*

formation (including statistical information) of public and private agencies and organizations, and individuals, in order that duplication of effort and expense may be avoided, thus assuring that the Council's activities will not unnecessarily overlap or conflict with similar activities authorized by law and performed by established agencies.

● ● ●

ENVIRONMENTAL QUALITY

RICHARD M. NIXON

Like those in the last century who tilled a plot of land to exhaustion and then moved on to another, we in this century have too casually and too long abused our natural environment. The time has come when we can wait no longer to repair the damage already done, and to establish new criteria to guide us in the future.

The fight against pollution, however, is not a search for villains. For the most part, the damage done to our environment has not been the work of evil men, nor has it been the inevitable by-product either of advancing technology or of growing population. It results not so much from choices made, as from choices neglected: not from malign intention, but from failure to take into account the full consequences of our actions.

Quite inadvertently, by ignoring environmental costs we have given an economic advantage to the careless polluter over his more conscientious rival. While adopting laws prohibiting injury to person or property, we have freely allowed injury to our shared surroundings. Conditioned by an expanding frontier, we came only late to a recognition of how precious and how vulnerable our resources of land, water, and air really are.

The tasks that need doing require money, resolve and ingenuity—and they are too big to be done by government alone. They call for fundamentally new philosophies of land, air and water use, for stricter regulation, for expanded government action, for greater citizen involvement, and for new programs to ensure that government, industry and individuals all are called on to do their share of the job and to pay their share of the cost.

Because the many aspects of environmental quality are closely interwoven, to consider each in isolation would be unwise. Therefore, I am today outlining a comprehensive, 37-point program, embracing 23 major legislative proposals and 14 new measures being taken by administrative action or Executive Order in five major categories:

SOURCE: Richard M. Nixon, "Environmental Quality," *Congressional Record*, Vol. 116, 91st Congress, Second Session, February 10, 1970 (Washington, D.C.: United States Government Printing Office, 1970), S1605–S1609, S1611.

—Water pollution control.
—Air pollution control.
—Solid waste management.
—Parklands and public recreation.
—Organizing for action.

As we deepen our understanding of complex ecological processes, as we improve our technologies and institutions and learn from experience, much more will be possible. But these 37 measures represent actions we can take *now*, and that can move us dramatically forward toward what has become an urgent common goal of all Americans: the rescue of our natural habitat as a place both habitable and hospitable to man.

WATER POLLUTION

Water pollution has three principal sources: municipal, industrial and agricultural wastes. All three must eventually be controlled if we are to restore the purity of our lakes and rivers.

Of these three, the most troublesome to control are those from agricultural sources: animal wastes, eroded soil, fertilizers and pesticides. Some of these are nature's own pollutions. The Missouri River was known as "Big Muddy" long before towns and industries were built on its banks. But many of the same techniques of pest control, livestock feeding, irrigation and soil fertilization that have made American agriculture so abundantly productive have also caused serious water pollution.

Effective control will take time, and will require action on many fronts: modified agricultural practices, greater care in the disposal of animal wastes, better soil conservation methods, new kinds of fertilizers, new chemical pesticides and more widespread use of natural pest control techniques. A number of such actions are already underway. We have taken action to phase out the use of DDT and other hard pesticides. We have begun to place controls on wastes from concentrated animal feedlots. We need programs of intensified research, both public and private, to develop new methods of reducing agricultural pollution while maintaining productivity. I have asked The Council on Environmental Quality to press forward in this area. Meanwhile, however, we have the technology and the resources to proceed *now* on a program of swift clean-up of pollution from the most acutely damaging sources: municipal and industrial wastes.

MUNICIPAL WASTES

As long as we have the means to do something about it, there is no good reason why municipal pollution of our waters should be allowed to persist unchecked.

In the four years since the Clean Waters Restoration Act of 1966 was passed, we have failed to keep our promises to ourselves: Federal appropriations for constructing municipal treatment plants have totaled only about one-third of authorizations. Municipalities themselves have faced increasing difficulty in selling bonds to finance their share of the construction costs. Given the saturated condition of today's municipal bond markets, if a clean-up program is to work it has to provide the means by which municipalities can finance their share of the cost even as we increase Federal expenditures.

The best current estimate is that it will take a total capital investment of about $10 billion over a five-year period to provide the municipal waste treatment plants and interceptor lines needed to meet our national water quality standards. This figure is based on a recently-completed nationwide survey of the deficiencies of present facilities, plus projections of additional needs that will have developed by then—to accommodate the normal annual increase in the volume of wastes, and to replace equipment that can be expected to wear out or become obsolete in the interim.

This will provide every community that needs it with secondary waste treatment, and also special, additional treatment in areas of special need, including communities on the Great Lakes. We have the industrial capacity to do the job in five years if we begin now.

To meet this construction schedule, I propose a two-part program of Federal assistance:

> —I propose a Clean Waters Act with $4 billion to be authorized immediately, for Fiscal 1971, to cover the full Federal share of the total $10 billion cost on a matching fund basis. This would be allocated at a rate of $1 billion a year for the next four years, with a reassessment in 1973 of needs for 1975 and subsequent years.

By thus assuring communities of full Federal support, we can enable planning to begin *now* for all needed facilities and construction to proceed at an accelerated rate.

> —I propose creation of a new Environmental Financing Authority, to ensure that every municipality in the country has an opportunity to sell its waste treatment plant construction bonds.

The condition of the municipal bond market is such that, in 1969, 509 issues totaling $2.9 billion proved unsalable. If a municipality cannot sell waste treatment plant construction bonds, EFA will buy them and will sell its own bonds on the taxable market. Thus, construction of pollution control facilities will depend not on a community's credit rating, but on its waste disposal needs.

Providing money is important, but equally important is where and how the money is spent. A river cannot be polluted on its left bank and clean on its right. In a given waterway, abating *some* of the pollution is often little better than doing nothing at all, and money spent on such partial efforts is often largely wasted. Present grant allocation formulas—those in the 1966 Act—have prevented the spending of funds where they could produce the greatest results in terms of clean water. Too little attention has been given to seeing that investments in specific waste treatment plants have been matched by other municipalities and industries on the same waterway. Many plants have been poorly designed and inefficiently operated. Some municipalities have offered free treatment to local industries, then not treated their wastes sufficiently to prevent pollution.

To ensure that the new funds are well invested, five major reforms are needed. One requires legislation: the other four will be achieved by administrative action.

—I propose that the present, rigid allocation formula be revised, so that special emphasis can be given to areas where facilities are most needed and where the greatest improvements in water quality will result.

Under existing authority, the Secretary of the Interior will institute four major reforms:

—Federally assisted treatment plants will be required to meet prescribed design, operation and maintenance standards, and to be operated only by State-certified operators.

—Municipalities receiving Federal assistance in constructing plants will be required to impose reasonable users' fees on industrial users sufficient to meet the costs of treating industrial wastes.

—Development of comprehensive river basin plans will be required at an early date, to ensure that Federally assisted treatment plants will in fact contribute to effective clean-up of entire river basin systems. Collection of existing data on pollution sources and development of effluent inventories will permit systems approaches to pollution control.

—Wherever feasible, communities will be strongly encouraged to cooperate in the construction of large regional treatment facilities, which provide economies of scale and give more efficient and more thorough waste treatment.

INDUSTRIAL POLLUTION

Some industries discharge their wastes into municipal systems; others discharge them directly into lakes and rivers. Obviously, unless we curb industrial as well as municipal pollution our waters will never be clean.

Industry itself has recognized the problem, and many industrial firms are making vigorous efforts to control their water-borne wastes. But strict standards and strict enforcement are nevertheless necessary—not only to ensure compliance, but also in fairness to those who have voluntarily assumed the often costly burden while their competitors have not. Good neighbors should not be placed at a competitive disadvantage because of their good neighborliness.

Under existing law, standards for water pollution control often are established in only the most general and insufficient terms: for example, by requiring all affected industries to install secondary treatment facilities. This approach takes little account of such crucial variables as the volume and toxicity of the wastes actually being discharged, or the capacity of a particular body of water to absorb wastes without becoming polluted. Even more important, it provides a poor basis for enforcement: with no effluent standard by which to measure, it is difficult to prove in court that standards are being violated.

The present fragmenting of jurisdictions also has hindered comprehensive efforts. At present, Federal jurisdiction generally extends only to interstate waters. One result has been that as stricter State-Federal standards have been imposed, pollution has actually increased in some other waters—in underground aquifers and the oceans. As controls over interstate waters are tightened, polluting industries will be increasingly tempted to locate on intrastate lakes and rivers—with a consequently increased threat to those waterways—unless they too are brought under the same strictures.

I propose that we take an entirely new approach: one which concerts Federal, State and private efforts, which provides for effective nationwide enforcement, and which rests on a simple but profoundly significant principle: that the Nation's waterways belong to us all, and that neither a municipality nor an industry should be allowed to discharge wastes into those waterways beyond their capacity to absorb the wastes without becoming polluted.

Specifically, I propose a seven-point program of measures we should adopt *now* to enforce control of water pollution from industrial and municipal wastes, and to give the States more effective backing in their own efforts.

> —I propose that State-Federal water quality standards be amended to impose precise effluent requirements on all industrial and municipal sources. These should be imposed on an expenditious timetable, with the limit for each based on a fair allocation of the total capacity of the waterway to absorb the user's particular kind of wastes without becoming polluted.
>
> —I propose that violation of established effluent requirements be considered sufficient cause for court action.
>
> —I propose that the Secretary of the Interior be allowed to proceed more swiftly in his enforcement actions, and that he be given new legal weapons including subpoena and discovery power.
>
> —I propose that failure to meet established water quality standards or implementation schedules be made subject to court-imposed fines of up to $10,000 per day.

—I propose that the Secretary of the Interior be authorized to seek immediate injunctive relief in emergency situations in which severe water pollution constitutes an imminent danger to health, or threatens irreversible damage to water quality.

—I propose that the Federal pollution-control program be extended to include all navigable waters, both inter- and intrastate, all interstate ground waters, the United States' portion of boundary waters, and waters of the Contiguous Zone.

—I propose that Federal operating grants to State pollution control enforcement agencies be tripled over the next five years—from $10 million now to $30 million in fiscal year 1975—to assist them in meeting the new responsibilities that stricter and expanded enforcement will place upon them.

AIR POLLUTION CONTROL

Air is our most vital resource, and its pollution is our most serious environmental problem. Existing technology for the control of air pollution is less advanced than that for controlling water pollution, but there is a great deal we can do within the limits of existing technology—and more we can do to spur technological advance.

Most air pollution is produced by the burning of fuels. About half is produced by motor vehicles.

MOTOR VEHICLES

The Federal Government began regulating automobile emissions of carbon monoxide and hydrocarbons with the 1968 model year. Standards for 1970 model cars have been made significantly tighter. This year, for the first time, emissions from new buses and heavy-duty trucks have also been brought under Federal regulation.

In future years, emission levels can and must be brought much lower.

The Secretary of Health, Education and Welfare is today publishing a notice of new, considerably more stringent motor vehicle emission standards he intends to issue for 1973 and 1975 models—including control of nitrogen oxides by 1973 and of particulate emissions by 1975.

These new standards represent our best present estimate of the lowest emission levels attainable by those years.

Effective control requires new legislation to correct two key deficiencies in the present law:

a) *Testing procedures.* Under present law, only manufacturers' prototype vehicles are tested for compliance with emission standards, and even this is voluntary rather than mandatory.

I propose legislation requiring that representative samples of actual production vehicles be tested throughout the model year.

b) *Fuel composition and additives.* What goes into a car's fuel has a major effect on what comes out of its exhaust, and also on what kinds of pollution-control devices can effectively be employed. Federal standards for what comes out of a car's engine should be accompanied by standards for what goes into it.

> I propose legislation authorizing the Secretary of Health, Education and Welfare to regulate fuel composition and additives.

With these changes, we can drastically reduce pollution from motor vehicles in the years just ahead. But in making and keeping our peace with nature, to plan only one year ahead or even five is hardly to plan at all. Our responsibility now is also to look beyond the Seventies, and the prospects then are uncertain. Based on present trends, it is quite possible that by 1980 the increase in the sheer number of cars in densely populated areas will begin outrunning the technological limits of our capacity to reduce pollution from the internal combustion engine. I hope this will not happen. I hope the automobile industry's present determined effort to make the internal combustion engine sufficiently pollution-free succeeds. But if it does not, then unless motor vehicles with an alternative, low-pollution power source are available, vehicle-caused pollution will once again begin an inexorable increase.

Therefore, prudence dictates that we move now to ensure that such a vehicle will be available if needed.

I am inaugurating a program to marshal both government and private research with the goal of producing an unconventionally powered, virtually pollution-free automobile within five years.

> —I have ordered the start of extensive Federal research and development program in unconventional vehicles, to be conducted under the general direction of the Council on Environmental Quality.
> —As an incentive to private developers, I have ordered that the Federal Government should undertake the purchase of privately produced unconventional vehicles for testing and evaluation.

A proposal currently before the Congress would provide a further incentive to private developers by authorizing the Federal government to offer premium prices for purchasing low-pollution cars for its own use. This could be a highly productive program once such automobiles are approaching development, although current estimates are that, initially, prices offered would have to be up to 200% of the cost of equivalent conventional vehicles rather than the 125% contemplated in the proposed legislation. The immediate task, however, is to see that an intensified program of research and development begins at once.

One encouraging aspect of the effort to curb motor vehicle pollution is the extent to which industry itself is taking the initiative. For example, the nation's principal automobile manufacturers are not only developing devices now to meet present and future Federal emission standards, but are also, on their own initiative, preparing to put on the market by 1972 automobiles which will not require and, indeed, must not use leaded gasoline. Such cars will not only discharge no lead into the atmosphere, but will also be equipped with still more effective devices for controlling emissions—devices made possible by the use of lead-free gasoline.

This is a great forward step taken by the manufacturers before any Federal regulation of lead additives or emissions has been imposed. I am confident that the petroleum industry will see to it that suitable non-leaded gasoline is made widely available for these new cars when they come on the market.

STATIONARY-SOURCE POLLUTION

Industries, power plants, furnaces, incinerators—these and other so-called "stationary sources" add enormously to the pollution of the air. In highly industrialized areas, such pollution can quite literally make breathing hazardous to health, and can cause unforeseen atmospheric and meteorological problems as well.

Increasingly, industry itself has been adopting ambitious pollution-control programs, and state and local authorities have been setting and enforcing stricter anti-pollution standards. But they have not gone far enough or fast enough, nor, to be realistic about it, will they be able to without the strongest possible Federal backing. Without effective government standards, industrial firms that spend the necessary money for pollution control may find themselves at a serious economic disadvantage as against their less conscientious competitors. And without effective Federal standards, states and communities that require such controls find themselves at a similar disadvantage in attracting industry, against more permissive rivals. Air is no respecter of political boundaries: a community that sets and enforces strict standards may still find its air polluted from sources in another community or another state.

Under the Clean Air Act of 1967, the Federal government is establishing air quality control regions around the nation's major industrial and metropolitan areas. Within these regions, states are setting air quality standards—permissible levels of pollutants in the air—and developing plans for pollution abatement to achieve those air quality standards. All state air quality standards and implementation plans require Federal approval.

This program has been the first major Federal effort to control air pollution. It has been a useful beginning. But we have learned in the past two years that it has shortcomings. Federal designation of air quality control regions, while necessary in areas where emissions from one state are polluting the air in another, has been a time-consuming process. Adjoining states within the same region often have proposed inconsistent air quality standards, causing further delays for compromise and revision. There are no provisions for controlling pollution *outside* of established air quality control regions. This means that even with the designation of hundreds of such regions, some areas of the country with serious air pollution problems would remain outside of the program. This is unfair not only to the public but to many industries as well, since those within regions with strict requirements could be unfairly disadvantaged with respect to competitors that are not within regions. Finally, insufficient Federal enforcement powers have circumscribed the Federal government's ability to support the states in establishing and enforcing effective abatement programs.

It is time to build on what we have learned, and to begin a more ambitious national effort. I recommend that the Clean Air Act be revised to expand the scope of strict pollution abatement, to simplify the task of industry in pollution abatement through more nearly uniform standards, and to provide special controls against particularly dangerous pollutants.

—I propose that the Federal government establish nationwide air quality standards, with the states to prepare within one year abatement plans for meeting those standards.

This will provide a minimum standard for air quality for all areas of the nation, while permitting states to set more stringent standards for any or all sections within the state. National air quality standards will relieve the states of the lengthy process of standard-setting under Federal supervision, and allow them to concentrate on the immediate business of developing and implementing abatement plans.

These abatement plans would cover areas both inside and outside of Federally designated air quality control regions, and could be designed to achieve any higher levels of air quality which the States might choose to establish. They would include emission standards for stationary sources of air pollution.

—I propose that designation of interstate air quality control regions continue at an accelerated rate, to provide a framework for establishing compatible abatement plans in interstate areas.

—I propose that the Federal government establish national emissions standards for facilities that emit pollutants extremely hazardous to health, and for selected classes of new facilities which could be major contributors to air pollution.

In the first instance, national standards are needed to guarantee the earliest possible elimination of certain air pollutants which are clear health hazards even in minute quantities. In the second instance, national standards will ensure that advanced abatement technology is used in constructing the new facilities, and that levels of air quality are maintained in the face of industrial expansion. Before any emissions standards were established, public hearings would be required involving all interested parties. The States would be responsible for enforcing these standards in conjunction with their own programs.

—I propose that Federal authority to seek court action be extended to include both inter- and intrastate air pollution situations in which, because of local non-enforcement, air quality is below national standards, or in which emissions standards or implementation timetables are being violated.

—I propose that failure to meet established air quality standards or implementation schedules be made subject to court-imposed fines of up to $10,000 per day.

SOLID WASTE MANAGEMENT

"Solid wastes" are the discarded leftovers of our advanced consumer society. Increasing in volume, they litter the landscape and strain the facilities of municipal governments.

New packaging methods, using materials which do not degrade and cannot easily be burned, create difficult new disposal problems. Though many wastes are potentially re-usable, we often discard today what a generation ago we saved. Most bottles, for example, now are "non-returnable." We re-process used paper less than we used to, not only adding to the burden on municipal sanitation services but also making wasteful use of scarce timberlands. Often the least expensive way to dispose of an old automobile is to abandon it—and millions of people do precisely that, creating eyesores for millions of others.

One way to meet the problem of solid wastes is simply to surrender to it: to continue pouring more and more public money into collection and disposal of whatever happens to be privately produced and discarded. This is the old way; it amounts to a public subsidy of waste pollution. If we are ever truly to gain control of the problem, our goal must be broader: to reduce the volume of wastes and the difficulty of their disposal, and to encourage their constructive re-use instead.

To accomplish this, we need incentives, regulations and research directed especially at two major goals: a) making products more easily disposable—especially containers, which are designed for disposal; and b) re-using and recycling a far greater proportion of waste materials.

As we look toward the long-range future—to 1980, 2000 and beyond—recycling of materials will become increasingly necessary not only for waste disposal but also to conserve resources. While our population grows, each one of us keeps using more of the earth's resources. In the case of many common minerals, more than half those extracted from the earth since time began have been extracted since 1910.

A great deal of our space research has been directed toward creating self-sustaining environments, in which people can live for long periods of time by re-processing, recycling and re-using the same materials. We need to apply this kind of thinking more consciously and more broadly to our patterns of use and disposal of materials here on earth.

Many currently used techniques of solid waste disposal remain crudely deficient. Research and development programs under the Solid Waste Disposal Act of 1965 have added significantly to our knowledge of more efficient techniques. The Act expires this year. I recommend its extension, and I have already moved to broaden its programs.

> I have ordered a re-direction of research under the Solid Waste Disposal Act to place greater emphasis on techniques for recycling materials, and on development and use of packaging and other materials which will degrade after use—that is, which will become temporary rather than permanent wastes.

Few of America's eyesores are so unsightly as its millions of junk automobiles.

Ordinarily, when a car is retired from use it goes first to a wrecker, who strips it of its valuable parts, and then to a scrap processor, who reduces the remainder to scrap for sale to steel mills. The prices paid by wreckers for junk cars often are less than the cost of transporting them to the wrecking yard. In the case of a severely damaged or "cannibalized" car, instead of paying for it the wrecker may even charge towing costs. Thus the final owner's economic incentive to deliver his car for processing is slight, nonexistent or even negative.

The rate of abandonment is increasing. In New York City, 2,500 cars were towed away as abandoned on the streets in 1960. In 1964, 25,000 were towed away as abandoned; in 1969, more than 50,000.

The way to provide the needed incentive is to apply to the automobile the principle that its price should include not only the cost of producing it, but also the cost of disposing of it.

> I have asked the Council on Environmental Quality to take the lead in producing a recommendation for a bounty payment or other system to promote the prompt scrapping of all junk automobiles.

The particular disposal problems presented by the automobile are unique. However, wherever appropriate we should also seek to establish incentives and regulations to encourage the re-use, recycling or easier disposal of other commonly used goods.

> I have asked the Chairman of the Council on Environmental Quality to work with the Cabinet Committee on the Environment, and with appropriate industry and consumer representatives, toward development of such incentives and regulations for submission to the Congress.

PARKS AND PUBLIC RECREATION

Increasing population, increasing mobility, increasing incomes and increasing leisure will all combine in the years ahead to rank recreational facilities among the most vital of our public resources. Yet land suitable for such facilities, especially near heavily populated areas, is being rapidly swallowed up.

Plain common sense argues that we give greater priority to acquiring now the lands that will be so greatly needed in a few years. Good sense also argues that the Federal Government itself, as the nation's largest landholder, should address itself more imaginatively to the question of making optimum use of its own holdings in a recreation-hungry era.

> —I propose full funding in fiscal 1971 of the $327 million available through the Land and Water Conservation Fund for additional park and recreational facilities, with increased emphasis on locations that can be easily reached by the people in crowded urban areas.
> —I propose that we adopt a new philosophy for the use of Federally-owned lands, treating them as a precious resource—like money itself—which should be made to serve the highest possible public good.

Acquiring needed recreation areas is a real estate transaction. One third of all the land in the United States—more than 750,000,000 acres—is owned by the Federal Government. Thousands of acres in the heart of metropolitan areas are reserved for only minimal use by Federal installations. To supplement the regularly-appropriated funds available, nothing could be more appropriate than to meet new real estate needs through use of presently-owned real estate, whether by transfer, sale or conversion to a better use.

Until now, the uses to which Federally-owned properties were put has largely been determined by who got them first. As a result, countless properties with enormous potential as recreation areas linger on in the hands of agencies that could just as well—or better—locate elsewhere. Bureaucratic inertia is compounded by a quirk of present accounting procedures, which has the effect of imposing a budgetary penalty on an agency that gives up one piece of property and moves to another, even if the vacated property is sold for 10 times the cost of the new.

The time has come to make more rational use of our enormous wealth to real property, giving a new priority to our newly urgent concern with public recreation—and to make more imaginative use of properties now surplus to finance acquisition of properties now needed.

> —By Executive Order, I am directing the heads of all Federal agencies and the Administrator of General Services to institute a review of all Federally-owned real properties that should be considered for other uses. The test will be whether a particular property's continued present use or another would better serve the public interest, considering both the agency's needs and the property's location. Special emphasis will be placed on identifying properties that could appropriately be converted to parks and recreation areas, or sold, so that proceeds can be made available to provide additional park and recreation lands.

—I am establishing a Property Review Board to review the GSA reports and recommend to me what properties should be converted or sold. This Board will consist of the Director of the Bureau of the Budget, the Chairman of the Council of Economic Advisers, the Chairman of the Council on Environmental Quality and the Administrator of General Services, plus others that I may designate.

—I propose legislation to establish, for the first time, a program for relocating Federal installations that occupy locations that could better be used for other purposes.

This would allow a part of the proceeds from the sales of surplus properties to be used for relocating such installations, thus making more land available.

—I also propose accompanying legislation to protect the Land and Water Conservation Fund, ensuring that its sources of income would be maintained and possibly increased for purchasing additional parkland.

The net effect would be to increase our capacity to add new park and recreational facilities, by enabling us for the first time to use surplus property sales in a coordinated three-way program: a) by direct conversion from other uses; b) through sale of presently-owned properties and purchase of others with the proceeds; and c) by sale of one Federal property, and use of the proceeds to finance the relocation and conversion costs of making another property available for recreational use.

—I propose that the Department of the Interior be given authority to convey surplus real property to State and local governments for park and recreation purposes at a public benefit discount ranging up to 100 percent.

—I propose that Federal procedures be revised to encourage Federal agencies to make efficient use of real property. This revision should remove the budgetary penalty now imposed on agencies relinquishing one site and moving to another.

As one example of what such a property review can make possible, a sizable stretch of one of California's finest beaches has long been closed to the public because it was part of Camp Pendleton. Last month the Defense Department arranged to make more than a mile of that beach available to the State of California for use as a State park. The remaining beach is sufficient for Camp Pendleton's needs; thus the released stretch represents a shift from low-priority to high-priority use. By carefully weighing alternative uses, a priceless recreational resource was returned to the people for recreational purposes.

Another vast source of potential parklands also lies untapped. We have come to realize that we have too much land available for growing crops and not enough land for parks, open space and recreation.

—I propose that instead of simply paying each year to keep this land idle, we help local governments buy selected parcels of it to provide recreational facilities for use by the people of towns in rural areas. This program has been tried, but allowed to lapse; I propose that we revive and expand it.

—I propose that we also adopt a program of long-term contracts with private owners of idled farmland, providing for its reforestation and public use for such pursuits as hunting, fishing, hiking and picnicking.

ORGANIZING FOR ACTION

The environmental problems we face are deep-rooted and widespread. They can be solved only by a full national effort embracing not only sound, coordinated planning, but also an effective follow-through that reaches into every community in the land. Improving our surroundings is necessarily the business of us all.

At the Federal level, we have begun the process of organizing for this effort.

The Council on Environmental Quality has been established. This Council will be the keeper of our environmental conscience, and a goad to our ingenuity; beyond this, it will have responsibility for ensuring that all our programs and actions are undertaken with a careful respect for the needs of environmental quality. I have already assigned it major responsibilities for new program development, and I shall look to it increasingly for new initiatives.

The Cabinet Committee on the Environment, which I created last year, acts as a coordinating agency for various departmental activities affecting the environment.

To meet future needs, many organizational changes will still be needed. Federal institutions for dealing with the environment and natural resources have developed piecemeal over the years in response to specific needs, not all of which were originally perceived in the light of the concerns we recognize today. Many of their missions appear to overlap, and even to conflict. Last year I asked the President's Advisory Council on Executive Organization, headed by Mr. Roy Ash, to make an especially thorough study of the organization of Federal environmental, natural resource and oceanographic programs, and to report its recommendations to me by April 15. After receiving their report, I shall recommend needed reforms, which will involve major reassignments of responsibilities among Departments.

For many of the same reasons, overlaps in environmental programs extend to the Legislative as well as the Executive branch, so that close consultation will be necessary before major steps are taken.

No matter how well organized government itself might be, however, in the final analysis the key to success lies with the people of America.

Private industry has an especially crucial role. Its resources, its technology, its demonstrated ingenuity in solving problems others only talk about—all these are needed, not only in helping curb the pollution industry itself creates but also in helping devise new and better ways of enhancing all aspects of our environment.

> I have ordered that the United States Patent Office give special priority to the processing of applications for patents which could aid in curbing environmental abuses.

Industry already has begun moving swiftly toward a fuller recognition of its own environmental responsibilities, and has made substantial progress in many areas. However, more must be done.

Mobilizing industry's resources requires organization. With a remarkable degree of unanimity, its leaders have indicated their readiness to help.

> I will shortly ask a group of the nation's principal industrial leaders to join me in establishing a National Industrial Pollution Control Council.

The Council will work closely with the Council on Environmental Quality, the Citizens' Advisory Committee on Environmental Quality, the Secretary of Commerce and others as appropriate in the development of effective policies for the curbing of air, water, noise and waste pollution from industrial sources. It will work to enlist increased support from business and industry in the drive to reduce pollution, in all its forms, to the minimum level possible. It will provide a mechanism through which, in many cases, government can work with key leaders in various industries to establish voluntary programs for accomplishing desired pollution-control goals.

Patterns of organization often turn out to be only as good as the example set by the organizer. For years, many Federal facilities have themselves been among the worst polluters. The Executive Order I issued last week not only accepts responsibility for putting a swift end to Federal pollution, but puts teeth into the commitment.

I hope this will be an example for others.

At the turn of the century, our chief environmental concern was to conserve what we had—and out of this concern grew the often embattled but always determined "conservation" movement. Today, "conservation" is as important as ever—but no longer is it enough to conserve what we have; we must also restore what we have lost. We have to go beyond conservation to embrace restoration.

The task of cleaning up our environment calls for a total mobilization by all of us. It involves governments at every level; it requires the help of every citizen. It cannot be a matter of simply sitting back and blaming someone else. Neither is it one to be left to a few hundred leaders. Rather, it presents us with one of those rare situations in which each individual everywhere has an opportunity to make a special contribution to his country as well as his community.

Through the Council on Environmental Quality, through the Citizens' Advisory Committee on Environmental Quality, and working with Governors and Mayors and county officials and with concerned private groups, we shall be reaching out in an effort to enlist millions of helping hands, millions of willing spirits—millions of volunteer citizens who will put to themselves the simple question: "What can I do?"

It is in this way—with vigorous Federal leadership, with active enlistment of governments at every level, with the aid of industry and private groups, and above all with the determined participation by individual citizens in every state and every community, that we at last will succeed in restoring the kind of environment we want for ourselves, and the kind the generations that come after deserve to inherit.

This task is ours together. It summons our energy, our ingenuity and our conscience in a cause as fundamental as life itself.

● ● ●

PRESIDENT'S MESSAGE TO THE CONGRESS ON THE ENVIRONMENT

I. The 37-Point Program

WATER POLLUTION. 1. Authorization of $4 billion to cover the Federal share of $10 billion needed for construction of municipal waste treatment plants. To be allocated at a rate of $1 billion per year over the next four years, with a reassessment in 1973 of further needs for 1973 and subsequent years.

2. Establishment of Environmental Financing Authority to ensure that every municipality can finance its share of treatment plant construction costs.

3. Revision of statutory formula governing allocation of grants for treatment plant construction, to permit construction of plants where need is greatest and where greatest improvements in water quality will result.

4. Requirement that treatment plants be built to prescribed design, operation and maintenance standards, and be operated only by certified operators.

5. Requirement that municipalities impose users fees on industrial users sufficient to meet costs of treating industrial wastes.

6. Requirement of comprehensive river basin plans, to assure that construction of municipal treatment plants is complimented by abatement of all other sources of water pollution.

7. Encouragement of construction of large-scale, regional treatment facilities.

8. Extension of Federal-State water quality standards to include precise effluent standards for all industrial and municipal sources.

9. Provision that violation of established water quality standards is sufficient cause for court action.

10. Revision of Federal enforcement procedures to permit swifter court action against those in violation of water quality standards.

11. Provision that violation of established water quality standards is subject to court-imposed fines of up to $10,000 per day.

12. Authorization for the Secretary of the Interior to seek immediate injunctions where severe water pollution threatens imminent danger to health or irreversible damage to water environment.

13. Extension of Federal pollution control authority to include all navigable waters, both inter- and intrastate, all interstate ground waters, the United States' portion of boundary waters, and waters of the Contiguous Zone.

14. Tripling of Federal operating grants to state pollution agencies—from $10 million now to $30 million in 1975.

AIR POLLUTION. 15. Publication of new, more stringent motor vehicle emissions standards for 1973 and 1975.

16. Revision of auto emissions enforcement procedures, to ensure that all new autos are in compliance with Federal standards.

17. Authorization for the Secretary of Health, Education and Welfare to regulate gasoline composition and additives.

18. Initiation of a research and development program to produce an unconventionally-powered, low-pollution auto within five years.

19. Initiation of testing and evaluation programs to assist private developers of unconventional, low-pollution autos.

20. Establishment of national air quality standards, with the states preparing abatement enforcement plans to meet national standards.

21. Accelerate designation of inter-state air quality control regions.

22. Establishment of national emissions standards for pollutants that are extremely hazardous to health and for specified classes of new facilities.

23. Extension of Federal air pollution control authority to both inter- and intrastate situations.

24. Provision that violation of air quality standards and national emissions standards are subject to court-imposed fines of up to $10,000 per day.

SOLID WASTE MANAGEMENT. 25. Re-direction of solid waste research toward techniques for recycling materials and producing packaging materials that are easily degradable.

26. Council on Environmental Quality to develop bounty payment or similar system to ensure prompt scrapping and recycling of junk automobiles.

27. Council on Environmental Quality to work with appropriate industry and consumer groups to develop other incentives or regulations for re-cycling or easier disposal of consumer goods.

INDUSTRIAL INVOLVEMENT. 28. Establishment of National Industrial Pollution Control Council.

29. Priority treatment for patent applications which could aid in curbing environmental abuses.

PARKS AND RECREATION. 30. Full funding of the $327 million available under the Land and Water Conservation Fund.

31. Review of all Federally-owned real estate to identify properties that can be converted to public recreational use, or sold, with proceeds used to acquire additional recreational areas.

32. Relocation of Federal installations that occupy locations that could better be used for other purposes.

33. Provision that the Land and Water Conservation Fund is maintained or increased as a source of funds for purchase of lands in future years.

34. Authorization for the Department of the Interior to convey surplus real property to State and local governments for park and recreational purposes at public benefit discounts of up to 100%.

35. Revision of budget accounting procedures to encourage Federal agencies to make more efficient use of their properties.

36. Assistance to State and local governments for making constructive recreational use of idled farmlands.

37. Authorization of long-term contracts with owners of idled farmlands for reforestation and other improvements for public recreational use.

CORPORATIONS AND POLLUTION

RALPH NADER

The modern corporation's structure, impact, and public accountability are the central issues in any program designed to curb or forestall the contamination of air, water, and soil by industrial activity. While there are other sources of pollution, such as municipalities dumping untreated or inadequately treated sewage, industrial processes and products are the chief contributors to the long-term destruction of natural resources that each year increases the risks to human health and safety.

Moreover, through active corporate citizenship, industry could soon overcome many of the obstacles in the way of curbing non-corporate pollution. The mighty automobile industry, centered around and in Detroit, never thought it part of its role to press the city of Detroit to construct a modern sewage treatment plant. The automobile moguls, whose products, according

SOURCE: Ralph Nader, "The Profits in Pollution," *The Progressive*, 34 (April 1970), 19–22. Copyright R. Nader. Reprinted by permission.

to Department of Health, Education and Welfare data, account for fifty-five to sixty per cent of the nation's air pollution, remained silent as the city's obsolete and inadequate sewage facilities dumped the wastes of millions into the Detroit River. Obviously, local boosterism does not include such elementary acts of corporate citizenship.

The toilet training of industry to keep it from further rupturing the ecosystem requires an overhaul of the internal and external levers which control corporations. There are eight areas in which policies must be changed to create the pressures needed to make corporate entities and the people who run them cease their destruction of the environment:

ONE—The conventional way of giving the public a share in private decisions that involve health and safety hazards is to establish mandatory standards through a public agency. But pollution control standards set by governmental agencies can fall far short of their purported objectives unless they are adequately drafted, kept up to date, vigorously enforced, and supported by sanctions when violated. Behind the adoption of such standards, there is a long administrative process, tied to a political infrastructure. The scientific-engineering-legal community has a key independent role to play in this vital and complex administrative-political process. Almost invariably, however, its talents have been retained on behalf of those to be regulated. Whether in Washington or in state capitals around the country, the experts demonstrate greater loyalty to their employers than to their professional commitments in the public interest.

This has been the regular practice of specialists testifying in behalf of coal and uranium mining companies on the latters' environmental contamination in Appalachia and the Rocky Mountain regions. Perhaps the most egregious example of willing corporate servility was a paper entitled "We've Done the Job—What's Next?" delivered by Charles M. Heinen, Chrysler's vehicle emissions specialist, at a meeting of the Society of Automotive Engineers last spring.

Heinen, whose paper bordered on technical pornography, said the auto industry had solved the vehicle pollution problem with an eighty per cent reduction of hydrocarbons and a seventy per cent reduction of carbon monoxide between the 1960 and 1970 model years. He avoided mentioning at least four other vehicle pollutants—nitrogen oxides, lead, asbestos, and rubber tire pollutants. He also failed to point out that the emissions control performance of new cars degrades after a few thousand miles, and that even when new they do not perform under traffic conditions as they do when finely tuned at a company test facility. The overall aggregate pollution from ever greater numbers of vehicles in more congested traffic patterns also escaped Heinen's company-indentured perceptions.

TWO—Sanctions against polluters are feeble and out of date, and, in any case, are rarely invoked. For example, the Federal air quality act has no criminal penalties no matter how willful and enduring the violations. In New Jersey, New York, and Illinois, a seventy-one year old Federal anti-water pollution law was violated with total impunity by industry until the Justice Department moved against a few of the violators in recent months. Other violators in other states are yet to be subjected to the law's enforcement. To be effective, sanctions should come in various forms, such as non-reimbursable fines, suspensions, dechartering of corporations, required disclosure of violations in company promotional materials, and more severe criminal penalties. Sanctions, consequently, should be tailored to the seriousness and duration of the violation.

It is expressive of the anemic and nondeterrent quality of existing sanctions that offshore oil leaks contaminating beaches for months, as in Santa Barbara, brought no penalty to any official of any offending company. The major controversy in Santa Barbara was whether the company—Union Oil—or the Government or the residents would bear the costs of cleaning up the mess. And even if the company bore the costs initially, the tax laws would permit a considerable shifting of this cost onto the general taxpayer.

THREE—The existing requirements for disclosure of the extent of corporate pollution are weak and flagrantly flouted. The Federal Water Pollution Control Administration (FWPCA) has been blocked since 1963 by industrial polluters (working with the Federal Bureau of the Budget) from obtaining information from these companies concerning the extent and location of discharges of pollutants into the nation's waterways. For three years, the National Industrial Waste Inventory has been held up by the Budget Bureau and its industry "advisers," who have a decisive policy role. Led by the steel, paper, and petroleum industries, corporate polluters have prevented the FWPCA from collecting specific information on what each company is putting into the water. Such information is of crucial importance to the effective administration of the water pollution law and the allocation of legal responsibility for violations.

Counties in California have been concealing from their citizens the identity of polluters and the amounts of pollution, using such weak, incredible arguments to support their cover-up as the companies' fear of revealing "trade secrets." California state agencies have refused to disclose pesticide application data to representatives of orchard workers being gradually poisoned by the chemicals. Once again the trade secret rationale was employed.

The real reason for secrecy is that disclosure of such information would raise public questions about why government agencies have not been doing their jobs—and would facilitate legal action by injured persons against the polluters. What must be made clear to both corporate and public officials is that no one has the right to a trade secret in lethality.

Massive and meticulous "fish bowl" disclosure requirements are imperative if citizens are to be alerted, at the earliest possible moment, to the flow of silent violence assaulting their health and safety, and that of unborn generations as well. This disclosure pattern, once established, must not lapse into a conspiracy between private and public officials, a conspiracy of silence against citizens and the public interest. A good place to start with such company-by-company disclosure is in the corporation's annual report, which now reveals only financial profits or losses; it should also reveal the social costs of pollution by composition and tonnage.

FOUR—Corporate investment in research and development of pollution controls is no longer a luxury to be left to the decision or initiative of a few company officers. Rather, such research and development must be required by law to include reinvestments of profits, the amount depending on the volume of pollution inflicted on the public. For example, in 1969 General Motors grossed $24 billion, yet last year spent less than $15 million on vehicle and plant pollution research and development, although its products and plants contribute some thirty-five per cent of the nation's air pollution by tonnage. A formula proportional to the size of a company and its pollution could be devised as law, with required periodic reporting of the progress of the company's research and its uses. A parallel governmental research and development program aimed at developing pollution-free product prototypes suitable for mass production, and a Federal procurement policy favoring the purchase of less-polluting products, are essential external impacts.

FIVE—Attention must be paid to the internal climate for free expression and due process within the corporate structure. Again and again, the internal discipline of the corporate autocracy represses the civic and professional spirit of employes who have every right to speak out or blow the whistle on their company after they have tried in vain, working from the inside, to bring about changes that will end pollution practices. Professional employes—scientists, engineers, physicians—have fewer due process safeguards than the blue collar workers in the same company protected by their union contract.

When Edward Gregory, a Fisher Body plant inspector for General Motors in St. Louis, publicly spoke out in 1966 on inadequate welding that exposed Chevrolet passengers to exhaust leakage, the company ignored him for a few years, but eventually recalled more than two million cars for correction. GM knew better than to fire Gregory, a member of the United Auto Workers.

In contrast, scientists and engineers employed by corporations privately tell me of their reluctance to speak out—within their companies or outside them —about hazardous products. This explains why the technical elites are rarely in the vanguard of public concern over corporate contamination. Demotion, ostracism, dismissal are some of the corporate sanctions against which there is little or no recourse by the professional employe. A new corporate constitutionalism is needed, guaranteeing employes' due process rights against arbitrary reprisals, but its precise forms require the collection of data and extensive study. Here is a major challenge to which college faculty and students can respond on the campus and in field work.

SIX—The corporate shareholder can act, as he rarely does, as a prod and lever for jolting corporate leaders out of their lethargy. The law and the lawyers have rigged the legal system to muffle the voice of shareholders, particularly those concerned with the broader social costs of corporate enterprise. However, for socially conscious and determined stockholders there are many functions that can be performed to help protect the public (including themselves) from industrial pollution.

Shareholders must learn to take full advantage of such corporate practices as cumulative voting, which permits the "single-shot" casting of all of a shareholder's ballots for one member of the board of directors. Delegations of stockholders can give visibility to the issues by lobbying against their company's ill-advised policies in many forums apart from the annual meeting—legislative hearings, agency proceedings, town meetings, and the news media, for example. These delegations will be in a position to expose company officers to public judgment, something from which executives now seem so insulated in their daily corporate activities.

SEVEN—Natural, though perhaps unexercised, countervailing forces in the private sector can be highly influential incentives for change. For example, the United Auto Workers have announced that pollution will be an issue in the collective bargaining process with automobile company management this year; the union hopes to secure for workers the right not to work in polluting activities, or in a polluted environment. Insurance companies could become advocates for loss prevention in the environmental field when confronted with policyholder, shareholder, and citizen demonstrative action. Through their political influence, their rating function in evaluating risks and setting premium charges, and their research and development capability, insurance companies could exert a key countervailing stress on polluters. Whether they do or not will first depend on citizen groups to whip them into action.

EIGHT—Environmental lawsuits, long blocked by a conservative judiciary and an inflexible judicial system, now seem to be coming into their own—a classic example of how heightened public expectations, demands, and the availability of facts shape broader applications of ancient legal principles. Environmental pollution is environmental violence—to human beings and to property. The common law has long recognized such violence against the person as actionable or enjoinable. What has been lacking is sufficient evidence of harm and avoidability to persuade judges that such hitherto invisible long-range harm outweighed the economic benefits of the particular plant activity in the community.

It now appears that such lawsuits will gain greater acceptance, especially as more evidence and more willing lawyers combine to breathe contemporary reality into long-standing legal principles. An amendment to the U.S. Constitution providing citizens with basic rights to a clean environment has been proposed; similar amendments to state constitutions are being offered. Such generic provisions can only further the judicial acceptance of environmental lawsuits. Imaginative and bold legal advocacy is needed here. The *forced consumption* of industrial pollutants by 200 million Americans must lead to a recognition of legal rights in environmental control such as that which developed with civil rights for racial minorities over the last two decades.

Three additional points deserve the attention of concerned citizens:

First, a major corporate strategy in combating antipollution measures is to engage workers on the company side by leading them to believe that such measures would threaten their livelihood. This kind of industrial extortion in a community—especially a company town—has worked before and will again unless citizens anticipate and confront it squarely.

Second, both industry spokesmen and their governmental allies (such as the President's Science Adviser, Lee DuBridge) insist that consumers will have to pay the price of pollution control. While this point of view may be an unintended manifestation of the economy's administered price structure, it cannot go unchallenged. Pollution control must not become another lever to lift up excess profits and fuel the fires of inflation. The costs of pollution control technology should come from corporate profits which have been enhanced by the use of the public's environment as industry's private sewer. The sooner industry realizes that it must bear the costs of cleanups, the more likely it will be to employ the quickest and most efficient techniques.

Finally, those who believe deeply in a humane ecology must act in accordance with their beliefs. They must so order their consumption and disposal habits that they can, in good conscience, preach what they actually practice. In brief, they must exercise a personal discipline as they advocate the discipline of governments and corporations.

The battle of the environmentalists is to preserve the physiological integrity of people by preserving the natural integrity of land, air, and water. The planet earth is a seamless structure with a thin slice of sustaining air, water, and soil that supports almost four billion people. This thin slice belongs to all of us, and we use it and hold it in trust for future earthlings. Here we must take our stand.

OUR POLLUTED PLANET

GAYLORD A. NELSON

Man lives on a limited, finite planet that spins in a mathematically precise orbit in the dead vacuum of space. The uniqueness of man's planet earth is that it is the only body in the solar system capable of supporting life.

SOURCE: Gaylord A. Nelson, "Our Polluted Planet," *The Progressive*, 33 (November 1969), 13–17. Reprinted by permission.

Just how long it will be able to sustain life, however, is a question that is causing increasing concern to many scientists and ecologists. Our planet has only a thin veneer of soil that is supporting rapidly diminishing forests and a dwindling variety of animal species.

The scientists and ecologists have been warning for years that earth's resources are not endless and that soaring population growth and blind disregard for the most vital resources of air and water could bring disaster. They have stepped up their warnings of pending disaster, because they believe that the end is virtually imminent. Every major watershed in America has been polluted by the unbridled expansion of business and industry and by municipalities unwilling to clean their wastes adequately before dumping. Lake Erie, an important fresh water supply for millions of people, is almost dead, and most other major bodies of water in the nation are close behind.

Even the vast oceans, which make up three-fourths of the surface of the globe, face disaster and destruction. Man has looked to the oceans as the future source of food protein when the land becomes too crowded and too overworked to produce enough. But the pollution of the seas has become so serious that one noted ecologist has flatly predicted that the end of life in the seas could come in ten years.

Evidence of nature in rebellion has already been seen in the oceans, as mysterious events take place which scientists have under study. In the South Pacific, a marauding starfish is destroying coral reefs; without these barriers, many islands, including the Hawaiian, will lie unprotected from the pounding seas. Scientists are guessing that dredging, underwater blasting, overuse of lingering pesticides, or even radioactive fallout have killed the starfish's natural enemies.

In the past year, other events have been observed that have brought death to thousands of creatures living in and around the sea. Some were killed by the ugly oil spills off the coasts of California and Southern England. Some, however, remain unexplained—with only the dead fish, birds, clams, or crabs, tumbling by the thousands in the surf, indicating that something serious was wrong.

There is almost no way to escape the poisons of pollution. Day after day the thin envelope of air that surrounds the earth is mixed with the belching smoke and soot of tens of thousands of industrial smokestacks and incinerators and the deadly fumes from millions of automobiles, buses, and trucks exhausting gases and lead particles from fuel into the air. Just how long the atmosphere will be able to absorb these pollutants cannot be predicted accurately.

The environmental threats have begun to jolt many Americans from their indifference and disregard for the severely limited natural resources of man. A recent Gallup Poll conducted for the National Wildlife Federation revealed that fifty-one per cent of all persons interviewed expressed "deep concern" about the effects of air pollution, water pollution, soil erosion, and the destruction of wildlife and natural resources. Most surprising was the fact that almost three out of every four of the persons interviewed said they would be willing to pay additional taxes to put a halt to these threats to life.

Even a limited survey of the ways in which man has been violating his environment demonstrates why the threat to life itself is so serious. The use of the deadly, long-lasting, poisonous pesticides is one of the most depressing examples. Each year, more than 600 million pounds of pesticides of all kinds are sprayed, dusted, fogged, or dumped in the United States—about three pounds for every man, woman, and child in the country.

The residues drift through the air, mingle with the waters to destroy aquatic life, and seep through the soil to contaminate the environment on a worldwide basis. Pesticide particles have been found, for example, in the tissues of reindeer in Alaska, in penguins in the Antarctic, and in the dust over the Indian Ocean. Several species of animal life, including the American bald eagle, the peregrine falcon, the osprey, and the Bermuda petrel are on the verge of extinction by pesticides.

A two-year national pesticide study completed recently by the U.S. Bureau of Sport Fisheries and Wildlife found DDT in 584 of 590 samples of fish taken from forty-four rivers and lakes across the United States. The study revealed DDT residues ranging up to forty-five parts per million in the whole fish, a count more than *nine times higher* than the current Food and Drug Administration guideline level for DDT in fish.

The threat of pesticides to public health and safety was made shockingly obvious last spring when the Food and Drug Administration seized 28,000 pounds of pesticide-contaminated Coho salmon in Lake Michigan. The concentration of DDT in the salmon was up to nineteen parts per million; the accumulation of dieldrin, a persistent and more toxic pesticide, up to 0.3 parts per million. Both levels are considered hazardous by the FDA and the World Health Organization.

Dangerous levels of DDT and other deadly pesticides have been found in tobacco and fruit, and vegetable producers constantly must take care to avoid having their crops banned from commercial markets.

An irony of the whole pesticide saga is that, time and again, the bugs have come out on top. Hit the insects with a pesticide, and a few hardy generations later, adaptation has developed a new breed that is immune to it. Rather than seeking the obvious answer of an alternative pest control, our response has usually been to use greater doses of the same old ineffective stuff.

Yet, despite the urgent warning by responsible scientists of imminent environmental disaster and health hazards from pesticides, Federal agencies have failed dismally to face the threatening problem. Not one agency has taken any significant action that would lead to the goal of "eliminating" the use of persistent, toxic pesticides that was established six years ago by President Kennedy's Science Advisory Commission on Pesticides.

The appalling fact is that the Federal Government has been perpetuating this grave environmental and health problem rather than working to resolve it.

The Department of Agriculture has virtually ignored the hazards of pesticides, and Department spokesmen have opposed state action to ban DDT and have supported the pro-pesticide arguments of the chemical companies with scandalous devotion. In spite of the obvious need for alternatives to DDT and other hard pesticides, the Department has failed to launch an all-out research effort in this area. One spokesman for the Agricultural Research Service admitted that the Department's program for improved means of non-chemical pest control is presently underfunded by at least $4 million.

It is obvious that the Department must research non-hazardous controls of pests and use its existing authority to place effective limitations on the use of all pesticides, including a complete cancellation of the registrations for the hard pesticides especially hazardous to the environment.

In the deepening national crisis facing our rivers and lakes, a dramatic new pollution source is developing—the massive discharges of heated water from nuclear power plants.

On Lake Michigan alone, seven nuclear power plants, several with capabilities larger than any in the history of power generation, are scheduled to be in operation by the mid-1970s. Together with the output around the lake of existing plants fueled by coal and oil, the higher volume of expelled heated water will raise the temperature of all of Lake Michigan by several degrees in the next few decades.

In addition to the threatened change in the taste and smell of drinking water near some of the plants, the delicate chain of Lake Michigan aquatic life, already severely threatened by other pollutants, could be further upset. Algae growth is already a problem that could be greatly increased by the warmer water. Yet, incredibly, not one of the plants is installing cooling towers to reduce the environmental impact of the heated water on this vital segment of the Great Lakes chain—a major resource of international importance.

On a nationwide basis, 120 nuclear power plants will be installed within the next six years. By 1980, the electric power industry—with both nuclear and fossil fuel plants—will be using one-fifth of the total fresh water run-off in the United States for cooling. But the Atomic Energy Commission, which is charged with regulating the development of the nuclear power plants, said it has absolutely no responsibility to assure that the gigantic heat discharges will be controlled.

The tragedy of what is happening to the Great Lakes is clearly one of the ugliest examples of stupidity and greed. The pollution sequence has reached the point where Lake Erie is nearly destroyed, with Lake Michigan close behind, and Lakes Huron and Ontario gravely threatened. Only Lake Superior, the third largest body of fresh water on earth—almost 3,000 cubic miles—is still clean.

Just how long Lake Superior will remain clean is highly questionable. The threat to its sparkling blue waters has begun. The Reserve Mining Company, owned by the Republic Steel and Armco Steel corporations, is dumping into these waters more than 60,000 tons of wastes daily from its taconite—low grade iron ore—processing plant. It has been computed that, if the plant operates at current levels for the next forty years, it will dump into the lake one trillion, 881 billion, 600 million pounds of taconite tailings.

A Federal report concluded last spring that the waste discharge is already damaging the fragile ecology in the lake, is affecting the mineral content and the clarity of the water, and is destroying the already limited fish spawning grounds. There seems to be little question that the wastes are polluting the lake.

The Water Quality Act of 1965 and the Clean Water Restoration Act of 1966 were Congressional declarations setting a national commitment to restore and protect the water quality of this country. Under the latter act, Congress authorized $3.4 billion in Federal aid for the period from 1968 to 1971 to begin the task. Congress recognized that the authorization was only for a minimal beginning and acknowledged that the job eventually would cost tens of billions of dollars.

Yet today, the water pollution control effort is in the same crisis condition as the waters of this nation. Efforts to implement the water quality standards face total collapse because the Federal aid commitment is not being met. In 1968, $450 million in Federal aid was authorized by Congress but only $203 million was appropriated. For 1969, $700 million was authorized, but less than one-third that figure was appropriated.

The backlog of need continues to climb to gigantic proportions. Recent figures disclosed that $2.2 billion in Federal aid has been requested under pending applications for the construction of effective municipal waste treatment plants. These plants are needed to eliminate one of the most continuous sources of water pollution—soaring population growth makes the best systems inadequate in a short time. For 1970, the Administration originally proposed spending only $214 million of the $1 billion authorized, but under great pressure from Congress agreed to a substantial increase, and the ultimate appropriation may come much closer to the authorized sum.

Last year, Congress recognized the hard fact that only a major infusion of new Federal funds would enable the creation of new national parks such as the Redwoods, and provide even a minimum of space and recreation for this nation's rampaging population growth. Congress amended the Land and Water Conservation Act to provide that revenues from outer continental shelf oil drillings—those beyond the three miles of shelf reserved to the states— would assure a minimum of $200 million a year for the next five years for the Land and Water Conservation fund.

But this year the Nixon Administration has requested only $124 million for the fund, and it is unlikely that more money will be added either by Congress or by the Administration. The supplemental oil revenues, which this year alone will total $76 million, are earmarked for the fund, but will be unappropriated and unspent, unless Congress and the Administration together take action. These oil funds could sit there indefinitely, as they cannot be spent for other purposes, while important available land is denuded of trees by chain saws and plowed into ugly, unplanned development by greedy real estate interests. Such delay destroys the encouraging starts made in conservation the last few years.

With demand for the nation's severely limited open space facilities already exceeding capacity, it is particularly disturbing to see Everglades National Park, one of the most valuable features of the National Park System, in grave danger of imminent destruction. In 1934, the 1.4 million acre park was set up by Congress to be "protected in perpetuity" as a unique subtropical wilderness in rapidly developing south Florida. The concept, "protected in perpetuity," in the National Park statutes has always been comforting because it seems to rule: "Here is where we draw the line. Here we are endowing a priceless natural resource with a sanctity not unlike that of a church."

But, as is so often the case, the commitment of words and statutes is being swept away by the frenzied pursuit of profit. The Everglades Park is on the brink of destruction, final and complete. One conservationist predicts that, within ten years, there will be an announcement by the Federal Government that the Park is no longer worthy of the name and, therefore, will be disbanded like an old military base, in the interest of economy.

It would be particularly appropriate for the Government to pronounce the doom of the Everglades because it has permitted Federal agencies—specifically the U.S. Army Corps of Engineers—working in direct opposition to the intent of Congress, to endanger the Park.

In 1962, the Corps of Engineers constructed a levee across the principal natural drainage way to the Everglades from the north and blocked the flow of water into the Park for two years. That water shortage brought the death of multitudes of fish, wildlife, and flora and began an unnatural succession of changes which may alter the unique ecology of the Everglades for all time. The only thing that saved the Park was a dramatic increase in rainfall in recent years, but that can be only a temporary respite.

Conservationists supported the Corps Flood Control Project, provided the Corps would insure that the flow of water would not be cut off from the Park. Without that protection, it is clear that the water—the life blood of the Park —will be choked off by the escalating industrial-municipal water demands of southern Florida or by drought.

In 1968, the Corps came before Congress for additional authorizations for the Flood Control Project and told the Department of Interior, in writing, that the project would be regulated by rules designed specifically to protect the Everglades Park. But one year later, now that the Corps has its new authorization, it is refusing to implement that agreement and says it will wait for the "crunch" it sees—in thirty or forty years—before it acts. Such response is a blatant about-face, with obvious consideration for the wealthy land developers of south Florida who won't be happy until every square mile of the Everglades is dredged, filled, put under the blade of the bulldozer, and subdivided into suburban lots around dead lagoons stocked with fish from someplace else.

The Army Corps has already spent $170 million of the public's money for the project that is steadily and rapidly destroying the Everglades—and it is asking for $160 million more to further despoil the Park. If Congress and the Administration refuse to require the Corps to establish protective measures before any further Federal funds are spent, we might as well admit that the Government has no sincere concern for protecting the environment of this country, even when it has authority to control the situation. The call for private development apparently is too enticing.

Perhaps man, with his rampaging breeding and indifference, has reached the point where much of the world he lives in will be nothing more than an area of poisonous waters and choking air surrounded by mountains of garbage and debris. With many municipalities already faced with a monumental problem of garbage disposal, it is estimated that every man, woman, and child in this country is now generating five pounds of refuse a day from household, commercial, and industrial uses. This refuse adds up to more than *365 billion pounds* a year.

Instead of using the country's impressive technology which made it possible to land man on the moon and develop super-mechanical devices capable of solving astronomical problems, the typically American approach is to take the easy way—dump the debris and garbage in the ocean.

Why shouldn't the municipal governments and business and industry believe the ocean would be a good dumping place? The sea bottom is already being used for dumping radioactive wastes, and until the Army was stopped recently, some thoughtful military bureaucrat decided it would be a great place to dump discarded poison gases. Perhaps previous dumping has caused some of the mysterious events and massive sea kills I have described.

The oceans are not a limitless funnel that take the chemical wastes and other debris to a magical "somewhere else" where they can be forgotten. More than twenty years ago, Los Angeles found that its beaches were contaminated and had to be closed to bathers because the city was not sterilizing its sewage. It was also discovered that wastes pumped by England into the North Sea were damaging Grand Banks fisheries off Newfoundland. The Japanese, concerned about their valuable fishing industry, have wisely banned dumping sewage into the sea.

It is the economic profit to be found in the sea that attracts and brings closer the threat of cataclysm which Dr. Paul Ehrlich, a noted ecologist, projected recently. He predicted that unless current trends are reversed, the oceans could end as a significant source of life in ten years with the end of man coming a short time later.

The massive oil leak off Santa Barbara, California, which killed fish and sea fowl could be the first dramatic warning of this end. Other commercial ventures are under consideration as developers look to the possibilities of rich returns from moving parts of crammed megalopolis to floating cities. One developer is planning a floating jetport in the ocean waters off New York City. Such a facility might well be beyond the reach of enforcement of any Federal agency regulations.

Unfortunately, there is a great deal of confusion and litigation concerning whether various ocean waters are public, private, national, or international. It seems to be a wild utopian dream that the world will be able to face the threat to the oceans in any reasonable way in the face of the fact that various government jurisdictions in this country cannot get together to develop responsible control programs for a simpler problem—domestic pollution.

Without agreements or strong regulations, the massive business and industrial corporations are at it again—this time it is frontier days on the high seas, and it's full speed ahead, damn the last clean environment on earth.

To date, 8,000 oil wells have been drilled on the outer continental shelf. And little mention is made of the fact that the outer shelf is really 823 thousand square miles of undersea public domain, *owned by the people of the United States*. This public domain was once much greater. But in 1953, with the Submerged Lands Act, Congress gave outright, to the states, the first three miles of offshore seabed.

Today, greedy over the prospect of trillions and trillions of dollars in potential continental shelf minerals, the East Coast states are banding together to fight the Federal government in court for the undersea booty beyond the states' three-mile territory in a mad scramble for the public domain frontier.

Our undersea domain is not the only ocean area that is threatened. Landward, our coastline environment is becoming an unmanageable tangle of conflicting, polluting uses that eliminate wetlands, destroy shellfish and other valuable sea life in sensitive estuaries, wipe out beaches with unwise development, and degrade the natural values that make our coastline areas perhaps the most vital recreation resource in the nation.

The one heartening sign so far has been the courageous move by the state of New Jersey to freeze all action on purchase, lease, and use of state lands fronting on coastal tidal waters until completion by the state of a master plan for managing the coastal environment.

The same freeze should immediately be adopted for public coastal lands on the Atlantic and Pacific coasts, the Great Lakes, and the Gulf of Mexico. The Federal government should halt all aid for development that would affect this environment until plans meeting national criteria are developed. And on the outer continental shelf—the vast undersea region extending beyond the coast —the Secretary of the Interior should grant no more leases of any kind until similar environmental criteria can be developed to protect this vital last frontier.

The President, with the advice and consent of the Senate, should appoint a group of independent specialists to develop the coastal land and water use criteria which the state plans would be required to meet. This group would also develop the outer continental shelf criteria. At least a three-year moratorium on continental shelf and public coastal land development will be required for orderly planning and adoption of the national criteria.

I will shortly propose legislation in Congress which will take these vital steps for protection of the coastline and ocean environments. Without such action, it will only be a brief time before the life-sustaining resources of our ocean are destroyed.

The real loser in man's greedy drive is the youth of this country and the world. Because of the stupidity of their elders, the children of today face an ugly world in the near future, with dangerously and deadly polluted air and water; overcrowded development; festering mounds of debris; and an insufficient amount of open space to get away from it all.

Since youth is again the great loser, perhaps the only hope for saving the environment and putting quality back into life may well depend on our being able to tap the energy, idealism, and drive of the oncoming generation that, otherwise, will inherit the poisonous air and deadly waters of the earth.

Biologist Barry Commoner, chairman of the St. Louis Committee for Environmental Information, warned recently that "we don't really know what the long-term effects of various types of environmental deterioration will be, and the kids are the guinea pigs."

Fortunately, the rising generation appears not to be content to be the guinea pigs of a society that has lost its sense of priority. One of the most dramatic developments of this decade has been the insistence of youth that in the last third of the Twentieth Century, the quality of life must have a much higher priority than the greed of past generations has permitted. A few random examples:

> • On learning that the United Nations is planning to hold a world conference on the environment in 1972, the youth of several nations have called for an International Youth Assembly on the environment in 1971 to give notice to the world's leaders that their generation realizes it is they who suffer most from a destroyed environment.
> • A group of high school juniors in Ashland, Wisconsin, recently showed concern for the growing threat to the ecology of Lake Superior by demonstrating in support of Duluth's Pollution Enforcement Conference. They were demanding a clean lake.
> • The same concern was voiced by a Washington, D.C., university student who, when told that a Congressional proposal to bring a complete halt to any Federal program that damaged the environment might be unconstitutional, asked: "Isn't polluting our rivers unconstitutional?"

The concern is there. I am convinced that all that is needed now is the trigger to activate the overwhelming insistence of the new generation on environmental quality. It is the young who can begin to stem the tide of disaster. To marshal such an effort, I am proposing a National Teach-In on the Crisis of the Environment to be held next spring on every university campus across the nation. The crisis is so imminent, in my opinion, that every university should set aside one day in the school year—the same day across the nation—for the Teach-In.

On that day, prominent ecologists, biologists, political scientists, publicists, public officials, and political leaders could meet with students and faculty in symposiums, convocations, and panel discussions to discuss environmental topics selected by the student body.

At the University of Southern California, it might be oil spills; at the University of Wisconsin, the devastation of the Great Lakes; at the University of Miami, it might be the Everglades; and at Yale, it might be the massive transportation snarl and urban sprawl. The topics could range widely; the list of critical subjects is virtually endless.

Each year new species of animals are added to the list of those soon to be extinct. Man in his arrogance appears to think that he can escape joining that list. The evidence is overwhelming, however, that it is much later than he realizes, that the species Man cannot long watch the animals disappear without seeing that his end, too, is coming. Man, ironically, may be the creature that left as his monument a planet nearly as incapable of sustaining life as its barren neighbors in the dead vacuum of the solar system we are now exploring at costs that are fantastically greater than we are prepared to spend to preserve our own planet.

Study Questions

1. Discuss the purposes of the National Environmental Act of 1969 and the duties of the Council on Environmental Quality. Does your state have an environmental act? If not, why? Discuss fully and critically.
2. Discuss the difficulties in solving our environmental problems. Outline and discuss the steps that must be taken if we are to stop polluting our environment. What actions have been taken in your community in this direction? Discuss fully and critically.
3. Comment on the statement that "When ecology engulfs economics, many of the dreams of imaginative engineers will be deliberately aborted because cost-benefit analysis will indicate an aggregate value that is negative."

Suggestions for Further Reading

Appleman, Philip, *The Silent Explosion.* Boston: Beacon Press, 1965.
Bernarde, Melvin A., *Our Precarious Habitat.* New York: W. W. Norton & Company, Inc., 1970.

Borgstrom, Georg, *The Hungry Planet.* New York: Collier Books, Collier-Macmillan Ltd., 1967.

Carson, Rachel, *Silent Spring.* Boston: Houghton Mifflin Co., 1962.

Commoner, Barry, *Science and Survival.* New York: Viking Press, Inc., 1967.

Day, Lincoln H., and Alice Taylor Day. *Too Many Americans.* New York: Delta Press, 1965.

Dorst, Jean. *Before Nature Dies.* Boston: Houghton Mifflin Co., 1970.

Ehrlich, Paul R. *Population Control or Race to Oblivion?* New York: Ballantine Books, Inc., 1968.

Ehrlich, Paul R., and Richard W. Holm, *The Process of Evolution.* New York: McGraw-Hill Book Company, Inc., 1963.

Ehrlich, Paul R., and Anne H. Ehrlich. *Population, Resources, Environment: Issues in Human Ecology.* San Francisco, California: W. H. Freeman and Company, 1970.

Graham, Frank, Jr. *Disaster by Default: Politics and Water Pollution.* New York: M. Evans & Company, 1966.

Graham, Frank, Jr. *Since Silent Spring.* Boston: Houghton Mifflin Co., 1970.

Hauser, Philip M. *The Population Dilemma.* Englewood Cliffs, New Jersey: Prentice-Hall, Inc., 1963.

Herber, Lewis. *Our Synthetic Environment.* New York: Alfred A. Knopf, Inc., 1962.

Hopcraft, Arthur. *Born to Hunger.* Boston: Houghton Mifflin Co., 1968.

Jaffee, Joyce. *Conservation: Maintaining the Natural Balance.* New York: Natural History Press/Doubleday and Company, 1970.

Linton, Ron. *Terracide—America's Destruction of Her Living Environment.* Boston: Little, Brown and Company, 1970.

Michelson, Max. *The Environmental Revolution.* New York: McGraw-Hill Book Company, Inc., 1970.

Ng, Larry K. Y., and Stuart Mudd (eds.) *The Population Crisis.* Bloomington, Indiana: Indiana University Press, 1965.

Paddock, William and Paul Paddock. *Famine 1975.* Boston: Little, Brown and Company, 1967.

Paddock, William and Paul Paddock. *Hungry Nations.* Boston: Little, Brown and Company, 1964.

Reid, Keith. *Nature's Network.* New York: Natural History Press/Doubleday and Company, 1970.

Reveille, Roger, and H. H. Landsberg (eds.) *America's Changing Environment.* Boston: Houghton Mifflin Co., 1970.

Roosevelt, Nicholas. *Conservation: Now Or Never.* New York: Dodd, Mead, 1970.

Sax, Karl. *Standing Room Only, The World's Exploding Population.* Boston: Beacon Press, 1955, 1960.

PART SIX

Political Dynamics:
Public Opinion, Pressure Groups
and Political Parties

In an open, democratic society public opinion shapes governmental policies. Decision-makers are influenced in one way or another by public opinion. Presidents and Congressmen pay a great deal of attention to public opinion polls and to what newspapers and television commentators are saying. Questions are raised concerning the proper role of public opinion in government. Scholars and politicians view public opinion in different ways. Some view it as a binding force; others hold a contemptuous view of it and fear the consequences of mob rule.

In recent years scholarly interest has focused on the nature and formation of public opinion. The nature and influence of public opinion is of interest to both democratic and non-democratic systems alike because it provides support to the ruling regime and gives it a sense of political legitimacy. In the following three selections we shall examine the role of public opinion in democracy and the foundations of political beliefs.

Bernard Berelson discusses the various characteristics demanded of the electorate in a free society such as (1) personality structure, and (2) interest and involvement in the political process and acceptance of responsibility. Moreover, he discusses the components of electorate decisions or the content of the decision. He states that the first requirement of electorate decisions is the possession of information and knowledge. It is assumed that informed citizens make wiser decisions. However, representative government does not require that everyone be equally informed about all issues all the time. The second component of decisions is the possession of political principles or moral standards.

Berelson examines other essential requirements of the democratic process. These requirements include: (1) objective perception of political reality, (2) communication and discussion, and (3) rationality. Each of these requirements is discussed at some length. Berelson concludes that these various requirements set a high standard for the political process. "And since this is a composite list . . . it is not necessarily a matter for disillusionment or even disappointment that the democratic electorate does not conform to every requirement in the full degree."

In his article "Public Opinion and the Decay of Democracy," V. O. Key, Jr. examines the role of public opinion on governmental actions and policies. He discusses the impact of public opinion on the conduct of foreign and domestic policies. Key goes on to say that although public opinion places some limitations upon governmental actions, the fact remains that within whatever limits opinion sets, government enjoys a wide latitude in determining whether to act, when to act, and what measures to take. Only a small proportion of the public maintains focus on public affairs. Furthermore, the government plays an important role in the molding of public opinion, for it seeks to change public opinion that it believes to be in error and it responds to opinion that it judges to be in the public interest. Key adds that public opinion is probably more affected by the impact of events than by the advocates of many causes.

Key also states that those who blame public opinion "for our ills hang the wrong villain." The influentials, a small proportion of the population, play a significant role in the formation of public opinion and in the creation of support for public policies. He writes: "Perhaps the policies of a democratic order depend ultimately on the outlooks and concerns of the more active citizenry rather than on mass opinion" and concludes that "the maintenance of a working democratic system requires the existence of a substantial sprinkling of persons throughout the population concerned with the public weal and animated by a faith in the system."

One of the simplest and most effective ways individuals can influence public officials is by participating in voluntary organizations or groups. A pressure group is a collection of individuals with one or more shared goals or attitudes who attempt to influence policy questions so that they are favorable to their interests by gaining access to the political process. In a pluralistic society such as ours, pressure groups place claims on the political system and on each other. The interests of the individual member, we should bear in mind, are not always in unanimous accord with the stated goals of the group; for instance, the American Medical Association reflects the interests of many doctors, but certainly not all doctors. In the next two selections, David Truman examines the meaning of interests and their role in society, and Norman Luttbeg and Harmon Zeigler analyze attitude consensus and conflict among the leaders and members of the Oregon Education Association.

Truman states that man is a social animal and cannot be viewed apart from the groups to which he belongs; that the groups to which an individual belongs shape and mold his opinions while giving voice in influencing and making public decisions. Truman defines an interest group as a group with shared attitudes toward what is needed in a given situation by making demands or claims on other groups in the society. Shared attitudes constitute interest. The governmental process, as viewed by Truman and other group theorists, is an *interaction* among groups. Political interest groups are those groups which place demands through or on the governmental system.

In the next article, Luttbeg and Zeigler examine attitude consensus and conflict among the leaders and members of the Oregon Education Association. They analyze leaders' perceptions of their rules, the extent to which leaders and followers are in agreement as to what the organization should do, and the relationships between sets of attitudes concerning the extent of satisfaction with the actual behavior of the leaders of the organization. Moreover, they examine whether or not the leaders represent the followers' values and discuss the political role of the teacher.

Their study shows that the leaders of OEA are more active, more liberal, and more willing to expand the activities of the organization than the followers. However, the leaders exaggerate the nature of their position for they view the followers as being more conservative and restrained than they actually are. The leaders are more emotionally committed to the organization than the followers. The study also shows that there is a discrepancy between leaders' attitudes and followers' attitudes. Therefore, "OEA leaders operating entirely upon their personal values would not be representatives of the values of their followers." However, if they were to take a purely representative role, they would become more restrained and conservative than the teachers would like.

Although pressure groups make substantial contributions to the operation of a democracy, they cannot do all that is required to make government function in a responsible manner. Political parties are essential to the working of the democratic process. They serve as the main link between pressure groups and the decision-makers. Moreover, political parties serve to: (1) crystallize opinion; (2) facilitate popular control over elected public officials; (3) offer the voters policy alternatives; (4) assist the voters to make more rational choices; (5) help in the peaceful resolution of conflicts; and (6) provide responsibility.

In the next essay, Herbert McClosky and others examine the relationship of ideology to party membership by comparing the attitudes of party leaders with those of followers. The authors discuss the various reasons for little ideological emphasis among American parties and the pressures which exist to promote uniformity and cleavage. They point out that although competition gives rise to certain similarities between the parties, it also impels them to diverge from each other. They contend that leaders of the Democratic and Republican parties differ on issues more sharply than followers possessing, for example, differing attitudes toward public ownership, regulation of the economy, equalitarian and human welfare, as well as tax policy and farm issues. The differences between party leaders on foreign policy issues seem to be the smallest.

The study indicates that rank and file members of the two parties are less divided than their leaders and explains the reasons for the consensus between rank and file members and the sharp division between party leaders.

Bayard Rustin in his article "Black Power and Coalition Politics" discusses the harm that might result from the advocacy of "black power," while expressing hope for possible transformation of the Democratic Party in the south as Negroes gain the right to vote. He prefers to see a labor-liberal coalition which would work to make the Democratic Party responsive to the demands of the poor. What "black power" advocates are urging "is the creation of a *new black establishment.*" Rustin points out that the Irish, Jews, and Italians have won power through alliances with other groups.

Rustin surveys Negro conditions and concludes that the lot of the ghetto Negro has not improved, despite legislative acts and judicial decisions. He states that the popularity of "black power" stems from the conviction of the Negroes that they cannot win. Why compromise with reluctant white allies, argue Negro militants, or have anything to do with the whites at all?

Rustin believes it would be unfortunate if white liberals allow hostile statements made by Negroes to drive them out of the civil rights movement. He feels that the issue of injustice is the main issue and that the "no-win" policy behind the slogan of "black power" will not help the Negro cause. We must not reject the Negro quest for equality by rejecting "black power." We must not only maintain the liberal-labor civil rights coalition but we must strengthen it. He concludes that: "It is up to the liberal movement to prove that coalition and integration are better alternatives" than "black power."

In the final article, Nathan Glazer examines the areas in which the new radicalism expresses itself and the approaches they follow in getting to the roots of our present evils in society. The New Left views the institutions as the cause of corruption of man and therefore must be overthrown. He discusses three major flaws in the position of the radical Left and states that "there can be no alternatives to institutionalization, the permanent bodies devoted to permanent problem areas, with all its consequences."

The New Left's major answer to the problem of institutionalization is "participatory democracy." Glazer points out how the masses are manipulated by those who object to "formal" democracy, tolerance, and public order. He also argues that there can be no substitute for institutions and that when institutions become inadequate for their tasks they must be supplemented or supplanted by new ones in order to meet the demands of the people.

Glazer turns his attention to the Vietnam war and states how his views and criticisms differ from those of the radical Left. He views radicalism "as a great reservoir of energy which moves the establishment to pay attention to the most serious and urgent problems, and tells it when it has failed." To some extent, he adds, radicalism can be viewed as a reservoir of political creativity.

DEMOCRATIC THEORY AND PUBLIC OPINION

BERNARD BERELSON

For a good many years the political scientists have been discussing the nature of public opinion and the role it plays in the political process. But somehow, in recent years, we have tended to overlook the related facts that there is a political content in what we call public opinion; that there exists a long and elegant intellectual tradition (in the form of the political theory of democracy) for dealing with opinion problems; and that this theory provides a helpful framework for the organization and conduct of opinion studies. The normative theory of political democracy makes certain requirements of the citizen and certain assumptions about his capacity to meet them. The tools of social research have made it possible, for the first time, to determine with reasonable precision and objectivity the extent to which the practice of politics by the citizens of a democratic state conforms to the requirements and the assumptions of the theory of democratic politics (insofar as it refers to decisions by the electorate). The closer collaboration of political theorists and opinion researchers should contribute new problems, new categories, and greater refinements and elaboration to both sides.

The theorists tell us how a democratic electorate is supposed to behave and we public opinion researchers claim to know something about how the democratic electorate in this country actually does behave. The task I have taken on myself is figuratively to confront the one with the other. Such an analysis should be useful not only in organizing the results of opinion studies in terms of an important body of theory, but also in revealing neglected and promising areas for further investigation. I bespeak the interest of both theorists and researchers in extending, refining, and, in general, improving this formulation. For even on the basis of my preliminary exploration, I am convinced that each side has a good deal to learn from the other and that joint work on this common problem can be valuable both for social science and for public policy.

Such collaboration, like most cross-disciplinary work, is not easy, but it is necessary since neither side can solve the problem alone. In this connection,

SOURCE: Bernard Berelson, "Democratic Theory and Public Opinion," *The Public Opinion Quarterly,* 16 (Fall 1952), 313–330. Reprinted by permission.

the deficiencies of the present formulation on the theoretical side will be particularly clear to the political theorist; I can only hope that the representation of theory, drawn as it is from a variety of sources, has not been caricatured, and that the theorists will themselves undertake the indicated corrections.

What, then, does democratic political theory assume or require of the democratic citizen, and to what extent are the assumptions or requirements realized? There are a number of ways of identifying and classifying the requirements, depending upon which political philosophers are given primary consideration. It has seemed most appropriate in this preliminary analysis to present a composite set of requirements, even though they may overlap at various points and thus not present a coherent system. While not all of them may be required in any single political theory of democracy, all of them are mentioned in one or another theory.

THE PREREQUISITES OF ELECTORATE DECISIONS

There appear to be two requirements in democratic theory which refer primarily to characteristics demanded of the electorate as it initially comes to make a political decision. These are the preconditions for electorate decisions.

The first is the possession of a suitable *personality structure:* within a range of variations, the electorate is required to possess the types of character which can operate effectively, if not efficiently, in a free society. Certain kinds of personality structures are not congenial to a democratic society, could not operate successfully within it, and would be destructive of democratic values. Others are more compatible with or even disposed toward the effective performance of the various roles which make up the democratic political system. Among the characteristics required—and this is not intended as anything more than an illustrative list—are a capacity for involvement in situations remote from one's face-to-face experience; a capacity to accept moral responsibility for choices; a capacity to accept frustration in political affairs with equanimity; self-control and self-restraint as reins upon the gross operation of self-interest; a nice balance between submissiveness and assertiveness; a reasonable amount of freedom from anxiety so that political affairs can be attended to; a healthy and critical attitude toward authority; a capacity for fairly broad and comprehensive identifications; a fairly good measure of self-esteem; and a sense of potency.

The distribution of such personality characteristics in the population, let alone their relationship to political behavior, is not known. What is more or less known is only a beginning of the problem. We know, for example, that contrary to common belief the incidence of psychosis has not increased in this country over the past century (Goldhamer and Marshall); on this score, at least, we are not less capable than past generations of governing ourselves. We know that the authoritarian personality is associated with social prejudice and restrictive politics (the Berkeley study of Adorno, Frenkel-Brunswick, *et al.*); that neuroticism limits attention to political matters (Elmira study); that a wide discrepancy between aspiration and achievement leads some persons to over-aggressive acts against the political environment and lowers their respect for political leaders (Bettelheim and Janowitz); that the "democratic character" is more flexible and adaptable than the authoritarian character (Lewin and Lippitt).

There is a great deal of work to be done on this problem; and it is here particularly that the psychologists can make an important contribution to the study of political behavior. The influence of character on political democracy has been perceived in general terms by a number of theorists, and some psychologists and sociologists have begun to work on the topic. The dependence of democratic processes upon the "democratic character" seems clear in general, but the nature of this relationship has been only slightly documented in the literature: Without doubt, a sympathetic and imaginative study of the literature of democratic theory will generate many important hypotheses for empirical investigation.

The second requirement is not only a prerequisite but also an outcome of electorate decisions. This is the factor of interest and participation;[1] the electorate is required to possess a certain degree of involvement in the process of political decision, to take an appropriate share of responsibility. Political democracy requires a fairly strong and fairly continuous level of interest from a minority, and from a larger body of the citizenry a moderate-to-mild and discontinuous interest but with a stable readiness to respond in critical political situations. Political disinterest or apathy is not permitted, or at least not approved.

Here the descriptive documentation provided by opinion studies is relatively good. The amount of political interest in the community, its fluctuations through time, its incidence among various population groups, its causes and its consequences—on all these topics we have reasonably systematic data. Less than one-third of the electorate is "really interested" in politics, and that group is by no means a cross-section of the total electorate. The more interested people are more likely to affect others and thus to exercise a greater influence upon the outcome of elections. The decreasing political interest in the population, viewed with alarm by some people who are distressed by the fact that a smaller proportion of eligible people vote now than did fifty years ago, is to some extent due to the increasing feeling people have that they are impotent to affect political matters in the face of the complexity and magnitude of the issues. Participation in the actual election is not only segmental but also partial; if everybody eligible to vote actually did vote, the distribution of sup-

[1] Included here is acceptance of the political sphere as one of the legitimate elements of social life. In a democratic society the political sphere must not be widely viewed as unclean or degraded or corrupt. Opinion studies have produced some data on the image of politics and of politicians among the citizenry.

port in recent national elections would have been measurably different. Finally, interest is not a simple unidimensional factor. A recent analysis identified three kinds of interest: spectator interest (regarding the campaign as a dramatic spectacle); citizen interest (deciding how to vote); and partisan interest (securing the election of one's own candidate). Of these, only the second is "pure" interest according to some theorists.

The major question raised by this requirement, both for political theory and for opinion research, is the fundamental one of its universality and intensity. People have always argued whether the vote is a duty or a privilege, and there have always been advocates of an unlimited and continuous requirement of interest. As early as the Athenian democracy it was said that "we regard a man who takes no interest in public affairs not as a harmless but as a useless character." But is he really so useless to the operation of democracy? Some recent theorists and studies have suggested that a sizable group of less interested citizens is desirable as a "cushion" to absorb the intense action of highly motivated partisans. For the fact is that the highly interested are the most partisan and the least changeable. If everyone in the community were highly and continuously interested, the possibilities of compromise and of gradual solution of political problems might well be lessened to the point of danger. It is an historical axiom that democracy requires a middle class for its proper operation. Perhaps what it really requires is a body of moderately and discontinuously interested citizens within and across social classes, whose approval of or at least acquiescence in political policies must be secured.

THE COMPONENTS OF ELECTORATE DECISIONS

The political theory of democracy also makes requirements regarding the components of electorate decisions; that is, the content of the decision.

The first requirement of electorate decisions is the possession of *information and knowledge;* the electorate must be informed about the matters under consideration. Information refers to isolated facts and knowledge to general propositions; both of them provide reliable insight into the consequences of the decision. This is a requirement nearly everyone sets down for a democratic electorate; politicians and statesmen, adult educators, journalists, professors of political science—all of them pay deference to the need for "enlightened public opinion."

This is another factor on which opinion researchers have assembled a good deal of data. What do they show? One persistent conclusion is that the public is not particularly well informed about the specific issues of the day. A recent survey of the current status of American public opinion states that "tests of information invariably show at least twenty per cent of the public totally uninformed (and usually the figure is closer to forty per cent)." And at that, most of the studies have been based upon simple and isolated questions of fact (i.e., information) and only seldom, if at all, upon the historical and general propositions (i.e., knowledge) which underlie political decisions. Perhaps the proportion of the knowledgeable would be even lower than the proportion of the informed. At the same time, it must be recognized that there is a significant middle ground—a kind of vaguely perceived impression which reveals to the possessor certain relationships which are very "real" to him, which form "reasonable" bases for his decision, yet which cannot be explicitly articulated by him in any detail. An obvious example is the difference between the Republican and Democratic parties, a difference visible to many partisans of both.

Thus it often appears that people express opinions on issues when they seem to know very little about them. Lack of information may be a bar to the holding of an opinion in the minds of the theorists but it does not seem to be among the electorate (where, of course, it is not experienced as lack of information at all). In most campaigns, whether political or informational, the people best informed on the issue are the ones least likely to change their minds. Much of this represents attitudinal stability; some of it may represent rigidity.

Information and knowledge are required of the electorate on the assumption that they contribute to the wisdom of the decision; informed citizens make wiser decisions. In this country it is clear that the better-educated people are the best informed and most knowledgeable, yet it is also clear that other variables are involved in the development of wise decisions, e.g., flexibility of predispositions, a wide range of identifications, a low level of aggressiveness, etc. Finally, it appears from most studies that information and knowledge are sought and used more often as rationalization and reinforcer than as data to be used in making what might be called a free decision.

The requirement thus does not seem to be met in any direct way. But this is really an oversimplified statement of the requirement. How can an electorate be expected to be informed on the wide range of issues which confront the modern public? For example, the front page of *The New York Times* for one day alone recently contained stories on the following events, in each of which is embedded an issue on which the public might be expected to inform itself: price ceilings, the Korean war and the British position in it, the American defense build-up, Communist riots in France, the Berlin crisis, a new disarmament proposal, American military aid to France, official Soviet spies in this country, and the Mutual Security Aid Bill. Clearly there is too little time for simply getting the relevant information, let alone digesting it into a generalized system of political opinions. Actually the major decisions the ordinary citizen is called upon to make in a modern representative democracy involve basic simplifications which need not rest upon a wide range of information so long as they are based upon a certain amount of crucial information, reasonably interpreted. After all, the voter's effective choice is limited; he can vote Republican, he can vote Democratic, or he can refrain from voting, and becoming informed on a number of minor issues usually does not tip the scales against the weight of the few things that really matter—employment, social security, the cost of living, peace.

If the theoretical requirement is "full" information and knowledge, then democratic practice does not conform. But for some theorists the requirement is more differentiated than that. Representative government with large-scale political organization does not require that everyone be equally informed on everything all the time. To such a differentiated standard, actual practice may conform reasonably well. Opinion studies should not only document this requirement, but also refine their inquiries into the actual ways in which information and knowledge are held and used by the citizen in his vote decision. At the same time, theorists should differentiate and elaborate their conceptions of the intellectual requirements for a democratic citizenry.

The second component required of decisions is the possession of *principle;* the electorate is required to possess a body of stable political principles or moral standards, in contrast with fluctuating impulses or whims, to which topical questions can be referred for evaluation and decision.

● ● ●

If it is nothing more, then, the requirements of principle or doctrine means that the electorate must genuinely accept the procedures and rules involved in democratic processes, that it must at least share the symbols describing the substantive ends to which political action is directed and in terms of which it is justified, and that it must make political decisions on the basis of relevant standards. The first two requirements are met to a greater extent than the third.

THE PROCESS OF ELECTORATE DECISION

The third set of essentials in democratic theory refers to the process by which decisions are made. Here there seem to be three requirements.

The first of the requirements relates to the process of perception of which information and knowledge are the end products. This is the requirement of *accurate observation;* the electorate is required to perceive political realities clearly and objectively, with an absence or only a small amount of subjective distortion. It is difficult indeed to see life steadily and see it whole, and in politics clarity of perception is made doubly hard on the one hand by the predispositional strength which the citizen brings to the matter and, on the other, by the deliberate and in many cases inevitable ambiguity which the political leader brings there.

There is no need to labor this point. Walter Lippmann made a reputation for himself thirty years ago by elaborating the differences between the "world outside and the pictures in our heads." For the most part, he said, "we do not first see and then define, we define first and then see." Recent studies provide some documentation which refines this general observation. According to data from the Elmira study, not only is the citizen's image of the candidate and the campaign subject to the influence of preconception, but so is his view

of group support for the candidates and even of the candidates' stand on political issues. Given just a minimum of ambiguity to work with—and that is
usually available—people tend to think their candidate agrees with them, or
at least they manage not to know where he stands on the particular issue
when they stand on the other side. The stronger the party affiliation, the
greater the misperception.

The consequences of such misperception are interesting to speculate about.
It seems to decrease the tension within the individual since it enables him to
bring his opinions into an internal consistency without disturbing his basic position. At the same time, it increases the internal solidarity of the parties and
thus increases political tension within the community by seeming to sharpen
the differences between the parties, particularly under the stress of a political
campaign. Thus political perception is by no means simply a matter of concrete observation; it also involves protective coloration from a total position.
And hence, that democratic theory which assumes clarity and objectivity of
political perception must be qualified at the outset.

The second important requirement of democratic process is *communication and discussion;* the electorate is required to engage in discussion and
communication on political affairs. Democratic decision-making requires free
examination of political ideas, and this means discussion. Democratic citizens
are supposed to listen to their political leaders arguing with one another, to
listen to them when they speak directly to the electorate, to talk back to
them, and to discuss among themselves the public issues of the day. According to many modern theorists, this requirement stands at the heart of the
democratic process. "Above all, if it is to be true to its own peculiar nature,
democracy must enlist the effective thought of the whole community in the
operation of discussion."

Now here again, as in the case of information, public opinion researchers
have assembled a sizable body of data, not only on the amount and kind of
communication and discussion within the community but also on the conditions under which it takes place. The overall picture presented by the opinion
studies looks something like this: There is a 20 per cent nucleus of people who
are active and regular political discussants, another group of 25 per cent who
engage in political discussion on occasion, another 25 per cent who are activated into discussion only by dramatic political events, and a residual group
of 25 or 30 per cent who do not engage in political discussion at all. Furthermore, it is particular groups within the community that give most attention to
politics: the better-educated, the men, the "joiners"—in short, those groups
most subject to social pressure translated into expectations of how "our kind
of people" should behave in this respect. And the people who read and listen
to political content in the mass media also talk and listen to other people, and
thus the concentration of political communication and discussion is carried
one step further.

To complete the picture we need to ask two other questions which together bring into consideration another aspect of this requirement. Democratic citizens are required not simply to discuss politics, but to discuss political alternatives in a genuine effort to clarify and refine public policy. The first question is, "Who talks to whom?", and the answer is that people mostly discuss politics with other people like themselves—"like" in such characteristics as social position, occupation, and attitude. Mainly this goes on inside the family, but even outside it there is a clear tendency for political discussions to be carried out intra- rather than inter-social groups. The second question is, "What do they see and hear and talk about?" The broad answer is, "What pleases them"; i.e., what is congenial to their own point of view. People usually read and listen to their own side. In person-to-person discussion of politics, about a third or more of the talk centers upon topics not directly involving political preferences—for example, predictions of and arguments about who will win an election—and the remainder consists overwhelmingly of exchange of mutually agreeable remarks. What this all means—and this is clearly documented—is that the people who do the most reading and listening and talking are the people who change their minds the least. Lowell did not say it first but he said it well: "To a great extent, people hear what they want to hear and see what they want to see. They associate by preference with people who think as they do, enter freely into conversation with them, and avoid with others topics that are controversial, irritating or unpleasant. This is not less true of what they read. To most people, that which runs counter to their ideas is disagreeable, and sought only from a sense of duty."

In summary, then, genuine political discussion—not acrimonious argumentation on the one hand or mutual admiration for right thinking on the other, but free and open discussion devoted to finding a solution to a problem through the clarification and modification of views—this is not marked by its magnitude. Perhaps it is naive to point this out once more; perhaps it is naive to require it in the first place. We cannot inquire here into what the requirement of discussion can really mean in a modern democracy; whether self-interested argument is improper, whether genuine discussion goes on a different level in the political process. But certainly democratic practice does not conform fully to the requirements of some theorists: "The person or party formulating political principles or policies in advance of discussion, and refusing to compromise under any circumstances; or settling such principles or policies before the process of discussion is completed and refusing to compromise further; renders discussion a farce in the first place, and in the second, limits its usefulness."

The third requirement under process is *rationality;* the electorate is required to exercise rational judgment in political decisions.

Philosophers and economists still talk professionally about "rational behavior," but sociologists never really used the concept, psychologists have given it up, and political scientists seem to be in the process of doing so. The problem of giving the term a clear meaning acceptable to others is partly responsible for this state of affairs. The term, says a recent writer on rational conduct, "has enjoyed a long history which has bequeathed to it a legacy of ambiguity and confusion . . . Any man may be excused when he is puzzled by the question how he ought to use the word and in particular how he ought to use it in relation to human conduct and to politics."

The difficulty, of course, is not that there is no reasonably clear definition for the term but that there are several definitions describing several different kinds of rationality. And the conformity of democratic practice varies with each definition. Let us review a few major meanings and their relationship to democratic practice. In the first place, we may distinguish between the rational decision as outcome and the rational decision as process. In the former case we speak of rationality as equivalent to a "right" decision. This assumes that there is one right answer to every problem, and that the power of reason can arrive at truths of policy which should be evident to all—all, that is, except those ruled by prejudice or emotion. When this is not simply a euphemism for describing decisions of which we approve, it presumably refers to a decision taken in conformity with an estimate of desirable ends (it thus assumes a valid analysis of whose interest lies where) and also in conformity with a correct estimate of which means will achieve the given ends. If we leave determination of self-interest up to the individual involved, then virtually all electorate decisions are rational by this definition; if we leave it up to the "objective observer" then the proportion will vary arbitrarily with his estimate of the present situation and the future. Even in philosophy, this meaning appears to be so ambiguous that it is difficult to see how we can design empirical research to test the extent of its observance by the electorate.

If we take rationality as referring to the process of decision—a more likely definition—then various possibilities are available. One meaning requires a certain independence of the rational process from the influence of predispositions broadly defined. Here rationality becomes the "free decision"—free from coercive imposition; free from blinding institutional loyalties; free from personal position (such as class or race); free from passions and impulses; free, in short, from any distorting or distracting pressures which prevent clear observation and calm, sober reflection. Here the term refers to logical, syllogistic ratiocination. But this seems to be an impractical, untenable, undesirable, and quite unreasonable definition; it takes the content heart out of politics and leaves the voter with no real basis on which to evaluate political proposals. By this standard, at least in its extreme version, there are almost no rational voters. As a social philosopher says, "individuals who on their own initiative form or change their fundamental beliefs through genuine critical reflection are so rare that they may be classed as abnormal."

A second meaning of rationality is close to, if not identical with, our requirement of information and knowledge: the voter should be aware of the correct state of public affairs at the present and of the "reasonable" consequences of alternative proposals for action. By this definition someone who made up his political mind on the basis of ends for which there are no present means of attainment would be making a non-rational decision, and so would the person whose estimates of the present situation or of the future were wrong. Also by this meaning the voter should be capable of indicating some relevant grounds for his decision, and most voters can cite such grounds. Here we meet the difficult question of rationalization, as against rationality, but we can suggest a partial answer. Rationality is limited by the individual's incapacity to deal with the real world in all its complexity, so it must allow for the legitimacy of dealing with simplified models of reality. In politics, the voter may "really" decide on the basis of one or two issues which are dominant for him (for example, peace or the New Deal) and use other issues as reinforcing rationalizations (for example, the military background of a candidate or corruption in the Federal administration).

A third definition requires the presence of convincibility or open-mindedness in consideration of political issues. This does not require the citizen to change his mind but only to be genuinely open to a change of mind. Here the time involved seems crucial. If this means, for example, that the citizen should be open-minded between June and November of an election year, then probably fewer than half the electorate is rational, and very few indeed in the South and parts of New England. If it includes the four years of a presidential administration or the "natural history" of a major political issue, from birth in controversy to death in near-unanimity, then the figure would become quite higher. It is hard for the researcher to be more specific because of the difficulty of determining just when "genuine consideration," as against rationalization, goes on.

Still another meaning of rationality as process requires that the decision be made in a state of low psychic tension; that is, that the decision not be an emotional one but be marked by a certain amount of detachment and freedom from passion. This poses a nice democratic dilemma; the people most rational by this definition are the people least interested in the political process and least involved in its outcome. The more interested people are the more emotional, in this sense, and the least detached; they are the ones who ascribe important consequences to the outcome of the decision and thus find enough psychic energy to be active about the matter. Here the rational voter is the independent voter, that is, the one without sufficient interest or investment in the election to get excited about it.

Still other meanings are available. There is the meaning in which rationality refers to the presence of deliberately directed behavior to consciously formulated purposes. Here again, almost all voters could qualify. There is the meaning in which rationality refers to a choice of behavior that is optimal in some sense, and this definition can be readily satisfied on the grounds of a subjective optimum if nothing more. There is the meaning in which a rational decision is a self-consistent decision. There are undoubtedly other meanings.

If it is not easy to say what is meant by a rational decision, it is somewhat easier to say what is not meant by it. A rational decision is not a capricious decision, or an impulsive one, or an unprincipled one, or a decision guided by custom or habit or tradition or sentiment alone. But the central problem is to relate the demand of rationality to the analysis of decision-making in terms of such sociopsychological concepts as the reference group; that is, to see the "rational decision" as imbedded in a social context which limits it at the same time that it gives it political meaning. While the types of rationality are not easy to define and while they are certainly never present in a pure or extreme form, they can be isolated empirically, clarified, and investigated as to their frequency, their functions, and their preconditions.

THE OUTCOME OF ELECTORATE DECISIONS

Finally, there is one basic requirement which might be included under the need for principle but which seems to deserve independent treatment in view of its central importance with reference to the outcome of the decision. This is the requirement of *community interest;* the electorate is supposed to come to political decisions on consideration of the common good rather than, or in addition to, self-interest.

In several formulations of democratic theory, the electorate is required to devote thought to what is good for the community as a whole instead of relying exclusively upon calculation of what is good for oneself or one's own group. The classical formulation comes from John Stuart Mill: "In any political election . . . the voter is under an absolute moral obligation to consider the interests of the public, not his private advantage, and give his vote, to the best of his judgment, exactly as he would be bound to do if he were the sole voter, and the election depended upon him alone."

Now here again the problem of definition is a central one. How is the researcher to distinguish between honest conclusion and forced rationalization, as in the slogan, "What's good for me is good for the country"? How distinguish the "immediate and apparent interest" from the "ultimate and real interest"? Does self-interest refer only to the criterion of direct self-gain or to that of benefit to one's group or class, and over what period of time? Does community interest refer to agreement on procedures, or to an outside criterion (and if so, what), or to the residual decision after the various self-interests have balanced themselves out, or to genuine concern for other groups, or to restraint upon self-interest, or to deviation from the predominant vote of one's group? The more one looks into the matter, the more it appears that one man's self-interest is another man's community interest, and that many people sincerely identify the one with the other. Nor have the theorists overlooked this. "Men come easily to believe that arrangements agreeable to themselves are beneficial to others," said Dicey. "A man's interest gives a bias to his judgment far oftener than it corrupts his heart." And from Schumpeter: "To different individuals and groups the common good is bound to mean different things. This fact, hidden from the utilitarian by the narrowness of his outlook on the world of human valuations, will introduce rifts on questions of principle which cannot be reconciled by rational argument."

In a current study of opinion formation (the Elmira study), we concluded that it is more satisfactory to analyze this question in terms of the forces making for political cleavage and political consensus within the community. The health of a democratic order depends on achieving a nice balance between them: enough cleavage to stimulate debate and action, enough consensus to hold the society together even under strain. Political parties in a democracy should disagree—but not too much, too sharply, nor too fundamentally. The evidences of cleavage are clear to everyone. Cleavage along class and religious and regional lines in addition to direct attitudinal differences on basic issues of foreign and domestic policy—these are so familiar as to require no elaboration. At the same time there are important evidences of consensus, of political cohesion, which deserve more attention than they usually get. In the first place, there is the basic fact that group memberships and identifications overlap political choices; sizable political minorities are found in various social groups and this provides a kind of glue to hold the community together. In addition, even at the height of a presidential campaign there are sizable attitudinal minorities within each party and each social group on political issues, and thus sizable attitudinal agreements across party and group lines. Such overlappings link various groups together and prevent their further estrangement. All of this means that democratic politics in this country is happily not total politics—a situation where politics is the single or central selector and rejector, where other social differences are drawn on top of political lines. Cross-pressures in political allegiances, based upon a pluralistic system of values, are thus highly important to the society.

So the question of self and community interest may best be seen as the question of cleavage and consensus. The multiplicity and the heterogeneity of identifications and associations in the great society develop an overlapping, pluralistic social organization which both sharpens and softens the impact and the consequences of political activity.

CONCLUSIONS

The political theory of democracy, then, requires that the electorate possess appropriate personality structures, that it be interested and participate in public affairs, that it be informed, that it be principled, that it correctly perceive political realities, that it engage in discussion, that it judge rationally, and that it consider the community interest.

Now this combination of requirements sets a high—an ideal—standard for the political process. And since this is a composite list, from a variety of sources, it is not necessarily a matter for disillusionment or even disappointment that the democratic electorate does not conform to every requirement in the full degree. There is always an appropriate observation from Lord Bryce:

> Orthodox political theory assumes that every citizen has, or ought to have, thought out for himself certain opinions, for example, ought to have a definite view, defensible by arguments, of what the country needs, what principles ought to be applied in governing it, of the men to whose hands the government ought to be entrusted. There are persons who talk, though certainly very few who act, as if they believed this theory, which may be compared to the theory of some ultra-Protestants that every good Christian has or ought to have, by the strength of his own reasons, worked out for himself from the Bible a system of theology.

Opinion studies in recent years have done much to fill in the picture of what actually happens in democratic decision-making. As is evident even from this brief survey, they have done so in three ways: first, by documenting the theoretical assumptions with facts about actual political behavior; second, by clarifying the concepts and assumptions of democratic theory, if in no other way simply by insisting upon researchable formulations; and third, by differentiating and reformulating the general theoretical propositions in more exact terms. Further systematic exploration of this subject within a sharper, more valid, and more sophisticated framework of political theory should make a rich contribution to each side. The difficulties of collaboration between political theorists on the one hand and opinion researchers on the other must not be allowed to stand in the way of joint work, for the theorists can provide a systematic statement in terms of which public opinion studies can be meaningfully organized, and the empirical researchers can document the theoretical requirements. The theorists can suggest new concepts and hypotheses to the researcher, and the researcher can force the theorists to sharpen and differentiate—yes, and quantify—their formulations.

Of course there are problems but they should be negotiated or overcome. For example, the theorists tend to use descriptive categories (e.g., rationality) and the researchers prefer predictive categories (e.g., group memberships) in "explaining" political preferences. Hard and joint thinking on such problems should bring returns.

The investigation of the realities of democratic processes at the level of the electorate is a useful service and it should be carried forward. Opinion studies can help a democracy not only to know itself in a topical and immediate way but also to evaluate its achievements and its progress in more general terms. In this framework, the study of public opinion can make a telling contribution in the basic, continuous struggle to bring democratic practice more and more into harmony with the requirements and the assumptions—that is, with the ideals—of democratic theory.

PUBLIC OPINION AND THE DECAY OF DEMOCRACY

V. O. KEY, JR.

I

Every age has its melancholy prophets who foresee the decay of the political order through the workings of irreversible processes which they identify with precision and assurance. We perhaps do not do enough honor to those oracles whose sensitive vision brings within their range a dark and forbidding future. Some of them we ignore because they are certifiable lunatics. Many of them are those who simply mistake the personal anxiety aroused by any novel public policy for a threat to the social order. Nevertheless, the unpleasant fact is that they turn out eventually to be right. They may be off in their timing. They may be dead wrong in their diagnosis of the causes of national decline. Yet sooner or later they are right. Nations, empires, and civilizations, in so far as history goes, incandesce in brief moments of glory only to decline into complacency, weakness, poverty. Portugal, let it be remembered, not so long ago ranked as one of the great powers of the globe.

II

The bleak prognostications that I propose to examine appear in many variants, but they have as a common denominator a simple proposition. They assert in one way or another that democratic systems contain within themselves an inner dynamic that must lead to their self-destruction. To the extent that governments are responsive to public opinion, to that extent are they destined to take steps that ultimately undermine their own foundations. That proposition, in turn, depends on the assumption that the mass of men, guided by their own ignorance or cupidity, in the long run throw their weight on the side of policies corrosive of the vitality of the great society. This motivational analysis is sometimes fortified by the observation that democracy, as we un-

SOURCE: V. O. Key, Jr., "Public Opinion and the Decay of Democracy," *The Virginia Quarterly Review*, 37 (Autumn 1961), 481–494. Copyright by *The Virginia Quarterly Review*, The University of Virginia. Reprinted by permission.

derstand it, has flourished for only a moment as history goes and then only among a small proportion of the people of this earth. More commonly tyranny and oppression have been the lot of mankind.

These general ideas find their most extended, and most plausible, elaborations in discussions of the management of the foreign politics of democracies. The gradual subjection of foreign offices to public opinion has mightily hampered them in the conduct of an effective foreign policy, or so it is said. Consideration of the probable nature of public response tempers policy when it should be forthright; makes it rigid when it should be flexible; imbues it with bellicosity when it should be restrained; and often makes wise decisions ineffective by delaying them beyond the moment of their timeliness. These consequences, the argument runs, flow from the tendency of the public to consider its own comfort and convenience and from its incapacity to estimate the long-run consequences for the nation of developments comprehensible only to those especially well informed and suitably trained.

These morbid hypotheses acquire plausibility from the episodes that are cited as illustrative. Chamberlain, on his return from Munich with "peace in our time," received the plaudits of the multitude to the astonishment of the experts who thought that he had compromised the national interest. Or, if we do not go beyond our own borders, it may be interesting, if not instructive, to ask what the course of history might have been had the American government not felt that it had to await the development of a supportive public opinion before it could take a firm stand in the events leading to World War II. Or to speculate ahead about how decisively our nation's leaders can be expected to act in moments of crisis when they remember the exploitation of the Korean issue in the presidential campaign of 1952 and the apparent response of the public to that question. Or to consider the fact that government is thought to be strait-jacketed by public opinion on some questions regardless of what course the national interest may prescribe. If, for example, it became certain that the admission of Red China to the UN would promote the national interest, what could our government do?

When the analysts turn their attention to domestic economic policy, they see ultimate consequences fatal for the polity as the substance of governmental action becomes more dependent upon public opinion. The basic psychology of the interpretation is a kind of Gresham's law: those who promise the most for the least will in the long run drive reasonable and just men from public life. Thus will be blotted up the incentives that give the system its vitality; thus the productive processes will be disrupted; thus freedom will be destroyed. Moreover, as the autonomous capacity of government itself shrinks, groups of brigands with comparatively small public followings may demand and obtain governmental action promotive of their indefensible ends. When good fortune smiles on the Republic, one group of brigands offsets another. Then we have countervailing power—and governmental paralysis. Though their motive may be the easy gains to be had from the genteel plunder feasible in a highly interdependent economy, these groups make a great show of deference to public opinion. At any rate they finance rituals calculated to generate a show of public support for their depredations.

In another phase of domestic politics responsiveness to public opinion puts government at the mercy of the paranoid sector of society, if we are to believe the amateur psychiatrists among the political scientists and the amateur political scientists among the psychiatrists. The McCarthyites with all their clamor did not bring government to a standstill, but they did make the United States of America look contemptible. And we are certain to have other movements that rise up to exploit human anxieties and in the process irreparably harm many of our citizens.

When all its elements are pieced together, the analysis produces a picture of government incapable of decisive and timely action in foreign politics for lack of assured capacity to command popular support; of a government hamstrung in domestic affairs by its forced preoccupation with the distribution of the loaves and fishes; of a government so responsive to even synthetic popular clamor that it must infringe the liberties of its citizens and commit wrongs that outrage the sense of decency of honorable men.

III

How should we regard the estimates of tendencies inherent in democracy that I have summarized? My initial disposition is to respond with an irreverent guffaw. Yet the analysis merits more respectful attention. It consists not of the reflections of a single person; it is rather an assembly of ideas from men widely reputed to be learned, men who have devoted their lives to study and speculation about the political tribulations of man. Moreover, as one reflects about the analysis, the uneasy hunch begins to take root that it may contain an occasional sliver of truth. It deserves careful if not sympathetic examination.

The essential components of the diagnosis, let us recall, are two. First, the linkage of government and public opinion is so intimate that public opinion determines the tenor of public policy, if not with minuteness, with firmness within a relatively narrow range. Second, public opinion by its very nature must demand of government the wrong actions. The public hesitates to face up to crises; it must be shortsighted because most men can see public problems only in terms of their experience as individuals; it may be greedy; and on occasion it is simply mad.

The only trouble with the analysis, or so it seems to me, is that it is wrong. One cannot deny that our government commits from time to time truly magnificent blunders nor that it is on occasion guilty of damaging, if not disastrous, errors of omission. Yet to attribute these shortcomings in any large measure to the stifling restraints of public opinion is a misreading of the relationships between popular attitudes and governmental action. Our systematic knowledge of public opinion is, one may concede, limited. Our knowledge of the interactions between government and popular attitudes is even thinner. Yet the evidence suffices to discount drastically the supposition of the dictatorship of public opinion.

A major difficulty with the hypothesis is that it errs in its identification of the villain. What is this public opinion that is supposed to compel government to conform to its own unwise judgments? The survey specialists have explored the public mind fairly extensively and we are no longer completely dependent upon excogitation as we seek the nature of public opinion. One conclusion that emerges from the survey data is that substantial proportions of the population remain both unconcerned and uninformed about a great many concrete policies of government. If people are asked whether they approve of the reciprocal trade program, for example, many of them will cheerfully confess that they never heard of it. That is the fate even of issues that have been as well ventilated as the Taft-Hartley Act or the Bricker Amendment. Senator Bricker's proposal received extended attention from the press and the electronic media and set off a debate that reached a high temperature. Of Mr. Gallup's sample of the population, though, 81 per cent said that they had neither heard nor read of the Senator's scheme to clip the wings of the President in foreign affairs.

Only a small proportion of the public maintains a sufficient focus of attention on public affairs to have much of an opinion about very many highly specific issues. On broadly stated issues, though, substantial proportions of the public have opinions. Heavy majorities, for example, approve of the idea that the government should do something or another to see that elderly persons are able to get adequate medical care. The public doubtless could be shown to be far less informed and far less opinionated about the relative merits of grants to the states, social security financing, or other means of achieving that end. When one is concerned about opinion on the details of public policy, if he is a skilled survey technician, he can frame questions to produce almost any picture of public opinion that he desires. And if you ask the right question, a great many people will say that the government ought to do what it thinks best rather than to be guided by mass opinion.

If we pursued this line of argument far enough, we would reach the position where we could contend that government is entirely free of restraints by public opinion because the public has, if any opinion, only a nebulous one. Such a position would deny the basic supposition of democracy that in one way or another governmental action should parallel popular wishes or at least meet with popular acceptance. Undoubtedly, at its margins governmental activity is policed by fairly firm opinions about what should and should not be done. But for the purposes of our argument the significant fact is that within whatever limits opinion fixes, government enjoys wide discretion in the determination whether to act, in the timing of action, and in the choice of the measures it takes. Only infrequently can government excuse its stupidities by pleading the hampering restrictions of the matrix of public opinion within which it acts.

The autonomy of government may be seen in another dimension if we examine the public's sanctions with respect to the actions of government. Opinion is supposed to express itself through elections, but it has long since been clear that the popular majority in an election does not constitute a set of congruent popular majorities on a series of discrete public issues. The motivation of the popular vote is by no means lacking in policy content, yet the fact that a candidate wins should not be taken to mean that a popular majority endorses all those measures he advocates. The public expresses itself prospectively only vaguely. In truth, the only genuine sanction of the public against governmental action contrary to its wishes is retrospective. It can throw from office that government whose policies displease it.

We are, of course, familiar with those confident interpretations of the public mind that appear on the day after an election. Reporters, columnists, campaign managers, and candidates attribute the outcome to the loser's action on a particular policy or bundle of policies, to the winner's position on a particular question, or to this factor or that factor. Even a cub reporter can put a tone of great assurance into such a piece. The studies of voting behavior by the scholars make us skeptical of all attributions of clear-cut policy determination to popular elections. In truth, the more I study elections the more disposed I am to believe that they have within themselves more than a trace of the lottery. That, of course, is not necessarily undesirable so long as all concerned abide by the toss of the coin. Be that as it may, the moral for our purposes is plain. Even when the public in manifest anger and disillusionment throws an Administration from office, it does not express its policy preferences with precision. The voice of the people may be loud but the enunciation is indistinct.

Another line of interpretation concedes that the general public speaks haltingly and unclearly but that segments of the public operating through pressure groups bring blocs of influential opinion to bear upon government in ways injurious to the common interest. That pressure groups can raise an awesome din there can be no doubt. That they deserve official deference because they can command the votes of their members at the next election the evidence makes doubtful. Certainly group interests determine the votes of some people at some times. Yet an impressive aspect of the evidence is the large proportion of, for example, industrial workers or farmers who are unaware of the policy positions of their own organizations. They do not have the rudimentary information necessary to respond to appeals to crack the whip over erring representatives. Moreover, as one examines the voting behavior of group members through time, it becomes apparent that the relevance of group membership for the vote differs markedly from election to election. The evidence points to the conclusion that the group leader who threatens to throw the vote of his members against a candidate asserts a power that he possesses only at some times and then usually only to a limited extent. Perhaps it is equally clear that leaders of pressure groups succeed in pushing outrageous measures through Congress and through state legislatures; yet their power must usually rest by and large on something other than their capacity to punish at future elections.

The rôle of public opinion vis-à-vis the actions of government appears in still another light when we reflect on the manner of formation of public opinion. The influences that bear upon our attitudes range from the effects of our family environment when we were children to what we read in yesterday's newspaper. Yet government itself is a major factor in the molding of popular attitudes. And it is as much the duty of government to seek to change a public opinion that it believes to be in error as it is to respond to an opinion that it judges to be in the public interest. The capacity of leadership to mold opinion appears to be closely related to the sense of identification of people with their political parties. The evidence suggests that, in the absence of compelling considerations to the contrary, people tend to adopt those opinions that seem to be appropriate for good Democrats or Republicans as the case may be. They seem to take their cues from their partisan leaders.

Opinion is shaped, too, and probably more effectively, by the impact of events than by the exhortations of the advocates of causes. For example, it is interesting to speculate whether in 1932 the American people would have voted for the New Deal if they had known in detail what it was going to be. This speculation is hampered by the fact that a majority would have voted against Hoover no matter who the Democratic candidate or what his program. But if we define that circumstance away it is possible that a majority would not have voted for the New Deal had it been spelled out in detail. People have no great yearning for the unknown. Yet once the people lived with the New Deal a while they learned to like it and in 1936 they rejected the Republican challenge to it by a vote astonishing in its decisiveness. In short, the way of the innovator is risky; people do not ordain innovation; they accept it or they reject it.

IV

The evidence on the interplay between mass opinion and government in the American democracy can lead only, I believe, to the conclusion that those who blame mass opinion for our ills hang the wrong villain. If we search further, though, another suspect appears. It may be that under the conditions of American democracy, politicians and political activists generally have perceptions of public opinion, perceptions of prospective public response to proposed action, and habits of behavior that lead them to act as if public opinion had all the deleterious effects and qualities that are ascribed to it. Their perceptions of mass opinion and their fears of mass wrath may move them to foolish actions on the plea that the public wants things that way even though in reality sensible actions would be acceptable to the public.

We have practically no systematic information about what goes on in the minds of public men as they ruminate about the weight to be given to public opinion in governmental decision. Yet in his gloomy moments the observer forms the impression that public men often act as if they thought the deciding margin in elections was cast by fools; moreover, by fools informed enough and alert enough to bring retribution to those who dare not demonstrate themselves to be equally foolish. In keeping with this impression we see a pervasive caution in action in fear of public opinion. A common posture is that of looking backward. Political battles tend to be fought from positions that have brought victory in the past. Or urgent matters may remain in abeyance until enough apparent opinion is generated to justify action. In other cases, public men assume that since they were elected their private predilections are in tune with public sentiment and therefore have a certified validity. Or in others, they may compound ignorance within the public by serving as its faithful but cynical advocate.

Speculation along these lines prompts the question whether to identify the roots of the ailments of the régime it may not be correct to look to the outlooks, beliefs, and habits of action of the political activists rather than to the opinions of the undifferentiated mass of people. This is not to say that the kinds of outlooks that the mass of people have are irrelevant. It is rather to contend that the populistic model of democracy departs from the reality and that perhaps a healthy democracy must contain within itself a suitable strain of political aristocracy. Our habitual emphasis upon equality in the voting booth and elsewhere may lead us to overlook the paradox of the inequality of duties, obligations, and rôles among citizens of a viable democratic order. Equality of opportunity is attractive only because of its promise of inequality of achievement. Perhaps neither can exist without the other.

The strain of "aristocracy" within an operating democracy consists of diverse sorts of people, not of a social or an economic upper crust. Broadly it includes the political influentials and the political activists. Public officials, candidates, defeated candidates, would-be candidates, and others engaged professionally and semi-professionally in politics would be included—and this is a varied lot. Included also are the journalists, the publicists, and others concerned with public information and education. And, perhaps more importantly, this strain includes those individuals who seem to be sprinkled throughout the social hierarchy who pay heed to public affairs, who have opinions, and who in turn shape the opinions of others. All these sorts of persons, who constitute a small proportion of the population, perform an important rôle in the formation of public opinion, in the creation of support for public policy, and in the maintenance of the morale of the citizenry. I do not mean to intimate that those I have labeled the political activists constitute a cohesive ruling class. They are by no means unified and they hold disparate views. They are of many types, some of them unsavory. But by their attention to public affairs and by their activities, they perform, as a class, a special rôle in the politics of a democracy. In the division of political labor others fill a far more passive role.

Perhaps the policies of a democratic order depend ultimately on the outlooks and concerns of the more active citizenry rather than on mass opinion. If so, any assessment of the vitality of a democratic system should rest on an examination of the outlooks, the sense of purpose, and the beliefs of this sector of society. Hard information on these matters is scarce; even scarcer is information on what changes have occurred over, say, the past century in the outlooks of the influentials.

Nevertheless, we have our impressions. The doctrines, beliefs, and catch phrases that are propagated among and by the influential sectors of the population manifest remarkably little concern about the problems which must be met by the community or by the nation as a whole if we are to continue the painfully slow process of lifting ourselves by our bootstraps from the primeval ooze. Instead, slogans are reiterated that deny the existence of public problems. Or the doctrine is that if there are problems of general concern they will be solved if we deny to government the power to deal with them. It is as if we blindfolded ourselves on the assumption that then all our communal problems would take care of themselves.

Consider, for example, the ideologies propagated by and apparently believed by businessmen. Apart from the focus on national development by a handful of executives of the largest corporations, businessmen, an extremely influential sector of the nation, seem by and large to believe that all solutions are contained within the magic phrase "free enterprise." The solemn incantation of this slogan is a poor substitute for thought about what we do to promote the national interest or the community interest on any concrete problem at any specific time. If by some miracle we should overnight establish a free enterprise system by wiping from the statute books all interferences with economic liberty, it would be regarded tomorrow as a catastrophe. The pressures on Congress to restore the status quo ante would be formidable. On hand to assert that they wanted none of free enterprise would be the lobbyists for the airlines, the steamship conferences, the investment trusts, the chambers of commerce, the banks, the truckers, the petroleum industry, the real estate developers, the cosmetologists, and the Nevada gamblers.

All this is not to berate businessmen. Like comments could be made about the popular political philosophy of doctors, lawyers, labor union leaders, or newspaper publishers. Nor is it to condemn freedom of enterprise. Sometimes freedom of enterprise is for the public weal; sometimes it is not.

The object of the illustration is only to raise a general inquiry about the nature of the outlook and the focus of attention of those who are influential, be they businessmen or something else, as they shape public opinion and influence public policy. Something can be said for the estimate that the influentials in large measure concentrate their attention on private ends. The consequence is an impressive neglect of problems of community concern and of matters that require collective action for their solution. To the extent that those opinion leaders scattered through the population impress their indifference about the common good upon the public generally, to that extent they may fix the form of public opinion and perhaps of public action or inaction.

One must cheerfully concede that our knowledge of the attitudes and outlooks of the, say, five to ten million influentials in the political system rests more upon hunch than upon careful inquiry. Nor can we say with any confidence whether the present state of affairs represents a change for the worse or merely a condition that has been with us for a long time. This broad class of men may have always given little attention to public questions. But the trends in their outlooks may be irrelevant for our problem. It may well be that the changes in the structure of power in the nation, the invention of new means for molding mass opinion, and the decline in the strength of the party system give a new significance to the network of influentials and political activists within the society. Their dedication to private ends and their neglect of the affairs of the commonwealth may have different consequences than they had earlier. Under the circumstances of our times, their apolitical, even antipolitical, orientations may generate forces with which governments cannot readily cope.

V

The entire analysis distills down, I suppose, to the contention that mass opinion tends to be formed by an inner core of influentials and activists, some millions in number but proportionately small in the total population. It follows, if this is true, that those who argue that democracy in the long run must fall because of the myopia and greed of the masses err in their identification of the sources of vitality of a democracy. The maintenance of a working democratic system requires the existence of a substantial sprinkling of persons throughout the population concerned with the public weal and animated by a faith in the system. The impression takes shape that the influentials may be in large measure attached to partial and special concerns and often believers in slogans with no great relevance for the problems of the day. If the American democracy has within itself a drive toward self-destruction, we might more accurately localize the trouble by looking among the best people than at the great mass of the people. I doubt that political systems, be they democratic or otherwise, are often destroyed by the self-corruption of the masses.

GROUPS AND SOCIETY

DAVID B. TRUMAN

Man is a social animal. Among other meanings involved in this Aristotelian statement is the observation that with rare exceptions man is always found in association with other men. John Dewey has observed: "Associated activity needs no explanation; things are made that way." [1] This association includes varying degrees of organization; that is, certain of the relationships among a collection of men regularly occur in certain consistent patterns and sequences. But there is another meaning in this classic proposition, closer to the one that Aristotle probably intended, namely, that men must exist in society in order to manifest those capacities and accomplishments that distinguish them from the other animals. These human accomplishments embrace not only the wonderous array of skills and creations that are thought of as civilization but also humbler and more fundamental developments such as primary intellectual growth and language.

We do not have to rely solely on Aristotle's confidence concerning the virtues of life in the city-state for support of the proposition that man is essentially social. The Robinson Crusoe hypothesis that men are best conceived of as isolated units is inadequate psychology as well as unfashionable economics. Accounts, at least partially authenticated, of children who by some chance of fate have been raised among animals, isolated from all contact with human beings, indicate not only that speech is not acquired under such circumstances but also that it is developed only very slowly after the child has been returned to human society. Cases of children who have been kept in solitary confinement during their early years illustrate the same point. An essentially human and social characteristic, speech, is not acquired, and, in fact, the very capacity to learn is apparently stunted or atrophied.[2] Man becomes characteristically human only in association with other men.

A more obvious sort of interdependence also requires man to live in soci-

---

[1] John Dewey: *The Public and Its Problems* (New York: Henry Holt & Company, Inc., 1927), p. 151. Copyright by and used with the permission of Henry Holt & Company, Inc.

[2] See Arnold Gesell: *Wolf Child and Human Child* (New York: Harper and Brothers, 1939) and Kingsley Davis: "Extreme Social Isolation of a Child," *American Journal of Sociology*, Vol. 45, no. 4 (January, 1940), pp.554–65.

SOURCE: David B. Truman, excerpts from *The Governmental Process: Political Interests and Public Opinion* (New York: Alfred A. Knopf, Inc., 1951), pp. 14–17, 33–44. Copyright 1951 by Alfred A. Knopf, Inc. Reprinted by permission of the publisher.

ety—purely physical dependence on others of his species. The family, the
most primitive social unit, the only one that man shares generally with other
mammals, exists in part to provide protection and training for the offspring
during their long period of helplessness. Furthermore, the division of labor or
specialization, which appears even in the simple family unit on the basis of
age and sex differences and on which a high degree of skill and large productivity fundamentally depend, almost by definition involves the mutual dependence of men. A modern urban dweller who has experienced the consequences of an interruption in the milk supply, in the public transportation
system, or in the distribution of electric power needs no introduction to the
implications of specialization.

In this chapter, as the remarks above suggest, we shall not focus our attention primarily upon "political" behavior. We shall rather examine groups of
all kinds and their significance in the social process generally. The point to
bear in mind is that the dynamics of groups are not essentially different because the groups are labeled "political." Basically they show the same regularities as do other continuing social patterns. In this connection we shall discuss the meaning of the terms "group" and "interest group" and shall
examine some of the characteristics of a peculiarly important type of group,
the association.

GROUP AFFILIATIONS AND INDIVIDUAL BEHAVIOR

In all societies of any degree of complexity the individual is less affected directly by the society as a whole than differentially through various of its subdivisions, or groups. In the first place, even in the simplest society, it is literally impossible for any one individual to function in all the groups of which
the society is made. Just as he can become highly skilled in only one or a few
techniques, so he can participate in only a limited number of the groups that
are formed about such specializations. In a society in which locality groupings
are important, an individual never "belongs" to more than a few and rarely to
more than one. In the second place, the positions occupied by the individual
in his society limit the effects upon him of society as a whole. The technical
term usually applied to these positions is *statuses*.[3] He may not participate in
those groups confined to persons of the opposite sex or of a differing age level.
Ordinarily he belongs to only one "extended" family, one church, one economic institution, and one political unit at a given level, such as the nation. At
any point in time and frequently over his entire life span he cannot belong to
more than one class or caste grouping.

To the extent that the range and type of behavior in these groupings vary
from one to another—and even in the simplest societies they inevitably vary

[3] Ralph Linton: *The Cultural Background of Personality* (New York: Appleton-Century-Crofts,
Inc., 1945), pp. 75–82.

to some degree—the patterns of action and attitude among individuals will differ from one another in large measure according to the clusters of group affiliations that the individuals have. In John Dewey's words: "The underlying and generative conditions of concrete behavior are social as well as organic: much more social than organic as far as the manifestation of *differential* wants, purposes and methods of operation is concerned." [4] Because such groups may come into conflict from time to time, various theorists have attempted to account for both the groups and the conflict in terms of "instincts." Gaetano Mosca, for example, asserts that men have an "instinct of herding together and fighting with other herds" that accounts not only for the conflicts between societies but also for "the formation of all the divisions and subdivisions . . . that arise within a given society and occasion moral and, sometimes, physical conflicts." [5] It is quite unnecessary to resort to any such crude *deus ex machina*, for, like the similar devices employed by the social contract philosophers of the seventeenth century to account for the origin of government and society, it implies the temporal priority of the individual over the group. That is, it implicitly assumes that individuals exist first in some degree of isolation and then form into societies or groups, a notion impossible to document.

It is simpler and more realistic to say with James Madison that the tendencies toward such groupings are "sown in the nature of man," meaning by that statement, as he apparently meant, that such tendencies are "sown" by the differing group experiences of individuals. When such groups become active, whether in conflict or not, that stage of development can be accounted for, again in Madison's words, in terms of "the different circumstances of civil society." [6] In slightly different terms: "The human being whom we fasten upon as individual *par excellence* is moved and regulated by his association with others; what he does and what the consequences of his behavior are, what his experience consists of, cannot even be described, much less accounted for, in isolation." [7]

● ● ●

INTEREST GROUPS
● ● ●

As used here "interest group" refers to any group that, on the basis of one or more shared attitudes, makes certain claims upon other groups in the soci-

---

[4] Dewey: *The Public and Its Problems*, p. 103. Copyright 1927 by and used with the permission of Henry Holt & Company, Inc.

[5] From *The Ruling Class* by Gaetano Mosca, translated from the Italian by Hannah D. Kahn, edited by Arthur Livingston, p. 163. Copyright 1939. Courtesy of McGraw-Hill Book Company, Inc.

[6] *The Federalist*, No. 10.

[7] Dewey: *The Public and Its Problems*, p. 188. Copyright 1927 by and used with the permission of Henry Holt & Company, Inc.

ety for the establishment, maintenance, or enhancement of forms of behavior that are implied by the shared attitudes. In earlier paragraphs of this chapter it was indicated that from interaction in groups arise certain common habits of response, which may be called norms, or shared attitudes. These afford the participants frames of reference for interpreting and evaluating events and behaviors. In this respect all groups are interest groups because they are shared-attitude groups. In some groups at various points in time, however, a second kind of common response emerges, in addition to the frames of reference. These are shared attitudes toward what is needed or wanted in a given situation, observable as demands or claims upon other groups in the society. The term "interest group" will be reserved here for those groups that exhibit both aspects of the shared attitudes.

The shared attitudes, moreover, constitute the interests. It has been suggested that a distinction be made between the two terms, reserving the latter to designate "the objects toward which these . . . [attitudes] are directed." [44] Such a distinction may be highly misleading. If, for example, reference were made to oil interests, one would presumably be referring, among other things, to certain elements in the physical environment, petroleum and its by-products. These features, however, have no significance in society apart from the activities of men. There were no oil attitudes prior to the time when the productive behaviors of men led them to do something with petroleum.[45] As a consequence of the use of oil, an array of attitudes with respect to that use has developed—that it should not be wasted, that it should be marketed in a particular way, that it should be produced by many small groups or enterprises, that it should be controlled by an international organization, and so on. Some of these attitudes are represented by interest groups asserting that the behaviors implied by the attitudes should be encouraged, discouraged, or altered. The physical features of oil production have no significance for the student of society apart from the attitudes, or interests, and the behaviors that they suggest.

Definition of the interest group in this fashion has a number of distinct advantages in the task of political analysis. In the first place, it permits the identification of various potential as well as existing interest groups. That is, it invites examination of an interest whether or not it is found at the moment as one of the characteristics of a particular organized group. Although no group that makes claims upon other groups in the society will be found without an interest or interests, it is possible to examine interests that are not at a particular point in time the basis of interactions among individuals, but that may become such. Without the modern techniques for the measurement of attitude and opinion, this position would indeed be risky, since it would invite

[44] Robert M. MacIver: "Interests," *Encyclopaedia of the Social Sciences*. Cf. Avery Leiserson: *Administrative Regulation: A Study in Representation of Interests* (Chicago: University of Chicago Press, 1942), pp. 1–10.

[45] Cf. Bentley: *The Process of Government*, pp. 193–4.

the error of ascribing an interest to individuals quite apart from any overt behavior that they might display.[46] In the scientific study of society only frustration and defeat are likely to follow an attempt to deal with data that are not directly observable. Even the most insistent defenders of the scientific position, however, admit that, although activity is the basic datum of social science, a "becoming" stage of activity must be recognized as a phase of activity if any segment of a moving social situation is to be understood. There are, in other words, potential activities, or "tendencies of activity." [47] These tendencies are the central feature of the most widely accepted social psychological definition of attitude. Gordon W. Allport, after examining a series of definitions, arrived at his own generally used statement: "An attitude is a mental and neural *state of readiness*, organized through experience, exerting a directive or dynamic influence upon the individual's response to all objects and situations with which it is related." [48] On the basis of widely held attitudes that are not expressed in interaction, therefore, it is possible to talk of potential interest groups.

In the second place, as these statements suggest, this concept of interest group permits attention to what Lundberg calls the "degree of integrative interaction." [49] The frequency, or rate, of interaction will in part determine the primacy of a particular group affiliation in the behavior of an individual and, as will be indicated in more detail later, it will be of major importance in determining the relative effectiveness with which a group asserts its claims upon other groups.[50] This approach affords all the advantages and none of the disadvantages that once accrued to the sociologists' concepts of "primary groups" and "secondary groups," meaning by the former face-to-face interaction as opposed to indirect contacts such as those made through the media of mass communication. Before the enormous expansion and development of the latter techniques, and still in societies where they have not penetrated, it was a verifiable fact that solidarity of group behavior depended largely upon physical proximity. Frequent face-to-face contact in no small measure accounted for the influence of such primary groups as the family, the neighborhood, and the like. As the social functions performed by the family institution in our society have declined, some of these secondary groups, such as labor unions, have achieved a rate of interaction that equals or surpasses that of certain of the primary groups. This shift in importance has been facilitated largely by the development of means of communication that permit frequent interaction among individuals not in face-to-face contact or not continuously so.

In this connection note the confidence that James Madison, in seeking re-

[46] Ibid., p. 213.
[47] Ibid., pp. 184 ff.
[48] Gordon W. Allport: "Attitudes," in Carl Murchison (ed.): *A Handbook of Social Psychology* (Worcester, Mass.: Clark University Press, 1935), chap. 17.
[49] Lundberg: *Foundations of Sociology*, p. 310.
[50] See below, chaps. 6 and 7.

straints upon the "mischiefs of faction" (interest groups), placed in "the greater obstacles opposed to the concert" of such groups by the "extent of the Union." [51] Such faith in physical dispersion had some basis in a period when it took a week to travel a distance of three hundred miles. It would not be true to say that primary groups no longer achieve the integration once ascribed to them. A recent study has indicated, for example, that the prolonged resistance of the German army in the face of repeated defeats in 1944 and 1945 was a result largely of the solidarity and continued structural integrity of such primary groups as the squad.[52] It is primarily from the degree of interaction that the face-to-face group fosters, however, that its influence is derived. A high degree may also be achieved through secondary means.

In the third place, this concept of the interest group permits us to evaluate the significance of formal organization. The existence of neither the group nor the interest is dependent upon formal organization, although that feature has significance, particularly in the context of politics. Organization indicates merely a stage or degree of interaction.[53] The fact that one interest group is highly organized whereas another is not or is merely a potential group— whether the interest involved is that of affording more protection to consumers, greater privileges for brunettes, or more vigorous enforcement of civil rights—is a matter of great significance at any particular moment. It does not mean, however, that the momentarily weaker group, or interest, will inevitably remain so. Events may easily produce an increased rate of interaction among the affected individuals to the point where formal organization or a significant interest group will emerge and greater influence will ensue. The point may be illustrated by noting that this increased rate of interaction is usually what is meant when the journalists speak of "an aroused public opinion."

Finally, this use of the concept also gives a proper perspective to the political activities of many interest groups that are the principal concern of this book. Although a characteristic feature of these groups is that they make claims upon other groups in the society, these claims may be asserted or enforced by means of a variety of techniques and through any of the institutions of the society, not merely the government. An interest group concentrating upon replacing the valuable shade trees in a village adjacent to a large gentleman's farm may achieve its objective by prevailing upon the baronial family to purchase the trees and pay for their planting. A group interested in the protection of certain moralities among the younger generation may secure the

[51] *The Federalist*, No. 10; see also No. 51 for similar arguments.

[52] Edward A. Shils and Morris Janowitz: "Cohesion and Disintegration in the Wehrmacht in World War II," *Public Opinion Quarterly*, Vol. 12, no. 2 (Summer, 1948), pp. 280–315.

[53] For an influential characterization along similar lines of the phenomenon of organization, see John M. Gaus: "A Theory of Organization in Public Administration" in John M. Gaus, Leonard D. White, and Marshall E. Dimock: *The Frontiers of Public Administration* (Chicago: University of Chicago Press, 1936), pp. 66–91.

behaviors they desire in part through inducing motion picture producers to permit its officers to censor films before they are released.[54] Whether a group operates in such fashions as these or attempts to work through governmental institutions, thereby becoming a political interest group, may be a function of circumstances; the government may have primary or exclusive responsibility in the area involved, as in the war-time allocation of scarce materials. Or the choice between political and other modes of operation may be a function of technique; it may be easier or more effective to achieve temperance objectives through the government than by prevailing upon people to sign pledges. The process is essentially the same whether the interest group operates through other institutions or becomes political.

To summarize briefly, an interest group is a shared-attitude group that makes certain claims upon other groups in the society. If and when it makes its claims through or upon any of the institutions of government, it becomes a political interest group. These are the meanings that we shall attach to these terms throughout this book. At times it will be convenient to omit the modifying term "political" in discussing interest group activity in the government. In such instances it will be clear from the context whether we are dealing with political interest groups or with groups that are making claims otherwise than through or upon the institutions of government.

It follows that any group in the society may function as an interest group and that any of them may function as political interest groups, that is, those that make their claims through or upon governmental institutions. An economic group, such as a corporation, that seeks a special tax ruling is in that respect functioning as a political interest group. Trade associations, labor unions, philatelic societies, world government societies, political parties, professional organizations, and a host of others can and do seek to achieve all or a portion of their objectives by operating through or upon the institutions of government. Even a family group, whose prestige or financial interests approach imperial proportions, may make such claims. It will be useful and significant to identify or classify such groups according to the regularity or the success with which such claims are advanced through these channels. Even the casual observer will give somewhat different places to the philatelic society that prevails upon the Postmaster General to provide special handling for letters bearing a new stamp issue and a trade association that seeks legislation to protect it against its competitors. These may sensibly be placed in separate subcategories, but they both display the fundamental characteristics of such groups.

Seen in these terms, is an interest group inherently "selfish"? In the first place, such judgments have no value for a scientific understanding of government or the operation of society. Schematically, they represent nothing more than the existence of a conflicting interest, possibly, but not necessarily, in-

[54] Ruth A. Inglis: *Freedom of the Movies* (Chicago: University of Chicago Press, 1947), chaps. 3–5.

volving another group or groups.[55] Judgments of this kind are and must be made by all citizens in their everyday life, but they are not properly a part of the systematic analysis of the social process. Secondly, many such political interest groups are from almost any point of view highly altruistic. One need only recall those groups that have consistently risen to defend the basic guarantees of the American constitution, to improve the lot of the underprivileged, or to diffuse the advantages stemming from scientific advance. Evaluations such as these may be made of particular groups, depending on the observer's own attitudes, but, as was indicated in the preceding chapter, they will not facilitate one's understanding of the social system of which the groups are a part.

Where does the term "pressure group" fit into this scheme? This expression, perhaps more than any other, has been absorbed into the language of political abuse. It carries a load of emotional connotations indicating selfish, irresponsible insistence upon special privileges. Any group that regards itself as disinterested and altruistic will usually repudiate with vigor any attempt to attach this label to it, a fact that suggests that the term has little use except to indicate a value judgment concerning those groups of which one disapproves. Some writers, however, in a courageous effort to reclaim for the term a core of neutral meaning, use it as a synonym for "political interest group." [56] This usage has certain disadvantages aside from the obvious possibility that many readers will be unable to accept the suggestion that "the objectives of the pressure group may be good or bad; the group may be animated by the highest moral purpose or it may be driving for the narrowest kind of class gain." [57] If the word "pressure" has more than a simply figurative meaning, it suggests a method or a category of methods that may be used by an interest group to achieve its objectives.[58] Even if the methods implied can be described precisely, unless we can demonstrate that all political interest groups use them, the term "pressure group" will indicate merely a stage or phase of group activity and will not serve as a satisfactory equivalent for "interest group" or "political interest group," as these have been defined.[59] In view of the improbability of satisfying the conditions specified, it will be avoided in these pages in favor of the more inclusive and more nearly neutral term.

[55] See, for example, the transparent interest preferences involved in the interesting popular treatment by Kenneth G. Crawford: *The Pressure Boys: The Inside Story of Lobbying in America* (New York: Julius Messner, Inc., 1939).

[56] See, for example, V. O. Key, Jr.: *Politics, Parties, and Pressure Groups* (2nd edition, New York: Thomas Y. Crowell Company, 1947). Key, however, uses the terms somewhat more narrowly, confining them to "private associations formed to influence public policy" (p. 15). A similar use of the term will be found in Ogburn and Nimkoff: *Sociology*, p. 287.

[57] Key: *Politics, Parties, and Pressure Groups*, pp. 16–17.

[58] Robert M. MacIver: "Pressures, Social," *Encyclopaedia of the Social Sciences.*

[59] Mary E. Dillon specifies the method of propaganda as the distinguishing characteristic of the pressure group, a usage that does not make it the equivalent of the political interest group. "Pressure Groups," *American Political Science Review*, Vol. 36, no. 3 (June, 1942), pp. 471–81. The best case for a specific meaning of the term "pressure" can be made in connection with the effect of a group on its own membership rather than on those outside its boundaries.

ASSOCIATIONS AS INTEREST GROUPS

Any group, as we have already seen, may function from time to time as an interest group. There is one type of group, which almost invariably operates as an interest group, that has become of such importance in our culture that it deserves special treatment. This type may be called the association. We are using this familiar term in a technical sense. The justification for doing so is that we are here making use of a recent and highly significant body of research in the measurement of human relations in which this concept has been developed to designate a type of group whose genesis and functions are unique.[60]

The association is a type of group that grows out of what have been called tangent relations.[61] In a society of any appreciable complexity we find many institutionalized groups and well-defined subdivisions within them. We also find in these cases that there are individuals who participate in or are common to more than one such group, or subdivision. Such groups or subdivisions are said to be tangent to one another through the individuals who participate in both. Thus, to use a simple example, a family and a school are tangent to one another through a child who interacts in both. The workers in the motor assembly department and those in the body stamping department of the Ford Motor Company are tangent to one another through the managers who direct both. The General Motors Corporation is tangent to the International Harvester Company through the officers of the United Automobile Workers of America, who lead labor unions in both companies. This tangency between groups may exist not only through an individual, but through a third group by which the tangent groups are similarly affected or through a common technique.

When a disturbance occurs within two or more of these tangent groups, or subdivisions, the affected individuals are likely to seek an adjustment through interaction with others in the tangent group, with whom they have "something in common." Thus in a family that is disturbed by a child's poor performance in school, the mother is likely to visit (interact with) the teacher or principal to discuss the problem. This interaction is called a tangent relation. Similar tangent relations may occur between workers in the departments of the Ford Motor Company in consequence of an unusual "speed-up" in the assembly lines. They may occur also between officials of General Motors and International Harvester as a result of extreme demands by the U.A.W. leaders.

An association is said to emerge when a considerable number of people

---

[60] See Chapple and Coon: *Principles of Anthropology*, chap. 17, from which this section is adapted; the items cited in note 31, above; and note 62, below.

[61] Chapple and Coon: *Principles of Anthropology*, pp. 337 ff.

have established tangent relations of the same sort and when they interact with one another regularly on that basis. It is a group, a continuing pattern of interactions, that functions as a "bridge" between persons in two or more institutionalized groups or subdivisions thereof. The word "tangent" is appropriate because it suggests a set of relationships that are in a sense peripheral to those that define the central functions of the institutionalized group. Thus, if, out of the family-school tangency mentioned above, a number of mothers and teachers interact fairly regularly with one another in consequence of their tangent relations, an association may be said to exist. Such is the nature of the Parent-Teachers Association that is a familiar feature of a great many American communities. The P.T.A. has its origins in disturbances in the equilibriums of individuals in two or more institutionalized groups. Mothers and teachers may interact in casual tangent relations for an indefinite period of time without an association (group) emerging. At some point a disturbance occurs in these casual relations—owing to a sudden increase in their frequency or to a crisis resulting from the failure of a number of students to be accepted by a university (if the school is a high school) or from an increase in juvenile delinquency, playground accidents or any number of such things—and it is felt that "something must be done." If that "something" involves establishing the teachers and mothers as an habitually interacting group, an association has been formed.

As the above example suggests, the function of an association is to stabilize the relations of individuals in tangent groups. This stability it may create at the expense of disturbing the accustomed behavior of those through whom the participant individuals are tangent. Thus the formation of the P.T.A. may result in restraining some of the disapproved behaviors of the school children, such as studying with the radio on, loafing at a pool room, or engaging in dangerous play. The formation of a labor union may similarly disturb the habitual actions of managers by preventing their paying whatever wages they wish to and by equivalent actions. The processes of the association—which may involve a formal constitution, officers, and meetings governed by Robert's *Rules of Order,* or which may depend upon certain largely informal techniques—facilitate among the participant individuals an adjustment of the equilibriums within the institutions disturbed by the events that gave rise to the association. If the association persists, that is, if it meets satisfactorily the needs of the participants that grow out of their tangent relations, similar and related disturbances in the institutional groups will also be adjusted by the association.

The simple example of the Parent-Teachers Association can be supplemented by hundreds and thousands in our society whose origins and functions are of the same type. A few additional cases will suffice here, since the development of these groups will be discussed in more detail in the following two chapters. The labor union organizes tangent relations among workers that are created by workers' contacts with management (or perhaps an employers' association). Thus, when the character or frequency of the customary interactions between workers and management is disturbed, the workers may increase the frequency of their tangent interactions. This increase may result in the formation of an association (labor union). Its function is that of a "compensatory mechanism" that stabilizes the relations among workers and tends to order those between management and workers through the union hierarchy. It is a "bridge" between workers in different plants or different departments of the same plant. Similarly, the merchants of a community are tangent to one another through their customers and through the town government. Consequently a disturbance in these relations, such as is reflected in a slogan like "patronize home enterprise" or such as might follow upon a drastic increase in taxes on business property, may result in the formation of a merchants association, chamber of commerce, or board of trade. This association would act as a bridge between the mercantile establishments, would stabilize their relationships, and would tend to order their relations with their customers or with the city government. Again, businessmen in a particular line have tangent relations through their customers (or "the market"), the government, the labor unions, and their specialty. Disturbances in the accustomed interactions in these areas are likely to produce a trade association or employers association. College students, also, have tangent relations through the officers of the school. In the 1830's these relations were disturbed by the resistance of college faculties to the introduction of "modern" secular literature and similar materials into the curricula. In part for this reason student associations—fraternities—developed as literary societies. They still constitute a means of stabilizing relations between their members and college authorities, though along somewhat different lines. Other fraternal societies, professional associations, political parties, philanthropic organizations, and a host of others are of the same type.

In all societies the association operates to relate and stabilize the interactions among persons in basic institutionalized groups.[62] The association also has the attitude-forming, behavior-influencing group functions that we discussed earlier in the chapter.

Because of their functions, moreover, associations are peculiarly likely to operate both as interest groups and as political interest groups. The political role constitutes their importance in the present context. In the process of affording a means of adjustment for the members of various institutionalized groups, they are likely to make claims upon other groups not part of the institutions of government—as the labor union upon management. They are equally likely to assert claims upon or through the government. So common is this tendency that some students choose to limit the concept of the political

[62] Ibid., pp. 424–5 and 426–9. See also Eliot D. Chapple: The Theory of Associations as Applied to Primitive and Civilized Communities with Special Emphasis Upon the Functional Approach (unpublished Ph.D. dissertation, Harvard University, 1933).

interest group to groups that qualify as associations.[63] Although a large proportion of the familiar political interest groups are of this type, it is not strictly
accurate, for the reasons indicated in an earlier paragraph, to omit from the
category other types of groups whose relations with governmental institutions
are of the same general character. The Standard Oil Company of New Jersey
is not an association. Nevertheless, it may operate as a significant political interest group. In addition, its officers may function through an association,
such as the National Association of Manufacturers, that is also a political interest group. Any group in the society may at one time or another operate as
a political interest group. The considerable political importance of associations, that is, the groups formed around tangent relations, lies not only in their
strong tendency to operate through or upon the institutions of government
but in their stabilizing functions, in the larger resources of various kinds that
they can command as compared with any of the participant elements, and in
their great numbers in our society.

CONCLUSION

Stating the argument of this chapter in general terms, we find that any society
is composed of groups, the habitual interactions of men. Any society, even
one employing the simplest and most primitive techniques, is a mosaic of
overlapping groups of various specialized sorts. Through these formations a
society is experienced by its members, and in this way it must be observed
and understood by its students. These group affiliations, with varying degrees
of completeness and finality, form and guide the attitudes and therefore the
behavior of their participants. How completely and finally a particular group
controls the attitudes and behavior of its members is a matter to be determined through observation of the degree to which habitual patterns of interaction persist. The frequency and persistence of interactions within a group
will determine its strength. The groups that form this mosaic emerge from the
particular techniques of the society. Some, especially associations, which constitute a major concern of these pages, develop more immediately out of
crises and disturbances within those groups in which the basic techniques of
the society are institutionalized. The moving pattern of a complex society
such as the one in which we live is one of changes and disturbances in the habitual subpatterns of interaction, followed by a return to the previous state of
equilibrium or, if the disturbances are intense or prolonged, by the emergence
of new groups whose specialized function it is to facilitate the establishment
of a new balance, a new adjustment in the habitual interactions of individuals.

[63] See Key: *Politics, Parties, and Pressure Groups.*

ATTITUDE CONSENSUS AND CONFLICT IN AN INTEREST GROUP: AN ASSESSMENT OF COHESION

NORMAN R. LUTTBEG AND HARMON ZEIGLER

In America, interest groups operate within the democratic frame of reference. Like all political organizations, they are accorded more legitimacy when they can show that they are representative of the attitudes and values of a particular segment of the population. Consequently, the leaders of interest groups frequently spend a great deal of time explaining just how democratic their organizations are. If one examines the testimony of interest group leaders at state and national legislative hearings, he is likely to find that much of it is begun with an introductory statement explaining that the leadership of the testifying group is merely the voice of the membership. The personal values of the interest group leader are played down, and his function as representative (as distinguished from delegate) is exaggerated.

On the other hand, relatively few political interest groups have systematic and formalized means of ascertaining the desires of members. We know that most of the devices used to solicit member opinion are not very effective. Truman has shown that the affairs of most interest groups are run on a day-to-day basis by a fraction of the total membership. The mass of the membership takes a relatively passive role with regard to the formation of public policies by the organization.[1]

Communication between leaders and followers is spasmodic and cannot provide efficient guidelines for the actions of leaders. Whether or not leadership of an organization seeks to become a manifestation of Michel's iron law of oligarchy, the realities of communication within an organization suggest that most of the communication undertaken by leaders will be with other members of the leadership clique rather than with the larger body of followers in the group.

[1] David B. Truman, *The Governmental Process* (New York: Alfred A. Knopf, Inc., 1951), pp. 129–139.

SOURCE: Norman R. Luttbeg and Harmon Zeigler, "Attitude Consensus and Conflict in an Interest Group: An Assessment of Cohesion," *The American Political Science Review*, 60 (September 1966), 655–666. Reprinted by permission.

This situation is not necessarily dysfunctional for the organization. By many criteria the leader's decision is superior to that of the average member. Leaders have more time to give to matters of special concern to the organization. The information on which they make their decisions is likely to be more extensive than that of the average member, and they are likely to be more cognizant of the long-term impact of a particular decision. Unlike the average member, however, the leader's decision is complicated by his need to consider the extra-group and intra-group impact of his various alternative decisions and actions.

In the area of extra-group considerations, he must estimate the probable responses of other actors in the political process and the effect of these responses upon the chances of achieving a desired goal, assuming that he does not possess all capabilities of realizing this goal himself. Concerning intra-group considerations he must consider how the followers will respond to a decision. Will they be aware of it? Do they care about the alternatives, and if so, how will they respond to a decision which is contrary to their desires?

Even in the absence of efficient consultative mechanisms, leaders and followers exist in a functional relationship.[2] That is to say, leaders are limited by the followers' expressed or latent values and expectations. Regardless of the efficiency of corrective mechanisms and apart from how extensive the violation of the followers' values must be before the corrective mechanism comes into play, the leader's position is less secure if he fails to satisfy the followers. If another leader is vying with him for the followers' support, the implications of failing to satisfy the followers are even more threatening. In a political interest group, the functional relationship of leaders to followers is keyed to the necessity for cohesion as a weapon in extra-group competition. The actuality or at least the appearance of unity is essential.[3]

Assuming that the leader desires to maintain an extra-group competitive position, he will therefore undertake efforts toward the fostering of intragroup cohesion. In a voluntary organization, one of the prime requisites for this cohesion is the extent to which the membership is satisfied with the performance of leaders.[4] There are three ways in which a leader may satisfy the desires of an organization's membership. First, he may unconsciously act consistently with their desires. For example, he may decide to act on the basis of his evaluation of extra-group factors in such a way that the membership will be entirely satisfied. Second, he may respond entirely in terms of his personal attitudes and beliefs and, because he so accurately reflects the attitudes of his membership, again satisfy their desires. Third, a leader may consciously seek to do what he believes the membership of the organization desires. His suc-

---

[2] William Haythorn, et al., "The Effects of Varying Combinations of Authoritarian and Equalitarian Leaders and Followers," Journal of Abnormal and Social Psychology, 53 (September, 1956), 210–219.

[3] Truman, op. cit., pp. 167–187.

[4] Herbert Simon, Administrative Behavior (New York: The Macmillan Co., 1957), pp. 110–122.

cess in satisfying the membership by this effort is dependent upon the accuracy of his perceptions of their attitudes and expectations.

RESEARCH DESIGN

In this paper we examine the latter two dynamics by which leaders can satisfy members. Our data were gathered from the membership of the Oregon Education Association. Three sets of information were collected: the beliefs and attitudes of the members of the Association, the beliefs and attitudes of the leaders of the Association, and the perception of the attitudes of the members as held by the leaders. The analysis consists of comparing these three sets of information and noting changes in their interrelationships on different attitudes. The nature of the analysis is illustrated by Figure 1.

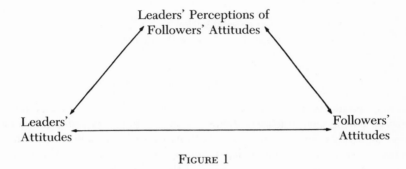

Leaders' Perceptions of Followers' Attitudes

Leaders' Attitudes

Followers' Attitudes

FIGURE 1

The sample of group members used in this study is a clustered stratified random sample of 803 high school teachers. This represents 14% of the high school teachers in Oregon.[5]

The sample of leaders includes all nine of the OEA's top administrative officials. These are the members of the executive staff, which is employed by the organization's Board of Trustees. Its official responsibility is to implement the policies of the Representative Council, which consists of 200 representatives elected by local teachers' organizations. The Representative Council is the official policy-making body of the Association. However, both the Representative Council, which meets only once a year, and the Board of Trustees, which is supposed to deal with the specifics of the council's directives, are part-time functions. Thus, the permanent administrative staff is often forced to act in areas in which directives are vague or nonexistent. As is frequently the case in formal organizations, therefore, the permanent administrative staff has great flexibility and is a major delineator of policy.

In interviewing the leaders, we used a majority of the questions included in

[5] Attitudes were assessed by personal interviews. There were 91 teachers in the original sample with whom interviews were not completed.

the teachers' interview schedule. Certain modifications in wording were made to allow for differences in organizational position. Leaders were first asked to answer the questions in terms of their own attitudes. They were then asked to take the point of view of the "average teacher" answering the same questions as they thought the "average teacher" would answer them. Only one of the leaders displayed any difficulty in assuming this attitude perspective; he had difficulty in keeping from answering questions in terms of what the teachers *should* believe rather than what he thought they actually *did* believe. The little difficulty the leaders experienced in answering these questions is evidence that the distinction between personal attitudes and the attitudes of the membership is a meaningful one for them.

These three sets of attitudes (teachers' attitudes, leaders' attitudes, and leaders' perceptions of teachers' attitudes) are studied in four attitudinal contexts. They are:

1. Mandates for organizational action,
2. Expectations and satisfaction with the direction of leadership behavior,
3. Abstract political values, and
4. Norms of teachers' political participation

The mandates for organizational action consist of two parts: expectations of behavior on the part of leaders themselves and expectations of action undertaken by teachers' organizations. In both cases, the satisfaction of the members with a particular action is dependent upon a congruence of the attitudes of the leaders with the actual attitudes of the followers.

Attitudes related to satisfaction with the direction of leadership are concerned with three of the Oregon Education Association's most strenuous activities; efforts toward salary improvement, efforts to raise teacher standards and accreditation, and efforts toward the establishment of a state sales tax with the revenues going to the public schools.

Abstract political values describe a set of attitudes, many of which are clichés often used by persons to persuade others to accept their position. They represent the basic "truths" of both the conservative and liberal points of view. A leader perceiving the membership as adhering to conservative values is ascribing conservatism to the membership and at the same time indicating that he believes an argument for action based upon these values would draw support from the membership.

The attitudes dealing with teachers' political participation concerned a broad set of politically related activities which might be undertaken by teachers in the classroom or during leisure time. The leadership's ability to satisfy members in this regard will be reflected in their efforts or lack of efforts to support teachers in trouble in their local communities for various political activities and in the formal or informal articulation of a professional ethic with respect to these activities.

Although it would be possible to analyze these data using contingency tables, the existence of 50 attitude items and three comparisons for each item would tax the reader's ability to follow the analysis. A single measure which characterizes the relationship on each comparison of attitudes is therefore required. Although numerous measures of association and correlation were considered for this purpose, we settled upon Kendall's tau chi (τ_c).[6] This measure has its faults, the principal one being that its maximum value is dependent upon the marginals of the table. Our tables frequently have marginals of 803 and 9 (the N's of our two samples). Such great differences will yield a correlation of only .044 for a perfect relationship on a 2×2 table. Since we are more interested in finding a measure to characterize the comparison of attitude distributions of leaders and followers than in using the measure as a test of statistical significance, it was decided to rely upon a new measure, τ_c over τ_c maximum.

As we are using this measure in comparing the distributions of attitudes of leaders and followers, a high correlation would indicate a strong relationship between attitudes and the person holding them. That is to say, a high correlation would indicate that leaders hold attitudes different from those of the followers. The sign of the measure will indicate the direction of this difference. Notice that a correlation of .000 indicates that leaders share the attitudes of the followers or that the two sets of attitudes compared have the same distribution.

Some may inquire of the statistical significance of the findings. There are two problems with the application of statistical significance tests to these data. First, one of the samples is not a sample at all but the universe of the administrative leaders of the Oregon Education Association. Thus, with no sampling error contributed by the leadership sample the comparing of leaders' and followers' attitudes does not necessitate as strong a relationship to achieve statistical significance as would be normally required. In the data comparing leaders' attitudes and their perceptions of followers' attitudes, clearly no statistical significance tests are applicable because the differences are real differences for the universe of leaders. Even if the leaders did consti-

---

[6] Our data justify the use of ordinal measures of association, but there are several characteristics of our data and properties of various measures of association which complicate the choice of such a measure. First, on some of the items only two responses are possible while others are seven-point Likert scales. Thus any measure which is sensitive to the shape of the contingency table from which it is computed will decrease the comparability of the data across items. A measure which reached unity when only one cell is zero is also undesirable, as instances in which the leaders are in perfect agreement while the followers differ are common in our data. Such measures would be insensitive to the degree of followers' disagreement with the leaders. The final difficulty is that some measures are sensitive to the marginals of the contingency table. No measure was discovered which did not have at least one of the characteristics. See Hubert Blalock, *Social Statistics* (New York: McGraw-Hill Book Co., 1960), p. 323; and Leo A. Goodman and William H. Kruskal, "Measures of Association for Cross Classifications," *Journal of the American Statistical Association*, 49 (December, 1954), p. 750.

tute a sample, their small number places an unnecessarily strict requirement on the strength of the relationship necessary to achieve statistical significance.[7] In general, therefore, greater reliance is placed upon the consistency of a relationship within an attitude area rather than on the statistical significance of any one item. However, those single-item relationships which are significant are indicated by a small "s" in the tables (the Kruskal-Wallis h test is used to test statistical significance).

FINDINGS

Leaders' perceptions of their roles. Before comparing the three sets of attitudes contained in this study, some discussion should be made of the leaders' perceptions of their roles within the organization. We refer here to the extent to which leaders believe they should act primarily in accordance with their own personal values rather than trying to reflect the desires of those whom they lead. We are asking whether leaders believe they should be delegates or representatives.[8]

Two questions were included in the leaders' interview schedule dealing with the problem of whose attitudes should be acted upon, those of the leaders or those of the followers. In one question the leaders were offered a brief dialogue between two persons, one arguing that a leader must do as the members wish and the other arguing that the leader must do what he personally believes to be correct. The leader was given the opportunity of selecting the argument which he found most satisfactory. Only one leader answered that the membership's desires should rule. Five answered that the leader should do what he personally believes to be right, although they added the comment that they thought the problem would occur very infrequently. Three of the leaders said that if this problem could not be resolved the leader should resign.

The second question approached the problem from a slightly different angle and achieved very dissimilar results. The leaders were asked if they felt the organization should do pretty much what the average teacher wants, what the more influential teachers want, what the school administrators want, or what they themselves want. The "pretty much" phrase in the first alternative

[7] David Gold, "Some Problems in Generalizing Aggregate Associations," *American Behavioral Scientists*, 8 (December, 1964), p. 18.

[8] The terms "delegate" and "representative" are borrowed from the literature on the legislative process, where they are applied to the role perceptions of legislators. Heinz Eulau presents three legislative role orientations in John C. Wahlke, Heinz Eulau, William Buchanan, and LeRoy C. Ferguson, *The Legislative System* (New York: John Wiley and Sons, Inc., 1962), pp. 267–286. The "trustee" of Eulau's scheme has traditionally been described as a "delegate" while the "delegate" corresponds to "representative." These roles are the extremes, with "politico" falling somewhere between them.

apparently was easier to accept than the wording in the other question, as five leaders chose this alternative. Two altered the second response to indicate that they believed they should do what the "more informed" teachers wanted while two indicated that they would prefer to do what they themselves thought best.

It would seem, therefore, that the leaders accept the maxim that they should do what the followers want, but they are also jealous of their autonomy to do what they think best. There appears to be a clear internalized conflict between the representative and delegate roles. Obviously the best of all possible worlds for the leaders would be perfect consensus between them and the members. In the absence of this consensus, they appear unable to reach a clear resolution of the conflict and to find a stable definition of their roles.

The leaders' acute awareness of the problem of communication with followers is indicated by a final question. Leaders were asked what policies of the Oregon Education Association they were most dissatisfied with. Seven volunteered the answer that the greatest problem was the OEA's failure to be true to the desires of its membership. Two of the leaders who gave this response explicitly criticized the administrative structure for not administering impartially the policy decisions of the Representative Council. It appears, therefore, that the representative nature of the organization is not only meaningful to leaders but is also potentially divisive of the leadership.

Expectations concerning organizational activity. The exact nature of this potential conflict within the organization will become clearer as we proceed to the analysis of the four attitude areas. We will first consider the mandates for organizational activity.

Table 1 presents the correlations for each of the attitude comparisons for each of the questions. In this, as in the tables which follow, the first column presents the objective attitudes, the "real world," and thus measures the extent of actual conflict. The second column shows the degree to which leaders are accurate in their perceptions of followers' attitudes, while the third column measures the extent of conflict as seen by the leaders. The negative sign of the correlation means that the bottom set of attitudes is more heavily weighted in the direction of believing that leaders of the organization *should* undertake a particular action. For example, in the first column a negative sign means that leaders believe more than the followers that they or the organization should undertake a given activity. In the second column the negative sign means that the leaders perceive the followers as being more in favor of undertaking a particular action than they actually are. The positive sign in the second column means that the followers are more in favor of undertaking a particular activity than the leaders believe them to be. A negative sign in the third column means that the leaders perceive the followers as more supportive of a particular activity than the leaders are. A positive sign in the third column indicates the reverse.

TABLE 1.

Comparison of the Three Attitude Sets in the Area of Mandate
for Actions by Leaders, Teachers' Organizations, and the OEA

	Sets of Attitudes Compared		
Questions	Followers' Attitudes vs. Leaders' Attitudes	Followers' Attitudes vs. Leaders' Perception of Followers' Attitudes	Leaders' Attitudes vs. Leaders' Perception of Followers' Attitudes
Leaders should:			
1. Fight attacks on educational principles and methods.	−.134	−.134	.000
2. Fight against dismissal of teachers.	−.073	−.073	.000
3. Defend teachers from public attacks from getting involved in controversial issues.	−.059	−.059	.000
4. Eliminate from staff political liberals.	+.284	+.061	−.222
5. Give helping hand to school board members coming up for election.	−.317(s)	+.211	+.528
Teachers' organizations should:			
6. Endorse political candidates.	−.419(s)	+.184	+.603
7. Take sides on public issues.	−.404(s)	+.221	+.625
OEA should:			
8. Endorse candidates in school elections.	−.387(s)	+.058	+.444
9. Try to influence legislation.	.000	.000	.000

The table indicates that, with the single exception of eliminating from the OEA staff people believed to be politically extreme, the leaders are more inclined to favor the involvement of the organization in each of the actions presented. This is shown by the fact that in seven of the nine cases the signs of the first column are negative. The first three of these items are the more clearly "professional" of the set. They involve the traditional academic values of freedom of expression and the protection of teachers against hostile forces in the community. These are at best *quasi* political activities. Yet even here the followers are more restrained than the leaders. Note that on the question of eliminating political liberals from the OEA staff the followers are more in favor of such action than are the leaders. However, it is true that the greatest discrepancy between followers' and leaders' attitudes occur on those questions involving the more purely political aspects of the organization, such as endorsing political candidates, taking sides on public issues, and taking part in the electoral activities of school board members.

With regard to these political activities, the followers are much more restrained than they are concerning more purely educational activities. Granted that the distinction between quasi-political and political is arbitrary at best, the followers do appear to make it. Thus, they are much more inclined to support the activities of the OEA if it defends teachers against public attacks than they would be if the teachers' organization endorsed political candidates.

The glaring exception to the general reluctance of the teachers to support the OEA's political activities is on the question of lobbying. Here there is nearly perfect agreement between leaders and followers. Lobbying is perceived by teachers to be an absolutely legitimate function of the organization. Teachers, therefore, are making a distinction between legislative politics and electoral politics.[9] The Association is currently engaged in a vigorous lobbying program at the state legislative level. With regard to lobbying, it is interesting to notice that not only do the attitudes of the leaders and followers converge, but also the leaders perceive that the followers support the lobbying activities. This is indicated by the zero correlation in the second and third columns.

Notice also that with regard to the first three activities (fighting attacks on educational principles and methods, fighting against the dismissal of teachers, and defending teachers from public attacks) the leaders see *more* support among the teachers than actually exists. Since the leaders overestimate the enthusiasm of followers, they see a consensus which does not hold true in the "real world." Hence the perfect correlation in the third column between the leaders' attitudes and their perceptions of teachers' attitudes is based upon faulty perceptions. This is not true with regard to the consensus about lobbying.

It is in the more purely electoral activities of the organization that discrepancies occur. Notice that on questions five, six, seven, and eight, the negative signs of the first column become positive signs in the second column. This means that, whereas leaders are more likely to want to engage in the electoral activities than are followers, the leaders perceive the followers as far more hesitant than the followers actually are. Consequently, these electoral activities can be contrasted with the professional and lobbying activities. In these professional and lobbying activities, the third column indicates that the leaders see little or no discrepancy between their point of view and the point

[9] Cf. Gabriel Almond and Sidney Verba, *The Civic Culture* (Boston: Little, Brown, and Co., 1965), pp. 250–251.

of view of the followers, whereas the correlations on items five, six, seven, and eight in the third column indicate that the leaders see a considerable conflict between their values and those of the followers. With regard to these political activities, the leaders are correct in perceiving conflict although conflict also exists in educational activities but is missed by the leaders.

At this point in its organizational history, the OEA is in fact more likely to engage in professional and lobbying activities than it is in electoral activities. It is these activities in which the leaders see the followers as being entirely supportive of the organization, although they are correct only with regard to lobbying. If the OEA were to increase its electoral activities, therefore, it would be engaging in practices which are less favored by the followers. However, the fact that the teachers are perceived as being more reluctant to support these activities than they actually are might result in the leaders engaging in these activities to a lesser extent than would be tolerated by the followers.

Evaluations of organizational performance. Turning from the extent to which leaders and followers are in agreement as to what the organization should do, we consider now the relationships between sets of attitudes concerning the extent of satisfaction with the actual behavior of the leaders of the organization. In Table 2 a negative sign indicates that the bottom set of attitudes is less satisfied with the performance of the teachers' organization. A positive sign indicates that the bottom set is more satisfied.

In the first analysis, we found that the leaders consistently underestimate the followers' activism. In Table 2 we find a similar tendency with several notable exceptions. On the question of the importance of the OEA's role in getting improved salaries and benefits in the past, we find a great discrepancy between leaders' and followers' attitudes: the followers are inclined to give the OEA less credit than are the leaders. However, the second column shows that the leaders' perception is accurate. Hence, they perceive followers as exhibiting more dissatisfaction with past performance than the leaders do. Leaders, intimately involved in the successes and failures of the organization, see their role as more significant than do the more passive followers. Only about one-third of the followers think that the OEA was "very important" in securing past benefits, whereas all the leaders are of this opinion.

With regard to current performance a different situation exists. The leaders are more dissatisfied with the performance of the organization and its constant fight for better salaries. Once again, however, they perceive more dissatisfaction among the followers than actually exists. Although accurate in their perceptions of teacher satisfaction with past performance, leaders fail in their evaluation of current satisfaction. In fact, 56% of the followers indicated that they think the OEA is doing enough about salaries. This is not exactly an overwhelming vote of confidence, but it is apparent that more satisfaction exists in reality than is perceived by the OEA leadership.

TABLE 2.

*Comparison of the Three Attitude Sets in the Areas of Expectations
and Satisfaction with Leaderships Actions*

Questions	Sets of Attitudes Compared		
	Followers' Attitudes vs. Leaders' Attitudes	Followers' Attitudes vs. Leaders' Perception of Followers' Attitudes	Leaders' Attitudes vs. Leaders' Perception of Followers' Attitudes
1. How important do you think has been the role played by the OEA in getting improved salaries and benefits?	+.556(s)	+.026	−.667
2. How about the Teachers' Union; how important do you think its role was in getting improved salaries and benefits?	−.297	−.098	+.185
3. Do you think the OEA is doing enough to improve teachers' salaries and benefits?	−.332	−.444	−.111
4. How about the Teachers' Union; is it doing enough in improving teachers' salaries and benefits?	−.396	−.396	.000
5. Do you think the OEA is doing enough in its support for higher teacher standards and accreditation to improve professional status?	−.016	−.016	.000
6. Do you think there should be a state sales tax with the revenue going to the schools?	+.253	+.364	+.111

In view of the current conflict between teachers' unions and professional organizations for the loyalties of teachers, it is interesting to note that the OEA leaders are more likely to denigrate the efforts of the teachers' union than are the teachers themselves. This is indicated by the negative sign of the correlations in column one considering the role of the union in past and present efforts toward salary increases. Again column two tells us that in both of these cases leaders perceive that followers are more dissatisfied with the union than they actually are. This distinction between past and present produces some curious results in the third column, showing the extent of conflict perceived by leaders. While they exaggerate the extent of dissatisfaction on the part of followers, perhaps projecting their own desires more than an objective evaluation would indicate, they recognize that the followers are more impressed with past union performance than they (the leaders) are. Yet they persist in seeing perfect agreement between themselves and teachers concerning current union performance, an agreement which does not exist. These distortions lead the leadership to assume a "what-have-you-done-for-me-lately" attitude somewhat along the lines of old fashioned bread and butter unionism. It seems likely that these perceptions will cause them to channel more of their resources into salary increase efforts at the risk of providing less satisfactory efforts in other areas. On the other hand this risk does not appear to be very great. For example, the leaders are extremely accurate in their perceptions of teacher satisfaction with regard to support for higher professional standards and accreditation. A consensus only slightly weaker than that regarding lobbying exists here.

The final item in the table dealing with the question of state sales tax enables us to return once again to lobbying. We may well ask "Lobbying for what?" The OEA has been strongly lobbying for a state sales tax with revenues going to the public schools, but only a slight majority (53%) of the teachers agree that a state sales tax should be enacted, while more than two-thirds of the leadership favor the tax. This is apparently an elite-derived effort enjoying only weak support from the followers. In this case, however, the leaders perceive far more support than actually exists. They actually believe that followers support their effort more than the leaders do, whereas the opposite is the case. Thus, although high consensus is achieved on the legitimacy of lobbying, leaders do not show a great capability of deciding how much effort should be devoted to the pursuit of certain policies by means of lobbying. The leaders want a sales tax, perceive the followers as wanting a sales tax, and pursue this effort vigorously. It is possible that if the efforts to achieve a sales tax are continued with increased intensity, membership support might be reduced beyond the bare majority it enjoys now, and intra-group conflict may result. If this happens the perceptual errors of the leaders could prove costly.

Abstract political values. Up to this point we have been considering the explicit programs of the Oregon Education Association, and the extent to which there is a congruence between leaders' and followers' values with regard to these programs. Members of organizations, however, may have values which are not directly translatable into explicit programs but which nevertheless color the relationship between leaders and followers. The overall ideological pattern of leaders and followers is, therefore, a component in determining the extent to which leaders represent the followers' values. It is this assumption which leads us to inquire about abstract political values. The items in Table 3 are offered as important in the leaders' evaluations as to what programs might appeal to the followers and also what the nature of appeals to the membership for support on a given issue might be. On the basis of their content, the items are separated into those indicating conservatism and those indicating liberalism. The first seven questions are the conservative questions, and the last six are the liberal questions. For each group, a negative sign indicates that the bottom set of attitudes shows greater acceptance of the item.

Looking at the first column, it can readily be seen that the leaders are more likely to disagree with the conservative items and more likely to agree with the liberal items than are the followers. Furthermore, the high correlations in the third column show that the leaders believe that the followers differ greatly from them with regard to these items. Once again, however, the leaders' perceptions of teachers' attitudes tends to exaggerate the differences. In eleven of the thirteen cases, leaders perceive followers to be more conservative and less liberal than they actually are. Thus, although the OEA leaders are a biased section of the teachers with respect to their political and economic values, they tend to perceive their atypical posture as more extreme than it actually is. This discrepancy in perception is likely to influence the leaders to use more conservative appeals to the followers in the urging support of particular programs than would be called for by an accurate inventory of their values.

Combined with the bread and butter perception described previously, this perceived conservatism of teachers leads the leaders into the path of heavy emphasis on salaries and other basic issues while at the same time forcing them to restrict their activities in the realm of expansion of organizational activities. If the leadership seeks to venture into untried areas which are not specifically related to educational problems, it may be hesitant to begin for fear that the programs are too liberal for the membership.

Of course, as Krech and Crutchfield point out, the degree of association between cognitive attitudes and action-orientated attitudes is not necessarily great.[10] Thus, a person holding conservative beliefs does not automatically favor conservative actions by government. To ascertain the extent to which abstract values are translatable into immediate preferences for governmental action, we administered the items from the Survey Research Center's domestic attitude scale.[11] As in the abstract value index, the leaders proved to be much more liberal than the followers. Also, the leaders saw the followers as not being as liberal as they actually are. In this case, however, the leaders are not so greatly more liberal and they do not see the followers as so greatly more conservative than they actually are. The main thrust of the conservatism scale is identical to that of the abstract political value index, but the discrepancies are not as great. It may be, therefore, that the leaders are less in

[10] David Krech and Richard Crutchfield, *Theory and Problems of Social Psychology* (New York: McGraw-Hill Book Co., 1948), p. 251.

[11] See Angus Campbell, *et al.*, *The American Voter* (New York: John Wiley and Sons, 1960), pp. 194–198. V. O. Key gives the items used in this scale. See V. O. Key, Jr., *Public Opinion and American Democracy* (New York: Alfred A. Knopf, 1961), p. 561.

TABLE 3.

Comparison of the Attitude Sets in the Area of Orthodox Values

Questions	Sets of Attitudes Compared		
	Followers' Attitudes vs. Leaders' Attitudes	Followers' Attitudes vs. Leaders' Perceptions of Followers' Attitudes	Leaders' Attitudes vs. Leaders' Perceptions of Followers' Attitudes
Conservative			
1. The American form of government may not be perfect, but it's the best type of government yet devised by man.	−.137	+.078	+.222
2. Democracy is considered the ideal form of government by most of the world.	−.160	−.658	−.407
3. Private enterprise could do better most of the things the government is now doing.	+.365	−.171	−.568
4. The participation of the federal government in local affairs leads to undesirable federal controls.	+.564(s)	−.389	−.926
5. Communism is a total evil.	+.142	−.466	−.630
6. People of most underdeveloped countries are by nature incapable of self-government.	+.303	−.226	−.506
7. Private enterprise is the only really workable system in the modern world capable of satisfying our economic needs.	+.257	−.182	−.469
Liberal			
8. Economic and social planning by government does not necessarily lead to dictatorship.	−.326	+.125	+.444
9. Man is the maker of his own society; such events as wars and depressions could be controlled by man.	−.122	+.161	+.259
10. The growth of large corporations make government regulation of business necessary.	−.190	+.088	+.309

TABLE 3. (Cont.)

Comparison of the Attitude Sets in the Area of Orthodox Values

| | | Sets of Attitudes Compared | |
Questions	Followers' Attitudes vs. Leaders' Attitudes	Followers' Attitudes vs. Leaders' Perceptions of Followers' Attitudes	Leaders' Attitudes vs. Leaders' Perceptions of Followers' Attitudes
11. We could increase spending for many government services without harming the nation's economy.	−.402	+.035	+.432
12. The federal government represents the needs of most people better than local government.	−.030	+.284	+.259
13. The government should increase its activities in matters of health, retirement, wages, and old-age benefits.	−.205	−.034	+.185

danger of undercutting the cohesion of the organization should they lend its support to an explicit governmental program outside the realm of education related issues. The danger to cohesion may be not so much in the undertaking of new programs but in the appeal to followers on the basis of their perceived conservatism.

The political role of the teacher. Teachers, like the holders of any social position, have perceptions of what is permissible behavior by holders of their social position. Others who do not hold this position also have expectations. The interaction of these two expectations constitutes a role. Table 4 presents the comparisons between the three sets of attitudes with regard to norms of teachers' political participation. A negative sign indicates that the bottom set of attitudes in the comparison favors teacher participation more than does the top set of attitudes.

Here we see a remarkably consistent pattern. Leaders are, in every case save one, more supportive of actions by teachers in these areas than are the teachers. This is even true of joining a teachers' union, but it is not true of striking to secure higher salaries and other benefits. In this latter case, the teachers are slightly more likely than leaders to be willing to undertake this activity and are much more likely to be willing to strike than leaders perceive them to be. This is the single example of followers being more "activist" than leaders to achieve liberal goals. In every other case, no matter what type of action is involved, leaders are more willing to take a risk, more willing to engage in controversial activity than are followers. When we examine the leaders' perception of followers' attitudes, we find once again the consistent pattern of underevaluation of the experimental nature of teachers. Leaders perceive teachers as being unlikely to engage in these activities whereas teachers themselves, although less anxious than leaders to take part in these activities, are more willing to do so than leaders believe them to be. Thus, the teachers are more willing to join teachers' unions, political party organizations, or racial organizations than leaders believe them to be.

CONCLUSIONS

To summarize the findings of this analysis, the following points may be offered. As is true of most organizations, the leaders of the Oregon Education Association are more active than the followers. They are more liberal than the followers and they are more willing than the followers to expand the activities of the organization, but they consistently exaggerate the atypical nature of their position. They see the followers as being more conservative and restrained than they actually are. These discrepancies, both in perception and in actual attitudes, lead us to speculate as to how they came about. Is the relative activisim of leaders a function of their social role, their organizational position, or their personality? It is certainly not feasible to argue that leadership positions somehow recruit more daring people. It is more feasible to seek explanations within the nature of the organization and the teaching profession. Consider, for example, the items dealing with political participation by teachers. Leaders would be subject to none of the pressures that teachers would feel from their community. Also, while teachers can recall relatively few cases in which the community made demands upon the school system for the dismissal of a teacher for engaging in controversial activity, those who can recall such incidents are of the opinion that the teachers' organization was ineffective in the defense of teachers. It is also true that the teachers look upon the local affiliates of the Oregon Education Association much more favorably than they look upon the statewide organization which employs the leaders considered in this study. In arguing for organizational position as a fundamental contributor to differential perception, we draw added support from the reaction of the leaders to the competition of the union. Leaders behave in much the same fashion as political party leaders.[12] They are more emotionally committed to the organization than are the rank and file. Hence, they find it difficult to comprehend the problems of teaching and the restrictions traditionally imposed upon teachers by the community.

[12] Herbert McClosky, "Consensus and Ideology in American Politics," this REVIEW, 58 (June, 1964), 361–382.

TABLE 4.

Comparison of the Attitude Sets in the Area of the
Norms of Teachers' Political Participation

Questions	Sets of Attitudes Compared		
	Followers' Attitudes vs. Leaders' Attitudes	Followers' Attitudes vs. Leaders' Perceptions of Followers' Attitudes	Leaders' Attitudes vs. Leaders' Perceptions of Followers' Attitudes
Teachers should if they want to:			
1. Join a teachers' union.	−.135	+.532(s)	+.667
2. Go on strike to secure higher salaries and other benefits.	+.067	+.317(s)	+.250
3. Join a political party organization.	−.036	+.186	+.222
4. Serve as party precinct worker in pre-election activities.	−.064	+.269	+.333
5. Publicly criticize local government officials.	−.268	+.510(s)	+.778
6. In a presidential election, outside school time, make speeches or give other services on the behalf of a candidate.	−.110	+.335(s)	+.444
7. Run for political office.	−.104	+.451(s)	+.556
8. In a presidential election, explain to class reasons for preferring one candidate.	−.055	+.279	+.333
9. Belong to the NAACP or CORE.	−.129	+.316(s)	+.444
10. Take part in a CORE or NAACP demonstration, such as public picketing.	−.112	+.460(s)	+.571
11. Allow an atheist to address the class.	−.126	+.430(s)	+.556
12. Argue in class against the censoring of literature by people who feel it is pornographic.	−.226	+.039	+.306
13. Speak out in class against the John Birch Society and groups like it.	−.153	+.180	+.333
14. Speak in favor of nationalizing the steel industry and the railroads.	−.249	+.307	+.556

TABLE 4. (Cont.)

Comparison of the Attitude Sets in the Area of the
Norms of Teachers' Political Participation

	Sets of Attitudes Compared		
Questions	Followers' Attitudes vs. Leaders' Attitudes	Followers' Attitudes vs. Leaders' Perceptions of Followers' Attitudes	Leaders' Attitudes vs. Leaders' Perceptions of Followers' Attitudes
15. Speak in class in favor of the Medicare program.	−.169	+.276	+.444
16. Speak in class in favor of the United Nations.	−.043	+.291	+.333
17. Allow the distribution of anti-communist literature put out by the National Association of Manufacturers.	−.254	+.191	+.444
18. Speak in class favorably about socialism.	−.105	+.229	+.333
19. Argue in class that labor unions should be more regulated or controlled by the government.	−.158	+.176	+.333
20. Allow the distribution of anti-communist literature put out by the John Birch Society.	−.443(s)	+.123	+.556

It might be useful to know something about the leaders' backgrounds. All have at one time been teachers and all have passed through some lower administrative position before achieving their present status. Most have taken graduate work, usually in educational administration. All earn in excess of ten thousand dollars per year. Thus, although they do have a teaching background, they are much more upwardly mobile than the average teacher and make more money. They are also substantially better educated. The upper mobility of the leaders of the OEA can be gleaned from the backgrounds of their fathers. Most of their fathers had less than a high school education and held low status occupations. Thus holding a position in the OEA marks more of a step up than does teaching. Perhaps, therefore, the leaders consider themselves as more sophisticated and advanced than teachers.

When we consider the fact that serving as an OEA administrator is in a sense moving beyond a teaching position, the explanation offered above becomes more plausible. Combine this with the fact that leaders have interaction with a more heterogeneous environment and their perception of teachers becomes even more understandable. Unlike the teachers, who interact mostly with teachers, students, principals, and parents, the OEA administrative staff interacts with lobbyists, legislators, state officials, and national educational officials.

As a final alternative to the explanation offered above, we considered the possibility that, whereas the leaders incorrectly perceive the political values and political role perceptions of teachers, they may base their reactions upon communication with a biased sample. There are, of course, many different shades of opinion among teachers just as there are among the general public. Is it true that the OEA leaders interact with a segment of the teaching population which is more conservative and more restrained? If this is true, then their perceptions of followers' attitudes might not be a function of their social position but might be the result of an unrepresentative sample of opinion being communicated to them. However, our evidence indicates quite clearly that there is no relationship between political conservatism and participation in organizational affairs. There is no evidence that the conservative teachers have any more interaction with OEA leaders than do the liberal teachers. Also, those teachers who take a restrained view of the political role of the teacher are no more likely to communicate with OEA leaders than are those teachers who take a more expansionist view.[13] Thus, we can say that there is no weighting of communication which comes to the attention of OEA leaders in favor of conservatism and restraint.

Assuming, therefore, that being a leader in an organization contributes to a discrepancy between leaders' and followers' attitudes, we may inquire finally into the possibility of having a democratic interest group without frequent and carefully supervised consultative mechanisms. Can leaders be representative simply because they intuitively comprehend what is required of them? In considering this question, let us note that, with the exception of the last table, the discrepancy between leaders' attitudes and followers' attitudes is generally *greater* than the errors made by leaders in perceiving these attitudes. Thus OEA leaders operating entirely upon their personal values would not be representative of the values of their followers. On the other hand, if they adopted a purely representative role, they would become more conservative and restrained than the teachers would prefer. Yet, with exception of the last set of attitudes, the error would be less than would be true if followers' wishes were ignored. That is to say, if they followed their understanding of followers' values, the resulting conservatism and restraint would be closer to the actual desires of teachers than would be true if leaders used their personal values as the sole criteria of judgment. "Virtual" representation in an interest group cannot serve as a substitute for actual representation, because the position of

---

[13] It is true, however, that there is more interaction between leaders and small town teachers; these teachers are considerably more.conservative and restrained than their big city counterparts.

group leader contributes to the development of attitudes which differ from those of the followers.

ISSUE CONFLICT AND CONSENSUS AMONG PARTY LEADERS AND FOLLOWERS

HERBERT McCLOSKY, PAUL J. HOFFMANN,

AND ROSEMARY O'HARA

American political parties are often regarded as "brokerage" organizations, weak in principle, devoid of ideology, and inclined to differ chiefly over unimportant questions. In contrast to the "ideological" parties of Europe—which supposedly appeal to their followers through sharply defined, coherent, and logically related doctrines—the American parties are thought to fit their convictions to the changing demands of the political contest.[1] According to this view, each set of American party leaders is satisfied to play Tweedledee to the other's Tweedledum.

1. PRESSURES TOWARD UNIFORMITY AND CLEAVAGE

Although these "conclusions" are mainly derived from *a priori* analysis or from casual observations of "anecdotal" data (little systematic effort having been made so far to verify or refute them), they are often taken as confirmed —largely, one imagines, because they are compatible with certain conspicuous features of American politics. Among these features is the entrenchment of a two-party system which, by affording both parties a genuine opportunity to win elections, tempts them to appeal to as many diverse elements in the electorate as are needed to put together a majority.[2] Since both parties want to attract support from the centrist and moderate segments of the electorate, their views on basic issues will, it is thought, tend to converge. Like giant

[1] Maurice Duverger, *Political Parties, their Organization and Activity in the Modern State* (New York, 1955), p. 102.

[2] The analysis of these and related tendencies associated with the American party system is ably set forth in Pendleton Herring, *The Politics of Democracy* (New York, 1940), p. 102 and *passim*. Also, James M. Burns, *Congress on Trial: The Legislative Process and the Administrative State* (New York, 1949), p. 34.

SOURCE: Herbert McClosky, Paul J. Hoffmann, and Rosemary O'Hara, "Issue Conflict and Consensus Among Party Leaders and Followers," *The American Political Science Review*, 54 (June 1960), 406–427. Reprinted by permission. Some footnotes have been deleted.

business enterprises competing for the same market, they will be led to offer commodities that are in many respects identical.[3] It is one thing for a small party in a multi-party system to preserve its ideological purity, quite another for a mass party in a two-party system to do so. The one has little hope of becoming a majority, and can most easily survive by remaining identified with the narrow audience from which it draws its chief supporters; the other can succeed only by accommodating the conflicting claims of many diverse groups—only, in short, by blunting ideological distinctions.[4]

Constraints against enlarging intellectual differences also spring from the loosely confederated nature of the American party system, and from each national party's need to adjust its policies to the competing interests of the locality, the state, and the nation.[5] Many party units are more concerned with local than with national elections, and prefer not to be handicapped by clear-cut national programs. Every ambitious politician, moreover, hopes to achieve a *modus vivendi* tailored to the particular and often idiosyncratic complex of forces prevailing in his constituency, an objective rarely compatible with doctrinal purity.[6] Often, too, local politics are largely nonpartisan or are partisan in ways that scarcely affect the great national issues around which ideologies might be expected to form.[7] The development and enforcement of a sharply delineated ideology is also hindered by the absence in either party of a firmly established, authoritative, and continuing organizational center empowered to decide questions of doctrine and discipline.[8] Party affiliation is loosely defined, responsibility is weak or non-existent, and organs for indoctrinating or communicating with party members are at best rudimentary.

Cultural and historical differences may also contribute to the weaker ideological emphasis among American, as compared with European, parties. Many of the great historical cleavages that have divided European nations for centuries—monarchism *vs.* republicanism; clericalism *vs.* anticlericalism; democracy *vs.* autocracy, etc.—have never taken root in this country. Apart from the slavery (and subsequently the race) issue, the United States has not experienced the intense class or caste conflict often found abroad, and contests of the capitalism *vs.* socialism variety have never achieved an important role in American politics. In addition, never having known a titled nobility,

---

[3] See especially E. E. Schattschneider, *Party Government* (New York, 1942), p. 92 and *passim;* and V. O. Key, *Politics, Parties, and Pressure Groups,* 4th ed. (New York, 1958), ch. 8; Howard R. Penniman, *Sait's American Parties and Elections,* 5th ed. (New York, 1952), p. 162.

[4] William Goodman, *The Two-Party System in the United States* (New Jersey, 1956), p. 43.

[5] Duverger, *op. cit.,* pp. 187, 418.

[6] Pendleton Herring, *op. cit.,* p. 133.

[7] *American State Legislatures,* ed. Belle Zeller (New York, 1954); but see also Malcolm E. Jewell, "Party Voting in American State Legislatures," *American Political Science Review,* Vol. XLIX (Sept. 1955), pp. 773–91.

[8] Report of the Committee on Political Parties, American Political Science Association, *Toward a More Responsible Two-Party System* (New York, 1950), *passim.*

we have largely been freed from the conflicts found elsewhere between the classes of inherited and acquired privilege.

Consider, too, the progress made in the United States toward neutralizing the forces which ordinarily lead to sharp social, and hence intellectual and political, differentiation. The class and status structure of American society has attained a rate of mobility equalling or exceeding that of any other long established society. Popular education, and other facilities for the creation of common attitudes, have been developed on a scale unequalled elsewhere. Improvements in transportation and communication, and rapid shifts in population and industry have weakened even sectionalism as a source of political cleavage. Rural-urban differences continue to exist, of course, but they too have been diminishing in force and have become less salient for American politics than the differences prevailing, for example, between a French peasant proprietor and a Parisian *boulevadier*.[9] In short, a great many Americans have been subjected in their public lives to identical stimuli—a condition unlikely to generate strong, competing ideologies.

The research reported here was designed not to refute these observations but to test the accuracy of the claim that they are sufficient to prevent differences in outlook from taking root in the American party system. We believed that the homogenizing tendencies referred to are strongly offset by contrary influences, and that voters are preponderantly led to support the party whose opinions they share. We further thought that the competition for office, though giving rise to similarities between the parties, also impels them to diverge from each other in order to sharpen their respective appeals. For this and other reasons, we expected to find that the leaders of the two parties, instead of ignoring differences alleged to exist within the electorate, would differ on issues more sharply than their followers would. We believed further that even in a brokerage system the parties would serve as independent reference groups, developing norms, values, and self-images to which their supporters could readily respond.[10] Their influence, we felt, would frequently exceed that of ethnic, occupational, residential and other reference groups. In sum, we proceeded on the belief that the parties are not simply spokesmen for other interest groups, but are in their own right agencies for formulating, transmitting, and anchoring political opinions, that they attract adherents who in general share those opinions, and that through a feedback process of mutual reinforcement between the organization and its typical supporters, the parties develop integrated and stable political tendencies. Other hypotheses will be specified as we present and analyze our findings.

[9] Data bearing on these generalizations will be presented in companion articles which specifically deal with sectional and rural-urban influences on issue outlook.

[10] Cf. James W. Prothro, Ernest Q. Campbell, and Charles M. Grigg, "Two Party Voting in the South: Class vs. Party Identification," *American Political Science Review*, Vol. LII (March 1958), pp. 131–39. Also, Peter H. Odegard and E. Allen Helms, *American Politics: A Study in Political Dynamics* (New York, 1947 ed.), pp. 200–221.

II. PROCEDURES

The questions considered in this paper were part of a large field study made in 1957–1958 on the nature, sources, and correlates of political affiliation, activity, and belief in the American party system (hereafter referred to as the PAB study). Pilot studies on Minnesota samples had led us to suspect that many "settled" notions about party affiliation and belief in America would not stand up under careful empirical scrutiny; further, we felt that little progress would be made in the exploration of this subject until a comprehensive portrait of party membership in America had been drawn. Accordingly, a nationwide study was launched to acquire a detailed description of party leaders and supporters, gathering data on their backgrounds, political experiences, personality characteristics, values, motivations, social and political attitudes, outlooks on key issues, and related matters.

For our samples of party "leaders" we turned to the Democratic and Republican national conventions, largely because they are the leading and most representative of the party organs, their delegates coming from every part of the United States and from every level of party and government activity. Our samples ranged from governors, senators, and national committeemen at the one end to precinct workers and local officials at the other. In the absence of comprehensive information about the characteristics of the party elites in America, no one can say how closely the convention delegates mirror the total party leadership. We felt it fair to assume, nevertheless, that the delegates represented as faithful a cross section of American party leadership as could be had without an extraordinary expenditure of money and labor. Using convention delegates as our universe of leaders also held some obvious advantages for research, since the composition of this universe (by name, address, party, state, sex, place of residence, and party or public office) can usually be ascertained from the convention calls. Of the 6,848 delegates and alternates available to be sampled, 3,193 actually participated; 3,020 (1,788 Democrats and 1,232 Republicans) completed and returned questionnaires that were usable in all respects.[11] The proportion of returns was roughly equivalent for both sets of party leaders.

The rank-and-file sample, which we wanted both for its intrinsic value and for its utility as a control group, was obtained by special arrangement with the American Institute of Public Opinion. In January 1958, Gallup interviewers personally distributed our questionnaire to 2,917 adult voters in two successive national cross-section surveys. Some 1,610 questionnaires were filled

[11] This gratifyingly large number of returns of so lengthy and detailed a questionnaire was attained through a number of follow-up mailings and special letters. These and other procedures designed to check the adequacy of the sample will be fully described in the volume containing the report of the overall study. The difference in the number of returns from the two parties was largely a result of the greater number of Democratic delegates to begin with.

out and returned, of which 1,484 were completely usable. This sample closely matched the national population on such characteristics as sex, age, region, size of city, and party affiliation, and, though it somewhat oversampled the upper educational levels, we considered it sufficiently large and representative for most of our purposes. Of the 1,484 respondents, 821 were Democratic supporters (629 "pure" Democrats, plus 192 whom we classified as "independent" Democrats) and 623 were Republican supporters (479 "pure" Republicans, plus 144 "independent" Republicans). Forty respondents could not be identified as adherents of either party.

The lengthy questionnaire developed for the study was designed to be self-administered. It contained, in addition to questions on the respondents' personal backgrounds, a number of queries on their political history and experience, their attitudes toward the party system and toward such related matters as party organization, discipline and responsibility, their self-images with regard to social class and liberalism-conservatism, their reference group identifications, and their views on party leadership and ideology. The largest part of the questionnaire consisted of 390 scale items, randomly arranged, which when sorted and scored fell into 47 scales for measuring the personality, attitude, and value characteristics of each of the respondents. We had validated and used all but three of these scales in earlier studies.

The questions most relevant for the present article were those which asked each respondent to express his attitudes toward twenty-four important national issues, and to state whether he believed support for each issue should be "increased," "decreased," or "remain as is." The list of issues and the responses of each sample will be found in Tables H2A through H2E, where for convenience of analysis, the issues have been grouped under five broad headings: Public Ownership, Government Regulation of the Economy, Equalitarianism and Human Welfare, Tax Policy and Foreign Policy.

In tabulating the results, we first scored each individual on each issue and then computed aggregate scores for all the members of a given sample. To begin with, percentages were used to show the proportion who favored increasing, decreasing, or retaining the existing level of support on each issue. But as it was clumsy to handle three figures for each issue, we constructed a single index or "ratio of support" which would simultaneously take account of all three scores. The index was built by assigning a weight of 1.0 to each "increase" response in the sample, of 0 to each "decrease" response, and of .50 to each "remain as is" (or "same") response. Thus the ratio-of-support score shown for any given sample is in effect a mean score with a possible range of 0 to 1.0, in which support for an issue increases as the scores approach 1.0 and decreases as they approach 0. In general, the scores can be taken to approximate the following overall positions: .0 to .25—strongly wish to reduce support; .26 to .45—wish to reduce support; .46 to .55—satisfied with the *status quo*; .56 to .75—wish to increase support; and .76 to 1.00—strongly wish to increase support. Note that the differences in degree suggested by these categories refer not to the *strength of feeling* exhibited by individuals toward an issue but rather to the *numbers of people* in a sample who hold points of view favoring or opposing that issue.

Because they include the "same" and "no code" as well as "increase" and "decrease" responses, our ratios of support sometimes flatten the differences between groups. Had we employed only the percentage scores for the "increase" or "decrease" responses, the differences between samples would in many instances have seemed larger. Nevertheless, the ratio of support offers so many advantages that we have employed it as our principal measure. For one thing, as the equivalent of a mean score, it takes into account all scores, omitting no respondent from the tabulation. For the same reason it enables us to assess the amount of dispersion or homogeneity exhibited by any sample and makes it easy to calculate significances of difference.[12] Reliance upon a single, uniform statistic also allows us to make ready comparisons not only *between* but *within* samples, and to determine quickly how large the differences actually are. By observing whether a ratio of support is above or below .50 we can see at once whether a particular group predominantly favors or opposes the issue in question, and how strongly it does so. The use of ratio scores also makes it possible to compare issues as well as groups, *e.g.*, to see whether one issue is more preferred than another.

For further information on the meaning of the issue responses, we also compared samples on a number of related scales and items. Tabulating and statistical operations were carried out to control for demographic influences like education, occupation, age, and sectionalism; to ascertain homogeneity of opinion within the several samples; to rank the issues according to the magnitude of the differences between samples; to compare members' positions on issues against official platform statements; and to determine whether leaders and followers are able to name the issues which actually divide the parties. Some of the findings yielded by these operations will be considered here, while others, for reasons of space, will have to be reserved for future publications.

A word of caution before we turn to the findings. The respondents were offered only the twenty-four issues that impressed us in February, 1957, as

---

[12] The measure of dispersion used for this purpose was the standard deviation, which was computed by using the scores of 0, .50 and 1.00 as intervals in the calculations. To avoid having to calculate separate significances of difference for each of the comparisons we wanted to observe, we simply made the assumption—erring on the side of caution—that the maximum variance of .50 had occurred in each instance. The magnitude of the significance of difference is, in other words, often greater than we have reported. The significance test used in this procedure was the critical ratio. Unless otherwise indicated, all the differences reported are statistically significant at or beyond the .01 level.

TABLE 1.

Average Differences in the Ratio-of-Support Scores among Party Leaders and Followers for Five Categories of Issues

Category of Issues	Democratic Leaders vs. Republican Leaders	Democratic Followers vs. Republican Followers	Democratic Leaders vs. Democratic Followers	Republican Leaders vs. Republican Followers	Democratic Leaders vs. Republican Followers	Republican Leaders vs. Democratic Followers
a. Public ownership of resources	.28	.04	.06	.18	.10	.22
b. Government regulation of the economy	.22	.06	.08	.10	.12	.16
c. Equalitarianism, human welfare	.22	.05	.08	.21	.06	.25
d. Tax policy	.20	.06	.06	.20	.04	.26
e. Foreign policy	.16	.02	.05	.08	.07	.10
Average differences in ratio scores for all categories	.21	.04	.07	.15	.08	.20

Sample Sizes: Democratic Leaders, 1,788; Republican Leaders, 1,232; Democratic Followers, 821; Republican Followers, 623.

most significant and enduring. However, they may not all be as salient today as they seemed at that time. Nor, within the limitations of a single questionnaire, could we explore every issue that informed observers might have considered important. Some presumably vital issues such as states rights, political centralization, and expansion of government functions could not be stated explicitly enough within our format to be tested properly. These are issues that are so generalized as to encompass many other specific issues, and so highly charged as to awaken a profusion of symbolic and emotive associations.

The *form* of our issue questions may also be open for criticism, for space limitations prevented our subjects from indicating how strongly they felt and how much they knew about each of the issues. This deficiency, however, may be less important than it appears, since for the groups we most wanted to compare (*e.g.*, Democratic *vs.* Republican leaders), the degree of political knowledge and intensity is likely to be rather similar. The difficulty is greater when comparing leaders with followers, but is somewhat offset by controlling for education and socio-economic status. Although some subtleties of interpretation are bound to be lost because these variables have been omitted, we are satisfied that our issue questions in their present form furnish a useful measure for assessing *group* (as distinguished from *individual*) opinion.

Finally, one may wonder about the value of opinions stated on a questionnaire compared with the worth of views formally expressed by an organization or implicit in the actions of its leaders. Advantages can be cited on both sides. The beliefs expressed in official party statements or in legislative roll calls, it might be claimed, represent the *operating* beliefs of the organization by virtue of having been tested in the marketplace or in the competition of legislative struggle. Positions taken on issues on which a party stakes its future may be more valid evidence of what the party truly believes than are the opinions expressed by individual members under conditions of maximum safety. On the other hand, the responses to the issue and attitude questions in the PAB study represent the anonymous, private opinions of party leaders and followers, uncomplicated by any need to make political capital, to proselytize, to conciliate critics, or to find grounds for embarrassing the opposition at the next election. Hence they may for some purposes represent the most accurate possible reflection of the "actual" state of party opinion. The controversy over the value of the two approaches is to some extent spurious, however, for they offer different perspectives on the same thing. In addition, considerable correspondence exists between the party positions evident in congressional roll calls and the privately expressed opinions of the party leaders in our study.[13]

III. FINDINGS: COMPARISONS BETWEEN LEADERS

No more conclusive findings emerge from our study of party issues than those growing out of the comparisons between the two sets of party leaders. Despite the brokerage tendency of the American parties, their active members are obviously separated by large and important differences. The differences, moreover, conform with the popular image in which the Democratic party is seen as the more "progressive" or "radical," the Republican as the more "moderate" or "conservative" of the two.[14] In addition, the disagreements are remarkably consistent, a function not of chance but of systematic points of view, whereby the responses to any one of the issues could reasonably have been predicted from knowledge of the responses to the other issues.

[13] See, for example, the congressional roll-call results reported by Julius Turner, *Party and Constituency: Pressures on Congress*, The Johns Hopkins University Studies in Historical and Political Science Series, Vol. LXIX, No. 1 (1951). The complexities affecting the determination of party votes in Congress are thoroughly explored in David B. Truman, *The Congressional Party: A Case Study* (New York, 1959).

[14] Conservatism is here used not in the classical but in the more popular sense, in which it refers to negative attitudes toward government ownership, intervention, and regulation of the economy; resistance to measures for promoting equalitarianism and social welfare through government action; identification with property, wealth, and business enterprise; etc.

Examination of Tables 2A–2E and 3 shows that the leaders differ significantly on 23 of the 24 issues listed and that they are separated on 15 of these issues by .18 or more ratio points—in short, by differences that are in absolute magnitude very large. The two samples are furthest apart in their attitudes toward public ownership and are especially divided on the question of government ownership of natural resources, the Democrats strongly favoring it, the Republicans just as strongly wanting it cut back. The difference of .39 in the ratio scores is the largest for any of the issues tested. In percentages, the differences are 58 per cent (D) vs. 13 per cent (R) in favor of increasing support, and 19 per cent (D) vs. 52 per cent (R) in favor of decreasing support. Both parties preponderantly support public control and development of atomic energy, but the Democrats do so more uniformly.

V. O. Key, among others, has observed that the Republican party is especially responsive to the "financial and manufacturing community," [15] reflecting the view that government should intervene as little as possible to burden

TABLE 2A.

Comparison of Party Leaders and Followers on "Public Ownership" Issues, by Percentages and Ratios of Support

	Leaders		Followers	
	Dem. N = 1,788	Repub. N = 1,232	Dem. N = 821	Repub. N = 623
Issues		(%s down)		
Public ownership of natural resources				
% favoring: Increase	57.5	12.9	35.3	31.1
Decrease	18.6	51.9	15.0	19.9
Same, n.c.*	23.8	35.2	49.7	49.0
Support ratio	.69	.30	.60	.56
Public control of atomic energy				
% favoring: Increase	73.2	45.0	64.2	59.4
Decrease	7.2	15.3	7.1	10.0
Same, n.c.	19.6	39.7	28.7	30.6
Support ratio	.83	.65	.79	.75
Mean support ratios for the public ownership category	.76	.48	.70	.66

* n.c. = no code.

[15] Key, *op. cit.*, p. 239.

or restrain prevailing business interests. The validity of this observation is evident throughout all our data, and is most clearly seen in the responses to the issues listed under Government Regulation of the Economy, Equalitarianism and Human Welfare, Tax Policy. Democratic leaders are far more eager than Republican leaders to strengthen enforcement of anti-monopoly laws and to increase regulation of public utilities and business. Indeed, the solidarity of Republican opposition to the regulation of business is rather overwhelming: 84 per cent want to decrease such regulation and fewer than .01 per cent say they want to increase it. Although the Democrats, on balance, also feel that government controls on business should not be expanded further, the differences between the two samples on this issue are nevertheless substantial.

The two sets of leaders are also far apart on the farm issue, the Democrats preferring slightly to increase farm supports, the Republicans wanting strongly to reduce them. The Republican ratio score of .20 on this issue is among the lowest in the entire set of scores. The magnitude of these scores somewhat surprised us, for while opposition to agricultural subsidies is consistent with Republican dislike for state intervention, we had expected the leaders to conform more closely to the familiar image of the Republican as the more "rural" of the two parties.[16] It appears, however, that the party's connection with business is far more compelling than its association with agriculture. The Republican desire to reduce government expenditures and to promote independence from "government handouts" prevails on the farm question as it does on other issues, while the Democratic preference for a more regulated economy in which government intervenes to reduce economic risk and to stabilize prosperity is equally evident on the other side. Party attitudes on this issue appear to be determined as much by ideological tendencies as by deliberate calculation of the political advantages to be gained by favoring or opposing subsidies to farmers. Comparison of our findings with Turner's earlier data on farm votes in Congress[17] suggests, in addition, that the sharp party difference on the farm issue is neither a recent development nor a mere product of the personal philosophy of the present Secretary of Agriculture.

Having implied that agricultural policies partly result from principle, we must note that on three other issues in this category (trade unions, credit, and tariffs), principle seems to be overweighed by old-fashioned economic considerations. In spite of their distaste for government interference in economic affairs, the Republicans almost unanimously favor greater regulation of trade

[16] The friendlier attitude toward farmers among Democratic leaders than Republican leaders is borne out in the responses to several other questions used in the study. For example, the Republican leaders list farmers as having "too much power" far more frequently than do the Democratic leaders. Equally, the Democrats are significantly more inclined to regard farmers as having "too little power."

[17] Turner, *op. cit.*, p. 64.

TABLE 2B.

Comparison of Party Leaders and Followers on "Government Regulation of the Economy" Issues, by Percentages and Ratios of Support

Issues	Leaders		Followers	
	Dem. $N = 1,788$	*Repub.* $N = 1,232$	*Dem.* $N = 821$	*Repub.* $N = 623$
	($\%$s down)			
Level of farm price supports				
% favoring: Increase	43.4	6.7	39.0	23.0
Decrease	28.1	67.4	27.6	40.3
Same, n.c.	28.5	25.8	33.4	36.7
Support ratio	.58	.20	.56	.41
Government regulation of business				
% favoring: Increase	20.2	0.6	18.6	7.4
Decrease	38.5	84.1	33.4	46.2
Same, n.c.	41.3	15.3	48.0	46.4
Support ratio	.41	.08	.43	.31
Regulation of public utilities				
% favoring: Increase	59.0	17.9	39.3	26.0
Decrease	6.4	17.6	11.1	12.0
Same, n.c.	34.6	64.5	49.6	62.0
Support ratio	.76	.50	.64	.57
Enforcement of anti-monopoly laws				
% favoring: Increase	78.0	44.9	53.2	51.0
Decrease	2.9	9.0	7.9	6.6
Same, n.c.	19.1	46.1	38.9	42.4
Support ratio	.88	.68	.73	.72
Regulation of trade unions				
% favoring: Increase	59.3	86.4	46.6	57.8
Decrease	12.4	4.5	8.9	10.6
Same, n.c.	28.3	9.2	44.5	31.6
Support ratio	.73	.91	.69	.74
Level of tariffs				
% favoring: Increase	13.0	19.2	16.6	15.2
Decrease	43.0	26.3	25.3	21.3
Same, n.c.	43.9	54.5	58.1	63.4
Support ratio	.35	.46	.46	.47
Restrictions on credit				
% favoring: Increase	24.8	20.6	26.1	25.7
Decrease	39.3	20.6	22.2	23.8
Same, n.c.	35.9	58.8	51.8	50.5
Support ratio	.43	.50	.52	.51
Mean support ratios for "government regulation of the economy" category	.59	.48	.58	.53

unions and they are more strongly disposed than the Democrats toward government intervention to restrict credit and to raise tariffs. Of course, party cleavages over the credit and tariff issues have a long history,[18] which may by now have endowed them with ideological force beyond immediate economic considerations.[19] The preponderant Democratic preference for greater regulation of trade unions is doubtless a response to recent "exposures" of corrupt labor practices, though it may also signify that the party's perspective toward the trade unions is shifting somewhat.

The closer Republican identification with business, free enterprise, and economic conservatism in general, and the friendlier Democratic attitude toward labor and toward government regulation of the economy, are easily observed in the data from other parts of our questionnaire. Republican leaders score very much higher than Democratic leaders on, for example, such scales as economic conservatism, independence of government, and business attitudes. On a question asking respondents to indicate the groups from which they would be most and least likely to take advice, 41 per cent of the Democratic leaders but only 3.8 per cent of the Republican leaders list trade unions as groups from which they would seek advice. Trade unions are scored in the "least likely" category by 25 per cent of the Democrats and 63 per cent of the Republicans. Similarly, more than 94 per cent of the Republican leaders, but 56 per cent of the Democratic leaders, name trade unions as groups that have "too much power." These differences, it should be noted, cannot be accounted for by reference to the greater number of trade union members among the Democratic party leadership, for in the 1956 conventions only 14 per cent of the Democrats belonged to trade unions, and while an even smaller percentage (4 per cent) of the Republicans were trade unionists, this disparity is hardly great enough to explain the large differences in outlook. The key to the explanation has to be sought in the symbolic and reference group identifications of the two parties, and in their underlying values.

Nowhere do we see this more clearly than in the responses to the Equalitarian and Human Welfare issues. The mean difference in the ratio scores for the category as a whole is .22, a very large difference and one that results from differences in the expected direction on all six issues that make up the category. On four of these issues—federal aid to education, slum clearance and public housing, social security, and minimum wages—the leaders of the two parties are widely separated, the differences in their ratio scores ranging from .36 to .21. The percentages showing the proportions who favor increased support for these issues are even more striking. In every instance the Democratic

[18] See John B. Johnson, Jr., *The Extent and Consistency of Party Voting in the United States Senate*, Ph.D. thesis, University of Chicago, 1943. By applying the Rice Index-of-Likeness to Senate votes, Johnson finds the tariff to have been the most partisan issue before the Congress in the years 1880–1940.

[19] Corinne Silverman, "The Legislator's View of the Legislative Process," *Public Opinion Quarterly*, Vol. 18 (1954–55), p. 180.

TABLE 2C.

Comparison of Party Leaders and Followers on "Equalitarian and Human Welfare" Issues, by Percentages and Ratios of Support

	Leaders		Followers	
	Dem. *N = 1,788*	*Repub.* *N = 1,232*	*Dem.* *N = 821*	*Repub.* *N = 623*
Issues		(%s down)		
Federal aid to education				
% favoring: Increase	66.2	22.3	74.9	64.8
Decrease	13.4	43.2	5.6	8.3
Same, n.c.	20.4	34.5	19.5	26.8
Support ratio	.76	.40	.85	.78
Slum clearance and public housing				
% favoring: Increase	78.4	40.1	79.5	72.5
Decrease	5.6	21.6	5.8	7.9
Same, n.c.	16.0	38.3	14.6	19.6
Support ratio	.86	.59	.87	.82
Social security benefits				
% favoring: Increase	60.0	22.5	69.4	57.0
Decrease	3.9	13.1	3.0	3.8
Same, n.c.	36.1	64.4	27.5	39.2
Support ratio	.78	.55	.83	.77
Minimum wages				
% favoring: Increase	50.0	15.5	59.0	43.5
Decrease	4.7	12.5	2.9	5.0
Same, n.c.	45.2	72.0	38.1	51.5
Support ratio	.73	.52	.78	.69
Enforcement of integration				
% favoring: Increase	43.8	25.5	41.9	40.8
Decrease	26.6	31.7	27.4	23.6
Same, n.c.	29.5	42.8	30.7	35.6
Support ratio	.59	.47	.57	.59
Immigration into United States				
% favoring: Increase	36.1	18.4	10.4	8.0
Decrease	27.0	29.9	52.0	44.6
Same, n.c.	36.9	51.7	37.6	47.4
Support ratio	.54	.44	.29	.32
Mean support ratios for "equalitarian and human welfare" category	.71	.50	.70	.66

percentages are considerably higher: 66 *vs.* 22 per cent (education); 78 *vs.* 40 per cent (slum clearance and housing); 60 *vs.* 23 per cent (social security); and 50 *vs.* 16 per cent (minimum wages). The Democratic leaders also are better disposed than the Republican leaders toward immigration: twice as many of them (36 per cent *vs.* 18 per cent) favor a change in policy to permit more immigrants to enter. The overall inclination of both party elites, however, is to accept the present levels of immigration, the Democratic ratio score falling slightly above, and the Republican slightly below, the midpoint.

More surprising are the differences on the segregation issue, for, despite strong southern influence, the Democratic leaders express significantly more support for enforcing integration than the Republicans do. Moreover, the difference between the two parties rises from .12 for the national samples as a whole to a difference of .18 when the southern leaders are excluded. In his study of Congress, Turner found that the Republicans gave more support to Negro rights than the Democrats did.[20] The reversal of this finding in our data does not necessarily mean that a change has occurred since Turner made his study, but only that the votes of the congressional parties do not always reflect the private feelings of the national party leadership. Then, too, southern influence is disproportionately stronger in the Democratic congressional party than in the national Democratic organization as a whole, and disproportionately weaker in the Republican congressional party than in the Republican organization as a whole.

Examination of the actual magnitude of the ratio scores in this category reveals that the Republicans want not so much to abrogate existing social welfare or equalitarian measures as to keep them from being broadened. The Democrats, by comparison, are shown to be the party of social equality and reform, more willing than their opponents to employ legislation for the benefit of the underprivileged. Support for these inferences and for the greater liberalism of the Democrats can be found elsewhere in our data as well. Analysis of the scale results show Republican leaders scoring higher than Democratic leaders on such measures as chauvinism, elitism, conservatism, and right-wing values, and lower on tolerance, procedural rights, and faith in democracy. No differences worth noting, however, were found for ethnocentrism, faith in freedom, or the California F scale. The Democrats had a slightly higher average score on the left-wing scale, but the number of leaders in either party who scored high on this measure was fairly small.

The self-images and reference group identifications of the two parties also should be noted in this connection. For example, many more Democratic than Republican leaders call themselves liberal and state that they would be most likely to take advice from liberal reform organizations, the Farmers' Union, and (as we have seen) from the trade unions; only a small number consider themselves conservative or would seek advice from conservative reform

[20] Turner, *op. cit.*, p. 54.

TABLE 2D.

Comparison of Party Leaders and Followers on "Tax Policy" Issues, by Percentages and Ratios of Support

| | Leaders | | Followers | |
| | Dem. $N = 1,788$ | Repub. $N = 1,232$ | Dem. $N = 821$ | Repub. $N = 623$ |
Issues		(%s down)		
Corporate income tax				
% favoring: Increase	32.3	4.0	32.0	23.3
Decrease	23.3	61.5	20.5	25.7
Same, n.c.	44.4	34.5	47.5	51.0
Support ratio	.54	.21	.56	.49
Tax on large incomes				
% favoring: Increase	27.0	5.4	46.6	34.7
Decrease	23.1	56.9	13.8	21.7
Same, n.c.	49.9	37.7	39.6	43.6
Support ratio	.52	.24	.66	.56
Tax on business				
% favoring: Increase	12.6	1.0	24.6	15.9
Decrease	38.3	71.1	24.1	32.6
Same, n.c.	49.1	27.8	51.3	51.5
Support ratio	.37	.15	.50	.42
Tax on middle incomes				
% favoring: Increase	2.7	0.8	4.5	3.0
Decrease	50.2	63.9	49.3	44.3
Same, n.c.	47.1	35.3	46.2	52.6
Support ratio	.26	.18	.28	.29
Tax on small incomes				
% favoring: Increase	1.4	2.9	1.6	2.1
Decrease	79.2	65.0	77.5	69.6
Same, n.c.	19.4	32.1	20.9	28.3
Support ratio	.11	.19	.12	.16
Mean support ratios for "tax policy" category	.36	.19	.42	.38

organizations, the National Association of Manufacturers, or the Farm Bureau Federation. The Republicans have in almost all instances the reverse identifications: only a handful regard themselves as liberal or would seek counsel from liberal organizations, while more than 42 per cent call themselves conservative and would look to the NAM or to conservative reform organizations for advice. Almost two-thirds of the Republicans (compared with 29 per cent of the Democrats) regard the Chamber of Commerce as an important source of advice. Businessmen are listed as having "too much power" by 42 per cent of the Democrats but by only 9 per cent of the Republicans. The Democrats are also significantly more inclined than the Republicans to consider Catholics, Jews, and the foreign born as having "too little power." While self-descriptions and reference group identifications often correspond poorly with actual beliefs—among the general population they scarcely correspond at all, in fact—we are dealing, in the case of the leaders, with a politically informed and highly articulate set of people who have little difficulty connecting the beliefs they hold and the groups that promote or obstruct those beliefs.

Our fourth category, Tax Policy, divides the parties almost as severely as do the other categories. The mean difference for the category as a whole is .20, and it would doubtless have been larger but for the universal unpopularity of proposals to increase taxes on small and middle income groups. Table 2D shows that the differences between the parties on the tax issues follow the patterns previously observed and that tax policy is for the Democrats a device for redistributing income and promoting social equality. Neither party, however, is keen about raising taxes for *any* group: even the Democrats have little enthusiasm for new taxes on upper income groups or on business and corporate enterprises. The Republican leaders are overwhelmingly opposed to increased taxes for *any* group, rich *or* poor. This can be seen in their low ratio scores on the tax issues, which range from only .15 to .24. But while they are far more eager than the Democratic leaders to cut taxes on corporate and private wealth, they are less willing to reduce taxes on the lower income groups. These differences, it should be remarked, are not primarily a function of differences in the income of the two samples. Although there are more people with high incomes among the Republican leaders, the disproportion between the two samples is not nearly great enough to account for the dissimilarities in their tax views.

Of the five categories considered, Foreign Policy shows the smallest average difference, but even on these issues the divergence between Democratic and Republican leader attitudes is significant. Except for defense spending the Democrats turn out to be more internationalist than the Republicans, as evidenced in their greater commitment to the United Nations and to American participation in international military alliances like NATO. Twice as many Democrats as Republicans want the United States to rely more heavily upon such organizations, while many more Republicans want to reduce our international involvements. Both parties are predominantly in favor of cutting back foreign aid—a somewhat surprising finding in light of Democratic public pronouncements on this subject—but more Republicans feel strongly on the subject. Our data thus furnish little support for the claim that the parties hold

TABLE 2E.

Comparison of Party Leaders and Followers on "Foreign Policy" Issues,
by Percentages and Ratios of Support

	Leaders		Followers	
	Dem.	Repub.	Dem.	Repub.
	N = 1,788	N = 1,232	N = 821	N = 623
Issues	(%s down)			
Reliance on the United Nations				
% favoring: Increase	48.9	24.4	34.7	33.4
Decrease	17.6	34.8	17.3	19.3
Same, n.c.	33.5	40.7	48.0	47.3
Support ratio	.66	.45	.59	.57
American participation in military alliances				
% favoring: Increase	41.5	22.7	39.1	32.3
Decrease	17.6	25.7	14.0	15.4
Same, n.c.	40.9	51.6	46.9	52.3
Support ratio	.62	.48	.62	.58
Foreign aid				
% favoring: Increase	17.8	7.6	10.1	10.1
Decrease	51.0	61.7	58.6	57.3
Same, n.c.	31.1	30.7	31.3	32.6
Support ratio	.33	.23	.26	.26
Defense spending				
% favoring: Increase	20.7	13.6	50.5	45.7
Decrease	34.4	33.6	16.4	15.4
Same, n.c.	44.8	52.8	33.0	38.8
Support ratio	.43	.40	.67	.65
Mean support ratios for "foreign policy" category (excl. defense spending)	.54	.39	.49	.47

the same views on foreign policy or that their seeming differences are merely
a response to the demands of political competition.[21]

•   •   •

[21] *Cf.* Turner, *op. cit.*, p. 56, in which he found differences on foreign policy difficult to assess in

Notice that the issues commonly thought to be most divisive do not always evoke the greatest cleavage between the parties. Immigration, tariffs, civil rights, monopoly control, and credit regulation fall toward the lower end of the rank order, while farm supports, federal aid to education, slum clearance, social security, minimum wages, public housing, and issues dealing with the regulation and taxation of business fall toward the upper end. Though by no means uniformly, the older, more traditional issues appear to have been superseded as sources of controversy by issues that have come into prominence chiefly during the New Deal and Fair Deal.

IV. COMPARISONS BETWEEN FOLLOWERS

So far we have addressed ourselves to the differences between Democratic and Republican *leaders*. In each of the tables presented, however, data are included from which the two sets of party *followers* may also be compared.

The observation most clearly warranted from these data is that the rank-and-file members of the two parties are far less divided than their leaders. Not only do they diverge significantly on fewer issues—seven as compared with 23 for the leader samples—but the magnitudes of the differences in their ratio scores are substantially smaller for every one of the 24 issues. No difference is larger than .14, and on the majority of the issues the disparity is smaller than .05. Insofar as they differ at all, however, the followers tend to divide in a pattern similar to that shown by the leaders, the correlation between their rank orders being .72. All the issues on which the followers significantly disagree are of the "bread and butter" variety, the more symbolic issues being so remotely experienced and so vaguely grasped that rank-and-file voters are often unable to identify them with either party. Policies affecting farm prices, business regulation, taxes, or minimum wages, by contrast, are quickly felt by the groups to whom they are addressed and are therefore more capable of arousing partisan identifications. It should also be noted that while the average differences are small for all five categories, they are smallest of all for foreign policy—the most removed and least well understood group of issues in the entire array.[24]

Democratic and Republican followers were also compared on a number of scales and reference group questions. The results, while generally consistent

---

Congress, partly because of its tie with the executive branch; see also, George Belknap and Angus Campbell, "Political Party Identification and Attitudes toward Foreign Policy," *Public Opinion Quarterly*, Vol. XV (Winter 1951–52), pp. 608–19.

[24] For comparative data on party affiliation and issue outlooks among rank-and-file voters, see Angus Campbell, Phillip E. Converse, Warren E. Miller, and Donald E. Stokes, *The American Voter* (New York, 1960), especially chs. 8 and 9 dealing with issues and ideology. The text of this important report on the 1956 election study carried out by the Michigan Survey Research Center unfortunately reached us too late to be used to full advantage in the present analysis. The

with the differences between the leaders, show the followers to be far more united than their leaders on these measures as well. Even on business attitudes, independence of government, and economic conservatism, the differences are small and barely significant. No differences were found on such scales as tolerance, faith in democracy, procedural rights, conservatism-liberalism (classical), the California F scale and isolationism. The average Democrat is slightly more willing than the average Republican to label himself a liberal or to seek advice from liberal organizations; the contrary is true when it comes to adopting conservative identifications. Only in the differential trust they express toward business and labor are the two sets of followers widely separated.

These findings give little support to the claim that the "natural divisions" of the electorate are being smothered by party leaders.[25] Not only do the leaders disagree more sharply than their respective followers, but the level of consensus among the electorate (with or without regard to party) is fairly high. Inspection of the "increase" and "decrease" percentage scores (Tables 2A–2E) shows that substantial differences of opinion exist among the electorate on only five of the 24 issues (credit restrictions, farm supports, segregatio.., and corporate and business taxes). Of course, voters may divide more sharply on issues at election time, since campaigns intensify party feeling and may also intensify opinions on issues. Available data from election studies allow no unequivocal conclusion on this point,[26] but even the party-linked differences found among voters during elections may largely be echoes of the opinions announced by the candidates—transient sentiments developed for the occasion and quickly forgotten.

V. LEADER CONFLICT AND FOLLOWER CONSENSUS: EXPLANATIONS

Considering the nature of the differences between the leader and follower samples, the interesting question is not why the parties fail to represent the "natural division" in the electorate (for that question rests on an unwarranted

findings of the Michigan and the PAB studies, relative to the role of issues and ideology among the general population, corroborate and supplement each other to a very great degree.

[25] Cf. Stephen K. Bailey, The Condition of Our National Parties (Monograph), Fund for the Republic, 1959.

[26] The data reported by the Elmira study of 1948 show the supporters of the two parties to be largely in agreement on issues. See ibid., pp. 186, 190, 194, 211. The findings of the 1956 Michigan Survey suggest strongly that most voters, even at election time, do not know much about issues and are unable to link the parties with particular issues. Campbell and his associates conclude, for example, that "many people fail to appreciate that an issue exists; others are insufficiently involved to pay attention to recognized issues; and still others fail to make connections between issue positions and party policy." The American Voter, op. cit., ch. 8.

assumption) but why the party elites disagree at all, and why they divide so much more sharply than their followers.

Despite the great pressures toward uniformity we have noted in American society, many forces also divide the population culturally, economically, and politically. The United States is, after all, a miscellany of ethnic and religious strains set down in a geographically large and diverse country. Many of these groups brought old conflicts and ideologies with them, and some have tried to act out in the new world the hopes and frustrations nurtured in the old. Then, too, despite rapid social mobility, social classes have by no means been eliminated. No special political insight is needed to perceive that the two parties characteristically draw from different strata of the society, the Republicans from the managerial, proprietary, and to some extent professional classes, the Democrats from labor, minorities, low income groups, and a large proportion of the intellectuals.[27] Partly because the leaders of the two parties tend to overrespond to the modal values of the groups with which they are principally identified, they gradually grow further apart on the key questions which separate their respective supporters.[28] The Republican emphasis on business ideology is both a cause and a consequence of its managerial and proprietary support; the greater Democratic emphasis on social justice, and on economic and social levelling, is both the occasion and the product of the support the party enjoys among intellectuals and the lower strata. These interrelationships are strengthened, moreover, by the tendency for a party's dominant supporters to gain a disproportionate number of positions in its leadership ranks.[29]

The differences which typically separate Democratic from Republican leaders seem also to reflect a deep-seated ideological cleavage often found among Western parties. One side of this cleavage is marked by a strong belief in the power of collective action to promote social justice, equality, humanitarianism, and economic planning, while preserving freedom; the other is distinguished by faith in the wisdom of the natural competitive process and in the supreme virtue of individualism, "character," self-reliance, frugality, and independence from government. To this cleavage is added another frequent source of political division, namely, a difference in attitude toward change between "radicals" and "moderates," between those who prefer to move quickly or slowly, to reform or to conserve. These differences in social philosophy and posture do not always coincide with the divisions in the social structure, and their elements do not, in all contexts, combine in the same way. But, however crudely, the American parties do tend to embody these competing points of view and to serve as reference groups for those who hold them.

[27] For an analysis of the connection between intellectuals and liberal politics, see Seymour M. Lipset, *Political Man* (New York, 1960), ch. 10; also Paul F. Lazarsfeld and Wagner Thielens, Jr., *The Academic Mind* (Glencoe, 1958), chs. 1 and 2.

[28] Samuel P. Huntington, "A Revised theory of American Party Politics," *American Political Science Review*, Vol. XLIV (1950), p. 676.

[29] PAB data supporting this generalization will be presented in a future publication.

Party cleavage in America was no doubt intensified by the advent of the New Deal, and by its immense electoral and intellectual success. Not only did it weld into a firm alliance the diverse forces that were to be crucial to all subsequent Democratic majorities, but it also made explicit the doctrines of the "welfare state" with which the party was henceforth to be inseparably identified. Because of the novelty of its program and its apparently radical threat to the familiar patterns of American political and economic life, it probably deepened the fervor of its Republican adversaries and drove into the opposition the staunchest defenders of business ideology. The conflict was further sharpened by the decline of left-wing politics after the war, and by the transfer of loyalties of former and potential radicals to the Democratic party. Once launched, the cleavage has been sustained by the tendency for each party to attract into its active ranks a disproportionate number of voters who recognize and share its point of view.

Why, however, are the leaders so much more sharply divided than their followers? The reasons are not hard to understand and are consistent with several of the hypotheses that underlay the present study.

1. Consider, to begin with, that the leaders come from the more articulate segments of society and, on the average, are politically more aware than their followers and far better informed about issues.[30] For them, political issues and opinions are the everyday currency of party competition, not esoteric matters that surpass understanding. With their greater awareness and responsibility, and their greater need to defend their party's stands, they have more interest in developing a consistent set of attitudes—perhaps even an ideology. The followers of each party, often ignorant of the issues and their consequences, find it difficult to distinguish their beliefs from those of the opposition and have little reason to be concerned with the consistency of their attitudes. Furthermore, the American parties make only a feeble effort to educate the rank-and-file politically, and since no central source exists for the authoritative pronouncement of party policy,[31] the followers often do not know what their leaders believe or on what issues the parties chiefly divide. In short, if we mean by ideology a coherent body of informed social doctrine, it is possessed mainly by the articulate leadership, rarely by the masses.

2. Differences in the degree of partisan involvement parallel the differences in knowledge and have similar consequences. The leaders, of course, have more party spirit than the followers, and, as the election studies make plain, the stronger the partisanship, the larger the differences on issues. The leaders are more highly motivated not only to belong to a party appropriate to their beliefs, but to accept its doctrines and to learn how it differs from the opposition party. Since politics is more salient for leaders than for followers, they develop a greater stake in the outcome of the political contest and are

[30] For the effects of education on issue familiarity, see Campbell *et al., op. cit.,* ch. 8.

[31] Schattschneider, *op. cit.; Toward a More Responsible Two-Party System, op. cit., passim.*

more eager to discover the intellectual grounds by which they hope to make victory possible. Through a process of circular reinforcement, those for whom politics is most important are likely to become the most zealous participants, succeeding to the posts that deal in the formation of opinion. Ideology serves the instrumental purpose, in addition, of justifying the heavy investment that party leaders make in political activity. While politics offers many rewards, it also makes great demands on the time, money, and energies of its practitioners—sacrifices which they can more easily justify if they believe they are serving worthwhile social goals. The followers, in contrast, are intellectually far less involved, have less personal stake in the outcome of the competition, have little need to be concerned with the "correctness" of their views on public questions, and have even less reason to learn in precisely what ways their opinions differ from their opponents'. Hence, the party elites recruit members from a population stratified in some measure by ideology, while the rank-and-file renews itself by more random recruitment and is thus more likely to mirror the opinions of a cross section of the population.

3. Part of the explanation for the greater consensus among followers than leaders resides in the nature and size of the two types of groups. Whereas the leader groups are comparatively small and selective, each of the follower groups number in the millions and, by their very size and unwieldiness, are predisposed to duplicate the characteristics of the population as a whole. Even if the Republicans draw disproportionately from the business-managerial classes and the Democrats from the trade union movement, neither interest group has enough influence to shape distinctively the aggregate opinions of so large a mass of supporters. Size also affects the nature and frequency of interaction within the two types of groups. Because they comprise a smaller, more selectively chosen, organized, and articulate elite, the leaders are apt to associate with people of their own political persuasion more frequently and consistently than the followers do. They are not only less cross-pressured than the rank-and-file but they are also subjected to strong party group efforts to induce them to conform. Because their political values are continually renewed through frequent communication with people of like opinions, and because they acquire intense reference group identifications, they develop an extraordinary ability to resist the force of the opposition's arguments. While the followers, too, are thrown together and shielded to some extent, they are likely to mingle more freely with people of hostile political persuasions, to receive fewer partisan communications, and to hold views that are only intermittently and inconsistently reinforced. Since, by comparison with the leaders, they possess little interest in or information about politics, they can more easily embrace "deviant" attitudes without discomfort and without challenge from their associates. Nor are they likely to be strongly rewarded for troubling to have "correct" opinions. The followers, in short, are less often and less effectively indoctrinated than their leaders. The group processes described here would function even more powerfully in small, sectarian, tightly organ-

ized parties of the European type, but they are also present in the American party system, where they yield similar though less potent consequences.

4. Political competition itself operates to divide the leaders more than the followers. If the parties are impelled to present a common face to the electorate, they are also strongly influenced to distinguish themselves from each other.[32] For one thing, they have a more heightened sense of the "national interest" than the followers do, even if they do not all conceive it in the same way. For another, they hope to improve their chances at the polls by offering the electorate a recognizable and attractive commodity. In addition, they seek emotional gratification in the heightened sense of brotherhood brought on by the struggle against an "outgroup" whose claim to office seems always, somehow, to border upon usurpation. As with many ingroup-outgroup distinctions, the participants search for moral grounds to justify their antagonisms toward each other, and ideologies help to furnish such grounds. Among the followers, on the other hand, these needs exist, if at all, in much weaker form.

VI. LEADERS VERSUS FOLLOWERS

In comparing each party elite with its own followers we were mainly interested in seeing how closely each body of supporters shared the point of view of its leaders, in order to test the hypothesis that party affiliation, even for the rank-and-file, is a function of ideological agreement. In predicting that the parties would tend to attract supporters who share their beliefs, we expected, of course, to find exceptions. We knew that many voters pay little attention to the ideological aspects of politics and that, in Gabriel Almond's phrase, a party's more "esoteric doctrines" are not always known to its followers.[33] Nevertheless we were not prepared for the findings turned up by this phase of the inquiry, for the differences between leaders and followers—among the Republicans at least—are beyond anything we had expected. Indeed, the conclusion is inescapable that the views of the Republican rank-and-file are, on the whole, much closer to those of the Democratic leaders than to those of the Republican leaders. Although conflicts in outlook also exist between Democratic leaders and followers, they are less frequent or severe.

● ● ●

In short, whereas Republican leaders hold to the tenets of business ideology and remain faithful to the spirit and intellectual mood of leaders like Robert A. Taft, the rank-and-file Republican supporters have embraced, along with their Democratic brethren, the regulatory and social reform measures of the Roosevelt and Truman administrations. This inference receives further sup-

[32] See E. E. Schattschneider, *Party Government, op. cit.*, p. 192.
[33] Gabriel Almond, *The Appeals of Communism* (Princeton, 1954), pp. 5–6, and ch. 3.

port from the scores on our Party Ideology scale where, on a variety of attitudes and values which characteristically distinguish the leaders of the two parties, the Republican followers fall closer to the Democratic than to the Republican side of the continuum. Thus, in addition to being the preferred party of the more numerous classes, the Democrats also enjoy the advantages over their opponents of holding views that are more widely shared throughout the country.

Assuming the findings are valid, we were obviously wrong to expect that party differentiation among followers would depend heavily upon ideological considerations.[34] Evidently, party attachment is so much a function of other factors (e.g., class and primary group memberships, religious affiliation, place of residence, mass media, etc.) that many voters can maintain their party loyalties comfortably even while holding views that contradict the beliefs of their own leaders.

Still, we are not entitled to conclude that issue outlook has no effect on the party affiliation of ordinary members. It is conceivable, for example, that the Republican party has come to be the minority party partly because the opinions of its spokesmen are uncongenial to a majority of the voters. We have no way of knowing from our data—collected at only a single point in time—how many "normally" Republican voters, if any, have defected to the Democrats or fled into independency because they disapprove of Republican beliefs. At the present stage of the analysis, we have no grounds for going beyond the proposition that political affiliation without conformity on issues is possible on a wide scale.

● ● ●

SUMMARY AND CONCLUSIONS

The research described in this paper—an outgrowth of a nationwide inquiry into the nature and sources of political affiliation, activity, and belief—was principally designed to test a number of hypotheses about the relation of ideology to party membership. Responses from large samples of Democratic and Republican leaders and followers were compared on twenty-four key issues and on a number of attitude questions and scales. Statistical operations were carried out to assess conflict and consensus among party groups and to estimate the size and significance of differences. From the data yielded by this inquiry, the following inferences seem warranted.

1. Although it has received wide currency, especially among Europeans, the belief that the two American parties are identical in principle and doc-

---

[34] See the discussion bearing on this conclusion in Campbell *et al.*, *op. cit.*, chs. 8 and 9. Also, Avery Leiserson, *Parties and Politics, An Institutional and Behavioral Approach* (New York, 1958), pp. 162–66.

trine has little foundation in fact. Examination of the opinions of Democratic and Republican leaders shows them to be distinct communities of co-believers who diverge sharply on many important issues. Their disagreements, furthermore, conform to an image familiar to many observers and are generally consistent with differences turned up by studies of Congressional roll calls. The unpopularity of many of the positions held by Republican leaders suggests also that the parties submit to the demands of their constituents less slavishly than is commonly supposed.

2. Republican and Democratic leaders stand furthest apart on the issues that grow out of their group identification and support—out of the managerial, proprietary, and high-status connections of the one, and the labor, minority, low-status, and intellectual connections of the other. The opinions of each party elite are linked less by chance than by membership in a common ideological domain. Democratic leaders typically display the stronger urge to elevate the lowborn, the uneducated, the deprived minorities, and the poor in general; they are also more disposed to employ the nation's collective power to advance humanitarian and social welfare goals (e.g., social security, immigration, racial integration, a higher minimum wage, and public education). They are more critical of wealth and big business and more eager to bring them under regulation. Theirs is the greater faith in the wisdom of using legislation for redistributing the national product and for furnishing social services on a wide scale. Of the two groups of leaders, the Democrats are the more "progressively" oriented toward social reform and experimentation. The Republican leaders, while not uniformly differentiated from their opponents, subscribe in greater measure to the symbols and practices of individualism, laissez-faire, and national independence. They prefer to overcome humanity's misfortunes by relying upon personal effort, private incentives, frugality, hard work, responsibility, self-denial (for both men and government), and the strengthening rather than the diminution of the economic and status distinctions that are the "natural" rewards of the differences in human character and fortunes. Were it not for the hackneyed nature of the designation and the danger of forcing traits into a mold they fit only imperfectly, we might be tempted to describe the Republicans as the chief upholders of what Max Weber has called the "Protestant Ethic." [36] Not that the Democrats are insensible to the "virtues" of the Protestant-capitalistic ethos, but they embrace them less firmly or uniformly. The differences between the two elites have probably been intensified by the rise of the New Deal and by the shift of former radicals into the Democratic party following the decline of socialist and other left-wing movements during and after the war.

3. Whereas the leaders of the two parties diverge strongly, their followers differ only moderately in their attitudes toward issues. The hypothesis that party beliefs unite adherents and bring them into the party ranks may hold

[36] Max Weber, *Protestant Ethic and the Spirit of Capitalism* (London, 1948), ch. V.

for the more active members of a mass party but not for its rank-and-file supporters. Republican followers, in fact, disagree far more with their own leaders than with the leaders of the Democratic party. Little support was found for the belief that deep cleavages exist among the electorate but are ignored by the leaders. One might, indeed, more accurately assert the contrary, to wit: that the natural cleavages between the leaders are largely ignored by the voters. However, we cannot presently conclude that ideology exerts no influence over the habits of party support, for the followers do differ significantly and in the predicted directions on some issues. Furthermore, we do not know how many followers may previously have been led by doctrinal considerations to shift their party allegiances.

4. Except for their desire to ingratiate themselves with as many voters as possible, the leaders of the two parties have more reason than their followers to hold sharply opposing views on the important political questions of the day. Compared with the great mass of supporters, they are articulate, informed, highly partisan, and involved; they comprise a smaller and more tightly knit group which is closer to the wellsprings of party opinion, more accessible for indoctrination, more easily rewarded or punished for conformity or deviation, and far more affected, politically and psychologically, by engagement in the party struggle for office. If the leaders of the two parties are not always candid about their disagreements, the reason may well be that they sense the great measure of consensus to be found among the electorate.

5. Finding that party leaders hold contrary beliefs does not prove that they *act* upon these beliefs or that the two parties are, in practice, governed by different outlooks. In a subsequent paper we shall consider these questions more directly by comparing platform and other official party pronouncements with the private opinions revealed in this study. Until further inquiries are conducted, however, it seems reasonable to assume that the views held privately by party leaders can never be entirely suppressed but are bound to crop out in hundreds of large and small ways—in campaign speeches, discussions at party meetings, private communications to friends and sympathizers, statements to the press by party officials and candidates, legislative debates, and public discussions on innumerable national, state, and local questions. If, in other words, the opinions of party leaders are as we have described them, there is every chance that they are expressed and acted upon to some extent. Whether this makes our parties "ideological" depends, of course, on how narrow we define that term. Some may prefer to reserve that designation for parties that are more obviously preoccupied with doctrine, more intent upon the achievement of a systematic political program, and more willing to enforce a common set of beliefs upon their members and spokesmen.

6. The parties are internally united on some issues, divided on others. In general, Republican leaders achieve greatest homogeneity on issues that grow out of their party's identification with business, Democratic leaders on issues that reflect their connection with liberal and lower-income groups. We find

no support for the hypothesis that the parties achieve greatest internal consensus on the issues which principally divide them from their opponents.

In a sequel to this paper we shall offer data on the demographic correlates of issue support, which show that most of the differences presented here exist independently of factors like education, occupation, age, religion, and sectionalism. Controlling for these influences furnishes much additional information and many new insights but does not upset our present conclusions in any important respect. Thus, the parties must be considered not merely as spokesmen for other interest groups but as reference groups in their own right, helping to formulate, to sustain, and to speak for a recognizable point of view.

"BLACK POWER" AND COALITION POLITICS

BAYARD RUSTIN

There are two Americas—black and white—and nothing has more clearly revealed the divisions between them than the debate currently raging around the slogan of "black power." Despite—or perhaps because of—the fact that this slogan lacks any clear definition, it has succeeded in galvanizing emotions on all sides, with many whites seeing it as the expression of a new racism and many Negroes taking it as a warning to white people that Negroes will no longer tolerate brutality and violence. But even within the Negro community itself, "black power" has touched off a major debate—the most bitter the community has experienced since the days of Booker T. Washington and W. E. B. Du Bois, and one which threatens to ravage the entire civil-rights movement. Indeed, a serious split has already developed between advocates of "black power" like Floyd McKissick of CORE and Stokely Carmichael of SNCC on the one hand, and Dr. Martin Luther King of SCLC, Roy Wilkins of the NAACP, and Whitney Young of the Urban League on the other.

There is no question, then, that great passions are involved in the debate over the idea of "black power"; nor, as we shall see, is there any question that these passions have their roots in the psychological and political frustrations of the Negro community. Nevertheless, I would contend that "black power" not only lacks any real value for the civil-rights movement, but that its propa-

SOURCE: Bayard Rustin, "Black Power and Coalition Politics," Commentary, 42 (September 1966), 35–40. Reprinted from Commentary, by permission; Copyright © 1966 by the American Jewish Committee.

gation is positively harmful. It diverts the movement from a meaningful debate over strategy and tactics, it isolates the Negro community, and it encourages the growth of anti-Negro forces.

In its simplest and most innocent guise, "black power" merely means the effort to elect Negroes to office in proportion to Negro strength within the population. There is, of course, nothing wrong with such an objective in itself, and nothing inherently radical in the idea of pursuing it. But in Stokely Carmichael's extravagant rhetoric about "taking over" in districts of the South where Negroes are in the majority, it is important to recognize that Southern Negroes are only in a position to win a maximum of two congressional seats and control of eighty local counties.[*] (Carmichael, incidentally, is in the paradoxical position of screaming at liberals—wanting only to "get whitey off my back"—and simultaneously needing their support: after all, he can talk about Negroes taking over Lowndes County only because there is a fairly liberal federal government to protect him should Governor Wallace decide to eliminate this pocket of black power.) Now there might be a certain value in having two Negro congressmen from the South, but obviously they could do nothing by themselves to reconstruct the face of America. Eighty sheriffs, eighty tax assessors, and eighty school-board members might ease the tension for a while in their communities, but they alone could not create jobs and build low-cost housing; they alone could not supply quality integrated education.

The relevant question, moreover, is not whether a politician is black or white, but what forces he represents. Manhattan has had a succession of Negro borough presidents, and yet the schools are increasingly segregated. Adam Clayton Powell and William Dawson have both been in Congress for many years; the former is responsible for a rider on school integration that never gets passed, and the latter is responsible for keeping the Negroes of Chicago tied to a mayor who had to see riots and death before he would put eight-dollar sprinklers on water hydrants in the summer. I am not for one minute arguing that Powell, Dawson, and Mrs. Motley should be impeached. What I am saying is that if a politician is elected because he is black and is deemed to be entitled to a "slice of the pie," he will behave in one way; if he is elected by a constituency pressing for social reform, he will, whether he is white or black, behave in another way.

Southern Negroes, despite exhortations from SNCC to organize themselves into a Black Panther party, are going to stay in the Democratic party—to them it is the party of progress, the New Deal, the New Frontier, and the Great Society—and they are right to stay. For SNCC's Black Panther perspective is simultaneously utopian and reactionary—the former for the by now obvious reason that one-tenth of the population cannot accomplish much by itself, the latter

[*] See "The Negroes Enter Southern Politics" by Pat Watters, *Dissent*, July-August 1966.

because such a party would remove Negroes from the main area of political struggle in this country (particularly in the one-party South, where the decisive battles are fought out in Democratic primaries), and would give priority to the issue of race precisely at a time when the fundamental questions facing the Negro and American society alike are economic and social. It is no accident that the two main proponents of "black power," Carmichael and McKissick, should now be co-sponsoring a conference with Adam Clayton Powell and Elijah Muhammad, and that the leaders of New York CORE should recently have supported the machine candidate for Surrogate—because he was the choice of a Negro boss—rather than the candidate of the reform movement. By contrast, Martin Luther King is working in Chicago with the Industrial Union Department of the AFL-CIO and with religious groups in a coalition which, if successful, will mean the end or at least the weakening of the Daley-Dawson machine.

The winning of the right of Negroes to vote in the South insures the eventual transformation of the Democratic party, now controlled primarily by Northern machine politicians and Southern Dixiecrats. The Negro vote will eliminate the Dixiecrats from the party and from Congress, which means that the crucial question facing us today is who will replace them in the South. Unless civil-rights leaders (in such towns as Jackson, Mississippi; Birmingham, Alabama; and even to a certain extent Atlanta) can organize grass-roots clubs whose members will have a genuine political voice, the Dixiecrats might well be succeeded by black moderates and black Southern-style machine politicians, who would do little to push for needed legislation in Congress and little to improve local conditions in the South. While I myself would prefer Negro machines to a situation in which Negroes have no power at all, it seems to me that there is a better alternative today—a liberal-labor-civil rights coalition which would work to make the Democratic party truly responsive to the aspirations of the poor, and which would develop support for programs (specifically those outlined in A. Philip Randolph's $100 billion Freedom Budget) aimed at the reconstruction of American society in the interests of greater social justice. The advocates of "black power" have no such programs in mind; what they are in fact arguing for (perhaps unconsciously) is the creation of a *new black establishment.*

Nor, it might be added, are they leading the Negro people along the same road which they imagine immigrant groups traveled so successfully in the past. Proponents of "black power"—accepting a historical myth perpetrated by moderates—like to say that the Irish and the Jews and the Italians, by sticking together and demanding their share, finally won enough power to overcome their initial disabilities. But the truth is that it was through alliances with other groups (in political machines or as part of the trade-union movement) that the Irish and the Jews and the Italians acquired the power to win their rightful place in American society. They did not "pull themselves up by their own bootstraps"—no group in American society has ever done so; and they most certainly did not make isolation their primary tactic.

In some quarters, "black power" connotes not an effort to increase the number of Negroes in elective office but rather a repudiation of nonviolence in favor of Negro "self-defense." Actually this is a false issue, since no one has ever argued that Negroes should not defend themselves as individuals from attack.° Non-violence has been advocated as a *tactic* for organized demonstrations in a society where Negroes are a minority and where the majority controls the police. Proponents of non-violence do not, for example, deny that James Meredith has the right to carry a gun for protection when he visits his mother in Mississippi; what they question is the wisdom of his carrying a gun while participating in a demonstration.

There is, as well, a tactical side to the new emphasis on "self-defense" and the suggestion that non-violence be abandoned. The reasoning here is that turning the other cheek is not the way to win respect, and that only if the Negro succeeds in frightening the white man will the white man begin taking him seriously. The trouble with this reasoning is that it fails to recognize that fear is more likely to bring hostility to the surface then respect; and far from prodding the "white power structure" into action, the new militant leadership, by raising the slogan of black power and lowering the banner of non-violence, has obscured the moral issue facing this nation, and permitted the President and Vice President to lecture us about "racism in reverse" instead of proposing more meaningful programs for dealing with the problems of unemployment, housing, and education.

"Black power" is, of course, a somewhat nationalistic slogan and its sudden rise to popularity among Negroes signifies a concomitant rise in nationalist sentiment (Malcolm X's autobiography is quoted nowadays in Grenada, Mississippi as well as in Harlem). We have seen such nationalistic turns and withdrawals back into the ghetto before, and when we look at the conditions which brought them about, we find that they have much in common with the conditions of Negro life at the present moment: conditions which lead to despair over the goal of integration and to the belief that the ghetto will last forever.

It may, in the light of the many juridical and legislative victories which have been achieved in the past few years, seem strange that despair should be so widespread among Negroes today. But anyone to whom it seems strange should reflect on the fact that despite these victories *Negroes today are in worse economic shape, live in worse slums, and attend more highly segregated*

° As far back as 1934, A. Philip Randolph, Walter White, then executive secretary of the NAACP, Lester Granger, then executive director of the Urban League, and I joined a committee to try to save the life of Odell Waller. Waller, a sharecropper, had murdered his white boss in self-defense.

schools than in 1954. Thus—to recite the appalling, and appallingly familiar, statistical litany once again—more Negroes are unemployed today than in 1954; the gap between the wages of the Negro worker and the white worker is wider; while the unemployment rate among white youths is decreasing, the rate among Negro youths has increased to 32 *per cent* (and among Negro girls the rise is even more startling). Even the one gain which has been registered, a decrease in the unemployment rate among Negro adults, is deceptive, for it represents men who have been called back to work after a period of being laid off. In any event, unemployment among Negro men is still twice that of whites, and no new jobs have been created.

So too with housing, which is deteriorating in the North (and yet the housing provisions of the 1966 civil-rights bill are weaker than the anti-discrimination laws in several states which contain the worst ghettos even with these laws on their books). And so too with schools: according to figures issued recently by the Department of Health, Education and Welfare, 65 per cent of first-grade Negro students in this country attend schools that are from 90 to 100 per cent black. (If in 1954, when the Supreme Court handed down the desegregation decision, you had been the Negro parent of a first-grade child, the chances are that this past June you would have attended that child's graduation from a segregated high school.)

To put all this in the simplest and most concrete terms: the day-to-day lot of the ghetto Negro has not been improved by the various judicial and legislative measures of the past decade.

Negroes are thus in a situation similar to that of the turn of the century, when Booker T. Washington advised them to "cast down their buckets" (that is to say, accommodate to segregation and disenfranchisement) and when even his leading opponent, W. E. B. Du Bois, was forced to advocate the development of a group economy in place of the direct-action boycotts, general strikes, and protest techniques which had been used in the 1880's, before the enactment of the Jim-Crow laws. For all their differences, both Washington and Du Bois then found it impossible to believe that Negroes could ever be integrated into American society, and each in his own way therefore counseled withdrawal into the ghetto, self-help, and economic self-determination.

World War I aroused new hope in Negroes that the rights removed at the turn of the century would be restored. More than 360,000 Negroes entered military service and went overseas; many left the South seeking the good life in the North and hoping to share in the temporary prosperity created by the war. But all these hopes were quickly smashed at the end of the fighting. In the first year following the war, more than seventy Negroes were lynched, and during the last six months of that year, there were some twenty-four riots throughout America. White mobs took over whole cities, flogging, burning, shooting, and torturing at will, and when Negroes tried to defend themselves, the violence only increased. Along with this, Negroes were excluded from unions and pushed out of jobs they had won during the war, including federal jobs.

In the course of this period of dashed hope and spreading segregation—the same period, incidentally, when a reorganized Ku Klux Klan was achieving a membership which was to reach into the millions—the largest mass movement ever to take root among working-class Negroes, Marcus Garvey's "Back to Africa" movement, was born. "Buy Black" became a slogan in the ghettos; faith in integration was virtually snuffed out in the Negro community until the 1930's when the CIO reawakened the old dream of a Negro-labor alliance by announcing a policy of non-discrimination and when the New Deal admitted Negroes into relief programs, WPA jobs, and public housing. No sooner did jobs begin to open up and Negroes begin to be welcomed into mainstream organizations than "Buy Black" campaigns gave way to "Don't Buy Where You Can't Work" movements. A. Philip Randolph was able to organize a massive March on Washington demanding a wartime FEPC; CORE was born and with it the non-violent sit-in technique; the NAACP succeeded in putting an end to the white primaries in 1944. Altogether, World War II was a period of hope for Negroes, and the economic progress they made through wartime industry continued steadily until about 1948 and remained stable for a time. Meanwhile, the non-violent movement of the 1950's and 60's achieved the desegregation of public accommodations and established the right to vote.

Yet at the end of this long fight, the Southern Negro is too poor to use those integrated facilities and too intimidated and disorganized to use the vote to maximum advantage, while the economic position of the Northern Negro deteriorates rapidly.

The promise of meaningful work and decent wages once held out by the anti-poverty programs has not been fulfilled. Because there has been a lack of the necessary funds, the program has in many cases been reduced to wrangling for positions on boards or for lucrative staff jobs. Negro professionals working for the program have earned handsome salaries—ranging from $14- to $25,000—while young boys have been asked to plant trees at $1.25 an hour. Nor have the Job Corps camps made a significant dent in unemployment among Negro youths; indeed, the main beneficiaries of this program seem to be the private companies who are contracted to set up the camps.

Then there is the war in Vietnam, which poses many ironies for the Negro community. On the one hand, Negroes are bitterly aware of the fact that more and more money is being spent on the war, while the anti-poverty program is being cut; on the other hand, Negro youths are enlisting in great numbers, as though to say that it is worth the risk of being killed to learn a trade, to leave a dead-end situation, and to join the only institution in this society which seems really to be integrated.

The youths who rioted in Watts, Cleveland, Omaha, Chicago, and Portland are the members of a truly hopeless and lost generation. They can see the alien world of affluence unfold before them on the TV screen. But they have already failed in their inferior segregated schools. Their grandfathers were sharecroppers, their grandmothers were domestics, and their mothers are domestics too. Many have never met their fathers. Mistreated by the local storekeeper, suspected by the policeman on the beat, disliked by their teachers, they cannot stand more failures and would rather retreat into the world of heroin than risk looking for a job downtown or having their friends see them push a rack in the garment district. Floyd McKissick and Stokely Carmichael may accuse Roy Wilkins of being out of touch with the Negro ghetto, but nothing more clearly demonstrates their own alienation from ghetto youth than their repeated exhortations to these young men to oppose the Vietnam war when so many of them tragically see it as their only way out. Yet there is no need to labor the significance of the fact that the rice fields of Vietnam and the Green Berets have more to offer a Negro boy than the streets of Mississippi or the towns of Alabama or 125th Street in New York.

The Vietnam war is also partly responsible for the growing disillusion with non-violence among Negroes. The ghetto Negro does not in general ask whether the United States is right or wrong to be in Southeast Asia. He does, however, wonder why he is exhorted to non-violence when the United States has been waging a fantastically brutal war, and it puzzles him to be told that he must turn the other cheek in our own South while we must fight for freedom in South Vietnam.

Thus, as in roughly similar circumstances in the past—circumstances, I repeat, which in the aggregate foster the belief that the ghetto is destined to last forever—Negroes are once again turning to nationalistic slogans, with "black power" affording the same emotional release as "Back to Africa" and "Buy Black" did in earlier periods of frustration and hopelessness. This is not only the case with the ordinary Negro in the ghetto; it is also the case with leaders like McKissick and Carmichael, neither of whom began as a nationalist or was at first cynical about the possibilities of integration.* It took countless beatings and 24 jailings—that, and the absence of strong and continual support from the liberal community—to persuade Carmichael that his earlier faith in coalition politics was mistaken, that nothing was to be gained from working with whites, and that an alliance with the black nationalists was desirable. In the areas of the South where SNCC has been working so nobly, implementation of the Civil Rights Acts of 1964 and 1965 has been slow and ineffective. Negroes in many rural areas cannot walk into the courthouse and register to vote. Despite the voting-rights bill, they must file complaints and the Justice Department must be called to send federal registrars. Nor do children attend integrated schools as a matter of course. There, too, complaints must be filed and the Department of Health, Education and Welfare must be notified. Nei-

* On Carmichael's background, see "Two for SNCC" by Robert Penn Warren in the April 1965 COMMENTARY—ED.

ther department has been doing an effective job of enforcing the bills. The feeling of isolation increases among SNCC workers as each legislative victory turns out to be only a token victory—significant on the national level, but not affecting the day-to-day lives of Negroes. Carmichael and his colleagues are wrong in refusing to support the 1966 bill, but one can understand why they feel as they do.

It is, in short, the growing conviction that the Negroes cannot win—a conviction with much grounding in experience—which accounts for the new popularity of "black power." So far as the ghetto Negro is concerned, this conviction expresses itself in hostility first toward the people closest to him who have held out the most promise and failed to deliver (Martin Luther King, Roy Wilkins, etc.), then toward those who have proclaimed themselves his friends (the liberals and the labor movement), and finally toward the only oppressors he can see (the local storekeeper and the policeman on the corner). On the leadership level, the conviction that the Negroes cannot win takes other forms, principally the adoption of what I have called a "no-win" policy. Why bother with programs when their enactment results only in "sham"? Why concern ourselves with the image of the movement when nothing significant has been gained for all the sacrifices made by SNCC and CORE? Why compromise with reluctant white allies when nothing of consequence can be achieved anyway? Why indeed have anything to do with whites at all?

On this last point, it is extremely important for white liberals to understand— as, one gathers from their references to "racism in reverse," the President and the Vice President of the United States do not—that there is all the difference in the world between saying, "If you don't want me, I don't want you" (which is what some proponents of "black power" have in effect been saying) and the statement, "Whatever you do, I don't want you" (which is what racism declares). It is, in other words, both absurd and immoral to equate the despairing response of the victim with the contemptuous assertion of the oppressor. It would, moreover, be tragic if white liberals allowed verbal hostility on the part of Negroes to drive them out of the movement or to curtail their support for civil rights. The issue was injustice before "black power" became popular, and the issue is still injustice.

In any event, even if "black power" had not emerged as a slogan, problems would have arisen in the relation between whites and Negroes in the civil-rights movement. In the North, it was inevitable that Negroes would eventually wish to run their own movement and would rebel against the presence of whites in positions of leadership as yet another sign of white supremacy. In the South, the well-intentioned white volunteer had the cards stacked against him from the beginning. Not only could he leave the struggle any time he chose to do so, but a higher value was set on his safety by the press and the government—apparent in the differing degrees of excitement generated by the imprisonment or murder of whites and Negroes. The white person's importance to the movement in the South was thus an ironic outgrowth of racism and was therefore bound to create resentment.

But again: however understandable all this may be as a response to objective conditions and to the seeming irrelevance of so many hard-won victories to the day-to-day life of the mass of Negroes, the fact remains that the quasi-nationalist sentiments and "no-win" policy lying behind the slogan of "black power" do no service to the Negro. Some nationalist emotion is, of course, inevitable, and "black power" must be seen as part of the psychological rejection of white supremacy, part of the rebellion against the stereotypes which have been ascribed to Negroes for three hundred years. Nevertheless, pride, confidence, and a new identity cannot be won by glorifying blackness or attacking whites; they can only come from meaningful action, from good jobs, and from real victories such as were achieved on the streets of Montgomery, Birmingham, and Selma. When SNCC and CORE went into the South, they awakened the country, but now they emerge isolated and demoralized, shouting a slogan that may afford a momentary satisfaction but that is calculated to destroy them and their movement. Already their frustrated call is being answered with counter-demands for law and order and with opposition to police-review boards. Already they have diverted the entire civil-rights movement from the hard task of developing strategies to realign the major parties of this country, and embroiled it in a debate that can only lead more and more to politics by frustration.

On the other side, however—the more important side, let it be said—it is the business of those who reject the negative aspects of "black power" not to preach but to act. Some weeks ago President Johnson, speaking at Fort Campbell, Kentucky, asserted that riots impeded reform, created fear, and antagonized the Negro's traditional friends. Mr. Johnson, according to the New York *Times*, expressed sympathy for the plight of the poor, the jobless, and the ill-housed. The government, he noted, has been working to relieve their circumstances, but "all this takes time."

One cannot argue with the President's position that riots are destructive or that they frighten away allies. Nor can one find fault with his sympathy for the plight of the poor; surely the poor need sympathy. But one can question whether the government has been working seriously enough to eliminate the conditions which lead to frustration-politics and riots. The President's very words, "all this takes time," will be understood by the poor for precisely what they are—an excuse instead of a real program, a cover-up for the failure to establish real priorities, and an indication that the administration has no real commitment to create new jobs, better housing, and integrated schools.

For the truth is that it need only take ten years to eliminate poverty—ten years and the $100 billion Freedom Budget recently proposed by A. Philip Randolph. In his introduction to the budget (which was drawn up in consultation with the nation's leading economists), Mr. Randolph points out: "The programs urged in the Freedom Budget attack all of the major causes of poverty—unemployment and underemployment, substandard pay, inadequate social insurance and welfare payments to those who cannot or should not be employed; bad housing; deficiencies in health services, education, and training; and fiscal and monetary policies which tend to redistribute income regressively rather than progressively. The Freedom Budget leaves no room for discrimination in any form because its programs are addressed to all who need more opportunity and improved incomes and living standards, not to just some of them."

The legislative precedent Mr. Randolph has in mind is the 1945 Full Employment bill. This bill—conceived in its original form by Roosevelt to prevent a postwar depression—would have made it public policy for the government to step in if the private economy could not provide enough employment. As passed finally by Congress in 1946, with many of its teeth removed, the bill had the result of preventing the Negro worker, who had finally reached a pay level about 55 per cent that of the white wage, from making any further progress in closing that discriminatory gap; and instead, he was pushed back by the chronically high unemployment rates of the 50's. Had the original bill been passed, the public sector of our economy would have been able to insure fair and full employment. Today, with the spiralling thrust of automation, it is even more imperative that we have a legally binding commitment to this goal.

Let me interject a word here to those who say that Negroes are asking for another handout and are refusing to help themselves. From the end of the 19th century up to the last generation, the United States absorbed and provided economic opportunity for tens of millions of immigrants. These people were usually uneducated and a good many could not speak English. They had nothing but their hard work to offer and they labored long hours, often in miserable sweatshops and unsafe mines. Yet in a burgeoning economy with a need for unskilled labor, they were able to find jobs, and as industrialization proceeded, they were gradually able to move up the ladder to greater skills. Negroes who have been driven off the farm into a city life for which they are not prepared and who have entered an economy in which there is less and less need for unskilled labor, cannot be compared with these immigrants of old. The tenements which were jammed by newcomers were way-stations of hope; the ghettos of today have become dead-ends of despair. Yet just as the older generation of immigrants—in its most decisive act of self-help—organized the trade-union movement and then in alliance with many middle-class elements went on to improve its own lot and the condition of American society generally, so the Negro of today is struggling to go beyond the gains of the past and, in alliance with liberals and labor, to guarantee full and fair employment to all Americans.

Mr. Randolph's Freedom Budget not only rests on the Employment Act of 1946, but on a precedent set by Harry Truman when he believed freedom was threatened in Europe. In 1947, the Marshall Plan was put into effect and 3 per cent of the gross national product was spent in foreign aid. If we were to allocate a similar proportion of our GNP to destroy the economic and social consequences of racism and poverty at home today, it might mean spending more than 20 billion dollars a year, although I think it quite possible that we can fulfill these goals with a much smaller sum. It would be intolerable, however, if our plan for domestic social reform were less audacious and less far-reaching than our international programs of a generation ago.

We must see, therefore, in the current debate over "black power," a fantastic challenge to American society to live up to its proclaimed principles in the area of race by transforming itself so that all men may live equally and under justice. We must see to it that in rejecting "black power," we do not also reject the principle of Negro equality. Those people who would use the current debate and/or the riots to abandon the civil-rights movement leave us no choice but to question their original motivation.

If anything, the next period will be more serious and difficult than the preceding ones. It is much easier to establish the Negro's right to sit at a Woolworth's counter than to fight for an integrated community. It takes very little imagination to understand that the Negro should have the right to vote, but it demands much creativity, patience, and political stamina to plan, develop, and implement programs and priorities. It is one thing to organize sentiment behind laws that do not disturb consensus politics, and quite another to win battles for the redistribution of wealth. Many people who marched in Selma are not prepared to support a bill for a $2.00 minimum wage, to say nothing of supporting a redefinition of work or a guaranteed annual income.

It is here that we who advocate coalitions and integration and who object to the "black-power" concept have a massive job to do. We must see to it that the liberal-labor-civil rights coalition is maintained and, indeed, strengthened so that it can fight effectively for a Freedom Budget. We are responsible for the growth of the "black-power" concept because we have not used our own power to insure the full implementation of the bills whose passage we were strong enough to win, and we have not mounted the necessary campaign for winning a decent minimum wage and extended benefits. "Black power" is a slogan directed primarily against liberals by those who once counted liberals among their closest friends. It is up to the liberal movement to prove that coalition and integration are better alternatives.

THE NEW LEFT AND ITS LIMITS

NATHAN GLAZER

For the last few years I have looked with increasing skepticism on the analyses and the actions of the radical Left in America. By the radical Left I mean those who believe there is something fundamentally and irredeemably wrong with our society, and who think the chief way of righting it lies in mobilizing the power of all the disadvantaged groups among us behind a drive for radical change, change going to the roots. My own skepticism in the face of so much passion and indeed accomplishment often troubles me, and it will certainly annoy radicals. They may say that to have been radical or liberal in one's youth, and to become relatively conservative in one's middle years, is so common an experience that it needs hardly any explanation at all. However, just as I would not explain the radical mood or outlook on psychological or temperamental grounds, so I would hope that radicals might suspend such easy judgments on my own outlook. There have been, after all, young conservatives and old radicals, even if not as many as the other way around. And just as I would accord the radical outlook full respect—as a perspective on the world that has its own rationale, its own roots, its own great thinkers, its own successes—so I would hope that radicals might for a while consider the point of view that is skeptical of their analyses, their programs, and their hopes.

There are three principal areas in which the new radicalism expresses itself: the problem of the Vietnam war, and by extension the whole question of the role of the United States in world affairs, and in the development of the poorer countries; the problem of achieving equality for Negroes, which now centers in the crisis of the great urban ghettos; and the problem of higher education—in particular the role of youth in the administration of the campus and the shaping of the curriculum. In none of these three areas can we point to much to be happy about. I need not describe the sense of catastrophe that hangs over us whether we consider the war, or the black-white conflict. I would not apply so grand a term as catastrophe to the campus situation, and yet there is a growing sense of the triviality of much of mass higher education; and while I would hesitate to go so far as to say that the hearts and minds of our young people are being destroyed, I think the crisis in the universities is as serious in its own right for American youth as are Vietnam and race for the larger society.

SOURCE: Nathan Glazer, "The New Left and Its Limits," *Commentary*, 46 (July 1968), 31–39. Reprinted from *Commentary*, by permission; Copyright © 1968 by the American Jewish Committee.

In all three areas, radicalism, true to the term, wishes to go to the roots because, it says, what is wrong in each case is wrong at the roots. To find a half-million Americans in Vietnam, killing and being killed, burning villages and destroying crops, is sufficiently outrageous to make it plausible that there is a horror within the bowels of our society which has called these outer horrors forth. To find in the ghettos vast numbers of poverty-stricken people who have lost all faith in society, their fellow man, and their own power, who present a picture of disinheritance that no other advanced industrial society can show us; and to find on the other hand among many whites a ferocious hatred of these unfortunates that again no other advanced society can show us—this too is sufficient cause to assume that the roots are poisoned. To confront, finally, in the colleges and universities a host of petty demands and restrictions irrelevant to understanding and education, makes it easy enough to believe that something very basic is the operative cause.

Faced with these evils, and the general sense that something fundamental is wrong, the radical chooses between two broad general approaches to getting at the roots. One is the whole grand scheme of Marxism, in its various modern formulations. Capitalism is too old-fashioned a term to arouse much interest—it is now replaced by imperialism. Similarly, the increasing misery of the working class is replaced by the increasing misery of the underdeveloped world, and by that of our own "colonials" at home, the Negroes and other minority groups. The machine presumed to be at the heart of the misery has also been modernized, but fundamental to it still is the selfishness of a ruling class which cannot or will not give up its power and which therefore must be smashed. The mechanisms of a better society are still not studied much—they fall under the ban Marx and Engels imposed on utopianism and reformism. Thus the Communist country where the most serious effort to establish such mechanisms has been made, Yugoslavia, is of no great interest to today's radicals. They are more concerned with Cuba and China, which still maintain a pre-institutional—or a post-institutional?—revolutionary vigor, in which the thought and decisions of the central leader of the revolution are capable of overturning the new and barely established social structures every other day.

The most attractive aspect of the new radicalism is that it has developed a second and more popular approach to getting at the roots—more pragmatic and empirical, more humanist, less mechanical and dogmatic. This is the approach suggested in the Port Huron statement of 1962, a document characteristic of the early spirit of Students for a Democratic Society (SDS). But the candid and open stance of the New Left in its first phase of development—that something deep was wrong but no one quite knew precisely what it was or what would change it—could not be maintained forever as a basis for action. Thus an explanation began to emerge. The simple analysis of the Old Left, that capitalism or imperialism is at the root of the matter, was not very satisfactory, if only because it was too easy to point to the example of capitalist countries like Sweden and England on the one side and Communist ones like Soviet Russia and East Germany on the other to prove that no necessary causal relation exists between oppression and the institutions of capitalism. Referring to real experience—"where am *I* bugged?, where do *I* feel the pinch?"—the New Left began to decide that the problem lies not in the institutions of capitalism as such but rather in all types of fixed and formal institutions. The university administrator is not involved in the search for private profit, nor is the indifferent slum school teacher, the insensitive social worker, the hypocritical mayor, the technologically minded general. Rather—so goes the new argument—they are all small men trapped into serving big and powerful institutions that have grown hopelessly distant from immediate human needs and satisfactions. The institutions nevertheless draw on strong personal motivations to achieve their inhuman ends—the desire for money and power and advancement, for security, for a comfortable home-life in suburbia. In the view of the New Left, the minor and more benign motivations of men emerge as having greater potentialities for evil than the grander ones. It is the man who wants to do his best for his wife and children, keep up the mortgage and buy a new car—it is this man who also releases the gas in the chambers and who makes the napalm containers. He may even be a good union member and vote Democratic.

When one sees institutions themselves as the source of our present evils, and when one sees these institutions fed not by the limited and distorted motivations of rampant capitalism, but by such ancient and well-rooted human impulses as the drives for comfort, security, and family, then one has forged an analysis which is indeed powerful.

Nevertheless, the New Left has an answer—a conception of democracy in which our traditional mix of civil liberties and elected legislatures and officials is supplemented or supplanted by new rights and new forms of democratic intervention in the process of decision-making and administration. Thus attempts have been made to establish such rights as those of the poor to direct representation in the institutions that affect their lives, to financial support with dignity, to legal counsel. These new conceptions have already scored remarkable successes. We have seen formerly unshakable Boards of Education begin to bow to demands that only a year or two ago may have seemed extremist and irrational—for example, the demand for community control of ghetto schools. We have seen "student power" in higher education reach levels that were inconceivable four years ago. To be sure, the forging of foreign policy still appears to lie beyond the reach of New Left ideas. And yet is it? In recent demonstrations we have seen revolutionary techniques employed that are justified less by resort to the traditional rhetoric of revolution than by the argument that new forms of "representation" of minority points of view are required in a democratic polity.

The question of how enduring these new developments will be still remains open, but it is clear that they already serve as extremely effective weapons to advance the argument that something fundamental is wrong with American society. Of course, the argument that something fundamental is wrong leads easily to the conclusion that something grand and apocalyptic is required to set it straight. And indeed, the two positions reinforce each other: given the inclination toward some tremendous change, some tremendous flaw must be found to justify it (just as the reverse is true). But a powerful analysis of what is wrong with society may be too powerful. The radical Left explains what is wrong by the tendency of men to act within institutions which develop their own dynamic, and a dynamic which may become irrelevant or positively subversive of the ends they are set up to realize. As instances, they point to the tendency of educational institutions to act in such ways as to inhibit education, welfare institutions in such ways as to reduce competence, defense institutions in such ways as to increase the likelihood and the ferocity of war. When I say that this analysis may be too powerful, I mean to raise the question: what alternative is there to institutions designed to deal with problems, calling upon the more common and everyday motivations, and developing their own rigidities and blinders?

There is an answer on the New Left even to that—and the answer is to release man's natural creativity and spontaneity, whether through revolution, or through participatory democracy, or through the smashing of the old institutions, and to hope that these newly released forces will finally lead to the overcoming of ancient social dilemmas. For the New Left believes that man is good by nature, and corrupted by institutions; that the earth and its riches are sufficient to maintain all men in comfort and happiness, and that only human selfishness and blindness prevent the emergence of this ideal state. One can appeal to the early Marx, who is so popular today, and his vision of a society in which man can fish in the morning, work in the afternoon, and criticize the arts in the evening, just as he will, and entirely according to the rhythms of his own being. Some on the New Left believe that only a violent overthrow of the institutions of society can bring such a world to birth; others believe that a steady and determined and unyielding pressure on power elites and power holders, if applied long enough, ingeniously enough, unflinchingly enough, will force these groups to give up their power and their goods and to desist in their willful obstruction of those who wish to create a better and more beautiful world.

There are, in my opinion, three serious flaws in this position.

The first is the assumption that the problems of bringing a better society into being are fundamentally problems of power. This has become a matter of gospel, and not only with the New Left. Yet the fact is that only certain basic problems can be settled, and even those only to a limited degree, by direct clashes between conflicting interests; and in advanced societies, the number of such problems grows progressively smaller and smaller. The natural history of social problems seems to involve an initial stage in which a selfish power monopoly must be defeated or overthrown. But clear evils to fight against are rapidly succeeded by increasingly ambiguous evils, whose causes and solutions are equally unclear. The minute we move to this later stage, we confront one important limitation of the radical perspective.

Let me be concrete. In the South not long ago, the resistance to equality for Negroes was centered in an irrational and inhuman racist ethos that denied to Negroes the most elementary rights of man in a democratic society, such as the right to a fair trial, to the security of life and property, and to the vote. The task of confronting these evils was simply to fight them, to organize to fight them, to insist that the Constitution be obeyed—even, if one was heroic enough, to die or risk death in the process.

But this was the initial stage of reform: equivalent in its moral clarity to earlier battles like those aimed at extending the franchise, banning child labor, establishing labor's right to organize, setting up systems of unemployment insurance and social security. After the principle has been established there comes a second stage, in which the problems are more complex, often more technical. It is in part for this reason that the administrators and the experts now take over, together with those whose interests are directly concerned, while the army of reformers moves off to issues in which the conflict between good and evil is still clear cut. This is precisely what happened after the victories of the civil-rights movement in the South and the shift of the movement to the North.

We are often very sympathetic to cynical explanations of human behavior, including our own, and we are thus attracted to the belief that when Southern whites only were affected by Negro demands, Northern whites could be staunchly militant in defense of Negro rights, but that when the Northerners themselves were affected, they fell silent or slunk off the battlefield. But something rather more important occurred as the battleground of the civil-rights movement shifted from the South to the North. In the South, the issues were civic equality and the vote; in the North, because both these goals had long been attained, the issues became employment and upgrading in jobs, income, education, housing. These are all highly complex matters that no simple law can settle. It cannot be decreed that Negroes and whites should have the same income regardless of their skills and education, or that they should have the same education regardless of their home backgrounds, or that they should have the same home backgrounds, regardless of their history, their culture, their experience.

Of course it is possible, even in this later stage of reform when the key element has ceased to be the obdurate political power of a selfish interest group, to insist that nothing has really changed. Thus, many who argue that it is "white racism" which is keeping the Negro down—an idea strongly encouraged by the Report of the National Advisory Commission on Civil Disorders —are in effect trying to cast the enormous problems of creating a true and widespread equality for American Negroes in the pattern of the heroic battles to change the cruel social structure of the South. Yet this interpretation flies in the face of the fact that racist attitudes have been in steady decline in this country for two decades. And if "white racism" refers to practices, it contradicts the reality that most of the major institutions in American life—government, big business, higher education, the foundations—have been engaged for years in a variety of efforts to increase and upgrade Negro participation in every area of American life. Paradoxically, "white racism" has become a rallying cry precisely at a moment when it has never been milder.

The truth is that it is not white racism but the difficulty of the problems which has so far frustrated us in finding satisfying jobs for the hard-core unemployed, or improving education and housing in the ghettos and slums. Not even the enactment of such legislative proposals as are being put forward by the Poor People's March on Washington would by itself settle matters—as, in its time, the enactment of the right to collective bargaining did. If the government were to become the "employer of last resort," there would still be thorny questions concerning rates of pay (certainly minimal wages would no longer be a solution, as they were with WPA in the depression), civil-service protection for these workers, and policies for dealing with incompetence and absenteeism—for after all we are speaking of people who cannot get jobs or will not take those which are available in a fairly brisk labor market.

If we consider education, no reform has yet been proposed or envisaged that can reasonably promise better education for ghetto youth, though we can passionately support community control of schools as a measure which *might* at least help to affect the tricky factor of the child's motivation. And even when we speak of housing and neighborhoods, where simple physical facilities alone are important, we have no easy solutions—as becomes evident once the question is raised of how much happier the poor have proved to be in public housing projects than in slums. In none of these major areas is there a major reform that can promise what social security or the right to collective bargaining promised. This is only an index to the increasing complexity of our problems, themselves the result of the increasing sophistication of social demands—not *any* job, but a good and meaningful job with security and promise of advancement; not merely free education, but education with certain effects; not just a minimally adequate dwelling, but one located within a network of social supports that we can often scarcely divine, let alone set out to create.

Even the demands for a guaranteed annual income, or a negative income tax, or a family allowance—demands that are, it is clear enough, pressed because there is no rapid and easy path to equality through good jobs—raise further technical questions that will not be solved by the passionate insistence that Congress decree an end to poverty or that communities do away with white racism. The guaranteed annual income or negative income tax would have serious and undetermined effects on those who work for rates at or near the legal minimum. If such workers (maids, messenger boys, janitors, hotel employees, restaurant employees, etc.) are to retain any incentive to work, the guaranteed annual income or negative income tax return must be set below the minimum wage—at which point we are back to welfare and the painful issues it involves (who qualifies, for how much, etc.?). The family allowance is less problematic, but as generally proposed it is too small to permit the abolition of the welfare system; nor can we be happy over the inevitable support it entails for population growth at a time when for other good reasons we might want to discourage large families.

At the moment it is fashionable among radicals to ignore these details and to justify their indifference by an assault on the idea that work is necessary to society. But anyone who looks concretely at what human beings in this country want, and what radicals feel is the least they should have (good housing, good education, various social services, good health care, recreational opportunities, etc.), and then simply adds up what that requires in the way of material and human resources, would soon be disabused of the notion that we can ignore the effects of various social measures on the incentive to work. Quite characteristically, the radical wants it both ways—he wants services that are enormously costly in manpower, and he wants social measures that will encourage fewer people to work.

If the issues become thus complex, when there are no simple slogans to proclaim—or, when such slogans are proclaimed, there are no visible routes to their immediate realization—then understandably the fervor and commitment of many reformers and radicals fall off. This is in part what happened when the issue of civil rights for Negroes in the South was replaced by the issue of achieving effective equality for the Negro throughout the nation. We can trace much the same development in all the earlier areas of reform; indeed, the advancement of a society can almost be measured by the extent to which political issues are transformed into technical issues—when this happens it is generally a sign that the central power struggle is over. In Scandinavia and England the provision of good medical care, for example, has come to involve such questions as how many doctors and nurses are needed, how they should be trained, how they can be kept from going to America or induced to move to small towns and distant rural areas, what kind of hospitals should be built, etc. Of course, politics enters into all this, with parties taking positions according to their class composition, their history, and their ideology. Yet such differences are relatively marginal, and only one element of many— among which they are by no means the most important—going into the framing of solutions.

To my mind, there are fewer and fewer major areas of American domestic policy in which the old-fashioned conflict between interests representing clearly reactionary forces, and the interests of the society in general, still remains central. One is the continued Southern resistance to legislation aimed at bettering the lot of the Negro; another is the continued resistance of organized medicine to an adequate program of medical care. In most other areas, I would argue, complex technical issues have superseded the crude power struggle between the forces of reaction and the forces of progress. This is not to deny that self-serving interests still operate throughout the political sphere, but so long as care is taken to pay them off, they do not constitute serious roadblocks in the way of improving our society. The drive for security is a massive one—in farmers, in businessmen, in workers—and I am not sure that our special interests are so much stronger than their counterparts in other societies which manage their problems pretty well, or in any imaginable future society.

A second argument against the perspective of radical leftism follows from this general point that in an industrially advanced society, whatever its background and history, social problems become more and more complex, more technical, and less political: Because change is continuous in such societies, no solution is ever complete or final, and consequently there is no alternative to bureaucracies, administrators, and experts. Of course, certain issues are on occasion structured so that solutions really can have a once-and-for-all character—in particular those issues which can be posed in strictly political or legal terms. Thus, the right to organize, when put into law and upheld by the courts, finally ended one great battle in American history. But most of the problems we face are not so simple and require continuous expert attention.

Consider, for example, public housing. No directly political measure, like a huge appropriation of money, could solve the problem of housing in this country; nor could the introduction of some new principle, like the once-new principle of public housing itself. For no matter what we might do on the political front, we would still have to decide what kind of housing to build, where to build it, in what size developments and at what scale; we would need to know the effect of setting different income limits, of excluding or not excluding those with criminal records, of accepting this proportion or that from the relief rolls; and we would have to determine the further effect of these and many other decisions on the balance of integration and segregation. There is no way of reaching such decisions from any large political position, radical or conservative: indeed, these questions (and they are increasingly becoming the ones that any advanced society must settle) make those very distinctions irrelevant. A few years ago I visited Warsaw and spoke to researchers in the field of housing and other social services. The problems we spoke about, that troubled them, were not very different from those of anyone dealing with housing in New York or Chicago, or, I would hazard, in Stockholm and Moscow.

Public welfare is another example. In the 1930's the basic issue was raised: is the government responsible for providing subsistence to those unable to earn it themselves? And the answer, after a struggle, was given: yes. It was, as is common in this politically complex nation, not as good or sharp an answer as other nations have given, but in the more advanced states of the Union, at any rate, public services of a standard commensurate with that of Northwestern Europe were established for the widowed and orphaned and abandoned and aged and disabled. The battle was over; reformers and radicals rested, or moved off to other fields. Twenty years later they were back, in force, denouncing the social workers, organizing the clients against them. What had happened? Had welfare services deteriorated or been cut back? Quite the contrary. More was being spent on them and they were probably being run more efficiently. Yet where it had once seemed the achievement of a generous society that those without income were no longer required to beg or to depend on private charity, but now received as of right some minimal level of subsistence, it seemed to the society of twenty years later an outrage that they were maintained on a dignity-destroying dole, that they were not rehabilitated, turned into productive and self-respecting citizens. Let me suggest that it is much easier to give someone money than to turn him into a productive and self-respecting citizen. The first task is also a much easier one to place on the banners of a political movement or to write into legislation than the second.

Or consider the poverty program. Within Congress, Left and Right both agree that something should be done about poverty, and that training the unemployed or the not-yet employed is a good idea; in consequence we have now developed a large range of training programs, of varying kinds, under varying auspices. When any one of these programs comes up for renewal, the technical people running it will always argue that theirs is the most important and should be maintained or expanded, and will try to convince their friends in Congress. Now it is true that congressmen, faced with conflicting expert opinion and pressure from differing interests, will tend to fall back on old prejudices and old political commitments—the liberals will generally say, spend more, the conservatives, spend less. But the combat takes place in a surprisingly restricted area. It is not yet as restricted as the area of political combat in England and Sweden, but it is much narrower than it was in this country twenty years ago.

Admittedly the overall scale of expenditures on housing or welfare or work-training programs is still an important political question in America, but this is not really what many on the radical Left are concerned about. For even if we were to spend twice as much in each of these areas as we do now, things would not really change that much, and no one—least of all the radical Leftists themselves—would believe that the millennium awaited by the radical Left had arrived.° But as a matter of fact, even the scope of politics as regards the scale of expenditure is remarkably restricted. In all advanced countries,

---

° New York City spends twice as much per child in its public schools as most other large cities do, yet these schools hardly serve as a model for the solution of the problems of urban education.

taxes are very high and not easily increased; similar proportions of the GNP are devoted to social welfare; and the increasing competition among equally worthy programs—health, education, welfare, work-training, scientific research, and the like—poses similarly perplexing decisions. We may come to a better understanding of these matters, but scarcely by following the assumptions and perspectives of the radical Left.

If, then, the need for reform and change is continuous, and depends on the expert knowledge of technicians continuously applied, there can be no alternative to institutionalization, the permanent bodies devoted to permanent problem areas, with all its consequences. I do not see how any sensible man can still think, as Lenin did in *State and Revolution,* that institutions and the state will wither away to the point where they can be run on a part-time and unspecialized basis by—in his term—cooks. Yet this is the vague, if not always expressed, hope of the New Left. Knowing that institutions corrupt, they hope to do away with them. One of the major grounds for my skepticism is my belief that, even though they corrupt, there is no chance of doing away with them.

I am aware, of course, of the common wisdom that to put education in the hands of the educators, housing in the hands of the professional housers, welfare in the hands of the social workers is to ensure that traditional practices will become institutionalized, that reformers will be fought, and that difficulties will pile up and get worse. But the fact is that judicious, flexible, creative people are always in short supply. Not every problem can be placed in the hands of the best men in the society—though this often seems to be what we are asked to achieve when we are told that our doctors must be better, our teachers must be better, our social workers must be better. Where after all are we to find a place for the people in our society who are less than the most imaginative, the most energetic, the most effective? The great majority of men, whether or not they lead lives of quiet desperation, certainly hope to lead lives of minimal security and moderate gratification. While we take it for granted that this is a reasonable and humane objective for Vietnamese peasants or Indian city-dwellers, we consider it reprehensible that most American doctors, teachers, social workers, and the like are of the same sort. No doubt this common human tendency seems reprehensible when viewed in the context of the suffering we are called upon to alleviate. But what solution is there? As far as I can see, only the normal political one—when the problems become bad enough, and enough people get angry and protest, new programs are started, new men and new ideas flow in, and hopefully all this leads to a new level of achievement, itself to become institutionalized in its turn, and to require at some later time another infusion of ideas, money, and innovators from the outside.

The New Left's main answer to the problem of institutionalization is participatory democracy, a concept derived from the Paris Commune in which, according to Marx's account, the people, permanently politicized, permanently in arms, met every day to settle their fate. This is a grand vision and one which makes it possible to argue that all established institutions, even if formally democratic, are actually undemocratic because they do not reflect the desires of the people at any given moment. I cannot imagine, however, how one can ever overcome the danger raised by a direct dependence on the people, permanently in session. For it inevitably means depending on that part of the people that is willing, for one reason or another, to stay permanently in session.

Participatory democracy is suited to truly revolutionary movements and moments—but only moments. No people as a whole has ever been ready to make a primary commitment to political action over a long period of time. Those who assert that formal democracy cannot be true democracy because many do not vote, many who vote do not know, the candidates do not reflect the full range of opinion and possibility, etc., ignore the fact that this limited interest on the part of most people most of the time is actually among the greatest defenses of democracy. It means, as Aaron Wildavsky has pointed out, that there are always enormous reserves to be mobilized whenever significant interests are affected. Wildavsky contends that one of the most critical resources in politics is time—time for talking, electioneering, canvassing—and the poor have as much of this resource as anyone else. Perhaps money decides only unimportant things, such as which of two not very different candidates will carry an election. But if important issues arise, reserves are available that can be brought into battle. Is it not such reserves that the organizers in the slums are now trying to mobilize? If they fail, as they sometimes do, it may be because they have not correctly diagnosed what is really troubling people in the slums, because they have been unable to convince them that the potential gains are worth their sacrifice of time and energy. And if issues are indeed becoming increasingly complex, it also becomes harder and harder to isolate and sloganize action that, if demanded and then taken, will result in a clear improvement of conditions.

In response to all these realities, we find new and astonishing doctrines coming into vogue. Herbert Marcuse, for example, attacks democracy and tolerance as themselves being barriers to the actions required for the overthrow of a monstrous society. In the past, even the Leninists, whatever their actual practices—the suppression of free speech and the murder of political opponents—usually tried to cover them up with such terms as "peoples' democracy" and with such justifications as the paramount need to defend the revolution from the violence of others. But lip service to the virtues of democracy and tolerance are now, it seems, to be abandoned by radicals on the ground that democracy and tolerance only protect an evil society—protect it precisely because they can be displayed as its virtues! We have come to such twisted arguments as one recently given by an American professor against accepting a Fulbright fellowship: he agreed that he was free to attack American foreign policy abroad, but by so doing he would mislead his foreign audience into believing that the United States was a free society and worthy of support by men of good will.

In the universities, participatory democracy has now been replaced by a new doctrine which decrees that when democratic procedures either do not exist (as indeed they do not in many sectors of many universities) or when a democratic system fails to respond to deeply felt needs (as with the Vietnam war) then it is quite legitimate to engage in disruption and disorder to bring about change. This argument has attracted the support of substantial minorities of students and even of faculties, though it has been less effective among the American people at large.

The new doctrine, which we see exemplified at Nanterre and Columbia, is a far cry from the ideals of participatory democracy, especially in the early days of the new Left when meetings were open to all, when discussions to gain consensus went on endlessly, when there was deep soul-searching about the morality of engaging in activity that provoked the violence of political opponents and police. Under the auspices of the new doctrine, the rights of the majority are held in derision, and political opponents are prevented from speaking or being heard. Tactics are worked out to strip authorities of dignity through staged confrontations, to arrange matters so that violence will erupt for the benefit of the press and television, to win over basically unsympathetic students who, owing to their commitment to fairmindedness, will almost always be "radicalized" by exposure to police intervention. In effect, we have moved from the ideal of the politicized masses with direct control over their fate—an unlikely form of organization in any case—to the quite cynical manipulation of the masses by those who themselves object to "formal" democracy and to the public order and tolerance that are its foundation. That small minorities are able to get so far with these tactics is attributable to two circumstances: first that they operate in an environment (the university) which is in fact undemocratic and which is also totally incapable of handling confrontation, disruption, and provocation; and second, that we have in the Vietnam war a case in which democratic processes most certainly do not work well, any more than they do in less explosive sectors of foreign policy in this country.

I think some good has and will come out of these tactics—university constitutions are being revised, and probably for the better—balanced by a good deal of evil. Alongside the wrong of university administrations which are unresponsive to faculty and student opinion, we now have the new wrong of groups of students who can impose their will on the university, regardless of what the majority of their colleagues and teachers want or think. Just recently, the students of Stanford University voted 70 per cent in favor of allowing the government agencies and Dow Chemical to recruit on campus— but on how many other campuses has policy been made by an aggressive minority, without a student vote to determine majority sentiment? The fact that our universities are not democratically organized has made it possible for small groups to instigate change and reform—and this is to the good. But the ultimate end of these changes and reforms will still have to be something on the order of formal democracy—universal suffrage, free discussion, free balloting, all of which seem remote from the affections of the passionate on the New Left. For when these democratic forms prevail, leftists can claim no greater rights than others, regardless of how strongly they feel they are right.

Through these changes in attitude and tactics, an anti-institutional bias remains at the heart of the New Left position; and at the heart of my own critique of that position is my belief that there can be no substitute for institutions, even though they may become tired, bureaucratic, and corrupt. Yet no more, in my view, can there be any substitute for the organized and aroused people when the institutions become, as they ineluctably will, inadequate to their task. At that point, they must be supplemented or supplanted by new institutions, which will hopefully respond more sensitively to the needs of their clients. I think in the host of proposals and experiments of the past six or seven years there have been many good ones—but then they eventually will become part of the institutionalized system too. We now have neighborhood law firms, which some people around the poverty program saw as the guarantor of a determinedly antagonistic and suspicious attitude toward all institutions. But why? How can they escape becoming institutions themselves? They will have to recruit staff, set limits to their work load, accept some cases and reject others, arrive at a modus vivendi with the rest of the institutionalized world, give security to their employees. And would we want it otherwise? Do we want to devote, each of us, full time to every problem—welfare, education, housing, legal rights, and what have you—or are we prepared to accept the subdivisions of a complex society, leaving some of our resources in reserve, to be called out against the worst problems, the most serious scandals?

One does feel rather like a Scrooge in insisting that spontaneity and feeling can never replace the institutions, with their bureaucrats, clerks, secretaries, forms, computers, regulations, and—hopefully—appeal boards. But there are to my mind more serious reasons than any I have yet suggested for thinking that this dream of the New Left must remain a limited one, and this brings me to the third major failing of the radical perspective. As I look to the future, I see that the expectation of more freedom, of more spontaneity, must be disappointed. Kenneth Boulding has pointed to three factors pushing us inexorably toward a more rather than a less organized society: one is the existence of the terribly destructive atomic weapons, the second is the growth of population, the third the exhaustion of natural resources. To these three might be added a fourth: the pollution of the environment.

The interesting thing about all these problems is that they take on roughly the same character in all advanced societies, and in each case the answer seems to come down to greater controls. Thus, once the atomic weapons emerge, there is no way of sweeping them under the rug. They are a reality, and to deal with them involves a species of considerations which makes the radical perspective all but entirely irrelevant. Perhaps I am wrong. Perhaps one can envisage the masses raging through the streets of Moscow and Washington demanding the absolute destruction of these horrible weapons, and with full faith in the good will of the other side. But even if we were to get this far, can anyone imagine the same thing happening in the streets of Peking, or Tel Aviv, or Cairo?

The population explosion—and I assume we are all frightened at the projections—constitutes a similar trap, for it means that the most basic of all forms of human spontaneity will have to be subjected to elaborate institutional controls if the world is ever to arrive at anything like the good life, or the good-as-possible life, that radicals so mistakenly tie to the overthrow of organized society. So too the gradual exhaustion of natural resources—which we are less concerned about today but which we will soon be forced to worry about constantly—sets another inexorable limit to the kind of society in which freedom is maximized and controls put at a minimum. As to environmental pollution, it is a more immediate concern, and one ironically linked to higher standards of living, in the form of insecticides, soaps, fertilizers, automobiles. Here too we can only foresee greater and more intrusive controls being imposed—not only in America but in all advanced countries, and not only under capitalism but under Communism (as a glance at the Russian response to these same problems quickly reveals). The radicals have offered no alternative to these imperatives, except the return to smaller communities, and lower standards of living. This I would regard as wholly consistent with their outlook, and one that makes sense in its own terms. Relatively few people, however, are willing to adopt it, and in the underdeveloped world it makes no sense at all.

My discussion up to now has concentrated solely on domestic affairs. Perhaps many might agree that our domestic problems are complex, require continuous and expert attention, and in large measure transcend or make irrelevant traditional political distinctions. But what about Vietnam? It is on this issue, after all, that the radical Left now principally expresses itself. Does not Vietnam point to some horrible illness in the American system—a sick reliance on technology as the solution to all problems, an outrageous view of the American role and prerogatives in the world, a suppressed violence which will out in the most grisly forms, an inhumanly narrow view of other societies and other peoples? I would agree that just as domestic politics stops at the water's edge, so my analysis in large measure is relevant only to our domestic problems. Many people look at the war and conclude, as I said at the beginning, that the roots are poisoned, that radical change is needed. Many other people —and this is a constant in the history of radicalism—begin with the idea that the roots are poisoned, and take the war as proof of their original conviction. Like the Talmudic scholar in the old story, they once ran through the streets shouting, "I have an answer! Does anyone have a question?" But now Vietnam has given them a very good question, too.

Nevertheless, I cannot accept the idea that the fundamental character of American society, its political or economic life, is the prime cause of the horrors of Vietnam. In the end, I cannot help believing, the Vietnam war must be understood as the result of a series of monumental errors. The key point to me is this: *America would not have had to be very different from what it now is for some President to have gotten us out of Vietnam rather than deeper and deeper into it.* Was America so much different or so much better under Eisenhower than it has been under Johnson? And yet all it took was a simple decision by Eisenhower to keep us from intervening in Vietnam in 1954.

The Vietnam war does to my mind point to something basically wrong with the American political system, but it is less apocalyptic than the analyses of the radical Left suggest. I believe—along with Senator Fulbright—that foreign policy, which was relatively marginal for the United States until the late 1930's, has become, or has remained, too exclusively the province of the President and his closest advisers. Whereas in domestic affairs the President must answer constantly to Congress, he has become literally irresponsible in the area of foreign affairs, where he must answer only to the electorate and only once every four years. If he is stubborn or stupid or makes mistakes and insists on sticking with them—and his position as head of a political party gives him every incentive to do so—he can destroy the country before being called to account. Since, moreover, we are still relatively insulated in our day-to-day national life from the world outside, the President can deceive the people as to the extent of his errors in foreign affairs much more effectively than he can in domestic affairs. This is a very serious matter indeed and the United States may be fatally damaged before we find a way out. But I cannot easily reconcile my own understanding as to how we have come to this terrible position with the basic perspectives and criticisms of the New Left. Nor are those perspectives particularly helpful in figuring out what we can do to repair the political system against a defect of this character and magnitude.

Ultimately, my disagreement with the radical Left comes down to this: I see no Gordian knot to be cut at a single stroke, the cutting of which would justify the greatest efforts (as in the past it has seemed to justify great horrors). Nationalizing the means of production, as Socialist countries have discovered, is no all-embracing answer; nor is permanent mobilization of the people, which is in any case fantastically difficult to accomplish, and which, if it were to be accomplished, as it has for a time in China, would create a society that we would find repulsive; nor is the destruction of the upper classes—in the advanced countries at any rate, whatever value such destruction might yield in underdeveloped nations—for the upper classes now consist of the managers, the organizers, and the highly skilled professionals, whom we would inevitably have to re-create.

From the point of view of the heroisms of the past, it is a gray world we are entering, in which technicians and interest groups, neither of whom can be said to bear the banner of humanity in its noblest form, will be the determining forces. The best we can do is to ensure that as things go wrong—and they inevitably will—the people will have an opportunity to protest. They will rarely know, I am afraid, quite what to do to set things right, but their complaints and their occasional rebellious fury will be important "inputs," to use the dreary language of the future, in setting the matter right. The logic of the situation—the size of our population, the number of our organizations, the extent of our problems, the interrelations among the different parts of our society, the development of science and technology—all point to this outcome. Under the circumstances, even reform and its traditions become part of the system. How much protest do we need to keep the system straight and keep it correcting itself? At what point will protest wreck the institutions altogether and prevent them from functioning? The system is necessary; not this system exactly, but some system, and one which, given the external forces that govern our lives, will turn out to be not so significantly different.

I view radicalism as a great reservoir of energy which moves the establishment to pay attention to the most serious and urgent problems, and tells it when it has failed. To a more limited degree, it is also a reservoir of potential creativity—a reaching for new solutions and new approaches. What radicalism is not, and what it can no longer be, is the great sword of vengeance and correction which goes to the source of the distress and cuts it out. There is no longer a single source, and no longer a single sword.

Study Questions

1. Compare and contrast the views of Berelson and Key concerning the role of public opinion in making public policies in a democratic system.
2. What is the difference between pressure groups and political parties? Discuss fully and critically.
3. Name the most influential pressure groups in your state. How effective do you think they are in attaining their goals? What methods do they use in seeking their objectives? Do they operate in the executive branch as well as the legislative? Give specific examples.
4. What are the reasons for the sharp differences between the leaders of the Democratic and Republican parties on such issues as public ownership, regulations of the economy, tax and farms policies? Do you think that our two major parties should be more ideologically oriented? Why?
5. On the basis of your reading of the Rustin and Glazer articles, do you think that such groups as the "Black Power" advocates and the "New Left" can be politically creative in the political system? Discuss fully and critically and give specific examples.

Suggestions for Further Reading

Bone, Hugh A. and Austin Ranney. *Politics and Voters.* New York: McGraw-Hill Company, 1963.

Burns, James MacGregor. *The Deadlock of Democracy: Four-Party Politics in America.* Englewood Cliffs, New Jersey: Prentice-Hall, 1963.

Campbell, Angus, Philip E. Converse, Warren E. Miller, and Donald Stokes. *The American Voter.* New York: John Wiley & Sons, Inc., 1960.

Childs, Harwood L. *Public Opinion: Nature, Function, and Role.* Princeton, New Jersey: D. Van Nostrand Company, Inc., 1965.

Eldersveld, Samuel J. *Political Parties: A Behavioral Analysis.* Chicago: Rand McNally and Company, 1964.

Eulau, Heinz. *The Behavioral Persuasion in Politics.* New York: Random House, 1965.

Flanigan, William H. *Political Behavior of the American Electorate.* Boston: Allyn and Bacon, Inc., 1968.

Greenstein, Fred I. *The American Party System and the American People.* Englewood Cliffs, New Jersey: Prentice-Hall, 1963.

Jennings, M. Kent and L. Harmon Zeigler (eds.). *The Electoral Process.* Englewood Cliffs, New Jersey: Prentice-Hall, 1966.

Kahn, Robert and Charles Cannel. *The Dynamics of Interviewing.* New York: John Wiley & Sons, Inc., 1957.

Key, V. O. Jr. *Politics, Parties, and Pressure Groups.* 5th ed. New York: Thomas Y. Crowell Company, 1964.

Key, V. O. Jr. *Public Opinion and American Democracy.* New York: Alfred A. Knopf, 1961.

Key, V. O. Jr. *The Responsible Electorate.* Cambridge, Mass.: Belknap Press, 1966.

Kish, Leslie. *Survey Sampling.* New York: John Wiley & Sons, Inc., 1965.

Lane, Robert E. and David O. Sears. *Public Opinion.* Englewood Cliffs, New Jersey: Prentice-Hall, 1964.

Lindblom, Charles E. *The Policy-Making Process.* Englewood Cliffs, New Jersey: Prentice-Hall, 1968.

Luttbeg, Norman R. (ed.) *Public Opinion and Public Policy: Models of Political Linkage.* Homewood, Illinois: The Dorsey Press, 1968.

Polsby, Nelson W., and Aaron B. Wildavsky. *Presidential Elections: Strategies of American Electoral Politics.* 2nd edition. New York: Charles Scribner's Sons, 1968.

Pomper, Gerald M. *Elections In America: Control and Influence in Democratic Politics.* New York: Dodd, Mead, & Company, 1968.

Rogers, Lindsay. *The Pollsters.* New York: Alfred A. Knopf, Inc., 1949.

Sindler, Allan P. *Political Parties In The United States.* New York: St. Martin's Press, 1966.

Truman, David. *The Governmental Process: Political Interests and Public Opinion.* New York: Alfred A. Knopf, 1951.

Zeigler, Harmon. *Interest Groups in American Society.* Englewood Cliffs, New Jersey: Prentice-Hall, 1964.

PART SEVEN

The Electoral Process

The electoral process with its rules and procedures governing the struggle in the political arena, and the conditions pertaining to candidacies and campaigns are of basic importance to the working of democracy. The rules and conditions under which the nominating and electoral processes are conducted deeply affect the resulting policies and the quality of representation. In these selections we shall examine the decision-making process at the national convention, the ballot and the political system in Presidential elections, and whether or not reforms are needed in our electoral system.

Nelson W. Polsby examines the roles of delegates at the national conventions and how they seek to maximize their power. Political power lies in the hands of the chief executive (mayor, governor, President). The incumbent President can control the national convention of his party if he chooses to do so. Polsby discusses the control of delegates and the unit rule. He states that the predisposition of delegates toward presidential aspirants depend upon their expectations of access to them, ideological affinities, historical accidents, and implicit or explicit "deals."

When the President chooses not to control the convention hierarchically or if he is from the opposite party, decision-making at the convention becomes a bargaining system. Moreover, Polsby points out that the two major parties compete for many of the same politically neutral, indifferent, and/or uncommitted groups and voters to win the Presidency. The Vice Presidential nominee must help the party win the Presidency. Polsby concludes by discussing five major strategies of participants.

Polsby and Aaron Wildavsky discuss coalitions in the American political system and state that coalitions mean bargaining. They point out the differences between Congressional and Presidential parties. Since power in Congress is diffused and party cohesion is lacking, legislative policy is approved or rejected by building coalitions through bargaining. The President, in order to get what he wants, may have to make policy concessions to influential interests in Congress. Coalitions are also formed in the executive branch of government.

They examine elections and public policies and state that in the American system, balloting, although important, does not often determine individual policies. "There are few clear mandates in our political system owing to the fact the elections are fought on so many issues and in so many incompletely over-lapping constituencies." They point out that "Presidential elections are not referenda" and discuss why our elections are not designed to confer mandate on specific public policies. They raise the question of what size of electorate victory confers upon the President a special mandate. They conclude that the American political system discourages extremism since extremist policies are ruled out by free elections and the two-party system.

Senator George McGovern states that the issue which brought the Democratic National Convention of 1968 to the edge of chaos was Vietnam and that the war showed that institutions which work satisfactorily in time of peace may not be sufficient in periods of stress. He believes that the defect of the convention system is a failure of democracy, that the existing political system failed to respond to the widely held popular commitment. Moreover, there were the frustrations caused by procedural abuses which prevented many rank-and-file Democrats from participating in the party's decision-making.

Senator McGovern discusses the reform movement and the findings of the Hughes Commission. One of the important conclusions of this Commission is that "state systems for selecting delegates to the national convention display considerably less fidelity to basic democratic principles than a nation which claims to govern itself can safely tolerate." McGovern also discusses in detail the findings of his (McGovern) Commission of the undemocratic pattern of delegate selection. For instance, the McGovern Commission found that "more than one-third of the delegates who attended the Convention in Chicago were selected, in effect, more than two years before, when the issues, to say nothing of the candidates, had not been clarified." The McGovern Commission offers several guidelines which will be binding on the states' delegate selection process. McGovern concludes that the failure of the convention system to respond to the demands of many people who were engaged in active dissent demonstrates to the extent to which the American parties are isolated from their constituencies.

DECISION-MAKING AT THE NATIONAL CONVENTIONS

NELSON W. POLSBY

Our national conventions are famous for puzzling casual observers, both foreign and domestic. It therefore seems especially worthwhile to show that a great many convention practices and events can be related to basic rules and circumstances of American politics.

THE CONVENTION AS A SOCIAL SYSTEM

1. *Delegates to national conventions are expected to behave in a way that will maximize their political power; that is, they are politicians.*

The rational dice player will place his bets in accordance with his chances of winning under the rules of the game he is playing. Similarly, the "rational" delegate will be expected to be reasonably well informed about how his behavior affects his chances of achieving his goals, and will behave in accordance with his information, his position in the game, and the goals he is intent upon achieving.

The goal "political power" can for our purposes be specified as the ability to make decisions, or to influence the making of decisions of government. Instrumental to this is the achievement of access to those offices and officials empowered to make governmental decisions, and instrumental to access, in turn, is the ability to staff the government, either by selecting officials to fill appointive offices (patronage) or by significantly influencing the nomination and election of elected officials. Since the latter are usually empowered to make appointments, access to this class of officials is often instrumental to the dispensation of patronage. "Access" we may define as the opportunity to press claims upon decision-makers. This does not imply that those who have more access are more successful in pressing their claims, but it is generally supposed that claims have a better chance of realization when they are presented repeatedly and auspiciously to decision-makers.

It may be well to emphasize that the term "politician" refers to but one of

SOURCE: Nelson W. Polsby, "Decision-Making at the National Conventions," *Western Political Quarterly*, 13 (September 1960), 609–619. Reprinted by permission of the University of Utah, copyright owners.

many roles that individuals play, and it is only insofar as these individuals are delegates to national conventions that they need be considered politicians here. If delegates are politicians in other contexts—members of Congress, for example—this fact may be expected to have impact on their behavior in the convention situation, and may predict channels of communication in the convention. This proposition, however, merely defines the frame of values within which delegates will be expected to calculate their gains and costs.

2. *At each level of government, party organization is controlled by the elected chief executive.*

Parties are organizations devoted to maximizing political power. At each level of government, the elected chief executive (mayor, governor, President) generally has the most political power, and as a result the party organizations depend more upon access to chief executives than on any other source for their political power. In addition, parties are accountable for the activities of chief executives elected with their endorsement. Accountability means that when the party endorses a man, it designates him as its agent before the electorate. The fortunes of the party depend on the success of party candidates. Candidates come and go, but parties and electorates remain, and it is assumed that the actions of a party's men in office will in the long run determine the extent and location of the party's appeal within the electorate, and its record of success at the polls.

Just as the party is greatly dependent, at any moment, upon its incumbent office-holders for its political power, these office-holders in turn often have great discretion in the distribution of indulgences to the party, and it is expected that they will seek to strengthen themselves within the party organization by the judicious dispensation of favors and patronage. This suggests that the elected chief executive comes closer than any other individual to possessing unilateral controls over the party organization, and that these unilateral controls may be used by the chief executive to impose his own preferences on the party organization.

We may consider it axiomatic that the presidency possesses more political power than any other national office, and that the governorship possesses more political power than any other state office. If we also take account of the fact that the national government as compared with state and local governments dominates American political life in the scope, comprehensiveness, and immediacy of its powers, we may deduce the following additional propositions: (1) the Presidency possesses more political power than any other office; (2) access to the Presidency is the most efficient means for politicians to realize their goals; and (3) the choice of a presidential candidate is the single decision dominating the national convention. If the powers of the President vis à vis the national party organization are all that previous propositions assert, they should be reflected in his control of a national convention.

3. *An incumbent President runs national conventions of his party hierarchically, if he chooses to do so.*

The presidential power over national conventions has historically extended to (1) the right to renomination, or to designate the party nominee, effectively exercised in seventeen of the nineteen conventions since the Civil War in which the President interested himself in the outcome; (2) the power to dictate the party platform; (3) the power to designate the officers of the convention; (4) the power to select many delegates—especially potent in the case of Republican delegations from the one-party Democratic South, where Republican Presidents, until the passage of the Hatch Act, drew upon a corporal's guard of federal patronage appointees to man this sizable convention bloc.

National conventions which are run hierarchically seem to be subject to the same costs of calculation and control as are most other hierarchies. Just as hierarchical price-fixing will tend to misrepresent real costs, this type of decision-making in conventions has historically miscalculated the bounds of the framework of consent within which the political party must function. Party accountability and federal patronage are powerful incentives to co-operation with the President, but this power is not unlimited. This was demonstrated when, in 1912 and 1948, several delegations walked out of national conventions and set up splinter parties to protest hierarchical decisions which threatened to inflict severe deprivations on factional and sectional politicians who acquiesced to them. This suggests that party splinters are much more likely to occur when a party is in power than when a party is out of power, as a possible consequence of hierarchical decision-making.

4. *A relatively few party leaders control the decisions of a large proportion of the delegates to conventions.*

Delegates to national conventions are chosen, after all, as representatives of the several state party organizations, apportioned according to a formula laid down by action of previous national conventions. While it is true that official decisions are made by majority vote of delegates, American party organizations are centralized at state and local levels. This means that such hierarchical controls as actually exist on the state and local levels will assert themselves in the national convention. Since the probabilities are fairly good that both major parties at any given time will have succeeded in electing a substantial number of governors and mayors of important cities, the chances are likewise fairly good that a substantial number of delegates will be controlled hierarchically. The tendency toward centralization is formally aided by the so-called unit rule, providing that a majority vote of a state delegation shall determine the way in which the vote of the entire delegation shall be cast.

The decision to adopt the unit rule is a difficult one for state political leaders faced with an intense, dissident minority within their delegations. While adoption of unit voting assures them of a solid bloc of votes with which they can bargain, hard feelings may linger on within the state. When a minority element within a state is strong enough to gain representation on a convention delegation, muzzling it by imposition of the unit rule is seldom wise. The unit rule is used to best advantage by those delegations whose members generally feel more strongly about preserving the bargaining advantages of a bloc vote than they do about any particular candidate. In a delegation firmly committed to a particular aspirant, the unit rule is superfluous. It is sometimes avoided by a leader who wants to reward delegates who stick together on the delegation's first choice. He releases them to vote as they individually please on their second choice, if the first choice is removed from contention. Hence state delegations governed by the unit rule are most often likely to be relatively uncommitted in their presidential preferences, and comparatively homogeneous in their political outlooks and allegiances. The following conclusions may therefore be drawn: (1) state delegations tend to be hierarchically controlled by state political leaders; (2) the chief political leader of state delegations will be the governor, or his agent; (3) if a state delegation puts forward a favorite son candidate, there is a higher probability that he will be the governor of the state than any other person; and (4) presidential nominees are more likely to be governors than any other persons.

These propositions all rest upon assumptions about who is likely to control access to political power. There may be significant deviations from these propositions in real life, however. For example, there are a few instances in recent years where party leaders controlled a majority of a state's delegation in opposition to the governor of the same party. Usually, the governor, if he is not a state's favorite son, is still the leader of the delegation and is likely to be allied with the favorite son as well. An example of this would be Governor Orville Freeman, who has long been a close ally of Minnesota's favorite son, Senator Humphrey. No doubt some of these coalitions between the leaders of a state are shotgun marriages, as may have been the case among Tennessee's Democrats in 1956, but for the purposes of the convention, these alliances seem to hold together despite centrifugal impulses.

5. *Politicians will have different preferences among those presidential aspirants having a chance of winning election.*

This proposition follows from the fact that politicians desire to maximize access to governmental decision-makers. But the probability is very high that they will differ in their relations with the various aspirants to the Presidency. A politician will naturally favor a presidential hopeful from his own state, or an aspirant with whom he has been on close personal or professional terms. Each presidential aspirant begins the convention with a cluster of connections of this sort with delegates and delegation leaders. The predispositions of delegates toward candidates are shaped by their expectations of access to them, which may depend upon historical accidents, ideological affinities, and/or explicit "deals."

6. *In the absence of hierarchical control by an incumbent President, decision-making at conventions is co-ordinated by a process of bargaining among party leaders.*

We may think of bargaining as a method by which activities are co-ordinated in situations where controls between individuals are bilateral or multi-lateral and approach equality. Bargainers may differ as to their goals. They are presumed to harbor the expectation that participating in the bargaining process (1) will aid them in achieving their goals and (2) will inform them of the goals and tactics of others, which in turn may help them in attaining their goals. Prerequisites to bargaining may be summarized as (1) non-hierarchical controls; (2) interdependence of bargainers; (3) disagreement among bargainers; and (4) expectation of gain.

When the President is of the opposite party, or chooses not to control the convention hierarchically, the convention becomes a bargaining system because no other political leader is in a position to control the national convention unilaterally. The interdependence of party leaders may be established by reference to the rule of American politics which provides that the voters may replace the elected officials of one party with those of another at general elections. In order to mobilize enough nationwide support to elect a President, party leaders from a large number of constituencies must be satisfied with the nominee. Without agreement on a nominee, none is likely to enjoy access to the eventual President; hence party leaders are interdependent and expect to gain from the outcome of the bargain. Because of the different access to different aspirants which delegates carry with them into the convention the preferences of delegates are likely initially to disagree.

Politicians seek to maximize their own political power, but in order to do so, must maximize the potential vote for candidates whom they sponsor. The more leaders who agree on a candidate, the more interest groups and state party organizations there are working for the election of the candidate; consequently, the greater are the chances that the candidate will win election and provide those politicians who supported him with access to political power. Therefore, we may postulate the following: (1) Party unity is perceived by politicians as prerequisite to the achievement of their goals. (2) Unless party leaders achieve a consensus among themselves, the chances are diminished that they will be able to elect a President. (3) Parties tend to nominate candidates who are (a) at the least, not obnoxious to, (b) at the most, attractive to, as many interest groups as possible. (4) Party platforms tend to be broad and vague. (5) Sanctions open to a dissident party faction revolve around its ability to destroy party unity.

7. *The parties are in direct competition for many of the same votes.*

Voters and interest groups are distributed between and outside the two parties, and parties must of necessity build a nationwide coalition of votes to win the Presidency. Politicians are uncertain as to the exact distribution of presidential preferences among groups in the population, however, and must make nominations and write platforms with the broadest possible constituency in mind. The two parties thus compete for many of the same politically neutral, apathetic, ambivalent and/or uncommitted interest groups and voters. Therefore, (1) party platforms tend to be similar, though not identical, and (2) presidential candidates are likely to come from states having a large electoral vote and which are politically competitive. This last proposition follows partly from what has been said above, with the addition of the electoral college rules which distribute presidential votes by states roughly according to population and give the whole electoral vote of a state to any candidate winning a majority within the state.

8. *Vice presidential nominees are calculated to help the party achieve the Presidency.*

Party nominees for President and Vice President always appear on the ballot together and are elected together. A vote for one is always a vote for the other. Yet the Vice President occupies a post in the legislative branch of the government which is formally honorific, and his powers and activities in the executive branch are determined by the President. The electoral interdependence of the two offices gives politicians an opportunity to gather votes for the Presidency, and from this we can deduce the criteria for the selection of the Vice President. A vice-presidential nominee must have the same qualities as a presidential nominee, with two additions: (a) he must possess those desirable qualities the presidential nominee lacks, and (b) he must be acceptable to the presidential nominee.

As we have seen, the selection of a presidential nominee is the business which dominates the convention. From this follow: (1) The importance of decisions preceding the presidential nomination in the convention is entirely dependent upon the implications of the outcomes for the presidential nomination. (2) Decisions not taken unanimously which precede the presidential nomination in the convention are tests of strength between party factions divided as to the presidential nomination.

The Strategies of Participants

The one route to political power open to all delegates in the convention is to contribute to the majority essential for the nomination of the man they believe will be the winner. This explains the so-called "band wagon" behavior, which can be seen in operation at many conventions.

1. *When delegates believe that one presidential aspirant is certain of nomination, they will attempt to record themselves as voting for that aspirant as quickly as possible. Delegates committed to a favorite son candidate will trade their votes for access to the candidate they think most likely to win nomination.*

Note the differences in the two statements above. In the first, delegates know which candidate will win, and hope to earn his gratitude by voting for him. In the corollary, delegates are less certain of the outcome, hence their commitment to an aspirant is more costly for the aspirant, who often makes explicit promises of access to delegates in return for their support.

2. *The most important consideration for a politican in choosing a presidential nominee is the expectation that he will win election.*

Clearly, if a candidate is given no chance of winning election, access to him is not instrumental to politicians' goals. Presidential aspirants claim victory and stimulate manifestations of public enthusiasm and support for themselves as a means of convincing delegates that they will win nomination and election. This follows from delegate behavior in the decision-making process outlined above. If delegates, because of their uncertainty about what other delegates will do, often are driven to band wagon behavior, the rational presidential aspirant will try to capitalize on this fact. The votes of a majority of delegates are indispensable to nomination, and, as we have seen, a prerequisite to getting these votes is the ability to stimulate the expectation of victory, that is, to generate a band wagon.

3. *Unexpected losses in primary elections usually doom an aspirant's chance of nomination, so the rational aspirant enters only those primaries he thinks he can win.*

Primary elections function largely as a means by which politicians inform themselves about the relative popularity of presidential aspirants. The expectations of delegates are of critical importance in determining the nominee, as the propositions above show, and the strategies of aspirants respond to these conditions. Some aspirants play a somewhat different game from the maximizing behavior postulated in the above proposition. An aspirant from a state with relatively few electoral votes and who has only a few votes from outside his state initially pledged to him may find it necessary to enter primaries where his chances are questionable, in order to come into the convention with enough first ballot votes pledged to him so that he is considered seriously for the nomination. Without this minimum number of votes, the aspirant from the small state stands little chance of consideration. He takes a chance on primaries not to maintain a preconvention record of success (since this is of little utility to him), but because he has nothing to lose.

4. *An aspirant who leads in votes for the nomination must actually win nomination by a certain point in time, after which his chances of eventually winning decline precipitously, even though he remains in the lead for the time being.*

This follows from the fact that much delegate support is given candidates because of the expectation of victory. When this victory falls short of quick materialization, delegates may question their initial judgment. Thus, the longer a candidate remains in the lead without starting a band wagon, the greater the chance that his supporters will reassess his chances of victory, and vote for someone else. In order to achieve access, delegates must support the eventual winner before he achieves a majority, as a general rule. They are therefore guided by what they expect other delegates to do, and are constantly on the alert to change their expectations to conform to the latest information. This information may be nothing more substantial than a rumor, which quickly takes on the status of a self-fulfilling prophecy, as delegates stampede in response to expectations—quickly realized—about how other delegates will respond. I have previously pointed out the costs of hierarchy in convention decision-making. In the fragmented situation there are also costs, since there is no guarantee that nominations made in this situation will reflect the best judgment of delegates or leaders, or even their second-best judgment as to the most acceptable party nominee. This is the case because delegates may stampede on reliable or unreliable information, with effects that may be highly prejudicial to the party's chances to elect a President.

Aspirants sometimes combine their voting strength in the convention in order to prevent a front-running candidate from gaining a majority. They will then negotiate the nomination among themselves. If the front-runner's victory promises other aspirants insufficient access, they may defeat him by preventing a band wagon in his favor. The rational aspirant who leads but lacks a majority will promise access to leaders representing the requisite number of votes. This is the rational response to the expectation that no band wagon will appear, unstimulated. The front-runner may reasonably expect to win without cost (i.e., without making such promises) unless leaders of opposing factions reach agreement on a ticket, and appear likely to combine against him. Early front-runners often win nominations, precisely because they face a divided opposition.

5. *There are conditions under which a rational delegate will vote for a candidate other than the probable winner, according to his calculations.*

If a politician is without hope of obtaining access to a particular candidate, for any of a variety of reasons, then there is no reason for voting for him, even if the politician calculates that the candidate is the probable winner. A second condition under which this obtains has already been mentioned. By withholding his vote temporarily from the probable winner, the delegate may obtain firm promises of access. A third condition may be classed as an irrationality, namely the force of primary law in some states which commits delegates to a candidate regardless of the promises of access other candidates make to the delegation. Since delegates may be released by the candidate they are bound by law to support, this transfers to the candidate significant bargaining power which may provide him with the access to more probable winners usually accorded to politicians within state delegations. Politicians bound by primary law are thus often severely handicapped in the bargaining process.

●　　●　　●

THE BALLOT AND
THE POLITICAL SYSTEM

NELSON W. POLSBY AND AARON WILDAVSKY

COALITIONS IN THE SYSTEM

In the American political system, powers and opportunities to act effectively on public policy are parceled out to the President, to Congress, to the courts, to independent regulatory agencies, to various of the Federal bureaucracies, to the political parties, and even, in some respects, to interest groups. It is clear that each of these agencies enjoys partial autonomy; but in most important areas of public policy formation, they share powers. And this means that it is possible for participants in policy making to achieve their desired ends only by entering into cooperation with other participants in the system, by making coalitions.

What sorts of behavior are encouraged in a system which requires coalitions? Coalitions mean bargaining. Participants must give something in order to get something. Those who start out with the most resources to give have an advantage. But skill also counts. The prizes tend to go to those individuals and groups who are skilled in using whatever resources they have to put together and maintain coalitions. They help themselves by finding ways in which the interests of others may also be served.

The most conspicuous problem that American political parties face is to achieve a record of advocacy and accomplishment in public policy while harmonizing the interests of Presidential and Congressional wings.

The parties that convene at the national conventions do not contain the same roster of personnel, the same coalitions of interests, or the same majorities as the parties that meet in Congress. These two different types of parties, though they bear the same party labels, represent different constituencies and perspectives. The national conventions are weighted according to the winning strategy dictated by the Electoral College; Congress is still somewhat weighted according to the overrepresentation in state legislatures (which de-

SOURCE: Nelson W. Polsby and Aaron B. Wildavsky, "The Ballot and the Political System," *Presidential Elections,* 2nd edition (New York: Charles Scribner's Sons, 1968), pp. 269–284. Copyright © 1968, 1964 by Charles Scribner's Sons. Reprinted with the permission of Charles Scribner's Sons.

termines the shape of Congressional districts) of rural interests,[1] according to the constitutional rule giving each state two Senators regardless of population, and according to the rules of seniority that govern the House and Senate and which tend to favor one-party areas. This explains why, for example, the conservative wing of the Republican party, though dominant in that party in Congress for many years, had for many years, until 1964, failed to nominate a candidate of its own choosing at the Republican National Convention. The difference on the Democratic side between the two party coalitions was made abundantly clear in 1956 when Senator Estes Kefauver defeated Senator John Kennedy for the Vice-Presidential nomination in the convention and lost to the man from Massachusetts in the Senate a few months later in a contest for a place on the prestigeful Foreign Relations Committee. Obviously, the same interests and considerations were not decisive in the national convention and the Senate.

Even when a President and a Congressional majority bear the same party identification, it may be, and often is, necessary in a Presidential election campaign to adjust their varying interests on particular policies. This is done through bargaining and the creation of a coalition including interests represented in both Congressional and Presidential parties.

Although the lack of cohesion and discipline attributed to American parties can be overemphasized, it is true that on many major policies the President cannot rely on support from the full complement of his party in Congress but must seek the support of at least some members of the other party. Thus, interparty coalitions are necessary and common in American national politics.

Power within Congress is fragmented and dispersed. Bits and pieces of influence are scattered, unequally to be sure, among committee chairmen, appropriations subcommittees, the Speaker of the House, the House Rules Committee, the Senate majority and minority leaders, the President's lobbyists, and others. How is legislation passed and defeated, then, if it is not done by a central body of cohesive leaders who are able to enforce their will on Congress?

Legislative policy is approved or rejected by building a majority coalition through a process of bargaining and the proposal of objectives appealing to a wide variety of interests. A series of bills may contain attractions for all; concessions may be offered, log-rolling may be attempted, and other bargaining techniques used. If the identical majority were required to pass every piece of legislation, however, and the diversity of interests in Congress prevented agreement on a comprehensive legislative program, the American political system could lead to stalemate and go the way of the French Fourth Republic. Actually, legislation in the various policy areas often requires somewhat different coalitions. Legislative politics, therefore, is largely concerned with constructing coalitions appropriate to each set of policies.

[1] *Wesberry* vs. *Sanders, Reynolds* vs. *Sims,* and the wave of reapportionment of state legislatures they set off may be expected to modify this condition somewhat over the next decade.

The President does not have sufficient power to accomplish all his purposes, and those the nation sets for him, by issuing orders. He must obtain the support of others. Congress holds the vital power of the purse and the general legislative authority which the President needs. But much of the time he cannot either help or harm legislators because they are nominated and elected in their own constituencies at the local and state levels. Consequently, to get some of the things he wants, the President may have to trade some top-level appointments and make policy concessions to influential interests in Congress or to interest groups or local party leaders who can exert influence in Congress.

Power is also fragmented and dispersed in the executive branch. Parts are held by bureau chiefs, department heads, interest groups, members of Congress, party leaders, coordinating committees, the Executive Office, independent regulatory commissions and, of course, by the President himself. With no central authority to dictate decisions, administrative politics require the formation of coalitions among the many dispersed centers of power.

"This does not mean," a contemporary student of the Presidency says, "that Presidents are powerless. . . ." If that were true they would have nothing with which to bargain. They do have a veto, powers over foreign policy and the armed forces, some executive authority and other resources at their disposal. "It does mean, though, that Presidential power must be exercised *ad hoc*, through the employment of whatever sources of support, whatever transient advantages can be found and put together, case by case." [2]

We may achieve some perspective on the American situation by noting how it differs from British and French experience. In Great Britain the major parties form their coalitions of interests before the national elections and, if victorious, the same coalition that won election governs in Parliament. In the Fourth Republic of France coalitions were generally not formed before, but only after the elections. Even in the Fifth Republic the alliances of convenience formed on the second ballot bear no necessary relationship to the coalition which governs France. In the United States coalitions are formed both before and after the national elections, but electoral and governing coalitions are different.

In characterizing each of our political parties as coalitions, we do not mean to suggest that they are entirely alike. In fact, they are coalitions having slightly different components, and these differences are in turn reflected in the very real differences that crop up from time to time in the platforms of the Presidential parties and in the policies the different party majorities favor in Congress.

The two political parties to a certain extent act as transmission belts for policy preferences in the general population. They perform this function

[2] Richard Neustadt, "The Presidency at Mid-Century," *Law and Contemporary Problems*, 21 (Autumn 1956), 614.

partly out of choice—as partisans, party leaders know more and care more about issues—but mostly out of necessity. In order to win the great prize of the Presidency, they must gather support from a variety of groups in the population. They gain support by offering inducements to the electorate and to the organized groups which represent its various interests. By giving this support at the polls to party winners, interest groups gain opportunities to participate in party and governmental decision-making.

ELECTIONS AND PUBLIC POLICY

We would argue that free and competitive elections discourage, though they cannot provide a complete guarantee against, extreme policies and political leaders and aid in making the political system free, open, and responsive to a great variety of people and groups in the population. But it would not be correct to say that our elections transmit unerringly the policy preferences of electorates to leaders or confer mandates upon leaders with regard to specific policies.

It is easy to be cynical and expect too little from elections, or to be euphoric and expect too much from them. A cynical view would hold that the United States was ruled by a power elite—a small group outside the democratic process. Under these circumstances the ballot would be a sham and a delusion. What difference can it make how voting is carried on or who wins if the nation is actually governed by other means? On the other hand, a euphoric view, holding that the United States was ruled as a mass democracy with equal control over decisions by all or most citizens, would enormously magnify the importance of the ballot. Through the act of casting a ballot, it could be argued, a majority of citizens would determine major national policies. What happened at the polls would not only decide who would occupy public office, it would also determine the content of specific policy decisions. In a way, public office would then be a sham because the power of decision in important matters would be removed from the hands of public officials. A third type of political system—a pluralist one in which numerous minorities compete for shares in policy making within broad limits provided by free elections—has more complex implications. It suggests that balloting is important but that it does not often determine individual policy decisions. The ballot both guides and constrains public officials who are free to act within fairly broad limits subject to anticipated responses of the voters and to the desires of the other active participants.

In fact, it is evident from our description of coalition politics that the American political system is of the pluralist type. Public officials do make major policy decisions but elections matter in that they determine which of two competing parties holds public office. In a competitive two-party situation such as exists in American Presidential politics, the lively possibility of change provides an effective incentive for political leaders to remain in touch with followers.

But it would be inaccurate to suggest that voters in Presidental elections transmit their policy preferences to elected officials with a high degree of reliability. There are few clear mandates in our political system owing to the fact that elections are fought on so many issues and in so many incompletely overlapping constituencies. Often the voters elect officials to Congress and to the Presidency who disagree on public policies. Thus, as we shall show, mandates are not only impossible to identify, but even if they could be identified they might well be impossible to enact because of inconsistency in the instructions issued to officials who must agree on legislation.[3]

Presidential elections are not referenda. The relationship between Presidential elections and policies is a great deal subtler than the relations between the outcomes of referenda and the policies they pertain to. In theory, the American political system is designed to work like this: two teams of men, one in office, the other seeking office, both attempt to get enough votes to win elections. In order to win, they go to various groups of voters and, by offering to pursue policies favored by these groups, hope to attract their votes. If there were only one office-seeking team, their incentive to respond to the policy preferences of groups in the population would diminish; if there were many such teams, the chances that any one of them could achieve a sufficient number of backers to govern would diminish. Hence the two-party system is regarded as a kind of compromise between the goals of responsiveness and effectiveness.

The proponents of a different theory would say that elections give the winning party a mandate to carry out the policies proposed during the campaign. Only in this way, they maintain, is popular rule through the ballot meaningful. A basic assumption in their argument is that the voters (or at least a majority of them) approve of all or most of the policies presented by the victorious candidate. No doubt this is plausible, but not in the sense intended because a vote for a Presidential candidate is usually merely an expression of a party habit and particular policy directions are not necessarily implied in the vote. Most voters in the United States are not ideologically oriented. That is, they do not see or make connections among issues. They do not seek to create or to adopt coherent systems of thought in which issues are related to one another in some logical pattern. If this is the case, then voters can hardly be said to transmit preferences for particular policies by electing candidates to public office.

Other basic objections to the idea that our elections are designed to confer mandates on specific public policies may also be raised. First, the issues debated in the campaign may not be the ones in which most voters are interested. These issues may be ones which interest the candidates, which they want to stress, or which interest segments of the press, but there is no neces-

---

[3] This parallels in many respects an argument to be found in Robert A. Dahl, *A Preface to Democratic Theory* (Chicago, 1956).

sary reason to believe that any particular issue is of great concern to voters just because it gets publicity. Time and time again, voting studies have demonstrated that what appear to be the major issues of a campaign turn out not to be significant for most of the electorate. In 1952, for example, three great Republican themes were Communism, Korea, and corruption. It turned out that the Communism issue, given perhaps the most publicity, had virtually no impact. Democrats simply would not believe that their party was the party of treason, and Republicans did not need that issue to make them vote the way they usually did. Korea and corruption were noticeable issues.[4] Yet how could anyone know, in the absence of a public opinion poll, which of the three issues were important to the voters and which constituted a mandate? There were, in any event, no significant policy differences between the parties on these issues—Democrats were also against Communism and corruption and also wanted an end to the war in Korea.

A second reason why voting for a candidate does not necessarily signify approval of his policies is that candidates pursue many policy interests at any one time with widely varying intensity, so that they may collect support from some voters on one issue and from other voters on another. It is possible for a candidate to get 100 per cent of the votes and still have every voter opposed to most of his policies, as well as having every one of his policies opposed by most of the voters.

Assume that there are four major issues in a campaign. Make the further, quite reasonable, assumption that the voting population is distributed in such a way that those people who care intensely about one major issue support the victorious candidate for that reason alone, although they differ with him mildly on the other three issues. Thus, voters who are deeply concerned about the problem of nuclear defense may vote for candidate Jones who prefers a minimum deterrence position, rather than Smith, who espouses the "no-city" doctrine which requires huge retaliatory forces.[5] This particular group of voters disagrees with Jones on the farm bill, on civil rights and on Federal aid to education, but they do not feel strongly about any of these matters. Another group, meanwhile, believes that farmers, the noble yeomanry, are the backbone of the nation and that if they are prosperous and strong, everything else will turn out all right. So they vote for Jones, too, although they prefer a "no-city" strategy and disagree with Jones's other policies. And so on for other groups of voters. Jones ends up with all the votes, yet each of his policies is preferred by less than a majority of the electorate. Since this is possible in any political system where many issues are debated at election time, it is hard to argue that our Presidential elections give unequivocal mandates on specific policies to the candidates who win.[6]

[4] Angus Campbell, Philip Converse, Warren E. Miller, and Donald Stokes, *The American Voter* (New York, 1960), pp. 525–527.

[5] An excellent popular treatment of this set of alternatives is contained in Richard Fryklund, *100 Million Lives* (New York, 1962).

[6] See Dahl, *A Preface to Democratic Theory*, pp. 124–131.

As we have seen, people go to the polls and vote for many reasons not directly connected with issues. They may vote on the basis of party identification alone. Party habits may be joined with a general feeling that Democrats are better for the common man or that Republicans will keep us safe—feelings too diffuse to tell us much about specific issues. Some people vote on the basis of a candidate's personality. Others follow a friend's recommendation. Still others may be thinking about policy issues but may be all wrong in their perception of where the candidates stand. It would be difficult to distinguish the votes of these people from those who know, care, and differentiate among the candidates on the basis of issues. We do know, however, that issue-oriented persons are usually in a minority while those who cast their ballots with other things in mind are generally in the majority.

Even if there is good reason to believe that a majority of voters do approve of specific policies supported by the victorious candidate, the mandate may be difficult or impossible to carry out. A man may get elected for a policy he pursued or preferred in the past which has no reference to present circumstances. One could have voted Republican because Dwight Eisenhower ended the war in Korea but this does not point to any future policy that is currently in the realm of Presidential discretion. "Corruption" in 1952 was a kind of issue where there was really no way of carrying out a supposed mandate other than determining to be honest, a course of action we may be pardoned for believing that Adlai Stevenson would have followed as well. John F. Kennedy promised in 1960 to get the nation moving. This was broad enough to cover a multitude of vague hopes and aspirations. More specifically, as President, Kennedy may dearly have wished to make good on this promise by increasing the rate of growth in the national economy, but no one was quite sure how to do this. Lyndon Johnson was able to make good many of his 1964 campaign promises on domestic policy, but saying he would be more responsible than Goldwater did not constitute a viable future policy for Vietnam.

Leaving aside all the difficulties about the content of a mandate, there is no accepted definition of what size electoral victory gives a President special popular sanction to pursue any particular policy. Would a 60% victory be sufficient? This is rarely achieved. Does 55 seem reasonable? What about 51 or 52, however, or the cases in which the winner receives less than half of the votes cast? And is it right to ignore the multitudes who do not vote and whose preferences are not directly being considered? One might ignore the nonvoters for the purpose of this analysis if they divided in their preferences between candidates in nearly the same proportions as those who do vote. But they often don't. In practice, this problem is easily solved. Whoever wins the election is allowed to pursue whatever policies he pleases, within the substantial constraints imposed by the rest of the political system. This, in the end, is all that a "mandate" is in American politics.

EXTREMISM

Among the most important things accomplished by a political system like ours is that it discourages the most extreme alternatives. Knowing that policies which would outrage significant groups in the country would result in a stream of protests leading to loss of the next election, the party in power is restrained from the worst excesses. For people in countries like America or Great Britain, this may be difficult to appreciate precisely because they rarely have occasion to witness these extremes; extreme policies are effectively ruled out by the party system and free elections. This is not so everywhere, and we can get an insight into what is possible when the ultimate restraint of free elections is missing. Imagine that in 1956 the United States repudiated its national debt on the ground that it was inflationary. Suppose that ten years previously our government had confiscated about nine-tenths of all savings by issuing new currency worth only a tenth of the old. No doubt there would have been riots in the streets, petitions galore, furious political participation by millions of formerly inactive citizens, and a complete change of government as soon as the election laws allowed. Can we conceive of a situation in which our government would ship millions of tons of wheat abroad while millions of our own people were starving? All these extreme policies have been pursued by the Soviet Union. We are more fortunate than we know if we can say that it is difficult or impossible to imagine extreme policies like these being carried out. Indeed, it is hard to imagine that anyone in a responsible position would think of such policies let alone attempt to promulgate them. Here we come to a key point. No one thinks about these things seriously, because everyone understands that they simply could not be done.

Extreme policies are discouraged in a more subtle way: Free elections discourage persons with extreme views from running for office because possible allies of such people know that they cannot win and that, if they do, their victories will last only until the next election. Extremists deprive too many people of too many of their preferred policies to win office easily. Thus we find that would-be Presidential aspirants do not get far if they are known publicly to hold bigoted views about racial or religious minorities or if they have done or said things which suggest that they are extremely hostile to large population groups such as laborers or small businessmen. Moreover, those who do attain office and wish to enjoy its benefits find that compromise and conciliation bring greater rewards than hostility and intransigence. The political system conditions those who accept the rules of free elections to moderate behavior.

PARTY COMPETITION AND POLICY

Aside from casting extremists out beyond the pale, free elections and a two-party system operate to bring governmental policy roughly in line with intense public preferences over a reasonable span of time. Through the trial and error of repeated electoral experiences, party leaders discover that certain policies must be excluded and others included if they are to have any hope of winning. The "out" party has a built-in incentive to propose policies more popular than the "in" party in order to assume office. And the "in" party is highly motivated to respond by adopting the policy itself or by proposing others which it believes may be even more popular. Party competition for votes brings public policy into accord with private preferences. This calculus of support is far from precise; it is necessarily based more on hunch and guesswork at any point in time than on hard facts. Party leaders undoubtedly have a number of policies which they know they must include or exclude, such as Social Security and veterans' benefits. Beyond that, however, they face considerable uncertainty in determining which policies will prove to be the most popular with the largest number of voters who are in a position to help them. Policies themselves may break down, subjecting proponents to charges of ineffectiveness. There may be consequences of consequences which turn what once looked like a good thing into a disaster. John Kennedy might have been helped by a successful Cuban invasion but how was he to know that it would turn into a rout? And how could he tell that a Soviet attempt to install missiles would enable him to act decisively and recoup his fortunes? President Johnson has found it possible to do much more than previous Presidents to improve relations with Communist countries in Eastern Europe. Yet the Vietnam war has certainly created all sorts of additional difficulties in dealing with the Soviet Union. So much for the effectiveness of the policy. How about the perhaps more difficult problem in our system of discovering whether particular policies are so widely preferred as to aid one's political fortunes?

Opinion polls may help the politician, but there are always lingering doubts as to the polls' reliability; it is not certain in any event that they tell the political leader what he needs to know. People who really have no opinion may give one just to satisfy the interviewer. People who have an opinion but who care little may be counted equally with those who are intensely concerned. Many people giving opinions may have no intention of voting for some politicians who heed them, no matter what. The result may be that the politician will get no visible support from a majority who agrees with him, but instead he will get complaints from an intense minority which disagrees. The people who agree with him may not vote while those who differ may take retribution at the ballot box. Those who are pleased may be the ones who would have voted for the public official anyway. And unless the poll is carefully done, it may leave out important groups of voters, overrepresent some, underrepresent others, and otherwise give a misleading impression. Other methods of determining voter sentiment are bound to be even more unreliable. Who knows whether opinions expressed in newspaper editorials or a mail campaign are representative of the majority of the voting populace?

Let us turn the question around for a moment. Suppose a candidate loses office. What does this tell him about the policies he should have preferred? If there were one or two key issues widely debated and universally understood, the election may tell him a great deal. But this is seldom the case. More likely there were many issues and it was difficult to separate out those which did or did not garner support for his opponent. Perhaps the election was decided on the basis of personality or some events in the economic cycle or a military engagement—points which were not debated in the campaign and which may not have been within anyone's control. The losing candidate may always feel that if he continues to educate the public to favor the policies he prefers, he will eventually win out. Should he lose a series of elections, however, his party would undoubtedly try to change something—policies, candidates, organization, maybe all three—in an effort to improve its fortunes.

Let us suppose that a candidate wins an election. What does this event tell him and his party about the policies he should prefer when in office? He can take it on faith that the policies he proposed during the campaign are the popular ones. Some were undoubtedly rather vague, and specfic applications of them may turn out quite differently than the campaign suggested. Others may founder on the rock of practicality; they sounded fine but they simply could not be carried out. Conditions change and policies which seemed appropriate but a few months before turn out to be irrelevant. As the time for putting policies into practice draws near, the new officeholder may discover that they generate a lot more opposition than when they were merely campaign oratory. And those policies he pursues to the end may have to be compromised considerably in order to get the support of other participants in the policy making process. Nevertheless, if he has even a minimal policy orientation, the newly elected candidate can try to carry out a few of his campaign proposals, seeking to maintain a general direction consonant with the approach that may—he cannot be entirely certain—have contributed measurably to his election.

Let us summarize. The role of Presidential elections has been found to be very important in keeping our political system open and competitive and in keeping public officials responsive to the preferences of a variety of interests in the general population. However, outcomes of these elections cannot by themselves transform the political system, nor can they register precisely all the nuances of policies preferred by the general public. In spite of this, our system of coalition politics, operating within and among the two parties, the President, Congress, state parties, and interest groups, does provide a kind of substitute for specific mandates by the electorate.

In the American political system, both inside and outside the formal government, it is necessary to receive multiple agreements and clearances from actors (bureaucrats, interest groups, legislators, the President) variously situated, having somewhat different roles to play and values to defend, in order to put new policies into effect. Alternatives which are fed into the political system and emerge as decisions are brought forth in a variety of ways, and all sorts of strategies and resources can be mobilized and focused on political decisions by interested parties. It is a system which encourages stability and discourages extremism, which sharply limits the choices available to the general public in the interests of finding agreement on only two alternatives, either of which can govern effectively. Very few people are perfectly satisfied with this framework within which our Presidential elections are held, but even fewer have devised ways of making the system better without simultaneously making it worse.

THE LESSONS OF 1968

GEORGE McGOVERN

The Democratic National Convention of 1968 already has settled into the folklore of American politics. Its mere mention evokes the vision of tumultuous floor debate, bloodshed and tear gas in the streets, demonstrators and delegates standing together, arm-in-arm, in confrontation with the police. To some it also evokes the image of rigged procedures, of a political party assembled to reach predetermined decisions. The Convention became the shame of the Democratic party, and in all likelihood assured its defeat in the November following. Wherever politicians meet—wherever Americans meet—they agree that the Convention imposed such a strain on the democratic system of government that a repetition would be intolerable.

Yet this Convention was governed by essentially the same rules as those which nominated Woodrow Wilson, Franklin Roosevelt, and John F. Kennedy. If anything, the rules in 1968 provided for more popular participation than in 1964, when the states were warned that delegations would not be seated unless chosen without regard to race. To be sure, discrimination was not absent from the 1968 Convention, but there were more black and brown Americans as delegates than ever before. Yet even in Chicago blacks were not represented in proportion to their numbers in the population, and even less so in proportion to their numbers in the Democratic party.

The issue which brought the convention to the edge of chaos, however, was not race but Vietnam. The war exposed the profound flaws in the American Convention system. It showed that institutions which work satisfactorily in times considered normal may be unequal to periods of stress. The Conven-

SOURCE: George McGovern, "The Lessons of 1968," *Harper's Magazine,* 240 (January 1970), 43–47. Copyright © 1969, by Harper's Magazine, Inc. Reprinted from the January, 1970 issue of Harper's Magazine by permission of the author.

tion which nominated Adlai Stevenson, for example, was not necessarily "healthier" than the Convention of 1968. Whatever illness became apparent at Chicago was present then, too, but the symptoms were concealed beneath the relative unity of objectives that the party enjoyed.

Delegates to those earlier conventions may have disagreed over the Presidential nominee, but they usually concurred on the basic questions of domestic and foreign policy. The assumption in those days seemed to be that the delegates had assembled to pick a winner, and it mattered very little how they went about their work. For several decades, of course, the deep South had not concurred in the party's objectives—and at every Democratic convention since 1948, blocs of Southerners have either defected or threatened to defect. These defections spotlighted the ugly racial exclusion practiced by many delegations. At successive conventions the majority took steps to correct that failing. In 1968, however, it was not the Southern minority but something like half the delegates who were profoundly disaffected. Feelings about the war ran so deep that it became impossible to hide the presence of a fundamental defect within the structure of the convention system itself. The defect was a failure of democracy, and went to the heart of the American political system.

The public began to sense that something was wrong when Senator McCarthy, soon joined by Senator Robert Kennedy, undertook to challenge President Johnson over the issue of Vietnam. McCarthy's early success indicated to the President that his conduct of the war was unpopular and contributed to his decision to withdraw as a candidate for renomination. Shortly afterward, Vice President Humphrey announced his candidacy, with the clear understanding that he supported the President's Vietnam stand. Though the Vice President chose to enter no primaries, partisans of his cause and of the war did seek to mobilize write-in support at the various primary way stations. In no election did the Vice President receive more than a tiny fraction of the votes. Yet he arrived at the Convention the clear favorite for the nomination, with perhaps 1,700 delegates out of a total of 2,500 pledged to him.

"I don't care who does the electing, so long as I can do the nominating," Boss Tweed once said. And, indeed, it looked as if a handful of party regulars were dictating their choice for the Democratic Presidential candidate to the Convention. Under other circumstances, the American people might not have been so stunned. After all, President Truman had handpicked Stevenson in 1952, though Senator Estes Kefauver had won the primaries. No one then challenged the assumption that the incumbent President should choose his own successor—especially when he was as obviously well-fitted for the responsibility as Adlai E. Stevenson. But 1968 was not 1952, and it surely was not the free-and-easy days of Tweed.

The rivalry between Senator McCarthy and Vice President Humphrey involved far more than the delegates' judgment of which man had superior credentials. Young Americans had blanketed New Hampshire not only for a man, but for an idea. Vast numbers of Americans believed that what was at stake was nothing less than the fundamental principles guiding our nation. In the primaries, Democrats had spoken out unmistakably against the war, yet now the party machinery was treating them with contempt. No wonder so many felt that the party had lost touch, had perhaps forfeited its very right to exist. However amiable Democrats felt about Stevenson's choice in 1952, they were not prepared in 1968 to have foisted upon them a nominee committed to the policies so many had voted to reject.

This kind of situation—in which the existing political system fails to respond to a widely held popular commitment—was not without precedent in American history. On two other occasions popular dissension within a political party had put the national convention as an institution of reconciliation to the test. Both times the institution failed. In 1860, slavery politics made a shambles of the Democratic party's two national conventions in Charleston and Baltimore and led to the election of Abraham Lincoln. In 1912, many Republicans were so deeply moved by the spirit of Progressivism that they broke away from their national convention to nominate Teddy Roosevelt, thereby assuring the election of Woodrow Wilson.

Certainly the stage was set for a similar walkout in Chicago. Added to the anxieties of a war imposed upon them by a President of their own party were the frustrations produced by procedural abuses which often made it virtually impossible for rank-and-file Democrats to participate in their party's decision making. But in 1968, unlike 1860 and 1912, those dissatisfied with the party opted to work for positive reform from within rather than to leave the party altogether.

Much credit for mobilizing the 1968 movement for party reform must go to Governor, now Senator, Harold Hughes of Iowa, who serves as Vice-Chairman of the Commission on Party Structure and Delegate Selection, which I chair. In midsummer of 1968, Hughes took the initiative in organizing a Commission on the Democratic Selection of Presidential Nominees to examine the manner in which the Democratic party nominated its Presidential candidates and the way state parties chose their delegates to national conventions. The Hughes Commission applied itself intelligently to the task, and was able to submit to the Convention a set of startling facts about how the Democratic party's delegates are selected. It is not so much that the facts had been a secret but that, curiously, no one—including the scholars of American politics —had ever bothered putting them together before. Even the best books on American government contained little information about the process of delegate selection. It was as if the American people, charmed by their electoral practices, cared nothing about the mystery of nominating a candidate.

What the Hughes Commission found was a widespread pattern of delegate selection by party bosses, small committees, and rigged conventions. It found that many of the delegates had been chosen by processes which started two or four years before the convention. And it established that minority representation was rendered impossible by the use of committees or conventions which abided by the unit rule at any level. While obviously only scratching the surface, the Commission had sufficient data to conclude: "State systems for selecting delegates to the national convention display considerably less fidelity to basic democratic principles than a nation which claims to govern itself can safely tolerate."

Given the atmosphere in Chicago in the summer of 1968, the Democratic National Convention could not ignore such evidence of disregard for popular expression. History is full of examples of human institutions that have died rather than be reformed. But the Democratic party, since New Deal days at least, has operated within a tradition of reform. In 1936 the Democrats eliminated the century-old "two-thirds rule" and thereby denied to a one-third minority the power of veto over Presidential nominations. In 1964, the party announced its intention to eliminate racial discrimination in all party affairs. For Democrats the way was clear: "The cure for the ills of democracy," it was long ago said, "is more democracy." So in the tumult of Chicago, even with Democrats at one another's throats, the reformers—who included the supporters of all the Presidential candidates—still were able to win a mandate for change.

A fight did ensue over how much power the Convention should use to compel the state parties to undertake reform. The Rules Committee, under Governor Sam Shapiro of Illinois, proposed that the Democratic National Committee appoint a commission to "give serious consideration" to certain reforms. The Credentials Committee under Governor Richard Hughes of New Jersey went a step further by proposing that a committee be appointed "to aid the state Democratic parties" in enacting reforms, and report its "efforts and findings" to the 1972 Convention. But a minority of the Rules Committee, with the active support of Harold Hughes, brought to the floor a still more rigorous resolution. They proposed that the 1972 Convention "shall require," in order to give "all Democratic voters . . . full and timely opportunity to participate" in nominating candidates, that (1) the unit rule be eliminated from all stages of the delegate selection process and (2) "all feasible efforts [be] made to assure that delegates are selected through party primary, convention, or committee procedures open to public participation within the calendar year of the national convention."

Amidst the madness of Chicago, the country hardly noticed that the motion of the Rules Committee minority—an indisputably tough mandate for procedural reform—was carried by a vote of 1,350 to 1,206. The victory was made possible by a coalition of supporters of McCarthy, Humphrey, and myself, the only such coalition of the entire Convention. But whatever the source of the majority, the favorable vote meant that the party had pledged, clearly and forthrightly, never again to deny full participation in its affairs to all Democrats.

In early February, Senator Fred Harris of Oklahoma, the new Chairman of the Democratic National Committee, acting on the Convention mandate, appointed the Commission on Party Structure and Delegate Selection, and invited me to serve as Chairman.

Beginning in April 1969, the Commission appointed to set minimum standards of popular participation in party affairs and to aid state parties in their efforts to comply with these standards, conducted public hearings in seventeen cities and heard the testimony of more than five hundred Democrats. They ranged from such established leaders as former National Chairman John Bailey and Governor John Connally of Texas to professors, party insurgents, Young Democrats, and one witness who was a member of both the New York State Democratic Central Committee and SDS. From Mayor Richard Daley of Chicago, despite his reputation as a party autocrat, came one of the most thoughtful proposals: that candidates for the Presidential nomination be required to enter at least a third of the state primaries, unless later relieved by a two-thirds vote of the convention. A small staff studied the testimony, and examined the maze of state laws and party regulations which determines how the national convention delegates are selected. The Commission found virtual unanimity that reform was essential. It also uncovered a pattern of delegate selection that was more appalling than had been suspected.

Let me offer some examples—all the more painful for being perfectly typical:

- More than one-third of the delegates who attended the Convention in Chicago were selected, in effect, more than two years before, when the issues, to say nothing of the candidates, had not been clarified. In many states, where delegates are actually selected within the calendar year of the Convention, the individuals empowered to appoint them were themselves selected two to four years before. This means, for example, that by the time President Lyndon B. Johnson announced his decision not to seek renomination, many delegates to the 1968 Convention had, in effect, already been chosen.

- Youth participation was a dramatic feature of the politics of 1968, yet in eighteen delegations to the Democratic Convention in Chicago, there were no voting delegates under thirty years of age. In thirteen other state delegations, there was only one voting delegate under thirty. The average age of the Delaware delegation was fifty-three years. Women also were substantially underrepresented, comprising only 13 per cent of the total delegates. Ten state delegations did not have the four women required to fill the places assigned to them on the four standing committees of the Convention. Only one delegation of the fifty-five had a woman as its chairman.

- In ten states, there were no codified party rules available to Democrats who wished to participate in the delegate selection process. In three more, there were no rules at all governing the selection process for delegates to the National Convention. In these cases, the rules were issued by the state committee. In many more states, rules, if they existed, were so inaccessible as to be useless to Democrats wishing to inform themselves of how to participate in party affairs.

• The costs of participation were often excessively high, and in some cases clearly discriminatory. In one state, the fees required of insurgent Democrats if they were to challenge for all delegate positions in the primary election exceeded $14,000, payable before they could even begin canvassing for petition signatures—which were also required for access to the ballot. Furthermore, the regular party slate in that state was automatically placed upon the ballot with an advantaged "official" designation. In several states, the party assessed all of its delegates, presumably to pay "hospitality" costs at the Convention, amounts which ranged from $15 to $250, with one state charging $500—exclusive of whatever personal expenses the delegates incurred while attending the Convention.

• In 1964, according to a study by the Citizens Research Foundation, the average expenses incurred by the delegates at the Atlantic City Convention was $455. The median income of the delegates who attended that Convention was more than $18,000 a year. The same study indicated that 55 per cent of the delegates to the 1964 Convention were officials of the Democratic party, and their annual contribution to the party was between $220 and $240.

• In many states, voters selected the party officers charged with choosing Convention delegates, without any notion that they were participating in the Presidential selection process. Even in some primary states, it is unlawful for candidates for delegate to the National Convention to list their Presidential preference on the ballot.

To be specific, I will go through the process by which a single state selects its delegates. I will not identify the state by name because I do not want to single it out unfairly for criticism. The Commission's inquiries have shown that its practices are far from unique.

The Democratic party of this state has no written constitution or set of rules, so the State Committee adopts procedures for choosing delegates early in each Presidential election year. In 1968, the State Committee decided to choose something more than 10 per cent of the state's delegates to the National Convention from among such dignitaries as the Governor, the Senators, and top party officers.

The Committee gave the Congressional District chairmen the power to conduct caucuses to select delegates. It further empowered the county chairmen to arrange for ward and township conventions at the lowest level, then county conventions at the next level, to elect delegates to the state convention. By custom, delegates to the state convention were also to serve as delegates to the Congressional District caucuses.

As a consequence of the absence of state or party rules, vast discretion was left to local leaders in the arrangement of conventions. Not surprisingly, the discretion was often abused. Although the State Committee said that the local conventions should be open to "Democrats," it was left to the county leaders to decide who "Democrats" were. This power became a device, in more than one instance, for simply excluding insurgents from convention sessions.

In one county the chairmen of four township conventions refused to disclose, despite repeated questioning from the press, where the meetings were being held. In another, the chairman refused to disclose the place of the meeting until the afternoon of the preceding day. The McCarthy Democrats, told to assemble at a local night spot, arrived to be informed by a bartender that the convention had been moved to another location unknown to him. In another instance, McCarthy backers were notified of a scheduled convention forty minutes before it was to meet; when they arrived, they found that the convention already had concluded its business.

In one township, where the meeting was genuinely open, a vote showed that McCarthy supporters outnumbered party regulars by a margin of 140 to 111. One of the regulars then stood up and voted 492 proxies for the regular Democratic organization. Observers could never remember an instance when proxies had been used at such a convention. Though the McCarthy people asked to examine the proxies, they were not permitted to do so. Nor did the organization ever reveal the proxies by name.

In several counties the required conventions were never held. The designated chairman merely forwarded a list of "approved" delegates to the next level in the nominating process.

On a number of occasions, McCarthy supporters did manage to get themselves elected to the delegation going to the county conventions. But in each case imposition of the unit rule effectively nullified their influence. As a result the impact of the McCarthy candidacy, on both the district caucuses and the state convention, was negligible. Nonetheless the state chairman demanded that the unit rule be observed by the delegation as a whole in Chicago. When the National Convention outlawed the use of the unit rule in the balloting for the Presidential nominee, some hidden McCarthy voting did emerge. But it amounted to about 6 per cent of the delegation, far less than the McCarthy strength in the state itself.

Apparently not impressed by the democratic nature of its own selection procedures, the party leaders in this state have established a state party reform commission. This commission already has begun its deliberations and has held public hearings on the adoption of a permanent set of party rules. Progress of this kind may indicate to some skeptics why I am genuinely optimistic about the possibilities for constructive reform within the party.

At the McGovern Commission, our problem was to write a standard which would assure the elimination of the abuses I have described, without at the same time circumscribing the right of the local Democratic organization to provide for the selection process most congenial to the people of the state.

The Commission is aware that many Americans believe the only genuinely democratic way to nominate Presidential candidates is through a national primary election. As of this time, our Commission has not considered the proposition. We have neither the authority from the Convention nor the power over Congress to make such a provision for 1972. I believe our nominating system should allow for leadership to be tested and would-be Presidential candidates to be publicly scrutinized in a variety of circumstances. Our present mixed system, properly conducted, is likely to perform these functions and ensure popular participation. My quarrel, in short, is not so much with the convention system as with its perversion. I find promising a proposal offered at the Commission's Denver hearing, incorporated into a bill by Senator Frank Moss, for a convention which designates the top two or three convention vote-getters as candidates for the party nomination in a national runoff.

Regardless of future modifications of the convention system, I believe that we can turn the nominating process over to the people. In November of 1969, our Commission met in Washington and adopted a series of official guidelines. These guidelines will be binding on the states' delegate selection process. They are based on the conviction that it is more important for the Commission to provide for easy access than to choose among different kinds of selection systems.

I will summarize a few of these guidelines here:

- All discriminatory costs, fees, and assessments on candidates and delegates are to be removed. In the future the process by which we nominate a President will not be inaccessible to any American by reason of financial incapacity to participate.
- All vestiges of discrimination on the grounds of age or sex are to be removed. Notably, state parties will be required to ensure that Democrats above the age of eighteen have the privilege of full participation in all party affairs, including the right to hold office and be elected as National Convention delegates.
- All minority group members must be guaranteed an opportunity to participate in the delegate selection process. The Commission further expected the state parties to overcome the effects of past discrimination by affirmative steps including specifically inviting black and brown Democrats to party meetings.
- All state parties must adopt readily accessible rules which prescribe the delegate selection procedures with clarity and detail and which en-

courage full popular participation in this process. Information about the time, place, and location of all Democratic party meetings should be publicized along with information on the Presidential preference of delegates who appear on the ballot in the course of the selection procedure.

• The nominating process must effectively begin after January 1 of the Presidential election year. All steps in the process, including the election of party officers who have special responsibilities in relation to delegate selection (including the nomination of a slate of delegates) must occur within the calendar year of the convention.

• The minimum standards set by the McGovern Commission include other regulations governing procedure, such as the elimination of proxy voting, the setting of reasonable quorums, the abolition of unit rule, the selection of alternates, and the filling of vacancies.

• Perhaps the two most important provisions of the Commission were those relating to apportionment of delegates and the fairer representation of minority views at all stages in the delegate selection process. The first of these recognizes that an apportionment formula based on one Democrat, one vote, will secure equitable representation for all Democrats. The second provides that political minority views should be preserved until the final stage of the selection process—the National Convention. These two provisions the Commission is urging, rather than requiring, of the states for 1972.

We know, of course, that the state parties, even with the best of intentions, cannot in all cases achieve these objectives by 1972. Some state laws cannot readily be overturned. In circumstances of this kind, our Commission has no plan to provoke a supremacy struggle between the party and state legislature. We recognize that conditions in some of the states may make such changes impossible. Although we do not expect state parties to violate state laws in order to satisfy the 1968 Convention mandate, there is one thing we do expect of them: simply put, we expect them to provide a party apparatus which allows for an effective test of leadership.

The most striking aspect of the politics of 1968 was that so many people who were engaged in active dissent from the policies of the incumbent Administration were using the traditional avenues of party politics to channel that dissent. The efforts of these people to make the system respond to their demands were instrumental in demonstrating how isolated the American parties are from their constituencies. Within the Democratic party, in state after state, rank-and-file efforts to participate in the first stage of the nominating process revealed that access was generally difficult, and, even when achieved, influence might still be minimal. Participation was often costly, sometimes completely illusory, and, in not a few instances, impossible.

The involvement of more people in the political process is a matter of life or death for our parties. Political parties are by no means the only way of organizing our political life. The media, especially television, offer direct access to the public. And some see an ominous alternative in the possibilities of the streets.

For too long now we have viewed our parties as private affairs—the property of the bosses, the large contributors, and the incumbent politicians. In the Progressive Era, people thought they could avoid boss politics by passing Presidential primary laws. They were wrong. History has shown that the primaries can be manipulated.

In 1968, parties—and specifically the nominating process—still belonged to the select few. Ed Costikyan, a respected New York politician long active in reform politics, has remarked that, "The first thing Presidential candidates should realize is that delegates are not free agents, nor are they individuals subject to persuasion. A delegate is the property of his leader." This was all too true in 1968. In more cases than we might care to admit, delegates were selected to nominate candidates for President of the United States without any opportunity for public participation.

But things are changing. The courts are beginning to take an interest in the business of political parties. And the work of our Commission is beginning to bear fruit. In over thirty states the Democratic party has established reform commissions which are exploring the hard questions of greater public access to party processes. In some of the most closed states of 1968, rules and laws have been changed to ensure more democratic procedures for the 1972 Convention.

I know that there is a long way to go. I also know that the vitality of the Democratic party will probably involve more than mere structural changes. Participation will increase only as people see the political parties as responsive to their needs and concerns.

Political parties must serve as more than just conduits by which people secure public office. They must address themselves seriously to the social problems and major issues of public policy which face our nation. But, as a first step, we must immediately open the door to all of those people who are or may be inclined to use political parties to serve the ends they seek. This is what reform of the Democratic party is all about.

We are in the process of invigorating our party with a massive injection of democracy. The day of the bosses is all but over. My optimism may be premature, but I do not think there will be another Chicago.

Study Questions

1. If the electoral college is abolished and the President is to be elected by direct vote, which areas of the nation would get more emphasis? Why? Would this change affect Presidential politics? Why? Would this change take away control from professional party leaders? Discuss.

2. In what ways does decision-making at the national party convention become a bargaining system? Give specific examples.
3. List the various electoral reforms. Discuss fully and critically the advantages and disadvantages of each proposal.
4. List and critically discuss the proposals suggested by the McGovern Commission.

Suggestions for Further Reading

Campbell, Angus, et al. The American Voter. New York: John Wiley & Sons, Inc., 1960.

Campbell, Angus, et al. The Voter Decides. New York: Harper & Row, Publishers, 1954.

David, Paul T., Malcolm Moos, and Ralph M. Goldman. Presidential Nominating Politics. Baltimore, Maryland: The Johns Hopkins Press, 1954, 5 volumes.

David, Paul T., Ralph M. Goldman, and Richard C. Bois. The Politics of National Party Conventions. Paperback edition, K. Sproul, (ed.) Washington, D.C.: The Brookings Institution, 1960.

Eulau, H., Samuel J. Eldersveld, and Morris Janowitz, (eds.) Political Behavior. New York: The Free Press, 1959.

Heard, Alexander. The Costs of Democracy. Chapel Hill, North Carolina: University of North Carolina Press, 1960.

Jennings, M. Kent, and L. Harmon (eds.) The Electoral Process. Englewood Cliffs, New Jersey: Prentice-Hall, Inc., 1966.

Key, V. O., Jr. The Responsible Electorate. Cambridge, Massachusetts: Harvard University Press, 1966.

Kelley, Stanley, Jr. Political Campaigning: Problems in Creating an Informed Electorate. Washington, D.C.: The Brookings Institution, 1960.

Lane, Robert E. Political Life. New York: The Free Press, 1959.

Lazarsfeld, Paul F., et al. The People's Choice: How the Voter Makes Up His Mind in a Presidential Campaign. New York: Duell, Sloan, and Pearce-Meredith Press, 1944.

Levin, Murray B. Kennedy Campaigning: The System and the Style as Practiced by Senator Edward Kennedy. Boston: Beacon Press, 1966.

Ogden, Daniel M., Jr., and Arthur L. Petersen. Electing the President. Rev. ed. San Francisco, California: Chandler Publishing Company, 1968.

Polsby, Nelson W. and Aaron B. Wildavsky, Presidential Elections: Strategies of American Electoral Politics. 2nd ed. New York: Charles Scribner's Sons, 1968.

Schattschneider, Elmer E. The Semisovereign People. New York: Holt, Rinehart and Winston, 1960.

Shadegg, Stephen. What Happened to Goldwater? New York: Holt, Rinehart and Winston, 1965.

Sorenson, Theodore C. Kennedy. New York: Harper & Row, 1965.

Stone, Irving. They Also Ran. New York: Pyramid Books, 1964.

Tillet, Paul (ed.) Inside Politics: The National Conventions. Dobbs Ferry, New York: Oceana Publishing Company, 1960.

U.S. Congress, Senate, 1956 General Election Campaigns. Washington: Government Printing Office, 1957.

White, F. Clifton. Suite 3505. New Rochelle, New York: Arlington House, 1967.

White, Theodore H. *The Making of the President, 1960.* New York: Atheneum Publishers, 1961.

White, Theodore H. *The Making of the President, 1964.* New York: Atheneum, 1965.

Wilmerding, Lucius. *The Electoral College.* Boston: Beacon Press, 1964.

PART EIGHT

The Congress

Congress, as the most representative branch within the American political system, is probably the major institutional symbol of the democratic creed. The Congressman represents a constituency to the extent he is authorized to speak for it in proposing policies or making binding commitments. Decentralization characterizes the legislative process. There are certain features of Congress which contribute to the fragmentation of power: bicameralism, federalism, partisan organization, and legislative procedures which can lead to delay and frustration. Decentralization of power, however, provides easy access to pressure groups to influence public policies.

In their article, "Constituency Influence in Congress," Warren E. Miller and Donald E. Stokes seek to test certain assumptions about representation made by classical political theorists. The authors attempt to assess the conditions of constituency influence and the control by those constituents over the congressman. The "model" or theory used—drawn from classical conceptions of representation—represents the constituent as affecting the representative both directly and through the representative's perception of the constituent's attitudes. In the context of a democratic representative system, it is important, of course to understand the manner in which a congressman (or other representative) does in fact represent his constitutents. To this end Miller and Stokes make a contribution to an understanding of the American system.

Former Senator Joseph S. Clark discusses what the Senate establishment means and how it operates. He believes that the Senate establishment is an undemocratic and a self-perpetuating oligarchy. He criticizes the seniority system and states that committee assignments are in the hands of the establishment, which is bipartisan. He feels that the rules of the Senate are obsolete and that liberal Democrats are represented sparsely, if at all, in the Senate establishment. He alludes to the 1913 revolution in the United States Senate and the failure of repeated efforts to change the present Senate rules.

Stephen K. Bailey examines congressional responsibility in terms of ethical standards for an individual Congressman and in terms of norms for Congress as a whole. He claims that congressmen by and large adhere to high standards of personal and group conduct. Bailey, however, points out two ethical problems: campaign finance and conflict of interest. He discusses the Bobby Baker case and some of the suggested reforms in campaign finance laws and in cases involving conflict of interest.

Congress has taken no action to revise laws governing campaign costs and conflict of interest. It is imperative that Congress retain public confidence. Bailey offers and discusses four measures of performance dealing with the following: (1) executive-legislative relations and party responsibility; (2) legislative review and oversight of administration; (3) representativeness of the House; and (4) the machinery of Congress.

Congress alone can work out acceptable and realistic guidelines to improve its performance. Congress is concerned with finding "rules and procedures which will make its new role possible and viable." Congress, to be sure, remains the major bastion of freedom.

CONSTITUENCY INFLUENCE IN CONGRESS

WARREN E. MILLER AND DONALD E. STOKES

Substantial constituency influence over the lower house of Congress is commonly thought to be both a normative principle and a factual truth of American government. From their draft constitution we may assume the Founding Fathers expected it, and many political scientists feel, regretfully, that the Framers' wish has come all too true. Nevertheless, much of the evidence of constituency control rests on inference. The fact that our House of Representatives, especially by comparison with the House of Commons, has irregular party voting does not of itself indicate that Congressmen deviate from party in response to local pressure. And even more, the fact that many Congressmen *feel* pressure from home does not of itself establish that the local constituency is performing any of the acts that a reasonable definition of control would imply.

SOURCE: Warren E. Miller and Donald E. Stokes, "Constituency Influence in Congress," *The American Political Science Review*, 57 (March 1963), 45–56. Reprinted by permission. Some footnotes have been deleted.

I. CONSTITUENCY CONTROL IN THE NORMATIVE
THEORY OF REPRESENTATION

Control by the local constituency is at one pole of *both* the great normative controversies about representation that have arisen in modern times. It is generally recognized that constituency control is opposite to the conception of representation associated with Edmund Burke. Burke wanted the representative to serve the constituency's *interest* but not its *will*, and the extent to which the representative should be compelled by electoral sanctions to follow the "mandate" of his constituents has been at the heart of the ensuing controversy as it has continued for a century and a half.

Constituency control also is opposite to the conception of government by responsible national parties. This is widely seen, yet the point is rarely connected with normative discussions of representation. Indeed, it is remarkable how little attention has been given to the model of representation implicit in the doctrine of a "responsible two-party system." When the subject of representation is broached among political scientists the classical argument between Burke and his opponents is likely to come at once to mind. So great is Burke's influence that the antithesis he proposed still provides the categories of thought used in contemporary treatments of representation despite the fact that many students of politics today would advocate a relationship between representative and constituency that fits *neither* position of the mandate-independence controversy.

The conception of representation implicit in the doctrine of responsible parties shares the idea of popular control with the instructed-delegate model. Both are versions of popular sovereignty. But "the people" of the responsible two-party system are conceived in terms of a national rather than a local constituency. Candidates for legislative office appeal to the electorate in terms of a *national* party program and leadership, to which, if elected, they will be committed. Expressions of policy preference by the local district are reduced to endorsements of one or another of these programs, and the local district retains only the arithmetical significance that whichever party can rally to its program the greater number of supporters in the district will control its legislative seat.

No one tradition of representation has entirely dominated American practice. Elements of the Burkean, instructed-delegate, and responsible party models can all be found in our political life. Yet if the American system has elements of all three, a good deal depends on how they are combined. Especially critical is the question whether different models of representation apply to different public issues. Is the saliency of legislative action to the public so different in quality and degree on different issues that the legislator is subject to very different constraints from his constituency? Does the legislator have a single generalized mode of response to his constituency that is rooted in a normative belief about the representative's role or does the same legislator respond to his constituency differently on different issues? More evidence is needed on matters so fundamental to our system.

II. AN EMPIRICAL STUDY OF REPRESENTATION

To extend what we know of representation in the American Congress the Survey Research Center of The University of Michigan interviewed the incumbent Congressman, his non-incumbent opponent (if any), and a sample of constituents in each of 116 congressional districts, which were themselves a probability sample of all districts. These interviews, conducted immediately after the congressional election of 1958, explored a wide range of attitudes and perceptions held by the individuals who play the reciprocal roles of the representative relation in national government. The distinguishing feature of this research is, of course, that it sought direct information from both constituent and legislator (actual and aspiring). To this fund of comparative interview data has been added information about the roll call votes of our sample of Congressmen and the political and social characteristics of the districts they represent.

Many students of politics, with excellent reason, have been sensitive to possible ties between representative and constituent that have little to do with issues of public policy. For example, ethnic identifications may cement a legislator in the affections of his district, whatever (within limits) his stands on issues. And many Congressmen keep their tenure of office secure by skillful provision of district benefits ranging from free literature to major federal projects. In the full study of which this analysis is part we have explored several bases of constituency support that have little to do with policy issues. Nevertheless, the question how the representative should make up his mind on legislative issues is what the classical arguments over representation are all about, and we have given a central place to a comparison of the policy preferences of constituents and Representatives and to a causal analysis of the relation between the two.

In view of the electorate's scanty information about government it was not at all clear in advance that such a comparison could be made. Some of the more buoyant advocates of popular sovereignty have regarded the citizen as a kind of kibitzer who looks over the shoulder of his representative at the legislative game. Kibitzer and player may disagree as to which card should be played, but they were at least thought to share a common understanding of what the alternatives are.

No one familiar with the findings of research on mass electorates could accept this view of the citizen. Far from looking over the shoulder of their Congressmen at the legislative game, most Americans are almost totally uninformed about legislative issues in Washington. At best the average citizen may be said to have some general ideas about how the country should be run, which he is able to use in responding to particular questions about what the government ought to do. For example, survey studies have shown that most people have a general (though differing) conception of how far government should go to achieve social and economic welfare objectives and that these convictions fix their response to various particular questions about actions government might take.[4]

What makes it possible to compare the policy preferences of constituents and Representatives despite the public's low awareness of legislative affairs is the fact that Congressmen themselves respond to many issues in terms of fairly broad evaluative dimensions. Undoubtedly policy alternatives are judged in the executive agencies and the specialized committees of the Congress by criteria that are relatively complex and specific to the policies at issue. But a good deal of evidence goes to show that when proposals come before the House as a whole they are judged on the basis of more general evaluative dimensions.[5] For example, most Congressmen, too, seem to have a general conception of how far government should go in the area of domestic social and economic welfare, and these general positions apparently orient their roll call votes on a number of particular social welfare issues.

It follows that such a broad evaluative dimension can be used to compare the policy preferences of constituents and Representatives despite the low state of the public's information about politics. In this study three such dimensions have been drawn from our voter interviews and from congressional interviews and roll call records. As suggested above, one of these has to do with approval of government action in the social welfare field, the primary domestic issue of the New Deal-Fair Deal (and New Frontier) eras. A second dimension has to do with support for American involvement in foreign affairs, a latter-day version of the isolationist-internationalist continuum. A third dimension has to do with approval of federal action to protect the civil rights of Negroes.[6]

Because our research focused on these three dimensions, our analysis of constituency influence is limited to these areas of policy. No point has been more energetically or usefully made by those who have sought to clarify the

---

[4] See Angus Campbell, Philip E. Converse, Warren E. Miller, and Donald E. Stokes, *The American Voter* (New York, 1960), pp. 194–209.

[5] This conclusion, fully supported by our own work for later Congresses, is one of the main findings to be drawn from the work of Duncan MacRae on roll call voting in the House of Representatives. See his *Dimensions of Congressional Voting: A Statistical Study of the House of Representatives in the Eighty-First Congress* (Berkeley and Los Angeles: University of California Press, 1958). . . .

[6] The content of the three issue domains may be suggested by some of the roll call and interview items used. In the area of social welfare these included the issues of public housing, public power, aid to education, and government's role in maintaining full employment. In the area of foreign involvement the items included the issues of foreign economic aid, military aid, sending troops abroad, and aid to neutrals. In the area of civil rights the items included the issues of school desegregation, fair employment, and the protection of Negro voting rights.

concepts of power and influence than the necessity of specifying the acts *with respect to which* one actor has power or influence or control over another.[7] Therefore, the scope or range of influence for our analysis is the collection of legislative issues falling within our three policy domains. We are not able to say how much control the local constituency may or may not have over *all* actions of its Representative, and there may well be pork-barrel issues or other matters of peculiar relevance to the district on which the relation of Congressman to constituency is quite distinctive. However, few observers of contemporary politics would regard the issues of government provision of social and economic welfare, of American involvement in world affairs, and of federal action in behalf of the Negro as constituting a trivial range of action. Indeed, these domains together include most of the great issues that have come before Congress in recent years.

In each policy domain we have used the procedures of cumulative scaling, as developed by Louis Guttman and others, to order our samples of Congressmen, of opposing candidates, and of voters. In each domain Congressmen were ranked once according to their roll call votes in the House and again according to the attitudes they revealed in our confidential interviews. These two orderings are by no means identical, nor are the discrepancies due simply to uncertainties of measurement. Opposing candidates also were ranked in each policy domain according to the attitudes they revealed in our interviews. The nationwide sample of constituents was ordered in each domain, and by averaging the attitude scores of all constituents living in the same districts, whole constituencies were ranked on each dimension so that the views of Congressmen could be compared with those of their constituencies. Finally, by considering only the constituents in each district who share some characteristic (voting for the incumbent, say) we were able to order these fractions of districts so that the opinions of Congressmen could be compared with those, for example, of the dominant electoral elements of their districts.

In each policy domain, crossing the rankings of Congressmen and their constituencies gives an empirical measure of the extent of policy agreement between legislator and district. In the period of our research this procedure reveals very different degrees of policy congruence across the three issue domains. On questions of social and economic welfare there is considerable agreement between Representative and district, expressed by a correlation of approximately 0.3. This coefficient is, of course, very much less than the limiting value of 1.0, indicating that a number of Congressmen are, relatively speaking, more or less "liberal" than their districts. However, on the question of foreign involvement there is no discernible agreement between legislator

---

[7] Because this point has been so widely discussed it has inevitably attracted a variety of terms. Dahl denotes the acts of *a* whose performance *A* is able to influence as the *scope* of *A*'s power. See Robert A. Dahl, "The Concept of Power," *Behavioral Science*, Vol. 2 (July 1957), pp. 201–215.

and district whatever. Indeed, as if to emphasize the point, the coefficient expressing this relation is slightly negative (−0.09), although not significantly so in a statistical sense. It is in the domain of civil rights that the rankings of Congressmen and constituencies most nearly agree. When we took our measurements in the late 1950s the correlation of congressional roll call behavior with constituency opinion on questions affecting the Negro was nearly 0.6.

The description of policy agreement that these three simple correlations give can be a starting-point for a wide range of analyses. For example, the significance of party competition in the district for policy representation can be explored by comparing the agreement between district and Congressman with the agreement between the district and the Congressman's non-incumbent opponent. Alternatively, the significance of choosing Representatives from single-member districts by popular majority can be explored by comparing the agreement between the Congressman and his own supporters with the agreement between the Congressman and the supporters of his opponent. Taking *both* party competition and majority rule into account magnifies rather spectacularly some of the coefficients reported here. This is most true in the domain of social welfare, where attitudes both of candidates and of voters are most polarized along party lines. Whereas the correlation between the constituency majority and congressional roll call votes is nearly +0.4 on social welfare policy, the correlation of the district majority with the non-incumbent candidate is −0.4. This difference, amounting to almost 0.8, between these two coefficients is an indicator of what the dominant electoral element of the constituency gets on the average by choosing the Congressman it has and excluding his opponent from office.

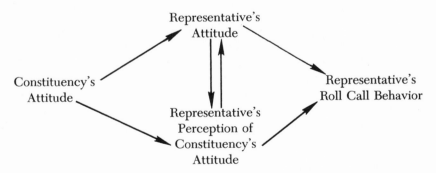

FIGURE 1. Connections between a Constituency's attitude and its Representative's roll call behavior

These three coefficients are also the starting-point for a casual analysis of the relation of constituency to representative, the main problem of this paper. At least on social welfare and Negro rights a measurable degree of congruence is found between district and legislator. Is this agreement due to constituency influence in Congress, or is it to be attributed to other causes? If this question is to have a satisfactory answer the conditions that are necessary and sufficient to assure constituency control must be stated and compared with the available empirical evidence.

III. THE CONDITIONS OF CONSTITUENCY INFLUENCE

Broadly speaking, the constituency can control the policy actions of the Representative in two alternative ways. The first of these is for the district to choose a Representative who so shares its views that in following his own convictions he does his constituents' will. In this case district opinion and the Congressman's actions are connected through the Representative's own policy attitudes. The second means of constituency control is for the Congressman to follow his (at least tolerably accurate) perceptions of district attitude in order to win re-election. In this case constituency opinion and the Congressman's actions are connected through his perception of what the district wants.[12]

These two paths of constituency control are presented schematically in Figure 1. As the figure suggests, each path has two steps, one connecting the constituency's attitude with an "intervening" attitude or perception, the other connecting this attitude or perception with the Representative's roll call behavior. Out of respect for the processes by which the human actor achieves cognitive congruence we have also drawn arrows between the two intervening factors, since the Congressman probably tends to see his district as having the same opinion as his own and also tends, over time, to bring his own opinion into line with the district's. The inclusion of these arrows calls attention to two other possible influence paths, each consisting of *three* steps, although these additional paths will turn out to be of relatively slight importance empirically.

Neither of the main influence paths of Figure 1 will connect the final roll call vote to the constituency's views if either of its steps is blocked. From this, two necessary conditions of constituency influence can be stated: *first,* the Representative's votes in the House must agree substantially with his own policy views or his perceptions of the district's views, and not be determined entirely by other influences to which the Congressman is exposed; and, *sec-*

---

[12] A third type of connection, excluded here, might obtain between district and Congressman if the Representative accedes to what he thinks the district wants because he believes that to be what a representative *ought* to do, whether or not it is necessary for re-election. We leave this type of connection out of our account here because we conceive an influence relation as one in which control is not voluntarily accepted or rejected by someone subject to it. Of course, this possible connection between district and Representative is not any the less interesting because it falls outside our definition of influence or control, and we have given a good deal of attention to it in the broader study of which this analysis is part.

ond, the attitudes or perceptions governing the Representative's acts must correspond, at least imperfectly, to the district's actual opinions. It would be difficult to describe the relation of constituency to Representative as one of control unless these conditions are met.[13]

Yet these two requirements are not sufficient to assure control. A *third* condition must also be satisfied: the constituency must in some measure take the policy views of candidates into account in choosing a Representative. If it does not, agreement between district and Congressman may arise for reasons that cannot rationally be brought within the idea of control. For example, such agreement may simply reflect the fact that a Representative drawn from a given area is likely, by pure statistical probability, to share its dominant values, without his acceptance or rejection of these ever having been a matter of consequence to his electors.

IV. EVIDENCE OF CONTROL: CONGRESSIONAL ATTITUDES AND PERCEPTIONS

How well are these conditions met in the relation of American Congressmen to their constituents? There is little question that the first is substantially satisfied; the evidence of our research indicates that members of the House do in fact vote both their own policy views and their perceptions of their constituents' views, at least on issues of social welfare, foreign involvement, and civil rights. If these two intervening factors are used to predict roll call votes, the prediction is quite successful. Their multiple correlation with roll call position is 0.7 for social welfare, 0.6 for foreign involvement, and 0.9 for civil rights; the last figure is especially persuasive. What is more, both the Congressman's own convictions and his perceptions of district opinion make a distinct contribution to his roll call behavior. In each of the three domains the prediction of roll call votes is surer if it is made from both factors rather than from either alone.

Lest the strong influence that the Congressman's views and his perception of district views have on roll call behavior appear somehow foreordained— and, consequently, this finding seem a trivial one—it is worth taking a sidewise glance at the potency of possible other forces on the Representative's vote. In the area of foreign policy, for example, a number of Congressmen are disposed to follow the administration's advice, whatever they or their districts think. For those who are, the multiple correlation of roll call behavior with the Representative's own foreign policy views and his perception of district

---

[13] It scarcely needs to be said that demonstrating *some* constituency influence would not imply that the Representative's behavior is *wholly* determined by constituency pressures. The legislator acts in a complex institutional setting in which he is subject to a wide variety of influences. The constituency can exercise a genuine measure of control without driving all other influences from the Representative's life space.

views is a mere 0.2. Other findings could be cited to support the point that the influence of the Congressman's own preferences and those he attributes to the district is extremely variable. Yet in the House as a whole over the three policy domains the influence of these forces is quite strong.

The connections of congressional attitudes and perceptions with actual constituency opinion are weaker. If policy agreement between district and

TABLE 1.

Correlations of Constituency Attitudes

Policy Domain	Correlation of Constituency Attitude with	
	Representative's Perception of Constituency Attitude	Representative's Own Attitude
Social welfare	.17	.21
Foreign involvement	.19	.06
Civil rights	.63	.39

Representative is moderate and variable across the policy domains, as it is, this is to be explained much more in terms of the second condition of constituency control than the first. The Representative's attitudes and perceptions most nearly match true opinion in his district on the issues of Negro rights. Reflecting the charged and polarized nature of this area, the correlation of actual district opinion with perceived opinion is greater than 0.6, and the correlation of district attitude with the Representative's own attitude is nearly 0.4, as shown by Table 1. But the comparable correlations for foreign involvement are much smaller—indeed almost negligible. And the coefficients for social welfare are also smaller, although a detailed presentation of findings in this area would show that the Representative's perceptions and attitudes are more strongly associated with the attitude of his electoral *majority* than they are with the attitudes of the constituency as a whole.

Knowing this much about the various paths that may lead, directly or indirectly, from constituency attitude to roll call vote, we can assess their relative importance. Since the alternative influence chains have links of unequal strength, the full chains will not in general be equally strong, and these differences are of great importance in the relation of Representative to constituency. For the domain of civil rights Figure 2 assembles all the intercorrelations of the variables of our system. As the figure shows, the root correlation of constituency attitude with roll call behavior in this domain is 0.57. How much of this policy congruence can be accounted for by the influence path involving the Representative's attitude? And how much by the path involving his perception of constituency opinion? When the intercorrelations of the sys-

Civil rights: intercorrelations

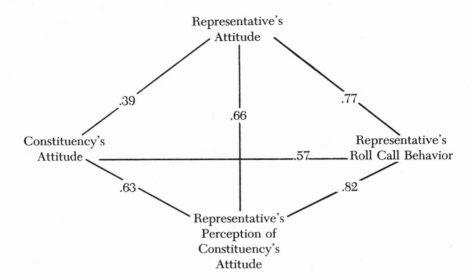

FIGURE 2. Intercorrelations of Variables pertaining to Civil Rights

tem are interpreted in the light of what we assume its causal structure to be,
it is influence passing through the Congressman's perception of the district's
views that is found to be preeminently important. Under the least favorable
assumption as to its importance, this path is found to account for more than
twice as much of the variance of roll call behavior as the paths involving the
Representative's own attitude. However, when this same procedure is applied
to our social welfare data, the results suggest that the direct connection of
constituency and roll call through the Congressman's own attitude is the most
important of the alternative paths. The reversal of the relative importance of
the two paths as we move from civil rights to social welfare is one of the most
striking findings of this analysis.

V. EVIDENCE OF CONTROL: ELECTORAL BEHAVIOR

Of the three conditions of constituency influence, the requirement that the
electorate take account of the policy positions of the candidates is the hardest
to match with empirical evidence. Indeed, given the limited information the
average voter carries to the polls, the public might be thought incompetent to
perform any task of appraisal. Of constituents living in congressional districts
where there was a contest between a Republican and a Democrat in 1958,
less than one in five said they had read or heard something about both candi-

dates, and well over half conceded they had read or heard nothing about either. And these proportions are not much better when they are based only on the part of the sample, not much more than half, that reported voting for Congress in 1958. The extent of awareness of the candidates among voters is indicated in Table 2. As the table shows, even of the portion of the public that was sufficiently interested to vote, almost half had read or heard nothing about either candidate.

Just how low a hurdle our respondents had to clear in saying they had read

TABLE 2.

Awareness of Congressional Candidates
among Voters, 1958

		Read or Heard Something About Incumbent[a]		
		Yes	No	
Read or Heard Something About Non-Incumbent	Yes	24	5	29
	No	25	46	71
		49	51	100%

[a] In order to include all districts where the House seat was contested in 1958 this table retains ten constituencies in which the incumbent Congressman did not seek re-election. Candidates of the retiring incumbent's party in these districts are treated here as if they were incumbents. Were these figures to be calculated only for constituencies in which an incumbent sought re-election, no entry in this four-fold table would differ from that given by more than two percent.

or heard something about a candidate is indicated by detailed qualitative analysis of the information constituents *were* able to associate with congressional candidates. Except in rare cases, what the voters "knew" was confined to diffuse evaluative judgments about the candidate: "he's a good man," "he understands the problems," and so forth. Of detailed information about policy stands not more than a chemical trace was found. Among the comments about the candidates given in response to an extended series of free-answer questions, less than two percent had to do with stands in our three policy domains; indeed, only about three comments in every hundred had to do with legislative issues of *any* description.[17]

This evidence that the behavior of the electorate is largely unaffected by knowledge of the policy positions of the candidates is complemented by evi-

[17] What is more, the electorate's awareness of Congress as a whole appears quite limited. A majority of the public was unable to say in 1958 which of the two parties had controlled the Congress during the preceding two years. Some people were confused by the coexistence of a Republican President and a Democratic Congress. But for most people this was simply an elementary fact about congressional affairs to which they were not privy.

dence about the forces that *do* shape the voters' choices among congressional candidates. The primary basis of voting in American congressional elections is identification with party. In 1958 only one vote in twenty was cast by persons without any sort of party loyalty. And among those who did have a party identification, only one in ten voted against their party. As a result, something like 84 percent of the vote that year was cast by party identifiers voting their usual party line. What is more, traditional party voting is seldom connected with current legislative issues. As the party loyalists in a nation-wide sample of voters told us what they liked and disliked about the parties in 1958, only a small fraction of the comments (about 15 percent) dealt with current issues of public policy.[18]

Yet the idea of reward or punishment at the polls for legislative stands is familiar to members of Congress, who feel that they and their records are quite visible to their constituents. Of our sample of Congressmen who were opposed for re-election in 1958, more than four-fifths said the outcome in their districts had been strongly influenced by the electorate's response to their records and personal standing. Indeed, this belief is clear enough to present a notable contradiction: Congressmen feel that their individual legislative actions may have considerable impact on the electorate, yet some simple facts about the Representative's salience to his constituents imply that this could hardly be true.

In some measure this contradiction is to be explained by the tendency of Congressmen to overestimate their visibility to the local public, a tendency that reflects the difficulties of the Representative in forming a correct judgment of constituent opinion. The communication most Congressmen have with their districts inevitably puts them in touch with organized groups and with individuals who are relatively well informed about politics. The Representative knows his constituents mostly from dealing with people who *do* write letters, who *will* attend meetings, who *have* an interest in his legislative stands. As a result, his sample of contacts with a constituency of several hundred thousand people is heavily biased: even the contacts he apparently makes at random are likely to be with people who grossly overrepresent the degree of political information and interest in the constituency as a whole.

But the contradiction is also to be explained by several aspects of the Representative's electoral situation that are of great importance to the question of constituency influence. The first of these is implicit in what has already been said. Because of the pervasive effects of party loyalties, no candidate for Congress starts from scratch in putting together an electoral majority. The Congressman is a dealer in increments and margins. He starts with a stratum of hardened party voters, and if the stratum is broad enough he can have a

[18] For a more extended analysis of forces on the congressional vote, see Donald E. Stokes and Warren E. Miller, "Party Government and the Saliency of Congress," *Public Opinion Quarterly*, Vol. 26 (Winter 1962), pp. 531–546.

measurable influence on his chance of survival simply by attracting a small additional element of the electorate—or by not losing a larger one. Therefore, his record may have a very real bearing on his electoral success or failure without most of his constituents ever knowing what that record is.

Second, the relation of Congressman to voter is not a simple bilateral one but is complicated by the presence of all manner of intermediaries: the local party, economic interests, the news media, racial and nationality organizations, and so forth. Such is the lore of American politics, as it is known to any political scientist. Very often the Representative reaches the mass public through these mediating agencies, and the information about himself and his record may be considerably transformed as it diffuses out to the electorate in two or more stages. As a result, the public—or parts of it—may get simple positive or negative cues about the Congressman which were provoked by his legislative actions but which no longer have a recognizable issue content.

Third, for most Congressmen most of the time the electorate's sanctions are potential rather than actual. Particularly the Representative from a safe district may feel his proper legislative strategy is to avoid giving opponents in his own party or outside of it material they can use against him. As the Congressman pursues this strategy he may write a legislative record that never becomes very well known to his constituents; if it doesn't win votes, neither will it lose any. This is clearly the situation of most southern Congressmen in dealing with the issue of Negro rights. By voting correctly on this issue they are unlikely to increase their visibility to constituents. Nevertheless, the fact of constituency influence, backed by potential sanctions at the polls, is real enough.

TABLE 3.

Awareness of Congressional Candidates among Voters in Arkansas Fifth District, 1958

		Read or Heard Something About Hays		
		Yes	No	
Read or Heard Something About Alford	Yes	100	0	100
	No	0	0	0
		100	0	100%

That these potential sanctions are all too real is best illustrated in the election of 1958 by the reprisal against Representative Brooks Hays in Arkansas'

Fifth District.[19] Although the perception of Congressman Hays as too moderate on civil rights resulted more from his service as intermediary between the White House and Governor Faubus in the Little Rock school crisis than from his record in the House, the victory of Dale Alford as a write-in candidate was a striking reminder of what can happen to a Congressman who gives his foes a powerful issue to use against him. The extraordinary involvement of the public in this race can be seen by comparing how well the candidates were known in this constituency with the awareness of the candidates shown by Table 2 above for the country as a whole. As Table 3 indicates, not a single voter in our sample of Arkansas' Fifth District was unaware of either candidate.[20] What is more, these interviews show that Hays was regarded both by his supporters and his opponents as more moderate than Alford on civil rights and that this perception brought his defeat. In some measure, what happened in Little Rock in 1958 can happen anywhere, and our Congressmen ought not to be entirely disbelieved in what they say about their impact at the polls. Indeed, they may be under genuine pressure from the voters even while they are the forgotten men of national elections.

VI. CONCLUSION

Therefore, although the conditions of constituency influence are not equally satisfied, they are met well enough to give the local constituency a measure of control over the actions of its Representatives. Best satisfied is the requirement about motivational influences on the Congressman: our evidence shows that the Representative's roll call behavior is strongly influenced by his own policy preferences and by his perception of preferences held by the constituency. However, the conditions of influence that presuppose effective communication between Congressman and district are much less well met. The Representative has very imperfect information about the issue preferences of his constituency, and the constituency's awareness of the policy stands of the Representative ordinarily is slight.

The findings of this analysis heavily underscore the fact that no single tradition of representation fully accords with the realities of American legislative politics. The American system *is* a mixture, to which the Burkean, instructed-delegate, and responsible-party models all can be said to have contributed elements. Moreover, variations in the representative relation are most likely

---

[19] For an account of this episode, see Corinne Silverman, "The Little Rock Story," Inter-University Case Program series, reprinted in Edwin A. Bock and Alan K. Campbell, eds., *Case Studies in American Government* (Englewood Cliffs, 1962), pp. 1–46.

[20] The sample of this constituency was limited to twenty-three persons of whom thirteen voted. However, despite the small number of cases the probability that the difference in awareness between this constituency and the country generally as the result only of sampling variations is much less than one in a thousand.

to occur as we move from one policy domain to another. No single, generalized configuration of attitudes and perceptions links Representative with constituency but rather several distinct patterns, and which of them is invoked depends very much on the issue involved.

The issue domain in which the relation of Congressman to constituency most nearly conforms to the instructed-delegate model is that of civil rights. This conclusion is supported by the importance of the influence-path passing through the Representative's perception of district opinion, although even in this domain the sense in which the constituency may be said to take the position of the candidate into account in reaching its electoral judgment should be carefully qualified.

The representative relation conforms most closely to the responsible-party model in the domain of social welfare. In this issue area, the arena of partisan conflict for a generation, the party symbol helps both constituency and Representative in the difficult process of communication between them. On the one hand, because Republican and Democratic voters tend to differ in what they would have government do, the Representative has some guide to district opinion simply by looking at the partisan division of the vote. On the other hand, because the two parties tend to recruit candidates who differ on the social welfare role of government, the constituency can infer the candidates' position with more than random accuracy from their party affiliation, even though what the constituency has learned directly about these stands is almost nothing. How faithful the representation of social welfare views is to the responsible-party model should not be exaggerated. Even in this policy domain, American practice departs widely from an ideal conception of party government. But in this domain, more than any other, political conflict has become a conflict of national parties in which constituency and Representative are known to each other primarily by their party association.

It would be too pat to say that the domain of foreign involvement conforms to the third model of representation, the conception promoted by Edmund Burke. Clearly it does in the sense that the Congressman looks elsewhere than to his district in making up his mind on foreign issues. However, the reliance he puts on the President and the Administration suggests that the calculation of where the public interest lies is often passed to the Executive on matters of foreign policy. Ironically, legislative initiative in foreign affairs has fallen victim to the very difficulties of gathering and appraising information that led Burke to argue that Parliament rather than the public ought to hold the power of decision. The background information and predictive skills that Burke thought the people lacked are held primarily by the modern Executive. As a result, the present role of the legislature in foreign affairs bears some resemblance to the role that Burke had in mind for the elitist, highly restricted *electorate* of his own day.

THE SENATE ESTABLISHMENT

JOSEPH S. CLARK

Mr. President, I desire to address the Senate on the subject of the Senate establishment and how it operates. Perhaps the first thing to do is to state what I mean by "the Senate establishment." Senators may recall that last May, Richard Rovere, the very able reporter who writes for magazines such as the New Yorker and Esquire . . . wrote an article on the establishment of the United States; and in the article he compared those who he thought ran America—although I suspect that to some extent he had his tongue in his cheek—with the British establishment, which is headed by the royal family, and includes the peers, whether hereditary or only for life, and most of the aristocracy, if not the plutocracy, of Great Britain and northern Ireland. . . .

● ● ●

I believe that the concept of an establishment in America is something which all of us who try to understand the sometimes almost inexplicable ways in which we in this country act would do well to contemplate. Just as Great Britain has its establishment and the United States of America perhaps has its establishment, so, the U.S. Senate has its establishment. I wish to discuss today what that establishment is, how it operates, and why in my opinion the present establishment is not operating in the interests of the future of the United States, or the future of the U.S. Senate, and certainly is not operating to the benefit of the future of the Democratic Party.

The Senate establishment, as I see it, after a relatively brief sojourn here—I am now in my seventh year—is almost the antithesis of democracy. It is not selected by any democratic process. It appears to be quite unresponsive to the caucuses of the two parties, be they Republican or Democratic. It is what might be called a self-perpetuating oligarchy with mild, but only mild, overtones of plutocracy. The way it operates is something like this:

There are a number of States, most of them Democratic, but one or two of them Republican, which inevitably and always return to the U.S. Senate members of one party, and under a custom which has grown up over the years of following the rule of seniority in making committee assignments, and in connection with the distribution of other perquisites of Senate tenure, the

SOURCE: Joseph S. Clark, "The Senate Establishment," *Congressional Record*, 88th Congress, First Session, Senate (February 19, 1963), pp. 2554–2555.

result has been that those who have been here longest have become chairmen of committees, and as such chairmen, have exercised virtual control over the distribution of favors, including committee assignments and other perquisites of office in the Senate, and largely—although not always, and not entirely, because there are exceptions—determine who shall be selected to posts of leadership in this body.

● ● ●

As I see it, the Senate establishment pretty well controls the assignment of Members to committees. How is that done? I think it is interesting to note that it is not only the present Senate establishment which does that. From time to time, going back at least to the early days of the present century, the same system prevailed. There have always been those who fought against the establishment, who thought that the Democratic caucus and the Republican caucus should determine who would select the members of committees and the other perquisites of office. One of the most eloquent men to speak in that vein was, at the time he spoke, a Republican. It was that very much revered and able Senator from Wisconsin, the elder Robert La Follette.

During the height of what was known as Aldrichism, referring to Nelson Aldrich, the eminent and conservative Senator from Rhode Island who left his mark for many years on the Senate, Senator La Follette said:

> Under the present system of choosing the standing committees of the U.S. Senate a party caucus is called. A chairman is authorized to appoint a committee on committees. The caucus adjourns. The committee on committees is thereafter appointed by the chairman of a caucus. It proceeds to determine the committee assignments of Senators. This places the selection of the membership of the standing committees completely in the hands of a majority of the committee on committees, because in practice the caucus ratifies the action of the committee and the Senate ratifies the action of the caucus. See now what has happened: The people have delegated us to represent them in the Senate. The Senate, in effect, has delegated its authority to party caucuses upon either side. The party caucus delegates its authority to a chairman to select a committee on committees. The committee on committees largely defers to the chairman of the committee on committees in the final decision as to committee assignments. The standing committees of the Senate as selected determine the fate of all bills; they report, shape, or suppress legislation practically at will.

That is what Robert La Follette had to say about the Senate establishment in the days around 1905 to 1910 and thereafter when Nelson Aldrich was the undoubted Republican leader of the Senate establishment of that day.

It was true then, as it is now, that the establishment was bipartisan. The senior ranking members of the minority party are a part of the establishment; and they, in conference—usually informal, always friendly—with their colleagues on the other side of the aisle pretty well decide who is going to do what to whom.

That is what is happening in the Senate today. That is what has happened in the Senate many times before. But it does not always happen in the Senate, and it need not happen in the Senate much longer. Whenever it does happen in the Senate, in a constantly shrinking world, in which change is inevitable, I suggest that the existence of that kind of oligarchical rule is a detriment to the national interest.

There was a very famous occasion when the rank and file of the Senate membership overturned the establishment and in a couple of years passed legislation—which had long been bottled up in previous Senates—as important to the welfare of the country as almost any other program in the long sweep of history.

I shall relate what happened in 1913, after Woodrow Wilson was elected President of the United States on a party platform which pledged to bring into legislative form the New Freedom—the program on which he defeated both William Howard Taft, seeking reelection to the Presidency, and Theodore Roosevelt, running on the Bull Moose ticket.

In 1913 the Democrats captured control of the Senate for the first time in 16 years. A majority of the Democratic Senators were progressive and espoused the progressive principles of the Baltimore platform, but the committee chairmanships and the important committee posts were to go to the conservative Democrats under the old seniority system in the Senate.

Note the striking analogy. A large majority of the Democratic Senators in the 88th Congress are also progressive. A majority of them support the Democratic platform adopted in Los Angeles in 1960. On that platform President Kennedy was swept into office by a very narrow majority.

We now stand at the beginning of the third session of what might be called a Kennedy Congress, but actually it is not a Kennedy Congress, and it seems to me that it is not going to be a Kennedy Congress. The principal reason why it is not going to be a Kennedy Congress, so far as the Senate is concerned, is, in my opinion, that we are operating under archaic, obsolete rules, customs, manners, procedures, and traditions—and because the operation under those obsolete and archaic setups is controlled by this oligarchical Senate establishment, a majority of the Members of which, by and large, are opposed to the program of the President.

I do not wish to overstate the case. There are able and effective Members of the establishment who will support the program of the President in many areas. There are a few Members of the establishment who will support the program of the President in some areas. But, by and large, the two-thirds majority of the Democratic Senators who are Kennedy men, and therefore liberals, and therefore want to get the country moving again, and therefore believe in the inevitability of change, are represented sparsely, if at all, in the Senate establishment.

I return now to a consideration of the situation of 1913. At that time, I point out again, the committee chairmanships and the important committee positions would have gone to conservative Democrats under the old seniority system in the Senate. The progressive Democrats, however, united to insure the passage of their progressive legislation and modified the Senate rules to aid in the translation of the Baltimore platform into legislation.

At that time there were 51 Democratic Senators, 44 Republicans, and 1 Progressive. Forty of the Democrats, 10 of the Republicans, and 1 Progressive—a total of 51—could be safely labeled as in sympathy with the important planks of the Baltimore platform and of the policy of President Woodrow Wilson. I refer to the currency, tariff, civil service reform, pure food, and health planks.

In all, the progressives of the three parties had a very slim majority in the Senate of 1913, but that majority was sufficient, and it enabled the Democratic Senators, with the aid of their Progressive colleague and of their friends in the Republican Party, to set aside the seniority system in the Senate, to displace senior committee chairmen, to replace the senior committee chairmen with young men, some of whom had not served in the Senate for more than 2 years; and, as a result of quiet meetings during different evenings in Washington they took over the Senate, reconstituted the membership of all committees, got rid of all the senior chairmen, and put their own men in.

A conference was held at Senator Luke Lea's home, to decide on a caucus leader, one who would be able to reconcile the differences with the conservative faction of the party and keep it united in the Senate with the progressive faction. Thirty Senators were present at that meeting at Senator Lea's home, and they agreed on John W. Kern, a Senator from Indiana with only 2 years' tenure in the Senate. Positions on certain important committees were given to men who deserved them because of seniority, but the memberships of various committees were packed with progressives, regardless of their seniority, and on several occasions the committee chairmen were themselves replaced. The old Senate procedures were changed to prevent a committee chairman from halting legislation arbitrarily. Instead of only the chairman, a majority of the committee might call the committee together at any time for consideration of a pending bill.

Mr. President, I have had before the Senate for the past 4 years a proposed rule which would do exactly that. It has been bottled up in the Committee on Rules and Administration. It has never seen the light of day.

In 1913 a majority of a majority of a committee was given power to name subcommittees to consider pending measures and to report to the full committee. I have had such a proposed rule pending in the Senate for the past 4 years, and it is still bottled up in the Committee on Rules and Administration.

A majority of a majority was given the power to name Members to confer with the House as to any bill over which the House and the Senate disagreed. I have had pending a proposed rule, bottled up in the Committee on Rules and Administration, which would accomplish the same result, although the text of the proposed rule is somewhat different.

The end results of the revolution of 1913 in the Senate of the United States were: First, emasculation of the old Senate seniority system; second, committee domination by the progressives, which meant the Wilson men; third, the Senate being democratized in terms of its rules and procedures; and fourth, the planks of the Baltimore platform being enacted into legislation.

I plead with my colleagues to do the same thing now—if not now, then next year—if not next year, then the year after—but let us get it done, while President Kennedy is still at the White House, if we want to preserve the Democratic Party for progressive principles, if we want to get the help of a number of our progressive friends on the Republican side—if we want to move this country forward and not be blocked by the hand of the past.

TOWARD A MORE RESPONSIBLE
CONGRESS

STEPHEN K. BAILEY

Responsibility is an ambiguous word. It may refer to the ethical behavior of individuals. It may refer to the collective behavior and accountability of a group or institution.

In this [essay] we shall take a brief look at both contexts: responsibility in terms of ethical standards for individuals in Congress; responsibility in terms of norms for the legislative branch as a whole.

CONGRESSIONAL ETHICS

In a tribute to Congress in June 1965, Vice President Hubert H. Humphrey said in part, "I have seen in the Halls of Congress more idealism, more humaneness, more compassion, more profiles of courage than in any other institution that I have ever known." [1] A decade and a half earlier, a U.S. senator

---

[1] Commencement Address, delivered at Syracuse University, Syracuse, New York, June 6, 1965.

SOURCE: Stephen K. Bailey, "Toward a More Responsible Congress," *The New Congress* (New York: St. Martin's Press, 1966), pp. 96–110. Reprinted by permission.

who had spent most of his life as a successful businessman said, "I have seen more [moral courage] in a day here in the Senate than the average business-man sees in a year, or even in a lifetime." [2]

Discounting the biases of club loyalty, these words of praise are reminders that the personal and public ethics of congressmen are far higher than cynics avow or than intermittent scandals in the press suggest. Like any other sampling of human beings, Congress has a few whose sense of probity is egregiously elastic. Like most social systems, Congress suffers from internal deferences and loyalties which are at times overly protective of wrongdoing. Like many professions (e.g., medicine, law, the ministry, business) politics sets or adjusts to standards of conduct that are internally comfortable and personally supportive even when they are socially harmful and/or ethically questionable. But faced with a myriad of temptations of power and money, congressmen by and large maintain high standards of personal and group conduct.

There are, however, two ethical jungles which need clearing: campaign finance and conflict of interest. Both areas are amenable to substantial improvement by adjustments in existing laws or by new laws providing for appropriate disclosure of extramural income and the external associations of congressmen and their staffs. Until such changes are made, Congress will bear a heavy, corrosive, and unnecessary burden of public suspicion and disapprobation, and in the case of campaign expenditures, will commit itself to a continuation of practices which violate the spirit if not the letter of the law.

A useful setting for a discussion of these issues may be found in the so-called "Bobby Baker investigations" held in the early 1960's. That case brought to light such a variety of questionable practices rooted in legislative influence that it furnishes a model of contemporary congressional practices needing correction. It also, by implication, indicates the major lines of essential reform.

Even an examination of the cast of characters is instructive. It included: (1) legislators and their powerfully situated assistants; (2) men identified with the money-raising end of political campaigns; (3) lobbyists acting as brokers between the buyers and sellers of influence; (4) outside interests and individuals standing to gain from association and affiliation with influence peddlers; (5) officials, public and private, whose discretionary judgment can grant or withhold things of value (licenses, loans, contracts, jobs, etc.). These were the interlocking roles played in the Bobby Baker drama. In a generic sense, it has ever been so.

[2] Senator William Benton. Testimony before the Douglas Subcommittee on Ethics. (U.S. Senate Committee on Labor and Public Welfare, *Hearings Before a Subcommittee to Study . . . the Establishment of a Commission on Ethics in Government*), 82nd Cong., 1st. Sess., June 19–July 11, 1951, p. 45.

Bobby Baker's Power

Bobby Baker's power derived from three sources: (1) his long and intimate knowledge of the Senate and of powerfully situated senators; (2) his position as Secretary of the Senate Majority; and (3) his position as Secretary-Treasurer of the Senate Democratic Campaign Committee. A word needs to be said about each of these.

He had first come to the Senate as a page at the age of 14. His talents of affability and shrewdness made him chief Democratic page at 16, chief of the Democratic cloakroom at 18, and Secretary of the Democratic Minority at 24. At 26, in 1955, he became Secretary to the Democratic Majority. Close to page-boy and cloakroom gossip for years, Baker absorbed a vast fund of information about the powerful men he observed. He came to know deference patterns and channels of influence. And he came to understand the horse trades of mutuality, compromise, and logrolling that at their best are the salvation of a free society, but at their worst are sinister and self-seeking.

To this knowledge of backstairs gossip Baker added an understanding of the substance and procedures of Senate business. After all, this was his business as clerk of the Democratic cloakroom and later Secretary of the Democratic Minority and then Majority. In this latter role he knew what bills were coming up on the floor and whether a particular senator's vote was needed. In the case of a senator's absence he arranged voting pairs, and usually he knew how individual senators would line up on any issue. On important roll calls he was available at the entrance to the floor of the Senate to give the Majority Leader's position. And on a host of matters, like office space, private bills, supplies, committee assignments, living quarters, or internal patronage, if Baker couldn't arrange matters, he knew who could.

The final ingredient in Baker's power came from his work for the Senate Democratic Campaign Committee. Here he was introduced to the realities of party finance; the expectations of large givers; the enormous return on investments supported by political influence; the availability of "credit" to those with proper connections.

With his intimate knowledge of the Senate, the string of indebtednesses owed him for favors rendered as Secretary of the Senate Majority, and his knowledge of the odorous financial fringe to the garment of politics, Baker parlayed his modest Senate salary into a $2,000,000 fortune.

Bobby Baker's Activities

A brief look at a few of the dozen or so cases investigated by Senate Committee on Rules and Administration in 1964 and 1965 yields some interesting lessons.[3]

[3] I have drawn particularly heavily upon the 1964 *Congressional Quarterly Almanac*, pp. 942–973, and upon the various relevant hearings and reports of the Senate Rules and Administration

Bobby Baker's activities came into the open as a result of the "Vending Contracts Case," a civil suit in which a former business associate charged that Baker had used influence to obtain contracts for Serv-U-Corp (a company in which Baker owned a substantial interest) in certain defense plants. The fact that there was no public registry of Senate employees' financial holdings or business associations had allowed Baker to function without the vigilant attention of members of the opposition party or of a sniffing and hungry press. Without the fortuitous circumstance of a private law suit, Baker's activities might have continued unnoticed.

The "Case of the D. C. Stadium" involved an insurance associate of Baker, Don B. Reynolds, who testified that Baker had helped him to secure a performance bond for a construction firm, in return for which Reynolds paid $4,000 (of the $10,000 commission) to Baker and $1,500 to the clerk of the House District of Columbia Committee. In addition, it was alleged that Baker had conspired with the contractor for the stadium, who happened to be Matthew McCloskey, treasurer of the Democratic National Committee, to make a sizable overpayment to Reynolds, of which $25,000 would be siphoned off for the 1960 Democratic Presidential campaign. Whether true or not, the testimony sketches a prototype of the symbiosis that links part of the construction industry to political influence via campaign contributions and personal pay-offs. No series of reforms can break entirely this kind of conspiracy. But changes in the methods of raising and reporting campaign money, and the proposed requirement of disclosure mentioned above, would go a long way toward improving the moral climate of American politics.

The "Case of the Freight Forwarders" concerned a lobbyist who, after successful passage of a bill favoring his clients, paid $5,000 to Baker's law partner. The latter deposited the check and wrote Baker another check for the same amount. The lobbyist testified that the payment to Baker was made for services unrelated to the passage of the bill. Here we see the outlines of perhaps the most widespread abuse of ethical standards: the practice of allowing one's law firm to benefit improperly from the office one holds. Congress has not even begun the process of sorting out effective bench marks to guide sound judgments in this area of ethical concern.

Another case involved the purchase of stock by Baker (through loans arranged for him by lobbyists) in a company whose value multiplied many times after a favorable tax ruling was secured from the Internal Revenue Service reportedly at the intervention of a congressman. Here again conflict of interest was the underlying issue.

In some ways the ethical lapses of Baker are less disturbing than the reaction of other senators to such deviations. At one point in the investigation when a transaction involving Senator George A. Smathers (D., Florida) was

Committee which conducted the Baker investigation over a sixteen-month period, from October 1963 to March 1965.

being discussed, Chairman B. Everett Jordan (D., North Carolina) was asked if Smathers would be called to testify. "We're not investigating Senators," replied the Chairman—leaving the problem of who will investigate senators if other senators will not. Perhaps the unhappiest aspect of the whole Bobby Baker episode was the sense conveyed to the public that the committee was attempting to cover up a situation which might be embarrassing to many influential people.

Recommendations for Reform: Conflicts of Interest

One result of the Baker affair was a resolution reported by the Senate Committee on Rules and Administration[4] which would require each senator and Senate employee earning more than $10,000 a year to file an annual report disclosing:

1. The businesses or professional activities in which he owned an interest equal to 50 percent or more of his annual rate of compensation;

2. The business or professional activities in which he served in a directing, managerial, or advisory capacity;

3. The professional firms in which he has a financial interest and which practice before any U. S. agency.

Senator Joseph S. Clark (D., Pennsylvania) wished to broaden the committee resolution. His suggested reforms included disclosure of other possible areas of conflict of interest (e.g., assets, liabilities, capital gains, spouse's finances) and prohibitions on joint ventures with or gifts from lobbyists. Senator Carl T. Curtis (R., Nebraska) criticized the resolution for its lack of enforcement provisions.

Even the mild resolution reported out by the committee still proved too strong for the Senate. A mild substitute measure was adopted, providing for a six-member bipartisan committee to investigate "allegations of improper conduct" by senators or Senate employees. Even in this case a delay of more than a year ensued before the members of the new committee were appointed.

Reform of Campaign Finance Laws

A number of federal statutes govern campaign finance, notably the Corrupt Practices Act of 1925, imposing limits on campaign expenditures, and the 1940 amendments to the Hatch Act, imposing limits on contributions. Additional laws prohibit both unions and corporations from donating money in connection with federal elections.

But the reporting requirements are unaccompanied by enforcement provisions and the intent of these laws is so easy to evade that they have been conspicuously ineffective. The Hatch Act, for example, sets a $5,000 annual limit on an individual's contributions to any candidate or committee, but it says

[4] U. S. Senate, Committee on Rules and Administration, Report No. 1125, 88th Congress, 2nd Sess., June 29, 1964, pp. 1–2.

nothing to prohibit every member of a large, wealthy family from contributing individually; nor does it preclude the formation of several committees for a particular candidate, to each of which an individual may contribute $5,000.

On the expenditure side, restrictions are equally meaningless, applying only to monies spent by the candidate himself, and having no application to monies spent or services rendered by others on the candidate's behalf. Furthermore, no restrictions apply to primary campaigns.

In recent years, suggestions for reform have come principally through studies made in 1956 and 1957 by the Privileges and Elections Subcommittee of the Senate Rules and Administration Committee; through the scholarly works of Alexander Heard and Herbert Alexander; and through President Kennedy's Commission on Campaign Costs. Perhaps the most systematic proposals have come from the Commission. Its most important recommendations were:

1. Tax credits or deductions up to a specified amount for individuals making political contributions. The purpose of this proposal is to increase the number of small gifts and thus reduce the influence of the few donors of large sums. In 1960 almost half the income of the two major parties came from donations of $500 or more.

2. Replacement of ceilings on contributions and expenditures by toughly written disclosure requirements, fearlessly enforced by a Registry of Elections Finance. The theory here is that unenforcible attempts at curbing campaign spending "serve only to demoralize the political climate and breed contempt for existing law." [5]

Other reforms proposed over the years, including a direct federal subsidy of certain kinds of campaign costs, have been aimed at the same basic questions: how to cut down on the lumpiness of political advantage which accrues to big contributors; and how to free elected officials from the indignities, illegalities, and temptations associated with present practice.

The unwillingness of Congress to clean house is discouraging. Perhaps there is a feeling that the present patterns of campaign finance insure a kind of functional representation that reflects the interests of major economic groups in our society, and that such representation is needed to offset alleged popular passions.

Whatever the reasons, excuses, or justification for inaction on revising laws governing campaign costs and conflicts of interest, Congress pays a heavy price in increased public cynicism. Moral courage and high ethical practice exist in Congress. Careful students of Congress believe this to be the rule rather than the exception. Politics ennobles more than it corrupts. If higher ethical standards are demanded of political figures than of others, it is right

[5] See Alexander Heard, The Costs of Democracy (Chapel Hill: University of North Carolina Press, 1960), and Herbert Alexander, [ed.], Studies in Money in Politics (Princeton: Citizens' Research Foundation, 1965).

that this be so, for politicians are the people's guardians quite as much as vice versa. The fact is, however, that the ethical reality is lower than it should be.

Public cynicism is not friendly to freedom. If Congress is to retain a position of strength in our federal system, it must retain the public's confidence. The public's confidence cannot be retained over time if the congressional image is tarnished by the misdeeds of a few, or by laws and practices that patently encourage law-breaking and inequities in political and economic advantage in our society.

The problems of congressional ethics, of course, go far beyond conflict of interest and campaign costs. But these are central.

TOWARD A MORE RESPONSIBLE CONGRESS

The United States enters the last third of the twentieth century as the most powerful nation on earth. Its military strength and its diplomatic and economic resources affect the lives and fortunes of the entire human race. It is the major guardian of territorial sovereignty and of free institutions the world around. Its perceived national interests lead it into infusive influences upon stability and change in scores of nations across the face of the globe. At home, the American government has become a major agent of economic growth and stability, of social amelioration, of cultural and educational adaptation and initiative, of scientific and technological advance.

It has been forced into these various responsibilities—domestic and international—by human interdependencies produced by technology and urbanization, and by the values and expectations of the preamble to its Constitution. The burden of government has never been more complex, the need for responsible and effective instruments of government never more insistent.

● ● ●

Four measures of performance suggest themselves:

1. Do present relations between the Congress and the executive branch provide responsible and rational answers to pressing national and international needs; and is each house politically accountable in the sense of having a visible partisan majority that controls organization and procedures and at the same time serves as a base for a responsible coalition on matters of substance?

2. Are sources of power in the Congress sufficiently independent to insure a critical and constructive review of presidential proposals and of bureaucratic performance, while at the same time they are not overly reflective of special and parochial interests?

3. Is the membership of the House of Representatives truly consonant with the Constitutional mandate for equality of representation?

4. Is the internal machinery of Congress sufficiently and rationally organ-

ized to provide an effective balance between deliberation and dispatch in handling the nation's business?

The only fair answer is that the new Congress represents progress on all of these fronts—but that there is still substantial room for improvement.

Executive-Legislative Relations and Party Responsibility

The first session of the 89th Congress, which ended October 23, 1965 was the most dramatic illustration in a generation of the capacity of the President and the Congress to work together on important issues of public policy. In part a mopping-up operation on an agenda fashioned at least in spirit by the New Deal, the work of the 89th Congress cut new paths through the frontier of qualitative issues: a beautification bill, a bill to create federal support for the arts and the humanities, vast increases in federal aid to education. These symbolized the beginning of a new agenda. Both parties responded to major presidential requests in the field of national security policy. Throughout, the policy leadership and the political skill of President Johnson found a ready and supportive response from a strengthened partisan leadership and a substantial, partisan, Democratic majority in both houses. A decade of incremental structural changes in the locus of power in both houses eased the President's task of consent building and of legislative implementation.

Yet Congress was far from a rubber stamp. On some issues the President met resounding defeat. On many issues, presidential recommendations were modified by exorcisms or additions—reflecting the power of particular committee chairmen, group interests, and bureaucratic pressures at odds with presidential perspectives.

One glaring deficiency emerged in the recent legislative output: lack of adequate attention to the *administrative* implications of "great society" legislation. Laws were passed and money provided without appropriate questions being asked and answered about the availability of trained manpower to carry out the programs; about optimum relationships between federal, state, local, and private jurisdictions; or about the effective interdepartmental coordination of old and new activities. Often it is too late to handle such questions by *post hoc* accounting and surveillance procedures. Congress must do more to raise administrative issues in the course of marking up enabling legislation. It can do this without limiting either the President or itself in responding to pressing national problems. The new Congress has proved its responsiveness. Responsiveness can be made more responsible by paying as much attention to instrumentation as to musical score.

Overall, the lessons of the 89th Congress were generally hopeful: that vigorous presidential leadership and a sizable partisan majority under strong partisan leadership in both houses can act in consonance and with dispatch in fashioning creative answers to major domestic and international issues. The nation's voters can pin responsibility upon a national party for the legislative output. If that partisan majority erred in judgment, it can be held accountable in ensuing congressional and presidential elections. Coalition, committee, and bureaucratic baronies unresponsible to presidential or partisan leadership are weaker on the general legislative front than in past years.

Will this last? Our constitutional and electoral structure precludes sanguinity. Partisan divisions between the Presidency and one or both houses of Congress will undoubtedly occur on occasions in the future as they have in the past. *Ad hoc,* inverted coalitions will continue to emerge intermittently. But reapportionment, the urbanization and pluralization of the American society, the increase in Negro voting in the South, and the force of international tensions will produce an increasing consistency between congressional and presidential views of the national interest. In consequence, we are likely to see in the years ahead fewer unresolvable confrontations between the President and the Congress than in recent decades. We are likely to see an increase in partisan identity between President and Congress, and an increase in benign as distinct from inverted coalitions in the Congress itself.

The areas of greatest tension and conflict are likely to occur not between the President and partisan leadership in both houses. The dangerous conflicts will be between the President and his partisan congressional leaders on the one hand, and executive-bureau/congressional-committee/interest-group coalitions on the other. This is the long engagement between the king and the barons which has given drama to so much of human history. Total victory for either side can produce either tyranny or a dangerous fragmentation of power. Tension between the two forces—with an edge to the king—is probably the key to achieving national purpose without loss of freedom.

The present balance is, however, sufficiently precarious to suggest that further measures are in order to strengthen centripetal forces within each house. The twin principles of seniority and committee autonomy—substantially weakened in the past decade—need to be modified even further. Majority membership controls within committees need to be increased vis-à-vis the power of committee chairmen. Majorities in each party in both houses need to develop more effective controls over their own caucuses, and through their leadership and their representative policy committees, more effective influence over committee assignments and floor calendars. If these oblique attacks prove to be inadequate, the evils of seniority may have to be attacked head on. But there is evidence to suggest that some of the advantages of seniority can be continued while conditions can be set to limit the more egregious manifestations of the practice.

Centripetal forces will be further strengthened by additional symbiotic linkages between the campaign committees in the Congress and the national committees of the two major parties.

Finally, the energy, skill, and understanding of the President will be a major factor in strengthening party leadership in each house. In the modern world, no parliament can function effectively without strong and continuing executive leadership.

The only rub here is that the American political system has never figured out an appropriate "shadow" President for the opposition party. The absence of an opposition leader looking toward a national contest with the incumbent President leaves the opposition party in America in substantial disarray. The Republican party can offer no effective opposition to the incumbent Democrats as long as there is no presidentially oriented leader to bridge the great gulf between the liberal and conservative wings of the GOP. The program of the Democratic President is not subject to review by an opposition party with a general alternative philosophy of the public interest. It is henpecked by special interests and special cliques in both parties in both houses of the Congress.

General alternatives to general legislation will be most effectively induced by strengthening the opposition party—and especially by strengthening its presidential wing. The absence of a shadow executive makes difficult the formation of a responsible opposition party in the Congress—or for that matter outside of it. If America is not to become a one-and-a-half party system, the opposition party must construct some institutional mechanism for developing national leadership and national policies of presidential caliber and perspective. The absence of such political machinery and leadership is America's most conspicuous institutional failure.

What the 89th Congress suggests is that when a strong and talented President can depend upon the support of partisan majorities in both houses, a responsive and responsible flow of public policy is likely to ensue, regardless of the weaknesses of the opposition party. But this is a short-range perspective. Over time, responsible policy-making requires a strong and constructively critical opposition party.

Legislative Review and the Oversight of Administration

When one turns from general directions of public policy, and partisan responsibility for general legislative output, to questions of legislative detail and administrative surveillance, the new Congress deserves lower marks. Parochialisms abound. Congress lacks adequate counterparts to the moralizing and rational forces of hierarchy in the executive branch. The presidential perspective may be wrong, but it is fashioned by the need to place a series of countervailing and parochial interests in the society and in the bureaucracy into some kind of general framework related to a national electoral majority. In the Congress, the unified programs of the President's State of the Union message, budget, and economic report are carved up into separate subcommittee and committee referrals and analyses. Too often bills are marked up by parochial pens. Too often patterns of internal deference in Congress lead to full committee and floor acceptance of myopic subcommittee amendments. Too often seniority gives undue personal, area, or functional advantage to a small number of powerfully situated legislators. The ideal editing of major legislative issues is not likely to come from compromises between general and parochial

views. It should come—at least in part—from a compromise between two
competing views of the general interest. The latter cannot be achieved by destroying the division of labor within the Congress. It can only be achieved by:

—promoting to positions of responsibility in the committee system what
Mazzini once called "the best and the wisest" rather than merely the
oldest in the Congress;

—periodically reorganizing the committee and subcommittee structure
of Congress to eliminate outmoded and limited jurisdictional interests;

—improving internal intercommittee communications within the Congress—perhaps by establishing one or two cross-cutting committees
for a general review of the President's program (e.g., a Joint Committee on the Budget; a Joint Committee on the State of the Union);

—continuing to strengthen the power of the staff of party leaders in
both houses; and

—improving the quality but not necessarily the quantity of staff aides to
individual congressional committees, and using university and other
external professional consultants far more extensively.

The Joint Committee on the Organization of the Congress addressed itself
to many of these issues in 1965. Their final recommendations merit the most
careful scrutiny and implementation.

The same therapy is called for in administrative surveillance. Whether surveillance takes place through advice and consent, through appropriations subcommittee hearings, through substantive committee hearings and investigations, or through control over executive branch organization, means must be
found within the Congress to broaden the perspective of nearsighted wielders
of parochial power. Politicians become statesmen as they are induced to react
to more inclusive interests. Scattered power can be constructive if the vision
and the accountability of each power-holder is broadly gauged and broadly
based. Whatever reforms of politics or congressional organization move in
this direction will tend to promote the public interest.

Perhaps the area in which Congress needs most general improvement in
deliberation is foreign affairs. The American people need the advantage of in-
telligent congressional debates over major foreign policy issues. Deferring to
the President on many national security issues is inevitable and prudent. But
Congress needs to do far more than this. It needs to serve as a forum for informed discussion about such long-range issues as our relations with China;
the future of nonwhites and whites in Southern Africa; the successes and failures of our Latin American policies; the development of the United Nations
system into a more effective world government. Individual speeches are not
enough, no matter how brave or eloquent. Committee hearings and the floor
of each house should be used far more extensively for general debates on for-

eign policy. Surely there are other options available to the Congress in its relations with the executive in foreign affairs than blind deference on the one hand or irresponsible, boat-rocking attack on the other. America's national interest is best served in foreign affairs when Presidents are given power to act, but Congress reserves the right to criticize and to search for long-range alternatives.

The Representativeness of the House

The struggle for equal representation among congressional districts has been all but won, although individual battles are still going on. By 1972 after redistricting that will follow the decennial census of 1970, the grossest illustrations of malapportionment will have been finally corrected. Minor distortions will continue to exist through the practice of gerrymandering—giving undue advantage to a party or to an ideology or interest. But *Wesberry* v. *Sanders* is forcing, and will continue to force, an equitable correspondence between population and representation in the House of Representatives.

Since suburbia will profit more than urbia from reapportionment, the effect of the *Wesberry* case will be to strengthen middle-class values. Whether this will be at the expense of the poor and the discriminated against in the central cities will depend upon the capacity of the President, party, education, civic leadership, and religion to broaden man's sense of community and social responsibility.

The Voting Rights Act of 1965 should hasten dramatically the political coming-of-age of the Southern Negro. In the spirit of the *Wesberry* decision, "one-man, one-vote" achieved through Negro registration can have a profound effect upon the representative character of the House and upon the nature of Southern politics. Increased political power for the Negro will move both urban and rural congressmen in the South to reconsider traditional attitudes and values. Within the House of Representatives, the traditional power of Southern congressmen will either be weakened or moved to the left on the political spectrum. The few arch conservatives who will undoubtedly emerge in the short run from the storm of change will be juniors on the totem pole of seniority, and they will find themselves alienated from both national political parties, which must look to a moderate national electorate for support. In this sense the Voting Rights Act of 1965 may be even more important than the *Wesberry* decision in producing a change in the long-run attitudes and power structures of the United States House of Representatives. Its effect may be no less dramatic in the United States Senate.

The Machinery of Congress

Finally, if Congress is to become a more responsible instrument of the public interest, both houses need to improve their internal machinery. As a functioning organism, Congress is woefully arthritic. In a study made by Arthur D.

Little, Inc., leading management consultants, for the NBC News in 1965, the conclusion was reached that Congress is "so overloaded with work it is not staffed or equipped to handle that it cannot function effectively in the twentieth century." [6] The Little study contrasts the methods congressmen must use with those used by such giant corporations as du Pont, "where accurate information on almost any subject relating to the company's activities is available through the use of computers and other electronic devices." [7]

It is of course fatuous to measure congressional organization and performance solely against the patterns of giant industry. Congress cannot mount either the internal sanctions or the clarity of goals of great private corporations. But Congress can and should borrow some of the techniques of efficient management from both public and private organizations. This need is especially valid in information retrieval, pay-roll practices, personnel management, communications systems, central housekeeping, clerical and mail services, and program evaluation and review. Management sciences have improved radically in recent years. Some improvements are not transferable to Congress without subverting basic legislative functions or prerogatives (e.g., in-house testing and measurement of individuals). But many management techniques and certain types of electronic hardware could undoubtedly improve the efficiency of congressional operations. These should be explored.

Certainly one field for rich exploration is the committee system itself. An increase in joint hearings—within each house and between each house—could save executive as well as congressional time. A central clearing house to help avoid conflicts in scheduling committee and subcommittee meetings would diminish frustration and increase the orderliness of conducting legislative business. Further encouragement of advance testimony with appropriate abstracts would cut the time of, and increase the quality of deliberation in, congressional hearings.

Floor procedures are in even greater need of attention. Traditional rules, or interpretations thereof, governing the reading of the *Journal*, quorum calls, unanimous consent, germaneness, cloture, and roll calls need critical review and amendment. Some procedural delays promote desirable deliberation. But many are anachronisms—the residue of a distant past or of unconscionable minority interests. The business of Congress is too massive in quantity and too important in quality to permit uncritically accepted tradition or precedent to govern the conduct of legislative business on the floor.

Only Congress itself, of course, can work out realistic and acceptable guidelines for improving its performance. One mark of the new Congress is a visible concern with finding an appropriate role in the American government system and with discovering rules and procedures which will make its new

[6] *New York Times*, Oct. 23, 1965, p. 63.
[7] *Ibid.*

role possible and viable. But in this search the Congress must have the sympathetic assistance of the President, the party system, the press, the universities,
and the concerned electorate. For Congress is an integral part of a larger society. In the words of Alfred North Whitehead, "those societies which cannot
combine reverence to their symbols with freedom of revision, must ultimately
decay either from anarchy or from the slow atrophy of a life stifled by useless
shadows." [8]

Congress and Freedom

For all of its weaknesses and inadequacies, Congress is a major bastion of
human freedom. This point would hardly need elaboration were it not so frequently and tragically forgotten in the mid-twentieth century.

If anything is clear in this fretful age, it is that legislative institutions which
gave freedom its birth and meaning have been eroded in power and denigrated in reputation the world around—eroded and denigrated, that is, where
they have not been totally destroyed. Necessary as the Gaullist revolution in
France may have been, nobody will pretend that the French National Assembly was upgraded in power or influence by the change. The first casualty of
wobbly novitiates in the family of nations seems to be their parliaments or
assemblies. In the past few years, a half-dozen new nations have abolished the
pretense of democracy, and have reverted to rule by tribal chieftains decked
out in modern military garb. Scrawled in invisible ink on the walls of the
empty parliament buildings are the words, "Parliaments, Go Home."

How short historical memories are! It was a congress of nobles that met at
Runnymede to make John Lackland sign the Magna Carta. It was a congress
of estates called "Parliament" that gradually reduced the prerogatives of the
English crown from absolutism to a benign symbol of spiritual and moral
unity. It was assemblies of free men which tempered and hamstrung the insolence of appointed royal governors during our own colonial days.

Of what does freedom consist, unless it is the atmosphere of human dignity
made possible by the existence of representative restraints upon rulers? Benevolent despots have dotted the pages of human history, but like the barking
dog who never bites, no one knows when a despot is going to stop being benevolent. And on this score, history is not encouraging.

It was with considerations of this sort in mind that our Founding Fathers,
after a brief preamble, began the Constitution of the United States with the
words, "All legislative Powers herein granted shall be vested in a Congress of
the United States, which shall consist of a Senate and House of Representatives."

That the first article of the Constitution deals with the Congress is no accident. Congress is first because, living in the long shadow of the Glorious Revolution of 1688 and of its great philosophical defender, John Locke, the

[8] Alfred North Whitehead, *Symbolism: Its Meaning and Effect.* (New York: Macmillan Company, 1927), p. 88.

Founding Fathers fully understood that although you could have government without a representative assembly, you could not have *free* government without a representative assembly.

Congress defends freedom by asking rude questions; by stubbornly insisting that technology be discussed in terms of its human effects; by eliciting new ideas from old heads; by building a sympathetic bridge between the bewildered citizen and the bureaucracy; by acting as a sensitive register for group interests whose fortunes are indistinguishable from the fortunes of vast numbers of citizens and who have a constitutional right to be heard.

Congress defends freedom by being a prudent provider; by carefully sifting and refining legislative proposals; by compromising and homogenizing raw forces in conflict; by humbling generals and admirals—and, on occasion, even Presidents.

For as far ahead as man can see, freedom is an eternal frontier. If not constantly cleared and defended it reverts to jungle where wild beasts play out their morbid and sullen dramas. As one of the great institutional forces in the life of modern man dedicated to the perpetuation of freedom, Congress in the last analysis deserves our respect and our reverence.[9]

Study Questions

1. Explain the model used by Miller and Stokes to describe the representative system.
2. Evaluate the normative theory of representation on the basis of the findings of Miller and Stokes.
3. Clark and Bailey examine the nature of the Senate establishment and Congressional ethics. What reforms are needed to make the Senate more democratic and Congress, on the whole, more responsible, especially in cases involving conflict of interest and campaign costs?
4. On the basis of your readings, what realistic guidelines would you propose in order to improve Congressional performance? Do you agree with Bailey's suggestions? Discuss fully.

Suggestions for Further Reading

Acheson, Dean. *A Citizen Looks at Congress.* New York: Harper & Row, Publishers, Inc., 1936.

Bailey, Stephen K. *Congress Makes a Law.* New York: Columbia University Press, 1950.

Bailey, Stephen K. *The New Congress.* New York: St. Martin's Press, 1966.

Baker, Gordon C. *The Reapportionment Revolution.* New York: Random House, 1966.

Barth, Alan. *Government by Investigation.* New York: The Viking Press, 1950.

Berman, Daniel M. *In Congress Assembled: The Legislative Process in the National Government.* New York: The Macmillan Company, 1964.

[9] The final six paragraphs are quoted from the author's "Is Congress the Old Frontier?" in Marian D. Irish (ed.), *The Continuing Crisis in American Politics,* © 1963, Prentice-Hall, Inc., Englewood Cliffs, N. J.

Bryce, James. *The American Commonwealth.* Rev. ed. New York: The Macmillan Company, 1911.

Byrnes, James M. *Congress on Trial.* New York: Harper & Row, Publishers, Inc., 1949.

Cater, Douglas. *Power in Washington.* New York: Random House, 1964.

Clark, Joseph S., *et al. The Senate Establishment.* New York: Hill and Wang, 1963.

Dahl, Robert A. *Congress and Foreign Policy.* New York: Harcourt, Brace & World, Inc., 1950.

Davidson, Roger, David M. Kovenack, and Michael K. O'Leary. *Congress in Crisis: Politics and Congressional Reform.* Belmont, California: Wadsworth Publishing Company, 1966.

Froman, Lewis A., Jr. *Congressmen and Their Constituencies.* Chicago: Rand McNally and Company, 1963.

Froman, Lewis, A., Jr. *The Congressional Process: Strategies, Rules, and Procedures.* Boston: Little, Brown and Company, 1967.

Galloway, George B. *The Legislative Process in Congress.* New York: Thomas Y. Crowell, 1953.

Hacker, Andrew. *Congressional Districting: The Issue of Equal Representation.* Washington, D.C.: The Brookings Institution, 1964.

Haynes, George H. *The Senate of the United States.* New York: Russell & Russell, 1960.

MacNeil, Neil. *The Forge of Democracy.* New York: David McKay Company, Inc., 1963.

Matthews, Donald R. *U.S. Senators and Their World.* New York: Vintage Books, 1960.

Miller, Clem. *Member of the House.* New York: Charles Scribner's Sons, 1962. Edited by John Baker.

Taylor, Telford. *Grand Inquest.* New York: Simon and Schuster, Inc., 1955.

Truman, David. *The Congressional Party.* New York: John Wiley & Sons, Inc., 1959.

Wahlke, J. C. and H. Eulau. *Legislative Behavior: A Reader in Theory and Research.* New York: The Free Press of Glencoe, 1959.

PART NINE

The Presidency

The Presidency of the United States is the central and most important position in the governmental system. The late President John F. Kennedy had succinctly described the American Presidency in his forward note in Theodore C. Sorensen's book, *Decision-Making in the White House: The Olive Branch or the Arrows,* in these terms:

> The American Presidency is a formidable, exposed, and somewhat mysterious institution. It is formidable because it represents the point of ultimate decision in the American political system. It is exposed because decision cannot take place in a vacuum: the Presidency is the center of the play of pressure, interest, and idea in the nation; and the presidential office is the vortex into which all the elements of national decision are irresistibly drawn. And it is mysterious because the essence of ultimate decision remains impenetrable to the observer—often, indeed, to the decider himself.[1]

The dominance of the Presidency may be attributed to rapid expansion in governmental activities and responsibilities, economic crisis, social revolution, tensions in the international arena, rapid means of communications, the need for political leadership, expert advice, and secrecy. Also, Congress finds it generally more convenient to deal with the broad principles of public policies and leave details to the Executive departments. Moreover, the cumbersome and slow procedures of Congress contribute to inefficiency in coping with the ever increasing demands (inputs) placed upon it in the last half of the twentieth century.

[1] Theodore C. Sorensen, *Decision-Making in the White House: The Olive Branch or the Arrows* (New York: Columbia University Press, 1963), p. 11.

434

The powers of the President as stated in Article II of the Constitution are vague and provide few guidelines on the jurisdiction of the President. This lack of precision gives the President an open mandate to exercise whatever powers he believes are essential for the performance of his duties. Since the Washington Administration, this uncertainty has touched off arguments as to whether the President is vested with independent powers (executive prerogative) or is simply an agent of Congress whose main function is to see that all the laws are faithfully executed.

In his article "The Presidency Under Scrutiny," New York *Times* associate editor Tom Wicker states that Richard Nixon takes a restrained view of his job. "I've always thought this country could run itself domestically, without a President," Candidate Nixon told Theodore H. White in 1968. "All you need is a competent Cabinet to run the country at home. You need a President for foreign policy; no Secretary of State is really important; the President makes foreign policy." Wicker states that the war in Vietnam ushered in the end of decades of liberal overreliance on the White House for it led to a reaction against Presidential government—at least the Johnsonian version of it. Wicker discusses several areas where Congress has imposed itself on President Nixon's policies. The President has the initiative in conducting foreign policy to a far greater extent than need be the case in domestic policy. Wicker concludes that the President may not be as free as he was. He is under scrutiny.

Saul K. Padover in his article "The Power of the President" calls for restraints over the powers of the President. He states that the President "is virtually a dictator in international affairs." The President shares this authority with no other person or group. The power of the President as Chief Diplomat has been established in practice and upheld by the courts. Padover gives several examples in which Presidents have sent armed forces into action without declaration of war. For instance, military steps were taken in recent years in Korea, Lebanon, Vietnam, and Dominican Republic at the President's direction, by virtue of the power inherent in him as Commander-in-Chief.

In this nuclear age, the President exercises power over the life and death of every American. Padover believes that what is needed is restraint over Presidential power and recommends several steps that must be taken if Congress, especially the Senate, is to restore its eroded powers.

In making his decisions the President relies upon the advice of White House specialists, Cabinet members, and experts from outside the government. Theodore C. Sorensen discusses Cabinet and National Security Council meetings. He points out that some advisers may mistake agreement for validity and coordination of policy. He claims that spirited debates can be stifling as well as stimulating and that although the President may be impressed by the experts' knowledge, his own common sense, balancing of priorities, and understanding of Congress and the country are more essential in reaching the right decision.

White House specialists are more likely to see problems in a broader perspective than Cabinet members. White House Staff members are chosen for
their ability to serve the President's needs. The President, however, may seek
advice from outside the Executive branch for outside advice may be more objective. Finally, Sorensen discusses the qualification of advisers and states that
personalities play an important role and political background is helpful. He
concludes that "there is no sure test of a good adviser."

The smooth transition of Presidential power from one political party to another is very important. In his article "Transition at the White House" Henry
F. Graff states that this transition is a uniquely American problem. In a parliamentary system there is always a shadow cabinet ready to step into office
overnight. Transfer of power is the shift of power to the next President in an
orderly manner. However, this transfer of power is usually painful. Graff discusses what takes place during the transition of authority by giving recent
examples of the transfer of power from Eisenhower to Kennedy and from
Johnson to Nixon. Every President, Graff states, leaves office with work incomplete.

THE PRESIDENCY UNDER SCRUTINY

TOM WICKER

It is only slightly unkind to suggest that President Nixon, once he got his first
White House view of the national situation, immediately dashed off to Europe; and that when he had had a few months to let American domestic problems really sink in, he leaped aboard Air Force One and headed for Asia. If
even in such an intractable world as this, with all its dangers and complexities, Mr. Nixon saw himself as more likely to get a few things done abroad
than at home, he could hardly be blamed.

The festering race problem, the decline of the cities, the pollution of the
American environment, the alienation of the young from American society,
the inflation of the dollar, the revolt of the taxpayer—after having got himself
elected not least by pointing with alarm to these matters, Mr. Nixon in the
White House has to face them at considerable disadvantage.

If legislation is required, he cannot surely control a Democratic Congress,
and his own supporters are those least likely to approve imaginative social

SOURCE: Tom Wicker, "The Presidency Under Scrutiny," *Harper's Magazine*, 239 (October 1969),
92–94. Copyright © 1969, by Harper's Magazine, Inc. Reprinted by permission of Paul R. Reynolds, Inc., 599 Fifth Avenue, New York, N.Y. 10017.

measures; if money is required, it is getting hard to squeeze out of taxpayers "fed up to here"; and before anything much can be done, Mr. Nixon has to retrieve the funds and the national unity of purpose for so long squandered in Vietnam.

Besides all that, Mr. Nixon takes a restrained view of his job. "I've always thought this country could run itself domestically, without a President," he told Theodore H. White in 1968. "All you need is a competent Cabinet to run the country at home. You need a President for foreign policy; no Secretary of State is really important; the President makes foreign policy."

That may not be so different from historic American attitudes but it is a moon-shot away from the accepted political theory of the mid- and late-twentieth century. Such an heretical notion would never have entered the head of Lyndon B. Johnson, who was eager to run everything, at home and abroad: and John Kennedy made a point of talking about the necessity for a President to be "in the forefront of the battle."

A strong Presidency, at the head of a powerful executive branch, has become dogma in the post-1932 liberal era of American politics; I sat in recently on a discussion among the small group of left-wing members of Congress, and their action plans kept coming back to the idea that they had to win the White House before they could have any hope of substantial social reform.

But time and circumstance already may have made the Nixonian idea of geared-down domestic responsibility for the Presidency more harmonious with a new cycle of decentralized politics in America; and if that is so, it is at least possible that even Mr. Nixon's confidently activist approach to his foreign-policy powers may not be fully warranted. Some close students of government believe that, in domestic affairs, it is an outmoded idea that only a dynamo in the White House, possessed of mysterious charismatic powers of leadership as well as super political skills and vast sums of federal dollars, can set the country right. Eugene McCarthy was much criticized in 1968 for his "relaxed" view of the Presidency; but Robert Kennedy, before his death, also was talking about the need for the federal executive to share responsibility with other areas of government and the private sector; and what apparently drew together Richard Nixon and Daniel Patrick Moynihan, a Democratic liberal of long standing, was their shared belief that a federal program was not necessarily the right answer to every problem.

In the first place, while an energetic President may wear with passable aplomb all those fancy hats assigned him in the civics books—chief executive, commander in chief, chief legislator, economic manager, party leader, etc.— the White House is a lousy place to look for a mayor. As demographic and economic forces have pushed the American population more and more into vast cities, the city is where virtually the whole range of domestic woes has come to a boil; and it is reasonably clear that the first thing needed to cope with the crisis is not more federal power, but more city power, including more money.

When, for example, the New York City subways are facing an operating deficit in fiscal 1970 of $120.5 million, on top of an $85 million deficit from fiscal 1969, with unknown new labor costs to be piled on top of that; and when the Nixon Administration has budgeted for fiscal 1970 only $250 million for mass-transportation programs, in which 99 cities hope to participate— then it is obvious that New York's transportation crisis is not going to be eased by such federal matching-grant programs, on which the Democratic liberal model of federal action depends. And transportation is only one of many domestic problems on which similar evidence could be cited.

In the second place, it is widely agreed that the federal government, which took, in 1966, about $117 billion of the total of only $175 billion collected in federal, state, and local taxes, and which gets the first and largest crack at the most lucrative and responsive revenue source, the income tax, has to find ways and means of getting more restricted, uncategorized money into the hands of states, cities, and localities, to use as *they* see fit. The Nixon Administration is at work on such a "revenue-sharing" plan and its beginnings can be foreseen. It is calculated to have a two-fold effect:

1. However modest the sums returned to lesser jurisdictions may be at first, they will ease the financial crisis of the cities and states to some extent and enable them to move more effectively into locally relevant action in fields that, for a quarter-century and more, have been regarded as federal—which is almost to say Presidential—territory. (The same effect ought to result from the Administration's plan to take over a greater share of welfare costs, which is another form of revenue-sharing.)

2. Since most states and practically all cities are not well organized and staffed for expanded social responsibilities, and since Congress knows they are not, the Congressional potentates of the federal purse are likely to demand guarantees that may result, eventually, in useful reforms and clarifications of authority in the federal system and an increase in local government effectiveness.

Critics contend that just the opposite may as easily happen; Congress might tie so many strings to the grants of funds as to create new tangles of federal bureaucracy and control, and the states and cities might use the money, however it comes, only to reduce their own taxes.

No doubt that *is* possible; but an effort to revitalize state and local government, as the next big development of American political theory and practice, is sure to be made in some fashion—because, in the third place, American social ills are so varied and complex, in what is, after all, one of the most diverse and sprawling and volatile nations in the world, that no central government can hope to deal effectively with all of them. The evidence, on the contrary, is that the vast, clanking machinery of the Washington agencies, with their huge snarl of matching-grant programs (anywhere from 140 to more than 400, depending on how you count them; when Melvin Laird was a mere Congressman, he said there were 190 grant-in-aid programs administered by HEW alone) and their intimidating tomes of rules and regulations and guidelines and procedures, to say nothing of their constant competition for too little money, concentrates neither energy nor funds on practical goals but dissipates both across the board.

All of these things, more or less inexorably, are making Mr. Nixon's view of the Presidency and its power in domestic affairs nearer the mark than, say, LBJ's; if the country cannot really "run itself" and if the Cabinet can't run it either, it now seems clear that there must be a better way than heaping every trouble on the White House portico. And the recognition of that fact has been sped along by the national, particularly the Congressional, reaction to the giantism of the Johnson Presidency, and particularly to the war in Vietnam.

To many members of Congress—including some who, like Senator J. W. Fulbright, admit to considerable hindsight in the matter—and to others as well, the war is the culmination of decades of liberal over-reliance on the White House and the "strength" of the man who sits there. Through the Thirties, Forties, Fifties and the first half of the Sixties, the United States developed a powerful Presidential form of government, while state and local authority atrophied and Congress swung politically between obstructionist and rubber-stamp periods.

Presidential government had its undeniable successes—the Social Security system climaxed by Medicare, the elimination of legal discrimination against blacks—but it had its damaging failures, too—Johnson's overblown "war on poverty"—and with our cities either strangling or blowing up, black militants arming themselves, our air and water poisoning us, the dollar flimsy and taxes astronomical, it is fair to ask what Presidential government of the Johnson type has done for us lately. Aside from that, it is necessary to ask whether the vast accretion in Presidential powers that took place from FDR to LBJ was entirely justified by the results—whether, indeed, the Presidency had not, by 1965, become almost a Frankenstein's monster that needed only the opportunity of Vietnam to turn on its creators.

Vietnam, surely, was the ultimate exercise of raw Presidential power in the twentieth century (Truman, in 1950, responded to the sort of aggression-across-a-border that Americans then and now abhor, and he immediately put himself under the U.N. flag); and even those who believe Johnson acted in the national interest in 1965 find it hard to defend the tactics by which he managed to act without any genuine Congressional sanction and against his own promises to the populace, or the subterfuge and stratagem by which the war was steadily expanded while its author insisted that Americans had to support it because the only President they had had launched it.

Had the war been "won," even so, things might be different today; but it was not won in any sense that can be understood, and so Johnson's war has become a powerful factor in the developing reaction against Presidential government—at least against that Johnsonian version of it, which, at last, made clear the lengths to which Presidential power could be carried. (Mr. Nixon's Attorney General, John Mitchell, is doing his bit by claiming that the President has the power to order, on his own authority and without a shred of sanction from any court, the wiretapping and bugging of any person or organization who might "foment violent disorders.")

The first consequence of all this is not only to be found in the Nixon Administration's welfare and revenue-sharing plans; for example, in a field where national policy had all but been abandoned to the executive—economic management through federal fiscal policy—Congress held up for nearly a year Johnson's request for an anti-inflationary surcharge on the income tax, until he agreed to a virtually unprecedented ceiling on federal spending.

Then, as if to show that this was not obstructionism but a new willingness to debate policy and priority matters, Congress went to the mat with Mr. Nixon when he asked for an anti-inflationary renewal of the surcharge for a second year. This time, the Congressional demand was for a real start on tax reform; and once again a President was forced at least partially to yield. Not only had Congress imposed itself on Mr. Nixon's policy in defense of the dollar; it also forced his hand on tax reform. This, in spite of the fact that the President—as Johnson had before him—pulled out all stops in demanding the surcharge as vital to that mysterious entity heretofore reserved only to Presidents to define and declare, and before which Congress used to flee in panic: "the national interest."

The long and bitter struggle over the Safeguard anti-ballistic missile system was similar in importance—a reaction against exclusive executive power, in this case backed by the military, to set costly national priorities, however disputed, in the name of that same "national interest." Most pointed of all was the Senate's passage of the so-called "commitments resolution"—a curious document that attempted to establish the doctrine that a President could not make a "national commitment" to another nation or group of nations without prior approval of Congress.

There is no way to enforce this doctrine, which Mr. Nixon rejects, and it runs clearly counter to most Constitutional and historical scholarship—which generally agrees that "the President makes foreign policy." What the resolution meant, nevertheless, was that it would be a long time before Congress would again tamely provide a President with anything like the Gulf of Tonkin resolution—a virtual blank check which went mostly unchallenged in 1964. Thus, the authors of the resolution sought to put Mr. Nixon and his successors, for at least the period during which the taste of Vietnam might linger on the national tongue, on notice that Congress would demand more justification and more consultation the next time it was asked to redeem a President's "national commitment" with planes and troops.

In fact, as the ABM debate suggested, Congress can influence foreign policy more powerfully than by passing admonitory resolutions. It can, that is, if it will screw its courage to the sticking place, which it does not often do. One of the reasons that the Tonkin Gulf resolution sailed so easily through House and Senate was the fact that Johnson shrewdly threw it on the table in the immediate aftermath of what he and the Pentagon believed was a North Vietnamese attack on American ships. It takes political courage to vote against a President who appears to be standing up for the flag and "our boys," particularly when you cannot pretend to have more information than he does, and it would have taken a lot more courage to vote restrictions on Johnson's power to wage the war once troops were committed to battle, carrying with them "the national prestige."

The Presidency's power in conducting foreign affairs, moreover, is so great that it is hard to conceive of its being more than peripherally restrained. The President has the initiative, to a far greater extent than need be the case in domestic policy, and the executive power. Whatever effect the ABM debate might have had on Soviet-American relations and the climate of disarmament, it was Mr. Nixon who delayed the start of strategic arms-limitation talks, who continued MIRV testing, who opted for the Safeguard system in the first place, who took on his own authority any number of other acts, large and small, such as his visit to Romania, that had their cumulative impact in the same areas.

And while earnest Mike Mansfield can interpret the President's statements at Guam last summer as an historic retreat from an interventionist policy in Asia, that means nothing more than a clue to current Congressional sentiment, which is plain anyway. And it is Richard Nixon alone who can actually head the nation along the line of policy disclosed at Guam—or on the more militantly anti-Communist path he suggested almost immediately thereafter in Bangkok.

So all that can be said with any certainty is that both at home and abroad, the President of the United States may not be quite as free as he was, only yesterday, to be, in Woodrow Wilson's phrase, "as big a man as he can." Suddenly, he is at least under scrutiny. Even Frankenstein got wise at last, although it is chilling to remember that it was quite a bit too late.

THE POWER OF THE PRESIDENT

SAUL K. PADOVER

"They talk about the power of the President," Harry Truman once complained, "how I can just push a button to get things done. Why, I spend most

SOURCE: Saul K. Padover, "The Power of the President," *Commonweal*, 88 (August 9, 1968), 521–525. Reprinted by permission of the Commonweal Publishing Company, Inc.

of my time kissing somebody's ass." And a similarly thwarted Lyndon B. Johnson exclaimed recently: "Power? The only power I've got is nuclear— and I can't use that."

But not so international affairs. The concentration of foreign-policy power in the White House, especially in the last three or four decades, has been of such a nature that the customary Constitutional and political checks have been made largely ineffective. For all practical purposes, the President is virtually a dictator in international affairs. His decisions are paramount and unrivalled. He occupies the field of decision and action by himself. He shares his authority and prerogative with no other person or group. The irony is that the President uses his preponderant authority legally, *within* the Constitutional framework, but is not bound by normally prescriptive constraints.

This development would have appalled the Founding Fathers. It is informative to recall that the framers of the Constitution, in their Convention of 1787, were deeply concerned with the question of Presidential power and were worried that the Chief Executive might become autocratic. They had in their minds the European models, all of whom they considered bad—including George III of England and the Stadtholder of Holland. Jefferson, who was not present at the Constitutional Convention, expressed a widely held American opinion of contemporary European Executives (monarchs whom he regarded as mostly fools or knaves panoplied in autocratic power), when, speaking of the "book of kings," he exclaimed fervently: "from all of whom the Lord deliver us. . . ."

In creating the Presidency, the framers of the Constitution were confronted by the age-old dilemma of those who appreciate the need for power and at the same time fear its use. "Make him too weak," said Gouverneur Morris, "—the legislature will usurp his power. Make him too strong—he will usurp the legislature."

On this issue, the debates in the Constitutional Convention are illuminating. One distinguished member, Roger Sherman of Connecticut, proposed that the Executive be chosen by Congress and be entirely accountable to it, because, he said: "an independence of the Executive over the Supreme Legislature was . . . the very essence of tyranny." Pierce Butler of South Carolina, expressing a dread of Executive power which, he said, "in all countries . . . is in constant increase," warned: "Gentlemen seem to think we had nothing to apprehend from an abuse of the Executive power. But why might not a Catiline or a Cromwell arise in this country as well as in others?"

The wise and aged (he was 81) Benjamin Franklin thought so too. Keeping George Washington in mind, Franklin said that the first Chief Executive "will be a good one," but what about his successors? "Nobody," he reminded his fellow-delegates, "knows what sort may come afterwards. The Executive will be increasing here, as elsewhere, till it ends in a monarchy." In those days, it should be remembered, "monarchy" had the connotation of "tyranny" or "absolutism."

The long and intermittent debates over the Presidency, which extended over a period of about 14 weeks, ended in a compromise. Thus the President was empowered to appoint "ambassadors, other public ministers and consuls," but each nomination was required to have the "advice and consent of the Senate." The President was made Commander in Chief of the armed forces of the United States, including the State militias in wartime, but had no authority to initiate war. The power "to declare war" was granted to Congress. It is interesting to note that during the Constitutional debates an early version stated that Congress shall have power "to make war." In subsequent years it was suggested that this changed phrasing *implied* that while Congress was empowered to "declare" war, it was left to the President to "make" it. The framers of the Constitution, however, did not seem to think so. Without defining the meaning of "war," they made specific enumerations of areas connected with all things military where Congress has exclusive authority. Article I, Section 8, of the Constitution provides that the "Congress shall have power. . . .

"To raise and support armies. . . .

"To provide and maintain a navy. . . .

"To make rules for the government and regulation of the land and naval forces. . . .

"To provide for calling forth the militia. . . .

"To provide for organizing, arming and disciplining the militia. . . .

"To exercise exclusive . . . authority over all places purchased for the erection of forts, magazines, arsenals, dock-yards, and other needful buildings. . . ."

In regard to the crucial problem of treaties—declared in the Constitution to be the "supreme law of the land"—the framers were equally wary about granting the Chief Executive extensive authority. This was particularly true in connection with peace treaties. Some of the delegates to the Constitutional Convention felt that the making of treaties of peace was a matter of such moment that it should be the prerogative of the Senate in cases where the President could not be trusted to end a war.

James Madison suggested that two-thirds of the Senate should have the power to make peace treaties, without Presidential concurrence. His reason for the proposal reveals the prevailing distrust of too much Executive power. Madison shrewdly argued that a wartime President would, of necessity, be in such a commanding position that he might be reluctant to terminate a conflict that had clothed him with so much authority and special eminence. In Madison's words, a President "would necessarily derive so much power and importance from a state of war that he might be tempted, if authorized [i.e. Constitutionally allowed], to impede a treaty of peace." In a compromise solution, the framers of the Constitution granted the President power "to make treaties," but with a specific reservation—"provided two-thirds of the Senators present concur."

Even so, the framers were not altogether at ease about Presidential power. The Congressional checks which they built into the Constitution did not allay their fear of some overbearing or corrupt Chief Executive in the future. They added a further safeguard—that of impeachment. As a guarantee for the "good behavior of the Executive," to quote North Carolina's William R. Davie, the framers thought it essential that the President (as well as the Vice President and other high officials) be made liable to impeachment, that is, legally tried (by the Senate sitting as a court) for certain stated causes. If found guilty, by two-thirds of the Senators present, he should be removed from office and then be subject "to indictment, trial, judgment and punishment, according to law." Benjamin Franklin added a wry note to the discussion on impeachment. He said that the provision was necessary to get rid of an "obnoxious Executive," because without it there would be "recourse . . . to assassination." Such an act, he felt was too drastic, since it would not only deprive the President of his life but also of "the opportunity of vindicating his character." Impeachment would give the Executive a chance of defending himself in a fair trial.

As the Constitutionally created Diplomatic Chief and Army Chief, the President has occupied a unique position in the Federal system, enjoying—and using—special powers not granted to any other person or political body. In practice, if not necessarily in theory (although there is some Constitutional theory here too), the Executive, beginning with George Washington, soon found that his functions as Chief Diplomat and Commander had to be performed in an arena that was, more or less, exclusively his own. As early as March 7, 1800, John Marshall, then a member of Congress, said in a speech in the House of Representatives: "The President is the sole organ of the nation in its external relations, and its sole representative with foreign nations . . . The demand of a foreign nation can only be made on him. He possesses the whole Executive power. He holds and directs the force of the nation. Of consequence, any act to be performed by the force of the nation is to be performed through him."

A similar position was taken by the Senate Committee on Foreign Relations on Feb. 15, 1816. In its report, the Committee confirmed Marshall's view when it stated: "The President is the Constitutional representative of the United States with regard to foreign nations." It affirmed that only the President "must necessarily be most competent to determine" the whole process of international negotiation; and while "he is responsible to the Constitution," nevertheless, any interference by the Senate would only "impair the best security for the national safety."

Over the years, the President's position of primacy as Chief Diplomat—as treaty-negotiator and treaty-maker—has been established in practice and confirmed in law. The Courts have not only upheld this power but have deepened and widened it in their interpretations. One Supreme Court decision (*Geofroy v. Riggs*, 1890) actually declared that the treaty-making power was virtually limitless in range and subject matter. The basic limit, according to that decision, was only that which the Constitution expressly prohibited. Otherwise, stated Justice Stephen J. Field in *Geofroy v. Riggs:* "The treaty power, as expressed in the Constitution, is . . . unlimited . . . It would not be contended that it extends so far as to authorize what the Constitution forbids . . . But with these exceptions, it is not perceived that there is any limit to the questions . . . touching any matter which is properly the subject of negotiation with a foreign country."

Furthermore, the Courts have been wary about putting restraints on the Executive's commanding prerogative in the realm of foreign affairs. They have taken the position that the Judicial branch was neither Constitutionally empowered nor administratively equipped to pass judgment in foreign policy matters, which they regarded as essentially political and not judicial. In the case of *Chicago and Southern Airlines v. Waterman Steamship Corp.* (1948), Justice Robert H. Jackson summarized the Supreme Court's opinion thus: "The President, both as Commander in Chief and as the Nation's organ for foreign affairs, has available intelligence services whose reports are not and ought not to be published to the world. It would be intolerable that Courts, without the relevant information, should review and perhaps nullify actions of the Executive taken on information properly held secret . . . But even if the Courts could require full disclosure, the very nature of Executive decisions as to foreign policy is political, not judicial . . . They are decisions of a kind for which the Judiciary has neither aptitude, facilities nor responsibility."

Justice Jackson concluded that foreign policy decisions, being the domain of political (Executive, primarily) power, were "not subject to judicial intrusion or inquiry."

As Presidential power in foreign affairs has grown and expanded, the originally designed Constitutional checks upon it have undergone a slow process of erosion. To a large extent, this development has been due to the ambiguity of the Constitutional provisions. In the 1967 Senate *Hearings on U.S. Commitments to Foreign Powers,* Senator J. William Fulbright, Chairman of the Senate's Foreign Relations Committee, frankly admitted that he was troubled by "the imprecision that exists in this field." Constitutionally, it is not even clear what a "war" is, or when it becomes one. Is chasing bandits across a foreign frontier "war" in the Constitutional sense? Is occupation by marines of foreign ports and customs houses "war"? Is large-scale fighting against Communists in Asia a "war" or a "police action"?

In a Supreme Court decision of 1936—*United States v. Curtiss-Wright Export Corp.*—Presidential domination in the foreign affairs field was summed up in sweeping terms. Speaking for the Court's majority (7 to 2), Justice George Sutherland stated, *inter alia*: "Not only . . . is the Federal power over external affairs in origin and essential character different from that over internal affairs, but participation in the exercise of the power is significantly limited. In this vast external realm, with its important, complicated, delicate and manifold problems, the President alone has the power to speak or listen as a representative of the nation. He *makes* treaties with the advice and consent of the Senate; but he alone negotiates. Into the field of negotiation the Senate cannot intrude; and Congress itself is powerless to invade it. . . ."

CIRCUMVENTING THE SENATE

Presidents have been able to circumvent Senatorial treaty power through the device of Executive Agreements. Such Agreements are of two types: those that require legislative implementation and those that are "pure," that is, require no Congressional action. Unlike a treaty, an Executive Agreement does not require the approval of the Senate. Presidents can make such Agreements, provided they do not infringe on the private rights of Americans, on any subject, ranging from recognition of foreign governments to barter deals. Among the better known Executive Agreements, one may mention: the destroyer-for-bases exchange with Great Britain in 1940; the Lend-Lease program in 1941; the Atlantic Charter Agreement in 1941; and the Allied Conferences of Yalta in 1944 and Potsdam in 1945, which involved postwar settlements. Executive Agreements, arranged between the President or his agents and foreign nations, have the binding force of treaties, as the Supreme Court has held in decisions such as *United States v. Belmont* (1937) and *United States v. Pink* (1942).

The number of treaties, requiring Senatorial concurrence, has decreased steadily while Executive Agreements, requiring none, have risen steeply. By 1939, out of 2,000 engagements made by the United States with foreign countries, 1,182 were Executive Agreements. In 1936, there were 8 treaties, and 16 Executive Agreements. In 1944, there was one treaty, and 74 Executive Agreements.

The vast, practically limitless, powers enjoyed by the President nowadays is seen most strikingly in the field of war making. From the very beginning, the "Commander in Chief" clause of the Constitution, not being defined or specifically limited, has provided the Executive with as much military authority as his personal discretion allowed. The main restraints have been the President's own character and political judgment. From the earliest days of the Republic to now, Presidents have sent armed forces into action—without Congressional authorization of war declaration—for the ostensible purposes of protecting life and property abroad. These have been recognized as legitimate steps in the defense of the "national interest." There have been at least 125 such instances, perhaps more.

John Adams waged an undeclared, although limited, war against France between 1798 and 1800. Jefferson sent a flotilla against the Algerian (Barbary) pirates in 1801. Polk ordered troops against Mexico in 1846, and Wilson in

1916. Presidents have dispatched marines to Central America on numerous occasions. More recently, Truman sent forces to Korea in 1950 (opening a large-scale war), Eisenhower to Lebanon in 1958, and Johnson to the Dominican Republic in 1966.

All these military steps were taken at the President's discretion, by virtue of the power inherent in him as Commander in Chief, without formal declarations of war. Occasionally there have been Congressional Resolutions, such as the Tonkin Gulf Resolution of 1964, but these must be construed as statements of support, not formal grants of power. A Congressional Resolution is in the nature of a politico-psychological tactic, to show the world that a certain Presidential step has national support or sometimes merely to nudge the Executive. But a Resolution as such adds little, if anything, to the President's inherent military prerogative.

Currently there is a claim in the Senate that the war in Vietnam is illegal because the Tonkin Gulf Resolution, which the President has used as his presumed authorization to initiate the bombing and to widen the conflict, was based on misleading information deliberately supplied by the Pentagon. The facts of the case may or may not be true. But even granting that the Senate was booby-trapped by the military agents of the Executive, the argument is of dubious Constitutional validity, although it may have great moral force. The truth is that the Commander in Chief does not actually need Congressional Resolutions. If and when he decides upon military action, he has a plenitude of authority and precedent behind him. He has, in fact, an awesome power in this field.

Is such power Constitutional? The answer is that it is not patently unconstitutional. There is nothing in the Constitution that says that the President may not wage war abroad at his discretion. The Constitution merely states that only Congress can "declare" war. But it does not say that a war has to be "declared" before it can be waged.

Vietnam is the culmination of this long-accumulating Executive power in the military domain. Where it differs from preceding Presidential commitments of armed forces abroad without war declaration is in scale—in numbers of troops committed, worldwide consequences, and soaring casualties. There is obviously a considerable difference between the three small frigates and one sloop of war that Jefferson dispatched against the Barbary pirates in 1801, and the current deployment in Vietnam. However, the principle of Presidential discretion in the use of force abroad remains the same.

We should remind ourselves that Vietnam is a Presidential war. It was initiated ("Americanized") with the bombing of 1964 and then steadily escalated and systematically conducted entirely by the President. The military heads and the chiefs of the Pentagon have acted, and legally may act, only at his orders. Whatever the reasons for the plunge into the Vietnam war there can be no question that the decision emanated from the Executive and has been his responsibility ever since. There is, moreover, no legal way to stop him.

Thus the fears that James Madison expressed in 1787 have actually come to pass, although under altered circumstances and under a different guise.

With luck, the war in Vietnam—now widely agreed to have been an American blunder—may end without global catastrophe. But what about the future?

Once in office, any man, by virtue of the power now inherent in the Presidency, is in absolute control over the levers of the mightiest military machine in the world, with an atomic-weapon capability of destroying much of humanity at his finger tips. That is a chance that this nation, or mankind as a whole, cannot afford to accept indefinitely.

The report of Senator Fulbright's Foreign Relations Committee, issued on Nov. 21, 1967 put the problem thus: "Already possessing vast powers over our country's foreign relations, the Executive, by acquiring the authority to commit the country to war, now exercises something approaching absolute power over the life and death of every living American—to say nothing of millions of other people all over the world. There is no human being or group of human beings alive wise and competent enough to be entrusted with such vast power. Plenary powers in the hands of any man or group threaten all other men with tyranny or disaster."

The situation is not only perilous in itself but it is also at variance with the philosophy of American democracy, which, in its governmental aspect, is based on the principle of "checked" and "balanced" powers. When one of the three coordinate branches of the national government is increasingly preponderant and unchecked, the structure is thrown out of kilter and creates a festering crisis that endangers the whole political system.

What is needed is not to take power in foreign affairs away from the President—the national security obviously requires that he has it—but to put manageable restraints upon it. What the situation requires is a counter-force to keep the overwhelming power of the Executive in acceptable balance. Only Congress can do that Constitutionally.

If Congress, especially the Senate, is to restore its eroded powers and reassert its originally assigned role as partner and balancer in foreign affairs, it will have to do it, not through the futility of accusatory speeches or committee reports, but through concrete legislation and institutionalized procedures. In the process, it may well have to reorganize itself. A number of steps come to mind:

> —Legislation putting specified limits on the size of forces committed to war abroad when there is no war declaration.
> —Legislation requiring Congressional authorization for any increase of forces under such circumstances.
> —Legislation requiring the Executive to consult the Congress before committing sizeable forces abroad.

—Legislation requiring a time limit on commitment of forces, subject to Congressional extension, or rescission.

—Reorganization of the Foreign Relations and Military Affairs Committees to small and wieldy size, with members making it their full-time occupation.

—Setting up of joint House-Senate Committees on the basis of continuous operations.

—Enlarging the professional and research staffs of those Committees.

—Establishing a Congressional intelligence service, not to compete with the gigantic apparatus available to the Executive (such as the CIA), but sufficiently equipped, trained and skilled to help the Congress evaluate properly the findings and recommendations of Presidential agencies.

These are, of course, merely indications of the kind of action required to strengthen Congress so that it could carry out properly its Constitutionally-assigned role. It is clear that without some such steps, future Vietnams may not be avoidable, and Congress will continue to be a paper tiger.

PRESIDENTIAL ADVISERS

THEODORE C. SORENSEN

. . . Article II, Section 2 provides that the President "may require the Opinion in writing of the principal Officer in each of the Executive Departments upon any subject relating to the Duties of their respective offices." But it does not prevent him from requiring their opinion *orally*. . . . It does not prevent him from obtaining a Cabinet member's opinion on subjects *not* relating to his respective office—if a Secretary of Defense has a business background, for example, that would be helpful in a dispute with the steel industry—or if a Secretary of the Treasury has experience in foreign affairs. Nor is the President prevented from seeking the opinions of those who are *not* principal officers of the Executive departments.

MEETING WITH ADVISERS

In short, each President must determine for himself how best to elicit and assess the advice of his advisers. Organized meetings, of the Cabinet and Na-

SOURCE: Theodore C. Sorensen, "Presidential Advisers," *Decision-Making in The White House* (New York: Columbia University Press, 1963), pp. 57–77. Reprinted by permission.

tional Security Council, for example, have certain indispensable advantages, not the least of which are the increased public confidence inspired by order and regularity and the increased esprit de corps of the participants.

President Kennedy, whose nature and schedule would otherwise turn him away from meetings for the sake of meeting, has sometimes presided over sessions of the full Cabinet and National Security Council held primarily for these two reasons. Regularly scheduled meetings can also serve to keep open the channels of communication. This is the primary purpose, for example, of the President's weekly breakfast with his party's legislative leaders.

But there are other important advantages to meetings. The interaction of many minds is usually more illuminating than the intuition of one. In a meeting representing different departments and diverse points of view, there is a greater likelihood of hearing alternatives, of exposing errors, and of challenging assumptions. It is true in the White House, as in the Congress, that fewer votes are changed by open debate than by quiet negotiation among the debaters. But in the White House, unlike the Congress, only one man's vote is decisive, and thorough and thoughtful debate *before* he has made up his mind can assist him in that task.

That meetings can sometimes be useful was proven by the deliberations of the NSC executive committee after the discovery of offensive weapons in Cuba. The unprecedented nature of the Soviet move, the manner in which it cut across so many departmental jurisdictions, the limited amount of information available, and the security restrictions which inhibited staff work, all tended to have a leveling effect on the principals taking part in these discussions, so that each felt free to challenge the assumptions and assertions of all others.

Everyone in that group altered his views as the give-and-take talk continued. Every solution or combination of solutions was coldly examined, and its disadvantages weighed. The fact that we started out with a sharp divergence of views, the President has said, was "very valuable" in hammering out a policy.

In such meetings, a President must carefully weigh his own words. Should he hint too early in the proceedings at the direction of his own thought, the weight of his authority, the loyalty of his advisers and their desire to be on the "winning side" may shut off productive debate. Indeed, his very presence may inhibit candid discussion. President Truman, I am told, absented himself for this reason from some of the National Security Council discussions on the Berlin blockade; and President Kennedy, learning on his return from a midweek trip in October, 1962, that the deliberations of the NSC executive committee over Cuba had been more spirited and frank in his absence, asked the committee to hold other preliminary sessions without him.

But no President—at least none with his firm cast of mind and concept of office—could stay out of the fray completely until all conflicts were resolved and a collective decision reached. For group recommendations too often put a premium on consensus in place of content, on unanimity in place of precision, on compromise in place of creativity.

Some advisers may genuinely mistake agreement for validity and coordination for policy—looking upon their own role as that of mediator, convinced that any conclusion shared by so many able minds must be right, and pleased that they could in this way ease their President's problems. They may in fact have increased them.

Even more severe limitations arise when a decision must be communicated, in a document or speech or diplomatic note. For group authorship is rarely, if ever, successful. A certain continuity and precision of style, and unity of argument, must be carefully drafted, particularly in a public communication that will be read or heard by many diverse audiences. Its key principles and phrases can be debated, outlined, and later reviewed by a committee, but basically authorship depends on one man alone with his typewriter or pen. (Had the Gettysburg address been written by a committee, its ten sentences would surely have grown to a hundred, its simple pledges would surely have been hedged, and the world would indeed have little noted or long remembered what was said there.)

Moreover, even spirited debates can be stifling as well as stimulating. The homely, the simple, or the safe may sound far more plausible to the weary ear in the Cabinet room than it would look to the careful eye in the office. The most formidable debater is not necessarily the most informed, and the most reticent may sometimes be the wisest.

Even the most distinguished and forthright adviser is usually reluctant to stand alone. If he fears his persistence in a meeting will earn him the disapprobation of his colleagues, a rebuff by the President, or (in case of a "leak") the outrage of the Congress, press, or public, he may quickly seek the safety of greater numbers. At the other extreme are those who seek refuge in the role of chronic dissenter, confining their analytical power to a restatement of dangers and objections.

Still others may address themselves more to their image than to the issues. The liberal may seek to impress his colleagues with his caution; idealists may try to sound tough-minded. I have attended more than one meeting where a military solution was opposed by military minds and supported by those generally known as peace-lovers.

The quality of White House meetings also varies with the number and identity of those attending. Large meetings are less likely to keep secrets—too many Washington officials enjoy talking knowingly at social events or to the press or to their friends. Large meetings are also a less flexible instrument for action, less likely to produce a meaningful consensus or a frank, hard-hitting debate. President Kennedy prefers to invite only those whose official views he requires or whose unofficial judgment he values, and to reserve crucial decisions for a still smaller session or for solitary contemplation in his own office.

The difficulty with small meetings, however, is that, in Washington, nearly everyone likes to feel that he, too, conferred and concurred. For years agencies and individuals all over town have felt affronted if not invited to a National Security Council session. The press leaps to conclusions as to who is in favor and who is not by scanning the attendance lists of meetings, speculating in much the same fashion (and with even less success) as the Kremlinologists who study the reviewing stand at the Russian May Day Parade or analyze which Soviet officials sat where at the opening of the Moscow ballet.

Yet in truth attendance at a White House meeting is not necessarily a matter of logic. Protocol, personal relations, and the nature of the forum may all affect the list. Some basic foreign policy issue, for example, may be largely decided before it comes to the National Security Council—by the appointment of a key official, or by the President's response at a press conference, or by the funds allocated in the budget. Yet personnel, press conference, and budget advice is generally given in meetings outside the National Security Council.

EXPERT ADVISERS

Many different types of advisers, with differing roles and contributions, attend these meetings. President Kennedy met on his tax policy in the summer of 1962, for example, with professional economists from both inside and outside the government, as well as with department heads and White House aides. To the key meetings on Cuba were invited highly respected Foreign Service officers as well as policy appointees, retired statesmen as well as personal presidential assistants.

There is no predictable weight which a President can give to the conclusions of each type. The technical expert or career specialist, operating below the policy-making level, may have concentrated knowledge on the issue under study which no other adviser can match. Yet Presidents are frequently criticized for ignoring the advice of their own experts.

The reason is that the very intensity of that expert's study may prevent him from seeing the broader, more practical perspective which must govern public policy. As Laski's notable essay pointed out, too many experts lack a sense of proportion, an ability to adapt, and a willingness to accept evidence inconsistent with their own. The specialist, Laski wrote, too often lacks "insight into the movement and temper of the public mind. . . . He is an invaluable servant and an impossible master."

Thus the atomic scientist, discussing new tests, may think largely in terms of his own laboratory. The career diplomat, discussing an Asian revolt, may think largely in terms of his own post. The professional economist, in urging lower farm price supports, may think more in terms of his academic colleagues than of the next presidential election.

But not all experts recognize the limits of their political sagacity, and they do not hesitate to pronounce with a great air of authority broad policy recommendations in their own field (and sometimes all fields). Any President would be properly impressed by their seeming command of the complex; but the President's own common sense, his own understanding of the Congress and the country, his own balancing of priorities, his own ability to analyze and generalize and simplify, are more essential in reaching the right decision than all the specialized jargon and institutionalized traditions of the professional elite.

The trained navigator, it has been rightly said, is essential to the conduct of a voyage, but his judgment is not superior on such matters as where it should go or whether it should be taken at all. Essential to the relationship between expert and politician, therefore, is the recognition by each of the other's role, and the refusal of each to assume the other's role. The expert should neither substitute his political judgment for the policy-maker's nor resent the latter's exercising of his own; and the policy-maker should not forget which one is the expert.

Expert predictions are likely to be even more tenuous than expert policy judgments, particularly in an age when only the unpredictable seems to happen. In the summer of 1962, most of the top economists in government, business, and academic life thought it likely that a recession would follow the stock-market slide—at least "before the snows melted" was the cautious forecast by one economist from a cold northern state. But, instead, this year's thaw brought with it new levels of production—and, naturally, a new set of predictions.

In the fall of 1962, most specialists in Soviet affairs believed that long-range Soviet missiles, with their closely guarded electronic systems, would never be stationed on the uncertain island of Cuba, nearly 6,000 miles away from Soviet soil and supplies. Nevertheless, each rumor to this effect was checked out; increasing rumors brought increased surveillance; and when, finally, the unexpected did happen, this did not diminish the President's respect for these career servants. It merely demonstrated once again that the only infallible experts are those whose forecasts have never been tested.

CABINET ADVISERS

In short, a Cabinet of politicians and policy-makers is better than a Cabinet of experts. But a President will also weigh with care the advice of each Cabinet official. For the latter is also bound by inherent limitations. He was not necessarily selected for the President's confidence in his judgment alone—considerations of politics, geography, public esteem, and interest-group pressures may also have played a part, as well as his skill in administration.

Moreover, each department has its own clientele and point of view, its own experts and bureaucratic interests, its own relations with the Congress and certain subcommittees, its own statutory authority, objectives, and standards of success. No Cabinet member is free to ignore all this without impairing the morale and efficiency of his department, his standing therein, and his relations with the powerful interest groups and congressmen who consider it partly their own.

The President may ask for a Secretary's best judgment apart from the department's views, but in the mind of the average Secretary (and there have been many notable exceptions) the two may be hardly distinguishable. Whether he is the captive or the champion of those interests makes no practical difference. By reflecting in his advice to the President his agency's component bureaus, some of which he may not even control, he increases both his prestige within the department and his parochialism without.

Bureaucratic parochialism and rivalry are usually associated in Washington with the armed services, but they in fact affect the outlook of nearly every agency. They can be observed, to cite only a few examples, in the jurisdictional maneuvering between the Park Service and the Forest Service, between the Bureau of Reclamation and the Army Engineers, between State and Treasury on world finance, or State and Commerce on world trade, or State and Defense on world disarmament.

They can also be observed in Cabinet autobiographies complaining that the President—any President—rarely saw things their way. And they can be observed, finally, in case studies of an agency head paying more heed to the Congress than to the President who named him. But it is the Congress, after all, that must pass on his requests for money, men, and authority. It is the Congress with which much of his time will be spent, which has the power to investigate his acts or alter his duties. And it is the Congress which vested many of his responsibilities directly in him, not in the President or the Executive branch.

WHITE HOUSE STAFF ADVISERS

The parochialism of experts and department heads is offset in part by a President's White House and executive staff. These few assistants are the only other men in Washington whose responsibilities both enable and require them to look, as he does, at the government as a whole. Even the White House specialists—the President's economic advisers or science adviser, for example—are likely to see problems in a broader perspective, within the framework of the President's objectives and without the constraints of bureaucratic tradition.

White House staff members are chosen, not according to any geographical, political, or other pattern, but for their ability to serve the President's needs and to talk the President's language. They must not—and do not, in this Administration—replace the role of a Cabinet official or block his access to the President. Instead, by working closely with departmental personnel, by spotting, refining, and defining issues for the President, they can increase governmental unity rather than splinter responsibility. A good White House staff can give a President that crucial margin of time, analysis, and judgment that makes an unmanageable problem more manageable.

But there are limiting factors as well. A White House adviser may see a departmental problem in a wider context than the Secretary, but he also has less contact with actual operations and pressures, with the Congress and interested groups. If his own staff grows too large, his office may become only another department, another level of clearances and concurrences instead of a personal instrument of the President. If his confidential relationship with the President causes either one to be too uncritical of the other's judgment, errors may go uncorrected. If he develops (as Mr. Acheson has suggested so many do) a confidence in his own competence which outruns the fact, his contribution may be more mischievous than useful. If, on the other hand, he defers too readily to the authority of renowned experts and Cabinet powers, then the President is denied the skeptical, critical service his staff should be providing.

OUTSIDE ADVISERS

Finally, a President may seek or receive advice from outside the Executive branch: from members of the Congress; from independent wise men, elder statesmen, academic lights; from presidentially named high-level commissions or special agents; or merely from conversations with friends, visitors, private interest leaders, and others. Inevitably, unsolicited advice will pour in from the mass media.

This is good. Every President needs independent, unofficial sources of advice for the same reasons he needs independent, unofficial sources of information. Outside advisers may be more objective. Their contact with affected groups may be closer. They may be men whose counsel the President trusts, but who are unable to accept government service for financial or personal reasons. They may be men who are frank with the President because, to use Corwin's phrase, their "daily political salt did not come from the President's table."

Whatever the justification, outside advice has its own limitations. As national problems become more complex and interrelated, requiring continuous, firsthand knowledge of confidential data and expert analysis, very few outsiders are sufficiently well informed. The fact that some simple recommendation, contained in an editorial or political oration or informal conversation, seems more striking or appealing or attention-getting than the intricate product of bureaucracy does not make it any more valid.

Moreover, once the advice of a distinguished private citizen or committee is sought and made public, rejection of that advice may add to the President's difficulties. The appointment by the last three Presidents of special advisory committees on civil rights, world trade, and foreign aid was, in that sense, a gamble—a gamble that the final views of these committees would strengthen, not weaken, the President's purpose. Should the outside report not be made public, the Gaither report being a well-known example, a President who rejects its advice may still have to face the consequences of its authors' displeasure.

QUALIFICATIONS OF ADVISERS

Finally, a President's evaluation of any individual's advice is dependent in part on the human characteristics of both men. Personalities play an intangible but surprisingly important role. Particular traits, social ties, recreational interests or occupational backgrounds may strengthen or weaken the bonds between them. Some Presidents pay more attention to generals, some to businessmen, some to politicians, some even to intellectuals who have "never met a payroll and never carried a precinct."

In truth, a political background, not necessarily at the precinct level, is helpful. It gives the adviser a more realistic understanding of the President's needs. Those without such experience will tend to assume that the few congressmen in touch with their agency speak for all the Congress, that one or two contacts at a Washington cocktail party are an index of public opinion, and that what looms large in the newspaper headlines necessarily looms large in the public mind.

Those with a political base of their own are also more secure in case of attack; but those with political ambitions of their own—as previous Presidents discovered—may place their own reputation and record ahead of their President's. (Such a man is not necessarily suppressing his conscience and forgetting the national interest. He may sincerely believe whatever it is most to his advantage to believe, much like the idealistic but hungry lawyer who will never defend a guilty man but persuades himself that all rich clients are innocent.)

Other advisers may also be making a record, not for some future campaign, but for some future publication. "History will record that I am right," he mutters to himself, if not to his colleagues, because he intends to write that history in his memoirs. The inaccuracy of most Washington diaries and autobiographies is surpassed only by the immodesty of their authors.

The opposite extreme is the adviser who tells his President only what he thinks the President wants to hear—a bearer of consistently good tidings but frequently bad advice.

Yet there is no sure test of a good adviser. The most rational, pragmatic-appearing man may turn out to be the slave of his own private myths, habits, and emotional beliefs. The hardest-working man may be too busy and out-of-touch with the issue at hand, or too weary to focus firmly on it. (I saw firsthand, during the long days and nights of the Cuban crisis, how brutally physical and mental fatigue can numb the good sense as well as the senses of normally articulate men.)

The most experienced man may be experienced only in failure, or his experience, in Coleridge's words, may be "like the stern lights of a ship which illumine only the track it has passed." The most articulate, authoritative man may only be making bad advice sound good, while driving into silence less aggressive or more cautious advisers.

All this a President must weigh in hearing his advisers. He need not weigh them equally. For toward some, he will have more respect. With some, he will communicate easier. For some, he will have more affection.

President Kennedy's confidence in the Attorney General, for example, on a wide variety of issues, is based not on fraternal ties alone but on long years of observing and testing his brother's judgment and dependability. The more active role taken by Secretary of Labor Goldberg, also assumed by his successor but in contrast with that of his predecessors, resulted not from an upgrading of that post but from a closer relationship with the President.

There are countless other examples. My emphasis on the role of the President has not made me a turncoat to the distinguished class of presidential advisers. On the contrary, while his perspective may be more limited, the career specialist, the Cabinet Secretary, the White House aide, or any other adviser still has a valuable contribution to make; and his limited perspective is a danger only if both he and the President are blind to that limitation.

TRANSITION AT THE WHITE HOUSE

HENRY F. GRAFF

The Presidential transition is now in full swing: The Cabinet has been designated, high-ranking officials are being named, and the shape of new policies in many fields is being hammered out. This transition is a uniquely American problem that recently has become more serious than in the past. In England and other countries governed under a Parliamentary system, where there is always a shadow cabinet ready to step into office, the transfer of governmental power can be accomplished overnight. In the United States there are less than 11 weeks between Election Day and Inauguration Day—a period that is too short to do thoroughly all that is required to shift the reins of government, and too long for any interregnum in a democratic age in a shrunken world.

The problem of transferring the Presidency used to take the form of assuring that the shift of power from one President to the next would be orderly, in the sense that it would be willing. At the beginning of Presidential history, the collective experience with monarchy that included false claimants to the throne as well as usurpations of power was never far from people's minds. When John Adams succeeded Washington peacefully to become the second

SOURCE: Henry F. Graff, "Transition at the White House," *The New Leader,* 51 (December 30, 1968), 3–7. Copyright © The American Labor Conference on International Affairs, Inc. Reprinted by permission.

President in 1797, Americans were delighted—and a few even amazed—that the process turned out to be friendly and smooth.

And so the turnovers of the Presidency have remained, although the meaning of the word friendly has sometimes been badly strained: Despite protestations to the contrary, the surrendering of power is usually painful. Being patriots, moreover, Presidents have an occupational fear that they leave the White House in less competent hands than their own.

President Polk, for example, wrote of his successor, the hero of Buena Vista: "General Taylor is, I have no doubt, a well-meaning old man. He is, however, uneducated, exceedingly ignorant of public affairs, and, I should judge, of very ordinary capacity. He will be in the hands of others. . . ." More recently, President Truman contemplated General Eisenhower's accession to the White House with comparable misgivings: "He'll sit here and he'll say, 'Do this! Do that!' And nothing will happen. Poor Ike—it won't be a bit like the Army."

But whatever the personal feelings of the President about the President-elect, the business of transferring the White House is now a complicated operation fraught with dangers and opportunities that did not exist in the early Presidency. The new President must in a trice find 70 Cabinet and subcabinet officials and approximately 2,000 additional people to fill other important posts. These men and women who will constitute "the Administration" must not only be moved to Washington; they must be supplied with policy directives for future programs, as well as be stuffed quickly with information that will enable them to function acceptably for the moment—usually in a field unfamiliar to them. The process is clearly vaster than the Founding Fathers ever dreamed, and more treacherous because this is the nuclear age and we live under the threat of instant crises at home and abroad.

Furthermore, since the passage of the Twentieth Amendment to the Constitution, establishing January 20 as Inauguration Day, the incoming Chief Executive arrives at his office for the first time after Congress has already been in session for two weeks or so. Congress awaits him formally organized and ready to zero in on the proposals he had had to whip into shape hastily, if not frenetically. Under the previous arrangements when Inauguration Day was March 4, the new President usually had a nine-month honeymoon before he had to face Congress—a bad system for many reasons but one which at least created the impression that a new President could ease into his responsibilities at a civilized pace.

The Presidential transition is comparable to the transfer of authority in any large corporative institution. But there is an important difference: The action and initiative are provided substantially by the group coming in, and the aim of the established group is to be helpful, not to instruct. Nor can the new President dawdle or take refuge in the idea that he is a "new boy" who does not know the ropes; he must begin his term at full tilt. He knows, too, that his historical "record" is being written indelibly from his first day in office, not from the time he finally feels ready.

The incoming President must rely on his predecessor's goodwill and control of subordinate officials in accepting the assistance and coaching available to him during the transition. The relationship between the arriving and departing chiefs is subtle and cannot always be judged immediately. Harry Truman and Dwight Eisenhower were quickly at loggerheads in the 1952–53 transfer period, Truman even concluding one letter to Eisenhower during the campaign with the tart words, "From a man who has always been your friend and who always intended to be!" Herbert Hoover and Franklin D. Roosevelt irritated each other so much that cooperation was impossible. One can only speculate as to whether the banking collapse in the early days of 1933 could have been cushioned by a friendlier transition.

President Eisenhower's first meeting with John F. Kennedy was correct and apparently surprising to Ike, who privately had referred to Kennedy as a "young whippersnapper." With a somewhat patronizing air Ike afterward wrote of the session: ". . . I must confess to considerable gratification in this visit with the young man who was to be my successor. Throughout the entire proceedings he conducted himself with unusual good taste. Resisting any temptation to flood the White House with his own retinue, he came riding in the back seat of an automobile completely by himself. In our conversation I was struck by his pleasing personality, his concentrated interest and his receptiveness."

When the President-to-be is entertained at the White House for the first time after his election he is, unavoidably, a listener. He is shifting his gears from being a candidate for office—full of promises and carping oratory—to another frame of mind in which he sees himself the proponent of a program and the President of all the people, eager to be persuasive to those who did not vote for him as well as satisfying to his supporters.

In this phase the President-elect discovers—if he did not know it all along —that men with minds and intentions as good as his own have been wrestling with the nation's problems. He finds out that the layers of public policy set by his predecessors are intractable indeed; that the room for maneuver in setting new courses for the nation is narrower than his friends hoped or his enemies feared, and perhaps than even he himself believed. The President-elect suddenly is tongue-tied on the central public questions, tensely determined to give no offense to any segment of the people at home or to those in his non-voting constituency in many parts of the world. He can protect himself in this silence partly because he must not intrude on the prerogatives of his predecessor, partly because he does not yet have access to the levers that control Presidential power.

The transition is also a trying time for the incumbent President. He must exercise his power until the last moment, counting on the declining days in office to press his program to the limit and to tidy the historical record of his era. He feels keenly the need not to bind his successor's hand, and at the same time not to yield a milligram of his authority until the day of departure arrives.

In the present transition, President Johnson is eager to offer President-elect Nixon the same kind of courtesy and helpfulness he would expect if the circumstances were reversed. Yet, he is protecting his prerogatives with a jealousy that is the oldest tradition of the office. He and the President-elect have known each other for years and the sparring periods in their relationship is long since over with. In addition, neither man can claim leverage on the other in consequence of a strangle hold on public popularity—a particular feature of the current transfer of office. They are in touch with each other on occasion, but they do not casually pick up the phone to engage in conversation. They only discuss personally what is described as "consequential business."

At the first Nixon-Johnson meeting a few days after the election, Secretary of State Dean Rusk asked the President-elect if he would approve a paragraph to be included in the Secretary's address to the NATO nations the following week, extending an invitation to them to meet in the United States next year on the 20th anniversary of the alliance. Rusk's deference, of course, was owing to the fact that the proposed event would take place during the Nixon administration. Nixon readily accepted the paragraph and the invitation it contained. When newsmen reported shortly afterward that Nixon had said he would have a veto on foreign-policy decisions of the Johnson Administration, the White House was both puzzled and irritated. The explanation for the misstatement that it accepts up to now is that Nixon had in mind Rusk's courteous gesture. The incident illustrates the type of problem the principals must face during the transition, and the sensitivities involved.

The quick appointment of the dean of diplomats, Robert D. Murphy, to be the liaison man between the Department of State and the new administration was greeted enthusiastically by the President. Nevertheless, the apparent slowness of the President-elect to name a Director of the Budget caused some eyebrow-lifting, among Nixon people as well as Administration people, for it is in the Bureau of the Budget that a President sets his priorities and the tone of his administration. Johnson has privately said, though, that he appreciated Nixon's desire to be cautious in making appointments.

Inevitably, there are points of conflict between the Nixon people and the Johnson people. The Johnson Administration so far has not turned over to its successor the reports on a number of critical issues prepared by special Presidential task forces in the last year. These reports contain the stuff for future legislation. The Nixon side is understandably eager to have these documents, and the matter is under discussion. The outgoing Administration is unwilling to see the newcomers reap whatever political reward may flow from the documents. (Vice President Humphrey has, though, turned over to the Nixon forces the position papers on foreign policy that were prepared for him during the campaign.)

In July, President Johnson named Charles S. Murphy, a soft-spoken elder statesman of the White House originally from North Carolina, who had served as special counsel to President Truman, to be in charge of transition matters from the Johnson side. The President publicly announced the fact September 5, and sent letters to the three major candidates inviting them to appoint representatives and expressing his wish to do all he could to make the transition cordial.

Vice President Humphrey appointed two spokesmen who visited with Murphy; former Governor Wallace appointed a representative to whom Murphy spoke once on the phone. Nixon's representative, now engaged in the task, was Franklin B. Lincoln Jr. Lincoln, who points out that his not seeking a position in the new administration helps fit him for the job, was an Assistant Secretary of Defense in the Eisenhower Administration and is at present a member of the law firm of which Nixon's is the senior name.

In a six-page memorandum to all the departments and agencies, Murphy set forth general transition procedures, including the instruction that they each prepare a two-volume basic reference book for the incoming head—actually modeled after the similar documents prepared by the Eisenhower Administration for the 1960–61 transition. The first volume, Murphy suggested, should contain statements on such matters as the agency's mission and statutory authorities, a chart of its basic organization, its budget arrangements including an account of budget planning for next year, biographical data on key personnel, the agency's statutory or administrative relationship to other agencies and to other governments, legislative procedures regarding the agency's affairs, and finally policy and program issues divided into three categories: those requiring immediate attention, those "coming into focus within 12 months," and those of "a longer range or continuing nature."

The second volume of "helps," Murphy prescribed, have information on these subjects: personal arrangements for the chief (including salary and benefits); personnel policies and administration; internal communications (including details about staff meetings, the clearance of documents, etc.); and program operations and administration. The volumes are now ready and await their users.

The Murphy memorandum further recommended to outgoing officials that their briefings of the newcomers "should be concise and devoted to essential information . . . Excessive length and detail . . . should be avoided. Similarly, incoming officials should not be overwhelmed with unsolicited advice and recommendations."

In the early exchanges between Murphy and Lincoln, the attention of the new administration was called to the value of subjecting all proposed major appointments to full field security investigations. This practice, followed since the days of the Truman Administration, was recommended to the Nixon people as a prudent procedure, for it is not a mandatory one. It was quickly adopted. To expedite clearances—and to prevent leaks of names—a special section has been established in the FBI under one of the Bureau's top officials, C. D. Deloach. A clearance that normally takes six weeks can be provided by this unit in one week. A similar arrangement was made available to Kennedy when he was the President-elect.

Lincoln and Murphy have established what both men regard as a warm and comfortable working relationship, aimed formally at maintaining orderly channels of communication. Lincoln has had ready access to Secretary of Defense Clark Clifford's file on transition affairs, Clifford having been in charge of the Truman side of the shift to Eisenhower and having helped Kennedy prepare for his takeover. Lincoln's relationship with Clifford is, therefore, a logical one; in addition, the two men have known each other well since both were young lawyers. Lincoln also confers with Lawson B. Knott Jr., the General Services Administrator, John W. Macy Jr., the Chairman of the Civil Service Commission and chief talent hunter for the Johnson Administration, and Charles Zwick, the Director of the Bureau of the Budget.

Knott is in the picture chiefly because he administers the $900,000 appropriated for the changeover under the Presidential Transition Act of 1963. This law was developed out of a recommendation that President Kennedy made to Congress to provide Federal funds for the work of future Presidents-elect. Kennedy's proposal was enthusiastically endorsed, too, by former Presidents Eisenhower and Truman. Both Eisenhower and Kennedy had been forced to use private and party funds to pay for their transitions to power.

The cost of transitions, inevitably hidden from public view, includes salaries and office space for staffs and for officials not yet legally installed. The $900,000 sum, based roughly on the cost of the transitions of 1952–53 and 1960–61, will be divided between the entering and the departing Administrations. Of the $450,000 allotted to each side, $75,000 will be earmarked for the Vice President involved—a figure based on Vice President Humphrey's transition costs in 1964–65.

Knott has arranged interim offices for the incoming administration in the new red-brick Executive Office building across the street from the old one. Up to now Nixon himself—who is established at the Hotel Pierre in New York—has not availed himself of their use, although his personnel operation is set up there.

John Macy's importance in the transition lies in the fact that he has about 30,000 names in his "talent bank." He has already made available to Nixon the 10,000 top names and biographies in his keeping. Other "banks" to which the new administration will have access include those of the Armed Services and the one in the Office of Emergency Planning. Eisenhower relied in substantial measure on at least two management consultant firms to find personnel, an arrangement that had several shortcomings. Having announced that he is conducting a nationwide hunt for the "right people," Nixon—and Lincoln—are being inundated with letters of inquiry and application.

The Nixon Group—a phrase that Lincoln uses to describe the President-elect and his chief advisers—has been working on its personnel problem for months now. Dr. Glenn Olds, former Dean of International Studies of the University of the State of New York, was engaged in "manpower development" early in the campaign. He was interviewing people even before the conventions, both as prospective jobholders and as sources of names. One day's appointments on his calendar in late September included David Lilienthal, the TVA planner; Douglas Dillon, a former Secretary of the Treasury; Winston Paul, the business executive; and Mitchell Sviridoff, the urban specialist, among others.

Many of the new appointees will soon be meeting informally with the chairman and members of the Senate committees responsible for approving their nominations. Since the names cannot be submitted by Nixon until he is sworn in, speed in confirmation will be essential. So tight is the schedule that in the same circumstances, President Kennedy spent some of the time between his inauguration ceremony and the beginning of the inaugural parade signing Presidential "commissions"—the prized diplomas done in copperplate script which signify that the persons named on them are Presidential appointees.

Lincoln says that if the new administration has 300 of its new people on hand on January 20, "it will be doing very well indeed." President Johnson will see to it that someone is left in charge of any agency whose new chief has not yet been named, or has not yet arrived on the scene. In some instances an Assistant Secretary or a political person may be asked to hold the fort until the Nixon administration moves its own man in. In making these assignments, Murphy is at pains to point out, the departing President is not pressing his influence beyond his time in office: "He is simply fulfilling his Constitutional obligation to see to it that the laws be faithfully executed."

The President's personal staff vacates the White House with him on Inauguration Day, but left behind is the permanent White House staff of about 200 people under the direction of William J. Hopkins, Executive Assistant to the President. Hopkins, who first came to the White House as a mail clerk in Hoover's Administration, is one of those rare men with "a passion for anonymity" that Franklin Roosevelt so much admired. Seldom photographed and never written about, Hopkins is a beloved and "indispensable" figure who will be on hand to greet the newcomers. In charge of the White House files and paperwork, he and his staff make the functioning of the Presidency administratively continuous.

Besides the staff under Hopkins, some of the secretaries now serving President Johnson's people will be staying on under President Nixon. In a modest way, the White House has been running an employment agency to find places for them with the newcomers. Thus audible evidence of the congeniality of the transition may be the few soprano Texas accents that will continue to be heard around the Executive offices.

President Eisenhower has entertained a fear that Inauguration Day—"a moment of practical dead center for the Federal government mechanism" is his phrase—is potentially a dangerous time for the nation. New officials with unfamiliar duties might respond to an emergency with confusion and irresolution. Ike declares that this concern was on his mind as he attended Kennedy's swearing-in ceremony in 1961, even though he had confidence in the alertness of the American Armed Forces and in the briefings that he and his staff had provided for the incoming administration.

Fears of a military attack on Inauguration Day are not commonly entertained in Washington. Nevertheless, the awareness is general that an administration is more likely to make mistakes and miscues in its early days than later on. The peculiar combination of misinformation and newness in office that made the Bay of Pigs adventure a fiasco in 1961 will always be the classic illustration.

To guard against disasters of this kind, the President and the President-elect must have very frank discussions. As Eisenhower has written soberly, the President can rely on "well-established procedures" in making major decisions, but he must know the procedures before he comes to office; there might not be sufficient time afterward. Kennedy, Eisenhower said, had to know for example, "the significance of the satchel filled with orders applicable to an emergency and carried by an unobstrusive man who would shadow [him] for all his days in office."

As the changing of the Presidents nears its climax, the Nixon people display the eagerness and the nervousness of brides going to the altar. The blank pages of the book of history that they gaze at lure them and dazzle them and give them pause. Meanwhile, the outgoing Administration begins to "decompress." During the next three weeks there will be farewell parties in every part of Washington: Department and agency heads will be presented with their desk chairs as mementos in ceremonies full of sentiment and nostalgia. Unmistakably, the heat is off, and the hour for drawing up a trial balance is at hand.

To aid in the fuller judgment by historians that can come only after the passage of time, President Johnson has already made detailed arrangements for the handling and management of his papers at the Presidential library being constructed on the campus of the University of Texas. Shortly, 2,000 or so filing cabinets containing them will be on their way to Austin to occupy secure warehouse space recently made available. The oral history of the Johnson era is being prepared under a distinguished historian, Joe B. Frantz of the University of Texas, formerly the chairman of its department of history. The interviewing in which Frantz is engaged in Washington will continue for a considerable time after the Johnsons return for good to the LBJ Ranch.

The President himself is serene—possibly more serene than at any time in his public life—and in good spirits, a manner that bespeaks his pride as well as his relief. His mind frequently turns to the subjects of the lectures he intends to deliver on college and university campuses next spring. He talks of his Administration's work in the past tense, and in taking stock of it he answers unhesitatingly a question about whether in retrospect he thinks he took any wrong turns: "Yes, we've made mistakes."

"We tried to do too much too quickly," he says of the domestic program, and he comments particularly on the problems of administering parts of it. He feels keenly that his Administration did not come to grips well enough with the problem of crime in the streets. He mentions the anger he feels every time he hears of new violence against persons in Washington itself, and contemplates that his wife, like other women, cannot be out at night and feel safe. Without criticizing his Attorney General, Ramsey Clark, he thinks that perhaps a Department of Justice prosecution in connection with the civil commotion during his Administration would have been helpful. He does not specify whether such a step would have been helpful in dealing with urban problems or only as a political stratagem.

And as the President faces South again, he muses on the cost of his program to "11 States, and 22 men"—a wistful reference to his native section and its Senatorial contingent, and the permanent changes for both that he was pivotal in fashioning. Then he sums up his prodigious labors simply and crisply: "I am well satisfied."

Every President leaves the Oval Office with the work incomplete. No one knows this better than Presidents. President Truman left behind in a locked drawer of the Presidential desk a set of urgent memoranda for President Eisenhower's immediate attention. In a figurative sense, each outgoing President makes the same kind of bequest to his successor. When Johnson is among friends in the White House and is in a wry mood about public questions, he says to them with mock-impatience in his voice, "I'll be so glad when Dick Nixon is in this room." Johnson knows that as the twilight deepens on his time in power, his chief duty is to pass on the problems of the nation to Nixon in comprehensible form.

Shortly after noon on January 20th, when President-elect Nixon takes the oath of office, the world will once more be witnessing America's stirring rite of political renewal. That the matchless burden and passion of the office will again change hands without rancor or reluctance remains a fact of national political life. The past is not less remarkable than the new possibilities for the solution of problems that always seem to shine so brightly on Inauguration Day.

Study Questions

1. How valid do you believe are the fears of Padover concerning the extension of Presidential powers? Do you share these fears? Are there any recent actions taken by a President to justify such a fear? If so, what remedies do you suggest?
2. Comment on Presidential transition using two or three previous administrations to illustrate your views.
3. On the basis of your reading, what are the various sources of Presidential power in foreign policy making?
4. What are the reasons for increased Presidential power in foreign policy making? Give specific examples.
5. Evaluate the role and influence of the White House staff.

Suggestions for Further Reading

Bailey, Thomas A. *Presidential Greatness: The Images and the Man from George Washington to the Present.* New York: Appleton-Century-Crofts, 1966.

Brown, Stuart Gerry. *The American Presidency: Leadership, Partisanship, and Popularity.* New York: The Macmillan Company, 1966.

Cornwell, Elmer E. *The American Presidency: Vital Center.* Chicago: Scott, Foresman, and Company, 1966.

Corwin, Edward S. *The President: Office and Powers 1787–1957.* 4th revised edition. New York: New York University Press, 1957.

Donovan, Robert J. *Eisenhower: The Inside Story.* New York: Harper & Row, Publishers, 1960.

Egger, Rowland and Joseph P. Harris. *The President and Congress.* New York: McGraw-Hill Book Company, Inc., 1963.

Eisenhower, Dwight D. *Mandate for Change: The White House Years.* New York: Doubleday and Company, Inc., 1963.

Fenno, Richard F., Jr. *The President's Cabinet: An Analysis in the Period from Wilson to Eisenhower.* New York: Vintage Books, 1959.

Finer, Herman. *The Presidency: Crisis and Regeneration.* Chicago: The University of Chicago Press, 1960.

Haight, David E. and Larry D. Johnston (eds.) *The President: Roles and Powers.* Chicago: Rand McNally Company, 1965.

Hargrove, Erwin C. *Presidential Leadership: Personality and Political Style.* New York: The Macmillan Company, 1966.

Heller, Francis H. *The Presidency: A Modern Perspective.* New York: Random House, 1960.

Henry, Laurin L. *Presidential Transitions.* Washington, D. C.: The Brookings Institution, 1960.

Herring, Pendleton. *Presidential Leadership.* New York: Holt, Rinehart and Winston, 1940.

Hughes, Emmet J. *The Ordeal of Power.* New York: Atheneum, 1963.

Koenig, Louis W. *The Chief Executive.* Rev. ed. New York: Harcourt, Brace & World, Inc., 1968.

Koenig, Louis W. *The Invisible Presidency*. New York: Holt, Rinehart and Winston, 1960.

Laski, Harold J. *The American Presidency*. New York: Harper & Row, Publishers, 1940.

Longaker, Richard P. *The Presidency and Individual Liberties*. Ithaca, New York: Cornell University Press, 1961.

McConnell, Grant. *The Modern Presidency*. New York: St. Martin's Press, 1967.

Neustadt, Richard E. *Presidential Power: The Politics of Leadership*. New York: John Wiley & Sons, Inc., 1960.

Roche, John P. and Leonard W. Levy. *The Presidency*. New York: Harcourt, Brace & World, Inc., 1964.

Rossiter, Clinton. *The American Presidency*. Rev. ed. New York: Harcourt, Brace & World, Inc., 1960.

Sorenson, Theodore C. *Decision-Making in the White House: The Olive Branch or the Arrows*. New York: Columbia University Press, 1963.

White, Theodore H. *The Making of the President, 1960*. New York: Atheneum, 1960.

PART TEN

The Judiciary

The judiciary, like Congress and the President, plays a significant role in shaping the public policies of the American political system. The influence of judges such as John Marshall, Oliver Wendell Holmes, Louis D. Brandeis, Benjamin N. Cardozo, Charles Evans Hughes, and Earl Warren, to mention a few, on the direction of American democracy is no less consequential than the impact of great Presidents and Congressmen.

No aspect of federal judicial power has been more subject to official and non-official criticism than that of judicial review—the power of the courts to pass on the constitutionality of legislative acts or any official act based on law. Today, judicial review is an accepted part of the American political system. The courts have the review power and exercise it.

We must understand that when the courts declare any legislative act unconstitutional they are indeed acting politically and concomitantly participating in the policy making process or "judicial legislation." For instance, in the famous case of *Brown* v. *Board of Education* (1954) the Supreme Court unanimously overruled the *Plessy* case and held that separate but equal accommodations for the two races are unconstitutional. Segregation in itself, the Court held, is a denial of equal protection to the Negroes. In this desegregation case the Court was not only saying that separate but equal was unconstitutional, but it was also charting a new direction in American social life. Moreover, the Court for many years refused to hear and pass on the question of reapportionment of state legislatures on the grounds that it was a "political question" and thus beyond its jurisdiction. It was not until the case of *Baker* v. *Carr* (1962) that the Court reversed itself and held that the reapportionment question is a justiciable one and that the plaintiffs in the case were deprived of their equal protection under the Fourteenth Amendment of the Constitution. This land-

468

mark decision left its impact on almost all state legislatures since it forced rural dominated legislatures to draw new district lines and afford urban voters their constitutional rights.

In the following articles we shall examine the role of the Supreme Court in policy-making, in extending and protecting the rights of the poor, and finally, the impact of pressure groups on the United States Supreme Court.

In the first article Robert A. Dahl states that the United States Supreme Court is not only a legal but also a political institution. Very often the cases before the Court involve alternatives about which there is disagreement in society such as segregation or economic regulation. The setting of such cases is political. From time to time the Court decides on cases where the legal criteria are not adequate to the task. It must "choose among controversial alternatives of public policy by appealing to at least some criteria of acceptability on questions of fact and value that cannot be found in or deduced from precedent, statute, and Constitution."

Dahl states that the policy views dominant in the Court are never for long out of step with the policy views dominant among the law-making majority. As a part of the dominant national alliance, the Court supports the major policies of the alliance. The Court, however, is not an *agent* of the alliance. "It is an essential part of the political leadership and possesses some bases of power of its own, the most important of which is the unique legitimacy attributed to its interpretation of the Constitution." Within limits set by the basic policy objectives of the dominant alliance, the Supreme Court *can* make public policy.

Few of the Supreme Court's policy decisions can be interpreted in terms of a "majority" versus "minority." The question is *minorities* rule. The main function of the Court is to confer legitimacy on the basic policies of the successful coalition.

Clement E. Vose in his article "Litigation as a Form of Pressure Group Activity" states that organizations may directly participate in court cases to protect their own rights and privileges or may support a member or officer in litigation. For instance, the National Association for the Advancement of Colored People (NAACP) has presented test cases before the Supreme Court and has made many gains protecting the rights of Negroes in many areas. Moreover, Vose draws attention to the activities of the American Liberty League and the National Consumers' League.

Judicial review in the United States allows interest groups whose efforts failed to defeat legislation to continue opposition by litigation. Organizations appeared as "friend of the court." This method is the most visible form of group representation in Supreme Court cases. Organizations play a less noticed role either by helping individuals in whose name "test cases" are brought to the Court or by providing assistance to government attorneys defending a statute in which the organization has an interest. The activities of organizations in courts are regulated in order to protect the integrity of the judicial process.

In his article "What to Do When The Judge Is Put Up Against the Wall" Louis Nizer discusses the tactics used by the defendants in the "Chicago Seven" trial in order to disrupt the judicial process. He claims that the new challenge to the judicial system must be met and offers several suggestions to meet this challenge. Nizer does not believe that defendants and their lawyers should be allowed to exploit the protective methods which the law provides for accused persons so as to obstruct judicial processes, because "We owe it to accused persons to preserve a trial procedure which is classic and protective."

DECISION-MAKING IN A DEMOCRACY: THE SUPREME COURT AS A NATIONAL POLICY-MAKER

ROBERT A. DAHL

To consider the Supreme Court of the United States strictly as a legal institution is to underestimate its significance in the American political system. For it is also a political institution, an institution, that is to say, for arriving at decisions on controversial questions of national policy. As a political institution, the Court is highly unusual, not least because Americans are not quite willing to accept the fact that it *is* a political institution and not quite capable of denying it; so that frequently we take both positions at once. This is confusing to foreigners, amusing to logicians, and rewarding to ordinary Americans who thus manage to retain the best of both worlds.

I

A policy decision might be defined as an effective choice among alternatives about which there is, at least initially, some uncertainty. This uncertainty may arise because of inadequate information as to (a) the alternatives that are thought to be "open"; (b) the consequences that will probably ensue from choosing a given alternative; (c) the level of probability that these conse-

SOURCE: Robert A. Dahl, "Decision-Making in a Democracy: The Supreme Court as a National Policy-Maker," *Journal of Public Law*, 6 (Fall 1957), 279–295. Reprinted by permission. Footnotes have been deleted.

quences will actually ensue; and (d) the relative value of the different alternatives, that is, an ordering of the alternatives from most preferable to least preferable, given the expected consequences and the expected probability of the consequences actually occurring. An *effective* choice is a selection of the most preferable alternative accompanied by measures to insure that the alternative selected will be acted upon.

No one, I imagine, will quarrel with the proposition that the Supreme Court, or indeed any court, must make and does make policy decisions in this sense. But such a proposition is not really useful to the question before us. What is critical is the extent to which a court can and does make policy decisions by going outside established "legal" criteria found in precedent, statute, and constitution. Now in this respect the Supreme Court occupies a most peculiar position, for it is an essential characteristic of the institution that from time to time its members decide cases where legal criteria are not in any realistic sense adequate to the task. . . .

Very often, then, the cases before the Court involve alternatives about which there is severe disagreement in the society, as in the case of segregation or economic regulation; that is, the setting of the case is "political." Moreover, they are usually cases where competent students of constitutional law, including the learned justices of the Supreme Court themselves, disagree; where the words of the Constitution are general, vague, ambiguous, or not clearly applicable; where precedent may be found on both sides; and where experts differ in predicting the consequences of the various alternatives or the degree of probability that the possible consequences will actually ensue. Typically, in other words, although there may be considerable agreement as to the alternatives thought to be open [(a)], there is very serious disagreement as to questions of fact bearing on consequences and probabilities [(b) and (c)], and as to questions of value, or the way in which different alternatives are to be ordered according to criteria establishing relative preferability [(d)].

If the Court were assumed to be a "political" institution, no particular problems would arise, for it would be taken for granted that the members of the Court would resolve questions of fact and value by introducing assumptions derived from their own predispositions or those of influential clienteles and constituents. But, since much of the legitimacy of the Court's decisions rests upon the fiction that it is not a political institution but exclusively a legal one, to accept the Court as a political institution would solve one set of problems at the price of creating another. Nonetheless, if it is true that the nature of the cases arriving before the Court is sometimes of the kind I have described, then the Court cannot act strictly as a legal institution. It must, that is to say, choose among controversial alternatives of public policy by appealing to at least some criteria of acceptability on questions of fact and value that cannot be found in or deduced from precedent, statute, and Constitution. It is in this sense that the Court is a national policy-maker, and it is this role that gives rise to the problem of the Court's existence in a political system ordinarily held to be democratic.

Now I take it that except for differences in emphasis and presentation, what I have said so far is today widely accepted by almost all American political scientists and by most lawyers. To anyone who believes that the Court is not, in at least some of its activities, a policy-making institution, the discussion that follows may seem irrelevant. But to anyone who holds that at least one role of the Court is as a policy-making institution in cases where strictly legal criteria are inadequate, then a serious and much debated question arises, to wit: Who gets what and why? Or in less elegant language: What groups are benefited or handicapped by the Court and how does the allocation by the Court of these rewards and penalties fit into our presumably democratic political system?

II

In determining and appraising the role of the Court, two different and conflicting criteria are sometimes employed. These are the majority criterion and the criterion of Right or Justice.

Every policy dispute can be tested, at least in principle, by the majority criterion, because (again: in principle) the dispute can be analyzed according to the numbers of people for and against the various alternatives at issue, and therefore according to the proportions of the citizens or eligible members who are for and against the alternatives. Logically speaking, except for a trivial case, every conflict within a given society must be a dispute between a majority of those eligible to participate and a minority or minorities; or else it must be a dispute between or among minorities only. Within certain limits, both possibilities are independent of the number of policy alternatives at issue, and since the argument is not significantly affected by the number of alternatives, it is convenient to assume that each policy dispute represents only two alternatives.

If everyone prefers one of two alternatives, then no significant problem arises. But a case will hardly come before the Supreme Court unless at least one person prefers an alternative that is opposed by another person. Strictly speaking, then, no matter how the Court acts in determining the legality or constitutionality of one alternative or the other, the outcome of the Court's decision must either (1) accord with the preferences of a minority of citizens and run counter to the preferences of a majority; (2) accord with the preferences of a majority and run counter to the preferences of a minority; or (3) accord with the preferences of one minority and run counter to the preferences of another minority, the rest being indifferent.

In a democratic system with a more or less representative legislature, it is unnecessary to maintain a special court to secure the second class of outcomes. A case might be made out that the Court protects the rights of national majorities against local interests in federal questions, but so far as I am aware, the role of the Court as a policy-maker is not usually defended in this fashion; in what follows, therefore, I propose to pass over the ticklish question of federalism and deal only with "national" majorities and minorities. The third kind of outcome, although relevant according to other criteria, is hardly relevant to the majority criterion, and may also be passed over for the moment.

One influential view of the Court, however, is that it stands in some special way as a protection of minorities against tyranny by majorities. In the course of its 167 years, in seventy-eight cases, the Court has struck down eighty-six different provisions of federal law as unconstitutional and by interpretation it has modified a good many more. It might be argued, then, that in all or in a very large number of these cases the Court was, in fact, defending the rights of some minority against a "tyrannical" majority. There are, however, some exceedingly serious difficulties with this interpretation of the Court's activities.

III

One problem, which is essentially ideological in character, is the difficulty of reconciling such an interpretation with the existence of a democratic polity, for it is not at all difficult to show by appeals to authorities as various and imposing as Aristotle, Locke, Rousseau, Jefferson, and Lincoln that the term democracy means, among other things, that the power to rule resides in popular majorities and their representatives. Moreover, from entirely reasonable and traditional definitions of popular sovereignty and political equality, the principle of majority rule can be shown to follow by logical necessity. Thus to affirm that the Court supports minority preferences against majorities is to deny that popular sovereignty and political equality, at least in the traditional sense, exist in the United States; and to affirm that the Court *ought* to act in this way is to deny that popular sovereignty and political equality *ought* to prevail in this country. In a country that glories in its democratic tradition, this is not a happy state of affairs for the Court's defenders; and it is no wonder that a great deal of effort has gone into the enterprise of proving that, even if the Court consistently defends minorities against majorities, nonetheless it is a thoroughly "democratic" institution. But no amount of tampering with democratic theory can conceal the fact that a system in which the policy preferences of minorities prevail over majorities is at odds with the traditional criteria for distinguishing a democracy from other political systems.

Fortunately, however, we do not need to traverse this well-worn ground; for the view of the Court as a protector of the liberties of minorities against the tyranny of majorities is beset with other difficulties that are not so much ideological as matters of fact and logic. If one wishes to be at all rigorous about the question, it is probably impossible to demonstrate that any particular Court decisions have or have not been at odds with the preferences of a "national majority." It is clear that unless one makes *some* assumptions as to the kind of evidence one will require for the existence of a set of minority and majority preferences in the general population, the view under consideration is incapable of being proved at all. In any strict sense, no adequate evidence exists, for scientific opinion polls are of relatively recent origin, and national elections are little more than an indication of the first preferences of a number of citizens—in the United States the number ranges between about forty and sixty per cent of the adult population—for certain candidates for public office. I do not mean to say that there is no relation between preferences among candidates and preferences among alternative public policies, but the connection is a highly tenuous one, and on the basis of an election it is almost never possible to adduce whether a majority does or does not support one of two or more policy alternatives about which members of the political elite are divided. For the greater part of the Court's history, then, there is simply no way of establishing with any high degree of confidence whether a given alternative was or was not supported by a majority or a minority of adults or even of voters.

TABLE 1.

The Interval Between Appointments to the Supreme Court

Interval in Years	Per Cent of Total Appointments	Cumulative Per Cent
Less than 1	21	21
1	34	55
2	18	73
3	9	82
4	8	90
5	7	97
6	2	99
—	—	—
12	1	100
Total	100	100

Note: The table excludes the six appointments made in 1789. Except for the four most recent appointments, it is based on data in the *Encyclopedia of American History,* 461–62 (Morris ed., 1953). It may be slightly inaccurate because the source shows only the year of appointment, not the month. The twelve-year interval was from 1811 to 1823.

In the absence of relatively direct information, we are thrown back on indirect tests. The eighty-six provisions of federal law that have been declared unconstitutional were, of course, initially passed by majorities of those voting in the Senate and in the House. They also had the president's formal approval.

We could, therefore, speak of a majority of those voting in the House and Senate, together with the president, as a "lawmaking majority." It is not easy to determine whether any such constellation of forces within the political elites actually coincides with the preferences of a majority of American adults or even with the preferences of a majority of that half of the adult population which, on the average, votes in congressional elections. Such evidence as we have from opinion polls suggests that Congress is not markedly out of line with public opinion, or at any rate with such public opinion as there is after one discards the answers of people who fall into the category, often large, labelled "no response" or "don't know." If we may, on these somewhat uncertain grounds, take a "lawmaking majority" as equivalent to a "national majority," then it is possible to test the hypothesis that the Supreme Court is shield and buckler for minorities against national majorities.

Under any reasonable assumptions about the nature of the political process, it would appear to be somewhat naive to assume that the Supreme Court either would or could play the role of Galahad. Over the whole history of the Court, on the average one new justice has been appointed every twenty-two months. Thus a president can expect to appoint about two new justices during one term of office; and if this were not enough to tip the balance on a normally divided Court, he is almost certain to succeed in two terms. Thus, Hoover had three appointments; Roosevelt, nine; Truman, four; and Eisenhower, so far, has had four. Presidents are not famous for appointing justices hostile to their own views on public policy nor could they expect to secure confirmation of a man whose stance on key questions was flagrantly at odds with that of the dominant majority in the Senate. Justices are typically men who, prior to appointment, have engaged in public life and have committed themselves publicly on the great questions of the day. As Mr. Justice Frankfurter has recently reminded us, a surprisingly large proportion of the justices, particularly of the great justices who have left their stamp upon the decisions of the Court, have had little or no prior judicial experience. Nor have the justices—certainly not the great justices—been timid men with a passion for anonymity. Indeed, it is not too much to say that if justices were appointed primarily for their "judicial" qualities without regard to their basic attitudes on fundamental questions of public policy, the Court could not play the influential role in the American political system that it does in reality play.

The fact is, then, that the policy views dominant in the Court are never for long out of line with the policy views dominant among the lawmaking majorities of the United States. Consequently it would be most unrealistic to suppose that the Court would, for more than a few years at most, stand against any major alternatives sought by a lawmaking majority. The judicial agonies of the New Deal will, of course, quickly come to mind; but Mr. Roosevelt's difficulties with the Court were truly exceptional. Generalizing over the whole history of the Court, the chances are about one out of five that a president will make one appointment to the Court in less than a year, better than one out of two that he will make one within two years, and three out of four that he will make one within three years. Mr. Roosevelt had unusually bad luck: he had to wait four years for his first appointment; the odds against this long an interval are four to one. With average luck, the battle with the Court would never have occurred; even as it was, although the "court-packing" proposal did formally fail, by the end of his second term Mr. Roosevelt had appointed five new justices and by 1941 Mr. Justice Roberts was the only remaining holdover from the Hoover era.

It is to be expected, then, that the Court is least likely to be successful in blocking a determined and persistent lawmaking majority on a major policy and most likely to succeed against a "weak" majority, e.g., a dead one, a transient one, a fragile one, or one weakly united upon a policy of subordinate importance.

TABLE 2.

Percentage of Cases Held Unconstitutional Arranged by Time Intervals Between Legislation and Decision

Number of Years	New Deal Legislation %	Other %	All Legislation %
2 or Less	92	19	30
3–4	8	19	18
5–8	0	28	24
9–12	0	13	11
13–16	0	8	6
17–20	0	1	1
21 or More	0	12	10
Total	100	100	100

TABLE 3.

Cases Holding Legislation Unconstitutional Within Four Years After Enactment

Interval in Years	New Deal No.	%	Other No.	%	Total No.	%
2 or Less	11	29	13	34	24	63
3 to 4	1	3	13	34	14	37
Total	12	32	26	68	38	100

IV

An examination of the cases in which the Court has held federal legislation unconstitutional confirms, on the whole, our expectations. Over the whole history of the Court, about half the decisions have been rendered more than four years after the legislation was passed.

Of the twenty-four laws held unconstitutional within two years, eleven were measures enacted in the early years of the New Deal. Indeed, New Deal measures comprise nearly a third of all the legislation that has ever been declared unconstitutional within four years after enactment.

● ● ●

The entire record of the duel between the Court and the lawmaking majority, in cases where the Court has held legislation unconstitutional within four years after enactment, is summarized in Table 6.

Thus the application of the majority criterion seems to show the following: First, if the Court did in fact uphold minorities against national majorities, as both its supporters and critics often seem to believe, it would be an extremely anomalous institution from a democratic point of view. Second, the elaborate "democratic" rationalizations of the Court's defenders and the hostility of its "democratic" critics are largely irrelevant, for lawmaking majorities generally have had their way. Third, although the Court seems never to have succeeded in holding out indefinitely, in a very small number of important cases it has delayed the application of policy up to as much as twenty-five years.

V

How can we appraise decisions of the third kind just mentioned? Earlier I referred to the criterion of Right or Justice as a norm sometimes invoked to describe the role of the Court. In accordance with this norm, it might be argued that the most important policy function of the Court is to protect rights that are in some sense basic or fundamental. Thus (the argument might run) in a country where basic rights are, on the whole, respected, one should not expect more than a small number of cases where the Court has had to plant itself firmly against a lawmaking majority. But majorities may, on rare occasions, become "tyrannical"; and when they do, the Court intervenes; and although the constitutional issue may, strictly speaking, be technically open, the Constitution assumes an underlying fundamental body of rights and liberties which the Court guarantees by its decisions.

Here again, however, even without examining the actual cases, it would appear, on political grounds, somewhat unrealistic to suppose that a Court whose members are recruited in the fashion of Supreme Court justices would long hold to norms of Right or Justice substantially at odds with the rest of the political elite. Moreover, in an earlier day it was perhaps easier to believe that certain rights are so natural and self-evident that their fundamental validity is as much a matter of definite knowledge, at least to all reasonable creatures, as the color of a ripe apple. To say that this view is unlikely to find many articulate defenders today is, of course, not to disprove it; it is rather to suggest that we do not need to elaborate the case against it in this essay.

TABLE 6.

Type of Congressional Action After Supreme Court Decisions Holding Legislation Unconstitutional Within Four Years After Enactment (Including New Deal Legislation)

Congressional Action	Major Policy	Minor Policy	Total
Reverses Court's Policy	17	2	19
None	0	12	12
Other	6	1	7
Total	23	15	38

In any event the best rebuttal to the view of the Court suggested above will be found in the record of the Court's decisions. Surely the six cases referred to a moment ago, where the policy consequences of the Court's decisions were overcome only after long battles, will not appeal to many contemporary minds as evidence for the proposition under examination. A natural right to employ child labor in mills and mines? To be free of income taxes by the federal government? To employ longshoremen and harbor workers without the protection of workmen's compensation? The Court itself did not rely upon such arguments in these cases, and it would be no credit to their opinions to reconstruct them along such lines.

So far, however, our evidence has been drawn from cases in which the Court has held legislation unconstitutional within four years after enactment. What of the other forty cases? Do we have evidence in these that the Court has protected fundamental or natural rights and liberties against the dead hand of some past tyranny by the lawmakers? The evidence is not impressive. In the entire history of the Court there is not one case arising under the First Amendment in which the Court has held federal legislation unconstitutional. If we turn from these fundamental liberties of religion, speech, press and assembly, we do find a handful of cases—something less than ten—arising under Amendments Four to Seven in which the Court has declared acts unconstitutional that might properly be regarded as involving rather basic liberties. An inspection of these cases leaves the impression that, in all of them, the lawmakers and the Court were not very far apart; moreover, it is doubtful that the fundamental conditions of liberty in this country have been altered by more than a hair's breadth as a result of these decisions. However, let us give the Court its due; it is little enough.

Over against these decisions we must put the fifteen or so cases in which the Court used the protections of the Fifth, Thirteenth, Fourteenth and Fifteenth Amendments to preserve the rights and liberties of a relatively privileged group at the expense of the rights and liberties of a submerged group: chiefly slaveholders at the expense of slaves, white people at the expense of colored people, and property holders at the expense of wage earners and other groups. These cases, unlike the relatively innocuous ones of the preceding set, all involved liberties of genuinely fundamental importance, where an opposite policy would have meant thoroughly basic shifts in the distribution of rights, liberties, and opportunities in the United States—where, moreover, the policies sustained by the Court's action have since been repudiated in every civilized nation of the Western world, including our own. Yet, if our earlier argument is correct, it is futile—precisely because the basic distribution of privilege *was* at issue—to suppose that the Court could have possibly acted much differently in these areas of policy from the way in which it did in fact act.

VI

Thus the role of the Court as a policy-making institution is not simple; and it is an error to suppose that its functions can be either described or appraised by means of simple concepts drawn from democratic or moral theory. It is possible, nonetheless, to derive a few general conclusions about the Court's role as a policy-making institution.

National politics in the United States, as in other stable democracies, is dominated by relatively cohesive alliances that endure for long periods of time. One recalls the Jeffersonian alliance, the Jacksonian, the extraordinarily long-lived Republican dominance of the post-Civil War years, and the New Deal alliance shaped by Franklin Roosevelt. Each is marked by a break with past policies, a period of intense struggle, followed by consolidation, and finally decay and disintegration of the alliance.

Except for short-lived transitional periods when the old alliance is disintegrating and the new one is struggling to take control of political institutions, the Supreme Court is inevitably a part of the dominant national alliance. As an element in the political leadership of the dominant alliance, the Court of course supports the major policies of the alliance. By itself, the Court is almost powerless to affect the course of national policy. In the absence of substantial agreement within the alliance, an attempt by the Court to make national policy is likely to lead to disaster, as the *Dred Scott* decision and the early New Deal cases demonstrate. Conceivably, the cases of the last three decades involving the freedom of Negroes, culminating in the now famous decision on school integration, are exceptions to this generalization; I shall have more to say about them in a moment.

The Supreme Court is not, however, simply an *agent* of the alliance. It is an essential part of the political leadership and possesses some bases of power of its own, the most important of which is the unique legitimacy attributed to its interpretations of the Constitution. This legitimacy the Court jeopardizes if it flagrantly opposes the major policies of the dominant alliance; such a course of action, as we have seen, is one in which the Court will not normally be tempted to engage.

It follows that within the somewhat narrow limits set by the basic policy goals of the dominant alliance, the Court *can* make national policy. Its discretion, then, is not unlike that of a powerful committee chairman in Congress who cannot, generally speaking, nullify the basic policies substantially agreed on by the rest of the dominant leadership, but who can, within these limits, often determine important questions of timing, effectiveness, and subordinate policy. Thus the Court is least effective against a current lawmaking majority —and evidently least inclined to act. It is most effective when it sets the bounds of policy for officials, agencies, state governments or even regions, a task that has come to occupy a very large part of the Court's business.

Few of the Court's policy decisions can be interpreted sensibly in terms of a "majority" versus a "minority." In this respect the Court is no different from the rest of the political leadership. Generally speaking, policy at the national level is the outcome of conflict, bargaining, and agreement among minorities; the process is neither minority rule nor majority rule but what might better be called *minorities* rule, where one aggregation of minorities achieves policies opposed by another aggregation.

The main objective of presidential leadership is to build a stable and dominant aggregation of minorities with a high probability of winning the presidency and one or both houses of Congress. The main task of the Court is to confer legitimacy on the fundamental policies of the successful coalition. There are times when the coalition is unstable with respect to certain key policies; at very great risk to its legitimacy powers, the Court can intervene in such cases and may even succeed in establishing policy. Probably in such cases it can succeed only if its action conforms to and reinforces a widespread set of explicit or implicit norms held by the political leadership; norms which are not strong enough or are not distributed in such a way as to insure the existence of an effective lawmaking majority but are, nonetheless, sufficiently powerful to prevent any successful attack on the legitimacy powers of the Court. This is probably the explanation for the relatively successful work of the Court in enlarging the freedom of Negroes to vote during the past three decades and in its famous school integration decisions.

Yet the Court is more than this. Considered as a political system, democracy is a set of basic procedures for arriving at decisions. The operation of these procedures presupposes the existence of certain rights, obligations, liberties and restraints; in short, certain patterns of behavior. The existence of these patterns of behavior in turn presupposes widespread agreement (particularly among the politically active and influential segments of the population) on the validity and propriety of the behavior. Although its record is by no means lacking in serious blemishes, at its best the Court operates to confer legitimacy, not simply on the particular and parochial policies of the dominant political alliance, but upon the basic patterns of behavior required for the operation of a democracy.

LITIGATION AS A FORM OF PRESSURE GROUP ACTIVITY

CLEMENT E. VOSE

The conventional judicial process is distinguished from legislative and administrative processes by features which forbid, conceal, or control the participation of organized pressure groups. Justice Robert H. Jackson warned that "perhaps the most significant and least comprehended limitation upon the judicial power is that this power extends only to cases and controversies." [1] This limitation has meant that the Supreme Court of the United States refuses to provide advisory opinions and avoids what judges are fond of calling "political questions." It cannot be overstressed that the Supreme Court's only power is to decide lawsuits between adversaries with real interests at stake. Under the case system that marks American jurisprudence, a court is a "substantially passive instrument, to be moved only by the initiative of litigants." [2] This contrasts with the power of the President and the Congress to deal with any subject as desired.

Despite this limiting prerequisite, the Supreme Court does possess considerable control over the particular cases to be decided. The Judiciary Act of 1925 gave the Court almost complete discretionary control of its appellate

[1] *The Supreme Court in the American System of Government* (Cambridge, Mass.: Harvard University Press, 1955), p. 11.

[2] *Ibid.*, p. 12.

SOURCE: Clement E. Vose, "Litigation as a Form of Pressure Group Activity," *The Annals of the American Academy of Political and Social Science*, 319 (September 1958), 20–31. Reprinted by permission.

business through grant or denial of the writ of certiorari. This statute settled the modern principle that the Supreme Court's function was

> not to see justice done in every case, but to decide the more important policy issues presented within the frame of a "case" or "controversy," concerning the federal balance, the relations of the branches of the federal government, or the fundamental rights of the individual in relation to government.[3]

Elaborating upon the function of deciding important policy issues, Chief Justice Fred M. Vinson, in 1949, told the bar that the Supreme Court is interested only in "those cases which present questions whose resolution will have immediate importance beyond the particular facts and parties involved."[4] Vinson added that "what the Court is interested in is the actual practical effect of the disputed decision—its consequences for other litigants and in other situations." This meant that lawyers whose petitions for certiorari were granted by the Supreme Court were representing not only their clients, "but tremendously important principles, upon which are based the plans, hopes and aspirations of a great many people throughout the country."

It is the thesis of this article that organizations—identifiable by letterhead —often link broad interests in society to individual parties of interest in Supreme Court cases. Since the American judicial system is built upon specific cases with specific facts, it is assumed that study of the role of specific organizations is relevant to understanding.[5]

REASONS ORGANIZATIONS GO TO COURT

Organizations support legal action because individuals lack the necessary time, money, and skill. With no delays a case takes an average of four years to pass through two lower courts to the Supreme Court of the United States. A series of cases on related questions affecting the permanent interest of a group may extend over two decades or more. The constant attention that litigation demands, especially when new arguments are being advanced, makes the em-

---

[3] James Willard Hurst, The Growth of American Law (Boston: Little, Brown 1950), p. 119.

[4] Vinson, "Work of the Federal Courts," 69 S. Ct. v (1949).

[5] For treatments of pressure groups in litigation, see Arthur F. Bentley, The Process of Government (Chicago: University of Chicago Press, 1908), pp. 382–399; David Truman, The Governmental Process (New York: Knopf, 1950), pp. 479–498; Donald C. Blaisdell, American Democracy Under Pressure (New York: Ronald, 1957), pp. 261–268; Jack W. Peltason, Federal Courts in the Political Process (Garden City, N.Y., Doubleday, 1955); Mark DeWolfe Howe, "Political Theory and the Nature of Liberty," Harvard Law Review, Vol. 67 (November, 1953), pp. 91–95; Joseph B. Robison, "Organizations Promoting Civil Rights and Liberties," The Annals of the American Academy of Political and Social Science, Vol. 275 (May, 1951), pp. 18–26; Comment, "Private Attorneys-General: Group Action in the Fight for Civil Liberties," Yale Law Journal, Vol. 58 (March, 1949), pp. 574–598. In criticism, see Walter Berns, Freedom, Virtue and the First Amendment (Baton Rouge: Louisiana State University Press, 1957), pp. 130–133, 160–162.

ployment of regular counsel economical. This may be supplemented by a legal staff of some size and by volunteer lawyers of distinction. Parties also pay court costs and meet the expense of printing the record and briefs. Organizations are better able to provide the continuity demanded in litigation than individuals. Some individuals do maintain responsibility for their own cases even at the Supreme Court level, but this is difficult under modern conditions.

The form of group participation in court cases is set by such factors as the type of proceeding, standing of the parties, legal or constitutional issues in dispute, the characteristics of the organization, and its interest in the outcome. Perhaps the most direct and open participation has been by organizations which have been obliged to protect their own rights and privileges. Robert A. Horn has shown that a modern constitutional law of association has developed out of Supreme Court cases concerning churches, trade unions, political parties, and other organizations.[6] The cases have sometimes placed organizations as parties, but more often the organization supports a member or an officer in litigation. One example must suffice.

The constitutional concept of religious freedom has been broadened in recent years by the Supreme Court decisions in cases involving members of the sect known as Jehovah's Witnesses. Most of the cases began when a Jehovah's Witness violated a local ordinance or state statute. Since 1938, the Witnesses, incorporated as the Watchtower Bible and Tract Society and represented by its counsel, Hayden Cooper Covington, have won forty-four of fifty-five cases in the United States Supreme Court. As a result Jehovah's Witnesses now enjoy

> the rights to solicit from house to house, to preach in the streets without a license, to canvass apartment buildings regardless of the tenants' or owners' wishes, to be recognized as ministers of an accredited religion and thus be exempt from the draft, to decline to serve on juries, and to refuse to salute or pledge allegiance to the flag.[7]

THE NAACP

Since 1909 the National Association for the Advancement of Colored People has improved the legal status of Negroes immeasurably by the victories it has won in more than fifty Supreme Court cases.[8] During its early years, the

[6] *Groups and the Constitution* (Stanford, Calif.: Stanford University Press, 1956). See also, Elias Lieberman, *Unions Before the Bar* (New York: Harper & Row, 1950).

[7] Richard Harris, "I'd Like to Talk with You for a Minute," *New Yorker*, June 16, 1956, pp. 72, 88.

[8] See Herbert Hill and Jack Greenberg, *Citizen's Guide to Desegregation* (Boston: Beacon, 1955); Clement E. Vose, "NAACP Strategy in the Covenant Cases," *Western Reserve Law Review*, Vol. 6 (Spring, 1955), pp. 101–145.

NAACP relied upon prominent volunteer lawyers like Moorfield Storey, Louis Marshall, and Clarence Darrow to represent Negroes in the courts. Limited success coupled with its failure to win gains from Congress led the NAACP in the 1930's to make court litigation fundamental to its program. A separate organization, the NAACP Legal Defense and Educational Fund, was incorporated for this purpose. The goal of the NAACP was to make Negroes "an integral part of the nation, with the same rights and guarantees that are accorded to other citizens, and on the same terms." [9] This ambition meant that beginning in 1938 Thurgood Marshall as special counsel for the NAACP Legal Defense and Educational Fund held what was "probably the most demanding legal post in the country." [10]

In aiming to establish racial equality before the law on a broad basis, the Legal Defense Fund has not functioned as a legal aid society. Limited resources have prevented the Fund from participating in all cases involving the rights of Negroes. As early as 1935 Charles Houston, an imaginative Negro lawyer who preceded Marshall as special counsel, set the tone of NAACP efforts when he declared that the legal campaign against inequality should be carefully planned "to secure decisions, rulings and public opinion on the broad principle instead of being devoted to merely miscellaneous cases." [11]

By presenting test cases to the Supreme Court, the NAACP has won successive gains protecting the right of Negroes in voting, housing, transportation, education, and service on juries.[12] Each effort has followed the development of new theories of legal interpretation and required the preparation of specific actions in the courts to challenge existing precedent. The NAACP Legal Defense Fund has accomplished these two tasks through the cooperation of associated and allied groups. First, as many as fifty Negro lawyers practicing in all parts of the country have been counsel in significant civil rights cases in the lower courts. Many of these men received their legal education at the Howard University Law School in Washington, D.C., and have shared membership in the National Bar Association since its founding in 1925. These common associations have contributed to the consensus among Negro lawyers on timing their quest for equality through litigation. Second, the NAACP has long benefited from its official advisory group, the National Legal Committee, composed of leading Negro and white lawyers. Today Lloyd Garrison is Chairman of the National Legal Committee of forty-five attorneys located in twenty-three cities. This is the nucleus of the many volunteers in many fields who have contributed ideas, often at national conferences, to the

---

[9] Roy Wilkins, "The Negro Wants Full Equality," in *What the Negro Wants*, Rayford W. Logan (ed.), (Chapel Hill: University of North Carolina Press, 1944), pp. 113, 118.

[10] Saunders Redding, *The Lonesome Road: The Story of the Negro's Past in America* (Garden City, N.Y.: Doubleday, 1958), p. 321.

[11] Hill and Greenberg, *op. cit.*, pp. 56–57.

[12] For a survey, see Robert E. Cushman, *Civil Liberties in the United States* (Ithaca: Cornell University Press, 1956), pp. 211–224.

planning of litigation. Third, other organizations with no direct connection with the Legal Defense Fund have sponsored a few cases. State and local chapters of the NAACP have often aided Negroes who were parties in cases, especially in the lower courts. The St. Louis Association of Real Estate Brokers was the chief sponsor of the important restrictive covenant case of Shelley v. Kraemer.[13] A Negro national college fraternity, Alpha Phi Alpha, sponsored quite completely the successful attack on discrimination in interstate railway dining cars.[14]

Individual Test Cases

Winning new constitutional protections for Negroes has depended on the development of individual test cases with a Negro as party in each. There is no chronicle of the human interest stories contained in the roles of Negroes in historic Supreme Court cases. But what is known reveals many difficulties to be inherent in improving the legal status of a group of fifteen million persons through individual court cases. In a suit by a single plaintiff, the case may become moot as the passage of time makes the remedy sought inapplicable. This danger, though avoided by the cooperation of state officials, was created in the Missouri Law School case of 1938 when the plaintiff, Lloyd Gaines, disappeared just as the case was completed.[15] Also the concerted efforts of authorities to deny Negroes participation in the Texas white Democratic primary kept Dr. L. A. Nixon from voting even though he was the plaintiff in two Supreme Court victories.[16] Furthermore there is always the temptation for compromise by the original plaintiff which would accomplish his narrow purpose but stop the litigation before the broad constitutional issue was before the appellate court.

These dangers were largely overcome in the School Segregation Cases[17] when federal court actions were instituted by individual plaintiffs both on their own behalf and on behalf of persons similarly situated. Since 1955, in the expanding litigation over race relations, the class action has become a procedural device of growing importance. Rule 23 (a) of the Federal Rules of Civil Procedure provides under certain circumstances that

> if persons constituting a class are so numerous as to make it impracticable to bring them all before the court, such of them, one or more, as will fairly insure the adequate representation of all may, on behalf of all, sue or be sued.[18]

[13] 334 U.S. 1 (1948).

[14] Henderson v. United States, 339 U.S. 816 (1950).

[15] Missouri ex rel. Gaines v. Canada, 305 U.S. 337 (1937). See Walter White, *A Man Called White* (New York: Viking, 1948), p. 162.

[16] Nixon v. Herndon, 273 U.S. 536 (1927); Nixon v. Condon, 286 U.S. 73 (1932). See Charles Reznikoff (ed.), *Louis Marshall, Champion of Liberty* (Philadelphia: Jewish Publication Society, 1957), pp. 426–447, *passim*.

[17] 347 U.S. 483 (1954).

[18] See "Class Actions: A Study of Group-Interest Litigation," *Race Relations Law Reporter,* Vol. 1 (October, 1956), pp. 991–1010.

One authority has said that "school segregation is a group phenomenon which is peculiarly suited to resolution in a class action." [19] As Negroes enter a new generation of litigation, their cases are apt increasingly to take the form of the class action.

THE AMERICAN LIBERTY LEAGUE

The experience of the American Liberty League, organized in 1934 by conservative businessmen to oppose the New Deal, provides another variation on the theme of organizations in litigation.[20] When the League proved unable to prevent enactment of economic regulation by Congress, a National Lawyers' Committee was formed to question the constitutionality of the legislation. In August 1935, the National Lawyers' Committee of fifty-eight members announced plans to prepare a series of reports to the public on whether particular federal laws were "consonant with the American constitutional system and American traditions." [21] These reports "would be of a strictly professional nature and would in no case go into the question of social and economic advisability or the need for constitutional change to meet new conditions." This intention led the Committee during the next two years to conclude that a dozen New Deal statutes were unconstitutional.

The most celebrated Liberty League "brief" prepared by the National Lawyers' Committee questioned the constitutionality of the National Labor Relations Act. That analysis was prepared by a subcommittee of eight attorneys under the chairmanship of Earl F. Reed. It was then submitted to the other members and made public by Raoul E. Desverine, Chairman of the entire group, on Constitution Day, 1935.[22] The reports of the Committee were given wide publicity through press releases, the distribution of pamphlets, and radio talks by leading conservative lawyers like James M. Beck. Critics of these reports feared that they had two purposes: "to influence the federal courts when such legislation shall be presented for consideration" and "to arouse public sentiment so that confidence in the courts will be impaired should the legislation be held constitutional." [23]

Members of the National Lawyers' Committee of the American Liberty League, but not the organization itself, participated in litigation. The Committee's first public announcement had stated that "it will also contribute its

---

[19] Robert B. McKay, " 'With All Deliberate Speed,' A Study of School Desegregation," *New York University Law Review*, Vol. 31 (June, 1956), pp. 992, 1086.

[20] See Benjamin R. Twiss, *Lawyers and the Constitution: How Laissez Faire Came to the Supreme Court* (Princeton, N.J.: Princeton University Press, 1942), pp. 241–249; Frederick Rudolph, "American Liberty League, 1934–1940," *American Historical Review*, Vol. 56 (October, 1950), pp. 19–33.

[21] For the announcement and list of members of the Committee, see *New York Times*, August 22, 1935, pp. 1, 6.

[22] *New York Times*, September 19, 1935, pp. 1, 10.

[23] Editorial in *United States Law Review* (October, 1935), quoted in Thomas Reed Powell, "Fifty-eight Lawyers Report," *New Republic*, December 11, 1935, p. 120.

services in test cases involving fundamental constitutional questions." Although the intention was to offer free legal services to citizens without funds to defend their constitutional rights, members of the National Lawyers' Committee actually represented major corporations which challenged the constitutionality of New Deal legislation in the Supreme Court. Earl F. Reed simply adapted the Liberty League report to apply to the specific facts of the case when he represented the Jones and Laughlin Steel Corporation against the National Labor Relations Board.[24] Another member of the National Lawyers' Committee, John W. Davis, represented the Associated Press in a companion case.[25]

AIDING THE GOVERNMENT DEFENSE

Judicial review in the United States constitutes an invitation for groups whose lobbying fails to defeat legislation to continue opposition by litigation. The NAACP has taken advantage of this in questioning state segregation laws, and, especially before 1937, business groups of various sizes—the American Liberty League, trade associations, and corporations—contested the constitutionality of state and federal regulatory legislation. This exploitation of judicial review has been balanced by the practice of victorious groups in legislation continuing to support administrative agencies in charge of enforcement. When statutes are challenged, organizations often support the Justice Department in Washington or a state Attorney General in defending them. This is to say that when losers in legislation have brought test cases in the courts, the legislative winners have aided the official legal defense.

THE NATIONAL CONSUMERS' LEAGUE

The efforts of the National Consumers' League to defend the validity of protective labor legislation affords an example of this private organizational aid to the public defense of legislation.[26] Organized by society women in 1899 to improve the lot of women and children in industry, the National Consumers' League sought first to boycott goods produced under substandard conditions and then to persuade state legislatures to control factory practices through legislation. When employers in the hotel and laundry business organized to defeat legislation in the courts, the National Consumers' League, in 1908, organized a Committee on Legislation and Legal Defense of Labor Laws to "assist in the defense of the laws by supplying additional legal counsel and other assistance." [27]

[24] N.L.R.B. v. Jones & Laughlin Steel Corp., 301 U.S. 1, 12 (1937).

[25] Associated Press v. N.L.R.B., 301 U.S. 103 (1937).

[26] Clement E. Vose, "The National Consumers' League and the Brandeis Brief," *Midwest Journal of Political Science*, Vol. 1 (November, 1957), pp. 267–290; Josephine Goldmark, *Impatient Crusader; Florence Kelley's Life Story* (Urbana: University of Illinois Press, 1953), pp. 143–179.

[27] National Consumers' League, *Sixth Annual Report* (1908). The first N.C.L. victory was in Muller v. Oregon, 208 U.S. 412 (1908).

The leaders of the National Consumers' League, especially Mrs. Florence Kelley and Miss Josephine Goldmark, learned to prod state Attorneys General in order to gain adequate defense for statutes under fire in the courts. They also made two positive contributions. First, arrangements were made to provide distinguished outside counsel—most importantly, Louis D. Brandeis; but also Felix Frankfurter, Newton D. Baker, and Dean Acheson—to supervise the preparation of briefs and to make oral arguments for a state. Second, the sociological material which was the mark of the Brandeis brief was prepared by Miss Josephine Goldmark and the staff of the National Consumers' League. The first four briefs that were successful were then collected with additional material and published by Miss Goldmark as *Fatigue and Efficiency*.[28] Attorneys General in states whose labor laws were under attack could then invite Consumers' League attorneys to manage the defense or else use the sociological materials prepared by the League in the preparation of their own brief. As a result, the League contributed to the successful defense of state statutes in more than fifteen important cases.

Like most organizations with a long-range interest in litigation, the National Consumers' League believed that publicity was vital. Criticizing the Illinois Supreme Court for invalidating an eight-hour law for women, Florence Kelley wrote in 1905 that when time

> shall have convinced the medical profession, the philanthropists, and educators, as experience has already convinced the factory employees themselves, that it is a matter of life and death to young people who form so large a proportion of their numbers, to have a working day of reasonable length guaranteed by law, it will be found possible to rescue the fourteenth amendment to the Constitution of the United States from the perverted interpretation upon which this decision rests.[29]

Mrs. Kelley's view was adopted in Illinois in 1910, but the full Consumers' League program of child labor, maximum hour, and minimum wage regulation was not accommodated by the United States Supreme Court for three more decades. In that period the League stressed education on the subject and for this purpose distributed extra copies of its briefs to law schools, colleges, and public libraries.

No catalogue exists of government relations with private interests concerned with the conduct of litigation. The National Consumers' League experience suggests similar practices on other subjects at all government levels. At the municipal level, an attorney for a local milk producers association acted "of counsel" on the city's brief defending a favorable ordinance.[30] At the state

[28] (New York: Russell Sage Foundation, 1912.)

[29] *Some Ethical Gains Through Legislation* (New York: Macmillan, 1905), p. 141. Mrs. Kelley was criticizing the decision in Ritchie v. People, 155, Ill. 98, 40 N.E. 454 (1895), *reversed by* Ritchie v. Wayman, 244 Ill. 509, 91 N.E. 695 (1910).

[30] Dean Milk Co. v. Madison, 340 U.S. 349 (1951).

level, the segregation interest has been closely associated with various Attorneys General in the South.[31] And a prominent attorney with national standing, John W. Davis, rendered free services to South Carolina in the School Segregation Cases.[32] At the federal level, the Justice Department has often been urged by organizations to initiate action to enforce federal statutes.[33]

ORGANIZATIONS AS "FRIENDS OF THE COURT"

The appearance of organizations as *amici curiae* has been the most noticed form of group representation in Supreme Court cases.[34] This does not concern the technical office of *amicus curiae* for which an attorney is appointed to assist the court in deciding complex and technical problems. Today, the Supreme Court does sometimes, as in formulating its decree in the School Segregation Cases, issue a special invitation to the Solicitor General or to State Attorneys General to act as *amici curiae*. Of interest here is the rule under which individuals, organizations, and government attorneys have been permitted to file briefs and/or make oral argument in the Supreme Court. During the last decade *amici curiae* have submitted an average of sixty-six briefs and seven oral arguments in an average total of forty cases a term.[35]

The frequent entrance of organizations into Supreme Court cases by means of the *amicus curiae* device has often given litigation the distinct flavor of group combat. This may be illustrated by the group representation in quite different cases. In 1943, when a member of the Jehovah's Witnesses challenged the constitutionality of a compulsory flag salute in the schools, his defense by counsel for the Watchtower Bible and Tract Society was supported by separate *amici curiae*, the American Civil Liberties Union and the Committee on the Bill of Rights of the American Bar Association.[36] The appellant state board of education was supported by an *amicus curiae* brief filed by the

[31] See Samuel Krislov, ". . . Southern Attorneys General and Their Stand on Desegregation," unpublished paper read before the American Political Science Association, New York City, September 7, 1957.

[32] The South Carolina case, Briggs v. Elliott, was joined with Brown v. Board of Education, and others, 347 U.S. 483 (1954). See *New York Times*, April 14, 1953, p. 11; "May It Please the Court," *Time*, December 21, 1953, p. 18.

[33] Philip B. Perlman, Solicitor General, 1947–1952, in a letter to the author, February 6, 1953. See Perlman's testimony, *Hearings Before Subcommittee of the House Committee on Appropriations*, January 12, 1950, 81st Cong., 2nd Sess. (1950), pp. 101, 105.

[34] Fowler V. Harper and Edwin D. Etherington, "Lobbyists Before the Court," *University of Pennsylvania Law Review*, Vol. 101 (June, 1953), pp. 1172–1177; Peter H. Sonnenfeld, "Participation of *Amici Curiae* . . . in Decisions of the Supreme Court, 1949–1957," Government Research Bureau, Working Papers, No. 2 (East Lansing, Mich., January, 1958); Johanna Bernstein, "Volunteer *Amici Curiae* in Civil Rights Cases," New York University *Student Law Review*, Vol. 1 (Spring, 1952), pp. 95–102.

[35] Sonnenfeld, *op. cit.*, p. 4.

[36] West Virginia State Board of Education v. Barnette, 319 U.S. 624 (1943).

American Legion. In 1951, in a case testing state resale price maintenance, the United States was an *amicus* against a Louisiana statute while the Commonwealth of Pennsylvania, the Louisiana State Pharmaceutical Association, American Booksellers, Inc., and the National Association of Retail Druggists entered *amici curiae* briefs in support of the statute.[37]

Many *amici curiae* briefs are workmanlike and provide the Court with helpful legal argument and material. Yet writers who favor their use by organizations and recognize that "the *amicus curiae* has had a long and respected role in our own legal system and before that, in the Roman law" believe that many briefs in recent years display a "timewasting character." [38] Another authority has said that after 1947 there were multiplying signs "that the brief *amicus curiae* had become essentially an instrumentality designed to exert extrajudicial pressure on judicial decisions." [39] Concern over this by the members of the Supreme Court was shown in 1946 when Justice Robert H. Jackson, in a dissenting opinion, criticized an *amicus curiae* brief by the American Newspaper Publishers Association:[40]

> . . . Of course, it does not cite a single authority not available to counsel for the publisher involved, and does not tell us a single new fact except this one: "This membership embraces more than 700 newspaper publishers whose publications represent in excess of eighty per cent of the total daily and Sunday circulation of newspapers published in this country. The Association is vitally interested in the issue presented in this case, namely, the right of newspapers to publish news stories and editorials pending in the courts."

Justice Jackson told his colleagues, "this might be a good occasion to demonstrate the fortitude of the judiciary."

REGULATION OF ORGANIZATIONS IN THE COURTS

Judges, lawyers, legislators, and citizens have reacted to appearances that organizational activity in court cases touches the integrity of the judicial process. A number of limitations have resulted. But in protecting the legal system against these dangers, regulations may be too harsh on organizations and interfere unduly with the freedom of association their functioning represents. Especially is this true when the barriers against group participation in litigation are erected by legislative bodies, but it is not entirely absent when the

---

[37] Schwegmann Brothers v. Calvert Distillers Corp., 341 U.S. 384 (1951).

[38] Harper and Etherington, *op. cit.*, p. 1172.

[39] Frederick Bernays Wiener, "The Supreme Court's New Rules," *Harvard Law Review*, Vol. 68 (November, 1954), pp. 20, 80.

[40] Craig v. Harney, 331 U.S. 367, 397 (1946).

rules are established by bar associations or by courts themselves. Some practices by organizations require control, but most of the practices of organizations in conducting litigation are perfectly compatible with an independent judiciary. Life tenure and other traditions of Anglo-American jurisprudence will attend to that. This should be borne in mind in evaluating controls placed on the practices discussed below.

Picketing of Federal Courthouses

During the trial of the leaders of the Communist party under the Smith Act in the Federal District Court for the Eastern District of New York located at Foley Square in New York City, picketing and parading outside the court was a daily occurrence. When the Senate Judiciary Committee was considering bills to limit this practice, it received many statements like the following: "Assuming under our form of representative government pressure groups must be tolerated in our legislative and executive branches, I feel there is no good reason why our courts should be subjected to such pressures." [41] In accord with this view, Congress, in 1950, enacted legislation prohibiting any person from parading, picketing, or demonstrating in or near a federal courthouse with the intent of "interfering with, obstructing, or impeding" the administration of justice or of "influencing any judge, juror, witness, or court officer" in the discharge of his duty.[42]

Mass Petitions to the Supreme Court

In 1953, the National Committee to Secure Justice in the Rosenberg Case addressed a petition claimed to have the support of 50,000 persons to the Supreme Court. Among many condemnations of this was one urging that "the Court must consult its own collective conscience on such matters without reference to the number of persons who are willing to sign a petition." [43] No rule prevents groups from such indecorous action, but Justice Hugo Black has expressed the intense disapproval of the Supreme Court. In 1951, when granting a stay of execution to Willie McGhee, a Negro under the death penalty in Mississippi, Justice Black lamented the "growing practice of sending telegrams to judges in order to have cases decided by pressure." [44] Declaring that he would not read them, he said that "the courts of the United States are not the kind of instruments of justice that can be influenced by such pressures." Justice Black gave an implied warning to the bar by noting that "counsel in this case have assured me they were not responsible for these telegrams."

[41] Communication of Judge F. Ryan Duffy (Federal Court of Appeals, 6th Circuit), Joint Hearings before the Subcommittee of the Committee on the Judiciary on S. 1681 and H.R. 3766, "To Prohibit the Picketing of Courts," 81st Cong., 1st Sess. (June 15, 1949), p. 5.

[42] 18 U.S.C. Sec. 1507 (1952), added in 1950 by 64 Stat. 1018; 63 Stat. 616 (1949), 40 U.S.C. Secs. 13f-p (1952).

[43] Harper and Etherington, op. cit., p. 1173, n. 4.

[44] New York Times, March 16, 1951, p. 1.

Organization Abuse of the Amicus Curiae Function

Supreme Court rules long provided that a "brief of an *amicus curiae* may be filed when accompanied by written consent of all parties to a case." [45] Until 1949 permission was freely granted. In that year, the filing of briefs by forty organizations in the case of the "Hollywood Ten" who had declined to testify before the House Un-American Activities Committee was widely regarded as an excessive use of the *amici curiae* procedure. [46] The Supreme Court thereupon called attention to the "rule of consent" by elaborating the procedures and permitting persons denied consent by a party to seek leave from the Court itself to act as *amici curiae*. The Solicitor General, as the legal representative of the United States in the Supreme Court, took the 1949 rule change to mean that he should exercise the "rule of consent" against persons or groups wishing to be *amici curiae* in all cases. Since the United States government is a party in approximately 50 per cent of all cases before the Supreme Court the universal refusal of consent cut the number of organizations filing *amici curiae* briefs rather drastically. This rigid policy was adhered to by a succession of Solicitors General until August 1952. Complaints by Justices Black and Frankfurter then led the Solicitor General to modify the practice and exercise administrative discretion in passing upon requests of organizations to file briefs *amici curiae*. [47] This practice satisfied a majority of the Supreme Court, for its 1949 rule change was incorporated into the full revision of the Court's rules which went into effect on July 1, 1954. However, Justice Black was still dissatisfied and, on adoption of the 1954 rules, declared:

> . . . I have never favored the almost insuperable obstacle our rules put in the way of briefs sought to be filed by persons other than the actual litigants. Most of the cases before this Court involve matters that affect far more than the immediate record parties. I think the public interest and judicial administration would be better served by relaxing rather than tightening the rule against *amicus curiae* briefs. [48]

The standard governing grant or denial of consent to file *amici curiae* briefs has been elaborated upon in a statement of policy issued by the Office of the Solicitor General. [49] While espousing a liberal attitude, the Solicitor General

[45] In the old Supreme Court Rules, effective February 27, 1939, section 27 (9), 306 U.S. 708–709 (1939). This section was amended on November 14, 1949, 338 U.S. 959–960 (1949). All existing provisions were rescinded when new Supreme Court Rules became effective on July 1, 1954, 346 U.S. 951 (1954). Rules 42 and 44 govern *amicus curiae* procedure, 346 U.S. 951, 993, 996.

[46] Lawson v. United States, 339 U.S. 934 (1949); Marshall v. United States, 339 U.S. 933 (1949). See Harper and Etherington, *op. cit.*, p. 1173.

[47] Sonnenfeld, *op. cit.*, pp. 2, 3, 8, 10. For criticism by the justices, see Lee v. United States, 343 U.S. 924 (1952); United States v. Lovknit, 342 U.S. 915 (1952).

[48] Justice Black's objection is appended to the Order Adopting Revised Rules of the Supreme Court, 346 U.S. 947 (1954).

[49] Statement of the Office of the Solicitor General, issued May 1957, quoted in Sonnenfeld, *op. cit.*, Appendix C, pp. 25–26.

frowns on applicants with "a general, abstract or academic interest" in a case and on "a brief which is 'a vehicle for propaganda efforts.'" Nor is a brief that merely repeats the arguments of the parties well regarded. On the other hand, consent is given "where the applicant has a concrete, substantial interest in the decision of the case, and the proposed brief would assist the Court by presenting relevant arguments or materials which would not otherwise be submitted." Furthermore, in recent years when the Solicitor General has refused consent, the Supreme Court in some cases has granted permission to an organization to file a brief *amicus curiae*.

Efforts to regulate the indiscriminate filing of *amici curiae* briefs prevent organizations on about ten occasions each term from participating in cases. For example, an American Legion post was refused consent to file an *amicus curiae* brief in the Steel Seizure Case while the Congress of Industrial Organizations was permitted to do so.[50] The most active organizations in filing *amici curiae* briefs in recent years have been the American Civil Liberties Union, the American Federation of Labor-Congress of Industrial Organizations, the American Jewish Congress, and the National Lawyers Guild. Yet under the "rule of consent" by parties to the case each of these organizations has sometimes been denied leave to file briefs.

Offer of Legal Aid by the Liberty League

The offer of the National Lawyers' Committee of the American Liberty League to donate its services in test cases led a critic to make a formal complaint to the American Bar Association. The League was charged with unethical conduct for having "organized a vast free lawyers service for firms and individuals 'bucking' New Deal laws on constitutional grounds." [51] The ABA Committee on Professional Ethics and Grievances ruled, in a formal opinion, that the activities of the Liberty League were perfectly proper, even laudable.[52] The Committee found that neither the substance of the offer, to provide legal defense for "indigent citizens without compensation," nor the "proffer of service," even when broadcast over the radio, was offensive to the ethical code of the American bar.

Barratry and the NAACP

Since 1954, eleven Southern states have acted separately through legislation or litigation to restrict the efforts of the National Association for the Advancement of Colored People to proceed with court cases aimed at ending

---

[50] Youngstown Sheet and Tube Co. v. Sawyer, 343 U.S. 579 (1952).

[51] *New York Times*, November 18, 1935, p. 15.

[52] Opinion 148 in *American Bar Association Canons of Professional and Judicial Ethics—Opinions of Committee on Professional Ethics and Grievances* (Chicago: American Bar Association, 1957), pp. 308–312.

segregation.[53] The NAACP frankly admits the deliberate and conscious use of litigation to secure economic, social, and political gains for Negroes. In some states, registration laws—similar to federal and state lobby registration provisions—require the filing of information by organizations which might participate in desegregation litigation. The common law crime of barratry, usually defined as the fomenting, soliciting, or inciting of unjustified litigation, has been outlawed by new statutes in other states. Legislative investigating committees have sought to expose NAACP practices in litigation as unethical and illegal. State Attorneys General have brought actions against the NAACP in state courts while the NAACP has brought suits in federal courts to secure declaratory judgments and injunctions against the enforcement of state statutes which would restrict their activities.

In June, the Supreme Court overruled as an unconstitutional violation of freedom of association a contempt fine of $100,000 imposed by Alabama on the NAACP for refusing to disclose its membership lists.[54] Two similar Virginia cases [were] docketed with petitions for certiorari awaiting action when the Supreme Court [convened] for its October 1958 term. In one, the NAACP . . . asked for review of a Supreme Court of Appeals of Virginia decision enabling a legislative committee to use subpoenas to secure the names of NAACP members and affiliates.[55] In the other case, Virginia . . . asked the Supreme Court to review the decision of a three-judge federal district court in which the majority concluded that acts punishing barratry and requiring registration could not constitutionally be applied to the normal activities of the NAACP.[56]

CONCLUSION

There is a logical relationship of organizational interest in litigation and the importance of courts in forming public policy. Although courts act only in cases between parties with concrete interests at stake, organizations concerned with the impact of the outcome may become quite active participants. Organizations may do this by sponsoring a "test case" brought in the name of a private party; they may aid the government attorney in a case, or they may

---

[53] For a three-year summary of developments, see *Race Relations Law Reporter*, Vol. 2 (August, 1957), pp. 892–894. Examples of the charges being made against the NAACP are seen in the Report of the Joint Committee on Offenses Against the Administration of Justice of the General Assembly of Virginia, filed on November 13, 1957, *Race Relations Law Reporter*, Vol. 3 (February, 1958), pp. 98–111. For defenses, see Robert L. Carter, "The Role of the NAACP in the School Segregation Cases," unpublished paper read before the American Political Science Association, New York City, September 6, 1957; American Jewish Congress, *Assault Upon Freedom of Association: A Study of the Southern Attack on the National Association for the Advancement of Colored People* (New York, 1957).

[54] NAACP v. Alabama, No. 91, U.S. Sup. Ct., June 30, 1958. (26 U.S. Law Week 4489).

[55] NAACP v. Committee on Offenses Against the Administration of Justice, 101 S. E. 2d 631 (Va. Sup. Ct. App., 1958).

[56] NAACP v. Patty (Harrison), 159 F. Supp. 503 (E. D. Va., 1958).

file a brief as an *amicus curiae*. Considering the importance of the issues resolved by American courts, the entrance of organizations into cases in these ways seems in order. Indeed the essential right of organizations to pursue litigation would appear to follow from the generous attitude of American society toward the freedom of individuals to form associations for the purpose of achieving common goals. Of course, traditional judicial procedures should be followed and the attorneys for organizations, as well as for individuals, must address their arguments to reason. If these standards of conduct are followed there is no incompatibility between the activity of organizations in litigation and the integrity or independence of the judiciary.

WHAT TO DO WHEN THE JUDGE IS PUT UP AGAINST THE WALL

LOUIS NIZER

In 1944, the United States Government tried 30 American Nazis and Fascists for undermining the morale of our armed forces then at war. Among the defendants were Gerhard Wilhelm Kunze, Fritz Kuhn's successor as head of the German-American Bund; Elizabeth Dilling, who had attended Hitler's giant 1938 Nuremberg rally; George Sylvester Viereck, a German agent; William Dudley Pelley, head of the Silver Shirts movement; Joseph E. McWilliams, head of the Christian Mobilizers; Lawrence Dennis, self-styled Nazi, who insisted on defending himself, and others. They had published leaflets hailing Hitler as a savior, and denouncing President Roosevelt as a Jew and warmonger. This printed material was being disseminated among American troops by devious means.

The trial took place in Washington, D. C., Justice Edward C. Eicher presiding. From the first moment that the case began, the defendants and their lawyers did not act as participants in a trial, but like storm troopers—spitting abuse at the judge and the judicial system. Some gave the Nazi salute. They kept the courtroom in an uproar.

Every obstructive device was used calculatingly. When a document was offered in evidence, each lawyer read it separately for 10 or 15 minutes. Then he would hand it to his client, who studied it leisurely. Then each of the 30 lawyers, in turn, would rise to make his objection—in as belligerent and insulting a manner as possible, engaging the court in lengthy polemics. The

SOURCE: Louis Nizer, "What to Do When the Judge Is Put Up Against the Wall," *The New York Times Magazine* (April 5, 1970), pp. 30, 122, 124, 126, 128. © 1970 by The New York Times Company. Reprinted by permission.

judge attempted to do what is often done in complex trials, such as antitrust suits with 20 or 30 defendants—to stipulate that the lead counsel's objection would protect all, unless one desired to add some special point. But no, that would not do. The prosecutor attempted to avoid the resulting delay by giving documents to each of the counsel in advance. That did no good, either.

Judge Eicher practiced restraint. He had been advised that if he retorted and struck back at counsel or the defendants, he would be playing into their hands because he might create reversible error. So, day after day, he listened patiently to abuse and insults directed at him.

On one occasion, he was provoked to act, and discharged a lawyer named James J. Laughlin who had been particularly abusive. Thereupon, his client, Robert Noble, set up a cry that he would accept none of the defense lawyers whom the judge assigned to him. He insisted that he had been denied his constitutional right to select his own lawyer. His screams prevented testimony from being heard. There was pandemonium in the courtroom. The prosecutor fell upon the device of severing Noble's case from that of the other defendants so that there would be a little peace in the courtroom. The judge granted the motion. So Noble was rewarded for his contumacy by walking out of the courtroom. He was never again brought to trial on this charge. The other defendants, encouraged by this successful maneuver, redoubled their unruliness.

Judge Eicher grew perceptibly weaker each day. At the end of seven months (the case could have been tried in about 20 days), after a particularly unnerving day, he collapsed. That night he died. His death automatically created a mistrial.

There were 18,000 pages in the record, only 1,000 of which contained testimony. The other 17,000 pages were filled with bickering and colloquy among counsel, the prosecutor and the judge. The Government prosecutor, O. John Rogge, decided not to try the case again because he did not know how he could cope with the defendants and their counsel in another such ordeal. So, the defendants walked out of this courtroom free (though some, including Noble, were sentenced in other trials on other charges). Their strategy to paralyze the judicial process had resulted in killing the judge. It had been a brilliant success.

A cynic once said that experience is a wonderful thing because it enables us to recognize our error every time we make it again. Let us move on from 1944 to 1949 and the Communist trial before Judge Harold Medina, in the Federal District Court in New York. It is interesting to observe that counsel and defendants in that trial patterned their battle plans precisely after the successful conduct of the defendants in the sedition trial of the Nazis. The same flanking movements of obstruction and procrastination were employed; the same frontal assault upon the judge to wear him down by insolence; the same gathering of batteries to cannonade the courtroom with furor and tumult.

When the witness Herbert A. Philbrick took the stand for the Government to offer in evidence a Communist party card, merely to illustrate that Communists referred to one another by first name only, each lawyer carefully studied the card at length, back and front, and then gave it to his client who did the same, and then turned it over to the next of the 11 defendants and counsel as if there were some great mystery to be unraveled. When Judge Medina protested the delay, they screamed that their constitutional rights were being denied and that he was a fascist.

When a telephone book was offered to identify a number, the defendants refused to accept it without authentication. An executive of the American Telephone and Telegraph Company was subpoenaed and put upon the stand, and each counsel for the defense proceeded to cross-examine him at length as to his birthplace, his education, his family and the kind of duties he performed at the telephone company. When the judge attempted to put an end to this farce, there were interminable protests and angry colloquies, until he was forced to call a recess.

On one day alone, 30 motions were made by defense counsel. They were picayune—for example, a motion to close the doors during lunch hour. But the resulting arguments lasted almost two days.

At another point, one of the defense lawyers charged Judge Medina with lying "particularly at 11:20 A.M. and 3:20 P.M. in the afternoon." The judge, intrigued by such specificity, asked: "What does the time element mean?" The lawyer said: "That is the deadline for the morning and afternoon editions."

"You have a terrible mind to make an accusation of that kind," Judge Medina replied, "but you will not goad me into making any statements which will create error in this courtroom. But I plead with you, stop it. You are wearing me down. I don't know whether I will be able to last through this trial, but I will do my utmost to do so." He called frequent recesses so that he could lie down in his anteroom to recuperate. At times, sedatives had to be administered.

As the barrage of invective and disobedience went on, the judge resorted to adjourning court at Friday noon, so that he could have a long weekend to recover. The defendants and their counsel feared that the judge might be slipping out of their hands, and—as the record shows—intensified their attacks on Friday mornings. Despite this venom, the judge was inhibited from retorting or defending himself, because to do so might achieve the defendants' purpose—reversible error. In short, our system lacks the common-sense means to deal with judicial sabotage.

Judge Medina, thanks to his vigor, survived. The trial was completed. The defendants were convicted. The judge went away for a long vacation to recover from his ordeal. When he returned, he was a popular hero. Isn't that sad, too? If a judge can last through one of these trials, we hail him as if he were a hero returning from Bataan. In order to preside at one of these trials, must the judge pass a rigorous physical test? If he is a scholar living a sedentary life, must he be disqualified because he won't be able to withstand the strain? Are we helpless to deal with this kind of situation?

In the recent Chicago trial, eight (later reduced to seven) defendants were charged with conspiring to incite a riot, and individually crossing state lines with that intent, during the 1968 Democratic National Convention, and of performing acts to achieve that purpose. They and their counsel not only imitated the tactics of the defendants in the sedition and Communist trials, but raised them to new peaks of audacity.

One of the defendants upbraided Judge Julius J. Hoffman for having a picture of George Washington on the wall behind him, because "George Washington and Benjamin Franklin [were] slave owners." They refused to stand when the judge entered the courtroom. They referred to him insolently as "Julie," "Hitler," "fascist pig," "liar," "sadist" and "executioner," and told him he "will go down in infamy." They screamed obscenities which, even in the most permissive circles, would be considered extreme. They brought a Vietcong flag into the courtroom. They ridiculed the court by putting on judicial robes.

The lawyers did nothing to quiet their clients; indeed, they supported and justified the outbursts. Early in the trial, Judge Hoffman appealed to them to control their clients: "In the circumstances of this case, this situation, sir, you, a lawyer in the United States District Court permitting your client to stand up in the presence of the jury and disrupt these proceedings. I don't know how to characterize it."

To which one of the defense lawyers, William Kunstler, replied: "Your Honor, we do not permit or not permit our clients. They are free independent human beings who have been brought by the Government to this courtroom."

At the end of the trial, the judge was able to state without contradiction: "I haven't heard either lawyer for the defendants try to quiet their clients during this trial when they spoke out, not once in four and a half months, not once."

Kunstler called the prosecutor "a dirty old man." The defense lawyers, despite instructions not to advise the jury of certain rulings (since these rulings would be reviewed by a higher court and should not, meanwhile, be brought to the attention of the jury), deliberately violated these instructions and informed the jury about them.

The defendants, with their counsel's connivance, indulged in antics of all sorts, intended to make impossible any decorum or dignity which should accompany the intellectual process of a trial. They insisted, for example, on their right to bring a birthday cake into the courtroom to celebrate the birthday of one of the defendants—who, incidentally, is under indictment in Connecticut for conspiring to commit murder.

The defendants packed the courtroom with partisans who yelled derisive comments at the prosecutor and the judge, joined in bursts of loud laughter by defendants at adverse testimony, and chanted, "Oink, oink," when the judge was called a pig. When any unruly spectator was ejected, curses, obscenities and threats were uttered by defendants and their adherents.

And now we have in New York the case of the Black Panthers indicted for the bombing of two police stations, attempts at murder, 20 counts for possessing bombs, pistols and guns without licenses and conspiracy to bomb local department stores during last year's Easter season. Since they claimed that some of the evidence had been seized illegally, they were entitled to a pretrial hearing of the issue of illegal seizure. The hearing was scheduled before Supreme Court Justice John Murtagh.

The defendants and their six counsel used the same tactics that had been used in the Chicago trial, with a few ingenious variations. When they entered the courtroom, they screamed: "Power to the people!" and adherents, who had packed the courtroom, yelled either: "Power to the people!" or "Right on!" They called Justice Murtagh "fascist pig," "faggot," "gangster," "greasy pig," "insane," "fascist lackey," "buzzard," "grandee vulture," "dried-up cracker in female robes," "Hitler" and other names and obscenities too lurid to repeat.

One of the defendants yelled: "If the courtroom doesn't give us justice, Mr. Murtagh, we are going to tear this raggedly, filthy, injustice pigpen out, every single day." These were not empty threats. On two occasions, they caused melees in which they threw tables and chairs around the room. While a witness was testifying, one defendant yelled: "We are going to go to your home and we will have M-14's for your ass."

They threatened the judge continuously with such phrases as: "We are going to get you, you —," or "We will settle this in the streets," "We don't take your b— law" and "There will be blood all over this room." There was. In one of the screaming scenes, they kicked and fought with court attendants. One detective and three policemen were hospitalized, one of them bleeding after being kicked in his kidneys. During these fights, spectators stood on their seats and screamed: "Kill the pigs." The defendants called the prosecutor, Joseph A. Phillips: "Old Phillips Magnesia—he's full of ——."

A bomb was thrown at the judge's home in upper Manhattan. The windows were blown out and the brick front scorched. There were riots near the courthouse. On the front sidewalk was painted: "Free the Panther 21." Autos were overturned. The rioters referred to the Chicago trial, screaming: "Pigs eat ——. —— Hoffman."

The defendants were represented by one black and five white attorneys. They approved the conduct of their clients as ideologically justified and necessary. One of them described himself as a "revolutionary lawyer" whose purpose was "to turn the courts upside down" and "—— up the courts."

Justice Murtagh was unable to proceed with the hearing because witnesses could not be heard and there were riotous conditions in the courtroom. He suspended proceedings and sent the defendants back to jail until they promised to behave. To solve the dilemma of an unending jail sentence, the prosecutor has adopted a suggestion which I have made—set forth below—as to how a case can be tried despite the rebellious determination of the defendants to prevent it.

When the Chicago trial is discussed, one hears much about Judge Hoffman's conduct, and the charges that he acted in a biased, prejudicial and unfair manner. The defendants and their counsel claim that their conduct must be understood in the light of Judge Hoffman's provocation. They ignore the provocation to which they subjected him.

When Seale was finally cross-examined, for example, he conceded that during the convention he had told the people in Lincoln Park: "Pick up a gun, pull the spike from the wall, because if you pull it out and you shoot well, all I am gonna do is pat you on the back, and say: 'Keep on shooting.' " Such a defendant cannot make credible his present claim that his peaceful disposition was stirred beyond control by the judge's "unfairness." Similarly, this remark by the defendant Abbie Hoffman to the judge—". . . stick it up [your] bowling ball. How is your war stock doing, Julie?"—hardly permits the contention that the defendants would have been courteous but for their resentment of legal rulings.

The reason I dismiss the criticism of Judge Hoffman's behavior is not that I endorse everything he did or ruled. On the contrary, his apparent resort to misstating counsel's name, and toying with sarcastic exchanges were often ineffectual as well as undignified exercises. Also, there may be serious questions about the correctness of his rulings in excluding certain witnesses and evidence.

The point is that there is full legal remedy for any error or misconduct by a judge. No judicial system in the world affords so many appeals to a convicted defendant to test the propriety of the judge's conduct and rulings—even any prejudicial comment by a prosecutor.

If the defendants and their counsel had been interested in acquittal rather than political incendiarism, they would have blessed the judge for what they claim was his open bias. The judge's alleged misbehavior was a boon to the defendants, because our protective judicial system would have turned it to their advantage.

But criticism of Judge Hoffman, even if justified, is irrelevant to the consideration of available procedure to preserve the judicial process. There is full remedy against a judge's misbehavior. There is no remedy at present for the kind of open treason to the judicial system which the defendants and their counsel committed in the cases we have been discussing here.

We have proceeded for centuries on the theory that all parties and their counsel in a trial will comply with certain rules. Those rules are sensitively constructed so that the *rights of the defendants* may be preserved. It was not anticipated that defendants would seek to escape justice by making it impossible to conduct a trial at all. That, and not Judge Hoffman's conduct, is the issue. It is this new challenge to our judicial system which must be met. I would like to propose some suggestions as to how to do so.

Before I do so, however, let me comment on two other aspects of the matter. The defendants and their counsel have proclaimed that the Chicago and Panther cases are "political trials" and one cannot expect them to be conducted in an orderly fashion, because the courts were not set up for such controversies.

This is nonsense. The defendants in the Chicago case were indicted under a statute passed by Congress and signed by the President of the United States. That trial was, therefore, no different from any other trial based upon a Federal law.

The defendants may, of course, contend that the law thus enacted is unconstitutional. They may succeed in this contention. It is for the Supreme Court of the United States to review this claim of unconstitutionality. But until the highest Court rules that a particular statute violates constitutional guarantees and is, therefore, invalid, the defendants cannot justify their open contempt of trial procedure. They cannot in advance decide for themselves that the law is invalid, and, therefore, that they have a right to misbehave and sabotage the trial.

The second observation is about Judge Hoffman's ruling at the end of the trial that the defendants should not be let out on bail since they were dangerous to the community. An upper court unanimously reversed, and did so immediately. This illustrates perfectly the fact that a judge's error—or even harsh exercise of discretion—can be corrected under our judicial system.

In the light of subsequent conduct of the defendants, the ruling of Judge Hoffman seems more reasonable than many of us thought at the time. A number of them, and their lawyers, have been going around the country making inflammatory speeches which were followed by violent outbursts. They have contributed, at least psychologically, to the bomb terror which has been sweeping the nation.

Before we condemn Judge Hoffman, we must recognize the plight of any man who must listen to personal insult and provocative vulgarity which, under other circumstances, might justify physical retort, but who must pretend that assaults upon his integrity, honor and self-respect do not reach him because the silk of his judicial robe is a sufficient shield. We can avoid this dilemma by providing the means to restore the courtroom to the judge's control, where it was always intended to be.

There is a joke about the American system of law: "This is the only country in the world in which the defendant goes home at night and the jury is locked up." We have constructed a cordon of protection around defendants. This admirable solicitude for the accused assumes that they will honor and cherish the judicial procedure which protects them. They must not be allowed to defile that procedure and then complain that it is tainted.

It is time that we free the judge—free him from the manacles of procedures and rules which were magnificent, and still remain so, for those who will comply with the exquisite machinery constructed and refined over centuries, but inadequate to meet a new assault upon it. The time has come to provide rules that will enable the judge to control the courtroom, prevent obstruction and not suffer the frustration of helplessness lest he commit reversible error. The challenge to our judicial system, to democracy and to our sense of decency can be met.

I make five suggestions:

First: Any defendant who deliberately and continuously violates decorum in the courtroom, whether by noisy outbursts, obscenities, insulting the judge or otherwise interfering with the normal conduct of the trial, may, after repeated unheeded warnings, be removed from the courtroom and placed in jail. The stenographic minutes of each day's trial shall be sent to him and his removal shall not be deemed a violation of his right not to be tried *in absentia.*

If we wish to be supermeticulous, we can arrange an open telephone line so that he can talk from jail to his lawyer; even a TV hookup, so that he can watch the proceedings. Technologically, he will be present in the courtroom.

It may be argued that this would still deprive the defendant of the right guaranteed by the Constitution to confront his accusers. If confrontation is interpreted to mean eyeball presence—yes. But if it means, as it should, full opportunity to hear the accusation, cross-examine accusing witnesses and rebut their testimony—no.

It has also been contended that a witness who sees the defendant staring at him may be inhibited from straying from the truth, and that jurors may form an impression of the defendant by watching him in the courtroom. Removing him from the courtroom deprives him of these advantages, it is said. These are questionable advantages at best, and they are far outweighed by the exigencies created by the defendant himself.

I reject the proposal that such a defendant be placed in an Eichmann-like Plexiglas booth in the court. He still could distract the jurors by gesticulating or pounding against the walls. Besides, the Eichmann booth was used not to prevent his disorder, but to protect him from possible injury.

As soon as the defendant realizes, and it will be soon, that he is not achieving his objective to prevent the trial's progress, and that he is better off enjoying the comfort of the courtroom and advises the court that he will behave, he should be returned to the courtroom.

The defendant is guaranteed the right to confront his accusers so that he can be assured a fair trial. But if, by his presence, he obstructs the trial, then he destroys the reason for his privilege, and can no longer claim it. The power of the Court to remove an uncontrollably obstreperous defendant from the courtroom, without violating his constitutional rights, would preserve decent conditions at a trial and make it unnecessary to resort to clumsy, cruel shackling and gagging of a defendant—as was done at the Chicago trial.

Second: Any lawyer who deliberately and continuously obstructs justice, collaborating with a client's misbehavior which prevents the orderly procedure of the court, may, after repeated, unheeded warnings, be removed from the trial by the judge, who may designate another defense counsel for the defendant.

This should not be deemed a violation of the defendant's constitutional right to select his own lawyer. The offending lawyer was his agent, and defendant approved his agent's defiance of the rules of the court. He cannot complain about the loss of his lawyer when he must share the responsibility for that loss.

It should be noted that we are here dealing with a rare instance. There are very few lawyers who will lend themselves to disorderly technique. They are either men who share the ideologies of their client or, for some other reason, are ready to violate their duty as officers of the court. Granting the court the authority to remove such a lawyer would be merely another step toward the court's proper preservation of the serenity of the courtroom, and would avoid the temptation for endless, vituperative exchanges.

Third: The practice of packing the courtroom with voluble adherents of the defendants must be controlled. The back of the courtroom is intended to be available for observers so that trials are public. But if partisans pre-empt the seats and applaud, cheer, scream and insult, sometimes in unison, the judicial process is prejudiced. Such behavior is a revolutionary tactic, violating the sanctity of reason and impartiality which should prevail in a court of justice.

Perhaps the Civil Liberties Union and similar groups should be invited to attend such trials, so as to preclude the charge that kangaroo proceedings are taking place.

Fourth: Whenever a man points an accusing finger at someone else, he has four fingers pointing at himself. We of the bar have a great responsibility which we have not met. The appellate divisions of the state and Federal Courts and bar associations, which have disciplinary powers over lawyers, must act firmly, promptly and quickly to suspend or disbar any lawyer who engages in unseemly conduct involving the honor and dignity of our profession. There are very few such offending lawyers, but they should be weeded out. Contempt charges are hardly enough; they raise more questions than they answer. Furthermore, they become effectual after the trial, and therefore do not solve the trial problem except as a deterrent for the future.

Although punishment for contempt is a classic power derived from Anglo-Saxon common law, it is subject to the charge that the judge who is offended acts as both prosecutor and judge. When a jail sentence is imposed, questions of due process arise—the right of a defendant to a trial with all the safeguards for one whose liberty is at stake. While Judge Hoffman kept within well-established precedents of two-month to six-month sentences for contemptuous conduct, he multiplied the sentences by treating each offense separately—and thus cumulatively reached four-year sentences for some of the defendants and lawyers. Thus, a whole series of new questions is posed by an attempt to apply the contempt remedy—whereas, as I have suggested, the procedure should really be preventive.

In normal circumstances, it is admirable that when there is a collision between lawyer and judge, the appellate courts guard the prerogatives and rights of the trial lawyer. However, the authorities who license lawyers must recognize the new and larger danger to the profession which disobedience of the law by its very practitioners presents.

Fifth: We should enact state and Federal legislation making the kind of conduct above described in a courtroom a felony—the felony of obstruction of justice. This will be the most effective deterrent of all.

If a defendant spirits away a witness, he is guilty of obstruction of justice. How much more so is there obstruction of justice by the defendants in their new tactics. If we had had such a law, the 30 Nazis and Fascists who walked out when Judge Eicher died could have been indicted and convicted of the separate crime of obstructing justice. Every lawyer who deliberately aided in that fiasco could have been indicted on the same ground—and, if found guilty, automatically disbarred.

If we meet the new challenge by such rules as I have suggested, or by equivalent ones, then neither defendants nor their lawyers will be able to exploit the magnificent protective devices which the law provides for accused persons, so as to prevent the judicial process from functioning. Otherwise, Mafia, narcotics and other organized groups, as well as individual defendants, may adopt these techniques to frustrate trial procedure and escape by default.

We owe it to accused persons to preserve a trial procedure which is classic and protective. Whenever reforms are suggested in judicial procedure, we may expect the charge that the new measures are "repressive." Aside from the meaninglessness of such labels, can it be said that taking stronger measures to preserve the judicial system is repressive rather than protective?

If those who are interested in preserving the rights of the accused, and the traditional role of the lawyer in fighting for human rights and justice, prevent the measures necessary to defeat the tactics of revolutionaries who are determined to destroy our democratic institutions, then there will be those who will submit far harsher countermeasures. Then we may have unnecessary repressive measures in the name of saving our system of justice. To make our democratic institutions effective, within clearly defined democratic and constitutional limits, is the least we can do. It is a noble task—one not to be decried as repression.

Study Questions

1. What is the relationship of organizational interest in litigation and the importance of courts in forming public policy?
2. Evaluate the present controversy concerning the Supreme Court ruling in the field of criminal law. Give examples.
3. Evaluate the impact of the Supreme Court decision in the case of *Baker* v. *Carr* (1962) on the composition of state legislatures? In your opinion why didn't the Court consider the reapportionment question a "political question"? Discuss fully and critically.
4. Evaluate fully and critically the proposals suggested by Louis Nizer.

Suggestions for Further Reading

Abraham, Henry J. *The Judicial Process.* 2nd edition. New York: Oxford University Press, 1968.

Abraham, Henry J. *The Judiciary: The Supreme Court in the Governmental Process.* Boston: Allyn and Bacon, Inc., 1965.

Danelski, David J. *A Supreme Court Justice Is Appointed.* New York: Random House, 1964.

Freund, Paul A. *The Supreme Court of the United States: Its Business, Purposes, and Performance.* New York: The World Publishing Company, 1961.

Friederich, Carl J., and John W. Chapman, (eds.) *Justice.* New York: Atherton Press, 1963.

Ginsberg, Morris. *On Justice in Society.* Baltimore: Penguin Books, 1965.

Jacob, Herbert. *Justice in America: Courts, Lawyers, and the Judicial Process.* Boston: Little, Brown and Company, 1965.

Krislov, Samuel. *The Supreme Court in the Political Process.* New York: The Macmillan Company, 1965.

Mason, Alpheus Thomas, and William M. Beaney. *The Supreme Court in a Free Society.* Englewood Cliffs, New Jersey: Prentice-Hall, 1963.

Mayers, Lewis. *The American Legal System.* Rev. ed. New York: Harper & Row, Publishers, 1964.

McClosky, Robert G. *The American Supreme Court.* Chicago: University of Chicago Press, 1960.

Murphy, Walter F. *Elements of Judicial Strategy.* Chicago: University of Chicago Press, 1964.

Murphy, Walter F., and C. Herman Pritchett. *Courts, Judges, and Politics.* New York: Random House, 1961.

Peltason, Jack W. *Federal Courts in the Political Process.* New York: Random House, 1955.

Roche, John P. *Courts and Rights: The American Judiciary in Action.* 2nd edition. New York: Random House, 1966.

Schubert, Glendon A. *Constitutional Politics: The Political Behavior of Supreme Court Justices and the Constitutional Policies That They Make.* New York: Holt, Rinehart and Winston, 1960.

Schubert, Glendon A. *Judicial Decision-Making.* New York: Free Press, 1963.

Schmidhauser, John R. *The Supreme Court.* New York: Holt, Rinehart and Winston, Inc., 1960.

Spaeth, Harold J. *The Warren Court: Cases and Commentary.* San Francisco: Chandler Publishing Company, 1966.

Westin, Alan F. (ed.) *The Supreme Court: Views from Inside.* New York: W. W. Norton & Company, Inc., 1961.

PART ELEVEN

United States Foreign Policy

Since 1945, the United States has become the major actor in Western Europe, the Middle East, Southeast Asia, and the Far East. Until recently, many of the countries in these regions were considered primarily within the British and/or French spheres of influence. However, due to an enfeebled French and British economy, and decline in power and prestige, the onus of solving many of the intricate problems facing these regions devolved primarily on the United States. The American effort to solve some of the problems of Asia, Europe, and the Middle East, was manifested in the Truman Doctrine, the Marshall Plan, NATO, the Point Four Program, SEATO, CENTO, and the Eisenhower Doctrine, to mention only a few.

The role of the United States in the world arena is derived from its economic strength, dynamic technology, security considerations, dedication to human freedom, and humanitarian concerns. Our global involvement, however, needs constant review in view of our current conditions and availability of resources.

The conduct of American foreign policy is influenced by the openness and pluralism of our society and institutions. It is shaped by domestic forces such as pressure groups, public opinion, the press, political parties, and by cultural values and belief systems. It is also shaped by external forces such as the international environment, distribution of power on the world scene and the aims and objectives of other great and small powers.

In the conduct of foreign policy, the United States, like other nation-states, is concerned primarily with the achievement of those objectives of national interest which it considers as vital. The foreign policy of a state, therefore, is the expression of its national interests vis-à-vis other sovereign states. The national interests of a state include the preservation of its territorial integrity, national institutions, economic and ideological integrity, and peace and security.

The objectives of United States foreign policy are the expression of its value system. Charles B. Marshall views the following as clearly in our national interest: "To avoid war; to preserve our institutions; to have strong allies; to avoid inflation; to have a prosperous civilian economy; to find common grounds on which to stand with the various nations which have newly come to responsibility; to preserve our access to strategic waterways and vital raw materials; and to protect our property and the safety of our nationals abroad." [1] To this partial list we can add the following important objectives: belief in peaceful change and the rule of law, assistance to developing and weak nations, cooperation in the economic, cultural and scientific spheres among all nations, and belief in the rights and freedom of individual men.

American policy in many regions of the world has encountered a series of dilemmas. Among them are the conflicting interests of the Western powers, the rise of national movements, internal subversion, regional conflicts, civil wars, and overt or covert threats. In the following selections we shall examine some of the problems that face the United States as a major power in a changing world.

William P. Bundy, former Assistant Secretary of State for Asian and Pacific Affairs, discusses the role of the President in foreign policy and states that the Cabinet is not an instrument for making foreign policy. The main advisory group to the President is the National Security Council (NSC). Presidents have used the NSC in the formation of basic policy decisions in different ways. Bundy discusses the use of the NSC by the Truman, Eisenhower, Kennedy and Johnson administrations.

Bundy also examines the various levels of decision-making in Washington and the role of our ambassadors in the field. He states that "experience will make things work and logic isn't necessarily the answer to all." Bundy examines the advantages and disadvantages of the Eisenhower style, the formal style, and the Kennedy-Johnson style, the informal and more personal style in using the NSC.

Bundy discusses the elements of success in foreign policy and cites several case histories such as the Cuban case, the Lebanon crisis, and Vietnam. Bundy turns his attention to the role of men—the military, and the Foreign Service. He concludes with a note on the role of Congress in the making of foreign policy. He states that Congress cannot "become an effective initiating body in the field of foreign policy. It is not that cohesive." Moreover, that Congress is not well-informed.

One of the major critics of our Vietnam policy is Senator J. W. Fulbright. Senator Fulbright believes that divergence between "old myths" and "cur-

---

[1] Eleanor Lansing Dulles, *American Foreign Policy in the Making* (New York: Harper & Row, Publishers, 1968), p. 3.

rent realities" is dangerous, especially in the conduct of foreign policy. Fulbright discusses the reason underlying such divergence and states that we have failed to adapt ourselves to new world realities and that "we are seeking to escape the contradiction by narrowing the permissible bounds of public discussion. . . ." There is an imperative need to start new thinking about the cold war and East-West relations and about the developing nations and particularly, Latin America, and to separate myths from current realities. He discusses the areas in which we can seek to reduce the tensions of the cold war.

Senator Fulbright discusses the crisis over the Panama Canal and the problem of Cuba. He believes that our policy toward Cuba has been a failure. In Latin America, he wants us to recognize the difficulties in bringing about change, and believes we should try to bring about peaceful change through the Alliance for Progress. In the Far East and particularly in China, we have been inflexible in our policies. We need to re-examine our policy and maintain an "open door" policy toward China. Moreover, we must avoid excessive moralism in the conduct of our foreign policy.

In a major speech of November 3, 1969, President Nixon discussed the origin and reasons behind our involvement in Vietnam, how his administration had changed the previous policy, what had happened in the Paris negotiations, the possible methods of bringing an end to the war, and finally, what he considered the prospects for peace. President Nixon rejected the call for immediate withdrawal of our forces; offering instead, several plans for achieving peace. He presented his Vietnamization plan and appealed to "the great silent majority" of Americans for support. "The more support I can have from the American people," said the President, "the sooner that pledge can be redeemed; for the more divided we are at home, the less likely the enemy is to negotiate at Paris."

In the last article John Kenneth Galbraith discusses the important question of how to control the military. He examines military power, assesses its strengths and weaknesses, and suggests guidelines of regaining control over the military. Also, he discusses the military-industrial complex and the payoffs involved. He states that closely associated with military power are the intelligence agencies, Foreign Service Officers, university scientists, and those scientists in such defense-oriented organizations as RAND, the Institute for Defense Analysis and the Hudson Institute. Moreover, there is the organized voice of the military in Congress, particularly, the Armed Services Committees in the House of Representatives and the Senate.

Galbraith states that the problem is that of unchecked rule; that is to say, bringing the military establishment under effective political control. Galbraith examines six major factors that have brought about the military-industrial bureaucracy to its present position of power. Congressmen and Senators are slow to criticize expenditures in their districts. "The military power," Galbraith states, "has been above challenge for so long that to attack still seems politically quixotic." He offers ten proposals as to what is needed to control the military.

Finally, Galbraith asserts that "The military power has reversed constitutional process in the United States—removed power from the public and Congress to the Pentagon."

HOW FOREIGN POLICY IS MADE—LOGIC AND EXPERIENCE

WILLIAM P. BUNDY

INTRODUCTION

I hope that what I am going to talk about this evening can properly be described as a part of the law. It surely can be described as a process by which a certain type of decision is made. What ruling principles are there about this process? What are the flesh and blood characteristics of it in terms of the human beings who enter into it, and how do they, in fact, interact with each other? In short: How does the process work?

My topic is: "How Foreign Policy Is Made—Logic and Experience." To the students or faculty of a Law School I need not say where the phrase "logic and experience" comes from—the opening sentences of Holmes' lecture on The Common Law in 1881: "The life of the law has not been logic, it has been experience." The same is true of foreign policy-making.

It is a concrete and identifiable subject. It is a subject that has been written about from a personal standpoint of exactly how this or that decision came to be made—at other times from a conceptual standpoint—here's the blueprint and this is the way it works. I would like to tackle it tonight from a viewpoint which, though personal, will attempt to combine and go beyond these two ways of looking at it.

● ● ●

Now let us look at this process—in effect a new part of the American Government—arising during the postwar period in response to needs for this country to have a thought-through foreign policy, a thought-through set of policies for individual situations, countries and areas, individual situations

SOURCE: William P. Bundy, "How Foreign Policy Is Made—Logic and Experience," *University of Pittsburgh Law Review*, 30 (Spring 1969), 437–458. Reprinted by permission.

defined functionally in trade, defense posture, and other areas. And let me say at the outset that I assume this country is going to have to have that kind of foreign policy in the future. We seem to be in the midst of a public opinion swing of some momentum toward withdrawing from responsibility. I hope that this tendency will be short and shallow. But even to the extent that it does take place, it will take the most careful thinking through, and the most careful handling of the instruments of foreign policy. So this is perhaps a good time to look at what has happened to a piece of our government over 23 years—to see what its problems are, to see how it might be made to work better.

In talking primarily about the Executive, and briefly about relations between the Executive and the Congress, I am not neglecting the fact that foreign policy in the last analysis depends upon public opinion. One could talk at length about that—it isn't my subject tonight—because it is a very broad one that is difficult to cover. Congress is, of course, a reflection of that public opinion, and Congress is whom you work with day in and day out in the foreign policy business, and that I *shall* talk about.

THE SUBSTANCE OF FOREIGN POLICY

When you talk about "foreign policy" you are in fact talking about a vast variety of things—the types of decisions that are made through this type of instrument and these types of people are the corpus, if you will, of this little corner of jurisprudence. This includes everything from an attempt to lay out a broad outline of our whole national policy—which would usually be dealt with in a major Presidential speech—to the definition of policy in key *areas*, be it NATO, the Middle East, or Southeast Asia, to policy in trade, policy in foreign aid (which, of course, gets back into specific countries) and, finally, policy defined in terms of individual areas and countries. In short, we are talking about a very broad sweep of decisions.

From the standpoint of the Executive Branch, decisions divide roughly into four categories:

1. high-level decisions reached by the President, with the personal and direct advice of his senior Cabinet officials, through the National Security Council, or otherwise;
2. the ongoing decisions that would be reached at a slightly lower level, *ad referendum*, subject to check by the President;
3. attempts to define long-range planning decisions and contingencies—a particular area of its own, and;
4. the day-to-day exercise of "policy" (as I see the word) in regard to countries and areas, handled largely by Assistant Secretaries.

I am going to talk first in terms of institutional machinery. It is not really machinery—it is not a blueprint—it is people. But you have to describe the names and numbers of the players and the style in which institutions have been used.

Secondly, I will talk in terms of what might be called the elements of due process, the fundamental elements for successful policy-making, irrespective of style.

And, third, I will discuss the importance, the key importance, of the men who operate the process. Who are they? How good are they? How can they be improved upon? This, I think, perhaps may be the most critical single part of the whole process.

Any discussion of foreign affairs in the Executive Branch starts with the powers of the President. We do not have a Cabinet system of government. The President is *the* single individual in charge of the Executive. Those of you who, as lawyers, have delved into the *Curtiss-Wright* case and its followers, know that there has developed over a long period a very great power in the Presidency in the field of foreign affairs, quite possibly going beyond anything contemplated by the Founding Fathers. But I think the bulk of the Bar, and certainly I, would regard this development as inevitable and inescapable. The President *is* the chief moving force, the Commander-in-Chief of the Armed Forces, the centerpiece in any discussion of how foreign policy is run. And all four Presidents under whom I have served in one capacity or another have been *the* decision-making and leading authorities in the government regarding foreign policy. It seems right to me. It seems impossible to run the government unless the President does assume this burden quite explicitly, and has the character and power of decision to make it work. I don't know whether the Presidency is now becoming very nearly an impossible job, but I do know that the conduct of foreign affairs is one duty which must rank at the very top of his priorities.

The structure that the President uses in foreign affairs is *not* the Cabinet. At no time in 17-plus years do I recall one single decision that effectively emerged from the President's discussion of matters with his Cabinet. The Cabinet *is* a useful mechanism for the President to convey what it is that has been decided in foreign policy, to mesh it together with domestic policy or to go over the Congressional program that may be very closely related to foreign policy. It is not an engine for making foreign policy. In fact, to labor the obvious, the Cabinet in our governmental system, unlike the British Cabinet, is a purely advisory group.

The famous story that is often told—perhaps many of you know it—is that of Lincoln deliberating the Emancipation Proclamation in the Fall of 1862, putting it before his Cabinet—seven members—and getting seven negative comments of one degree or another, and announcing wryly at the end: "The motion has been made. The ayes one. The nays seven. The ayes have it." That is the Cabinet system in this country. But the Cabinet as a label, as a group, is not of any significance whatsoever in foreign policy.

Rather, it is perfectly clear in the law what the principle advisory group to the President *is*. It is the National Security Council, defined in the National Security Act of 1947.

I have always thought this particular Act a very interesting bit of legislation. It set up the Department of Defense. It set up the Director of Central Intelligence and the Central Intelligence Agency. It defined certain powers in the Joint Chiefs of Staff, including the right of direct personal access to the President for their requests, and also the right to state military views to the Congress, on demand, as they saw the matter—a right not accorded to civilians in the government. It proceeded finally to say that the President, in considering what are broadly defined as national security matters, should do so in a council which will consist of the Secretary of State, the Secretary of Defense, and other stated officials.

To me, viewed in any manner other than a purely advisory one, this particular provision of the Act is clearly unconstitutional and would be so held if anybody, for example, were to contest a particular decision of the government, on the grounds that it had not been reviewed or voted upon by the National Security Council. I submit that to any enterprising third-year student for research. I have considerable confidence in the result. The executive power in the Presidency under the Constitution is not subject to change by a law telling him who he should see or not see. In point of fact, the National Security Council has been used very heavily by each of the four Presidents I have known, but in very different ways.

Let me run through some of these differences. I am speaking now principally, of course, of the NSC's use in what you might call the formulation of basic policy decisions; that is, broad policy, a definition of policy worldwide, a definition of policy by region, perhaps most conspicuously, and certainly most dramatically, policy as it may relate to Vietnam at present, Cuba in 1962, a crisis such as Lebanon in 1958, Korea and the ending of the Korean War in 1953. These are dramatic cases where the government has had to make a decision to cope with a set of circumstances that has arisen or has had to take a new initiative. For these decisions the President does indeed call on the members of the NSC, but it is entirely at his pleasure whether he calls on the NSC *as such*. And in these four Presidencies, I, at least, identified two very distinctly different ways of styling the procedure, which I will happen to define in terms of the party identification of the President involved. I don't think it is necessarily that way. However, it seems to me to have worked that way.

Under all Presidents, the Secretaries of State and the Secretaries of Defense, and their departments, have had paramount importance as fully participating members of the NSC in whatever form. Under all administrations the Joint Chiefs of Staff as military advisors and the Central Intelligence Agency, as the "puller-together" of all the intelligence functions and as conveyor of the best judgment that men can make, fallible as it may be, have been fundamental cornerstones. You will notice I leave out the covert functions of the

Agency that are dealt with in an entirely different way; in any event, they are much less important today.

Beyond this point, styles have diverged sharply. The position of Special Assistant to the President for National Security Affairs has been of great importance under Presidents Kennedy and Johnson, of largely ministerial significance in the Eisenhower Administration, and, as far as I can determine, nonexistent in the Truman Administration. The presence of the President's speech writer—a very, very important individual because so many decisions culminate in what the President says—has been much more marked in the last two administrations. In the Eisenhower Administration the Secretary of the Treasury played a much greater role; the Director of the Bureau of the Budget also played a greater role—neither of these are defined by the statute, incidentally, as members of the NSC. So you can see very important differences in the weightings of the individuals.

There have been tremendously important differences in the way that the Security Council has been used. Under the Truman Administration, its meetings were formal, infrequent and intended to be held for the purpose of nailing down vital state papers, which were already effectively agreed to by discussions between the State and the Defense Departments. It was a ratifying organization to be sure, but an organization used to put the Presidential stamp on what had been worked out among the departments, submitted to and argued before the President and approved by him. I betray in my description my partiality for this particular style.

In the Eisenhower Administration formal meetings were held quite frequently, almost once a week for the first two years. And substantive attempts to define policy systematically were made: "Have we got a policy for . . . (I caricature it—Baluchistan)? If not, let's get cracking and have one." Really, an attempt was made to codify the national policy all across the board and to use the NSC as a real meeting point and decision-making body. In the Eisenhower Administration, the decisions were made in the room with the NSC present to a greater degree than has been the case in any of the other administrations.

Then in the Kennedy and Johnson Administrations, there were really two types of meetings. The first was informal, very frequent, and quite often did not include all of the membership—meetings on the substance, the guts of decisions; meetings that in the Johnson Administration have been termed the "Tuesday lunches." In the Kennedy Administration, these were held on, usually, very short notice. The second and much rarer type of NSC meeting was formal, substantive, and rather like those of the Truman Administration in ratifying that which had already been decided.

Those are interesting differences in styles, I think. And the substance has varied enormously, but with a common thread. At no time has any President acted without having gone through the matter thoroughly with his Secretaries of State and Defense, gotten military and intelligence advice, and consulted the people he wanted to. But the framework in which that has been done and the whole style of it has been enormously different.

Now we come to another layer of decisions, the ongoing decisions of government which are not very dramatic but which in the aggregate constitute the enormous percentage of effective foreign policy decisions. I refer to decisions, for example, on the totality of an aid budget—now so slashed by the Congress, to my great regret, and I hope to many of yours. The basic information policy—how are you going to handle that? Major area policies—Europe, and so on, within guidelines understood, if not stated, from the top—essentially carrying on things.

Here again there was a difference in style. In the Eisenhower Administration these were treated as if they were the *execution* of policy, as though there were a clear distinction between policy and its execution, a distinction I for one don't for a moment accept because the way you carry something out can make a sea of change in it. In that Administration there was an Operations Coordinating Board which in effect was supposed to take a codified body of law, if you will, handed down by the National Security Council, and carry it into execution. That was one style.

Then there was the style of the Truman-Kennedy-Johnson Administrations which did not have a central coordinating committee of this sort, but vested the power to see that the necessary decisions were made, in effect, in the State Department. These decisions were the medium-grade, next to top-grade ones, all the action decisions—budgets, and all the rest, which are of the greatest importance. That responsibility has been formalized since 1966 in a group called the Senior Interdepartmental Group (SIG), headed by the Under Secretary of State with subordinate Interdepartmental Regional Groups (IRG's) headed by the Assistant Secretary for each region. In short, exemplified there, as in many other parts of the description I am giving, is a contrast between two ways of looking at the process:

> —One method, in which the agencies concerned with foreign policy abroad—the State Department, the Defense Department, the Joint Chiefs, and CIA, but also the Treasury, Agriculture, Interior, whoever it may be, are somewhat equal. Each has a stake and a right to be consulted in very great degree—a group method.
> —And secondly, a method that puts the State Department very much *primus inter pares*, taking the lead, calling the shots, subject to appeal to the President, as always exists for any Cabinet officer, but taking the lead in trying to mold the whole into a more coherent policy.

These arguments were made at length in Senator Jackson's subcommittee on this subject. Thomas Gates, now with Morgan Guaranty but then Secretary of Defense, spoke on the side of the group system, saying that Defense had at least an equal stake in every decision around the world with the State Department. Paul Nitze, now Deputy Secretary of Defense, spoke on behalf of the theory that the State Department must take the real lead. It is a very important distinction and one where I have already made clear that my sympathies are entirely with the Nitze point of view, while respecting the other.

Then we get into the third type of policy that I defined at the outset: long-range planning and contingency work. That is very well done today, in the Joint Chiefs and in the Department of Defense where the factors are finite and you can grasp them. In my judgment, at least since the days of George Kennan and Paul Nitze, we have not had real generalized policy planning in the State Department. There have been, I think, occasional distinguished initiatives on a limited scale which emerged from the situation as it was felt. One such occasion that my own deputy, Mr. Barnett, played a great part in was the formation of the policy announced by the President in April, 1965, of really large-scale, long-term help to Southeast Asian economic development, including the Mekong Delta of Vietnam. It had lain on the drawing boards for years, and it had come to fruition at that time because the facts had fallen into place and it had become practical. In short, *practical*, long-term contingency planning, I think, has been done effectively in the State Department. I don't think long-term conceptual planning has been well done, and I am frankly very doubtful that it can be very well done. Today at least (it may not have been the case in the immediate post-war years) I think most initiatives emerge from the felt necessities of the situation.

Now I come to the lowest point, in terms of status, of policy-making, and that is country and area policies. It is institutionalized now under the IRG's chaired by the Assistant Secretaries and it really depends on a daily, close network of contact between the Department of State and the Department of Defense primarily, but also between the Department of State and the Agriculture Department for food, the Commerce Department for trade policy and the Treasury Department for balance of payments and any financial implications. The whole structure flows out in that way. There again style does come into play. In the Eisenhower years these Departments tended to be treated as more nearly equal. In the last two Administrations, and I think rightly, the process was pulled together much more under the Department of State.

Now, I have been talking far too much about Washington, and not enough about what happens in the field. Contrary to popular superstition, and I hope not contrary to the beliefs of young men contemplating a career in the Foreign Service, the fact is that Ambassadors serving abroad have tremendous responsibility today all across the board. This is true above all in the action posts, just about every one in East Asia that I deal with, and also in the greater majority of the posts around the world. Even in the field, intragovernmental relations used to be on a "treaty basis" to an excessive degree, with the military reporting in their channels and the CIA in their channels; in short, a situation creating a great deal of separation and diffusion. President Kennedy rightly moved in on this in May, 1961, and made the Ambassador *the* top man in the field. The very significant and important letter of May 29,

1961, establishing the ground rules, was part of the overall effort to give the State Department a real pulling-together power as a *primus inter pares*.

Today, in practice, an Ambassador in an action post *is* the center of policy. Some of you may have seen Arthur Schlesinger's book on Kennedy. I remember Ambassador Reischauer saying to me wryly: "There are only two references in that book to Japan." The fact is that in those years, and in Reischauer's tenure through 1966—and the same has held true since—we have had an enormously successful policy toward Japan, not only in ironing out frictions between us, but in working together to the point where Japan is now assuming a much greater economic role in Asia which can have the very greatest future significance. In bringing that about, Ambassador Reischauer played the key part. Our policy toward Japan—and it was a *very* important policy—was to do what Ed Reischauer recommended, so that it didn't happen to hit the White House, and didn't happen to fall under Arthur Schlesinger's nose. Nonetheless, it was an extraordinarily effective demonstration of policy coming from the field, operating the way it should; operating, above all, with a unity of substance and style which in many countries of the world is the essence of success.

This is so because (and I say this as a truism to any of you who follow foreign affairs) style is going to be a very important part of our policy—an increasingly important part—in the coming years. We have been, in wide areas of the world, and necessarily so, the *one* source of economic and military assistance. We are no longer, and should not be. Much more should be done by Japan in Asia, by European countries in Asia, by European countries in other parts of the world. Therefore we can afford to find, and should find, a new style. And it is our Ambassadors who will find that style.

THE MERITS OF THE TWO APPROACHES

I have talked a lot about the ways in which different administrations have operated, dividing them into two different types. One, the Eisenhower Administration style, which was far more systematic, group-oriented, tending to put people together in a sort of equal board-of-directors relation; the other in varying degree—less formal, oriented toward the leadership of the State Department, less dependent on institutions and committees. Those are extremes, but characteristic of a very important difference, and one that an incoming Administration will be choosing between to one degree or another.

Now what are the pros and cons—I am not saying either one is better, abstractly, than the other. In fact, the essence of the point is, as logic and experience was intended to convey, that experience will make things work and logic isn't necessarily the answer at all.

In behalf of the more systematic Eisenhower approach: Everybody knows where you stand. The records are excellent. Security, I think, has a better chance of being preserved. That is, people don't talk outside the circle because it operates in a defined area. There is a certain magic in putting "NSC Paper" on something, and people keep it secret. Not that I am an enemy of the Press, you understand, but I do think that the government has got to operate with discretion in this area until it makes up its mind. And lastly, the committee system brings the institutional judgment, the military judgment, the intelligence judgment and the political judgment into play properly and with less dependence on the personal factor. Those are its big advantages.

On the opposite side of the coin, although you may know where you stand, where you stand may be fudged. Time after time I can recall policy papers of the Eisenhower period which, after being litigated in endless fashion and endless pain, emerged saying that we would take a certain action "as appropriate" or "if feasible," leaving the entire discussion on whether you did or didn't do that to some future time, with each fellow clinging to the remnants that he had of the legislative record—a process, I believe, familiar in the practice of law in legislative interpretation (there are parallels to the law in so many of these matters). But, it's fudged. And that won't do any good, really. Too many committees, and a waste of time. I think this became acute and was felt by everybody at the end of the Eisenhower Administration—less scope for debate and initiative—the erasure of differences of view under an often synthetic consensus. And this tendency to false equality, in which the Budget Bureau was as entitled to express itself on the political situation in Japan or Western Europe as the State Department, or on the military feasibility of a course of action as the Joint Chiefs of Staff is nonsense, basically.

Now that isn't to say that the other style is not free of major flaws in itself— the more personal and informal style of the Kennedy and Johnson Administrations. It has more individual responsibility; it puts more stress on contacts between individuals, the State Department and the Defense Department, and so on, where the day-to-day work will be done. It puts the weights of influence where, in my judgment, they should be: with the State Department, usually more important unless the issue is a particularly Defense-oriented one. It therefore gets away from false equality. It allows for differences to come to the President—indeed both President Kennedy and President Johnson have used their special assistants deliberately to present different points of view. And President Johnson, as is well known in the case of Vietnam, used George Ball specifically as a devil's advocate to present different views to him on that subject. Real differences occur, a situation which did not arise in the Eisenhower Administration, at least visibly. Also, decision relates directly to action, and is clearer. You are not deciding hypothetical cases, you are deciding an actual case, and action immediately flows.

On the other hand, I think it is only fair to say, very categorically, that this style is much less clear in the records it produces, and that is a very important part of the ongoing nature of government. It is less systematic. And it may lend itself—I don't think it has, but it may—to making small decisions without assessing their long-range consequences. I will come to that charge as it relates to Vietnam a little later.

So I would come out, as I said earlier, somewhere between the two but more toward the less formal style. That is, the primacy of the Department of State and less reliance on the White House staff, with an adequate degree of system so that everybody understands what you are doing. Under any system, the State and Defense Departments are the keys.

THE ELEMENTS OF SUCCESS

Now that may be too much about machinery. I want to extract the sort of underlying principles that will work. If you achieve them, it doesn't matter what system you use.

First of all, you have got to frame the question properly. Define the objectives—see what the question is you are talking about. These are going to sound so much like what any good court in the land would do that I am afraid the gentlemen of the Bench here present will think they are extraordinarily simple—framing the question and defining the objective.

You have to get the fullest advice and judgment of the professionals in their professional fields. I don't think Mr. Caplan would be insulted if it were said that he has an absolutely first-rate legal mind. And I would not feel insulted if I were told that I have a reasonably adequate grasp of diplomatic factors. I don't regard it as an insult if I say to some of my military friends that they have absolutely first-rate military minds, or that there is another fellow who is an expert on information. That doesn't limit them—it does describe what they are trained to bring together. And I think, in the first instance, you have got to have advice that is based on solid professional input. So that is point two.

Third, you must have a real presentation of the options. However you do it, you must have the possible canvas fully explored, laid out and prepared to be argued—if necessary, with the use of devil's advocates, whoever they may be.

Then, fourth, this being in progressively narrowing circles, the President and his senior advisors must get together. At that point the senior advisors serve two different purposes.

First, they represent the professional, final mouthpiece of their own considered views: the Chairman of the Joint Chiefs to say: "Here is the military consequence, cost, all the rest"; the Intelligence man to say: "Here are all the intelligence factors"; the State Department to talk about the diplomacy and the political element; the Secretary of Defense to talk broadly, in addition to straight military factors, on all the additional elements that enter in on that standpoint. Professionals, in the first instance, in the shoes of the President in the second. In other words, they move over, in effect, and say to the President: "Here is what I tell you from the State Department standpoint. Here is what, on an overall basis, I believe you should do." I think that is the right concept of responsibility at that point. I say that with diffidence because I haven't operated at that level.

At that point, if not before, the President must call on outsiders, as he sees fit. Call on the leaders of the Congress. Call, if he wants to, on senior citizens outside the government with experience. That, I think is a suggestion made by Professor Reischauer in a recent meeting of the Political Science Association. I have doubts about this as a regular practice, however. I have seen again and again senior groups of great experience pulled together. By the time you get them really educated to the problem, chances are that you have, in some way, so described the problem that you have twisted their judgment —and it isn't really as though they had soaked in it and given it the kind of attention they would have done when they were in office.

I feel the same way about academic groups coming in from the outside. It is immensely useful to have, as we have done in the Department in the last two years, periodic meetings with the Asian experts, particularly the China experts—we meet with them separately—to go over policy broadly. However, in that I do not think that outside consulting groups are really a very useful tool of government other than as a check-up. I respectfully differ from Reischauer on that point.

But the point is that the President gets the advice he needs on the broader aspects that only he can put into the process. And that is above all public opinion. There are specific Congressional factors. It is getting outside the whole thing, getting away, thinking about it, brooding about it, that every President I have known has done in the clinch. That is the crucial part of the whole process and is done by talking to anybody he wishes to talk to, at that point. That is quite apart from anything that anybody can prescribe.

All of that being done, you come to decision. It should be clear and it should be recorded. And it should then be presented to the American people, which rounds out the process.

CASE HISTORIES

Now I want to consider some case histories, briefly. Thinking over a long period of time about the decisions that were made and whether there were defects in the process that contributed to whether the decisions were right or wrong, I have chosen three. First, two very clearly successful ones: the decisions in the Cuban missile crisis in 1962, and the decision to go into Lebanon in 1958. Then, for contrast, and to be blunt in an appraisal of the machinery, take the successive major decisions on whether to get into Vietnam, on which, of course, the returns aren't in—I hold one set of views, others might hold different ones. At any rate it is an undecided case and a much argued one.

Take the successful cases:

Cuba in 1962 is one that has been written about more than I care to add to.

Robert Kennedy's estate is coming out with what will probably be a definitive book on it. Obviously, it was a brilliant success. And as I think his book will reveal and other treatments have not, because they have been from the wings, it was a success because from the very beginning there was a recognition by all concerned that it was not a clear-cut case, that you could make an argument for a range of action from mere protest to the blockade that was used, to air attack, to invasion. Therefore, from the very beginning, a systematic bloc of supporting data was built up on important alternatives. It was a rare case, in a sense, because this whole policy was carried through at a time when the whole country didn't know there was even an issue. That is, the evidence came in on a Monday, the 15th of October, and the decision on it came out on the following Monday. It was all utterly secret, and kept so. It was a sort of hothouse case, but a perfectly conducted one, and one that in the result seems to me to have been brilliantly vindicated, where all the fundamentals were observed—a real textbook example—and a case where nobody doubted that you had to act. For all practical purposes there was no option of not acting.

The second case, the Lebanon crisis in 1958, was a case where we went in and, I think, got a good result, at least for a time, in stabilizing the area and so on. I rate it as a success case. Again, it was considered from the beginning— through the NSC machinery—in terms of the two basic alternatives which were, if the contingency arose, to act or not to act. You looked down the pike. And I recall vividly that we in intelligence were told to look. What happens if we do go in? What do we get into? What happens if we don't go in? How does it play out a month, two months, a year, two years, down the line?

These were two first-rate cases, then, where the machinery worked. I have deliberately chosen one where the machinery was that of the Johnson-Kennedy style—the Kennedy style particularly, but it would have been the same in the Johnson Administration—and one where it was under the Eisenhower style. So both can work. That is perfectly obvious.

The third case, the Vietnamese decisions, the ones I know well—1954, 1961, early 1965 and the middle of 1965—are going to be debated at great length in history as they are today. I would only say that I do not think the fault, if fault there be, will be found to have lain in the process. For at each of those points—in a way going far beyond the recollections of people who were at the outskirts of the process (even a person as close to President Johnson as Bill Moyers seems to me quite wrong on this) there was a looking down the pike.

By 1965 or even 1961, there was a situation where we were in whether we willed it or not, to a certain degree. We had been committing limited assets in an effort to preserve South Vietnam's right to run its affairs. The question was, in the face of greater opposition and declining odds of success, whether we should put more assets in. And in the successive cases that I watched, 1954 from a distance, and both the 1961 and 1965 decisions at fairly close range, the record will show that the matter was considered very thoroughly, that at each stage we looked as hard as we knew how at what would happen if we did and what would happen if we didn't pursue a given course. I won't say we estimated the costs as high as they have become on the "What if we did?" question. But we always weighed that with a considerable recognized margin of error on the upward side. In other words, we recognized that this was a new venture in the most difficult area in the world that you could possibly tackle. And above all, we looked at the judgment of what happened if we did not—a hard judgment to validate in the eye of history because, of course, that wasn't the turn you took, in Frost's words, and that has made all the difference. But as nearly as we could judge, the consequences of not doing what we did were extraordinarily black. And while we could not paint the shade of blackness of acting affirmatively, we thought, on balance, it was likely to be less black than if we did not act. And I think it will be found that it was at least thought through in that sense.

There are certain things that float through these examples on the *nature* of foreign policy decisions as they arise for the United States Government in this period of history. Irving Kristol summed them up, eloquently, in an article in "Foreign Affairs" about two years ago. As a great power—certainly as the only worldwide super-power—we must face the fact that our *not* acting is a tremendous decision in its own right. If we don't take the lead on trade policy, there won't be a Kennedy Round; there won't be any world trade policy. If we don't act in foreign aid, worldwide foreign aid from the northern group of countries to the southern group of countries will be far less than it should be. And so, if we had not acted in Southeast Asia, Southeast Asia would have been left to the naked play of the elements. We, and we alone, could have a policy that would act on that. And almost every choice you have, and all the choices that I have posed as examples, are going to be choices where there are marked drawbacks to the possibilities that are put before you. We have got to face it: there is no easy road.

I say that because there is a certain school of thought commenting in foreign affairs that seems to me to fall into the error suggested by one of the old Viennese stories about a character usually described as Count Boddie, a dilettante in Vienna in the old days. In this story, he gets married and his Countess eventually goes to the hospital to have an accouchement, and the Count is waiting there. The nurse comes out with a large basket containing three bustling infants and goes up to the Count, who adjusts his monocle, and says: "Please give the Countess my compliments and tell her, I'll take *this* one."

It isn't that way. And there is no point pretending that it is. There is no point pretending that there is in substance going to be that kind of choice for a President. You are going to have grave costs in either direction. You are going to have to take a lot together. And there isn't any point pretending that your machinery doesn't have to come to that.

GOOD MEN—THE REAL KEY

Now I come to the factor of men. Because I think this is something that an incoming Administration, whoever its leader may be, will have to face acutely.

The machinery works as well as the men. The machinery is important, but really good men would make almost anything work, I suspect.

Of course, in any circumstance, there will be a very large change in senior cabinet men in a new Administration, be it Democratic or Republican. Then you come to the professional services, the constant underpinning of the foreign policy process.

The military services I think have moved ahead in a most extraordinary fashion. And I say that most particularly to the younger members of this audience who may subscribe to the view that there is a military-industrial complex. I am not saying there are not influences of that sort. But if you take the military men who are acting in the field of policy today, they are men who have broadened their training, broadened their outlook, and are still, as they must be, professional military men who give you the military answer first. They are not afflicted by bias—they hate war as much as any of us. They are trained in what power can do, but the great bulk at the top have a shrewd sense of its limitations, and have accepted the limitation imposed on them in this war, as in Korea, with a discipline that must win the praise beyond the stint of any student of military or political history. I think that the military institution is in very solid shape.

The other great institution is the one that I am associated with, and to which I am deeply devoted, the Foreign Service, which includes the State Department, the men who man AID and USIA. These men have also come a tremendous distance. The cross-fertilization of military and civilian men through the Service schools, through the State Department Senior Seminar, through the attendance of State Department people at the War College, through the civilianization, if you want to call it that, of the curricula of the National War College and the Service colleges, has done a tremendous amount to create a group of professionals on the civilian as well as on the military side. At the same time—and without going into detail in terms of the kind of role I have sketched out for the Department of State and what I believe is the right way to run the policy of this country—the Foreign Service would be the first to admit that it has a great deal to do. This is indeed the theme of a report that is coming out next week, by senior members of the Foreign Service. This is so because the senior members, to some degree, had their formative years when the United States was an observer, and not a participant in world affairs. The executive and political responsibilities that have been thrust upon the Department have fallen on shoulders that were not trained or personally oriented in this direction. And I think a great deal more needs to be done. I think the newer breed in the Foreign Service, the men who are coming up in their 40's and below, will change this very rapidly, and it needs to be brought along just as fast as it can.

Then there is a group in between. Men next to the top. The fact is that a new President will not be appointing just a Cabinet after November. He must have, and these are the most conservative figures I have seen, at least 10 senior and 10 to 20 junior people in the Department of State that are *his* men, and he must have double the numbers of each in the Department of Defense, just to take those two.

Now, you may ask, why can this not be the professional services, the civilian career service in the Department of Defense, if not serving officers, and the Foreign Service in the Department of State? The answer is twofold: first, that you have not gotten a full development of the needed policy training. Too much of the time—and this has been changed tremendously in a decade, but still needs changing—too much of the time of a foreign service officer is spent abroad and outside the processes of government in Washington.

But it is more basic than that, and gets to the root of this whole process, so that the second part of the answer is that the defense of a policy in the Congress and its articulation to the public must, at a certain point, be the task of men politically associated with the Administration. A man holding my position in this Administration could not, frankly, be a career man. That simply could not be the case. I happen to be somebody who has tried to know as much as he can, but who is still political. That is the best you can expect. You have *got* to have *this* kind of person. And they will be new.

It is as if you took a major bank in Pittsburgh and changed not only the President and the Vice President, but also all the assistant vice presidents, all across the board. Now you might have the run of the whole city of Pittsburgh or all of Pennsylvania to do it, and get some mighty bright fellows, with a lot of "oomph," and all the rest. But I think all of you who were executives would recognize that you would go through a period when they would be salting down. And then you would go through a period when they would start to come into fruition, and you would get the advantage of their energy and their novelty, their looking at the thing with a fresh eye. And this would take hold. Then, if they all went back to business or to teaching, you would have another drop.

That, in fact, is what does happen in government, very, very markedly—especially in foreign policy. And how a new Administration gets the plus of this, the new blood, the men from business, law firms, teaching, academic experience, and cranks them in—men who don't expect to make their careers in government but who have a tremendous amount to contribute, and holds them long enough by inducements that are mostly the excitement but that should include very much greater salaries (as my brother, among others, has argued)—how you do that personal thing is perhaps as crucial as anything else to what will make foreign policy work in the coming years.

I should like at some leisurely moment to do a graph of the effectiveness of government in these terms as I have seen it over 17 years, but I can say categorically that it has the same characteristic. It will start low, because of inexperience at the beginning of an Administration; it will go up very rapidly for two or three years, and then it will tend to drop off. I think it can be said that the Kennedy and Johnson Administrations managed to hold people longer than the Eisenhower Administration, and this may be something for Republicans to think about, but I won't carry any partisan thoughts further than that. At any rate, this getting of people and getting them to work on this subject, is at the core of it.

A WORD ON CONGRESS

As you can see, I have done more of an essay than a treatise, but this is not a systematic subject. At every point you are dealing with elements of quality and style.

Now I do want to close by just a word on the situation respecting the Congress. The Congress in legal terms is in effect an appellate court with partial jurisdiction. The Executive can do a great many things on its own, and put the Congress in the position where it really *must* support them. This has been increasingly true throughout history. The cases multiply in terms of committing American forces to conflict and so on, including Korea, including Vietnam. That is only one aspect of it.

The Congress, however, can, at a certain point, fail to support these actions. And, above all, it has the power to vote money for the ongoing sinews of policy: for aid, for information, indeed the appropriation of the State Department itself, which includes cultural exchanges, many matters of that sort. Congress, in short, has enormous power to, in blunt terms, take you off at the ankles, if you look at it from the standpoint of someone serving in the Executive Branch. Congress can do this and, I am afraid, does do it in extraneous ways, and in the reflection of a mood of frustration at times. And one of those times is today when you have major and deeply felt, and honest of course, disagreement with a major policy, particularly in the Senate. This is Vietnam, and all that is assumed to go with it in terms of interventionism and "playing the world's policeman," and the other broad charges that are made. A deep difference of philosophy.

And I say frankly to you that this is having a very serious effect, and is a problem that a new President will have to tackle as perhaps his greatest single problem. I myself believe that while the pendulum may swing back to the point of a greater and quicker interposition of the Congressional will than has been the case in some past instances, the Congress cannot really become an effective initiating body in the field of foreign policy. It is not that cohesive. It is by no means that well-informed. It simply doesn't have the staff. It simply cannot do it, and I think it would be disastrous if it tried.

But, given that statement, the fact is that we need a great deal more teamwork than we are now able to achieve.

CONCLUSION

That is only a sketch of a very large area of terrain. I hope I have given you some feeling of the personal and institutional factors that go into the making of our foreign policy. You may disagree totally with the foreign policies we have followed—particularly in recent years. I myself believe that our record over the last 23 years—scarred as it may be by error—will rank as one of the great accomplishments of any nation in history. I think major historians would incline now in that direction. We may be wrong now—who can say—we cannot possibly really know for ten or fifteen years, in some instances. And that is another thing that you have to learn to live with in the field of foreign policy —that you make the best decision you can. This is like a judge, I assume, not knowing whether his decisions in their unfolding will turn out to have been right or not.

But you will find you have got to *have* a foreign policy—a foreign policy that reaches out into all the areas of the world, that may seek to use its assets differently, that may seek to rely less or more on military power, more on economic means, other things of that sort. But you are going to have to have a major foreign policy. You are going to have to learn to use the tools and the men and to find the new men to do it.

I think we can. I think what we have done as a nation in understanding more about this is already impressive. And the exposure of Americans of all ages to the world abroad, through going there, through receiving students from abroad here, has brought us into the world in a sense that will be reflected in growing maturity and in growing effectiveness in the future—in judging our own national interests and in making effective use of the kind of machinery I have tried to describe.

OLD MYTHS AND NEW REALITIES

J. WILLIAM FULBRIGHT

There is an inevitable divergence, attributable to the imperfections of the human mind, between the world as it is and the world as men perceive it. As long as our perceptions are reasonably close to objective reality, it is possible for us to act upon our problems in a rational and appropriate manner. But when our perceptions fail to keep pace with events, when we refuse to believe something because it displeases or frightens us, or because it is simply

SOURCE: J. William Fulbright, "Old Myths and New Realities," *Congressional Record*, Vol. 110, 88th Congress, Second Session, (March 25, 1964), 6227–6232.

startingly unfamiliar, then the gap between fact and perception becomes a chasm and action becomes irrelevant and irrational.

There has always—and inevitably—been some divergence between the realities of foreign policy and our ideas about it. This divergence has in certain respects been growing, rather than narrowing; and we are handicapped, accordingly, by policies based on old myths, rather than current realities. This divergence is, in my opinion, dangerous and unnecessary—dangerous, because it can reduce foreign policy to a fraudulent game of imagery and appearances; unnecessary, because it can be overcome by the determination of men in high office to dispel prevailing misconceptions by the candid dissemination of unpleasant, but inescapable, facts.

Before commenting on some of the specific areas where I believe our policies are at least partially based on cherished myths, rather than objective facts, I should like to suggest two possible reasons for the growing divergence between the realities and our perceptions of current world politics. The first is the radical change in relations between and within the Communist and the free world; and the second is the tendency of too many of us to confuse means with ends and, accordingly, to adhere to prevailing practices with a fervor befitting immutable principles.

Although it is too soon to render a definitive judgment, there is mounting evidence that events of recent years have wrought profound changes in the character of East-West relations. In the Cuban missile crisis of October 1962, the United States proved to the Soviet Union that a policy of aggression and adventure involved unacceptable risks. In the signing of the test ban treaty, each side in effect assured the other that it was prepared to forego, at least for the present, any bid for a decisive military or political breakthrough. These occurrences, it should be added, took place against the background of the clearly understood strategic superiority—but not supremacy—of the United States.

It seems reasonable, therefore, to suggest that the character of the cold war has, for the present, at least, been profoundly altered: by the drawing back of the Soviet Union from extremely aggressive policies; by the implicit repudiation by both sides of a policy of "total victory"; and by the establishment of an American strategic superiority which the Soviet Union appears to have tacitly accepted because it has been accompanied by assurances that it will be exercised by the United States with responsibility and restraint. These enormously important changes may come to be regarded by historians as the foremost achievements of the Kennedy administration in the field of foreign policy. Their effect has been to commit us to a foreign policy which can accurately—though perhaps not prudently—be defined as one of "peaceful coexistence."

Another of the results of the lowering of tensions between East and West is that each is now free to enjoy the luxury of accelerated strife and squabbling within its own domain. The ideological thunderbolts between Washington and Moscow which until a few years ago seemed a permanent part of our daily lives have become a pale shadow of their former selves. Now, instead, the United States waits in fascinated apprehension for the Olympian pronouncements that issue from Paris at 6-month intervals while the Russians respond to the crude epithets of Peiping with almost plaintive rejoinders about "those who want to start a war against everybody."

These astonishing changes in the configuration of the postwar world have had an unsettling effect on both public and official opinion in the United States. One reason for this, I believe, lies in the fact that we are a people used to looking at the world, and indeed at ourselves, in moralistic rather than empirical terms. We are predisposed to regard any conflict as a clash between good and evil rather than as simply a clash between conflicting interests. We are inclined to confuse freedom and democracy, which we regard as moral principles, with the way in which they are practiced in America—with capitalism, federalism, and the two-party system, which are not moral principles but simply the preferred and accepted practices of the American people. There is much cant in American moralism and not a little inconsistency. It resembles in some ways the religious faith of the many respectable people who, in Samuel Butler's words, "would be equally horrified to hear the Christian religion doubted or to see it practiced."

Our national vocabulary is full of "self-evident truths" not only about "life, liberty, and happiness," but about a vast number of personal and public issues, including the cold war. It has become one of the "self-evident truths" of the postwar era that just as the President resides in Washington and the Pope in Rome, the Devil resides immutably in Moscow. We have come to regard the Kremlin as the permanent seat of his power and we have grown almost comfortable with a menace which, though unspeakably evil, has had the redeeming virtues of constancy, predictability, and familiarity. Now the Devil has betrayed us by traveling abroad and, worse still, by dispersing himself, turning up now here, now there, and in many places at once, with a devilish disregard for the laboriously constructed frontiers of ideology.

We are confronted with a complex and fluid world situation and we are not adapting ourselves to it. We are clinging to old myths in the face of new realities and we are seeking to escape the contradictions by narrowing the permissible bounds of public discussion, by relegating an increasing number of ideas and viewpoints to a growing category of "unthinkable thoughts." I believe that this tendency can and should be reversed, that it is within our ability, and unquestionably in our interests, to cut loose from established myths and to start thinking some "unthinkable thoughts"—about the cold war and East-West relations, about the underdeveloped countries and particularly those in Latin America, about the changing nature of the Chinese Communist threat in Asia and about the festering war in Vietnam.

The master myth of the cold war is that the Communist bloc is a monolith composed of governments which are not really governments at all but organized conspiracies, divided among themselves perhaps in certain matters of tactics, but all equally resolute and implacable in their determination to destroy the free world.

I believe that the Communist world is indeed hostile to the free world in its general and long-term intentions but that the existence of this animosity in principle is far less important for our foreign policy than the great variations in its intensity and character both in time and among the individual members of the Communist bloc. Only if we recognize these variations, ranging from China, which poses immediate threats to the free world, to Poland and Yugoslavia, which pose none, can we hope to act effectively upon the bloc and to turn its internal differences to our own advantage and to the advantage of those bloc countries which wish to maximize their independence. It is the responsibility of our national leaders, both in the executive branch and in Congress, to acknowledge and act upon these realities, even at the cost of saying things which will not win immediate widespread enthusiasm.

For a start, we can acknowledge the fact that the Soviet Union, though still a most formidable adversary, has ceased to be totally and implacably hostile to the West. It has shown a new willingness to enter mutually advantageous arrangements with the West and, thus far at least, to honor them. It has, therefore, become possible to divert some of our energies from the prosecution of the cold war to the relaxation of the cold war and to deal with the Soviet Union, for certain purposes, as a normal state with normal and traditional interests.

If we are to do these things effectively, we must distinguish between communism as an ideology and the power and policy of the Soviet state. It is not communism as a doctrine, or communism as it is practiced within the Soviet Union or within any other country, that threatens us. How the Soviet Union organizes its internal life, the gods and doctrines that it worships, are matters for the Soviet Union to determine. It is not Communist dogma as espoused within Russia but Communist imperialism that threatens us and other peoples of the non-Communist world. Insofar as a great nation mobilizes its power and resources for aggressive purposes, that nation, regardless of ideology, makes itself our enemy. Insofar as a nation is content to practice its doctrines within its own frontiers, that nation, however repugnant its ideology, is one with which we have no proper quarrel. We must deal with the Soviet Union as a great power, quite apart from differences of ideology. To the extent that the Soviet leaders abandon the global ambitions of Marxist ideology, in fact if not in words, it becomes possible for us to engage in normal relations with them, relations which probably cannot be close or trusting for many years to come but which can be gradually freed of the terror and the tensions of the cold war.

In our relations with the Russians, and indeed in our relations with all nations, we would do well to remember, and to act upon, the words of Pope John in the great Encyclical, Pacem in Terris:

"It must be borne in mind," said Pope John, "that to proceed gradually is the law of life in all its expressions, therefore, in human institutions, too, it is not possible to renovate for the better except by working
from within them, gradually. Violence has always achieved only destruction, not construction, the kindling of passions, not their pacification, the accumulation of hate and ruin, not the reconciliation of the
contending parties. And it has reduced men and parties to the difficult
task of rebuilding, after sad experience, on the ruins of discord."

Important opportunities have been created for Western policy by the development of "polycentrism" in the Communist bloc. The Communist nations, as George Kennan has pointed out, are, like the Western nations, currently caught up in a crisis of indecision about their relations with countries
outside their own ideological bloc. The choices open to the satellite states are
limited but by no means insignificant. They can adhere slavishly to Soviet
preferences or they can strike out on their own, within limits, to enter into
mutually advantageous relations with the West.

Whether they do so, and to what extent, is to some extent at least within
the power of the West to determine. If we persist in the view that all Communist regimes are equally hostile and equally threatening to the West, and
that we can have no policy toward the captive nations except the eventual
overthrow of their Communist regimes, then the West may enforce upon the
Communist bloc a degree of unity which the Soviet Union has shown itself to
be quite incapable of imposing—just as Stalin in the early postwar years
frightened the West into a degree of unity that it almost certainly could not
have attained by its own unaided efforts. If, on the other hand, we are willing
to reexamine the view that all Communist regimes are alike in the threat
which they pose for the West—a view which had a certain validity in Stalin's
time—then we may be able to exert an important influence on the course of
events within a divided Communist world.

We are to a great extent the victims, and the Soviets the beneficiaries, of
our own ideological convictions, and of the curious contradictions which they
involve. We consider it a form of subversion of the free world; for example,
when the Russians enter trade relations or conclude a consular convention or
establish airline connections with a free country in Asia, Africa, or Latin
America—and to a certain extent we are right. On the other hand, when it is
proposed that we adopt the same strategy in reverse—by extending commercial credits to Poland or Yugoslavia, or by exchanging Ambassadors with a
Hungarian regime which has changed considerably in character since the revolution of 1956—then the same patriots who are so alarmed by Soviet activities in the free world charge our policymakers with "giving aid and comfort to
the enemy" and with innumerable other categories of idiocy and immorality.

It is time that we resolved this contradiction and separated myth from reality. The myth is that every Communist state is an unmitigated evil and a re-

lentless enemy of the free world; the reality is that some Communist regimes pose a threat to the free world while others pose little or none, and that if we will recognize these distinctions, we ourselves will be able to influence events in the Communist bloc in a way favorable to the security of the free world.

It could well be argued . . . —

Writes George Kennan—

That if the major Western Powers had full freedom of movement in devising their own policies, it would be within their power to determine whether the Chinese view, or the Soviet view, or perhaps a view more liberal than either would ultimately prevail within the Communist camp. George Kennan, "Polycentrism and Western Policy," Foreign Affairs, January 1964, page 178.

There are numerous areas in which we can seek to reduce the tensions of the cold war and to bring a degree of normalcy into our relations with the Soviet Union and other Communist countries—once we have resolved that it is safe and wise to do so. We have already taken important steps in this direction: the Antarctic and Austrian treaties and the nuclear test ban treaty, the broadening of East-West cultural and educational relations, and the expansion of trade.

On the basis of recent experience and present economic needs, there seems little likelihood of a spectacular increase in trade between Communist and Western countries, even if existing restrictions were to be relaxed. Free world trade with Communist countries has been increasing at a steady but unspectacular rate, and it seems unlikely to be greatly accelerated because of the limited ability of the Communist countries to pay for increased imports. A modest increase in East-West trade may nonetheless serve as a modest instrument of East-West detente—provided that we are able to overcome the myth that trade with Communist countries is a compact with the Devil and to recognize that, on the contrary, trade can serve as an effective and honorable means of advancing both peace and human welfare.

Whether we are able to make these philosophic adjustments or not, we cannot escape the fact that our efforts to devise a common Western trade policy are a palpable failure and that our allies are going to trade with the Communist bloc whether we like it or not. The world's major exporting nations are slowly but steadily increasing their trade with the Communist bloc and the bloc countries are showing themselves to be reliable customers. Since 1958 Western Europe has been increasing its exports to the East at the rate of about 7 percent a year, which is nearly the same rate at which its overall world sales have been increasing.

West Germany—one of our close friends—is by far the leading Western nation in trade with the Sino-Soviet bloc. West German exports to bloc countries in 1962 were valued at $749.9 million. Britain was in second place —although not a close second—with exports to Communist countries amounting to $393 million in 1962. France followed with exports worth $313.4 million, and the figure for the United States—consisting largely of surplus food sales to Poland under Public Law 480—stood far below at $125.1 million.

Our allies have made it plain that they propose to expand this trade, in nonstrategic goods, wherever possible. West Germany, in the last 16 months, has exchanged or agreed to exchange trade missions with every country in Eastern Europe except Albania. Britain has indicated that she will soon extend long-term credits to Communist countries, breaching the 5-year limit which the Western allies have hitherto observed. In the light of these facts, it is difficult to see what effect the tight American trade restrictions have other than to deny the United States a substantial share of a profitable market.

The inability of the United States to prevent its partners from trading extensively with the Communist bloc is one good reason for relaxing our own restrictions, but there is a better reason: the potential value of trade—a moderate volume of trade in nonstrategic items—as an instrument for reducing world tensions and strengthening the foundations of peace. I do not think that trade or the nuclear test ban, or any other prospective East-West accommodation, will lead to a grand reconciliation that will end the cold war and usher in the brotherhood of man. At the most, the cumulative effect of all the agreements that are likely to be attainable in the foreseeable future will be the alleviation of the extreme tensions and animosities that threaten the world with nuclear devastation and the gradual conversion of the struggle between communism and the free world into a safer and more tolerable international rivalry, one which may be with us for years and decades to come but which need not be so terrifying and so costly as to distract the nations of the world from the creative pursuits of civilized societies.

There is little in history to justify the expectation that we can either win the cold war or end it immediately and completely. These are favored myths, respectively, of the American right and of the American left. They are, I believe, equal in their unreality and in their disregard for the feasibilities of history. We must disabuse ourselves of them and come to terms, at last, with the realities of a world in which neither good nor evil is absolute and in which those who move events and make history are those who have understood not how much but how little it is within our power to change.

● ● ●

Latin America is one of the areas of the world in which American policy is weakened by a growing divergency between old myths and new realities.

The crisis over the Panama Canal has been unnecessarily protracted for reasons of domestic politics and national pride and sensitivity on both sides—for reasons, that is, of only marginal relevance to the merits of the dispute. I think the Panamanians have unquestionably been more emotional about the dispute than has the United States. I also think that there is less reason for emotionalism on the part of the United States than on the part of Panama. It is important for us to remember that the issue over the canal is only one of a great many in which the United States is involved, and by no means the most important. For Panama, on the other hand, a small nation with a weak economy and an unstable government, the canal is the preeminent factor in the nation's economy and in its foreign relations. Surely in a confrontation so unequal, it is not unreasonable to expect the United States to go a little farther than halfway in the search for a fair settlement.

We Americans would do well, for a start, to divest ourselves of the silly notion that the issue with Panama is a test of our courage and resolve. I believe that the Cuban missile crisis of 1962, involving a confrontation with nuclear weapons and intercontinental missiles, was indeed a test of our courage, and we acquitted ourselves extremely well in that instance. I am unable to understand how a controversy with a small and poor country, with virtually no military capacity, can possibly be regarded as a test of our bravery and will to defend our interests. It takes stubbornness but not courage to reject the entreaties of the weak. The real test in Panama is not of our valor but of our wisdom and judgment and commonsense.

We would also do well to disabuse ourselves of the myth that there is something morally sacred about the treaty of 1903. The fact of the matter is that the treaty was concluded under circumstances that reflect little credit on the United States. It was made possible by Panama's separation from Colombia, which probably could not have occurred at that time without the dispatch of U.S. warships to prevent the landing of Colombian troops on the isthmus to put down the Panamanian rebellion. The United States not only intervened in Colombia's internal affairs but did so in violation of a treaty concluded in 1846 under which the United States had guaranteed Colombian sovereignty over the isthmus. President Theodore Roosevelt, as he boasted, "took Panama," and proceeded to negotiate the canal treaty with a compliant Panamanian regime. Panamanians contend that they were "shot-gunned" into the treaty of 1903 as the price of U.S. protection against a possible effort by Colombia to recover the isthmus. The contention is not without substance.

It is not my purpose here to relate the events of 60 years ago but only to suggest that there is little basis for a posture of injured innocence and self-righteousness by either side and that we would do much better to resolve the issue on the basis of present realities rather than old myths.

The central reality is that the treaty of 1903 is in certain respects obsolete. The treaty has been revised only twice, in 1936 when the annual rental was raised from $250,000 to $430,000 and other modifications were made, and in 1955 when further changes were made, including an increase in the annual rental to $1.9 million, where it now stands. The canal, of course, contributes far more to the Panamanian economy in the form of wages paid to Panamanian workers and purchases made in Panama. The fact remains, nonetheless, that the annual rental of $1.9 million is a modest sum and should probably be increased. There are other issues, relating to hiring policies for Panamanian workers in the zone, the flying of flags, and other symbols of national pride and sovereignty. The basic problem about the treaty, however, is the exercise of American control over a part of the territory of Panama in this age of intense nationalist and anticolonialist feeling. Justly or not, the Panamanians feel that they are being treated as a colony, or a quasi-colony, of the United States, and this feeling is accentuated by the contrast between the standard of living of the Panamanians, with a per capita income of about $429 a year, and that of the Americans living in the Canal Zone—immediately adjacent to Panama, of course, and within it—with a per capita income of $4,228 a year. That is approximately 10 times greater. It is the profound social and economic alienation between Panama and the Canal Zone, and its impact on the national feeling of the Panamanians, that underlies the current crisis.

Under these circumstances, it seems to me entirely proper and necessary for the United States to take the initiative in proposing new arrangements that would redress some of Panama's grievances against the treaty as it now stands. I see no reason—certainly no reason of "weakness" or "dishonor"— why the United States cannot put an end to the semantic debate over whether treaty revisions are to be "negotiated" or "discussed" by stating positively and clearly that it is prepared to negotiate revisions in the canal treaty and to submit such changes as are made to the Senate for its advice and consent.

I think it is necessary for the United States to do this even though a commitment to revise the treaty may be widely criticized at home. It is the responsibility of the President and his advisers, in situations of this sort, to exercise their own best judgment as to where the national interest lies even though this may necessitate unpopular decisions.

An agreement to "negotiate" revisions is not an agreement to negotiate any particular revision. It would leave us completely free to determine what revisions, and how many revisions, we would be willing to accept. If there is any doubt about this, one can find ample reassurance in the proceedings at Geneva, where several years of "negotiations" for "general and complete disarmament" still leave us with the greatest arsenal of weapons in the history of the world.

The problem of Cuba is more difficult than that of Panama, and far more heavily burdened with the deadweight of old myths and prohibitions against "unthinkable thoughts." I think the time is overdue for a candid reevaluation of our Cuban policy even though it may also lead to distasteful conclusions.

There are and have been three options open to the United States with respect to Cuba: First, the removal of the Castro regime by invading and occupying the island; second, an effort to weaken and ultimately bring down the regime by a policy of political and economic boycott; and finally, acceptance of the Communist regime as a disagreeable reality and annoyance but one which is not likely to be removed in the near future because of the unavailability of acceptable means of removing it.

The first option, invasion, has been tried in a halfhearted way and found wanting. It is generally acknowledged that the invasion and occupation of Cuba, besides violating our obligations as a member of the United Nations and of the Organization of American States, would have explosive consequences in Latin America and elsewhere and might precipitate a global nuclear war. I know of no responsible statesman who advocates this approach. It has been rejected by our Government and by public opinion and I think that, barring some grave provocation, it can be ruled out as a feasible policy for the United States.

The approach which we have adopted has been the second of those mentioned, an effort to weaken and eventually bring down the Castro regime by a policy of political and economic boycott. This policy has taken the form of extensive restrictions against trade with Cuba by United States citizens, of the exclusion of Cuba from the inter-American system and efforts to secure Latin American support in isolating Cuba politically and economically, and of diplomatic efforts, backed by certain trade and aid sanctions, to persuade other free world countries to maintain economic boycotts against Cuba.

This policy, it now seems clear, has been a failure, and there is no reason to believe that it will succeed in the future. Our efforts to persuade our allies to terminate their trade with Cuba have been generally rebuffed. The prevailing attitude was perhaps best expressed by a British manufacturer who, in response to American criticisms of the sale of British buses to Cuba, said: "If America has a surplus of wheat, we have a surplus of buses."

In cutting off military assistance to Great Britain, France, and Yugoslavia under the provisions of section 620 of the Foreign Assistance Act of 1963, the United States has wielded a stuffed club. The amounts of aid involved are infinitesimal; the chances of gaining compliance with our boycott policy are nil; and the annoyance of the countries concerned may be considerable. What we terminated with respect to Britain and France, in fact, can hardly be called aid; it was more of a sales promotion program under which British and French military leaders were brought to the United States to see—and to buy—advanced American weapons. Terminating this program was in itself of little importance; Britain and France do not need our assistance. But terminating the program as a sanction against their trade with Cuba can have no real effect other than to create an illusory image of "toughness" for the benefit of our own people.

Free world exports to Cuba have, on the whole, been declining over recent years, but overall imports have been rising since 1961.

● ● ●

. . . The exports from Cuba to various allies of ours, particularly Japan, the United Kingdom, Morocco, and others, have been going up, and have been very substantial. This reflects, I believe, the importation from Cuba of sugar to a great extent, and also accounts for the accumulation by Cuba of substantial foreign aid as a result of the dramatic increase in the price of sugar during the past couple of years.

The exports from the free world to Cuba have been going up in similar instances, in the case of Japan, but generally speaking they have not been increasing. Of course, since 1958, when we accounted for more than half of Cuba's exports, they have gone down rather dramatically.

I should like to make it very clear that I am not arguing against the desirability of an economic boycott against the Castro regime but against its feasibility. The effort has been made and all the fulminations we can utter about sanctions and retaliation against free world countries that trade with Cuba cannot long conceal the fact that the boycott policy is a failure.

The boycott policy has not failed because of any "weakness" or "timidity" on the part of our Government. This charge, so frequently heard, is one of the most pernicious myths to have been inflicted on the American people. The boycott policy has failed because the United States is not omnipotent and cannot be. The basic reality to be faced is that it is simply not within our power to compel our allies to cut off their trade with Cuba, unless we are prepared to take drastic sanctions against them, such as closing our own markets to any foreign company that does business in Cuba, as proposed by Mr. Nixon. We can do this, of course, but if we do, we ought first to be very sure, as apparently Mr. Nixon is, that the Cuban boycott is more important than good relations with our closest allies. In fact, even the most drastic sanctions are as likely to be rewarded with defiance as with compliance. For practical purposes, all we can do is to ask other countries to take the measures with respect to Cuba which we recommend. We have done so and in some areas have been successful. In other areas, notably that of the economic boycott, we have asked for the full cooperation of other free world countries and it has been largely denied. It remains for us to decide whether we will respond with a sustained outburst of hollow and ill-tempered threats, all the while comforting ourselves with the myth that we can get anything we want if we only try hard enough—or, in this case, shout loud enough—or we can acknowledge the failure of our efforts and proceed, coolly and rationally, to reexamine the policies which we now pursue in relation to the interests they are intended to serve.

The prospects of bringing down the Castro regime by political and economic boycott have never been very good. Even if a general free world boycott were successfully applied against Cuba, it is unlikely that the Russians would refuse to carry the extra financial burden and thereby permit the only Communist regime in the Western Hemisphere to collapse. We are thus compelled to recognize that there is probably no way of bringing down the Castro regime by means of economic pressures unless we are prepared to impose a blockade against nonmilitary shipments from the Soviet Union. Exactly such a policy has been recommended by some of our more reckless politicians, but the preponderance of informed opinion is that a blockade against Soviet shipments of nonmilitary supplies to Cuba would be extravagantly dangerous, carrying the strong possibility of a confrontation that could explode into nuclear war.

Having ruled out military invasion and blockade, and recognizing the failure of the boycott policy, we are compelled to consider the third of the three options open to us with respect to Cuba: the acceptance of the continued existence of the Castro regime as a distasteful nuisance but not an intolerable danger so long as the nations of the hemisphere are prepared to meet their obligations of collective defense under the Rio Treaty.

In recent years we have become transfixed with Cuba, making it far more important in both our foreign relations and in our domestic life than its size and influence warrant. We have flattered a noisy but minor demogog by treating him as if he were a Napoleonic menace. Communist Cuba has been a disruptive and subversive influence in Venezuela and other countries of the hemisphere, and there is no doubt that both we and our Latin American partners would be better off if the Castro regime did not exist. But it is important to bear in mind that, despite their best efforts, the Cuban Communists have not succeeded in subverting the hemisphere and that in Venezuela, for example, where communism has made a major effort to gain power through terrorism, it has been repudiated by a people who in a free election have committed themselves to the course of liberal democracy. It is necessary to weigh the desirability of an objective against the feasibility of its attainment, and when we do this with respect to Cuba, I think we are bound to conclude that Castro is a nuisance but not a grave threat to the United States and that he cannot be gotten rid of except by means that are wholly disproportionate to the objective. Cuban communism does pose a grave threat to other Latin American countries, but this threat can be dealt with by prompt and vigorous use of the established procedures of the inter-American system against any act of aggression.

I think that we must abandon the myth that Cuban communism is a transitory menace that is going to collapse or disappear in the immediate future and face up to two basic realities about Cuba: first, that the Castro regime is not on the verge of collapse and is not likely to be overthrown by any policies which we are now pursuing or can reasonably undertake; and second, that the continued existence of the Castro regime, though inimical to our interests and policies, is not an insuperable obstacle to the attainment of our objectives, unless we make it so by permitting it to poison our politics at home and to divert us from more important tasks in the hemisphere.

The policy of the United States with respect to Latin America as a whole is predicated on the assumption that social revolution can be accomplished without violent upheaval. This is the guiding principle of the Alliance for Progress and it may in time be vindicated. We are entitled to hope so and it is wise and necessary for us to do all that we can to advance the prospects of peaceful and orderly reform.

At the same time, we must be under no illusions as to the extreme difficulty of uprooting long-established ruling oligarchies without disruptions involving lesser or greater degrees of violence. The historical odds are probably against the prospects of peaceful social revolution. There are places, of course, where it has occurred and others where it seems likely to occur. In Latin America, the chances for such basic change by peaceful means seem bright in Colombia and Venezuela and certain other countries; in Mexico, many basic changes have been made by peaceful means, but these came in the wake of a violent revolution. In other Latin American countries, the power of ruling oligarchies is so solidly established and their ignorance so great that there seems little prospect of accomplishing economic growth or social reform by means short of the forcible overthrow of established authorities.

I am not predicting violent revolutions in Latin America or elsewhere. Still less am I advocating them. I wish only to suggest that violent social revolutions are a possibility in countries where feudal oligarchies resist all meaningful change by peaceful means. We must not, in our preference for the democratic procedures envisioned by the Charter of Punta del Este, close our minds to the possibility that democratic procedures may fail in certain countries and that where democracy does fail violent social convulsions may occur.

We would do well, while continuing our efforts to promote peaceful change through the Alliance for Progress, to consider what our reactions might be in the event of the outbreak of genuine social revolution in one or more Latin American countries. Such a revolution did occur in Bolivia, and we accepted it calmly and sensibly. But what if a violent social revolution were to break out in one of the larger Latin American countries? Would we feel certain that it was Cuban or Soviet inspired? Would we wish to intervene on the side of established authority? Or would we be willing to tolerate or even support a revolution if it was seen to be not Communist but similar in nature to the Mexican revolution or the Nasser revolution in Egypt?

These are hypothetical questions and there is no readily available set of answers to them. But they are questions which we should be thinking about because they have to do with problems that could become real and urgent with great suddenness. We should be considering, for example, what groups in particular countries might conceivably lead revolutionary movements, and if we can identify them, we should be considering how we might communicate with them and influence them in such a way that their movements, if successful, will not pursue courses detrimental to our security and our interests.

The Far East is another area of the world in which American policy is handicapped by the divergence of old myths and new realities. Particularly with respect to China, an elaborate vocabulary of make-believe has become compulsory in both official and public discussion. We are committed, with respect to China and other areas in Asia, to inflexible policies of long standing from which we hesitate to depart because of the attribution to these policies of an aura of mystical sanctity. It may be that a thorough reevaluation of our Far Eastern policies would lead us to the conclusion that they are sound and wise, or at least that they represent the best available options. It may be, on the other hand, that a reevaluation would point up the need for greater or lesser changes in our policies. The point is that, whatever the outcome of a rethinking of policy might be, we have been unwilling to undertake it because of the fear of many Government officials, undoubtedly well founded, that even the suggestion of new policies toward China or Vietnam would provoke a vehement public outcry.

I do not think the United States can, or should, recognize Communist China, or acquiesce in its admission to the United Nations under present circumstances. It would be unwise to do so, because there is nothing to be gained by it so long as the Peiping regime maintains its attitude of implacable hostility toward the United States. I do not believe, however, that this state of affairs is necessarily permanent. As we have seen in our relations with Germany and Japan, hostility can give way in an astonishingly short time to close friendship; and, as we have seen in our relations with China, the reverse can occur with equal speed. It is not impossible that in time our relations with China will change again—if not to friendship, then perhaps to "competitive coexistence." It would therefore be extremely useful if we could introduce an element of flexibility, or, more precisely, of the capacity to be flexible, into our relations with Communist China.

We would do well, as former Assistant Secretary Hilsman has recommended, to maintain an "open door" to the possibility of improved relations with Communist China in the future. For a start, we must jar open our minds to certain realities about China, of which the foremost is that there really are not "two Chinas," but only one—mainland China; and that it is ruled by Communists, and is likely to remain so for the indefinite future. Once we accept this fact, it becomes possible to reflect on the conditions under which it might be possible for us to enter into relatively normal relations with mainland China. One condition, of course, must be the abandonment by the Chinese Communists, tacitly, if not explicitly, of their intention to conquer and incorporate Taiwan. This seems unlikely now; but far more surprising changes have occurred in politics, and it is quite possible that a new generation of leaders in Peiping and Taipei may put a quiet end to the Chinese civil war, thus opening the possibility of entirely new patterns of international relations in the Far East.

Should such changes occur, they will open important opportunities for American policy; and it is to be hoped that we shall be able and willing to take advantage of them. It seems possible, for instance, that an atmosphere of reduced tensions in the Far East might make it possible to strengthen world peace by drawing mainland China into existing East-West agreements in such fields as disarmament, trade, and educational exchange.

These are long-range prospects, which may or may not materialize. In the immediate future, we are confronted with possible changes in the Far East resulting from recent French diplomacy.

French recognition of Communist China, although untimely and carried out in a way that can hardly be considered friendly to the United States, may nonetheless serve a constructive long-term purpose, by unfreezing a situation in which many countries, none more than the United States, are committed to inflexible policies by long-established commitments and the pressures of domestic public opinion. One way or another, the French initiative may help generate a new situation in which the United States, as well as other countries, will find it possible to reevaluate its basic policies in the Far East.

The situation in Vietnam poses a far more pressing need for a reevaluation of American policy. Other than withdrawal, which I do not think can be realistically considered under present circumstances, three options are open to us in Vietnam: First, continuation of the antiguerrilla war within South Vietnam, along with renewed American efforts to increase the military effectiveness of the South Vietnamese Army and the political effectiveness of the South Vietnamese Government; second, an attempt to end the war, through negotiations for the neutralization of South Vietnam, or of both North and South Vietnam; and, finally, the expansion of the scale of the war, either by the direct commitment of large numbers of American troops or by equipping the South Vietnamese Army to attack North Vietnamese territory, possibly by means of commando-type operations from the sea or the air.

It is difficult to see how a negotiation, under present military circumstances, could lead to termination of the war under conditions that would preserve the freedom of South Vietnam. It is extremely difficult for a party to a negotiation to achieve by diplomacy objectives which it has conspiciously failed to win by warfare. The hard fact of the matter is that our bargaining position is at present a weak one; and until the equation of advantages between the two sides has been substantially altered in our favor, there can be little prospect of a negotiated settlement which would secure the independence of a non-Communist South Vietnam.

Recent initiatives by France, calling for the neutralization of Vietnam, have tended to confuse the situation, without altering it in any fundamental way. France could, perhaps, play a constructive mediating role if she were willing to consult and cooperate with the United States. For somewhat obscure reasons, however, France has chosen to take an independent initiative. This is puzzling to Americans, who recall that the United States contributed $1.2 billion to France's war in Indochina of a decade ago—which was 70 percent of the total cost of the conflict. Whatever its motivation, the problem posed by French intervention in southeast Asia is that while France may set off an unforeseeable chain of events, she is neither a major military force nor a major economic force in the Far East, and is therefore unlikely to be able to control or greatly influence the events which her initiative may precipitate.

It seems clear that only two realistic options are open to us in Vietnam in the immediate future: the expansion of the conflict in one way or another, or a renewed effort to bolster the capacity of the South Vietnamese to prosecute the war successfully on its present scale. The matter calls for thorough examination by responsible officials in the executive branch; and until they have had an opportunity to evaluate the contingencies and feasibilities of the options open to us, it seems to me that we have no choice but to support the South Vietnamese Government and Army by the most effective means available. Whatever specific policy decisions are made, it should be clear to all concerned that the United States will continue to meet its obligations and fulfill its commitments with respect to Vietnam.

These, I believe, are some, although by no means all, of the issues of foreign policy in which it is essential to reevaluate longstanding ideas and commitments in the light of new and changing realities. In all the issues which I have discussed, American policy has to one degree or another been less effective than it might have been because of our national tendency to equate means with ends and therefore to attach a mythological sanctity to policies and practices which in themselves have no moral content or value except insofar as they contribute to the achievement of some valid national objective. I believe that we must try to overcome this excessive moralism, which binds us to old myths and blinds us to new realities and, worse still, leads us to regard new and unfamiliar ideas with fear and mistrust.

We must dare to think about "unthinkable" things. We must learn to explore all of the options and possibilities that confront us in a complex and rapidly changing world. We must learn to welcome rather than fear the voices of dissent and not to recoil in horror whenever some heretic suggests that Castro may survive or that Khrushchev is not as bad a fellow as Stalin was. We must overcome our susceptibility to "shock"—a word which I wish could be banned from our newspapers and magazines and especially from the *Congressional Record*.

If Congress and public opinion are unduly susceptible to "shock," the executive branch, and particularly the Department of State, is subject to the malady of chronic and excessive caution. An effective foreign policy is one which concerns itself more with innovation abroad than with conciliation at home. A creative foreign policy—as President Truman, for one, knew—is not necessarily one which wins immediate general approval. It is sometimes necessary for leaders to do unpleasant and unpopular things, because, as Burke pointed out, the duty of the democratic politician to his constituents is not to comply with their every wish and preference but to give them the benefit of, and to be held responsible for, the exercise of his own best judgment.

We must dare to think about "unthinkable things," because when things become "unthinkable," thinking stops and action becomes mindless. If we are to disabuse ourselves of old myths and to act wisely and creatively upon the new realities of our time, we must think and talk about our problems with perfect freedom, remembering, as Woodrow Wilson said, that "The greatest freedom of speech is the greatest safety because, if a man is a fool, the best thing to do is to encourage him to advertise the fact by speaking."

THE PURSUIT OF PEACE

RICHARD M. NIXON

Good evening, my fellow Americans:

Tonight I want to talk to you on a subject of deep concern to all Americans and to many people in all parts of the world—the war in Vietnam.

I believe that one of the reasons for the deep division about Vietnam is that many Americans have lost confidence in what their government has told them about our policy. The American people cannot and should not be asked to support a policy which involves the overriding issues of war and peace unless they know the truth about that policy.

Tonight, therefore, I would like to answer some of the questions that I know are on the minds of many of you listening to me.

How and why did America get involved in Vietnam in the first place?

How has this Administration changed the policy of the previous Administration?

What has really happened in the negotiations in Paris and on the battle-front in Vietnam?

What choices do we have if we are to end the war?

What are the prospects for peace?

Let me begin by describing the situation I found when I was inaugurated on January 20.

> The war had been going on for four years.
>
> 31,000 Americans had been killed in action.
>
> The training program for the South Vietnamese was behind schedule.
>
> 540,000 Americans were in Vietnam with no plans to reduce the number.
>
> No progress had been made at the negotiations in Paris and the United States had not put forth a comprehensive peace proposal.
>
> The war was causing deep division at home and criticism from many of our friends as well as our enemies abroad.

SOURCE: Richard M. Nixon, "The Pursuit of Peace," an address delivered on November 3, 1969. Department of State Publication 8502, pp. 1–17.

In view of these circumstances there were some who urged I end the war at once by ordering the immediate withdrawal of all American forces.

From a political standpoint this would have been a popular and easy course to follow. After all, we became involved in the war while my predecessor was in office. I could blame the defeat which would be the result of my action on him and come out as the peacemaker. Some put it quite bluntly: This was the only way to avoid allowing Johnson's war to become Nixon's war.

But I had a greater obligation than to think only of the years of my Administration and the next election. I had to think of the effect of my decision on the next generation and on the future of peace and freedom in America and in the world.

Let us all understand that the question before us is not whether some Americans are for peace and some Americans are against peace. The question at issue is not whether Johnson's war becomes Nixon's war.

The great question is: How can we win America's peace?

Let us turn now to the fundamental issue. Why and how did the United States become involved in Vietnam in the first place?

Fifteen years ago North Vietnam, with the logistical support of Communist China and the Soviet Union launched a campaign to impose a Communist government on South Vietnam by instigating and supporting a revolution.

In response to the request of the government of South Vietnam, President Eisenhower sent economic aid and military equipment to assist the people of South Vietnam in their efforts to prevent a Communist takeover. Seven years ago, President Kennedy sent 16,000 military personnel to Vietnam as combat advisors. Four years ago, President Johnson sent American combat forces to South Vietnam.

Now, many believe that President Johnson's decision to send American combat forces to South Vietnam was wrong. And many others—I among them—have been strongly critical of the way the war has been conducted.

But the question facing us today is—now that we are in the war, what is the best way to end it?

In January I could only conclude that the precipitate withdrawal of American forces from Vietnam would be a disaster not only for South Vietnam but for the United States and for the cause of peace.

For the South Vietnamese, our precipitate withdrawal would inevitably allow the Communists to repeat the massacres which followed their takeover in the North 15 years before.

—They then murdered more than 50,000 people and hundreds of thousands more died in slave labor camps.

—We saw a prelude of what would happen in South Vietnam when the Communists entered the City of Hue last year. During their brief rule, there was a bloody reign of terror in which 3,000 civilians were clubbed, shot to death, and buried in mass graves.

—With the sudden collapse of our support, these atrocities of Hue would become the nightmare of the entire nation—and particularly for the million and a half Catholic refugees who fled to South Vietnam when the Communists took over in the North.

For the United States, this first defeat in our nation's history would result in a collapse of confidence in American leadership, not only in Asia but throughout the world.

Three American Presidents have recognized the great stakes involved in Vietnam and understood what had to be done.

—In 1963, President Kennedy, with his characteristic eloquence and clarity, said, "we want to see a stable government there carrying on the struggle to maintain its national independence. We believe strongly in that. We're not going to withdraw from that effort. In my opinion for us to withdraw from that effort would mean a collapse not only of South Vietnam, but Southeast Asia, so we're going to stay there."

President Eisenhower and President Johnson expressed the same conclusion during their terms of office.

For the future of peace, precipitate withdrawal would thus be a disaster of immense magnitude.

> A nation cannot remain great if it betrays its allies and lets down its friends.
>
> Our defeat and humiliation in South Vietnam would without question promote recklessness in the councils of those great powers who have not yet abandoned their goals of world conquest.
>
> This would spark violence wherever our commitments help maintain peace—in the Middle East, in Berlin, eventually even in the Western Hemisphere.
>
> Ultimately, this would cost more lives.
>
> It would not bring peace but more war.

For these reasons, I rejected the recommendation that I should end the war by immediately withdrawing all our forces. I chose instead to change American policy on both the negotiating front and the battlefront.

In order to end a war fought on many fronts, I initiated a pursuit for peace on many fronts.

In a television speech on May 14, in a speech before the United Nations, and on a number of other occasions I set forth our peace proposals in great detail.

> We have offered the complete withdrawal of all outside forces within one year.
>
> We have proposed a cease-fire under international supervision.
>
> We have offered free elections under international supervision with

the Communists participating in the organization and conduct of the elections as an organized political force. The Saigon Government has pledged to accept the result of the elections.

We have not put forth our proposals on a take-it-or-leave-it basis. We have indicated that we are willing to discuss the proposals that have been put forth by the other side. We have declared that anything is negotiable except the right of the people of South Vietnam to determine their own future. At the Paris peace conference, Ambassador Lodge has demonstrated our flexibility and good faith in 40 public meetings.

Hanoi has refused even to discuss our proposals. They demand our unconditional acceptance of their terms, which are that we withdraw all American forces immediately and unconditionally and that we overthrow the government of South Vietnam as we leave.

We have not limited our peace initiatives to public forums and public statements. I recognized, in January, that a long and bitter war like this usually cannot be settled in a public forum. That is why in addition to the public statements and negotiations I have explored every possible private avenue that might lead to a settlement.

Tonight I am taking the unprecedented step of disclosing to you some of our other initiatives for peace—initiatives we undertook privately and secretly because we thought that we thereby might open a door which publicly would be closed.

I did not wait for my inauguration to begin my quest for peace.

> Soon after my election through an individual who is directly in contact on a personal basis with the leaders of North Vietnam I made two private offers for a rapid, comprehensive settlement. Hanoi's replies called in effect for our surrender before negotiations.

> Since the Soviet Union furnishes most of the military equipment for North Vietnam, Secretary of State Rogers, my Assistant for National Security Affairs, Dr. Kissinger, Ambassador Lodge, and I, personally, have met on a number of occasions with representatives of the Soviet Government to enlist their assistance in getting meaningful negotiations started. In addition we have had extended discussions directed toward that same end with representatives of other governments which have diplomatic relations with North Vietnam. None of these initiatives have to date produced results.

> In mid-July, I became convinced that it was necessary to make a major move to break the deadlock in Paris talks. I spoke directly in this office, where I am now sitting, with an individual who had known Ho Chi Minh on a personal basis for 25 years. Through him I sent a letter to Ho Chi Minh.

> I did this outside of the usual diplomatic channels with the hope that

with the necessity of making statements for propaganda removed, there might be constructive progress toward bringing the war to an end. Let me read from that letter:

"Dear Mr. President:

"I realize that it is difficult to communicate meaningfully across the gulf of four years of war. But precisely because of this gulf, I wanted to take this opportunity to reaffirm in all solemnity my desire to work for a just peace. I deeply believe that the war in Vietnam has gone on too long and delay in bringing it to an end can benefit no one—least of all the people of Vietnam.

●　　●　　●

"The time has come to move forward at the conference table toward an early resolution of this tragic war. You will find us forthcoming and open-minded in a common effort to bring the blessing of peace to the brave people of Vietnam. Let history record that at this critical juncture, both sides turned their face toward peace rather than toward conflict and war."

I received Ho Chi Minh's reply on August 30, three days before his death. It simply reiterated the public position North Vietnam had taken in the Paris talks and flatly rejected my initiative.

The full text of both letters is being released to the press.

In addition to the public meetings I referred to, Ambassador Lodge has met with Vietnam's chief negotiator in Paris in 11 private meetings.

We have taken other significant initiatives which must remain secret to keep open some channels of communication which may still prove to be productive.

But the effect of all the public, private and secret negotiations which have been undertaken since the bombing halt a year ago and since this Administration came into office on January 20, can be summed up in one sentence—

No progress whatever has been made except agreement on the shape of the bargaining table. Now who is at fault?

It has become clear that the obstacle in negotiating an end to the war is not the President of the United States. And it is not the South Vietnamese.

The obstacle is the other side's absolute refusal to show the least willingness to join us in seeking a just peace. It will not do so while it is convinced that all it has to do is to wait for our next concession, and the next until it gets everything it wants.

There can now be no longer any question that progress in negotiation depends only on Hanoi's deciding to negotiate, to negotiate seriously.

I realize that this report on our efforts on the diplomatic fronts is discouraging to the American people, but the American people are entitled to know the truth—the bad news as well as the good news, where the lives of our young men are involved.

Now let me turn, however, to a more encouraging report on another front.

At the time we launched our search for peace I recognized we might not succeed in bringing an end to the war through negotiation. I, therefore, put into effect another plan to bring peace—a plan which will bring the war to an end regardless of what happens on the negotiating front.

It is in line with a major shift in U.S. foreign policy which I described in my press conference at Guam on July 25. Let me briefly explain what has been described as the Nixon Doctrine—a policy which not only will help end the war in Vietnam, but which is an essential element of our program to prevent future Vietnams.

We Americans are a do-it-yourself people. We are an impatient people. Instead of teaching someone else to do a job, we like to do it ourselves. And this trait has been carried over into our foreign policy.

In Korea and again in Vietnam, the United States furnished most of the money, most of the arms, and most of the men to help the people of those countries defend their freedom against the Communist aggression.

Before any American troops were committed to Vietnam, a leader of another Asian country expressed this opinion to me when I was traveling in Asia as a private citizen. He said, "When you are trying to assist another nation defend its freedom, U.S. policy should be to help them fight the war but not to fight the war for them."

Well, in accordance with this wise counsel, I laid down in Guam three principles as guidelines for future American policy toward Asia:

First, the United States will keep all of its treaty commitments.

Second, we shall provide a shield if a nuclear power threatens the freedom of a nation allied with us or of a nation whose survival we consider vital to our security.

Third, in cases involving other types of aggression, we shall furnish military and economic assistance when requested in accordance with our treaty commitments. But we shall look to the nation directly threatened to assume the primary responsibility of providing the manpower for its defense.

After I announced this policy, I found that the leaders of the Philippines, Thailand, Vietnam, South Korea, and other nations which might be threatened by Communist aggression, welcomed this new direction in American foreign policy.

The defense of freedom is everybody's business—not just America's business. And it is particularly the responsibility of the people whose freedom is threatened. In the previous Administration, we Americanized the war in Vietnam. In this Administration, we are Vietnamizing the search for peace.

The policy of the previous Administration not only resulted in our assuming the primary responsibility for fighting the war but even more significantly did not adequately stress the goal of strengthening the South Vietnamese so that they could defend themselves when we left.

The Vietnamization Plan was launched following Secretary Laird's visit to

Vietnam in March. Under the plan, I ordered first a substantial increase in the training and equipment of South Vietnamese forces.

In July, on my visit to Vietnam, I changed General Abrams' orders so that they were consistent with the objectives of our new policies. Under the new orders, the primary mission of our troops is to enable the South Vietnamese forces to assume the full responsibility for the security of South Vietnam.

Our air operations have been reduced by over 20 percent.

And now we have begun to see the results of this long overdue change in American policy in Vietnam.

> After five years of Americans going into Vietnam, we are finally bringing American men home. By December 15, over 60,000 men will have been withdrawn from South Vietnam—including 20 percent of all of our combat forces.
>
> The South Vietnamese have continued to gain in strength. As a result they have been able to take over combat responsibilities from our American troops.

Two other significant developments have occurred since this Administration took office.

> Enemy infiltration, infiltration which is essential if they are to launch a major attack, over the last three months is less than 20 percent of what it was over the same period last year.
>
> Most important—United States casualties have declined during the last two months to the lowest point in three years.

Let me now turn to our program for the future.

We have adopted a plan which we have worked out in cooperation with the South Vietnamese for the complete withdrawal of all U.S. combat ground forces, and their replacement by South Vietnamese forces on an orderly scheduled timetable. This withdrawal will be made from strength and not from weakness. As South Vietnamese forces become stronger, the rate of American withdrawal can become greater.

I have not and do not intend to announce the timetable for our program. There are obvious reasons for this decision which I am sure you will understand. As I have indicated on several occasions, the rate of withdrawal will depend on developments on three fronts.

> One of these is the progress which can be or might be made in the Paris talks. An announcement of a fixed timetable for our withdrawal would completely remove any incentive for the enemy to negotiate an agreement.
>
> They would simply wait until our forces had withdrawn and then move in.

The other two factors on which we will base our withdrawal decisions are the level of enemy activity and the progress of the training program of the South Vietnamese forces. I am glad to be able to report tonight progress on both of these fronts has been greater than we anticipated when we started the program in June for withdrawal. As a result, our timetable for withdrawal is more optimistic now than when we made our first estimates in June. This clearly demonstrates why it is not wise to be frozen in on a fixed timetable.

We must retain the flexibility to base each withdrawal decision on the situation as it is at that time rather than on estimates that are no longer valid.

Along with this optimistic estimate, I must—in all candor—leave one note of caution.

If the level of enemy activity significantly increases we might have to adjust our timetable accordingly.

However, I want the record to be completely clear on one point.

At the time of the bombing halt just a year ago, there was some confusion as to whether there was an understanding on the part of the enemy that if we stopped the bombing of North Vietnam they would stop the shelling of cities in South Vietnam. I want to be sure that there is no misunderstanding on the part of the enemy with regard to our withdrawal program.

We have noted the reduced level of infiltration, the reduction of our casualties, and are basing our withdrawal decisions partially on those factors.

If the level of infiltration or our casualties increase while we are trying to scale down the fighting, it will be the result of a conscious decision by the enemy.

Hanoi could make no greater mistake than to assume that an increase in violence will be to its advantage. If I conclude that increased enemy action jeopardizes our remaining forces in Vietnam, I shall not hesitate to take strong and effective measures to deal with that situation.

This is not a threat. This is a statement of policy which as Commander-in-Chief of our Armed Forces I am making in meeting my responsibility for the protection of American fighting men wherever they may be.

My fellow Americans, I am sure you recognize from what I have said that we really only have two choices open to us if we want to end this war.

> I can order an immediate, precipitate withdrawal of all Americans from Vietnam without regard to the effects of that action.
>
> Or we can persist in our search for a just peace through a negotiated settlement if possible, or through continued implementation of our plan for Vietnamization if necessary—a plan of which we will withdraw all of our forces from Vietnam on a schedule in accordance with our program, as the South Vietnamese become strong enough to defend their own freedom.

I have chosen the second course.

It is not the easy way.

It is the right way.

It is a plan which will end the war and serve the cause of peace—not just in Vietnam but in the Pacific and in the world.

In speaking of the consequences of a precipitate withdrawal, I mentioned that our allies would lose confidence in America.

Far more dangerous, we would lose confidence in ourselves. The immediate reaction would be a sense of relief that our men were coming home. But as we saw the consequences of what we had done, inevitable remorse and divisive recrimination would scar our spirit as a people.

We have faced other crises in our history and have become stronger by rejecting the easy way out and taking the right way in meeting our challenges. Our greatness as a nation has been our capacity to do what had to be done when we knew our course was right.

I recognize that some of my fellow citizens disagree with the plan for peace I have chosen. Honest and patriotic Americans have reached different conclusions as to how peace should be achieved.

In San Francisco a few weeks ago, I saw demonstrators carrying signs reading: "Lose in Vietnam, bring the boys home."

Well one of the strengths of our free society is that any American has a right to reach that conclusion and to advocate that point of view. But as President of the United States, I would be untrue to my oath of office if I allowed the policy of this nation to be dictated by the minority who hold that point of view and who try to impose it on the nation by mounting demonstrations in the street.

For almost 200 years, the policy of this nation has been made under our Constitution by those leaders in the Congress and in the White House selected by all of the people. If a vocal minority, however fervent its cause, prevails over reason and the will of the majority this nation has no future as a free society.

And now I would like to address a word if I may to the young people of this nation who are particularly concerned, and I understand why they are concerned about this war.

I respect your idealism.

I share your concern for peace.

I want peace as much as you do.

There are powerful personal reasons I want to end this war. This week I will have to sign 83 letters to mothers, fathers, wives and loved ones of men who have given their lives for America in Vietnam. It is very little satisfaction to me that this is only one-third as many letters as I signed the first week in office. There is nothing I want more than to see the day come when I do not have to write any of those letters.

I want to end the war to save the lives of those brave young men in Vietnam.

But I want to end it in a way which will increase the chance that their younger brothers and their sons will not have to fight in some future Vietnam someplace in the world.

And I want to end the war for another reason. I want to end it so that the energy and dedication of you, our young people, now too often directed into bitter hatred against those responsible for the war, can be turned to the great challenges of peace, a better life for all Americans, a better life for all people on this earth.

I have chosen a plan for peace. I believe it will succeed.

If it does not succeed, what the critics say now won't matter. Or, if it does succeed, what the critics say now won't matter. If it does not succeed, anything I say then won't matter.

I know it may not be fashionable to speak of patriotism or national destiny these days. But I feel it is appropriate to do so on this occasion.

Two hundred years ago this nation was weak and poor. But even then, America was the hope of millions in the world. Today we have become the strongest and richest nation in the world. The wheel of destiny has turned so that any hope the world has for the survival of peace and freedom will be determined by whether the American people have the moral stamina and the courage to meet the challenge of free world leadership.

Let historians not record that when America was the most powerful nation in the world we passed on the other side of the road and allowed the last hopes for peace and freedom of millions of people to be suffocated by the forces of totalitarianism.

And so tonight—to you, the great *silent majority* of my fellow Americans— I ask for your support.

I pledged in my campaign for the Presidency to end the war in a way that we could win the peace. I have initiated a plan of action which will enable me to keep that pledge.

The more support I can have from the American people, the sooner that pledge can be redeemed; for the more divided we are at home, the less likely the enemy is to negotiate at Paris.

Let us be united for peace. Let us also be united against defeat. Because let us understand: *North Vietnam cannot defeat or humiliate the United States. Only Americans can do that.*

Fifty years ago, in this room and at this very desk, President Woodrow Wilson spoke words which caught the imagination of a war-weary world. He said, "This is the war to end wars." His dream for peace after World War I was shattered on the hard realities of great power politics and Woodrow Wilson died a broken man.

Tonight I do not tell you that the war in Vietnam is the war to end wars. But I do say this:

I have initiated a plan which will end this war in a way that will bring us closer to that great goal to which Woodrow Wilson and every American President in our history has been dedicated—the goal of a just and lasting peace.

As President I hold the responsibility for choosing the best path to that goal and then leading the nation along it.

I pledge to you tonight that I shall meet this responsibility with all of the strength and wisdom I can command in accordance with your hopes, mindful of your concerns, sustained by your prayers.

Thank you and good night.

HOW TO CONTROL THE MILITARY

JOHN KENNETH GALBRAITH

In January as he was about to leave office, Lyndon Johnson sent his last report on the economic prospect to the Congress. It was assumed that, in one way or another, the Vietnam war, by which he and his Administration had been destroyed, would come gradually to an end. The question considered by his economists was whether this would bring a decrease or an increase in military spending. The military budget for fiscal 1969 was $78.4 billions; for the next year, including pay increases, it was scheduled to be about three billions higher. Thereafter, assuming peace and a general withdrawal from Asia, there would be a reduction of some six or seven billions. But this was only on the assumption that the Pentagon did not get any major new weapons—that it was content with what had already been authorized. No one really thought this possible. The President's economists noted that plans already existed for "a package" consisting of new aircraft, modern naval vessels, defense installations, and "advanced strategic and general purpose weapons systems" which would cost many billions. This would wipe out any savings from getting out of Vietnam. Peace would now be far more expensive than war.

With Richard Nixon the prospect for increased arms spending would seem superficially to be better. During the election campaign he promised to establish a clear military superiority over the Soviets, an effort that he could not believe would escape their attention. Their response would also be predictable and would require a yet larger effort here. (At his first press conference Mr. Nixon retreated from "superiority" to "sufficiency.")

SOURCE: John Kenneth Galbraith, "How to Control the Military," *Harper's Magazine*, 238 (June 1969), 32–46. Copyright © 1969 by John Kenneth Galbraith. Used by permission of Doubleday & Company, Inc.

Melvin Laird, the new Secretary of Defense, while in the Congress was an ardent spokesman for the military viewpoint, which is to say for military spending. And his Under Secretary of Defense, David Packard, though the rare case of a defense contractor who had spoken for arms control, was recruited from the very heart of the military-industrial complex.

Just prior to Mr. Nixon's inauguration the Air Force Association, the most eager spokesman for the military and its suppliers, said happily that "If the new Administration is willing to put its money where its mouth is in national defense some welcome changes are in the offing." And speaking to a reporter, J. Leland Atwood, president and chief executive officer of North American Rockwell, one of the half-dozen biggest defense firms, sized up the prospect as follows: "All of Mr. Nixon's statements on weapons and space are very positive. I think he has perhaps a little more awareness of these things than some people we've seen in the White House." Since no one had previously noticed the slightest unawareness, Mr. Atwood considered the prospect very positive indeed.

Yet he could be wrong. Browning observed of Jove that he strikes the Titans down when they reach the peak—"when another rock would crown the work." When I started work on this paper some months ago, I hazarded the guess that the military power was by way of provoking the same public reaction as did the Vietnam war. Now this is no longer in doubt. If he remains *positive*, the military power will almost certainly do for President Nixon what Vietnam did for his predecessor. But it might also lead him to a strenuous effort to avoid the Johnson fate. Mr. Nixon has not, in the past, been notably indifferent to his political career. The result in either case would be an eventual curb on the military power—either from Mr. Nixon or his successor.

Or so it would seem. What is clear is that a drastic change is occurring in public attitudes toward the military and its industrial allies which will not for long be ignored by politicians who are sensitive to the public mood. And from this new political climate will come the chance for reasserting control.

The purpose of this article is to see the nature of the military power, assess its strengths and weaknesses, and suggest the guidelines for regaining control. For no one can doubt the need for doing so.

II

The problem of the military power is not unique; it is merely a rather formidable example of the tendency of our time. That is for organization, in an age of organization, to develop a life and purpose and truth of its own. This tendency holds for all great bureaucracies, both public and private. And their action is not what serves a larger public interest, their belief does not reflect the reality of life. What is done and what is believed are, first and naturally, what serve the goals of the bureaucracy itself. Action in the organization interest, or in response to the bureaucratic truth, can thus be a formula for public disservice or even public disaster.

There is nothing academic about this possibility. There have been many explanations of how we got into the Vietnam war, an action on which even the greatest of the early enthusiasts have now lapsed into discretion. But all explanations come back to one. It was the result of a long series of steps taken in response to a bureaucratic view of the world—a view to which a President willingly or unwillingly yielded and which, until much too late, was unchecked by any legislative or public opposition. This view was of a planet threatened by an imminent takeover by the unified and masterful forces of the Communist world, directed from Moscow (or later and with less assurance from Peking) and coming to a focus, however improbably, some thousands of miles away in the activities of a few thousand guerrillas against the markedly regressive government of South Vietnam.

The further bureaucratic truths that were developed to support this proposition are especially sobering. What was essentially a civil war between the Vietnamese was converted into an international conflict with rich ideological portent for all mankind. South Vietnamese dictators became incipient Jeffersonians holding aloft the banners of an Asian democracy. Wholesale graft in Saigon became an indispensable aspect of free institutions. An elaborately rigged election became a further portent of democracy. One of the world's most desultory and impermanent armies became, always potentially, a paragon of martial vigor. Airplanes episodically bombing open acreage or dense jungle became an impenetrable barrier to men walking along the ground. An infinity of reverses, losses, and defeats became victories deeply in disguise. Such is the capacity of bureaucracy to create its own truth.

There was nothing, or certainly not much, that was cynical in this effort. Most of the men responsibly involved accepted the myth in which they lived a part. For from the inside it is the world outside which looks uninformed, perverse, and very wrong. Throughout the course of the war there was bitter anger in Washington and Saigon over the inability of numerous journalists to see military operations, the Saigon government, the pacification program, the South Vietnam army in the same rosy light as did the bureaucracy. Why couldn't they be indignant instruments of the official belief—like Joseph Alsop?

As many others have observed, the epitome of the organization man in our time was Secretary of State Dean Rusk. Few have served organization with such uncritical devotion. A note of mystification, even honest despair, was present in his public expression over the inability of the outside world to accept the bureaucratic truths just listed. Only the eccentrics, undisciplined or naïve, failed to accept what the State Department said was true. His despair was still evident as he left office, his career in ruins, and the Administration of which he was the ranking officer destroyed by action in pursuit of these beliefs. There could be no more dramatic—or tragic—illustration of the way organization captures men for its truths.

But Vietnam was not the first time men were so captured—and the country suffered. Within this same decade there was the Bay of Pigs, now a textbook case of bureaucratic self-deception. Organization needed to believe that Castro was toppling on the edge. Communism was an international conspiracy; hence it could have no popular local roots; hence the Cuban people would welcome the efforts to overthrow it. Intelligence was made to confirm these beliefs, for if it didn't it was, by definition, defective information. And, as an unpopular tyranny, the Castro government *should* be overthrown. Hence the action, thus the disaster. The same beliefs played a part in the military descent, against largely nonexistent Communists, on the Dominican Republic.

But the most spectacular examples of bureaucratic truth are those that serve the military power—and its weapons procurement. These have not yet produced anything so dramatic as the Vietnam, Bay of Pigs, or Dominican misadventures but their potential for disaster is far greater. These beliefs and their consequences are worth specifying in some detail.

There is first the military belief that whatever the dangers of a continued weapons race with the Soviet Union these are less than those of any agreement that offers any perceptible opening for violation. If there is such an opening the Soviets will exploit it. Since no agreement can be watertight this goes far to protect the weapons race from any effort at control.

Secondly, there is the belief that the conflict with Communism is man's ultimate battle. Accordingly, one would not hesitate to destroy all life if Communism seems seriously a threat. This belief allows acceptance of the arms race no matter how dangerous. The present ideological differences between industrial systems will almost certainly look very different and possibly rather trivial from a perspective of fifty or a hundred years hence if we survive. Such thoughts are eccentric.

Third, the national interest is total, that of man inconsequential. So even the prospect of total death and destruction does not deter us from developing new weapons systems if some thread of national interest can be identified in the outcome. We can accept 75 million casualties if it forces the opposition to accept 150 million. This is the unsentimental calculation. Even more unsentimentally, Senator Richard Russell, the leading Senate spokesman of the military power, argued on behalf of the Army's Sentinel Anti-Ballistic Missile System (ABM) that, if only one man and one woman are to be left on earth, it was his deep desire that they be Americans. It was part of the case for the Manned Orbiting Laboratory (MOL) that it would maintain the national position in the event of extensive destruction down below.

Such, not secretly but as they have been articulated, are the organization truths of the military power. The beliefs that got us into (and keep us in) Vietnam in their potential for disaster pale as compared with these doctrines. We shall obviously have accomplished little if we get out of Vietnam but leave unchecked in the government the capacity for this kind of bureaucratic truth. What, in tangible form, is the organization which avows these truths?

III

It is an organization or a complex of organizations and not a conspiracy. Although Americans are probably the world's least competent conspirators—partly because no other country so handsomely rewards in cash and notoriety the man who blows the whistle on those with whom he is conspiring—we have a strong instinct for so explaining that of which we disapprove. In the conspiratorial view, the military power is a collation of generals and conniving industrialists. The goal is mutual enrichment; they arrange elaborately to feather each other's nest. The industrialists are the *deus ex machina;* their agents make their way around Washington arranging the payoff. If money is too dangerous, then alcohol, compatible women, more prosaic forms of entertainment or the promise of future jobs to generals and admirals will serve.

There is such enrichment and some graft. Insiders do well. H. L. Nieburg has told the fascinating story of how in 1954 two modestly paid aerospace scientists, Dr. Simon Ramo and Dr. Dean Wooldridge, attached themselves influentially to the Air Force as consultants and in four fine years (with no known dishonesty) ran a shoestring of $6,750 apiece into a multimillion-dollar fortune and a position of major industrial prominence.° (In 1967 their firm held defense contracts totaling $121 million.) Senator William Proxmire, a man whom many in the defense industries have come to compare unfavorably to typhus, has recently come up with a fascinating contractual arrangement between the Air Force and Lockheed for the new C-5A jet transport. It makes the profits of the company greater the greater its costs in filling the first part of the order, with interesting incentive effects. A recent Department of Defense study reached the depressing conclusion that firms with the poorest performance in designing highly technical electronic systems—and the failure rate was appalling—have regularly received the highest profits. In 1960, 691 retired generals, admirals, naval captains, and colonels were employed by the ten largest defense contractors—186 by General Dynamics alone. A recent study made at the behest of Senator Proxmire found 2,072 employed in major defense firms with an especially heavy concentration in the specialized defense firms.† It would be idle to suppose that presently serving officers—those

---

° *In the Name of Science* (Chicago, Quadrangle Press, 1966). This is a book of first-rate importance which the author was so unwise as to publish some three years before concern for the problems he discusses became general. But perhaps he made it so.

† General Dynamics 113, Lockheed 210, Boeing 169, McDonnell Douglas 141, North American Rockwell 104, Ling-Temco-Vought 69. All of these firms are heavily specialized to military busi-

for example on assignment to defense plants—never have their real income improved by the wealthy contractors with whom they are working, forswear all favors, entertain themselves, and sleep austerely alone. Nor are those public servants who show zeal in searching out undue profits or graft reliably rewarded by a grateful public. Mr. A. E. Fitzgerald, the Pentagon management expert who became disturbed over the C-5A contract with Lockheed and communicated his unease and its causes to the Proxmire Committee, had his recently acquired civil-service status removed and was the subject of a fascinating memorandum (which found its way to Proxmire) outlining the sanctions appropriate to his excess of zeal. Pentagon officials explained that Mr. Fitzgerald had been given his civil-service tenure as the result of a computer error (the first of its kind) and the memorandum on appropriate punishment was a benign gesture of purely scholarly intent designed to specify those punishments against which such a sound public servant should be protected.

Nonetheless the notion of a conspiracy to enrich and corrupt is gravely damaging to an understanding of the military power. It causes men to look for solutions in issuing regulations, enforcing laws, or sending people to jail. It also, as a practical matter, exaggerates the role of the defense industries in the military power—since they are the people who make the most money, they are assumed to be the ones who, in the manner of the classical capitalist, pull the strings. The armed services are assumed to be in some measure their puppets. The reality is far less dramatic and far more difficult of solution. The reality is a complex of organizations pursuing their sometimes diverse but generally common goals. The participants in these organizations are mostly honest men whose public and private behavior would withstand public scrutiny as well as most. They live on their military pay or their salaries as engineers, scientists, or managers or their pay and profits as executives and would not dream of offering or accepting a bribe.

The organizations that comprise the military power are the four Armed Services, and especially their procurement branches. And the military power encompasses the specialized defense contractors—General Dynamics, McDonnell Douglas, Lockheed, or the defense firms of the agglomerates—of Ling-Temco-Vought or Litton Industries. (About half of all defense contracts are with firms that do relatively little other business.) And it embraces the defense division of primarily civilian firms such as General Electric or AT&T. It draws moral and valuable political support from the unions. Men serve these organizations in many, if not most, instances, because they believe in what they are doing—because they have committed themselves to the bureaucratic truth. To find and scourge a few malefactors is to ignore this far more important commitment.

ness; General Dynamics, Lockheed, McDonnell Douglas and North American Rockwell almost completely so.

The military power is not confined to the Services and their contractors—what has come to be called the military-industrial complex. Associate membership is held by the intelligence agencies which assess Soviet (or Chinese) actions or intentions. These provide, more often by selection than by any dishonesty, the justification for what the Services would like to have and what their contractors would like to supply. Associated also are Foreign Service Officers who provide a civilian or diplomatic gloss to the foreign-policy positions which serve the military need. The country desks at the State Department, a greatly experienced former official and ambassador has observed, are often "in the hip pocket of the Pentagon—lock, stock, and barrel, ideologically owned by the Pentagon." °

Also a part of the military power are the university scientists and those in such defense-oriented organizations as RAND, the Institute for Defense Analysis, and Hudson Institute who think professionally about weapons and weapons systems and the strategy of their use. And last, but by no means least, there is the organized voice of the military in the Congress, most notably on the Armed Services Committees of the Senate and House of Representatives. These are the organizations which comprise the military power.

The men who comprise these organizations call each other on the phone, meet at committee hearings, serve together on teams or task forces, work in neighboring offices in Washington or San Diego. They naturally make their decisions in accordance with their view of the world—the view of the bureaucracy of which they are a part. The problem is not conspiracy or corruption but unchecked rule. And being unchecked, this rule reflects not the national need but the bureaucratic need—not what is best for the United States but what the Air Force, Army, Navy, General Dynamics, North American Rockwell, Grumman Aircraft, State Department representatives, intelligence officers, and Mendel Rivers and Richard Russell believe to be best.

In recent years Air Force generals, perhaps the most compulsively literate warriors since Caesar, have made their views of the world scene a part of the American folklore. These in all cases serve admirably the goals of their Service and the military power in general. Similarly with the other participants.

Not long ago, Bernard Nossiter, the brilliant economics reporter of the Washington *Post,* made the rounds of some of the major defense contractors to get their views of the post-Vietnam prospect. All, without exception, saw profitable tension and conflict. Edward J. Lefevre, the vice-president in charge of General Dynamics' Washington office, said "One must believe in

---

° Ralph Dungan, formerly White House aide to Presidents Kennedy and Johnson and former Ambassador to Chile. Quoted in George Thayer, *The War Business* (Simon and Schuster). The appearance of the State Department as a full-scale participant in the military power may have been the hopefully temporary achievement of Secretary Rusk. Apart from a high respect for military acumen and need, he in some degree regarded diplomacy as subordinate to military purpose. In time such attitudes penetrate deeply into organization.

the long-term threat." James J. Ling, the head of Ling-Temco-Vought, reported that "Defense spending has to increase in our area because there has been a failure to initiate—if we are not going to be overtaken by the Soviets." Samuel F. Downer, one of Mr. Ling's vice-presidents, was more outspoken. "We're going to increase defense budgets as long as those bastards in Russia are ahead of us." A study of the Electronics Industries Association also dug up by Mr. Nossiter (to whom I shall return in a moment) discounted the danger of arms control, decided that the "likelihood of limited war will increase" and concluded that "for the electronic firms, the outlook is good in spite [sic] of [the end of hostilities in] Vietnam."

From the foregoing beliefs, in turn, comes the decision on weapons and weapons systems and military policy generally. No one can tell where the action originates—whether the Services or the contractors initiate decisions on weapons—nor can the two be sharply distinguished. Much of the plant of the specialized defense contractors is owned by the government. Most of their working capital is supplied by the government through progress payments—payments made in advance of completion of the contract. The government specifies what the firm can and cannot charge to the government. The Armed Services Procurement Regulation states that "Although the government does not expect to participate *in every management* decision, it may reserve the right to review the contractor's management efforts. . . ." (Italics added.)

In this kind of association some proposals will come across the table from the military. Some will come back from the captive contractors. Nossiter asked leading contractors, as well as people at the Pentagon, about this. Here are some of the answers.

From John W. Bessire, General Manager for Pricing, General Dynamics, Fort Worth: "We try to foresee the requirements the military is going to have three years off. We work with their requirements people and therefore get new business."

From Richard E. Adams, Director of Advanced Projects, Fort Worth Division of General Dynamics, who thought the source was the military: "Things are too systematized at the Pentagon for us to invent weapons systems and sell them on a need."

On the influence of the military he added: "We know where the power is [on Capitol Hill and among Executive Departments]. There's going to be a lot of defense business and we're going to get our share of it."

From John R. Moore, President of Aerospace and Systems Group of North American Rockwell: "A new system usually starts with a couple of military and industry people getting together to discuss common problems."

After noting that most of his business came from requirements "established by the Defense Department and NASA," he concluded: "But it isn't a case of industry here and the government here. They are interacting continuously at the engineering level."

And finally from a high civilian in the Pentagon: "Pressures to spend more. . . . In part they come from the industry selling new weapons ideas and in part from the military here. Each military guy has his own piece, tactical, antisubmarine, strategic. Each guy gets where he is by pushing his particular thing."

He added: "Don't forget, too, part of it is based on the perception of needs by people in Congress."

The important thing is not where the action originates but in the fact that it serves the common goals of the military and the defense contractors. It is, in the language of labor relations, a sweetheart deal between those who sell to the government and those who buy. Once competitive bidding created an adversary relationship between buyer and seller sustained by the fact that, with numerous sellers, any special relationship with any one must necessarily provoke cries of favoritism. But modern weapons are bought overwhelmingly by negotiation and in most cases from a single source of supply. (In the fiscal year ending in 1968, General Accounting Office figures show that 57.9 per cent of the $43 billion in defense contracts awarded in that year was by negotiation with a single source of supply. Of the remainder 30.6 per cent was awarded by negotiation where alternative sources of supply had an opportunity to participate and only 11.5 per cent was open to advertised competitive bidding.)° Under these circumstances the tendency to any adversary relationship between the Services and their suppliers is minimal. Indeed, where there are only one or two sources of supply for a weapons system, the interest of the Services in sustaining a source of supply will be no less than that of the firm in question in being sustained.

Among those who spoke about the sources of ideas on weapons needs, no one was moved to suggest that public opinion played any role. The President, as the elected official responsible for foreign policy, was not mentioned. The Congress came in only as an afterthought. And had the Pentagon official who mentioned the Congress been pressed, he would have agreed that its "perception of needs" is a revelation that almost always results from prompting by either the military or the defense industries. It was thus, for example, that the need for a new generation of manned bombers was perceived (and provided for) by Congress though repeatedly vetoed as unnecessary by Presidents Kennedy and Johnson. But in the past the role of the Congress has been overwhelmingly acquiescent and passive. As Senator Gaylord Nelson said in the Senate in February 1964:

> . . . an established tradition . . . holds that a bill to spend billions of
> dollars for the machinery of war must be rushed through the House and
> the Senate in a matter of hours, while a treaty to advance the cause of

---

° Testimony of Elmer B. Staats, Comptroller General, before Senator Proxmire's Committee (November 11, 1968).

peace, or a program to help the underdeveloped nations . . . guarantee the rights of all our citizens, or . . . to advance the interests of the poor must be scrutinized and debated and amended and thrashed over for weeks and perhaps months.

IV

We see here a truly remarkable reversal of the American political and economic system as outlined by the fathers and still portrayed to the young. That view supposes that ultimate authority—ultimate sovereignty—lies with the people. And this authority is assumed to be comprehensive. Within the ambit of the state the citizen expresses his will through the men—the President and members of the Congress—whom he elects. Outside he accomplishes the same thing by his purchases in the market. These instruct supplying firms— General Motors, General Electric, Standard Oil of New Jersey—as to what they shall produce and sell. But here we find the Armed Services or the corporations that supply them making the decisions and instructing the Congress and the public. The public accepts whatever is so decided and pays the bill. This is an age when the young are being instructed, in my view rightly although with unnecessary solemnity, to respect constitutional process and seek change within the framework of the established political order. And we find the assumed guardians of that order, men with no slight appreciation of their righteousness and respectability, calmly turning it upside down themselves.

How did this remarkable reversal in the oldest of constitutional arrangements come about? How, in particular, did it come about in a country that sets great store by individual and citizen rights and which traditionally has been suspicious of military, industrial, and bureaucratic power? How did it come to allow these three forces to assert their authority over a tenth of the economy and something closer to ten-tenths of our future? °

V

Six things brought the military-industrial bureaucracy to its present position of power. To see these forces is also to be encouraged by the chance for escape.

First there has been, as noted, the increasing bureaucratization of our life. In an economically and technologically complex society, more and more tasks

° I have argued elsewhere (*The New Industrial State*, Houghton Mifflin, 1967) that with increasing industrialization the sovereignty of the consumer or citizen yields to the sovereignty of the producer or public bureaucracy. Increasingly the consumer or citizen is made subordinate to their needs. I have been rather sharply challenged. But in the very important area of military production, about 10 per cent of the total, we see that producer sovereignty is accepted and avowed. Not even my most self-confident critics would be wholly certain of my error here.

are accomplished by specialists. Specialists must then have their knowledge and skills united by organization. Organization, then, as we have seen, proceeds to assert its needs and beliefs. These will not necessarily be those of the individual or community.

In what Ralph Lapp has called the weapons culture, both economic and technological complexity are raised to the highest power. So, accordingly, are the scope and power of organization. So, accordingly, is the possibility of self-serving belief.

It is a power, however, which brings into existence its own challenge. The same technical and social complexity that requires organization requires that there be large numbers of trained and educated people. Neither these people nor the educational establishment that produces them are docile in the face of organization. So with organization come people who resist it—who are schooled to assert their individual beliefs and convictions. No modern military establishment could expect the disciplined obedience which sent millions (in the main lightly schooled lads from the farm) against the machine guns as late as World War I.

The reaction to organization and its beliefs may well be one of the most rapidly developing political moods of our time. Clearly it accounted for much of the McCarthy strength in the last year—for if Dean Rusk or General Westmoreland were the epitome of the organization man, Eugene McCarthy was its antithesis. Currently one sees it sweeping ROTC off the campuses—or out of the university curricula. It is causing recruiting problems for big business—and not alone the defense firms. One senses, if the draft survives, that it will cause trouble for the peacetime Armed Forces.

But so far the impressive thing is the power that massive organization has given to the military industrial complex and not the resistance it is arousing. The latter is for the future.

Second in importance in bringing the military-industrial complex to power were the circumstances and images of foreign policy in the late Forties, Fifties and early Sixties. The Communist world, as noted, was viewed as a unified imperium mounting its claim to every part of the globe. The postwar pressure on Eastern Europe and on Berlin, the Chinese revolution, and the Korean war, seemed powerful evidence in the case. And, after the surprisingly early explosion of the first Soviet atomic bomb, followed within a decade by the even more astonishing flight of the first Sputnik, it was easy to believe that the Communist world was not only politically more unified than the rest but technologically stronger as well.

The natural reaction was to delegate power and concentrate resources. The military Services and their industrial allies were given unprecedented authority—as much as in World War II—to match the Soviet technological initiative. And the effort of the nation's scientists (and other scholars) was concentrated in equally impressive fashion. None or almost none remained outside.

Robert Oppenheimer was excluded, not because he opposed weapons development in general or the hydrogen bomb in particular, but because he thought the latter unnecessary and undeliverable. That anyone, on grounds of principle, should refuse his services to the Pentagon or Dow Chemical was nearly unthinkable. Social scientists responded eagerly to invitations to spend the summer at RAND. They devoted their winters to seminars on the strategy of defense and deterrence. The only question in this time was whether a man could get a security clearance. The extent of a man's access to secret matters measured his responsibility and influence in public affairs and prestige in the community.

The effect of this concentration of talent was to add to the autonomy and power of the organizations responsible for the effort. Criticism or dissent requires knowledge; the knowledgeable men were nearly all inside. The Eisenhower Administration affirmed the power of the military by appointing Secretaries of Defense who were largely passive except as they might worry on occasion about the cost. The Democrats, worrying about a nonexistent missile gap and fearing, as always, that they might seem soft on Communism, accorded the military more funds and power, seeking principally to make it more efficient.

This enfranchisement of the military power was in a very real sense the result of a democratic decision—it was a widely approved response to the seemingly fearsome forces that surrounded us. With time those who received this unprecedented grant of power came to regard it as a right. Where weapons and military decision were concerned, their authority was meant to be plenary. Men with power have been prone to such error.

Third, secrecy confined knowledge of Soviet weapons and responding American action to those within the public and private bureaucracy. No one else had knowledge, hence no one else was qualified to speak. Senior members of the Armed Services, their industrial allies, the scientists, the members of the Armed Services Committees of the Congress were in. It would be hard to imagine a more efficient arrangement for protecting the power of a bureaucracy. In the academic community and especially in Congress there was no small prestige in being a member of this club. So its influence was enhanced by the sense of belonging and serving. And, as the experience of Robert Oppenheimer and other less publicized persons showed, it was possible on occasion to exclude the critic or skeptic as a security risk.

Fourth, there was the disciplining effect of personal fear. A nation that was massively alarmed about the unified power of the Communist world was not tolerant of skeptics or those who questioned the only seemingly practical line of response. Numerous scientists, social scientists, and public officials had come reluctantly to accept the idea of the Communist threat. This history of reluctance could now involve the danger—real or imagined—that they might be suspected of past association with this all-embracing conspiracy. The late

Senator Joseph R. McCarthy would not have been influential in ordinary times; but he and others saw or sensed the opportunity for exploiting national and personal anxiety. The result was further and decisive pressure on anyone who seemed not to concur in the totality of the Communist threat. (McCarthy was broken only when he capriciously attacked the military power.)

Fear provided a further source of immunity and power. Accepted Marxian doctrine holds that a cabal of capitalists and militarists is the cutting edge of capitalist imperialism and the cause of war. Anyone who raised a question about the military-industrial complex thus sounded suspiciously like a Marxist. So it was a topic that was avoided by the circumspect. Heroism in the United States involves some important distinctions. It requires a man to stand up fearlessly, at least in principle, to the prospect for nuclear extinction. But it allows him to proceed promptly to cover if there is risk of being called a Communist, a radical, an enemy of the system. Death we must face but not social obloquy or political ostracism. The effect of such discriminating heroism in the Fifties and Sixties was that most potential critics of the military power were exceptionally reticent.

In 1961, in the last moments before leaving office, President Eisenhower gave his famous warning: "In the councils of government we must guard against the acquisition of unwarranted influence, whether sought or unsought, by the military-industrial complex. The potential for the disastrous rise of misplaced power exists and will persist." This warning was to become by a wide margin the most quoted of all Eisenhower statements. This was principally for the flank protection it provided for all who wanted to agree. For many years thereafter anyone (myself included) who spoke to the problem of the military power took the thoughtful precaution of first quoting President Eisenhower. He had shown that there were impeccably conservative precedents for our concern.

Fifth, in the Fifties and early Sixties the phrase "domestic priority" had not yet become a cliché. The civilian claim on federal funds was not, or seemed not, to be overpowering. The great riots in the cities had not yet occurred. The appalling conditions in the urban core that were a cause were still unnoticed. Internal migration had long been under way but millions were yet to come from the rural into the urban slums. Poverty had not yet been placed on the national agenda, with the consequence that we would learn how much and how abysmal it is. And promises not having been made to end poverty, expectations had not been aroused. The streets of Washington, D.C., were still safer than those of Saigon. Travel by road and commuter train was only just coming to a crawl. The cities' air and water were dirty but not yet lethally so.

In this innocent age, in 1964, taxes were reduced because there seemed to be danger of economic stagnation and unemployment from raising more federal revenue than could quickly be spent. The then Director of the Budget, Kermit Gordon, was persuaded that if an excess of revenue were available the military would latch on to it. Inflation was not a pressing issue. Military expenditures, although no one wished to say so, did sustain employment. Circumstances could not have been better designed, economically speaking, to allow the military a clear run.

Sixth and finally, in these years, both conservative and liberal opposition to the military-industrial power was muted. Nothing could be expected, in principle, to appeal less to conservatives than a vast increase in bureaucratic power at vast cost. In an earlier age the reaction would have been apoplectic. Some conservatives in an older tradition—men genuinely concerned about the Leviathan State—were aroused. Ernest Weir, the head of National Steel and the foe of FDR and the New Deal, Alf M. Landon, the much-underestimated man who opposed Roosevelt in 1936, Marriner Eccles, banker and longtime head of the Federal Reserve, and a few others did speak out. But for most it was enough that the Communists—exponents of a yet more powerful state and against private property too—were on the other side. One accepted a lesser danger to fight a greater one. And, as always, when many are moderately aroused some are extreme. It became a tenet of a more extreme conservatism that civilians should never interfere with the military except to provide more money. Nor would there be any compromise with Communism. It must be destroyed. Their military doctrine, as Daniel Bell has said, was "that negotiation with the Communists is impossible, that anyone who discusses the possibility of such negotiation is a tool of the Communists, and that a 'tough policy'—by which, *sotto voce*, is meant a preventative war of a first strike—is the only means of forestalling an eventual Communist victory." ° To an impressive extent, in the Fifties and Sixties this new conservatism, guided by retired Air Force generals and the redoubtable Edward Teller, became the voice of all conservatism on defense policy.

The disappearance of liberal criticism was almost as complete—and even more remarkable. An association of military and industrial power functioning without restraint would have been expected to arouse liberal passion. So also the appropriation of public power for private purpose by defense contractors, some of them defining missions for the Services so as to require what they had to sell. But liberals did not react. Like conservatives they accepted a lesser threat to liberty to forestall a greater one. Also it was not easy for a generation that had asked for more executive power for FDR and his successors over conservative opposition to see danger in any bureaucracy or remedy in stronger legislative control. This was a too radical reversal of liberal form.

The generation of liberals which was active in the Fifties and Sixties had also been scarred by the tactics of the domestic Communists in politics and the trade-union movement. And members of this generation had seen what happened to friends who had committed themselves to the wartime alliance with the Soviets and had nailed their colors to its continuation after the war.

° Quoted by Ralph E. Lapp in *The Weapons Culture* (Norton, 1968).

Stalin had let them down with a brutal and for many a mortal thump. Those who escaped, or many of them, made common cause with the men who were making or deploying weapons to resist Communism, urging only, as good liberals, that there was a social dimension to the struggle. As time passed it was discovered that many good and liberal things—foreign aid, technical assistance, travel grants, fellowships, overseas libraries—could be floated on the Communist threat. Men of goodwill became accomplished in persuading the more retarded to vote for foreign-aid legislation, not as a good thing in itself but as an indispensable instrument in the war against Communism. Who, having made this case, could then be critical of military spending for the same purpose?

Additionally in the Fifties and Sixties American liberals were fighting for the larger federal budget not for the things it bought but for the unemployment it prevented. Such a budget, with its stabilizing flow of expenditures and supported by personal income taxes which rose and fell with stabilizing effect, was the cornerstone of the New or Keynesian Economics. And this economics of high and expanding employment, in turn, was the cornerstone of the liberal position. As noted it was not easy for liberals to admit that defense expenditures were serving this benign social function; when asked they (*i.e.* we) always said that spending for education, housing, welfare, and civilian public works would serve just as well and be much welcomed as an alternative.

But there was then no strong pressure to spend for these better things. Accordingly it was not easy for liberals to become aroused over an arms policy which had such obviously beneficent effects on the economy.

By the early Sixties the liberal position was beginning to change. From comparatively early in the Kennedy Administration—the Bay of Pigs was a major factor in this revelation—it became evident that a stand would have to be made against policies urged by the military and its State Department allies—against military intervention in Cuba, military intervention in Laos, military intervention in Vietnam, an all-out fallout shelter program, unrestricted nuclear testing, all of which would be disastrous for the President as well as for the country and world. A visible and sometimes sharp division occurred between those who, more or less automatically, made their alliance with the military power, and those—Robert Kennedy, Adlai Stevenson, Theodore Sorensen, Arthur Schlesinger, Averell Harriman, and, though rendering more homage to the organizations of which they were a part, George Ball and Robert McNamara—who saw the dangers of this commitment. With the Johnson Administration this opposition disappeared or was dispersed. The triumph of those who allied themselves with the bureaucracy was the disaster of that Administration.

The opposition, much enlarged, then reappeared in the political theater. Suspicion of the military power in 1968 was the most important factor uniting the followers of Senators Kennedy, McCarthy, and McGovern. Along with the more specific and more important opposition to the Vietnam conflict, it helped to generate the opposition that persuaded Lyndon Johnson not to run. And the feeling that Vice President Humphrey was not sufficiently firm on this issue—that he belonged politically to the generation of liberals that was tolerant of the military-industrial power—unquestionably diluted and weakened his support. Conceivably it cost him the election.

VI

To see the sources of the strength of the military-industrial complex in the Fifties and Sixties is to see its considerably greater vulnerability now. The Communist imperium, which once seemed so fearsome in its unity, has broken up into bitterly antagonistic blocks. Moscow and Peking barely keep the peace. Fear in Czechoslovakia, Yugoslavia, and Romania is not of the capitalist enemy but the great Communist friend. The more intimate calculations of the Soviet High Command on what might be expected of the Czech (or for that matter the Romanian or Polish or Hungarian) army in the event of war in Western Europe must not be without charm. Perhaps they explain the odd military passion of the Soviets for the Egyptians. The Soviets have had no more success than has capitalism in penetrating and organizing the backward countries of the world. Communist and capitalist jungles are indistinguishable. Men of independent mind recognize that after twenty years of aggressive military competition with the Soviets our security is not greater and almost certainly less than when the competition began. And although in the Fifties it was fashionable to assert otherwise ("a dictator does not hesitate to sacrifice his people by the millions") we now know that the Soviets are as aware of the totally catastrophic character of nuclear war as we are—and more so than our more articulate generals.

These changes plus the adverse reaction to Vietnam have cost the military power its monopoly of the scientific community. This, in turn, has damaged its claim to a monopoly of knowledge including that which depends on security classification. Informed critics are amply available outside the military-industrial complex. When earlier this year Under Secretary of Defense Packard sought, in an earlier tradition, to discredit the opposition of Dr. Herbert A. York, former Director of Defense Research and Engineering, to the ABM, on the grounds that the latter did not have access to secret information, the effort backfired. The only person whose credibility was damaged was Secretary Packard. In consequence men are now available to distinguish between what weapons are relevant to an equilibrium with the Soviets, what destroys this balance by encouraging a new competitive round, and what serves primarily the prestige of the Services and the prestige and profits of the contractors. The attack on the Sentinel-Safeguard ABM system could never have been mounted in the Fifties.

Additionally, civilian priority has become one of the most evocative words in the language. Everywhere—for urban housing and services, sanitation, schools, police, urban transportation, clean air, potable water—the needs are huge and pressing. Because these needs are not being met the number of people who live in fear of an urban explosion may well be greater than those who are alarmed by the prospect of nuclear devastation. For many years I have lived in summers on an old farm in southern Vermont. In the years following Hiroshima we had the advance refugees from the atomic bomb. Now we have those who are escaping the ultimate urban riot. The second migration is much bigger than the first and has had a far more inflationary effect on local real-estate values.

Certainly the day when military spending was a slightly embarrassing alternative to unemployment is gone and, one imagines, forever.

With all of these changes has come a radical change in the political climate. Except in the darker reaches of Orange County and suburban Dallas (where defense expenditures also have their influence) fear of Communism has receded. We have lived with the Communists on the same planet now for a half-century. An increasing number are disposed to believe we *can* continue doing so. Communism seems somewhat less triumphant than twenty years ago. Perhaps the Soviet Union is yet another industrial state in which organization—bureaucracy—is in conflict with the people it must educate in such numbers for its tasks. Mr. Nixon in his many years as a political aspirant was not notably averse to making capital out of the Communist menace. But neither, if a little belatedly, was he a man to resist a trend. Many must have noticed that his warnings overt or implied of the Communist menace in his Inaugural Address were rather less fiery than those of John F. Kennedy eight years earlier.

The anxiety which led to the great concentration of military and industrial power in the Fifties having dissipated, the continued existence of that power has naturally become a political issue. There are many who think that Mr. Nixon sacrificed some, perhaps much, of his lead when, in the closing days of the Presidential campaign, he promised to revitalize the arms race with an effort to establish clear superiority over the Soviets. There can be little question that General Curtis LeMay, far from attracting voters to Governor George Wallace in 1968, was a disaster. At a somewhat lower level than Eisenhower, MacArthur, Patton, and Bradley, LeMay was one of the *bona fide* heroes in the American pantheon. But his close association with the military power, especially his long efforts to make nuclear warfare palatable, if not altogether appetizing, to the American public, was unnerving. As noted a stand-up-to-it heroism is combined with a deep sensitivity when the nuclear nerve is touched.

If the potential followers of Governor Wallace were capable of alarm over the military power, then the potential opposition is not confined to the bearded and barefoot left. (This, as in the case of Vietnam, will be the first assumption of the bureaucracy.) Nor is it. Concern reaches deeply into the suburban middle class and business community. During the summer of 1968, if I may recur once more to personal experience, I was concerned with raising money for Eugene McCarthy. We raised a great deal: the efforts with which I was at least marginally associated produced some $2.5 million. Overwhelmingly we got that money from businessmen. Opposition to the Vietnam war was, of course, the prime reason for this support. But concern over the military power was a close (and closely affiliated) second. When one is asking for money one very soon learns what evokes response.

Social concern, however inappropriate for a businessman, was most important but there were also very good business reasons for being aroused. In 1968, the hundred largest defense contractors had more than two-thirds (67.4 per cent) of all the defense business and the smallest fifty of these had no more in the aggregate than General Dynamics and Lockheed. A dozen firms specializing in military business (e.g., McDonnell Douglas, General Dynamics, Lockheed, United Aircraft) together with General Electric and AT&T had a third of all the business. For the vast majority of businessmen the only association with the defense business is through the taxes they pay. Not even a subcontract comes their way. And they have another cost. They must operate in communities that are starved for revenue, where, in consequence, their business is exposed to disorder and violence and where materials and manpower are preempted by the defense contractors. They must also put up with inflation, high interest rates, and regulation on overseas investment occasioned by defense spending. The willingness of American businessmen to suffer on behalf of the big defense contractors has been a remarkable manifestation of charity and self-denial.

Two other changes have altered the position of the military power. In the Fifties the military establishment of the United States was still identified in the public mind with the great captains of World War II—with Eisenhower, Marshall, MacArthur, Bradley, King, Nimitz, Arnold. And many members of a slightly junior generation—Maxwell Taylor, James Gavin, Matthew Ridgway, Curtis LeMay—were in positions of power. Some of these soldiers might have done less well had they been forced to fight an elusive and highly motivated enemy in the jungle of Vietnam encumbered by the leisurely warriors of the ARVN. (At one time or another, Eisenhower, MacArthur, Gavin all made it explicitly clear that they would never have got involved in such a mistake.) The present military generation is intimately associated with the Vietnam misfortune. And its credibility has been deeply damaged by its fatal association with the bureaucratic truths of that war—with the long succession of defeats that became victories, the victories that became defeats, and brilliant actions that did not signify anything at all. In the Fifties it required courage for a civilian to challenge Eisenhower on military matters. Anyone is allowed to doubt the omniscience of General Westmoreland.

Finally, all bureaucracy has a mortal weakness; it cannot respond effectively to attack. The same inertial guidance which propels it into trouble—which sends it mindlessly into the Bay of Pigs or Vietnam even when disaster is evident—renders it helpless in self-defense. It can, in fact, only mimic itself. Organization could not come up with any effective response to its critics on Vietnam. The old slogans—we must resist worldwide Communist aggression, we must not reward aggression, we must stand by our brave allies—were employed not only after repetition had robbed them of all meaning but after they had been made ludicrous by events. In the end Secretary of State Rusk was reduced to mnemonic speeches about our commitments. Organized thought was incapable of anything better.

So with the military power—only more so. One of the perquisites of great power is that its use need not be defended. In consequence kings, czars, dictators, capitalists, even union leaders—when their day of accounting comes have rarely been able to speak for themselves. As the military power comes under scrutiny, it will be reduced to asserting that its critics are indifferent to Soviet or Chinese intentions, unacquainted with the most recent intelligence, militarily inexperienced, naïve, afraid to look nuclear destruction in the eye. Or it will be said that they are witting or unwitting tools of the Communist conspiracy. Following Secretary Laird's effort on behalf of the ABM (when he deployed from new intelligence an exceptionally alarming generation of Soviet missiles) a special appeal will be made to fear. A bureaucracy under attack is a fortress with thick walls but fixed guns.

VII

It is a cliché, much beloved of those who supply the diplomatic gloss for the military power, that not much can be done to limit the latter—or its budget—so long as "American responsibilities" in the world remain unchanged. And for others it is a persuasive point that to reduce the military budget will require a change in foreign policy.

But these changes have already occurred. In the years following World War II there was a spacious view of the American task in the world. We guarded the borders of the non-Communist world. We prevented subversion there and put down wars of liberation elsewhere. In pursuit of these aims we maintained alliances, deployed forces, provided military aid on every continent. This was the competition of the superpowers. We had no choice but to meet the challenge of that competition.

We have already found that the world so depicted does not exist. Superpowers there are but superpowers cannot much affect the course of life within the countries they presume to see as on their side. In part that was the lesson of Vietnam; annual expenditures of $30 billion, a deployment of more than half a million men, could not much affect the course of development in one small country. In lands as diverse as India, Indonesia, Peru, and the

Congo we have found that our ability to affect the development is even less. We have also found, as in the nearby case of Cuba, that a country can go Communist without inflicting any overpowering damage.

What we have not done is accommodate our military policy to this reality. Military aid, bases, conventional force levels, weapons requirements still assume superpower omnipotence. (And the military power still projects this vision of our task.) Our foreign policy has, in fact, changed. It is the Pentagon that hasn't.

VIII

To argue that the military-industrial complex is now vulnerable is not to suggest that it is on its last legs. It spends a vast amount of public money, which insures the support of many (though by no means all) of those who receive it. Many Senators and Congressmen are slow to criticize expenditures in their districts even though for most of their supporters the cost vastly exceeds the gain. (Defense contracts are even more concentrated geographically than by firm. In 1967 three favored states out of fifty—California and New York and Texas—received one-third. Ten states accounted for a full two-thirds. In all but a handful of cases the Congressman or Senator who votes for military spending is voting for the enrichment of people he does not represent at the expense of those who elect him.) And there is the matter of habit and momentum. The military power has been above challenge for so long that to attack still seems politically quixotic. One recalls, however, that it once seemed quixotic to be against the Vietnam war.

Nonetheless control is possible. I come to my final task. It is to offer a political decalogue of what is required. It is as follows.

1. *The goal, all must remember, is to get the military power under firm political control. This means electing a President on this issue next time. This, above all, must be the issue in the next election.*

However, for the next three and a half years, not much can be done about the Presidency. Also if Mr. Nixon does not resist the military power he will follow President Johnson into oblivion—conceivably taking quite a few others with him. This one must suppose he will see. So while all possible moral pressure must be kept on the President, the immediate target is Congress.

2. *Congress will not be impressed by learned declamation on the danger of the military power. There must be organization.* The last election showed the power of that part of the community—the colleges, universities, concerned middle class, businessmen—which was alert to the Vietnam war. Now in every possible Congressional District there must be an organization alert to the military power. Anciently, legislators up for election have pledged themselves to an "adequate national defense," a euphemism for according the Pentagon a blank check. In the next election everyone must be pressed for a promise to resist military programs and press relentlessly for negotiations

along lines indicated below. Any Senator or Congressman who does not believe that the Congress should exercise strict supervision over the Pentagon, that the latter should be strictly answerable to Congress both for its actions and its expenditures, confesses his indifference to the proper role of the legislative body. He will be better at home.

This effort must not be confined to the North, the Middle West, or West. In the last five years there has been a rapid liberalization of the major college and university centers of the South. Nowhere did McCarthy or Kennedy draw larger and more enthusiastic crowds than in the big Southern universities. Mendel Rivers, Richard Russell, Strom Thurmond, John Tower, and the other sycophants of the military from the South must be made sharply aware of this new constituency—and if possible be retired by it.

3. *The Armed Services Committees of the two houses must obviously be the object of a special effort.* They are now, with the exception of a few members, a rubber stamp for the military power. Some liberals have been reluctant to serve on these fiefs. No effort, including an attack on the seniority system itself, should be spared to oust the present functionaries and to replace them with acute and independent-minded members. Here too it is important to get grass-roots expression from the South.

4. *The goal is not to make the military power more efficient or more righteously honest. It is to get it under control.* These are very different objectives. The first seeks out excessive profits, high costs, poor technical performance, favoritism, delay, or the other abuses of power. The second is concerned with the power itself. The first is diversionary for it persuades people that something is being done while leaving power and budgets intact.

5. *This is not an antimilitary crusade. Generals and admirals and soldiers, sailors, and airmen are not the object of attack. The purpose is to return the military establishment to its traditional position in the American political system.* It was never intended to be an unlimited partner in the arms industry. Nor was it meant to be a controlling voice in foreign policy. Any general or admiral who rose to fame before World War II would be surprised and horrified to find that his successors in the profession of arms are now commercial accessories of General Dynamics.

6. *Whatever its moral case there is no political future in unilateral disarmament.* And the case must not be compromised by wishful assumptions about the Soviets which the Soviets can then destroy. It can safely be assumed that nuclear annihilation is as unpopular with the average Russian as it is with the ordinary American, and that their leaders are not retarded in this respect. But it is wise to assume that within their industrial system, as within ours, there is a military-industrial bureaucracy committed to its own perpetuation and growth. This governs the more precise objectives of control.

7. *Four broad types of major weapons systems can be recognized.* There are first those that are related directly to the existing balance of power or the balance of terror vis-à-vis the Soviets. The ICBMs and the Polaris submarines are

obviously of this sort; in the absence of a decision to disarm unilaterally, re-striction or reduction in these weapons requires agreement with the Soviets. There are, secondly, those that may be added within this balance without tip-ping it drastically one way or the other. They allow each country to destroy the other more completely or redundantly. Beyond a certain number, more ICBMs are of this sort. Thirdly there are those that, in one way or another, tip the balance or seem to do so. They promise, or can be thought to promise, de-struction of the second country while allowing the first to escape or largely es-cape. Inevitably, in the absence of a prospect for agreement, they must pro-voke response. An ABM, which seems to provide defense while allowing continued offense, is of this sort. So are missiles of such number, weight, and precision as to be able to destroy the second country's weapon without possi-bility of retaliation.

Finally there are weapons systems and other military construction and gadgetry which add primarily to the prestige of the Armed Services, or which advance the competitive position of an individual branch.

The last three classes of weapons do not add to such security as is provided under the balance of terror.° Given the response they provoke, they leave it either unchanged or more dangerous. But all contribute to the growth, em-ployment, and profits of the contractors. All are sought by the Armed Forces. The Army's Sentinel (now Safeguard) Anti-Ballistic Missile system is urged even though it is irrelevant and possibly dangerous as a defense. As Mr. Rus-sell Baker has said, it is based at least partly on the assumption that the Chi-nese would "live down to our underestimates of their abilities and produce a missile so inferior that even a Sentinel can shoot it down." But it holds a posi-tion for the Army in this highly technological warfare. The Air Force wants a new generation of manned bombers, their vulnerability notwithstanding, be-cause an Air Force without such bombers—with the key fighting men sitting silently in underground command posts—is much less interesting. And Boeing, General Dynamics, Lockheed, North American Rockwell, Grumman, and McDonnell Douglas are naturally glad that this is so. The Navy wants nu-

° Charles L. Schultze, the former Director of the Budget under President Johnson and his asso-ciate William M. Capron, neither of them radicals in this matter, have recently observed that "Once we have achieved a minimum deterrent, plus an ample margin of safety and a healthy R & D program to be prepared for the future, it is difficult to conceive of any value the United States could gain from additional 'superiority' in nuclear forces. . . . we cannot attain a first-strike capa-bility. And if we can retaliate with devastating force against a Soviet attack, what do we gain by having twice or three times that force? It adds nothing to our diplomatic strength in situations short of nuclear war. It does not add to deterence—devastation twice over is no greater deterrent than devastation once. We can, to some extent, limit damage to the United States by having the capability, in a retaliatory strike, to target Soviet missiles and bombers withheld in a first strike. But the 'ample margin of safety' described above gives us such a capability already. Excessive su-periority, in other words, gains us little of value, costs substantially in budget terms, and almost inevitably forces a Soviet response which eliminates the superiority temporarily gained." Unpub-lished memorandum. A valuable recent document on this whole subject is George W. Rathjens' *The Future of the Strategic Arms Race* (Carnegie Endowment for International Peace, 1969).

clear carriers and their complement of aircraft, their vulnerability also not-withstanding, for the same reason.

A prime objective of control is to eliminate from the military budget those things which contribute to the arms race or are irrelevant to the present balance of terror. This includes the second, third, and fourth classes of weapons mentioned above. The ABM and the MIRV (the Multiple Independently-targeted Reentry Vehicle), both of which will spark a new competitive round of a peculiarly uncontrollable sort, as well as manned bombers and nuclear carriers are all of this sort. Perhaps as a simple working goal, some five billions of such items should be eliminated in each of the next three years for a total reduction of fifteen billion.°

8. *The second and more important objective of control is to win agreement with the Soviets on arms control and reduction.* This means, in contrast with present military doctrine, that we accept that the Soviets will bargain in good faith. And we accept also that an imperfect agreement—for none can be watertight—is safer than continuing competition. It means, as a practical matter, that the military role in negotiations must be sharply circumscribed. Military men—prompted by their industrial allies—will always object to any agreement that is not absolute, self-enforcing, and watertight. Under such circumstances arms-control negotiations become, as they have been in recent times, a charade. Instead of halting the arms race they may even have the effect of justifying it. "After all we are trying for agreement with the bastards." The Congress and the people must make the necessity for this control relentlessly clear to the Executive.

9. *Independent scientific judgment must be mobilized in this effort–as guidance to the political effort, for advice to Congress, and of course, within the Executive itself.* The arms race, in its present form, is a scientific and mathematical rather than a military contest. Those military can no longer barricade themselves behind claims of military expertise or needed secrecy, opposing views must be reliably available.

But decisions on military needs are still made in a self-serving compact between those who buy weapons and those who sell. So the time has come to constitute a special body of highly qualified scientists and citizens to be called, perhaps, the Military Audit Commission. Its function would be to advise the Congress and inform the public on military programs and negotiations. It should be independently, *i.e.* privately, financed. It would be the authoritative voice on weapons systems that add to international tension or

---

° I would urge leaving the space race out of this effort. The gadgetry involved is not uniquely lethal; on the contrary it channels competition with the Soviets, if such there must be, into comparatively benign channels. It has so far been comparatively safe for the participants—strikingly so as compared with early efforts at manned flight in the atmosphere and across the oceans. One observes, between ourselves and the Soviets, a gentlemanly obligation to admire each other's accomplishments which, on the whole, compares favorably with similar manifestations at the Olympic games or involving music and the ballet.

competition or serve principally the competitive position and prestige of the Services or the profits of their suppliers. It would have the special function of serving as a watchdog on negotiations to insure that the military power is excluded.

10. *Control of the military power must be an ecumenical effort.* Obviously no one who regards himself as a liberal can any longer be a communicant of the military power. But the issue is one of equal concern to conservatives—to the conservative who traditionally suspects any major concentration of public power. It is also an issue for every businessman whose taxes are putting a very few of his colleagues on the gravy train. But most of all it is an issue for every citizen who finds the policy images of this bureaucracy—the Manned Orbiting Laboratory preserving the American position when all or most are dead below—more than a trifle depressing.

IX

A few will find the foregoing an unduly optimistic effort. More, I suspect, will find it excessively moderate, even commonplace. It makes no overtures to the withdrawal of scientific and other scholarly talent from the military. It does not encourage a boycott on recruiting by the military contractors. It does not urge the curtailment of university participation in military research. These, there should be no mistake about it, will be necessary if the military power is not brought under control. Nor can there be any very righteous lectures about such action. The military power has reversed constitutional process in the United States—removed power from the public and Congress to the Pentagon. It is in a poor position to urge orderly political process. And the consequences of such a development could be very great—they could amount to an uncontrollable thrust to unilateral disarmament. But my instinct is for action within the political framework. This is not a formula for busy ineffectuality. None can deny the role of those who marched or picketed on Vietnam. But, in the end, it was political action that arrested the escalation and broke the commitment of the bureaucracy to this mistake. Control of the military power is a less easily defined and hence more difficult task. (To keep the military and its allies and spokesmen from queering international negotiations will be especially difficult.) But if sharply focused knowledge can be brought to bear on both weapons procurement and negotiation; if citizen attitudes can be kept politically effective by the conviction that this is the political issue of our time; if there is effective organization; if in consequence a couple of hundred or even a hundred members of Congress can be kept in a vigilant, critical, and aroused mood; and if for the President this becomes visibly the difference between success and failure, survival and eventual defeat, then the military-industrial complex will be under control. It can be made to happen.

Study Questions

1. Compare and contrast the use of the National Security Council by the Truman, Eisenhower, Kennedy, and Johnson administrations and state the advantages and disadvantages of the style of each administration.
2. What is Senator Fulbright's major criticism of our foreign policy? Do you agree or disagree with him? Explain why.
3. In view of Nixon's speech and actions, do you think that Fulbright's criticism of our Vietnam policy is still valid? Explain fully and critically.
4. What is meant by the industrial-military complex? In what ways does the industrial-military bureaucracy pose a threat to our democratic processes? Do you agree or disagree with Galbraith's criticisms and his suggestions for control over the military establishment?
5. Why haven't the American public and Congress questioned military requests and actions in the past? To what factors would you attribute the present demands for more effective controls over the military establishment? Discuss fully and critically.

Suggestions for Further Reading

Appleton, Sheldon. *United States Foreign Policy: An Introduction with Cases.* Boston: Little, Brown and Company, 1968.

Armacost, Michael H. *The Foreign Relations of the United States.* Belmont, California: Dickenson Publishing Company, Inc., 1969.

Aron, Raymond. *The Great Debate: Theories of Nuclear Strategy.* New York: Doubleday and Company, 1965.

Bader, William B. *The United States and the Spread of Nuclear Weapons.* New York: Pegasus, 1968.

Beloff, Max. *Foreign Policy and the Democratic Process.* Baltimore: Johns Hopkins University Press, 1955.

Bemis, Samuel Flagg. *A Diplomatic History of the United States.* 5th ed. New York: Holt, Rinehart and Winston, 1965.

Carleton, William G. *The Revolution in American Foreign Policy: Its Global Range.* New York: Random House, 1963.

Crabb, Cecil V., Jr. *American Foreign Policy in The Nuclear Age.* 2nd ed. New York: Harper & Row, 1965.

Dulles, Eleanor Lansing. *American Foreign Policy In the Making.* New York: Harper & Row, Publishers, 1968.

Frankel, Joseph. *The Making of Foreign Policy: An Analysis of Decision-Making.* New York: Oxford University Press, 1963.

Fulbright, J. William. *Old Myths and New Realities.* New York: Random House, 1964.

Goldwin, Robert A., (ed.) *America Armed: Essays on the United States Military Policy.* Chicago: Rand McNally, 1963.

Kennan, George F. *American Diplomacy: 1900–1950.* Chicago: University of Chicago Press, 1951.

Kissinger, Henry A. *American Foreign Policy.* New York: W. W. Norton & Company, Inc., 1969.

Kissinger, Henry A. *Nuclear Weapons and Foreign Policy.* New York: Harper & Row, Publishers, 1957.

Kissinger, Henry A. *The Necessity for Choice.* New York: Harper & Row, Publishers, 1961.

Lerche, Charles O. *Foreign Policy of the American People.* 3rd ed. Englewood Cliffs, New Jersey: Prentice-Hall, 1967.

Morganthau, Hans J. *In Defense of the National Interest.* New York: Alfred A. Knopf, Inc., 1951.

Morgenthau, Hans J. *The Purpose of American Politics.* New York: Alfred A. Knopf, Inc., 1960.

Needler, Martin C. *Dimensions of American Foreign Policy.* Princeton, New Jersey: D. Van Nostrand Company, Inc., 1966.

Needler, Martin C. *Understanding Foreign Policy.* New York: Holt, Rinehart and Winston, 1966.

Plischke, Elmer. *Conduct of American Diplomacy.* 3rd ed. Princeton, New Jersey: D. Van Nostrand Company, Inc., 1967.

Robinson, James A. *Congress and Foreign Policy-Making.* Rev. ed. Homewood, Illinois: The Dorsey Press, 1967.

Rosenau, James N. *Public Opinion and Foreign Policy: An Operational Formulation.* New York: Random House, 1961.

Rostow, Walt W. *View from the Seventh Floor.* New York: Harper & Row, Publishers, 1964.

Spanier, John. *American Foreign Policy Since World War II.* 2nd rev. ed. New York: Frederick A. Praeger, 1965.

Williams, William Appleman. *The Tragedy of American Diplomacy.* Revised and enlarged ed. New York: Dell Publishing Company, Inc., 1962.